STEP-BY-STEP RESUMES

For All

CONSTRUCTION TRADES

Laborer & Contractor Positions

First Edition

PAGE PUBLISHING, INC.
New York, NY

First originally published by Page Publishing, Inc. 2015

ISBN 978-1-68213-163-3 (paperback)
ISBN 978-1-68213-164-0 (digital)

Printed in the United States of America

EMAIL: CareerCatapult@aol.com | **PHONE:** 631-698-7777 | **WEBSITE:** StepByStepResumes.com

Dedicated to my husband, John C. Salvador, who is there to encourage me and cheer me on as I continue to author each profession-specific book in the Step-by-Step Resumes book series in which this multiyear endeavor required forgoing much of my regular resume writing income stream.

ABOUT THE AUTHOR

EVELYN U. SALVADOR, NCRW, JCTC

Certified Resume Writer & Career Coach | Personal Branding Pioneer

Multiaward-winning Resume Product Innovator | Author

EVELYN U. SALVADOR, ***Certified Resume Writer and Career Coach,*** is a Personal Branding pioneer *(since 1990)* and the world's leading, multiaward-winning resume product innovator who has helped revolutionize the resume writing industry. She is the author of ***Step-by-Step Resumes: Build an Outstanding Resume in 10 Easy Steps!*** and ***Step-by-Step Cover Letters: Build a Cover Letter in 10 Easy Steps Using Personal Branding*** *(both published by JIST Publishing).* She is also a contributing author to ***Interview Magic*** *(Susan Britton-Whitcomb, JIST Publishing)* and ***The Complete Job Search Guide for Latinos*** *(Murray Mann, Barons Publishing)* and has been interviewed for and/or quoted in various other books, numerous publications, talk shows, and Websites.

As a credentialed career management expert and thought leader, Evelyn is one of the top Professional Resume Writers in the world. She is a former ***National Resume Writers' Association*** *Advertising and Public Relations Chair* as well as its *Eastern Regional Representative.* Her award-winning resume and career products used worldwide by professional resume writers, career coaches, colleges and universities, the military, Departments of Labor, jobseekers, and others can be found at CareerCatapult.com.

Evelyn has been positioning careerists in the top 2 percent in their industry for 25 years. As such, her clients succeed a lot quicker and earn more than their average counterparts. She achieves this by identifying and defining their Personal Brands and leveraging it across all marketing platforms through marketing-savvy wordsmithing and design that compels hiring managers to seek them out over other candidates. This Book shows you step by step how to do this for yourself.

Evelyn is the founder of CreativeImageBuilders.com a personal and business-branding firm in Coram, NY, where she spearheads the development of visionary strategies and innovative solutions to meet her clients' target audiences' needs that help position businesses and individuals at the top. She develops self-promotional marketing materials that sell the product...*you.* Whether "you" are a business or an individual and whether your marketing communications are your resume or brochure, web portfolio or website, or LinkedIn or company profile.

When Evelyn first started her practice in 1990, she created branding materials for businesses. When she was asked by family and friends to craft their resumes, she did. When they immediately received calls for interviews, she first chalked it up to being "lucky." When that occurred time and again and became the norm, she realized it wasn't luck at all. Their success was due to her applying the same methodology to writing and designing resumes as she was for businesses in creating their marketing materials—that is, selling their features, benefits, competitive edge, value proposition, and return on investment along with their matching achievements—in a designer resume format.

She imparts upon you in this ***Step-by-Step Resumes*** Book how to define and leverage your own unique brand and has put her resume-writing verbiage and methods into each of the scientific tools it contains so you can do the same to position yourself head and shoulders above your peers. Her own brand characteristics of being visionary, scientific, creative / artistic, strategic, marketing savvy, comprehensive, detail-oriented, and organized is what helps her showcase her clients and readers so desirably to their target audience. *(You will identify your own top 10 brand attributes in Step 3: Check Off Your Personal Attributes and Capabilities.)*

Evelyn's work in the career management field has been referred to as *"revolutionary," "groundbreaking," "a labor of love,"* and *"I don't know how I did without it"* by her resume writer peers. Jobseekers refer to her books as *"amazing," "right-on,"* and *"very easy."* And clients state their resumes have helped them *"realize their own worth,"* made them feel *"confident and empowered"* in their job search and that human resource professionals have told them they had *"the best resume"* they had ever seen.

Evelyn attended New York Institute of Technology and started her career in banking where she progressed to Assistant Vice President in charge of bank policies and procedures, after which she worked for a top advertising agency as a Graphic Designer prior to starting her business. She is a member of The National Resume Writers' Association and Career Directors International. Her creative talents encompass writing and editing, design, fine art, and photography. *(Evelyn's Web Portfolio and resume are viewable at EvelynSalvador.com.)*

Construction Trades
START
EASY STYLE
DISPLAY PROPERTIES
SCALABLE

POSITION TITLES
THIS BOOK COVERS

ADMINISTRATIVE

- *Administrator & Coordinator*
- *Construction & Service Coordinator*
- *Construction Administrative Coordinator*
- *Construction Administrator*
- *Construction Coordinator*
- *Construction Customer Service Manager*
- *Construction Expeditor*
- *Construction Materials Technician*
- *Construction Office Manager*
- *Construction Project Administrator*
- *Construction Project Coordinator*
- *Construction Project Specialist*
- *Construction Project Supervisor*
- *Construction Representative*
- *Construction Services Assistant*
- *Construction Services Manager*
- *Contract Administrator*
- *Customer Service Representative – Construction*
- *Customer Service Superintendent*
- *Inventory Control Assistant – Construction*
- *Inventory Control Manager – Construction*
- *Lead Project Coordinator*
- *Material Coordinator*
- *Office Administrator – Construction*
- *Office Manager – Construction*
- *Planning & Coordination Specialist*
- *Project Control Coordinator*
- *Project Coordination Specialist*
- *Project Coordinator*
- *Project Management Administrator*
- *Project Material Coordinator*
- *Project Principal Work Planner*
- *Project Scheduler*
- *Project Specialist*
- *Resident Project Representative*
- *Services Manager*
- *Support Specialist*
- *Other related positions*

BUILDING OPERATIONS

- *General Manager – Construction*
- *Operations Manager – Construction*
- *Building Engineer*
- *Building Operations Supervisor*
- *Building Operations Manager*
- *Building Program Specialist*
- *Commercial Construction Office Manager*
- *Construction Operations Manager*
- *Operations Manager – Construction*
- *Operations Supervisor*
- *Other related positions*

BUILDING MAINTENANCE

- *Area Maintenance Supervisor*
- *Assistant Building Superintendent*
- *Building & Grounds Laborer*
- *Building & Grounds Mechanic*
- *Building Handyman*
- *Building Maintenance Attendant*
- *Building Maintenance Engineer*
- *Building Maintenance Manager*
- *Building Maintenance Mechanic*
- *Building Maintenance Supervisor*
- *Building Maintenance Technician*
- *Building Maintenance Worker*
- *Building Manager*
- *Building Service Engineer*
- *Building Technician*
- *Custodian*
- *Custodian Engineer*
- *Facilities Maintenance Mechanic*
- *General Maintenance Mechanic*
- *General Maintenance Technician*
- *General Maintenance Worker*
- *Janitor*
- *Maintenance & Operations Supervisor*
- *Maintenance Engineer*
- *Maintenance Helper*
- *Maintenance Journeyman*
- *Maintenance Mechanic*
- *Maintenance Project Superintendent*
- *Maintenance Project Supervisor*
- *Maintenance Repair Worker*
- *Maintenance Repair Worker Assistant*
- *Maintenance Specialist*
- *Plant Maintenance Mechanic*

BUILDING MAINTENANCE
(Cont'd)

- *Senior Building Facilities Technician*
- *Senior Building Maintenance Mechanic*
- *Senior Building Maintenance Technician*
- *Senior Building Maintenance Worker*
- *Senior Building Technician*
- *Senior Facilities Maintenance Mechanic*
- *Senior Maintenance Mechanic*
- *Senior Plant Maintenance Mechanic*
- *Superintendent of Facilities Maintenance*
- *Other related positions*

CARPENTRY

- *Acoustical Carpenter*
- *Acoustical Ceiling Installer*
- *Acoustical Ceiling Technician*
- *Acoustical Ceiling Mechanic*
- *Cabinetmaker*
- *Carpenter*
- *Carpenter / Crew Leader*
- *Carpenter / Form Setter*
- *Carpenter / Repairman*
- *Carpenter Apprentice*
- *Carpenter Assistant*
- *Carpenter Lead Hand*
- *Carpenter, General Foreman*
- *Carpenter-Contractor*
- *Carpentry Contractor*
- *Carpentry Foreman*
- *Carpentry Supervisor*
- *Carpet Fitter*
- *Carpet Installer*
- *Carpet Layer*
- *Ceiling Installer*
- *Ceiling Tile Installer*
- *Commercial / Industrial Painter*
- *Commercial Construction Carpenter*
- *Commercial Glazing Estimator*
- *Commercial Project Manager*
- *Craftsman*
- *Deck Builder*
- *Deck Installer*
- *Deck Worker*
- *Demolition Foreman*
- *Demolition Worker*

POSITION TITLES COVERED *(Continued)*

CARPENTRY *(Cont'd)*

- *Door & Window Installer*
- *Driller Drywall & Ceiling Tile Installer*
- *Drywall & Make-ready Technician*
- *Drywall Applicator*
- *Drywall Boardhanger*
- *Drywall Carpenter*
- *Drywall Finisher*
- *Drywall Hanger*
- *Drywall Installer*
- *Drywall Mechanic*
- *Drywall Metal Stud Worker*
- *Drywall Sander*
- *Drywall Stripper*
- *Drywall Taper*
- *Drywall Worker*
- *Drywaller*
- *Elevator Installer*
- *Fence Builder*
- *Finish Carpenter*
- *Finish Superintendent*
- *Fire Sprinkler Designer*
- *Fire Sprinkler Fitter*
- *Fire Sprinkler Helper*
- *Fire Sprinkler Installer*
- *Flat Glass Glazier Technician*
- *Floor Installer*
- *Floor Layer*
- *Floor Systems Carpenter*
- *Foreman*
- *Framer*
- *Framing Carpenter*
- *Furniture Maker*
- *General Construction Laborer*
- *General Foreman*
- *Glass Combo Technician*
- *Glass Fitter*
- *Glass Installer*
- *Glass Setter*
- *Glass Technician*
- *Glazier*
- *Glazier Contractor*
- *Glazier Supervisor*
- *Glazing Project Manager*
- *Handyman*
- *Handyman / Service Technician*
- *Installation / Service Technician*
- *Installation Supervisor*
- *Installer*
- *Installer Technician*
- *Insulation Installer*
- *Insulation Worker*
- *Interior Finish Carpenter*
- *Journeyman Carpenter*
- *Journeyman Construction Carpenter*

CARPENTRY *(Cont'd)*

- *Journeyman Fire Sprinkler Fitter*
- *Labor Foreman*
- *Labor Supervisor*
- *Laborer*
- *Lath & Plaster*
- *Lath Hand*
- *Lather*
- *Lather Apprentice*
- *Lead Carpenter*
- *Lead Glazer*
- *Maintenance Carpenter*
- *Master Carpenter*
- *Metal Framer*
- *Metal Furrer*
- *Metal Lather*
- *Metal Roofing Technician*
- *Metal Stud Framer*
- *Multiskilled Craftsman / Remodeler*
- *Painter*
- *Painter – Commercial*
- *Painter – Industrial*
- *Painter – Residential*
- *Painter / Crew Leader*
- *Painter Helper / Prepper*
- *Painter Leader*
- *Painting Contractor*
- *Painting Foreman*
- *Plaster Lather*
- *Plasterer*
- *Prefabricated Structures Carpenter*
- *Remodeling Tradesman*
- *Restoration Carpenter*
- *Rock Lather*
- *Rockboard Lather*
- *Roofer*
- *Roofing Apprentice*
- *Roofing Carpenter*
- *Roofing Foreman*
- *Scaffold Builder*
- *Scaffold Construction Manager*
- *Scaffold Erector*
- *Scenic Carpenter*
- *Sheetrock Applicator*
- *Sheetrock Applier*
- *Sheetrock Finisher*
- *Sheetrock Hanger*
- *Sheetrock Installer*
- *Sheetrock Layer*
- *Sheetrock Nailer*
- *Sheetrock Sander*
- *Sheetrock Worker*
- *Sheetrocker*
- *Siding Foreman*
- *Skilled Carpenter*

CARPENTRY *(Cont'd)*

- *Solar Heating Cooling System Installer*
- *Solar Installation / Production Manager*
- *Solar Photovoltaic Installer*
- *Tile Installer*
- *Window Washer*
- *Wire Lather*
- *Wood Lather*
- *Working Foreman*
- *Other related positions*

CONCRETE WORK

- *Cement Gun Operator*
- *Cement Mason*
- *Cement Mason Apprentice*
- *Cement Patcher*
- *Cementer*
- *Concrete & Terrazzo Finisher*
- *Concrete Finisher*
- *Concrete Finisher Apprentice*
- *Concrete Floater*
- *Concrete Floor Installer*
- *Concrete Form Setter*
- *Concrete Form Laborer*
- *Concrete Grinder Operator*
- *Concrete Installer*
- *Concrete Laborer*
- *Concrete Layer*
- *Concrete Materials Tester*
- *Concrete Placement Equipment Operator*
- *Concrete Pointer*
- *Concrete Polisher*
- *Concrete Smoother*
- *Concrete Safety Manager*
- *Concrete Stone Finisher*
- *Concrete Swimming Pool Installer*
- *Concreting Supervisor*
- *Construction Form Setter*
- *Curb Builder*
- *Finish-Pour Assistant*
- *Joint Finisher*
- *Joint Setter*
- *Structural Concrete Superintendent*
- *Swimming Pool Installer*
- *Other related positions*

CONSTRUCTION

- *Apprentice Lineman*
- *Apprenticeship Manager*
- *Assistant Builder*
- *Assistant Commercial Construction Superintendent*
- *Assistant Construction Manager*
- *Assistant Multifamily Superintendent*

POSITION TITLES COVERED *(Continued)*

CONSTRUCTION *(Cont'd)*

- *Assistant Superintendent*
- *Building Construction Laborer*
- *Cement Finisher*
- *Cement Laborer*
- *Civil Foreman*
- *Civil Superintendent*
- *Commercial Construction Laborer*
- *Commercial Construction Manager*
- *Commercial Construction Superintendent*
- *Concrete Foreman*
- *Construction Area Manager*
- *Construction Assistant Superintendent*
- *Construction Carpenter*
- *Construction Field Engineer*
- *Construction Field Estimator*
- *Construction Field Supervisor*
- *Construction Foreman*
- *Construction Journeyman*
- *Construction Journeyman Electrician*
- *Construction Laborer*
- *Construction Manager*
- *Construction Operations Supervisor*
- *Construction Site Manager*
- *Construction Site Superintendent*
- *Construction Supervisor*
- *Construction Tradesman*
- *Construction Trainee*
- *Construction Worker*
- *Contract (Site) Manager*
- *Contractor*
- *Crew Chief*
- *Demolition Superintendent*
- *Dirt Foreman / Superintendent*
- *Drilling Foreman*
- *Field Foreman*
- *Foreman / Foreperson*
- *General Contractor*
- *General Foreman – Civil*
- *General Laborer*
- *General Superintendent*
- *Hazardous Materials Removal Worker*
- *Heavy Civil Project Engineer*
- *Home Building Superintendent*
- *Independent Contractor*
- *Job Superintendent*
- *Journey Lineworker*
- *Junior Site Surveyor*
- *Junior Superintendent*
- *Land Construction Manager*
- *Land Development Manager*
- *Lead Superintendent*
- *Leadman / Lead Person*
- *Leadman Construction Laborer*

CONSTRUCTION *(Cont'd)*

- *Multifamily Construction Project Supervisor*
- *Multifamily Superintendent*
- *New Homes Superintendent*
- *Preconstruction Manager*
- *Preconstruction Manager – Renovation*
- *Project Superintendent*
- *Property Manager – Construction*
- *Public Works Manager*
- *Regional Property Manager*
- *Residential Construction Project Manager*
- *Retail Construction Manager*
- *Sheet Metal Helper*
- *Sheet Metal Worker*
- *Site Manager*
- *Site Superintendent*
- *Site Supervisor*
- *Site Surveyor*
- *Sitework Manager*
- *Skilled Trades Apprentice*
- *Skilled Trades Specialist*
- *Skilled Trades Worker*
- *Structural Trades Superintendent*
- *Structural Tradesworker*
- *Superintendent – Concrete*
- *Superintendent – Installation*
- *Superintendent – Specialty Construction*
- *Superintendent – Steel*
- *Superintendent – White Paving*
- *Supervisor of Building Trades*
- *Tile Setter*
- *Trade Professional Manager*
- *Union Carpenter*
- *Utility Line Locator*
- *Utility Maintenance Worker*
- *Vocational Assistant / General Laborer*
- *Waterproofer*
- *Working Superintendent*
- *Working Superintendent – Retail / Commercial*
- *Other related positions*

ELECTRICAL WORK

- *Apprentice Electrician*
- *Commercial Electrician*
- *Construction Electrician Journeyman*
- *Electric Service Worker*
- *Electrical Apprentice*
- *Electrical Construction Foreman*
- *Electrical Design Engineer*
- *Electrical Engineering Technician*
- *Electrical Foreman*

ELECTRICAL WORK *(Cont'd)*

- *Electrical Project Manager*
- *Electrical Systems Design Engineer*
- *Electrical Systems Supervisor*
- *Electrician*
- *Electrician Apprentice*
- *Electrician Contractor*
- *Electrician Foreman*
- *Electrician Helper*
- *Electrician Supervisor*
- *Engineer – Electrical Systems Design*
- *Industrial Electrician*
- *Journeyman Electrician*
- *Lead Electrician*
- *Licensed Journeyman Electrician*
- *Maintenance Electrician*
- *Master Electrician*
- *Residential Electrical Foreman*
- *Wiring Technician*
- *Other related positions*

EQUIPMENT OPERATIONS

- *Asphalt Paving Equipment Operator*
- *Asphalt Paving-Patching Equipment Operator*
- *Backhoe / Loader Operator*
- *Backhoe Operator / Excavator*
- *Bulldozer Operator*
- *CDL Driver / Equipment Operator*
- *Certified Crane Operator*
- *Compact Track Loader Operator*
- *Concrete & Asphalt Equipment Operator*
- *Construction Equipment Operator*
- *Construction Labor / Equipment Operator*
- *Crane Manager*
- *Crane Operator*
- *Crane Rigger*
- *Directional Bore Operator*
- *Directional Drill Operator*
- *Dragline Operator*
- *Dredge Operator*
- *Dredger*
- *Dump Truck Backhoe Operator*
- *Dump Truck Driver*
- *Engineering Equipment Operator*
- *Equipment Operator*
- *Excavating Machine Operator*
- *Excavator Operator*
- *Forklift Operator*
- *Front-End Loader Operator*
- *General Construction Equipment Operator*
- *Gradall Operator*
- *Grader Operator*

POSITION TITLES COVERED *(Continued)*

EQUIPMENT OPERATIONS *(Cont'd)*

- *Heavy Equipment Operator*
- *Heavy Equipment Operator Apprentice*
- *Horizontal Directional Drill Operator*
- *Landfill Heavy Equipment Operator*
- *Loader Operator*
- *Loading Machine Operator*
- *Low Boy Driver*
- *Motor Grader Operator*
- *Multiterrain Loader*
- *Paving Equipment Operator*
- *Pay Loader Operator*
- *Pile-Driver Operator*
- *Side Boom Tractor Operator*
- *Skid Steer Loader Operator*
- *Surfacing Equipment Operator*
- *Tamping Equipment Operator*
- *Track Hoe Operator*
- *Trencher Operator*
- *Truck Driver / Equipment Operator*
- *Utility Worker – Heavy Equipment*
- *Other related positions*

ESTIMATING

- *Assistant Estimator – High-end General Construction*
- *Chief Commercial Roofing Estimator*
- *Commercial Flooring Estimator*
- *Construction & Estimator Assistant*
- *Construction Cost Estimator*
- *Construction Estimator*
- *Commercial Estimator*
- *Cost Analyst*
- *Cost Estimator*
- *Estimator*
- *Estimator – High-end General Construction*
- *Estimator Project Manager*
- *Estimating / Bidding Assistant*
- *Estimating / Change Manager*
- *Estimating Assistant*
- *Estimating Supervisor*
- *Estimator – Specialty Construction*
- *Estimator – Structural & Miscellaneous Steel Fabrication*
- *Estimator / Assistant Project Manager*
- *Estimator / Purchaser*
- *Junior Construction Estimator*
- *Junior Estimator*
- *Mid-level Estimator*
- *Residential Construction Estimator*
- *Senior Estimator*
- *Senior Estimator, Home Building Commercial Construction*

ESTIMATING *(Cont'd)*

- *Senior Project Manager / Estimator*
- *Other related positions*

FACILITIES

- *Facilities Construction Trades Worker*
- *Facilities Construction Coordinator*
- *Facilities Foreperson*
- *Facilities Generalist*
- *Facilities Construction Project Specialist*
- *Facilities Superintendent*
- *Facility Maintenance Specialist*
- *Facility Operations Project Manager*
- *Manager Construction Projects, Facility Engineering*
- *Territory Facilities Manager*
- *Other related positions*

FIELD WORK

- *Field Construction Coordinator*
- *Field Helper*
- *Field Install Site Supervisor*
- *Field Manager*
- *Field Manager – Homebuilding*
- *Field Manager – Residential Construction*
- *Field Operations Supervisor*
- *Field Representative*
- *Field Superintendent*
- *Field Supervisor*
- *Field Survey Specialist*
- *Field-based Construction Manager*
- *Field-based Facilities Manager*
- *Senior Field Manager*
- *Other related positions*

GENERAL CONTRACTING

- *Commercial Contractor*
- *Concrete Contractor*
- *Demolition Contractor*
- *Electrical Contractor*
- *Excavating Contractor*
- *Excavator Foreman*
- *Floor Laying Contractor*
- *General Building Contractor*
- *General Contractor*
- *General Engineering Contractor*
- *Glass & Glazing Contractor*
- *Home Improvement Contractor*
- *Home Remodeling Contractor*
- *HVAC Contractor*
- *Maintenance Contractor*
- *Masonry & Stone Setting Contractor*
- *Owner / Operator (Contractor)*

GENERAL CONTRACTING *(Cont'd)*

- *Painting Contractor*
- *Plastering, Drywall, Acoustical & Insulation Contractor*
- *Plumbing Contractor*
- *Plumbing, Heating & Air Conditioning Contractor*
- *Remodel Contractor*
- *Residential General Contractor*
- *Roofing & Siding Contractor*
- *Roofing Contractor*
- *Sheet Metal Contractor*
- *Special Trade Contractor*
- *Specialty Contractor*
- *Structural Contractor*
- *Subcontractor*
- *Other related positions*

GROUNDSKEEPING & GREENSKEEPING

- Athletic Field Custodian
- Cemetery Warden
- Greens Foreman
- Greens Superintendent
- Greenskeeper Foreman
- Groundskeeper Foreman
- Park Foreman
- Property Manager – Groundskeeping
- Brush Cutter
- Building & Grounds Attendant
- Building & Grounds Technician
- Cemetery Keeper
- Cemetery Laborer
- Cemetery Worker
- Golf Course Keeper
- Golf Course Laborer
- Grass Cutter
- Grass Mower
- Greens Cutter
- Greens Laborer
- Greenskeeper
- Ground Crewman
- Ground Worker
- Grounds Caretaker
- Grounds Cleaner
- Groundskeeper
- Groundskeeping Maintenance Worker
- Hedge Trimmer
- Maintenance Groundsman
- Park Caretaker
- Park Caretaker Keeper
- Park Caretaker Worker
- Park Crew Chief
- Park Keeper

POSITION TITLES COVERED *(Continued)*

GROUNDSKEEPING & GREENSKEEPING *(Cont'd)*

- Pesticide Handler
- Pesticide Sprayer
- Pruner
- Shrub Trimmer
- Tree Maintenance Worker
- Tree Pruner
- Tree Specialist
- Tree Surgeon
- Tree Trimmer
- Weed Controller
- Weed Inspector
- Weed Sprayer
- Weeder
- Yard Work Laborer
- Yard Worker
- *Other related positions*

See also **"Landscaping."**

HIGHWAY & BRIDGE WORK

- *Bridge Construction Laborer*
- *Bridge Foreman*
- *Bridge Maintenance Mechanic*
- *Bridge Superintendent*
- *Crew Leader – Maintenance*
- *General Highway Worker*
- *Highway Construction Inspector*
- *Highway Foreman*
- *Highway Maintenance Foreman*
- *Highway Maintenance Laborer*
- *Highway Maintenance Lead Worker*
- *Highway Maintenance Technician*
- *Highway Maintenance Worker*
- *Highway Safety Specialist*
- *Highway Technician*
- *Maintenance of Traffic*
- *Roadway Construction Laborer*
- *Tradesworker – Bridges*
- *Other related positions*

INSPECTIONS & COMPLIANCE

- *Boiler Inspector*
- *Bridge Inspector*
- *Build-It-Back Plumbing Inspector*
- *Building & Housing Inspector*
- *Building & Safety Inspector*
- *Building & Trade Inspector*
- *Building Engineering Inspector*
- *Building Equipment Inspector*
- *Code Inspector*
- *Combination Inspector*
- *Commercial Building Inspector*
- *Commercial Inspector*

INSPECTIONS & COMPLIANCE *(Cont'd)*

- *Commissioning Engineer*
- *Construction & Building Inspector*
- *Construction Inspector*
- *Construction Quality Assurance / Quality Control Engineer*
- *Construction Quality Assurance Inspector*
- *Construction Quality Control Manager*
- *Construction Quality Specialist*
- *Dredging Inspector*
- *Electrical Inspector*
- *Field Inspector*
- *Gas Inspector*
- *Grade Checker*
- *Highway Inspector*
- *Home Inspector*
- *Housing Inspector*
- *HVAC-R Inspector*
- *Inspecting Engineer*
- *Inspector*
- *Paving Inspector*
- *Plumbing Inspector*
- *Plumbing / Mechanical Inspector*
- *Plumbing Inspector / Plans Reviewer*
- *Property Compliance Inspector*
- *Public Works Inspector*
- *Other related positions*

LABOR RELATIONS

- *Chief Steward*
- *Director, Labor Relations*
- *Labor Business Representative*
- *Labor Organization Representative*
- *Labor Organizer*
- *Labor Relations Director*
- *Labor Union Business Representative*
- *Shop Steward*
- *Steward*
- *Trade Union Representative*
- *Union Business Representative*
- *Union Negotiator*
- *Union Organizer*
- *Union Representative*
- *Union Staff Representative*
- *Union Steward*
- *Other related positions*

LANDSCAPING

- *Crew Leader*
- *Greenhouse Foreman*
- *Landscape Foreman*
- *Landscape Management Technician*

LANDSCAPING *(Cont'd)*

- *Nursery Manager*
- *Planting Foreman*
- *Property Manager – Landscaping*
- *Principal Landscape Architect*
- *Garden Center Worker*
- *Gardener*
- *Greenhouse Worker*
- *Horticulturist*
- *Indoor Gardener*
- *Irrigation Project Superintendent*
- *Landscape Gardener*
- *Landscape Laborer*
- *Landscape Irrigation Project Superintendent*
- *Landscape Maintenance Worker*
- *Landscape Technician*
- *Landscaper*
- *Landscaper Helper*
- *Landscape Design & Build Project Manager*
- *Lawn Caretaker*
- *Lawn Maintenance Laborer*
- *Lawn Mower Operator*
- *Lawn Service Worker*
- *Lawn Sprinkler Installer*
- *Lawn Sprinkler Servicer*
- *Maintenance Aide*
- *Maintenance Worker*
- *Nursery Helper*
- *Plant-Care Worker*
- *Property Maintenance Worker*
- *Shrub Planter*
- *Sprinkler Fitter*
- *Other related positions*

See also **"Groundskeeping & Greenskeeping."**

HVAC / HVAC-R

- *Air Conditioning Foreman*
- *Air Conditioning Installer*
- *Air Conditioning Mechanic*
- *Air Conditioning Specialist*
- *Air Conditioning Technician*
- *Commercial HVAC Foreman*
- *Commercial HVAC Technician*
- *Heating Foreman*
- *Heating Installer*
- *Heating Mechanic*
- *Heating Specialist*
- *Heating Technician*
- *HVAC / Skilled Tradesman*
- *HVAC Foreman*
- HVAC Helper
- *HVAC Installer & Service Technician*

POSITION TITLES COVERED *(Continued)*

HVAC / HVAC-R *(Cont'd)*

- *HVAC Mechanic*
- *HVAC Project Manager*
- *HVAC Service Technician*
- *HVAC Specialist*
- *HVAC Systems Foreman*
- *HVAC Technician*
- *HVAC/R Service Technician*
- *HVAC/R Mechanic*
- *HVAC/R Specialist*
- *HVAC/R Technician*
- *Refrigeration Apprentice*
- *Refrigeration Foreman*
- *Refrigeration Installer*
- *Refrigeration Mechanic*
- *Refrigeration Specialist*
- *Refrigeration Technician*
- *Trades Specialist – HVAC*
- *Zone Chief (HVAC)*
- *Other related positions*

MASONRY

- *Block Mason*
- *Blocklayer*
- *Blocklayer Apprentice*
- *Brick Laborer*
- *Brick Mason*
- *Brick Mason Foreman*
- *Brick Mason Laborer*
- *Bricklayer*
- *Bricklayer Apprentice*
- *Carpentry & Masonry Specialist*
- *Cement Contractor*
- *Cement Mason*
- *Commercial Journeyman Mason*
- *Commercial Masonry Foreman*
- *Concrete Finisher*
- *Construction Mason*
- *Industrial Brick Mason Foreman*
- *Marble Setter*
- *Mason*
- *Mason Carpenter*
- *Mason Laborer*
- *Mason Tender*
- *Mason-Plasterer*
- *Masonry Contractor*
- *Masonry Foreman*
- *Masonry Outfitter*
- *Masonry Specialist*
- *Masonry Superintendent*
- *Masonry Tuck-pointer Laborer*
- *Masonry Worker*
- *Stonemason*
- *Stonesetter*
- *Swimming Pool Installer*

MASONRY *(Cont'd)*

- *Terrazzo Contractor*
- *Terrazzo Finisher*
- *Terrazzo Grinder*
- *Terrazzo Setter*
- *Terrazzo Worker*
- *Other related positions*

PLUMBING

- *Apprentice Plumber*
- *Lead Plumber*
- *Licensed Plumber*
- *Master Plumber*
- *Plumber*
- *Plumber Apprentice / Helper*
- *Plumbing Contractor*
- *Plumbing Designer*
- *Plumbing Foreman*
- *Plumbing Foreman (Multifamily)*
- *Plumbing Installer*
- *Service Plumber*
- *Other related positions*

PURCHASING

- *Assistant Purchasing Estimator – Construction*
- *Assistant Purchasing Manager – Construction*
- *Purchasing / Estimating Assistant*
- *Purchasing Administrator*
- *Purchasing Agent – Construction*
- *Purchasing Manager – Construction*
- *Purchasing Trade Agent*
- *Regional Purchasing Administrator*
- *Regional Purchasing Manager*
- *Other related positions*

PROJECT MANAGEMENT

- *Assistant Project Superintendent / Engineer*
- *Commercial Project Manager*
- *Commercial Solar Project Manager*
- *Construction Manager*
- *Construction Project Engineer*
- *Construction Project Manager*
- *Construction Project Manager / Designer*
- *Construction Project Manager / Site Superintendent*
- *Construction Superintendent*
- *Construction Supervisor*
- *Land Assistant Project Manager*
- *Project Assistant – Jobsite*
- *Project Associate – Construction*

PROJECT MANAGEMENT *(Cont'd)*

- *Project Engineer – Electrical*
- *Project Engineer / Finish Carpenter*
- *Project Environmental Engineer*
- *Project Foreman*
- *Project Lead*
- *Project Leader*
- *Project Manager*
- *Project Manager – Electrical*
- *Project Manager – HVAC*
- *Project Manager – Metal Construction*
- *Project Manager – Plumbing*
- *Project Manager – Residential Remodeling*
- *Project Manager – Sheet Metal*
- *Project Manager / General Contractor*
- *Project Manager / Installation Manager*
- *Project Manager / Site Superintendent*
- *Project Manager Assistant*
- *Project Superintendent*
- *Project Superintendent / Engineer*
- *Project Supervisor*
- *Solar Project Manager*
- *Structural Superintendent*
- *Other related positions*

NOTE: For other Project Management positions, refer to the ARCHITECTURE & ENGINEERING Book.

WELDING / STEAMFITTING

- *Arc Welder*
- *Blowtorch Operator*
- *Blowtorch Welder*
- *Boiler Welder*
- *Combination Welder*
- *Gas Welder*
- *Hand Arc Welder*
- *Helliarc Welder*
- *Iron Worker*
- *Lead Welder*
- *Metal Welder*
- *Pipe Welder*
- *Pipefitter*
- *Pipefitter Helper*
- *Pipefitter Trade Foreman*
- *Spot Welder*
- *Steamfitter*
- *Tack Welder*
- *Torch Welder*
- *Tradesworker – Welding*
- *Welder*
- *Welding Contractor*
- *Other related positions*

THE INDEX IN THE BACK OF THE BOOK CONTAINS ALL POSITION TITLES LISTED ALPHABETICALLY.

TABLE OF CONTENTS

Next: See how easy it is to use this book!

HOW TO USE THIS BOOK

Congratulations. You have taken the first, most important step towards advancing your career and becoming more successful!

INTRODUCTION

You are about to embark on a self-discovery process that will help you to not only craft an exemplary resume step by step but better understand what you have to offer prospective employers in order to land the job you seek quickly and garner your highest salary. And so that you don't have in your hands an outstanding resume without the guidance on what to do with it, it also includes chapters on how to develop your personal brand, market yourself, conduct your job search, network, and prepare for and ace your interviews.

The ***Step-by-Step Resumes*** Book series is an extension of Evelyn Salvador's more generalized ***Step-by-Step Resumes: Build an Outstanding Resume in 10 Easy Steps!*** book *(JIST Publishing)* in that it is profession specific to not only your field and position, but contains numerous functions for each position, resume bullets for each function, and achievement samples. In essence, this Book includes everything you need to easily craft an exemplary resume to help position you in the top percentage in your field—as if you hired a Certified Resume Writer to craft it for you—as well as the necessary steps to help you obtain the job you want. You can use it time and again to update your resume throughout your career.

Everything in this book is written in its "lowest common denominator," that is, extremely content rich but in the most concise way possible so you don't have to do a lot of reading, writing, or research.

WHAT YOU NEED TO SUCCEED

Years ago, an excellent resume got a jobseeker's foot in the door. In today's world of work, careerists need three things to succeed: (1) an outstanding resume that highlights your skills and achievements, (2) a well-defined, unique personal brand that showcases your value proposition, and (3) a positive online identity for when employers check your Web presence prior to calling you in for an interview or making a job offer. This Book covers the content you will need for all three.

THE DIFFERENCE BETWEEN A TEMPLATE AND A FOUNDATION

Templates are generally very basic. They provide a starting point where you must fill in all relative information in your own words. They do not help you write an interview-generating resume. Unlike resume templates where you have to ponder what you did, Evelyn Salvador's books contain *foundations*. These foundations provide not only the framework that shapes and structures your resume, but all possible options that may be relative to a particular function. Each bullet foundation in this Book includes all of the necessary information required to complete it, whereas very little writing is necessary. As a Certified Resume Writer and Career Coach, Evelyn has written everything out for you. All you need to do is just check off what is relative to your own background.

HOW TO USE THIS BOOK

This resource is best used as a workbook by identifying everything that is applicable to you. The tools in each chapter will take you step by step to complete your resume in order to highlight your strengths and showcase your value proposition in the best of light to hiring managers. The more thoroughly you complete the sections, the better your end result, the more interviews you will receive, the faster your job turnaround can be, and the higher your salary potential.

Thousands of hours of research and writing went into creating the ***Step-by-Step Resumes*** Books so that most everything prospective employers seek in a job candidate would be covered—from your scope of work to each job function and achievement you perform(ed)—and includes the largest resource of all relative and current keywords in your industry to help your resume be "screened in" by human resources professionals. Since achievement statements are the most powerful in every resume, Evelyn has included numerous achievement samples throughout the Book. Each individual, however, will have his or her own unique set of accomplishments, so be sure to include any you may not see by viewing samples of similar achievements.

YOUR ACHIEVEMENTS

The most important rule in resume development—*and this is where 98% of the general public falls short*—is to include **CAR *(Challenge–Action–Result)* Statements**. To the extent possible, this is already done for you.

Don't just say what you did, state how well you accomplished it, the actions you took to make it happen, the end results it derived, and the benefits to your employer and/or its clients (in dollars and percentages wherever possible).

Following are the Chapters this book contains:

THE EASY STEP-BY-STEP PROCESS

INTRODUCTION

This ***Step-by-Step Resumes*** Book is divided into ten sections, or primary steps. The first six steps show you how to develop your personal brand and write your resume, while the last four help you to market yourself, conduct your job search, network, and prepare for and ace your interviews. In ***Step 6: Pull Your Resume Together,*** you will tie everything together that you worked up in steps one through five to create your exemplary resume that will help position you in the top two percent of candidates.

The ***Resume Worksheet*** in this step is where you will start to compile your resume. This section covers your employment, responsibilities, achievements, education and training, professional affiliations, and other related information. During the course of the Book, you will be selecting and transferring over applicable information (such as your professional summary, keywords, and resume bullets) to complete your resume.

Resume Keywords are critical to include in your resume so it can get in the hands of hiring managers. Scroll through the category lists and check off those core competencies you are proficient and knowledgeable in as they relate to your targeted position. You will be including your Primary Keywords within your *"Professional Summary,"* your Secondary Keywords listed in a *"Core Competencies"* or *"Areas of Expertise"* section, and all remaining keywords infused within the body of your resume. Applicable keywords are already included for you in all of the ***Resume ClipBullets*** found in ***Step 5***, and additional keyword instructions are contained in ***Step 6: Pull Your Resume Together***.

In this step you will be identifying your personal attributes (your assets / features) and honing in on your top ten attributes that match your prospective employer's needs. Those would be your unique qualities, characteristics, attributes, capabilities, and skills that can be valuable to an employer. You will use these attributes in ***Step 4: Develop Your Personal Brand and Professional Summary***.

Personal Branding is what puts you head and shoulders above your peers and helps position you in the top percentage in your field of expertise. You will first complete the ***Personal Branding Worksheet*** that will allow you to identify your ***Personal Brand*** components *(your assets, benefits, competitive edge, value proposition, and return on investment),* then develop your brand message that includes those elements in five formats: your personally branded ***Biography, LinkedIn Profile, Elevator Pitch, Slogan,*** and ***Professional Summary***. This step is thought provoking because it allows you to delve into yourself as to what you have to offer prospective employers. *Don't skip it*...take the time you need to really get to understand your own unique value you bring to the table. The end result will empower you to obtain the job you seek!

Resume ClipBullets™ are prewritten, customizable bullet foundations for the *"Professional Experience"* section of your resume. This step covers most all of the functions, responsibilities, and achievements you will be using to compile your employment information. Select applicable bullets and options as they relate to your specific position(s). You will include those bullets under your applicable employers / job titles in ***Step 6: Pull Your Resume Together.***

This step provides step-by-step instructions to compile and edit the information you completed throughout this Book to construct and finalize your resume. It contains a list of ***Action Verbs*** and ***Descriptive Adjectives*** and ***Adverbs*** to infuse within your resume, how to write your ***Company and Position Descriptors***, ***Resume Design Layout Samples,*** and a ***Resume Foundation***. And to be sure you've left no stone unturned, read the article *"100 Components of an Exemplary Resume: How Does Your Resume Fare?"* at the end. Just follow the instructions and you're done!

This step covers various ways you can market yourself—online and in print—including how to develop or enhance your positive online identity, everything you need to know about your social networking profiles and posts, creating a blog in your area of expertise, developing a Web Portfolio, and compiling a Career Portfolio. It also includes additional ways to market and brand yourself, such as logos, business cards, stationery, and more. Keep in mind that the more methods you use, the better your chances for success in getting the position you want quickly—*and* at your highest earnings potential.

This step includes various methods to conduct an effective job search including targeting companies of interest to you, mailing and emailing your career marketing materials to hiring managers, using your social media platforms to locate positions, posting your resume to job boards, joining industry-specific professional associations, and registering with an employment agency. Again, the more methods you use to get your resume in the hands of hiring managers, the quicker you can obtain a position.

Networking is about building new contacts and nurturing relationships that can ultimately lead to word-of-mouth referrals. It allows you to make connections and develop genuine, lasting relationships that can help you achieve your career goals. Since most positions are filled through networking *outside* of job boards and position postings, you should network everywhere you go when you meet up with people. This chapter takes the "scare" out of networking and simplifies the process for you by providing many resources, methods, and ways to network.

This step covers how to prepare for and ace your interviews, Informational Interviews, job interview types and styles, effective salary negotiation strategies, the follow-up steps you should take after the interview, Thank You Letters, and additional interview resources.

Ready? Grab yourself a cup of coffee, and let's get started!

STEP 1

START YOUR RESUME

CONTENTS OF STEP 1

☐ Fill in the Resume Worksheet

- Personal Information
- Licenses & Certifications
- Professional Summary
- Core Competencies / Skills
- Professional Experience (Your Employment History)
- Education & Training
- Professional Affiliations
- Other Categories (such as Publications, Community Activities, Military, Foreign Languages, or Related Hobbies)

FILL IN THE RESUME WORKSHEET

INSTRUCTIONS

The ***Resume Worksheet*** you are about to complete will start your resume compilation process. It includes areas for your skills, education, employment, responsibilities, achievements, licenses and certifications, professional affiliations, and other related information. During the course of this Book, you will be adding your *"Core Competencies"* from ***Step 2: Check Off Your Resume Keywords***, the *"Professional Summary"* from ***Step 4: Develop Your Personal Brand and Professional Summary***, and your *"Professional Experience"* bullets from ***Step 5: Select Your Resume ClipBullets***. Even though some contents will be brought in from other steps, it is recommended that—with the exception of your *"Professional Summary"*—you complete the Worksheet to the best of your ability at this stage so you can be sure that all of your pertinent information has been included when you get to ***Step 6: Pull Your Resume Together*** where you will be finalizing and editing your resume.

Personal Information

NAME: ADDRESS:

HOME PHONE: CELL PHONE: EMAIL:

WEB PORTFOLIO: LINKEDIN:

TWITTER: FACEBOOK:

Licenses & Certifications *(if any)*

TITLE	YEAR OBTAINED

Professional Summary

This information will be garnered from ***Step 4: Develop Your Personal Brand and Professional Summary****.*

Core Competencies / Areas of Expertise

List below all of your core competencies / areas of expertise as they relate to your targeted position. In ***Step 2: Check Off Your Resume Keywords,*** *you will be developing a comprehensive list of these keywords.*

CORE COMPETENCIES / AREAS OF EXPERTISE

________	________	________	________
________	________	________	________
________	________	________	________
________	________	________	________
________	________	________	________
________	________	________	________

TECHNICAL SKILLS

________	________	________	________
________	________	________	________

Personal Attributes / Soft Skills

List below all of your personal attributes / soft skills you have that are helpful to you in your targeted position. In ***Step 3: Check Off Your Personal Attributes & Capabilities,*** *you will be developing a comprehensive list of these keywords.*

PERSONAL ATTRIBUTES / SOFT SKILLS

________	________	________	________
________	________	________	________
________	________	________	________
________	________	________	________

Professional Experience (Your Employment History)

List your current and former positions starting with your most recent. It is not necessary to go back further than 10 to 15 years unless your relevant experience is not shown within that timeframe or position progression is important to note.

JOB #1 – POSITION TITLE: ________________________

COMPANY: **CITY, STATE:** **START & END YEARS:**

Type of Firm: Revenues: $ No. Locations: No. Employees:

No. Direct Reports & Titles: No. Indirect Reports & Titles:

Your scope of responsibility / main job functions:

Describe all of your job functions and how well you accomplished each against company or industry standards.

1.

2.

3.

4.

5.

6.

7.

8.

9.

10.

11.

12.

13.

14.

15.

Fully explain each of your achievements in terms of the challenges you were faced with, the actions you took, and end results.

ACHIEVEMENT #1

YOUR CHALLENGE:

YOUR ACTIONS:

YOUR RESULTS

ACHIEVEMENT #2

YOUR CHALLENGE:

YOUR ACTIONS:

YOUR RESULTS

ACHIEVEMENT #3

YOUR CHALLENGE:

YOUR ACTIONS:

YOUR RESULTS

ACHIEVEMENT #4

YOUR CHALLENGE:

YOUR ACTIONS:

YOUR RESULTS

ACHIEVEMENT #5

YOUR CHALLENGE:

YOUR ACTIONS:

YOUR RESULTS

OTHER ACHIEVEMENTS

JOB #2 – POSITION TITLE: ____________________

COMPANY: **CITY, STATE:** **START & END YEARS:**

Type of Firm: Revenues: $ No. Locations: No. Employees:

No. Direct Reports & Titles: No. Indirect Reports & Titles:

Your scope of responsibility / main job functions:

Describe all of your job functions and how well you accomplished each against company or industry standards.

1.
2.
3.
4.

5.

6.

7.

8.

9.

10.

11.

12.

Fully explain each of your achievements in terms of the challenges you were faced with, the actions you took, and end results.

ACHIEVEMENT #1

YOUR CHALLENGE:

YOUR ACTIONS:

YOUR RESULTS

ACHIEVEMENT #2

YOUR CHALLENGE:

YOUR ACTIONS:

YOUR RESULTS

ACHIEVEMENT #3

YOUR CHALLENGE:

YOUR ACTIONS:

YOUR RESULTS

ACHIEVEMENT #4

YOUR CHALLENGE:

YOUR ACTIONS:

YOUR RESULTS

OTHER ACHIEVEMENTS

JOB #3 – POSITION TITLE:

COMPANY: **CITY, STATE:** **START & END YEARS:**

Type of Firm: Revenues: $ No. Locations: No. Employees:

No. Direct Reports & Titles: No. Indirect Reports & Titles:

Your scope of responsibility / main job functions:

Describe all of your job functions and how well you accomplished each against company or industry standards.

1.
2.
3.
4.
5.
6.
7.
8.
9.
10.

Fully explain each of your achievements in terms of the challenges you were faced with, the actions you took, and end results.

ACHIEVEMENT #1

YOUR CHALLENGE:

YOUR ACTIONS:

YOUR RESULTS

ACHIEVEMENT #2

YOUR CHALLENGE:

YOUR ACTIONS:

YOUR RESULTS

ACHIEVEMENT #3

YOUR CHALLENGE:

YOUR ACTIONS:

YOUR RESULTS

OTHER ACHIEVEMENTS

JOB #4 – POSITION TITLE: ____________

COMPANY: **CITY, STATE:** **START & END YEARS:**

Type of Firm: Revenues: $ No. Locations: No. Employees:

No. Direct Reports & Titles: No. Indirect Reports & Titles:

Your scope of responsibility / main job functions:

Describe all of your job functions and how well you accomplished each against company or industry standards.

1.

2.

3.

4.

5.

6.

7.

8.

9.

10.

Fully explain each of your achievements in terms of the challenges you were faced with, the actions you took, and end results.

ACHIEVEMENT #1

YOUR CHALLENGE:

YOUR ACTIONS:

YOUR RESULTS

ACHIEVEMENT #2

YOUR CHALLENGE:

YOUR ACTIONS:

YOUR RESULTS

ACHIEVEMENT #3

YOUR CHALLENGE:

YOUR ACTIONS:

YOUR RESULTS

OTHER ACHIEVEMENTS

JOB #5 – POSITION TITLE: ____________________

COMPANY: **CITY, STATE:** **START & END YEARS:**

Type of Firm: Revenues: $ No. Locations: No. Employees:

No. Direct Reports & Titles: No. Indirect Reports & Titles:

Your scope of responsibility / main job functions:

Describe all of your job functions and how well you accomplished each against company or industry standards.

1.
2.
3.
4.
5.
6.
7.
8.

Fully explain each of your achievements in terms of the challenges you were faced with, the actions you took, and end results.

ACHIEVEMENT #1

YOUR CHALLENGE:

YOUR ACTIONS:

YOUR RESULTS

ACHIEVEMENT #2

YOUR CHALLENGE:

YOUR ACTIONS:

YOUR RESULTS

OTHER ACHIEVEMENTS

Education & Training

COLLEGE / UNIVERSITY	CITY & STATE	DEGREE / COURSEWORK	GPA	YEAR(S)

TRAINING / SEMINAR TITLES	SPONSORED BY	CITY & STATE	YEAR(S)

Professional Affiliations

Use this section to include all memberships and affiliations related to your targeted position.

ORGANIZATIONS	MEMBERSHIP / OFFICES HELD	YEAR(S)

Other

Use this section for other categories such as Publications, Community Activities, Military, Foreign Languages, Related Hobbies, etc.

STEP 2

CHECK OFF YOUR RESUME KEYWORDS

(CORE COMPETENCIES)

CONTENTS OF STEP 2

- ☐ Resume Keyword Instructions
- ☐ List Your Resume Keywords
  - Primary Keywords
  - Secondary Keywords
  - Remaining Keywords
- ☐ Resume Keywords for Your Profession
  - Bidding Process
  - Business & Administrative Functions
  - Construction
  - Electrical
  - General Contracting / Trades Management
  - Inspections & Compliance
  - Masonry
  - Trades – General
  - Building Maintenance
  - Carpentry
  - Contracts & Negotiations
  - Environmental Compliance
  - Heavy Equipment Operation
  - Labor Relations
  - Plumbing
  - Welding / Steamfitting
  - Building Services
  - Ceiling, Lathing, Insulation & Drywall Installation
  - Cost Management
  - Equipment, Machinery, Tools & Testing Devices
  - HVAC / HVAC-R
  - Landscaping & Groundskeeping
  - Project Management
  - Technical Skills
- ☐ Technical Skills

RESUME KEYWORD INSTRUCTIONS

INTRODUCTION

Resume Keywords are industry buzz words and phrases that prospective employers use to search resumes for the right candidates to fill their open positions. Keywords include core competencies *(your areas of expertise)*, position titles you've held, job-specific skills, soft skills *(personal attributes and capabilities)*, industry credentials *(licenses, certifications, degrees, training)*, and knowledge areas.

Resume Keywords are essential to include in your resume as most hiring managers use Applicant Tracking Software (ATS) to determine whether to "screen in" or "screen out" job candidates by scanning for keywords that match the position they wish to fill. They also search Internet job sites and LinkedIn profiles to find suitable candidates using these job-related keywords. If your resume does not contain important keywords relative to the position you seek, it may never be seen by human eyes. This Book contains the largest keywords resource available for your profession. The more applicable keywords you include in your resume, the higher your probability of being called in for interviews.

INSTRUCTIONS

Scroll through the category lists in this chapter and check off all core competencies you are proficient and/or knowledgeable in as they relate to your targeted position. Then to be sure you've left no stone unturned, search job boards for positions that interest you to ensure you have captured all keywords contained in those postings. In Step 3: Check Off Your Personal Attributes, you will determine your soft skills.

You will be including your primary keywords in your *"Professional Summary,"* your secondary keywords under *"Core Competencies,"* and remaining keywords within your employment bullets under *"Professional Experience."* You can also include a personally branded slogan containing some of your primary keywords under your resume header.

SAMPLE USE OF KEYWORDS IN YOUR RESUME

Following is an example of how resume keywords *(underlined)* can be infused within the various sections of your resume:

YOUR NAME

123 FIRST AVENUE, TOWN, ST 00000 | (000) 000-0000

Email: xxxx@xxxxxx.com | LinkedIn: linkedin.com/xxxxxx | Web Portfolio: YourName.com

Completing Quality Projects on Time and Within Budget…Every Time

PROFESSIONAL SUMMARY

A results-oriented, profitability-conscious Project Manager with more than 12 years of experience spanning all aspects of project management, trades coordination, labor relations management, and structural problem solving via action-driven leadership, direction, and support. Extensive background in managing major commercial construction projects including high-rise buildings, corporate offices, colleges and universities, public buildings, hospitals, and shopping malls. Adept at coordinating multiple subcontractors simultaneously and in developing tactical action plans that direct high-producing teams to overcome boundaries and successfully meet all challenges.

CORE COMPETENCIES

- Full Project Lifecycle Management
- Functional Specifications Development
- Project Time Tracking
- Quality Management
- Cost Estimate Preparation
- Proposals Review & Approval
- Client Presentations
- Scope Change Requests
- Budget Monitoring & Control
- Resource Allocation
- Customer Satisfaction
- Change Management

PROFESSIONAL EXPERIENCE

2012-Present: CONSTRUCTION PROJECT MANAGER | ABC Company | Town, ST

- Provide construction management leadership and direction in the design and build of commercial building projects ranging $1.5 to $5 million for this multimillion-dollar leading construction management firm with three locations.
- Effectively plan, manage, and lead commercial projects from inception through close-out, directing the activities of all trades to ensure projects are completed with high quality on time and within budget.
- Facilitate various project management functions including the review and/or modification of construction drawings, development of job estimates, securing competitive bids, handling contract negotiations, scheduling and coordinating trades, and processing change orders—to the customers' complete satisfaction.

...and so on

Let's get started selecting your Resume Keywords...

LIST YOUR RESUME KEYWORDS

INSTRUCTIONS

After you check off your applicable keywords in this section, come back to this page to list them, as follows:

- Your ***Primary Keywords*** are those functions you are most proficient in as they relate to your targeted field. They will be included within your *"Professional Summary"* section at the top of your resume (as described in ***Step 6: Pull Your Resume Together***) as well as in your Personally Branded Bio and LinkedIn Profile.
- Your ***Secondary Keywords*** are more "explanatory" as to what your primary keywords involve. These will be listed in your *"Core Competencies"* section of your resume.
- All ***Remaining Keywords*** should be infused within the bullets in your *"Professional Experience"* section where they are applicable to the functions you handled. These are already included in the bullets contained in ***Step 5: Select Your Resume ClipBullets***. *(See sample on preceding page.)*

Note: Less important keywords—such as those performed in lower-level positions—can be omitted unless, for example, hands-on performance of those skills are mentioned as "required" in the job descriptions you researched.

PRIMARY KEYWORDS

________	________	________	________
________	________	________	________
________	________	________	________
________	________	________	________
________	________	________	________
________	________	________	________

SECONDARY KEYWORDS

________	________	________	________
________	________	________	________
________	________	________	________
________	________	________	________
________	________	________	________
________	________	________	________
________	________	________	________

REMAINING KEYWORDS

________	________	________	________
________	________	________	________
________	________	________	________
________	________	________	________
________	________	________	________
________	________	________	________
________	________	________	________
________	________	________	________
________	________	________	________

SELECT RESUME KEYWORDS FOR YOUR PROFESSION

INSTRUCTIONS: *Place one "X" before all areas of expertise in which you are knowledgeable. Place "XX" before all areas in which you are highly proficient and they directly target your profession.*

Bidding Process

☐ BIDDING PROCESS

- ☐☐ Acquisition Methods
- ☐☐ Construction Methods Compliance
- ☐☐ Cost Estimating
- ☐☐ Price Change Evaluations
- ☐☐ Product Delivery Resolution
- ☐☐ Vendor Performance Monitoring
- ☐☐ Vendor Reliability Cost Analyses
- ☐☐ Bid Specification Preparation
- ☐☐ Construction Proposals
- ☐☐ Customer Satisfaction
- ☐☐ Pricing & Payment Terms
- ☐☐ Production Bids
- ☐☐ Solutions Development
- ☐☐ Weighted Value Procedures
- ☐☐ Awards Issuance
- ☐☐ Contract Negotiation
- ☐☐ Lifecycle Costing
- ☐☐ Materials Costing
- ☐☐ Proposal Evaluations
- ☐☐ Value Analysis
- ☐☐ Vendor Evaluations
- ☐☐ Construction Bids
- ☐☐ Contractor Selection
- ☐☐ Manufacturing Bids
- ☐☐ Product Requirements
- ☐☐ Purchasing Alternatives
- ☐☐ Vendor Bids
- ☐☐ Other: ______

Building Maintenance

*See also **"Facilities Management."***

☐ BUILDING MAINTENANCE

- ☐☐ Boiler & Chiller Inspections & Repair
- ☐☐ Carpentry/Construction Work
- ☐☐ Construction Oversight
- ☐☐ Cost Reductions & Savings
- ☐☐ Emergency Lighting System
- ☐☐ Executive Office Facilities
- ☐☐ Facility Surveys
- ☐☐ Generator Operations
- ☐☐ Inspections & Compliance
- ☐☐ Machinery Maintenance & Repair
- ☐☐ Office Relocations
- ☐☐ Painting
- ☐☐ Renovations
- ☐☐ Safety & Responsibility for Others
- ☐☐ Sprinkler System Installation / Repair
- ☐☐ Work Collaboration
- ☐☐ Building Maintenance & Repair
- ☐☐ Client Relations
- ☐☐ Continuous Office Space Planning
- ☐☐ Custodial Services
- ☐☐ Environmental, Health & Safety
- ☐☐ Facility Functioning
- ☐☐ Furniture & Equipment Purchasing
- ☐☐ Groundskeeping
- ☐☐ Inventory Control
- ☐☐ Messenger & Courier Services
- ☐☐ Office Renovation & Furnishing
- ☐☐ Plumbing
- ☐☐ Repairs
- ☐☐ Security Systems
- ☐☐ Telecommunications Systems
- ☐☐ Work Inspections
- ☐☐ Building Management
- ☐☐ Company Relocations
- ☐☐ Corporate Office Relocations
- ☐☐ Electrical Wiring
- ☐☐ Equipment Installation & Moves
- ☐☐ Facility Record Maintenance
- ☐☐ Floor Plans
- ☐☐ HVAC Operations
- ☐☐ Maintenance & Repair Reports
- ☐☐ Mailroom Operations
- ☐☐ OSHA Compliance
- ☐☐ Productivity Improvement
- ☐☐ Roofing Repairs
- ☐☐ Special Event Set-ups
- ☐☐ Warehousing
- ☐☐ Other: ______

☐ BUILDING MAINTENANCE SYSTEM TYPES

- ☐☐ Boilers (Gas / Electric / Open Flame)
- ☐☐ Commercial Plumbing Systems
- ☐☐ Energy Management Control System (EMCS)
- ☐☐ Energy Related Equipment & Control Systems
- ☐☐ Gas & Electric Heating Systems
- ☐☐ Heating, Cooling & Ventilation Systems
- ☐☐ Industrial Plumbing Systems
- ☐☐ Residential Plumbing Systems
- ☐☐ Water Systems
- ☐☐ Building Management Systems
- ☐☐ Distribution Systems & Controls
- ☐☐ Domestic Plumbing Systems
- ☐☐ Fire Sprinkler Systems
- ☐☐ HVAC Electric Systems
- ☐☐ In-Door Plumbing Systems
- ☐☐ Refrigeration Systems
- ☐☐ Split Systems
- ☐☐ Winterizing Systems
- ☐☐ Cooling Systems
- ☐☐ Drainage Systems
- ☐☐ Gas Systems
- ☐☐ Heating Systems
- ☐☐ HVAC Systems
- ☐☐ Piping Systems
- ☐☐ Plumbing Systems
- ☐☐ Sprinkler Systems
- ☐☐ Other: ______

Building Services

☐ BUILDING SERVICES ENGINEERING

- ☐☐ BREEAM (BRE Environmental Assessment Method)
- ☐☐ CIBSE Low Carbon Consultants (LCC) Status
- ☐☐ Construction Suitability Assessments
- ☐☐ Energy Management
- ☐☐ Building Sustainability
- ☐☐ Conservation Methods
- ☐☐ Energy Assessors (LCEA) Status
- ☐☐ Engineering Integration
- ☐☐ Carbon Emissions Reduction
- ☐☐ Cost Efficiency
- ☐☐ Energy Distribution
- ☐☐ Engineering Systems

- ☐☐ Environmental Impact Minimization
- ☐☐ Fire Detection & Protection
- ☐☐ Information Technology Networking
- ☐☐ Whole Lifecycle Costing Techniques
- ☐☐ Environmentally Friendly Operation
- ☐☐ Health & Safety Compliance
- ☐☐ Low Carbon Technologies
- ☐☐ Other: ______
- ☐☐ Environmentally Sustainable
- ☐☐ Lightning Protection
- ☐☐ Sustainable & Green Design

☐ BUILDING SERVICES SPECIALIZATIONS

- ☐☐ Construction
- ☐☐ Monitoring
- ☐☐ Design
- ☐☐ Operation
- ☐☐ Development
- ☐☐ Other: ______
- ☐☐ Implementation
- ☐☐ Maintenance

☐ BUILDING ENGINEERING SYSTEMS

- ☐☐ Air Filtration
- ☐☐ Distribution Boards
- ☐☐ Low Voltage (LV) Systems
- ☐☐ Refrigeration
- ☐☐ Water, Draining & Plumbing
- ☐☐ Alarm Systems
- ☐☐ Electrical
- ☐☐ Mechanical
- ☐☐ Renewable Energy
- ☐☐ Ventilation
- ☐☐ Building Facades
- ☐☐ Environmental
- ☐☐ Natural & Artificial Lighting
- ☐☐ Security
- ☐☐ Others: ______
- ☐☐ Communication Lines
- ☐☐ HVAC
- ☐☐ Plumbing
- ☐☐ Sustainable Energy

☐ BUILDING MAINTENANCE SYSTEM TYPES

- ☐☐ Boilers (Gas / Electric / Open Flame)
- ☐☐ Commercial Plumbing Systems
- ☐☐ Energy Management Control System (EMCS)
- ☐☐ Energy Related Equipment & Control Systems
- ☐☐ Gas & Electric Heating Systems
- ☐☐ Heating, Cooling & Ventilation Systems
- ☐☐ Industrial Plumbing Systems
- ☐☐ Residential Plumbing Systems
- ☐☐ Water Systems
- ☐☐ Building Management Systems
- ☐☐ Distribution Systems & Controls
- ☐☐ Domestic Plumbing Systems
- ☐☐ Fire Sprinkler Systems
- ☐☐ HVAC Electric Systems
- ☐☐ In-Door Plumbing Systems
- ☐☐ Refrigeration Systems
- ☐☐ Split Systems
- ☐☐ Winterizing Systems
- ☐☐ Cooling Systems
- ☐☐ Drainage Systems
- ☐☐ Gas Systems
- ☐☐ Heating Systems
- ☐☐ HVAC Systems
- ☐☐ Piping Systems
- ☐☐ Plumbing Systems
- ☐☐ Sprinkler Systems
- ☐☐ Other: ______

Business & Administrative Functions

This section is provided primarily for General Contractors.

☐ ADMINISTRATION & GENERAL BUSINESS

- ☐☐ Account Servicing
- ☐☐ Administrative Support
- ☐☐ Benefits Administration
- ☐☐ Bookkeeping
- ☐☐ Budget Development
- ☐☐ Business Plans
- ☐☐ Claims Avoidance Handling
- ☐☐ Client Interface
- ☐☐ Communications
- ☐☐ Contract Development & Review
- ☐☐ Contract Records & Reports
- ☐☐ Customer Handling
- ☐☐ Database Maintenance
- ☐☐ Deposits Preparation
- ☐☐ Document Preparation
- ☐☐ Emailing
- ☐☐ Expense Reporting
- ☐☐ Financial Data Research
- ☐☐ Goods Transfers
- ☐☐ Internet Research
- ☐☐ Job Assignments
- ☐☐ Legal Records Maintenance
- ☐☐ Maintenance Activities
- ☐☐ Materials Distribution
- ☐☐ Negotiations
- ☐☐ Office Services
- ☐☐ Operations Management
- ☐☐ Payroll Issues Resolution
- ☐☐ Administration
- ☐☐ Appointment Scheduling
- ☐☐ Bids Preparation
- ☐☐ Budget Administration
- ☐☐ Building / Lease Contracts
- ☐☐ Certificates of Insurance Monitoring
- ☐☐ Claims & Litigations Research
- ☐☐ Client Needs Assessment
- ☐☐ Compliance Oversight
- ☐☐ Contract Issue Resolution
- ☐☐ Correspondence Composition
- ☐☐ Customer Service
- ☐☐ Deliveries
- ☐☐ Dispute Resolution
- ☐☐ Document Processing
- ☐☐ Executive Assistance
- ☐☐ Facility Management
- ☐☐ Fulfillment
- ☐☐ Grant Applications Development
- ☐☐ Inventory Management & Control
- ☐☐ Job Cost Reporting
- ☐☐ Logistics Management
- ☐☐ Management Support
- ☐☐ Materials Scheduling
- ☐☐ Networking
- ☐☐ Office Space Planning
- ☐☐ Order Processing
- ☐☐ Pricing Strategies Development
- ☐☐ Administration Management
- ☐☐ Back-office Operations
- ☐☐ Billing
- ☐☐ Budget Database Updating
- ☐☐ Business Analysis
- ☐☐ Cash Receipts Recording
- ☐☐ Client Correspondence
- ☐☐ Client Relations
- ☐☐ Computer Troubleshooting
- ☐☐ Contract Negotiations
- ☐☐ Cost Reductions & Savings
- ☐☐ Data Entry
- ☐☐ Departmental Support
- ☐☐ Document Filing
- ☐☐ Document Scanning
- ☐☐ Expense Report Processing
- ☐☐ Faxing
- ☐☐ General Office Administration
- ☐☐ Interdisciplinary Team Meetings
- ☐☐ Invoicing
- ☐☐ Labor Relations
- ☐☐ Mail Processing
- ☐☐ Material Requisitioning
- ☐☐ Meeting Agenda
- ☐☐ Office Management
- ☐☐ Office Supplies Purchasing
- ☐☐ Payment Requisition Processing
- ☐☐ Printing

- ☐☐ Procedures Development
- ☐☐ Progress Update Reports
- ☐☐ Project Management Support
- ☐☐ Quality Assurance
- ☐☐ Records Management
- ☐☐ Risk Management
- ☐☐ Shipping & Receiving
- ☐☐ Subcontracts Monitoring
- ☐☐ Switchboard Operations
- ☐☐ Transportation
- ☐☐ Vendor Relations
- ☐☐ Work Flow Coordination
- ☐☐ Procurement
- ☐☐ Project Planning & Coordination
- ☐☐ Project Scheduling / Timelines
- ☐☐ Quality Control
- ☐☐ Report Generation
- ☐☐ Sales Progress Tracking
- ☐☐ Spreadsheets Preparation
- ☐☐ Supplies Reordering
- ☐☐ Time Cards Approval
- ☐☐ Travel Arrangements
- ☐☐ Word Processing
- ☐☐ Workflow Management
- ☐☐ Productivity Improvement
- ☐☐ Project Life Cycle
- ☐☐ Purchasing
- ☐☐ Recordkeeping
- ☐☐ Research & Analysis
- ☐☐ Security
- ☐☐ Stock Distribution
- ☐☐ Support Staff Training
- ☐☐ Trades Work Direction
- ☐☐ Vendor Communications
- ☐☐ Work Collaboration
- ☐☐ Other: ______

☐ ADMINISTRATIVE MANAGEMENT

- ☐☐ Accounting & Financial Recordkeeping
- ☐☐ Budget Development & Expenditure Control
- ☐☐ Contracts Administration
- ☐☐ Cost Reductions & Savings
- ☐☐ Employee Benefit Programs Administration
- ☐☐ Health & Safety Program Development
- ☐☐ Inventory Management & Control
- ☐☐ Permit Issuance Verification
- ☐☐ Productivity Improvement
- ☐☐ Presentation Preparation
- ☐☐ Staff Management
- ☐☐ Workflow Management
- ☐☐ Administrative Management
- ☐☐ Compensation Management
- ☐☐ Contract Negotiations
- ☐☐ Customer Service Management
- ☐☐ Dispute Resolution
- ☐☐ Human Resource Management
- ☐☐ Office Space Planning
- ☐☐ Policies & Procedures Development
- ☐☐ Purchasing Management
- ☐☐ Risk Management
- ☐☐ Staff Training
- ☐☐ Other: ______
- ☐☐ Change Management
- ☐☐ Contractor Bids Issuance
- ☐☐ Contract Issue Resolution
- ☐☐ Database Set-up & Management
- ☐☐ Facility Management
- ☐☐ Office Management
- ☐☐ Operations Management
- ☐☐ Personnel Management
- ☐☐ Records Management
- ☐☐ Sales Progress Tracking
- ☐☐ Time Cards Approval

☐ INVENTORY MANAGEMENT & CONTROL

- ☐☐ Access Control Installation
- ☐☐ Access Control Support
- ☐☐ Bookkeeping Assistance
- ☐☐ Collaborative Vendor Forecasting
- ☐☐ Control Inventory Management System
- ☐☐ Customer Access Control
- ☐☐ Digital Video
- ☐☐ Electronic Security Systems
- ☐☐ File Organizing & Maintenance
- ☐☐ Integrated Systems
- ☐☐ Inventory Accounting Tools Software
- ☐☐ Inventory Control Management
- ☐☐ Inventory Control Software
- ☐☐ Inventory Control Spreadsheet
- ☐☐ Inventory Management Software
- ☐☐ Office Practices & Procedures
- ☐☐ Personnel Accountability
- ☐☐ Policies, Procedures, Processes & Forms
- ☐☐ Production Planning Inventory Control
- ☐☐ Software License Transactions
- ☐☐ Spreadsheet & Database Tools
- ☐☐ Access Control Inventory
- ☐☐ Asset Protection
- ☐☐ Business Letter Writing
- ☐☐ Computer Networking
- ☐☐ Control Inventory Module Software
- ☐☐ Detailed Clerical Work Accurately
- ☐☐ Direct Importing
- ☐☐ Employee Safety
- ☐☐ Grammar & Punctuation
- ☐☐ Inventory Access Control
- ☐☐ Inventory Accuracy Software
- ☐☐ Inventory Control Processing
- ☐☐ Inventory Control System
- ☐☐ Inventory Shrinkage Reduction
- ☐☐ Inventory Tracking Software
- ☐☐ Online Stock Control
- ☐☐ Quality Control Access Inventory
- ☐☐ Recordkeeping
- ☐☐ Security & Asset Protection
- ☐☐ Spare Parts Inventory Control
- ☐☐ Statistical Process Control
- ☐☐ Access Control Maintenance
- ☐☐ Bill Paying
- ☐☐ Card Control Inventory
- ☐☐ Control Form Inventory
- ☐☐ Correct English Usage
- ☐☐ Customer Service
- ☐☐ Distribution Process
- ☐☐ Facilities
- ☐☐ Human Resources
- ☐☐ Inventory Accounting
- ☐☐ Inventory Control Point
- ☐☐ Invoice Process
- ☐☐ Loss Reduction
- ☐☐ Order Entry
- ☐☐ Operating Equipment
- ☐☐ Order Processing
- ☐☐ Quality Control
- ☐☐ Secure Asset Storage
- ☐☐ Stock Control
- ☐☐ Tool Control & Inventory
- ☐☐ Other: ______

☐ OFFICE SUPPORT

- ☐☐ Activity Coordination
- ☐☐ Assignment Oversight
- ☐☐ Budget Monitoring
- ☐☐ Conference Coordination
- ☐☐ Customer Complaint Handling
- ☐☐ Document Processing
- ☐☐ Event Coordination
- ☐☐ Financial Transactions
- ☐☐ Keyboarding
- ☐☐ Management Liaison
- ☐☐ Administrative Functions
- ☐☐ Billing
- ☐☐ Complex Tasks
- ☐☐ Confidential Matters
- ☐☐ Customer Service & Support
- ☐☐ Discretion Exercising
- ☐☐ Filing
- ☐☐ Greeting Visitors
- ☐☐ Legal Secretarial Support
- ☐☐ Medical Secretarial Support
- ☐☐ Appointment Scheduling
- ☐☐ Bookkeeping
- ☐☐ Complex Info. Interpretation
- ☐☐ Correspondence Writing
- ☐☐ Dictation & Transcription
- ☐☐ Email Generation
- ☐☐ Financial Record Keeping
- ☐☐ Independent Judgment
- ☐☐ Letter Composition
- ☐☐ Medical Terminology

☐☐ Memoranda
☐☐ Multiple Projects Handling
☐☐ Office Support
☐☐ Public Relations Contacts
☐☐ Report Preparation
☐☐ Screening Callers & Visitors
☐☐ Support Staff Supervision
☐☐ Meeting Scheduling
☐☐ Nonroutine Secretarial Functions
☐☐ Problem Resolution
☐☐ Record Keeping
☐☐ Research & Analysis
☐☐ Shorthand
☐☐ Telephone Answering
☐☐ Minutes of Meetings
☐☐ Office Management
☐☐ Procedure Development
☐☐ Report Generation
☐☐ Sales Contracts
☐☐ Spreadsheets
☐☐ Other: ______

☐ PURCHASING

☐☐ Acquisition Management
☐☐ Bidding
☐☐ Client Interface
☐☐ Competitive Bidding
☐☐ Delivery Scheduling
☐☐ Expediting
☐☐ Leasing
☐☐ Office Supplies
☐☐ Order Processing
☐☐ Production Materials
☐☐ Request for Proposal (RFP)
☐☐ Supplier Management
☐☐ Vendor Relations
☐☐ Warehouse Management
☐☐ Adjustments
☐☐ Blanket Orders
☐☐ Client & Vendor Records Maintenance
☐☐ Computer Equipment
☐☐ Contract Terms & Negotiations
☐☐ High Volume Processing
☐☐ Logistics Management
☐☐ Materials Replenishment Ordering
☐☐ Pricing Negotiations
☐☐ Promotional Items
☐☐ Request for Quotation (RFQ)
☐☐ Trade Shows
☐☐ Vendor Partnerships
☐☐ Other: ______
☐☐ Barter Arrangements
☐☐ Capital Equipment Acquisition
☐☐ Comparative Cost Analyses
☐☐ Contract Change Orders
☐☐ Distribution Management
☐☐ Inventory Control / Management
☐☐ Materials Management
☐☐ Office Machinery
☐☐ Procurement
☐☐ Purchase Orders
☐☐ Strong Follow-up
☐☐ Vendor Bids
☐☐ Warehousing

Carpentry

☐ CARPENTRY / CONSTRUCTION SPECIALIZATIONS

☐☐ Acoustical Ceilings
☐☐ Color Concrete Surfaces
☐☐ Ceilings / Lathing
☐☐ Concrete & Steel Reinforcement
☐☐ Concrete Beams & Forms
☐☐ Excavation & Fill Operations
☐☐ Exposed Aggregate Walls
☐☐ Floor-to-Floor Build-outs
☐☐ Irrigation Systems
☐☐ Maintenance & Repair Projects
☐☐ Masonry (Brick/Stone/Cement)
☐☐ Paving & Grading
☐☐ Reinforced Concrete Structures
☐☐ Roof-top Installations
☐☐ Sidewalks & Walkways
☐☐ Smoke Control Systems
☐☐ Steel & Concrete Construction
☐☐ Structural Insulated Wall Panels
☐☐ Waterproofing
☐☐ Alarms Systems
☐☐ Brattices
☐☐ Concrete Foundations
☐☐ Concrete Castings
☐☐ Ditches & Dredging
☐☐ Doors & Door Jambs
☐☐ Fire Sprinklers
☐☐ Foundations
☐☐ Hardware
☐☐ Materials Transport
☐☐ Painting
☐☐ Platforms
☐☐ Refractory Tile
☐☐ Security Systems
☐☐ Skylights
☐☐ Steel Reinforcement
☐☐ Taping & Spackling
☐☐ Weather Stripping
☐☐ Windows / Glazing
☐☐ Asbestos Abatement
☐☐ Cabinet Making
☐☐ Copper Flashings
☐☐ Demolition
☐☐ Drywall Installation
☐☐ Escalators
☐☐ Firebrick Linings
☐☐ Framing
☐☐ Insulation
☐☐ Metal Stud Framing
☐☐ Paneling
☐☐ Podiums
☐☐ Roofing
☐☐ Sheetrocking
☐☐ Soaking Pits
☐☐ Steps / Stairs
☐☐ Tiling
☐☐ Walls & Partitions
☐☐ Other: ______
☐☐ Blueprint Reading
☐☐ Carpeting
☐☐ Columns
☐☐ Decking
☐☐ Elevators
☐☐ Fences
☐☐ Flooring
☐☐ Gratings
☐☐ Landscaping
☐☐ Millwork
☐☐ Partitions
☐☐ Ramps
☐☐ Scaffolding
☐☐ Siding Installation
☐☐ Solar Panels
☐☐ Stone Walls
☐☐ Trim work
☐☐ Wall Coverings

☐ CARPENTRY & MASONRY MATERIALS

☐☐ Black Iron
☐☐ Cement Products
☐☐ Face Brick
☐☐ Hardy Shake
☐☐ Mortar
☐☐ Stucco
☐☐ Other: ______
☐☐ Brick
☐☐ Concrete
☐☐ Flashing
☐☐ Limestone
☐☐ Plywood
☐☐ Terrazzo
☐☐ Brick Veneer
☐☐ Concrete Pavers
☐☐ Glass
☐☐ Marble
☐☐ Sheetrock
☐☐ Tiles
☐☐ Cal Shake
☐☐ Copings
☐☐ Granite
☐☐ Metal Studs
☐☐ Stone
☐☐ Vinyl Siding
☐☐ Cedar Shake
☐☐ Drainage Supplies
☐☐ Grout
☐☐ Masonry Ties
☐☐ Structural Steel
☐☐ Wood Studs

Ceiling, Lathing, Insulation & Drywall Installation

☐ CEILING, LATHING, INSULATION & DRYWALL INSTALLATION

☐☐ Acoustical Tiles Mounting
☐☐ Decorative Trim Installation
☐☐ Drywall Installation
☐☐ Energy Consumption Reductions
☐☐ Installation Methods
☐☐ Joint Sealing
☐☐ Masonry Inspections
☐☐ Metal Frame Support Welding
☐☐ Plaster, Drywall, Paneling Removal
☐☐ Sealing Compound
☐☐ Tile Installation
☐☐ Wire-Tie Lathing
☐☐ Ceiling Framing
☐☐ Dry Lines Hanging
☐☐ Drywall Mounting
☐☐ Furring Inspections
☐☐ Installation Preparation
☐☐ Lathing Installation
☐☐ Materials Determination
☐☐ One-Person Drywall Ceiling Installations
☐☐ Productivity Improvement
☐☐ Shock-Absorbing Materials
☐☐ Wall Framing
☐☐ Work Coordination
☐☐ Ceiling Installation
☐☐ Drywall & Plaster Applications
☐☐ Drywall Mounting
☐☐ Furring Strips Installation
☐☐ Insulation Installation
☐☐ Man Hour Time Reductions
☐☐ Metal Casings Installation
☐☐ Partition Framing
☐☐ Safety Guidelines
☐☐ Surface Measurement & Marking
☐☐ Wallboard Fitting & Fastening
☐☐ Other: ______

☐ INSULATION TYPES

☐☐ Cellulose
☐☐ Fiberglass
☐☐ Foam
☐☐ Rock Wool Batt
☐☐ Other: ______

☐ PROJECTS

☐☐ Attics
☐☐ Ceiling Joists
☐☐ Paneling
☐☐ Tanks
☐☐ Boilers
☐☐ Ceiling Partitions
☐☐ Plaster Walls
☐☐ Vats
☐☐ Buildings
☐☐ Ceilings
☐☐ Steam & Hot Water Pipes
☐☐ Other: ______
☐☐ Ceiling Concrete Surfaces
☐☐ Exterior Walls
☐☐ Storage Rooms

Construction

☐ CONSTRUCTION – GENERAL

☐☐ Administrative Management
☐☐ Budget Development & Expense Control
☐☐ Building & Safety Codes Enforcement
☐☐ Business Conduct Policies & Practices
☐☐ Construction Management Staff Supervision
☐☐ Construction Leadership & Oversight
☐☐ Construction Submittals Approval
☐☐ Contracts Development & Review
☐☐ Corporate Governance Systems Management
☐☐ Design Guidelines Development
☐☐ Employment Policies & Procedures Oversight
☐☐ Environmental Services Management
☐☐ Financial Recordkeeping Oversight
☐☐ Geospatial Information Services Oversight
☐☐ Long-range Goals Establishment
☐☐ Municipal Permit Attainment
☐☐ New Business Development Initiatives
☐☐ New Division / Department Start-up
☐☐ Performance Recognition Leadership
☐☐ Materials Procurement Oversight
☐☐ Policies & Procedures Development
☐☐ Project Lifecycle Oversight
☐☐ Project Planning & Coordination
☐☐ Project Resource Requirements
☐☐ Project Management Practices
☐☐ Resource Acquisition Direction
☐☐ Senior-level Construction Planning
☐☐ Specifications Standards Development
☐☐ Asset Utilization Management
☐☐ Bidding Process Oversight
☐☐ Capital Improvement Projects
☐☐ Business Goals & Priorities Setting
☐☐ Claims Negotiation & Settlement
☐☐ Client Meeting & Strategizing
☐☐ Client Presentations & Proposals
☐☐ Client Relationship Building
☐☐ Construction Risk Mitigation
☐☐ Cost Reductions & Savings
☐☐ Distribution Support
☐☐ Engineer Management
☐☐ Field Supervision Oversight
☐☐ Increased Sales & Profitability
☐☐ Inspections & Compliance
☐☐ Job Bidding Oversight
☐☐ Key Customer Management
☐☐ Operating Plans Execution
☐☐ Profit & Loss Accountability
☐☐ Project Prioritization
☐☐ Project Development & Initiation
☐☐ Procurement Management
☐☐ Project Lifecycle Management
☐☐ Proposed Land Developments
☐☐ Regulatory Inspections
☐☐ Regulatory & Legal Standards
☐☐ Safety & Health Promotion
☐☐ Safety Program Execution
☐☐ Approval Management
☐☐ Closeout Processing
☐☐ Construction Inspections
☐☐ Construction Timetables
☐☐ Corporate Affairs
☐☐ Contract Negotiations
☐☐ Cost Control
☐☐ Cost Estimating
☐☐ Cost Management
☐☐ Employee Retention
☐☐ Estimating Oversight
☐☐ Ethics & Compliance
☐☐ Field Quality Assurance
☐☐ Financial Management
☐☐ Increased Account Base
☐☐ Management Recruitment
☐☐ New Business Start-up
☐☐ Productivity Improvement
☐☐ Operations Management
☐☐ Organization Strategy
☐☐ Project Team Leadership
☐☐ Report Monitoring
☐☐ Research Management
☐☐ Property Management
☐☐ Property Purchases
☐☐ Proposal Presentations
☐☐ Quality Assurance
☐☐ Risk Assessment

☐☐ Team Leadership & Direction
☐☐ Strategy Execution
☐☐ Site Analysis
☐☐ Other: ______
☐☐ Strategic Planning

☐ RESIDENTIAL PROJECTS

☐☐ Apartment Buildings
☐☐ Extensions
☐☐ Finished Basements
☐☐ Room Additions
☐☐ Other: ______
☐☐ Condominiums
☐☐ Interior Design
☐☐ Home Construction
☐☐ Patios & Decks
☐☐ Custom-built Baths
☐☐ High-Rise Buildings
☐☐ Home Improvements
☐☐ Room Remodeling
☐☐ Custom-built Kitchens
☐☐ Finished Attics
☐☐ Landscape Design
☐☐ Playgrounds

☐ COMMERCIAL PROJECTS

☐☐ Building Complexes
☐☐ Clean Rooms
☐☐ Corporate Offices
☐☐ Financial Institutions
☐☐ Industrial Parks
☐☐ Landmark Restorations
☐☐ Office Space Planning
☐☐ Renovations
☐☐ Shopping Malls
☐☐ Building Lobbies
☐☐ Commercial Buildings
☐☐ Drive-Up Units
☐☐ Government Agencies
☐☐ Interior Design
☐☐ Landscape Design
☐☐ Private Buildings
☐☐ Restaurants
☐☐ Stores
☐☐ Churches & Temples
☐☐ Communities
☐☐ Elevators
☐☐ Healthcare Facilities
☐☐ Interior Renovation
☐☐ Manufacturing Plants
☐☐ Public Buildings
☐☐ Restorations
☐☐ Universities
☐☐ College Campuses
☐☐ Corporate Buildings
☐☐ Escalators
☐☐ Hotels / Resorts
☐☐ Laboratories
☐☐ New Construction
☐☐ Public / Private Schools
☐☐ Retail Stores
☐☐ Other: ______

☐ PUBLIC WORKS PROJECTS

☐☐ Aerospace / Aeronautical
☐☐ Atmospheric Sciences
☐☐ Buildings
☐☐ Construction
☐☐ Earthquake
☐☐ Energy Management Systems
☐☐ Environmentally-friendly Systems
☐☐ Ground Water Systems
☐☐ High-Voltage Underground Cables
☐☐ Manufacturing Plants
☐☐ Metering Systems
☐☐ Monorails
☐☐ Pedestrian Safety Management System
☐☐ Power Generation Systems
☐☐ Railroads
☐☐ Pressure Reducing Chambers
☐☐ Sewage Treatment Facilities
☐☐ Stand-by Power Generation
☐☐ Storage & Delivery Systems
☐☐ Storm Water Treatment Facilities
☐☐ Sub-Soil Investigation & Earthing Systems
☐☐ Water Resource Management Systems
☐☐ Water Storage Tanks & Delivery Systems
☐☐ Agricultural Systems
☐☐ Bicycle Paths
☐☐ Canals
☐☐ Dams
☐☐ Embankments
☐☐ Flood Control projects
☐☐ Government Buildings
☐☐ Highway Maintenance
☐☐ Highways & Roadways
☐☐ Materials Management
☐☐ Metros
☐☐ Municipal Projects
☐☐ Parking Facilities
☐☐ Power Plants
☐☐ Retaining Walls
☐☐ River Basin Systems
☐☐ Surveying
☐☐ Transit Systems
☐☐ Transportation Systems
☐☐ Water Distribution Systems
☐☐ Surface & Ground Water Systems
☐☐ Water Quality Systems
☐☐ Water Transmission & Distribution Mains
☐☐ Airport Runways
☐☐ Biomechanics
☐☐ Coastal & Ocean
☐☐ Disposal Systems
☐☐ Environmental
☐☐ Geodesy
☐☐ Geotechnical
☐☐ High-Speed Trains
☐☐ Irrigation Systems
☐☐ Maritime Facilities
☐☐ Military
☐☐ Municipal Pumps
☐☐ Pipelines
☐☐ Public Buildings
☐☐ Rights-of-Way
☐☐ Sewage Systems
☐☐ Tolling
☐☐ Tunnels
☐☐ Urban Centers
☐☐ Water Main Crossings
☐☐ Water Pumping Stations
☐☐ Water Supply Systems
☐☐ Other: ______
☐☐ Airport Terminals
☐☐ Bridges
☐☐ Complexes
☐☐ Earth Science
☐☐ Forensic
☐☐ Geophysics
☐☐ Harbors
☐☐ Light Rails
☐☐ Marinas & Docks
☐☐ Materials Science
☐☐ Mining
☐☐ Museums
☐☐ Ports
☐☐ Public Utilities
☐☐ Structural
☐☐ Traffic Control
☐☐ Water Systems
☐☐ Wells

Contracts & Negotiations

☐ CONTRACTUAL PROCESS

☐☐ Contract Administration
☐☐ Contract Closeout Processing
☐☐ Contract Development
☐☐ Contract Editing
☐☐ Contract Interpretation
☐☐ Contract Language
☐☐ Contract Modifications
☐☐ Contract Regulations
☐☐ Contract Set-Up
☐☐ Contract Writing
☐☐ Contract Analysis
☐☐ Contract Practices & Procedures
☐☐ Contract Documentation
☐☐ Contract Execution
☐☐ Contract Issues Response
☐☐ Contract Law
☐☐ Contract Negotiations
☐☐ Contract Review Process
☐☐ Contract Templates
☐☐ Document Review & Redlining
☐☐ Contract Approval
☐☐ Contract Consistency
☐☐ Contract Drafting
☐☐ Contract Guidelines
☐☐ Contract Key Element Extraction
☐☐ Contract Management
☐☐ Contract Performance Monitoring
☐☐ Contract Revisions
☐☐ Contract Terms & Conditions
☐☐ Financial Aspects of Contracts

☐☐ Other: ______

☐ CONTRACT & LEGAL DOCUMENT TYPES

☐☐ Agreements
☐☐ Bids
☐☐ Briefings
☐☐ Client Agreements
☐☐ Contractual Documents
☐☐ Grant Requests
☐☐ Legal Correspondence
☐☐ License Agreements
☐☐ Plans
☐☐ Proposals
☐☐ Software Agreements
☐☐ Side Letters Preparation
☐☐ Specifications
☐☐ Subcontractor Agreements
☐☐ Technology Services
☐☐ Amendments
☐☐ Bidding Process, Formal
☐☐ Business Initiatives Support
☐☐ Clinical Trial Agreements
☐☐ Estimates
☐☐ Integrated Requirements Documents
☐☐ Legal Documents
☐☐ Maintenance Services
☐☐ Nondisclosure Agreements (NDAs)
☐☐ Requests for Comment (RFC)
☐☐ Risk Mitigation & Management
☐☐ Requests for Proposal (RFP)
☐☐ Subcontract Agreements
☐☐ Teaming Agreements
☐☐ Warrantees
☐☐ Best Practices
☐☐ Bidding Review Procedures
☐☐ Client Estimates
☐☐ Consulting Services
☐☐ Government Contracts
☐☐ Guarantees
☐☐ Legal Standards
☐☐ Memoranda of Understanding
☐☐ Price Negotiation Memoranda
☐☐ Requests for Information (RFI)
☐☐ Service Agreements
☐☐ Source Selection Reports
☐☐ Subcontracting Procedures
☐☐ Technical Documents
☐☐ Other: ______

☐ CONTRACTS ADMINISTRATION

☐☐ Architectural Principles
☐☐ Client Interface
☐☐ Data Entry
☐☐ Bids Preparation
☐☐ Facility Service Contracts
☐☐ Leasing Options
☐☐ Monitoring Contract Status
☐☐ Proposal Terms Preparation
☐☐ Real Estate Leases
☐☐ Updating Budget Databases
☐☐ Pricing Strategy Development
☐☐ Contractor Claims & Litigation Research
☐☐ Claims Avoidance
☐☐ Dispute Resolution Methods
☐☐ Fire & Life Safety Codes
☐☐ License Agreements & Amendments
☐☐ Negotiating Contracts
☐☐ State & Local Building Codes
☐☐ Uniform Building Code
☐☐ Risk Mitigation Strategies
☐☐ Contractor Claims & Litigations
☐☐ Construction Requirements
☐☐ Design & Construction Law
☐☐ Electrical & Plumbing Codes
☐☐ Identifying Risks
☐☐ Legal Obligations Records
☐☐ Payment Vouchers Processing
☐☐ Rental Payment Amounts
☐☐ Terms & Conditions Interpretation
☐☐ Other: ______

☐ CONTRACT AREAS OF EXPERTISE

☐☐ Acquisition Documentation
☐☐ Acquisition Process Automated Tools
☐☐ Approved Acquisition Strategies Development
☐☐ Approved Acquisition Strategies Execution
☐☐ Cost Accounting Principals
☐☐ Cost Accounting Standards (CAS)
☐☐ Cost Proposal Preparation & Coordination
☐☐ Evaluation Criteria Development
☐☐ Federal Acquisition Regulations (FAR)
☐☐ Network Real Estate Principles & Practices
☐☐ Post-Award Contract Management
☐☐ Pre-Award Contract Management
☐☐ Service Contract Administration
☐☐ Source Selection Plans Development
☐☐ Subcontract Administration
☐☐ Other: ______
☐☐ Award Fee Plans Development
☐☐ Business Writing
☐☐ Clinical Development
☐☐ Commercial Contracting
☐☐ Cost Components & Factors
☐☐ Cost Proposal Oversight
☐☐ CSA Contracts Structure
☐☐ Facility Contract Management
☐☐ Legal Correspondence Drafting
☐☐ Paralegal Certification
☐☐ Pre-Solicitation Documentation
☐☐ Quality Criteria Adherence
☐☐ Security Clearance
☐☐ Service Contract Management
☐☐ Terms & Conditions Negotiation
☐☐ Accounting Principles
☐☐ Claims Avoidance
☐☐ Clinical Trials
☐☐ Cost/Price Analysis
☐☐ Customer Interface
☐☐ Data Entry
☐☐ Fixed Price Contracts
☐☐ Government Contracting
☐☐ Negotiations & Mediation
☐☐ Partner Management
☐☐ Proposal Preparation
☐☐ Risk Mitigation
☐☐ Software Licensing
☐☐ Task Order Closeouts
☐☐ Subcontractor Proposal Evaluation

☐ CONTRACT COMPLIANCE / QUALITY CONTROL

☐☐ Accounting Principles
☐☐ Claims Litigation
☐☐ Contractual Issues
☐☐ Data Security
☐☐ Issue Identification
☐☐ Pricing Strategies
☐☐ Proposal Evaluations
☐☐ Federal Acquisition Regulations (FAR)
☐☐ FAR & DFAR, Agency FAR Supplements
☐☐ Best Practices Compliance
☐☐ Contract Management
☐☐ Corporate Policies
☐☐ Departmental Practices
☐☐ Past Performance Factors
☐☐ Proactive Quality Monitoring
☐☐ Proposals Development
☐☐ Risk Mitigation
☐☐ Government Contracts Administration
☐☐ Change Control
☐☐ Contractual Appropriations
☐☐ Cost Evaluations
☐☐ Federal Contracting Law
☐☐ Preproposal Conferences
☐☐ Project Scope & Requirements
☐☐ Regulations Compliance
☐☐ Service Contract Act (SCA)
☐☐ Other: ______

☐ TYPE OF CONTRACTS & LEGAL DOCUMENTS

- ☐☐ Agreements
- ☐☐ Bids
- ☐☐ Briefings
- ☐☐ Client Agreements
- ☐☐ Contractual Documents
- ☐☐ Grant Requests
- ☐☐ Legal Correspondence
- ☐☐ License Agreements
- ☐☐ Plans
- ☐☐ Proposals
- ☐☐ Software Agreements
- ☐☐ Side Letters Preparation
- ☐☐ Specifications
- ☐☐ Subcontractor Agreements
- ☐☐ Technology Services
- ☐☐ Amendments
- ☐☐ Bidding Process, Formal
- ☐☐ Business Initiatives Support
- ☐☐ Clinical Trial Agreements
- ☐☐ Estimates
- ☐☐ Integrated Requirements Documents
- ☐☐ Legal Documents
- ☐☐ Maintenance Services
- ☐☐ Nondisclosure Agreements (NDAs)
- ☐☐ Requests for Comment (RFC)
- ☐☐ Risk Mitigation & Management
- ☐☐ Requests for Proposal (RFP)
- ☐☐ Subcontract Agreements
- ☐☐ Teaming Agreements
- ☐☐ Warrantees
- ☐☐ Best Practices
- ☐☐ Bidding Review Procedures
- ☐☐ Client Estimates
- ☐☐ Consulting Services
- ☐☐ Government Contracts
- ☐☐ Guarantees
- ☐☐ Legal Standards
- ☐☐ Memoranda of Understanding
- ☐☐ Price Negotiation Memoranda
- ☐☐ Requests for Information (RFI)
- ☐☐ Service Agreements
- ☐☐ Source Selection Reports
- ☐☐ Subcontracting Procedures
- ☐☐ Technical Documents
- ☐☐ Other: ______

Cost Management

☐ COST MANAGEMENT

- ☐☐ Alternative Design Solutions
- ☐☐ Bills of Quantities & Materials
- ☐☐ Change Management
- ☐☐ Commercial Returns Analysis
- ☐☐ Cost Estimate System Development
- ☐☐ Cost Forecasting & Reporting
- ☐☐ Cost-to-Complete Reports
- ☐☐ Financing Arrangements
- ☐☐ Invoice Validation
- ☐☐ Mediation & Arbitration Costs
- ☐☐ Profit Improvement Activities
- ☐☐ Project Budget Requirements
- ☐☐ Project Cost Estimations
- ☐☐ Project Execution Cost Management
- ☐☐ Project Viability Determination
- ☐☐ Requests for Proposals (RFPs)
- ☐☐ Risk Analysis
- ☐☐ Other: ______
- ☐☐ Analytical Costing Studies
- ☐☐ Budget Development
- ☐☐ Change Management Processes
- ☐☐ Corrective Actions
- ☐☐ Cost Estimates
- ☐☐ Cost Management Processes
- ☐☐ Expenditure Control
- ☐☐ Functional Cost Analysis
- ☐☐ Market Analysis
- ☐☐ Procurement Management
- ☐☐ Profitability Analysis
- ☐☐ Project Change Management System
- ☐☐ Project Earned Value Analyses
- ☐☐ Project Management Costs
- ☐☐ Property Condition Reports
- ☐☐ Reserve Fund Studies
- ☐☐ Tentative Budget Establishment
- ☐☐ Bid Analysis Preparation
- ☐☐ Change Impact Estimations
- ☐☐ Closeout Administration
- ☐☐ Cost Control Estimates
- ☐☐ Cost Estimates
- ☐☐ Cost Reporting
- ☐☐ Feasibility Studies
- ☐☐ Insurance Replacement Cost Assessments
- ☐☐ Material Costs
- ☐☐ Procurement Services
- ☐☐ Project Budget Establishment
- ☐☐ Project Controls System Establishment
- ☐☐ Project Economic Viability
- ☐☐ Project Outcome Predictions
- ☐☐ Reimbursable Cost Determination
- ☐☐ Revenue Forecasts
- ☐☐ Value Engineering

Electrical

*See also **"Electrical Engineering."***

☐ ELECTRICIAN, GENERAL

- ☐☐ Atmospheric Dynamics
- ☐☐ Electrical Contract Specifications
- ☐☐ Electrical Controls Diagnoses & Repair
- ☐☐ Electrical Maintenance & Repair
- ☐☐ Electrical Testing & Inspections
- ☐☐ Emergency Customer Callbacks
- ☐☐ Engineering Proposals
- ☐☐ Estimating Job Costs
- ☐☐ Industrial Motor Control Centers
- ☐☐ Installation Process Oversight
- ☐☐ Inventory Management & Control
- ☐☐ Material Lists Compilation
- ☐☐ Parts Specifications
- ☐☐ Preventive & Seasonal Maintenance
- ☐☐ Programmable Logic Controllers
- ☐☐ Contractor Bid Selections
- ☐☐ Electrical Construction Practices
- ☐☐ Electrical Formula Computations
- ☐☐ Electrical Parts Ordering
- ☐☐ Electrical Tools & Equipment Usage
- ☐☐ Electrician Job Preparation
- ☐☐ Equipment Adaptation
- ☐☐ First Aid & CPR
- ☐☐ Inspections & Compliance
- ☐☐ Inventory Control Programs
- ☐☐ Maintenance Staff Assistance
- ☐☐ Operating Efficiency
- ☐☐ Physical Principles & Laws
- ☐☐ Process Control Application
- ☐☐ Scheduling Electrical Work
- ☐☐ Cost Estimates Preparation
- ☐☐ Defect Isolation
- ☐☐ Electrical Installations
- ☐☐ Electrical Principles
- ☐☐ Electrician Training
- ☐☐ Engineering Data
- ☐☐ Equipment Improvements
- ☐☐ Flaw Detection & Repair
- ☐☐ Instrumentation Theory
- ☐☐ Measuring Instruments
- ☐☐ Operating Cost Reduction
- ☐☐ Parts & Materials Ordering
- ☐☐ Project Time Tracking
- ☐☐ Purchasing Requests
- ☐☐ Record Keeping

- ☐☐ Safety & Responsibility for Others
- ☐☐ Seasonal Maintenance & Repair Work
- ☐☐ Telemetry Theory & Application
- ☐☐ Trades Coordination & Oversight
- ☐☐ Work Orders Preparation
- ☐☐ Seasonal Overhauls
- ☐☐ Sewer Rooters
- ☐☐ Technical Devices
- ☐☐ Tools & Testing Devices
- ☐☐ Other: ______
- ☐☐ Seasonal Transitions
- ☐☐ Shop Drawings
- ☐☐ Technology Design
- ☐☐ Work Collaboration

☐ ELECTRICAL PROJECTS

- ☐☐ Electrical Systems
- ☐☐ Electronic Facilities
- ☐☐ Cable Systems
- ☐☐ Cargo Systems
- ☐☐ Electromagnetic Systems
- ☐☐ Electronic Products
- ☐☐ Voltage Transformers
- ☐☐ Power Systems
- ☐☐ Electronic Systems
- ☐☐ Exterior Lighting
- ☐☐ Proximity Systems
- ☐☐ Other: ______
- ☐☐ Electronic Equipment
- ☐☐ Interior Lighting
- ☐☐ Fuel Systems

☐ ELECTRICAL FUNCTIONS

- ☐☐ Adjusting
- ☐☐ Calibrating
- ☐☐ Disconnects
- ☐☐ Fabrication
- ☐☐ Lubricating
- ☐☐ Preventive Maintenance
- ☐☐ Replacement
- ☐☐ Testing
- ☐☐ Specialized Electrical Work
- ☐☐ Air Balancing
- ☐☐ Climate Control
- ☐☐ Electrical Wiring
- ☐☐ Fine-Tuning
- ☐☐ Machinery Testing
- ☐☐ Regulating
- ☐☐ Rewiring
- ☐☐ Time Scheduling
- ☐☐ Other: ______
- ☐☐ Alteration
- ☐☐ Cost Estimating
- ☐☐ Equipment Testing
- ☐☐ Inspections
- ☐☐ Maintenance
- ☐☐ Remodeling
- ☐☐ Temperature Balancing
- ☐☐ Troubleshooting
- ☐☐ Cable Splicing
- ☐☐ Diagnosis
- ☐☐ Estimating
- ☐☐ Installation
- ☐☐ Overhauling
- ☐☐ Repair
- ☐☐ Servicing
- ☐☐ Winterizing

☐ ELECTRICIAN MANAGEMENT

*Refer to **"General Contracting."***

☐ ELECTRICAL SYSTEMS

- ☐☐ Bus Bar Systems
- ☐☐ Computer Systems
- ☐☐ Electrical Communications Systems
- ☐☐ Energy Management Systems
- ☐☐ High-Tension Distribution Systems
- ☐☐ Industrial Systems
- ☐☐ Low-Voltage Electrical Systems
- ☐☐ Public Address Systems
- ☐☐ Signaling Systems
- ☐☐ Other: ______
- ☐☐ Climate Control Systems
- ☐☐ Conduit Systems
- ☐☐ Electrical Systems
- ☐☐ Fiber Optic Electrical Systems
- ☐☐ High-Voltage Electrical Systems
- ☐☐ Intercom Systems
- ☐☐ Motor Control Systems
- ☐☐ Refrigeration Systems
- ☐☐ Telephone Systems
- ☐☐ Communications Systems
- ☐☐ Digital Systems
- ☐☐ Electronic Systems
- ☐☐ Fire Alarm Systems
- ☐☐ Heating Systems
- ☐☐ Lighting Systems
- ☐☐ Pneumatic Tube Systems
- ☐☐ Security Systems
- ☐☐ Video Systems

☐ ELECTRICAL WORK / EQUIPMENT & COMPONENT TYPES

- ☐☐ AC & DC Motors
- ☐☐ Above-ground Conductors
- ☐☐ Conductors
- ☐☐ Data Communications Devices
- ☐☐ Double-phase Electric Cables
- ☐☐ Electrical Accessories
- ☐☐ Electrical Equipment
- ☐☐ Electrical Instruments
- ☐☐ Electrical Switches
- ☐☐ Generator Equipment
- ☐☐ High-voltage Electrical Work
- ☐☐ Inside Electrical Services
- ☐☐ Lighting Fixtures
- ☐☐ Low-voltage Electrical Work
- ☐☐ Motor Controllers
- ☐☐ Overhead Lines
- ☐☐ Power Lines & Poles
- ☐☐ Programmable Controllers
- ☐☐ Secondary Service Laterals
- ☐☐ Transmission Equipment
- ☐☐ Underground Cable Locators
- ☐☐ Air Compressors
- ☐☐ Above-ground Conduit
- ☐☐ Cables
- ☐☐ Conduits
- ☐☐ DC Speed Control
- ☐☐ Electronic Controllers
- ☐☐ Electrical Components
- ☐☐ Electrical Motors
- ☐☐ Electronic Controls
- ☐☐ Generators
- ☐☐ Heating Units
- ☐☐ Outside Conductors
- ☐☐ Junction Boxes
- ☐☐ Plumbing Components
- ☐☐ Motor Controls
- ☐☐ Phase Electric Cables
- ☐☐ Primary Power Lines
- ☐☐ Receptacles
- ☐☐ Switchboards
- ☐☐ Underground Conduit
- ☐☐ Outside Electrical Services
- ☐☐ Air Conditioning Units
- ☐☐ Circuit Breakers
- ☐☐ Circuit Breakers
- ☐☐ Connectors
- ☐☐ Electric Lines
- ☐☐ Electrical Fuses
- ☐☐ Electrical Controls
- ☐☐ Electrical Panels
- ☐☐ Electronic Controllers
- ☐☐ Fiber-optic
- ☐☐ Inside Conductors
- ☐☐ Outside Conduit
- ☐☐ Mechanical Equipment
- ☐☐ Primary Power Lines
- ☐☐ Motors
- ☐☐ Plumbing Equipment
- ☐☐ Pull Boxes
- ☐☐ Street Lights
- ☐☐ Terminations
- ☐☐ Transformers
- ☐☐ Specialized Electrical Work
- ☐☐ Bus Bar
- ☐☐ Control Wiring
- ☐☐ Coax Cables
- ☐☐ Conveyors
- ☐☐ Electrical Apparatus
- ☐☐ Fire Alarms
- ☐☐ Electrical Fixtures
- ☐☐ Electrical Starters
- ☐☐ Elevators
- ☐☐ Fuses
- ☐☐ Inside Conduit
- ☐☐ Overhead Lines
- ☐☐ Microprocessors
- ☐☐ Power Circuits
- ☐☐ Outlet Boxes
- ☐☐ Power Circuits
- ☐☐ Pumps
- ☐☐ Switches
- ☐☐ Traffic Signals
- ☐☐ Water Heaters
- ☐☐ Water Pumps

☐☐ Single-phase Electric Cables
☐☐ Triple-phase Electric Cables
☐☐ Secondary Service Laterals
☐☐ Telecommunications Wiring/Cable
☐☐ Underground Conductors
☐☐ Underground Electrical Services
☐☐ Other: ______

☐ ELECTRICAL COMPLIANCE TESTING & QUALITY CONTROL

☐☐ Assembly & Installation Inspections
☐☐ Building Codes Compliance
☐☐ Company Policies

☐☐ Compliance Monitoring
☐☐ Customer Specifications
☐☐ Electrical Codes Compliance
☐☐ Electrical Installation Tracking
☐☐ Electrical Standards & Practices
☐☐ Life-Safety Codes Compliance
☐☐ National Electric Code Compliance
☐☐ Proper Operation Testing
☐☐ Specifications Conformance
☐☐ Underground Faults Location
☐☐ Component Safety
☐☐ Defect Detection
☐☐ Electrical Compatibility
☐☐ Environmental Regulations
☐☐ Handicap Accessibility
☐☐ Occupational Hazards Avoidance
☐☐ On-Site Field Inspections
☐☐ Quality Compliance
☐☐ Safety Precautions
☐☐ Worksite Inspections
☐☐ Contract Compliance
☐☐ Emergency Procedures
☐☐ Faulty Wires Detection
☐☐ Facilities Inspection
☐☐ Maintenance Logs Upkeep
☐☐ Loose Connections Repair
☐☐ OSHA Compliance
☐☐ Quality Control Standards
☐☐ Safety Regulations
☐☐ Other: ______

☐ ELECTRICIAN TOOLS & EQUIPMENT USAGE

*Refer to **"Equipment, Machinery, Tools & Testing Devices."***

Environmental Compliance

☐ ENVIRONMENTAL COMPLIANCE REGULATIONS

☐☐ Abandoned Mine Lands (AML)
☐☐ Continuous Emission Monitoring System (CEMS)
☐☐ CERCLA Hazardous Substances Sec. 101(14)
☐☐ Chemical Compliance
☐☐ Clean Water Act (CWA)
☐☐ Contract Laboratory Program (CLP)
☐☐ Contract Required Quantitation Limit (CRQL)
☐☐ Designated for Drinking Water Use [Sec. 305(a)
☐☐ Emergency Planning and Community Right-to-Know Act
☐☐ Environmental Protection Agency (EPA)
☐☐ Federal Insecticide, Fungicide & Rodenticide Act
☐☐ Hazard Ranking System Guidance Manual (HRSGM)
☐☐ Maximum Contaminant Level (MCL)
☐☐ Method Detection Limit (MDL)
☐☐ National Ambient Air Quality Standard (NAAQS)
☐☐ National Environmental Policy Act (NEPA)
☐☐ National Institute for Occupational Safety & Health (NIOSH)
☐☐ National Pollution Discharge Elimination System (NPDES)
☐☐ Oil Pollution Act (OPA)
☐☐ OSHA Hazard Communication Standard
☐☐ RC14001 Implementation
☐☐ Reciprocating Internal Combustion Engine (RICE)
☐☐ Resource Conservation & Recovery Act (RCRA)
☐☐ Safe Drinking Water Act (SDWA)
☐☐ Superfund Accelerated Cleanup Model (SACM)
☐☐ Superfund Chemical Data Matrix (SCDM)
☐☐ Title V
☐☐ Wastewater Compliance
☐☐ Ambient Aquatic Life Advisory Concentration (AALAC)
☐☐ CERCLA Environmental Data Management
☐☐ CERCLA Pollutant or Contaminant Sec. 101(33)
☐☐ Clean Air Act (CAA)
☐☐ Code of Federal Regulations (CFR)
☐☐ Contract Required Detection Limit (CRDL)
☐☐ EDM Operations & Process of the Clean Water Act
☐☐ Environmental Management System (EMS)
☐☐ Environmental Protection Act (EPA)
☐☐ Environmental Site Assessments (ESAs)
☐☐ Hazardous Air Pollutants (HAP)
☐☐ Maximum Achievable Control Technology (MACT)
☐☐ Maximum Contaminant Level Goal (MCLG)
☐☐ National Contingency Plan (NCP)
☐☐ National Emission Standards for Hazardous Air Pollutants (NESHAP)
☐☐ National Security Personnel System (NSPS)
☐☐ National Pollutant Discharge Elimination System (NPDES)
☐☐ Occupational Safety & Health Act (OSHA)
☐☐ OSHA Air Quality Regulations
☐☐ Pollution Prevention Act (PPA)
☐☐ RCRA Permitting
☐☐ Remedial Investigation Work Plan (RIWP)
☐☐ Resource Conservation & Recovery Act (RCRA)
☐☐ SARA Title III - Community Right to Know
☐☐ Superfund Amendments & Reauthorization Act
☐☐ Title 27 Permitting
☐☐ Toxic Substances Control Act (TSCA)
☐☐ Other: ______
☐☐ Comprehensive Environmental Response, Compensation & Liability Act (CERCLA)

☐ ENVIRONMENTAL COMPLIANCE – GENERAL

☐☐ Air Emissions
☐☐ Chemical, Biological, & Radiological Hazards
☐☐ Cost Effective Remediation Methods
☐☐ Environmental Assessments
☐☐ Environmental Cost Estimating
☐☐ Air Pollution
☐☐ Compliance Permitting
☐☐ Emission Inventory
☐☐ Environmental Engineering
☐☐ Environmental Field Work
☐☐ Compliance Issues
☐☐ Compliance Systems
☐☐ Engineering Analysis
☐☐ Environmental Audits
☐☐ EPA Performance

☐☐ Environmental Field Investigations
☐☐ Environmental Investigations
☐☐ Equipment Changes

- ☐☐ Environmental Modeling
- ☐☐ Environmental Regulations
- ☐☐ Federal & State Environmental Laws
- ☐☐ Federal Facilities Environmental Compliance
- ☐☐ Indoor And Outdoor Air & Water Systems
- ☐☐ Phase II Investigations
- ☐☐ Process Safety Management
- ☐☐ Remediation Services
- ☐☐ Scenario Development & Evaluation
- ☐☐ Soil & Groundwater Sampling
- ☐☐ Tank Removal & Installation
- ☐☐ Watershed Analysis
- ☐☐ Environmental Principles
- ☐☐ Environmental Report Writing
- ☐☐ OSHA Monitoring
- ☐☐ Legal Due Process System
- ☐☐ OSHA HAZWOPER Training
- ☐☐ Plant Site Compliance
- ☐☐ Project Installations
- ☐☐ Remediation Systems
- ☐☐ Risk Management Plans
- ☐☐ Soil & Water Cleanup
- ☐☐ Toxic Industrial Chemicals
- ☐☐ Wetland Restoration
- ☐☐ Environmental Sciences
- ☐☐ New Regulations
- ☐☐ Permit Obtainment
- ☐☐ Permit Applications
- ☐☐ Phase I Assessments
- ☐☐ Pollution Monitoring
- ☐☐ Regulatory Reports
- ☐☐ Risk Assessments
- ☐☐ Site Assessments
- ☐☐ Waste Disposal
- ☐☐ Waste Management
- ☐☐ Other: ______

☐ ENVIRONMENTAL PROTECTION OFFICES

- ☐☐ Nuclear Regulatory Commission (NRC)
- ☐☐ Office of Air Quality (OARM)
- ☐☐ Office of Environmental Justice (OEJ)
- ☐☐ Office of Regulatory Enforcement (ORE)
- ☐☐ Other: ______
- ☐☐ Office of Administration & Resource Management (OARM)
- ☐☐ Office of Compliance (OC)
- ☐☐ Office of General Counsel (OGC)
- ☐☐ Office of Solid Waste & Emergency Response (OSWER)

Equipment, Machinery, Tools & Testing Devices

See also "Heavy Equipment Operations."

☐ CARPENTRY & CONSTRUCTION TOOLS

- ☐☐ Atlas Machines
- ☐☐ Carpet Knives & Shears
- ☐☐ Grinders
- ☐☐ Loop Pile Cutters
- ☐☐ Mechanical Soil Compactors
- ☐☐ Mattocks
- ☐☐ Power Stretchers
- ☐☐ Sanding Machines
- ☐☐ Sledge Hammers
- ☐☐ Torches
- ☐☐ Axes
- ☐☐ Chainsaws
- ☐☐ Hammers
- ☐☐ Heliarc
- ☐☐ Machine Saws
- ☐☐ Picks
- ☐☐ Power Tools
- ☐☐ Saws
- ☐☐ Stages
- ☐☐ Trowels
- ☐☐ Brush Hooks
- ☐☐ Drill Presses
- ☐☐ Hand Shovels
- ☐☐ Knee Kickers
- ☐☐ Mallets
- ☐☐ Post Hole Diggers
- ☐☐ Power Wet Saws
- ☐☐ Screw Guns
- ☐☐ Staple Guns
- ☐☐ Wall Trimmers
- ☐☐ Bush Axes
- ☐☐ Drills
- ☐☐ Heat Irons
- ☐☐ Lathes
- ☐☐ Manifolds
- ☐☐ Power Ladders
- ☐☐ Rakes
- ☐☐ Sheathing Guns
- ☐☐ Testing Devices
- ☐☐ Other: ______

☐ CEILING, LATHING, INSULATION & DRYWALL TOOLS & EQUIPMENT

- ☐☐ Brushes
- ☐☐ Pliers
- ☐☐ T-Braces
- ☐☐ Compressor Hoses
- ☐☐ Power Saws
- ☐☐ Trowels
- ☐☐ Insulation Compressors
- ☐☐ Saws
- ☐☐ Welding Machines
- ☐☐ Knives
- ☐☐ Stapling Guns
- ☐☐ Other: ______

☐ ELECTRICIAN EQUIPMENT, TOOLS & TESTING DEVICES

- ☐☐ Ampmeters
- ☐☐ Cable Locating Meters
- ☐☐ Digger Derricks
- ☐☐ Equipment Threading
- ☐☐ Hacksaws
- ☐☐ Hydraulic Pipe Benders
- ☐☐ Measuring Devices
- ☐☐ Pickup Trucks
- ☐☐ Portable Generators
- ☐☐ Skill Saws
- ☐☐ Volt-Ohm Meters
- ☐☐ Bead Blasters
- ☐☐ Cement Cutters
- ☐☐ Drill Presses
- ☐☐ Fault Locators
- ☐☐ Hand & Power Tools
- ☐☐ Jackhammers
- ☐☐ Megger Meters
- ☐☐ Pipe Cutters
- ☐☐ Propane Torches
- ☐☐ Test Lamps
- ☐☐ Welding Equipment
- ☐☐ Boom Trucks
- ☐☐ Conduit Bending
- ☐☐ Drills
- ☐☐ Forklifts
- ☐☐ Hoists
- ☐☐ Knockout Punches
- ☐☐ Ohmmeters
- ☐☐ Pipe Threaders
- ☐☐ PVC Benders
- ☐☐ Testing Instruments
- ☐☐ Wire & Cable Winches
- ☐☐ Bucket Trucks
- ☐☐ Cutting Torches
- ☐☐ Electric Drills
- ☐☐ Grinders
- ☐☐ Hydraulic Boom Lifts
- ☐☐ Lift Trucks
- ☐☐ Oscilloscopes
- ☐☐ Portable Compressors
- ☐☐ Sand Blasters
- ☐☐ Voltmeters
- ☐☐ Other: ______

☐ GLAZIER EQUIPMENT

- ☐☐ Beveling Machines
- ☐☐ Grinders
- ☐☐ Suction Cups
- ☐☐ Drills
- ☐☐ Polishing Machines
- ☐☐ Other: ______
- ☐☐ Glass Cutters
- ☐☐ Power Saws
- ☐☐ Glazing Knives
- ☐☐ Sanding Machines

☐ HVAC EQUIPMENT, TOOLS & TESTING DEVICES

☐☐ Acetylene Torches	☐☐ Backhoes	☐☐ Electric Drills	☐☐ Forklifts
☐☐ Hand Tools	☐☐ Manometers	☐☐ Measurement Gauges	☐☐ Metal Snips
☐☐ Pipe Benders	☐☐ Pipe Cutters	☐☐ Power Tools	☐☐ Pressure Gauges
☐☐ Propane Torches	☐☐ Sewer Rooters	☐☐ Thermometers	☐☐ Trenchers
☐☐ Voltmeters	☐☐ Welding Equipment	☐☐ Other: ______	

☐ LANDSCAPING & MASONRY EQUIPMENT & MACHINERY

☐☐ Backhoes / Loaders	☐☐ Boom Trucks	☐☐ Bulldozers	☐☐ Cement Mixers
☐☐ Cement Trucks	☐☐ Compressors	☐☐ Cranes	☐☐ Crawlers
☐☐ Dozers	☐☐ Dump Bodies	☐☐ Force-feed Loaders	☐☐ Forklifts
☐☐ Front Loaders	☐☐ Gear-cutting Machines	☐☐ Graders	☐☐ Heavy Dump Trucks
☐☐ Hoists	☐☐ Hook Lift Hoists	☐☐ Hook Lifts	☐☐ Hydraulic Excavators
☐☐ Mowers	☐☐ Municipal Dump Bodies	☐☐ Orange Peelers	☐☐ Paving Equipment
☐☐ Payloaders	☐☐ Pick-up Trucks	☐☐ Piggy-back Forklifts	☐☐ Platforms
☐☐ Plow Trucks	☐☐ Rand paving Equipment	☐☐ Rear Loaders	☐☐ Road Milling Machines
☐☐ Roadrangers	☐☐ Roll-offs	☐☐ Roof Mowers	☐☐ Sewer Jets
☐☐ Side Loaders	☐☐ Snow Plows	☐☐ Spreaders	☐☐ Steam Rollers
☐☐ Street Sweepers	☐☐ Sweepers	☐☐ Tiger Mowers	☐☐ Tractors
☐☐ Trenchers	☐☐ Truck Loaders	☐☐ Truck-mounted Lifts	☐☐ Other: ______

☐ LANDSCAPING & MASONRY TOOLS

☐☐ Axes	☐☐ Chain Saws	☐☐ Clippers	☐☐ Electric Clippers
☐☐ Handsaws	☐☐ Hedge Trimmers	☐☐ Power Pruners	☐☐ Power Tools
☐☐ Pruning Hooks	☐☐ Pruning Saws	☐☐ Rakes	☐☐ Saws
☐☐ Shears	☐☐ Shovels	☐☐ Snow Blowers	☐☐ Sod Cutters
☐☐ Other: ______			

☐ PLUMBING TOOLS & EQUIPMENT

☐☐ Acetylene Torches	☐☐ Backhoes	☐☐ Carbon Dioxide Testers	☐☐ Electric Drills
☐☐ Equipment Maintenance	☐☐ Equipment Safety	☐☐ Equipment Use	☐☐ Forklifts
☐☐ Hand & Power Tools	☐☐ Hand & Power Tools	☐☐ Measurement Gauges	☐☐ Metal Snips
☐☐ Oxygen Testers	☐☐ Pipe Benders	☐☐ Plumbing Machinery	☐☐ Pipe Cutters
☐☐ Propane Torches	☐☐ Sewer Rooters	☐☐ Trenchers	☐☐ Welding Equipment
☐☐ Other: ______			

☐ WELDING / STEAMFITTING MACHINERY, TOOLS & TESTING DEVICES

☐☐ Acetylene Torches	☐☐ Atlas Machines	☐☐ CNC Machines	☐☐ Drill Presses
☐☐ Carbon Dioxide Testers	☐☐ Gear Cutting Machines	☐☐ Electric Drills	☐☐ Hand & Power Tools
☐☐ Centrifugal Chiller Machines	☐☐ Measurement Gauges	☐☐ Metal Snips	☐☐ Micrometers
☐☐ Metal Forming Equipment	☐☐ Milling Machines	☐☐ Oxygen Testers	☐☐ Pipe Benders
☐☐ Metal-removing Machines	☐☐ Pipe Cutters	☐☐ Propane Torches	☐☐ Protractors
☐☐ Steam Absorption Machines	☐☐ Vernier Calipers	☐☐ Welding Devices	☐☐ Other: ______

General Contracting / Trades Management

☐ GENERAL CONTRACTING MANAGEMENT

☐☐ Accident Reports Preparation	☐☐ Accounts Payable & Receivable	☐☐ Advertising Campaigns
☐☐ Accounting & Financial Recordkeeping	☐☐ Administrative Management	☐☐ Bid Development
☐☐ Architectural Planning & Design	☐☐ Asbestos Removal / Abatement	☐☐ Bid Specifications
☐☐ Blueprint Reading & Interpreting	☐☐ Bidding Process	☐☐ Business Analysis
☐☐ Blueprint Review &/or Modification	☐☐ Business Development	☐☐ Business Start-up
☐☐ Budget Development & Expense Control	☐☐ Building Maintenance & Repair	☐☐ Cash Control
☐☐ Capital Improvements & Expansions	☐☐ Building Operations Management	☐☐ Client Invoicing
☐☐ Carpentry / Construction Projects Oversight	☐☐ Client Meeting & Strategizing	☐☐ Client Relations
☐☐ Change Order Negotiation & Processing	☐☐ Client Needs Assessment	☐☐ Closeout Processing
☐☐ Computer Hardware & Software	☐☐ Client Presentations & Proposals	☐☐ Competitive Analysis

- ☐☐ Construction Leadership & Direction
- ☐☐ Construction Oversight & Supervision
- ☐☐ Construction Project Management
- ☐☐ Contracts Development & Review
- ☐☐ Cost Estimate Preparation
- ☐☐ Cost Reductions & Savings
- ☐☐ Customer Service & Problem Resolution
- ☐☐ Database Set-up & Management
- ☐☐ Employee Benefit Programs Administration
- ☐☐ Environment & Safety Health Management Compliance
- ☐☐ Estimating Material & Labor Costs
- ☐☐ Field Labor & Subcontractor Supervision
- ☐☐ General Contractor Office Management
- ☐☐ Increased Sales & Profitability
- ☐☐ Interdisciplinary/Project Team Member
- ☐☐ Machinery & Equipment Maintenance
- ☐☐ Maintenance & Repair Projects
- ☐☐ New Business Development
- ☐☐ On-site Construction Supervision
- ☐☐ Operations Management
- ☐☐ Performance Recognition Leadership
- ☐☐ Preventive & Seasonal Maintenance
- ☐☐ Project Coordination with Contractors
- ☐☐ Project Lifecycle Management
- ☐☐ Project Resources & Staffing Requirements
- ☐☐ Profit & Loss Responsibility
- ☐☐ Project Planning & Coordination
- ☐☐ Punch List Preparation & Completion
- ☐☐ Quality Control Programs Development
- ☐☐ Safety & Responsibility for Others
- ☐☐ Safety Practices Compliance
- ☐☐ Staff Collaboration & Team Influence
- ☐☐ Strategic Planning & Direction
- ☐☐ Subcontractor Influence & Collaboration
- ☐☐ Subcontractor Negotiations
- ☐☐ Team Building & Development
- ☐☐ Team Leadership & Direction
- ☐☐ Trades Coordination & Oversight
- ☐☐ Work Area Inspections
- ☐☐ Workers' Compensation Program Administration
- ☐☐ Workflow Planning & Coordination
- ☐☐ Compensation Management
- ☐☐ Computer Layout & Design
- ☐☐ Contract Negotiations
- ☐☐ Contracts & Leases
- ☐☐ Cost Management
- ☐☐ Crew Assignments
- ☐☐ Customer Service Management
- ☐☐ Design-and-Build Projects
- ☐☐ Dispute Mediation & Resolution
- ☐☐ Estimating Timeframes
- ☐☐ Facilities Management
- ☐☐ Floor-to-Floor Build-outs
- ☐☐ Hiring & Coordinating Trades
- ☐☐ Human Resource Management
- ☐☐ Inspections & Compliance
- ☐☐ Inventory Management & Control
- ☐☐ Job Bidding
- ☐☐ Job Site Preparation
- ☐☐ New Business Start-up
- ☐☐ Labor Supervision
- ☐☐ Long-range Planning
- ☐☐ Materials Purchasing
- ☐☐ Office Management
- ☐☐ Payroll Processing
- ☐☐ Post Construction Services
- ☐☐ Productivity Improvement
- ☐☐ Project Development
- ☐☐ Project Management
- ☐☐ Project Time Tracking
- ☐☐ Purchasing
- ☐☐ Quality Control
- ☐☐ Research & Analysis
- ☐☐ Scheduling & Coordinating Trades
- ☐☐ Space Planning
- ☐☐ Staff Training & Development
- ☐☐ Subcontractor Project Coordination
- ☐☐ Supply Requests Monitoring
- ☐☐ Technical Construction Assistance
- ☐☐ Training & Development
- ☐☐ Trend Forecasting
- ☐☐ Work Collaboration
- ☐☐ Work Scheduling
- ☐☐ Competitive Bids
- ☐☐ Construction Drawings
- ☐☐ Contracting Costs
- ☐☐ Cost Analyses
- ☐☐ Cost Factoring
- ☐☐ Crew Supervision
- ☐☐ Customer Satisfaction
- ☐☐ Design Conceptualization
- ☐☐ Employee Retention
- ☐☐ Expense Control
- ☐☐ Final Cost Estimates
- ☐☐ Forecasting Costs
- ☐☐ Increased Account Base
- ☐☐ Inspecting Work Areas
- ☐☐ Insurance Costs
- ☐☐ Invoicing / Client Billing
- ☐☐ Job Estimating
- ☐☐ Job Preparation
- ☐☐ Job Scheduling
- ☐☐ Land & Building Surveys
- ☐☐ Low Staff Turnover
- ☐☐ Media Analysis
- ☐☐ Overhead Costs
- ☐☐ Permits Obtainment
- ☐☐ Procedure Development
- ☐☐ Project Initiation
- ☐☐ Project Estimating
- ☐☐ Project Prioritization
- ☐☐ Project Time Tracking
- ☐☐ Quality Assurance
- ☐☐ Recordkeeping
- ☐☐ Sales Forecasting
- ☐☐ Site Locating
- ☐☐ Staff Recruitment
- ☐☐ Staff Supervision
- ☐☐ Strategizing Client Needs
- ☐☐ Tools & Equipment Usage
- ☐☐ Trades Scheduling
- ☐☐ Trades Supervision
- ☐☐ Welding/Steamfitting
- ☐☐ Work Order Completion
- ☐☐ Other: ______

Glazier Projects & Functions

☐ GLAZIER PROJECTS

- ☐☐ Aluminum Curtain Walls
- ☐☐ Blast Resistant Windows
- ☐☐ Display Cases
- ☐☐ Glass Panels
- ☐☐ Mounting Sashes
- ☐☐ Skylights
- ☐☐ Tempered Glass
- ☐☐ Other: ______
- ☐☐ Aluminum Storefronts
- ☐☐ Commercial Projects
- ☐☐ Entrance Enclosures
- ☐☐ Glass Railing Systems
- ☐☐ Residential Projects
- ☐☐ Storefronts
- ☐☐ Unique Designs
- ☐☐ Automotive Projects
- ☐☐ Decorative Finishes
- ☐☐ Glass Doors
- ☐☐ Metal Framework Extrusions
- ☐☐ Security Windows
- ☐☐ Sun Rooms
- ☐☐ Windows
- ☐☐ Backsplashes
- ☐☐ Decorative Room Dividers
- ☐☐ Glass Insulations
- ☐☐ Mirrors
- ☐☐ Shower Enclosures
- ☐☐ Table Tops
- ☐☐ Windshields

☐ GLAZIER – GENERAL

- ☐☐ Benchmark Setting
- ☐☐ Calculation Measurement
- ☐☐ Contract Review & Approval
- ☐☐ Equipment Costing
- ☐☐ Bid Proposal Preparation
- ☐☐ Change Order Processing
- ☐☐ Contractual Obligations
- ☐☐ Equipment Requirements Estimating
- ☐☐ Blueprints Reading & Interpreting
- ☐☐ Closeout Processing
- ☐☐ Customer Satisfaction
- ☐☐ Frames Installation

☐☐ Industry Standards
☐☐ Manufacturer's Installation Instructions
☐☐ Materials Lead Time Planning
☐☐ Photographing Progress & Results
☐☐ Project Cost Estimating
☐☐ Project Scheduling
☐☐ Project Status Reports
☐☐ Quality Work Standards
☐☐ Safety Program Compliance
☐☐ Work Monitoring & Inspections
☐☐ Invoice Approval
☐☐ Material Deliveries Scheduling
☐☐ Materials Ordering & Scheduling
☐☐ Precision-Cutting Methods
☐☐ Project Drawings Review & Verification
☐☐ Project Scope & Requirements
☐☐ Purchase Orders Issuance
☐☐ Records Management
☐☐ Scope Changes
☐☐ Work Scheduling
☐☐ Labor Coordination
☐☐ Material Quotes
☐☐ Negotiating Vendor Pricing
☐☐ Progress Records
☐☐ Project Management
☐☐ Project Specifications
☐☐ Quality Installations
☐☐ Risks & Liabilities Determination
☐☐ Specifications Interpretation
☐☐ Other: ______

Heavy Equipment Operations

*See also "**Equipment, Machinery, Tools & Testing Devices.**"*

☐ HEAVY EQUIPMENT – GENERAL

☐☐ Airport Runways Lighting
☐☐ Athletic Field Lighting
☐☐ Brush & Tree Stumps Clearing
☐☐ Concrete Pouring & Paving
☐☐ Data Verification
☐☐ Distribution Powerlines
☐☐ Energy Conducting
☐☐ Equipment Maintenance & Repair
☐☐ Equipment Safety
☐☐ Excavating, Backfilling & Grading
☐☐ High-voltage Transmission Systems
☐☐ Land Reclamation
☐☐ Materials Handling
☐☐ Mobile Equipment
☐☐ Personnel Resource Management
☐☐ Quarrying
☐☐ Road-building
☐☐ Soil Compacting
☐☐ Systems Operation & Control
☐☐ Underground Services Locating
☐☐ Weight Handling
☐☐ Asphalt Batching & Paving
☐☐ Blueprint Reading & Understanding
☐☐ Building Construction
☐☐ Concrete Spreading & Leveling
☐☐ Demolishing & Rebuilding
☐☐ Driveway Construction
☐☐ Equipment Cleaning & Lubricating
☐☐ Equipment Operation & Control
☐☐ Equipment Selection
☐☐ Foundation Pouring & Leveling
☐☐ Highway & Roadway Construction
☐☐ Low-Voltage Lighting Systems
☐☐ Materials Loading & Moving
☐☐ Outdoor Areas
☐☐ Piers Construction
☐☐ Records Maintenance
☐☐ Safety Protocols
☐☐ Stationary Equipment
☐☐ Taxiways Lighting
☐☐ Water Wells
☐☐ Other: ______
☐☐ Asphalt Spreading & Leveling
☐☐ Bridge Construction
☐☐ Concrete Batch Plant Operations
☐☐ Data Compilation
☐☐ Demolition
☐☐ Earth Moving
☐☐ Equipment Inspections
☐☐ Equipment Operation Monitoring
☐☐ Equipment Troubleshooting
☐☐ Curves & Shoulders Grading
☐☐ Information Compiling
☐☐ Map Reading
☐☐ Mechanized Equipment & Devices
☐☐ Parking Lots
☐☐ Preoperational Equipment Checks
☐☐ Retaining Walls
☐☐ Sand, Rock & Gravel Removal
☐☐ Structures Erecting
☐☐ Traffic Signal Systems
☐☐ Waterways Excavation

☐ HEAVY EQUIPMENT OPERATIONS

☐☐ 10-wheelers
☐☐ A-frame Mowers
☐☐ Backup Trucks
☐☐ Bush Hogs
☐☐ Compressors
☐☐ Crawlers
☐☐ Distributors
☐☐ Excavators
☐☐ Gradalls
☐☐ Hook Lifts
☐☐ Hydraulic Cranes
☐☐ Landfill Heavy Equipment
☐☐ Loading Machines
☐☐ Multiterrain Loaders
☐☐ Paving Equipment
☐☐ Pile-Drivers
☐☐ Pneumatic Asphalt Tampers
☐☐ Roadmilling Machines
☐☐ Scrubbing Machines
☐☐ Sewer Jets
☐☐ Single-blade Plows
☐☐ Snow Plows
☐☐ 18-Ton Hydraulic Crane
☐☐ Airport Sweepers
☐☐ Belly Dumpers
☐☐ Catch Basin Cleaners
☐☐ Concrete Equipment
☐☐ Crysteel Dump Bodies
☐☐ Draglines
☐☐ Forcefeed Loaders
☐☐ Graders
☐☐ Hooklift Hoists
☐☐ Hydraulic Excavators
☐☐ Lane Closure Trucks
☐☐ Low Boys
☐☐ Municipal Dump Bodies
☐☐ Payloaders
☐☐ Pilot Cars
☐☐ Post Pounders
☐☐ Roadrangers
☐☐ Seeders
☐☐ Side Boom Tractors
☐☐ Skid Steer Loaders
☐☐ Sprayers
☐☐ 18-wheel Semi-trucks
☐☐ Asphalt Paving Equipment
☐☐ Boom Trucks
☐☐ Cement Mixers
☐☐ Crane Riggers
☐☐ Directional Bores
☐☐ Dredgers
☐☐ Forklifts
☐☐ Heavy Dump Trucks
☐☐ Horizontal Directional Drills
☐☐ Hydraulic Truck Cranes
☐☐ Large Rollers
☐☐ Mechanical Sweepers
☐☐ Orange Peelers
☐☐ Pick-up Trucks
☐☐ Platforms
☐☐ Rear Loaders
☐☐ Roll-offs
☐☐ Semi-truck Trailers
☐☐ Side Loaders
☐☐ Skid Steer Machines
☐☐ Spreaders
☐☐ 6-wheelers
☐☐ Backhoes
☐☐ Bulldozers
☐☐ Churn Drills
☐☐ Cranes
☐☐ Directional Drills
☐☐ Dump Truck Backhoes
☐☐ Front-end Loaders
☐☐ Hoists
☐☐ Hydraulic Boom Trucks
☐☐ Land Drilling Rigs
☐☐ Loaders
☐☐ Motorgraders
☐☐ Patch Rollers
☐☐ Piggyback Forklifts
☐☐ Plow Trucks
☐☐ Road Watering Equipment
☐☐ Roof and Tiger Mowers
☐☐ Sewer Cleaners
☐☐ Single Axle Dump Trucks
☐☐ Skip Loaders
☐☐ Steam Rollers

- ☐☐ Street Sweepers
- ☐☐ Tamping Equipment
- ☐☐ Tractor Mowers
- ☐☐ Vertical Drills
- ☐☐ Wing Plows
- ☐☐ Stump Grinders
- ☐☐ Tandem Axle Dump Trucks
- ☐☐ Tractors
- ☐☐ Viking Plows
- ☐☐ Others: ______
- ☐☐ Surfacing Equipment
- ☐☐ Tankers
- ☐☐ Trenchers
- ☐☐ Water Trucks
- ☐☐ Sweepers
- ☐☐ Track Hoes
- ☐☐ Truck Loaders
- ☐☐ Wideners

HVAC / HVAC-R

☐ HVAC LICENSES & CERTIFICATIONS

- ☐☐ HVAC-related Journeyman's License
- ☐☐ Other: ______
- ☐☐ ICBO HVAC Inspector Certification
- ☐☐ HVAC Certificate

☐ HVAC / HVAC-R *(Heating, Ventilation, Air Conditioning, Refrigeration)*

- ☐☐ Air Balancing
- ☐☐ Air Quality Testing
- ☐☐ Air Quality Control
- ☐☐ Boiler, Pump & Valve Maintenance
- ☐☐ Central Air Conditioning Systems
- ☐☐ Compressors / Compressor Overhauls
- ☐☐ Digital HVAC Systems
- ☐☐ Energy Management Equipment
- ☐☐ Filter & Duct Replacements
- ☐☐ Freon / Refrigerant Charging
- ☐☐ Generator Testing & Maintenance
- ☐☐ Heating Seasonal Performance Factor (HSPF)
- ☐☐ High Pressure Steam Boilers
- ☐☐ HVAC Installation
- ☐☐ HVAC Fans, Piping, Gauges & Indicator Lights
- ☐☐ HVAC Maintenance & Repair Work
- ☐☐ Microprocessor Fan Control
- ☐☐ Pneumatic Piping Systems
- ☐☐ Preventive & Seasonal Maintenance
- ☐☐ Preventive Maintenance Program Development
- ☐☐ Production & Injection Systems
- ☐☐ Seasonal Energy Efficiency Ratio (SEER)
- ☐☐ Solid Fuel Heating Systems
- ☐☐ Supplies & Equipment Ordering
- ☐☐ Temperature & Humidity Control
- ☐☐ Water Softener Adjustments
- ☐☐ Chlorofluorocarbon & Hydrochlorofluorocarbon Refrigerant Control
- ☐☐ Electrical Wiring of Furnaces, Unit Heaters & Cooling Units
- ☐☐ HVAC / HVAC-R & Plumbing Tools & Equipment Usage
- ☐☐ Air Conditioning Systems
- ☐☐ Air Distribution Systems
- ☐☐ Air Quality Testing
- ☐☐ Attic Duct Work
- ☐☐ Compliance with Regulations
- ☐☐ Customer Service & Support
- ☐☐ Duct Work & Cleaning
- ☐☐ Electric Burners
- ☐☐ Firing & Fuel Ratio Controls
- ☐☐ Fuel System Components
- ☐☐ Gas Burners
- ☐☐ Heat Exchangers
- ☐☐ HVAC System Balancing
- ☐☐ Improved Energy Efficiency
- ☐☐ Installation, Service & Repair
- ☐☐ HVAC Monitoring & Testing
- ☐☐ New HVAC System Designing
- ☐☐ Oil Burners
- ☐☐ Pipe Calibration
- ☐☐ Refrigerant Lines & Air Ducts
- ☐☐ Sand Traps
- ☐☐ Service & Maintenance Contracts
- ☐☐ Sump & Chemical Pumps
- ☐☐ Switches & Light Fixtures
- ☐☐ Water Treatment Testing
- ☐☐ Water Tower Treatment
- ☐☐ Air Conditioning Servicing
- ☐☐ Air Handlers
- ☐☐ Airborne Contaminants
- ☐☐ Climate Control
- ☐☐ Coil & Condenser Cleaning
- ☐☐ Condensing Units
- ☐☐ Duct Flow Readings
- ☐☐ Evaporators
- ☐☐ Fuel & Water Supply Lines
- ☐☐ Furnaces
- ☐☐ Geothermal Pumps
- ☐☐ Heating Systems
- ☐☐ Hot Water Heaters
- ☐☐ HVAC Testing
- ☐☐ HVAC Installations
- ☐☐ Metal & Fiberglass Ducts
- ☐☐ Natural Gas Piping
- ☐☐ Outlet Box Installations
- ☐☐ Refrigerant Systems
- ☐☐ Roof-top Installations
- ☐☐ Solar Panels
- ☐☐ Split Systems
- ☐☐ Testing Devices
- ☐☐ Thermostat Inspections
- ☐☐ Water Loops
- ☐☐ Ventilation
- ☐☐ Inspections & Compliance
- ☐☐ Project Time Tracking
- ☐☐ Other: ______

☐ HVAC / HVAC-R SYSTEM TYPES

- ☐☐ Air Conditioning Systems
- ☐☐ Commercial Plumbing Systems
- ☐☐ Energy Management Control System (EMCS)
- ☐☐ Energy Related Equipment & Control Systems
- ☐☐ Heating, Cooling & Ventilation Systems
- ☐☐ Industrial Plumbing Systems
- ☐☐ Refrigeration Systems
- ☐☐ Residential Plumbing Systems
- ☐☐ Ventilation Systems
- ☐☐ Other: ______
- ☐☐ Building Management Systems
- ☐☐ Distribution Systems & Controls
- ☐☐ Domestic Plumbing Systems
- ☐☐ Gas & Electric Heating Systems
- ☐☐ HVAC Electric Systems
- ☐☐ In-Door Plumbing Systems
- ☐☐ Piping Systems
- ☐☐ Split Systems
- ☐☐ Water Systems
- ☐☐ Cooling Systems
- ☐☐ Drainage Systems
- ☐☐ Fire Sprinkler Systems
- ☐☐ Gas Systems
- ☐☐ Heating Systems
- ☐☐ HVAC Systems
- ☐☐ Plumbing Systems
- ☐☐ Sprinkler Systems
- ☐☐ Winterizing Systems

☐ HVAC EQUIPMENT

*Refer to **"Equipment, Machinery, Tools & Testing Devices."***

Inspections & Compliance

☐ INSPECTIONS & COMPLIANCE – GENERAL

☐☐ Alarms & Smoke Control Systems
☐☐ Asbestos Abatement Requirements
☐☐ Asphalt Paving & Grading Operations
☐☐ Building Code Regulations Compliance
☐☐ Code Requirements Verification
☐☐ Compliance Awareness Training
☐☐ Construction Contract Administration
☐☐ Contract Specifications Compliance
☐☐ Design Specifications Compliance
☐☐ Energy Efficiency Measures
☐☐ Energy Conservation Requirements
☐☐ Environmental Regulations Compliance
☐☐ Government Regulations
☐☐ Energy Conservation Requirements
☐☐ Environmental, Health & Safety Standards
☐☐ Hazardous Materials Pollution Control
☐☐ Health & Safety Program Administration
☐☐ Health & Safety Program Development
☐☐ International Code Council (ICC) Compliance
☐☐ Internal & External Review Processes
☐☐ Policies & Procedures Compliance
☐☐ Quality Testing of Construction Materials
☐☐ QA / QC Implementation
☐☐ Quality Control Process Development
☐☐ Record Accuracy Verification
☐☐ Safety Practices
☐☐ Safety Regulations Compliance
☐☐ State & Local Building Codes
☐☐ Structural Quality & Safety
☐☐ Uniform Building Code (UBC) Compliance
☐☐ Other: ______
☐☐ Air Quality Testing
☐☐ Audit Plan Development
☐☐ Audit Studies & Analyses
☐☐ Building Inspections
☐☐ Comprehensive Final Inspections
☐☐ Construction Site Development
☐☐ Corporate Operations
☐☐ Documentation Review
☐☐ Electrical Codes Compliance
☐☐ Enforcement Activities
☐☐ HVAC Systems Compliance
☐☐ Fire Protection Equipment
☐☐ Life-safety Codes Compliance
☐☐ Health Care Quality
☐☐ Inventory Audits
☐☐ Manual Procedures
☐☐ Operations Audits
☐☐ OSHA Standards Compliance
☐☐ P&L Statements Analysis
☐☐ Plumbing Codes Compliance
☐☐ Project Progress Meetings
☐☐ QA / QC Conceptualization
☐☐ QA / QC Programs & Systems
☐☐ QA Performance Reports
☐☐ Quality Assurance Audits
☐☐ Security Systems
☐☐ Specifications Compliance
☐☐ Survey Instruments, Use of
☐☐ Stop Work Orders
☐☐ Work Logs & Reports Maintenance
☐☐ Audit Management
☐☐ Audit Reports
☐☐ Automated Procedures
☐☐ Control Programs
☐☐ Corrective Actions
☐☐ Cost Reductions
☐☐ Data Integrity
☐☐ Efficiency Evaluations
☐☐ Energy Audits
☐☐ Financial System Audits
☐☐ Investigations
☐☐ Operational Compliance
☐☐ Fire Regulations
☐☐ In-process Testing
☐☐ Management Protocols
☐☐ Methods Development
☐☐ Ordinance Violations
☐☐ Policy Effectiveness
☐☐ Preventive Maintenance
☐☐ QA / QC Documentation
☐☐ Quality Control
☐☐ Site Inspections
☐☐ Specifications Compliance
☐☐ Records Examinations
☐☐ Regulatory Compliance
☐☐ Stability Studies
☐☐ Standards Compliance
☐☐ Workmanship Quality
☐☐ Testing Systems
☐☐ Zoning Laws

☐ BUILDINGS & STRUCTURES COMPLIANCE

☐☐ Air Quality
☐☐ Commercial Construction & Repair Practices
☐☐ Commercial Construction Materials & Equipment
☐☐ Corrective Actions Recommendations
☐☐ Drain, Waste & Vent Lines
☐☐ Elevator & Escalator Inspections
☐☐ Environmental, Health & Safety Standards
☐☐ Fire Protection Equipment
☐☐ Footings Positioning & Depth
☐☐ Gas-fired & Oil-fired Appliances
☐☐ Handicap Accessibility Compliance
☐☐ Hazardous Materials Pollution Control Methods
☐☐ Irrigation Systems
☐☐ Plan Change Architectural Negotiations
☐☐ Quality Testing of Construction Materials
☐☐ Reinforced Concrete Structures
☐☐ Sewer & Water System Inspections
☐☐ Structural Quality, Stability & Safety
☐☐ Waste & Vent Lines
☐☐ Water Supply & Distribution Systems
☐☐ Alarm Systems
☐☐ Commercial Roofing Systems
☐☐ Construction Problems Identification
☐☐ Disposal Systems
☐☐ Drainage Systems
☐☐ Energy Conservation Requirements
☐☐ Excavation & Fill Operations
☐☐ Fire Exits
☐☐ Fire Sprinklers
☐☐ Gas & Oil Piping
☐☐ Grading Operations
☐☐ HVAC Systems & Equipment
☐☐ Ordinance Violations
☐☐ Plumbing Fixtures, Traps & Systems
☐☐ Quality Assurance
☐☐ Roofing Systems
☐☐ Security Systems
☐☐ Soil Conditions
☐☐ Water Distribution Systems
☐☐ Zoning Laws & Regulations
☐☐ Concrete Forms & Foundations
☐☐ Corporate Buildings
☐☐ Demolition & Remodel Procedures
☐☐ Ditches & Dredging
☐☐ Electrical Wiring
☐☐ Energy Efficiency Measures
☐☐ Enforcement Activities
☐☐ Fire Regulations
☐☐ Food Product Safety
☐☐ Gasoline & Butane Tanks
☐☐ Home Systems
☐☐ Insulation
☐☐ OSHA Standards
☐☐ Preventive Maintenance
☐☐ Quality Control
☐☐ Safety Practices
☐☐ Smoke Control Systems
☐☐ Stop Work Orders
☐☐ Water Rights Adjudication
☐☐ Other: ______

Labor Relations

☐ LABOR RELATIONS

- ☐☐ Adherence to Labor Codes
- ☐☐ Bargaining Table Meetings
- ☐☐ Capacity-building Objectives Development
- ☐☐ Collective Bargaining Agreement Enforcement
- ☐☐ Complex Contract Language Interpretation
- ☐☐ Contract Settlement Administration
- ☐☐ Contractual Terms Compliance
- ☐☐ Employee Engagement Increase
- ☐☐ Employee Engagement Advice
- ☐☐ Employee Engagement Programs
- ☐☐ Employee Rights & Responsibilities
- ☐☐ Employer | Employee-related Concerns
- ☐☐ External Communications Strategy
- ☐☐ Grievance Procedures Execution
- ☐☐ Grievance Research & Evaluation
- ☐☐ Health & Safety Issues Resolution
- ☐☐ Health & Safety Procedures Development
- ☐☐ Labor Agreement Interpretation
- ☐☐ Labor Agreements Administration
- ☐☐ Legally Compliant Job Descriptions
- ☐☐ Member Development Goals Establishment
- ☐☐ Membership Rallies Organization
- ☐☐ National Labor Relations Board Liaison
- ☐☐ National Occupational Standards
- ☐☐ New Union Activists Identification
- ☐☐ Operations Management Oversight
- ☐☐ Organizing Campaigns Implementation
- ☐☐ Policy Change Recommendations
- ☐☐ Press Representatives Relationships
- ☐☐ Program Goals Establishment
- ☐☐ Regulatory Compliance Oversight
- ☐☐ Safety & Health Measures Development
- ☐☐ Union Contract Specifications Adherence
- ☐☐ Union Member Job Performance Enhancement
- ☐☐ Union Membership Benefits Meetings
- ☐☐ Work Lives Quality Improvement
- ☐☐ Workers Compensation Board Regulations
- ☐☐ Workplace Issues Resolution
- ☐☐ Workplace Organization
- ☐☐ Arbitration Hearings
- ☐☐ Budget & Expense Proposals
- ☐☐ Circumstance Mitigation
- ☐☐ Communication Networks
- ☐☐ Contract Campaigns
- ☐☐ Contract Negotiations
- ☐☐ Demonstrations Organizing
- ☐☐ Departmental Operations
- ☐☐ Employee Advocate
- ☐☐ Employer Relations
- ☐☐ Fair Wages & Benefits
- ☐☐ Health & Safety Regulations
- ☐☐ Human Resources Oversight
- ☐☐ Innovative Problem-solving
- ☐☐ International Labor Relations
- ☐☐ Labor Laws
- ☐☐ Labor Organization Direction
- ☐☐ Labor Relations Support
- ☐☐ Liability Reports Review
- ☐☐ Membership Coordination
- ☐☐ Local Membership Promotion
- ☐☐ New Union Activists Training
- ☐☐ Memorandum Agreements
- ☐☐ Negotiations with Stakeholders
- ☐☐ New Employees Orientation
- ☐☐ New Union Membership Growth
- ☐☐ Organizing Campaigns Planning
- ☐☐ OSHA Compliance Ensurance
- ☐☐ OSHA Standards & Compliance
- ☐☐ Past Practices Establishment
- ☐☐ Plant Production Measures
- ☐☐ Protection of Employee Rights
- ☐☐ Program Goals Formulation
- ☐☐ Side Letter Agreements (SLA)
- ☐☐ Sponsored Events & Rallies
- ☐☐ Union | Management Meetings
- ☐☐ Union Policies & Activities
- ☐☐ Work Site Visits
- ☐☐ Other: ______
- ☐☐ Benefits Orientations
- ☐☐ Coalition Building
- ☐☐ Collective Agreements
- ☐☐ Collective Bargaining
- ☐☐ Contract Enforcement
- ☐☐ Contract Ratification
- ☐☐ Cost Determinations
- ☐☐ Dispute Resolution
- ☐☐ Employee Relations
- ☐☐ Employment Laws
- ☐☐ Grievance Handling
- ☐☐ Investigations
- ☐☐ Job Placement
- ☐☐ Job Safety Workshops
- ☐☐ Job Security Provisions
- ☐☐ Labor Movement
- ☐☐ Labor Relations
- ☐☐ Local Labor Relations
- ☐☐ Mediation
- ☐☐ Meeting Arrangements
- ☐☐ National Labor Relations
- ☐☐ Negotiations
- ☐☐ Organization Counseling
- ☐☐ Organizing Plans
- ☐☐ Personnel Policies
- ☐☐ Productivity Improvement
- ☐☐ Political Activity
- ☐☐ Program Cost Monitoring
- ☐☐ Research Compilation
- ☐☐ Pro-employer Campaigns
- ☐☐ Release Agreements
- ☐☐ Risk Mitigation Solutions
- ☐☐ Shop Steward Meetings
- ☐☐ Solutions Development
- ☐☐ Subject Matter Expert
- ☐☐ Union Leadership
- ☐☐ Union Meetings
- ☐☐ Union Relationships

Landscaping & Groundskeeping

☐ LANDSCAPING MANAGEMENT

*Refer to **"General Contracting / Trades Management."***

☐ LANDSCAPE ARCHITECTURE

*See also **"CAD Drafting."***

- ☐☐ 3D & Sectional Views
- ☐☐ Architectural Design / Drawings
- ☐☐ Budget Development & Administration
- ☐☐ Client Presentations & Proposals
- ☐☐ Civil Landscape Drafting
- ☐☐ Competitive Bid Solicitation & Analysis
- ☐☐ Contract / Agreement Enforcement
- ☐☐ Contracts Development & Review
- ☐☐ Contract Change Order Preparation
- ☐☐ Contractor Selection
- ☐☐ Aesthetic & Functional Design
- ☐☐ Architectural Rendering Drafting
- ☐☐ Client Consultation & Interface
- ☐☐ Client Invoicing
- ☐☐ Client Relations
- ☐☐ Client Meeting & Strategizing
- ☐☐ Client Needs Assessments
- ☐☐ Contract Negotiations
- ☐☐ Contract Award Procedures
- ☐☐ Cross-section Plotting
- ☐☐ Bidding Process
- ☐☐ Blueprints Preparation
- ☐☐ CAD Drawings
- ☐☐ Client Presentations
- ☐☐ Closeout Processing
- ☐☐ Client Satisfaction
- ☐☐ Contract Administration
- ☐☐ Cost Management
- ☐☐ Contract Negotiations
- ☐☐ Cost Analyses

- ☐☐ Customer Service & Problem Resolution
- ☐☐ Design / Build Project Management
- ☐☐ Dimension Preparation
- ☐☐ Environmental Impact Studies
- ☐☐ Hazardous Conditions Evaluations
- ☐☐ Horizontal & Vertical Grounds Design
- ☐☐ Interior Landscaping Design
- ☐☐ Landscaping Construction Direction
- ☐☐ Landscaping Site Inspections
- ☐☐ Long-range Planning
- ☐☐ Print, Mylar & Sepia Preparation
- ☐☐ Priority Establishment & Scheduling
- ☐☐ Project Resources & Staffing Requirements
- ☐☐ Quality Work Standards
- ☐☐ Topographical & Relief Map Overlays
- ☐☐ Structural Features
- ☐☐ Trades Scheduling
- ☐☐ Use of Sun, Earth & Water Power
- ☐☐ Working Plan Development
- ☐☐ Cost Reductions & Savings
- ☐☐ Design Conceptualization
- ☐☐ Documents Preparation
- ☐☐ Feasibility Studies
- ☐☐ Field Work Coordination
- ☐☐ Hiring and Coordinating Trades
- ☐☐ Land Development
- ☐☐ Landscaping Management
- ☐☐ Landscaping Plans
- ☐☐ On-site Inspections
- ☐☐ Post Construction Services
- ☐☐ Project Coordination
- ☐☐ Project Life Cycle
- ☐☐ Project Time Tracking
- ☐☐ Scheduling
- ☐☐ Structural Inspections
- ☐☐ Surveying
- ☐☐ Sketches & Thumbnails
- ☐☐ Other: ______
- ☐☐ Design Development
- ☐☐ Electrical Drafting
- ☐☐ Estimating
- ☐☐ Fee Negotiations
- ☐☐ Issue Defining
- ☐☐ Land Use Studies
- ☐☐ Landscape Bidding
- ☐☐ Landscape Design
- ☐☐ Layout Diagrams
- ☐☐ Permit Obtaining
- ☐☐ Plumbing Systems
- ☐☐ Project Estimating
- ☐☐ Project Planning
- ☐☐ Project Prioritization
- ☐☐ Schematics
- ☐☐ Recordkeeping
- ☐☐ Wiring Diagrams
- ☐☐ Zoning Laws

☐ LANDSCAPING EQUIPMENT & MACHINERY

Refer to ***"Equipment, Machinery, Tools & Testing Devices."***

☐ LANDSCAPING & GROUNDSKEEPING

- ☐☐ Account Servicing & Administration
- ☐☐ Blueprint Interpreting & Updating
- ☐☐ Cost / Expenditure Estimates
- ☐☐ Dethatching & Aerating Lawns
- ☐☐ Full-service Landscape Maintenance
- ☐☐ Commercial Landscape Maintenance Services
- ☐☐ Landscaping Equipment Operation & Maintenance
- ☐☐ Painting Outdoor Furniture & Structures
- ☐☐ Plant Damage Resolution
- ☐☐ Property Potential Maximizing
- ☐☐ Snow Removal / Plowing
- ☐☐ Swimming Pool Maintenance
- ☐☐ Trades Coordination & Oversight
- ☐☐ Transplanting Trees & Shrubs
- ☐☐ Weed, Disease & Insect Control
- ☐☐ Work Functions Coordination
- ☐☐ Other: ______
- ☐☐ Cash Management
- ☐☐ Grounds Maintenance
- ☐☐ Customer Service Inquiries
- ☐☐ Inspections & Compliance
- ☐☐ Landscape Installations
- ☐☐ Lawn Mowing & Edging
- ☐☐ Mulching Planting Areas
- ☐☐ New Garden Plantings
- ☐☐ Pest Management Techniques
- ☐☐ Raking / Mulching Leaves
- ☐☐ Soil Composition Testing
- ☐☐ Sprinkler Systems
- ☐☐ Trades/Crew Supervision
- ☐☐ Troubleshooting
- ☐☐ Weekly Grounds Maintenance
- ☐☐ Pesticide, Herbicide, Fungicide, Insecticide Applications
- ☐☐ Client Database
- ☐☐ Fertilizing
- ☐☐ Irrigation Systems
- ☐☐ Landscape Design
- ☐☐ Lighting Systems
- ☐☐ Masonry Projects
- ☐☐ Property Grading
- ☐☐ Purchasing
- ☐☐ Safety Practices
- ☐☐ Raw Material Use
- ☐☐ Shrub Pruning
- ☐☐ Sod Harvesting
- ☐☐ Work Collaboration
- ☐☐ Sod Planting
- ☐☐ Tree Trimming

Masonry

☐ MASONRY PROJECT TYPES

- ☐☐ Landscape Designs
- ☐☐ Sidewalks, Walkways & Paths
- ☐☐ Concrete Casting & Forms
- ☐☐ Ponds & Waterfalls
- ☐☐ Stone Walls
- ☐☐ Walls & Partitions
- ☐☐ Retainer Walls
- ☐☐ Concrete Foundations
- ☐☐ Flooring
- ☐☐ Retaining Walls
- ☐☐ Solar Panels
- ☐☐ Other: ______
- ☐☐ Decorative Patios
- ☐☐ Fireplaces
- ☐☐ Refractory Tile
- ☐☐ Roof-top Installations
- ☐☐ Tiling
- ☐☐ Driveways
- ☐☐ Chimneys
- ☐☐ Steps
- ☐☐ Roadways
- ☐☐ Trim Work

☐ MASONRY WORK

- ☐☐ Blueprint Reading
- ☐☐ Color Concrete Surfaces
- ☐☐ Concrete & Steel Reinforcement
- ☐☐ Excavation & Fill Operations
- ☐☐ Steel & Concrete Construction
- ☐☐ Masonry (Brick/Stone/Cement)
- ☐☐ Brattices
- ☐☐ Concrete Foundations
- ☐☐ Concrete Beams & Forms
- ☐☐ Exposed Aggregate Walls
- ☐☐ Job Estimating
- ☐☐ Paving & Grading
- ☐☐ Concrete Castings
- ☐☐ Ditches & Dredging
- ☐☐ Firebrick Linings
- ☐☐ Irrigation Systems
- ☐☐ Job Scheduling
- ☐☐ Refractory Tile
- ☐☐ Columns
- ☐☐ Demolition
- ☐☐ Foundations
- ☐☐ Job Bidding
- ☐☐ Millwork
- ☐☐ Painting

☐☐ Reinforced Concrete Structures
☐☐ Soaking Pits
☐☐ Structural Insulated Wall Panels
☐☐ Other: ______

☐ MASONRY EQUIPMENT & MACHINERY

*Refer to **"Equipment, Machinery, Tools & Testing Devices."***

Plumbing

☐ PLUMBING LICENSES & CERTIFICATIONS

☐☐ EPA - CFC Certification
☐☐ Master plumber's License
☐☐ Plumbing Contractor License
☐☐ HVAC-Related Journeyman's License
☐☐ Plumber Apprenticeship Certificate
☐☐ Universal CFC Certification
☐☐ Licensed Journeyman Plumber
☐☐ Plumber's License
☐☐ Other: ______

☐ PLUMBING AREAS OF EXPERTISE

☐☐ Air Conditioning
☐☐ Apprentice Monitoring
☐☐ Bid Coordination & Selection
☐☐ Building & Safety Codes
☐☐ Building Code Specifications
☐☐ Building Plans Interpretation
☐☐ Client Meeting & Strategizing
☐☐ Contracting / Subcontracting
☐☐ Control System Efficiency
☐☐ Direct Digital Controls
☐☐ Engineering Drawings
☐☐ Estimating Job Times, Materials & Costs
☐☐ Federal & State Laws & Regulations
☐☐ Grounds, Top-Out & Finish
☐☐ Hazardous Waste Handling & Disposal
☐☐ Hazardous Waste Transportation
☐☐ HVAC Heat Return & Main Water Lines
☐☐ HVAC Maintenance & Repair
☐☐ HVAC Systems, Digitally Controlled
☐☐ Inspecting Piping Systems
☐☐ Material Shipment Monitoring
☐☐ Material Handling
☐☐ OSHA, EPA, MSDS & ADA
☐☐ Performance Monitoring
☐☐ Piping System Inspections
☐☐ Plumbing Equipment
☐☐ Plumbing Kitchen Facilities
☐☐ Plumbing Plans Interpretation
☐☐ Plumbing Tools, Materials & Supplies
☐☐ Preventive Maintenance Scheduling
☐☐ Quality Standards
☐☐ Refrigerant Recovery
☐☐ Safety Procedure Enforcement
☐☐ Specifications
☐☐ Temperature Adjustment
☐☐ Temperature Controls Verification
☐☐ Water System Inspections
☐☐ Winterizing Piping Systems
☐☐ HVAC Computer-Based Monitoring & Control Devises
☐☐ Air Handlers
☐☐ Architectural Drawings
☐☐ Blueprint Interpretation
☐☐ Building Automation
☐☐ Building Systems Repair
☐☐ Client Emergency Response
☐☐ Code Violations Assessment
☐☐ Contract Negotiations
☐☐ Cooling Water
☐☐ Dampers
☐☐ Equipment Inspections
☐☐ Fabrication
☐☐ Faucet & Valve Repair
☐☐ Gas Line Installation
☐☐ HVAC / HVAC-R
☐☐ HVAC Equipment
☐☐ HVAC Troubleshooting
☐☐ In-Ground Pools Installation
☐☐ Inventory Ordering & Issuing
☐☐ Job Cost Accountability
☐☐ Materials & Hardware Selection
☐☐ Materials Shipping
☐☐ Microelectronics
☐☐ National Plumbing Code
☐☐ Plumbing Codes
☐☐ Plumbing Installation
☐☐ Plumbing Practices & Techniques
☐☐ Plumbing Tools & Equipment
☐☐ Plumbing Safety Practices
☐☐ Punch List Handling
☐☐ PVC / EPDM
☐☐ Radiant Heating
☐☐ Regulatory Requirements
☐☐ Safety Requirements
☐☐ Sewer Inspections
☐☐ Uniform Plumbing Code
☐☐ Water Consumption
☐☐ Winterizing Sprinkler Systems
☐☐ Plumbing Systems Compatibility Determination
☐☐ Air Quality
☐☐ Asbestos Removal
☐☐ Blueprint Modification
☐☐ Client Billing
☐☐ Client Relations
☐☐ Combustion Analyses
☐☐ Compressed Air
☐☐ Contract Specifications
☐☐ Cost Estimating
☐☐ Diffusers
☐☐ Equipment Monitoring
☐☐ Fans
☐☐ Gas Consumption
☐☐ Humidification
☐☐ HVAC Codes
☐☐ HVAC Installation
☐☐ HVAC Parts
☐☐ Isometric Drawings
☐☐ Job Preparation
☐☐ Job Scheduling
☐☐ Material Bids Review
☐☐ Mechanical Operations
☐☐ Multi-Family Dwellings
☐☐ Plumbing Agreements
☐☐ Plumbing Construction
☐☐ Plumbing Permits
☐☐ Plumbing Specifications
☐☐ Potable Water
☐☐ Procurement Policies
☐☐ Purchasing
☐☐ Materials Estimates
☐☐ Registers
☐☐ Safety Practices
☐☐ Schematics
☐☐ Technical Drawings
☐☐ Ventilation
☐☐ Water Heaters
☐☐ Other: ______

☐ PLUMBING SYSTEM TYPES

☐☐ Boilers (Gas / Electric / Open Flame)
☐☐ Commercial Plumbing Systems
☐☐ Distribution Systems & Controls
☐☐ Energy Management Control System (EMCS)
☐☐ Energy Related Equipment & Control Systems
☐☐ Heating, Cooling & Ventilation Systems
☐☐ In-Door Plumbing Systems
☐☐ Residential Plumbing Systems
☐☐ Water Systems
☐☐ Building Management Systems
☐☐ Domestic Plumbing Systems
☐☐ Fire Sprinkler Systems
☐☐ Gas & Electric Heating Systems
☐☐ Industrial Plumbing Systems
☐☐ HVAC Electric Systems
☐☐ Piping Systems
☐☐ Split Systems
☐☐ Winterizing Systems
☐☐ Cooling Systems
☐☐ Drainage Systems
☐☐ Gas Systems
☐☐ Heating Systems
☐☐ HVAC Systems
☐☐ Plumbing Systems
☐☐ Refrigeration Systems
☐☐ Sprinkler Systems
☐☐ Other: ______

☐ PLUMBING COMPONENTS & DEVICES

☐☐ Air Compressors
☐☐ Building Mechanical Systems
☐☐ Chlorine Gas Feeders
☐☐ Cooling System Maintenance
☐☐ Electronic Controls
☐☐ Emergency Lighting System
☐☐ Gas & Electric Stoves & Ovens
☐☐ Heating System Boilers
☐☐ Monitoring & Control Devices
☐☐ Pipes, Fittings, Valves & Fixtures
☐☐ Plumbing System Equipment
☐☐ Plumbing Malfunction Source Identification
☐☐ Programmable Logic Controls
☐☐ Pump Seals, Bearings & Couplings
☐☐ Sewage Collection Systems
☐☐ Soda Ash & Chlorine Gas Feeders
☐☐ Standard Inspection Procedures
☐☐ Swimming Pool Filtration Pumps
☐☐ Water Supply & Drain Lines
☐☐ Backflow Devices
☐☐ Boiler & Steam Controls
☐☐ Commodes
☐☐ Dishwashers
☐☐ Emergency Generator
☐☐ Fixtures
☐☐ Freezers
☐☐ Gas & Oil Piping
☐☐ Heat Return Lines
☐☐ Main Water Lines
☐☐ Open Flame Boilers
☐☐ Pneumatic Valves
☐☐ Roof Drains
☐☐ PVC Pipe Installation
☐☐ Sheet Metal Handling
☐☐ Specialty Plumbing Items
☐☐ Steam Lines & Controls
☐☐ Toilets / Urinals
☐☐ Water Heaters
☐☐ Other: ______
☐☐ Bearing Assemblies
☐☐ Circulation Pumps
☐☐ Compressors
☐☐ Electric Boilers
☐☐ Filtration Pumps
☐☐ Flush Valves
☐☐ Garbage Disposals
☐☐ Heat Exchangers
☐☐ Heating Pipes
☐☐ Mixing Valves
☐☐ Package Units
☐☐ Pressure Testing
☐☐ Rooftop Units
☐☐ Sewer Lines
☐☐ Steam Boilers
☐☐ Steam Lines
☐☐ Storm Drains
☐☐ Univents
☐☐ Water Softeners
☐☐ Cesspool Lines
☐☐ Coils
☐☐ Condensers
☐☐ Electric Motors
☐☐ Fittings
☐☐ Fountains
☐☐ Gas Boilers
☐☐ Grills
☐☐ Microwaves
☐☐ Pumps
☐☐ Refrigerators
☐☐ Retro-Fittings
☐☐ Septic Tanks
☐☐ Sinks & Faucets
☐☐ Steam Cookers
☐☐ Steam Traps
☐☐ Thermostats
☐☐ Valves

☐ PLUMBING ASSOCIATED SERVICES

☐☐ Computer Programming
☐☐ Consulting
☐☐ Facilities Maintenance
☐☐ Home Heating Conversions
☐☐ Pipe Cutting & Threading
☐☐ Preventive Maintenance
☐☐ Time & Materials Estimating
☐☐ Work Assignment Delegating
☐☐ Carpentry
☐☐ Copper Soldering
☐☐ Engineering
☐☐ Maintenance & Repair
☐☐ Plumbing Inspections
☐☐ Servicing
☐☐ Trades Coordination
☐☐ Work Prioritization
☐☐ Connecting
☐☐ Dismantling
☐☐ Installations
☐☐ Pipe Soldering
☐☐ Plumbing Repairs
☐☐ Supplies Ordering
☐☐ Troubleshooting
☐☐ Work Scheduling
☐☐ Construction
☐☐ Duct Work
☐☐ Outdoor Plumbing
☐☐ Pipefitting
☐☐ Project Planning
☐☐ Take-offs
☐☐ Welding
☐☐ Other: ______

☐ PLUMBING EQUIPMENT

*Refer to **"Equipment, Machinery, Tools & Testing Devices."***

Project Management

☐ PROJECT LIFECYCLE MANAGEMENT

☐☐ Project Budgeting
☐☐ Project Definition
☐☐ Project Planning
☐☐ Project Scope
☐☐ Project Timelines
☐☐ Full Lifecycle Project Integration
☐☐ Project Close-out
☐☐ Project Deliverables
☐☐ Project Prioritization
☐☐ Project Specifications
☐☐ Project Time Tracking
☐☐ Project Resources & Staffing Requirements
☐☐ Project Coordination
☐☐ Project Development
☐☐ Project Resource Allocation
☐☐ Project Strategizing
☐☐ Project Strategizing & Initiation
☐☐ Project Costing
☐☐ Project Objectives
☐☐ Project Scheduling
☐☐ Project Time Frames
☐☐ Other: ______

☐ PROJECT MANAGEMENT FUNCTIONS

- ☐☐ Change Management Plan Development
- ☐☐ Cross-Disciplinary Project Management
- ☐☐ Cross-Functional Solutions Development
- ☐☐ Cross-Functional Team Coordination
- ☐☐ Cross-Organizational Project Deployment
- ☐☐ Functional Specifications Development
- ☐☐ Full-Scope Solutions Plan Development
- ☐☐ Management Consulting Support
- ☐☐ Operational Specifications Development
- ☐☐ Plan Development Facilitation
- ☐☐ Project Deliverables Coordination & Control
- ☐☐ Project Financial Administration
- ☐☐ Project Financial Development & Planning
- ☐☐ Project Logistical Support & Planning
- ☐☐ Project Management Coordination
- ☐☐ Project Management Plan Development
- ☐☐ Project Management Repository Establishment
- ☐☐ Project Performance Management
- ☐☐ Project Proposals Review & Approval
- ☐☐ Project Resource Deployment & Management
- ☐☐ Project Scoping & Estimating
- ☐☐ Quality Standards Compliance
- ☐☐ Reengineering Management
- ☐☐ Risk Management Strategizing
- ☐☐ Schedule Creation & Management
- ☐☐ Subcontract Agreements Preparation
- ☐☐ System Integration
- ☐☐ Team Selection
- ☐☐ Tracking & Reporting
- ☐☐ Work Plan Management
- ☐☐ Budget Control
- ☐☐ Business Case Reviews
- ☐☐ Client Relationship Building
- ☐☐ Global Project Management
- ☐☐ Issue Escalation & Resolution
- ☐☐ Issues Escalation Management
- ☐☐ Materials Submittal Management
- ☐☐ New Work Process Development
- ☐☐ Payment Applications Coordination
- ☐☐ Project Activity Management
- ☐☐ Project Closure & Acceptance
- ☐☐ Project Design & Development
- ☐☐ Project Issues & Risks Tracking
- ☐☐ Project Logistics Determination
- ☐☐ Project Objectives Setting
- ☐☐ Project Operational Development
- ☐☐ Project Plan Development
- ☐☐ Project Resource Interdependence
- ☐☐ Project Risk Deliverables
- ☐☐ Project Tracking & Reporting
- ☐☐ Project Variance Management
- ☐☐ Quality Deliverables Control
- ☐☐ Risk Identification & Mitigation
- ☐☐ Risks & Controls Management
- ☐☐ Scope Change Management
- ☐☐ Solutions Development
- ☐☐ Task Management
- ☐☐ Time Management
- ☐☐ Use Cases Development
- ☐☐ Other: ______
- ☐☐ Change Control
- ☐☐ Cost Assessments
- ☐☐ Cost Control
- ☐☐ Efficiency Reviews
- ☐☐ Logistics Planning
- ☐☐ Materials Procurement
- ☐☐ Process Improvement
- ☐☐ Partnership Leveraging
- ☐☐ Process Modeling
- ☐☐ Project Communication
- ☐☐ Project Documentation
- ☐☐ Project Execution
- ☐☐ Project Initiation
- ☐☐ Project Implementations
- ☐☐ Project Needs Analysis
- ☐☐ Project Plan Execution
- ☐☐ Project Prioritization
- ☐☐ Project Scheduling
- ☐☐ Project Testing
- ☐☐ Quality Management
- ☐☐ Requirements Elicitation
- ☐☐ Resource Allocation
- ☐☐ Resource Management
- ☐☐ Scope Change Requests
- ☐☐ Scope Management
- ☐☐ Status Reporting
- ☐☐ Task Planning & Scheduling
- ☐☐ Time Management
- ☐☐ Value Proposition

☐ PROJECT RESOURCE ALLOCATION

- ☐☐ Equipment & Supplies Purchasing
- ☐☐ Human Resource Planning
- ☐☐ New Hire Administrative Processing
- ☐☐ Performance Management & Planning
- ☐☐ Project Team Meeting Facilitation
- ☐☐ Project Team Roles & Responsibilities
- ☐☐ Resource Acquisition Plan Preparation
- ☐☐ Resource Allocation Management
- ☐☐ Resource Management System (RMS)
- ☐☐ Resource Relationship Outsourcing
- ☐☐ Skill Set Requirements Identification
- ☐☐ Time & Budget Deliverables
- ☐☐ High Performing Work Teams
- ☐☐ Large Teams Management
- ☐☐ Performance Recognition Leadership
- ☐☐ Project Resource Management
- ☐☐ Project Team Member Mentoring
- ☐☐ Project Team Sourcing & Building
- ☐☐ Project Timeline Development
- ☐☐ Resource Allocation Usage Monitoring
- ☐☐ Resource Mix Assessment
- ☐☐ Resource Supply & Demand
- ☐☐ Staffing Requirements Identification
- ☐☐ Training Needs Identification
- ☐☐ Cost/Benefit Analysis
- ☐☐ Project Task Assignments
- ☐☐ Purchase Order Preparation
- ☐☐ Resource Analysis
- ☐☐ Resource Identification
- ☐☐ Resource Management
- ☐☐ Resource Modeling
- ☐☐ Resource Optimization
- ☐☐ Resource Utilization
- ☐☐ Team Building
- ☐☐ Team Management
- ☐☐ Other: ______

☐ PROJECT MANAGEMENT ANALYSIS

- ☐☐ Alternatives Analysis
- ☐☐ Customer-Centric Analytics
- ☐☐ Portfolio Theory Analysis
- ☐☐ Risk Analysis and Management
- ☐☐ Conjoint Measurement Analysis
- ☐☐ Portfolio Analyzer
- ☐☐ Return on Investment Analysis
- ☐☐ Value and Risk Analysis
- ☐☐ Cost/Benefit Analysis
- ☐☐ Portfolio Level Analysis
- ☐☐ Value and Cost Analysis
- ☐☐ Other: ______

☐ PROJECT MANAGEMENT METHODOLOGIES

- ☐☐ Analytical Problem-Solving Methodology
- ☐☐ Project Management Framework
- ☐☐ Project Methodology
- ☐☐ Structure-Disciplined Project Management
- ☐☐ Change Management Methodologies
- ☐☐ Deliverables-based PM Methodology
- ☐☐ Mitigation Strategies
- ☐☐ Best Practice Leveraging
- ☐☐ Facilities Methodology
- ☐☐ Other:______

☐ PROJECT MANAGEMENT, OTHER

- ☐☐ ANSI Standards
- ☐☐ Complexity Management
- ☐☐ Complex Business Problems Resolution
- ☐☐ Contingency Planning Orchestration
- ☐☐ Dual Reporting Relationships
- ☐☐ Earned Value Management Systems
- ☐☐ Functional Requirements Documentation
- ☐☐ Information Technology Outsourcing
- ☐☐ Large Multichannel Retailer Interface
- ☐☐ Management & Scheduling Techniques
- ☐☐ Multiple & Large Project Execution
- ☐☐ Operating Level Agreements (OLAs)
- ☐☐ Planning & Scheduling Techniques
- ☐☐ Project Team Management
- ☐☐ Risk Management Framework
- ☐☐ Schedule Performance Indexing
- ☐☐ Skills Categorization Hierarchies
- ☐☐ Strategic Initiatives Implementation
- ☐☐ Tactical Elements Organization
- ☐☐ Vendor Negotiations
- ☐☐ Other: ______
- ☐☐ Change Orders Estimating
- ☐☐ Communications Channels & Tools
- ☐☐ Conjoint Measurement Systems
- ☐☐ Contract Negotiations
- ☐☐ Cost Performance Indexing
- ☐☐ Functional Improvement Changes
- ☐☐ Functional Managers' Priorities
- ☐☐ Management by Objectives
- ☐☐ Management by Exception
- ☐☐ Manual Processing Procedures
- ☐☐ On-Time Delivery Ensurance
- ☐☐ Organizational Change Management
- ☐☐ Planned Versus Actual Variance
- ☐☐ Process & Data Flow Modeling
- ☐☐ Relationship Management
- ☐☐ Service Level Agreements
- ☐☐ Strategic Business Planning
- ☐☐ Supply Chain Management
- ☐☐ Underpinning Contracts (UCs)
- ☐☐ Work Prioritization
- ☐☐ Client Relations Management
- ☐☐ Computer Science
- ☐☐ Conflict Resolution
- ☐☐ Contract Writing
- ☐☐ Efficient Frontiers
- ☐☐ Methodology Adoption
- ☐☐ Multi-Month Timelines
- ☐☐ Multi-Year Timelines
- ☐☐ Order Management
- ☐☐ Portfolio Management
- ☐☐ Proactive Management
- ☐☐ Program Management
- ☐☐ Project Charter
- ☐☐ Service Delivery
- ☐☐ Service Management
- ☐☐ Storyboards Creation
- ☐☐ Vendor Management
- ☐☐ Vendor Relations
- ☐☐ Vendor Bids
- ☐☐ Workflow Processes

Trades Coordination & Oversight

☐ TRADES COORDINATION & OVERSIGHT

- ☐☐ Carpentry
- ☐☐ Construction
- ☐☐ Concrete Pouring
- ☐☐ Dismantling
- ☐☐ Electrical
- ☐☐ Facilities Maintenance
- ☐☐ HVAC / HVAC-R
- ☐☐ Landscaping
- ☐☐ Masonry
- ☐☐ Plumbing
- ☐☐ Welding / Steamfitting
- ☐☐ Other: ______

☐ ELECTRICAL SYSTEMS

- ☐☐ Bus Bar Systems
- ☐☐ Climate Control Systems
- ☐☐ Conduit Systems
- ☐☐ Electrical Systems
- ☐☐ Exterior Lighting
- ☐☐ Fuel Systems
- ☐☐ High-Voltage Electrical Systems
- ☐☐ Interior Lighting
- ☐☐ Motor Control Systems
- ☐☐ Proximity Systems
- ☐☐ Security Systems
- ☐☐ Video Systems
- ☐☐ Cable Systems
- ☐☐ Communications Systems
- ☐☐ Digital Systems
- ☐☐ Electromagnetic Systems
- ☐☐ Fiber Optic Electrical Systems
- ☐☐ Heating Systems
- ☐☐ Industrial Systems
- ☐☐ Lighting Systems
- ☐☐ Pneumatic Tube Systems
- ☐☐ Public Address Systems
- ☐☐ Signaling Systems
- ☐☐ Voltage Transformers
- ☐☐ Cargo Systems
- ☐☐ Computer Systems
- ☐☐ Electrical Communications Systems
- ☐☐ Energy Management Systems
- ☐☐ Fire Alarm Systems
- ☐☐ High-Tension Distribution Systems
- ☐☐ Intercom Systems
- ☐☐ Low-Voltage Electrical Systems
- ☐☐ Power Systems
- ☐☐ Refrigeration Systems
- ☐☐ Telephone Systems
- ☐☐ Other: ______

☐ HVAC / HVAC-R SYSTEMS

- ☐☐ Air Conditioning Systems
- ☐☐ Commercial Plumbing Systems
- ☐☐ Energy Management Control System (EMCS)
- ☐☐ Energy Related Equipment & Control Systems
- ☐☐ Heating, Cooling & Ventilation Systems
- ☐☐ Industrial Plumbing Systems
- ☐☐ Refrigeration Systems
- ☐☐ Residential Plumbing Systems
- ☐☐ Ventilation Systems
- ☐☐ Other: ______
- ☐☐ Building Management Systems
- ☐☐ Distribution Systems & Controls
- ☐☐ Domestic Plumbing Systems
- ☐☐ Gas & Electric Heating Systems
- ☐☐ HVAC Electric Systems
- ☐☐ In-Door Plumbing Systems
- ☐☐ Piping Systems
- ☐☐ Split Systems
- ☐☐ Water Systems
- ☐☐ Cooling Systems
- ☐☐ Drainage Systems
- ☐☐ Fire Sprinkler Systems
- ☐☐ Gas Systems
- ☐☐ Heating Systems
- ☐☐ HVAC Systems
- ☐☐ Plumbing Systems
- ☐☐ Sprinkler Systems
- ☐☐ Winterizing Systems

☐ MASONRY & LANDSCAPE PROJECTS

- ☐☐ Landscape Designs
- ☐☐ Sidewalks, Walkways & Paths
- ☐☐ Concrete Casting & Forms
- ☐☐ Ponds & Waterfalls
- ☐☐ Stone Walls
- ☐☐ Walls & Partitions
- ☐☐ Retainer Walls
- ☐☐ Concrete Foundations
- ☐☐ Flooring
- ☐☐ Retaining Walls
- ☐☐ Solar Panels
- ☐☐ Other: ______
- ☐☐ Decorative Patios
- ☐☐ Fireplaces
- ☐☐ Refractory Tile
- ☐☐ Roof-top Installations
- ☐☐ Tiling
- ☐☐ Driveways
- ☐☐ Chimneys
- ☐☐ Steps
- ☐☐ Roadways
- ☐☐ Trim Work

☐ PLUMBING SYSTEMS

- ☐☐ Boilers (Gas / Electric / Open Flame)
- ☐☐ Commercial Plumbing Systems
- ☐☐ Distribution Systems & Controls
- ☐☐ Energy Management Control System (EMCS)
- ☐☐ Energy Related Equipment & Control Systems
- ☐☐ Heating, Cooling & Ventilation Systems
- ☐☐ In-Door Plumbing Systems
- ☐☐ Residential Plumbing Systems
- ☐☐ Water Systems
- ☐☐ Building Management Systems
- ☐☐ Domestic Plumbing Systems
- ☐☐ Fire Sprinkler Systems
- ☐☐ Gas & Electric Heating Systems
- ☐☐ Industrial Plumbing Systems
- ☐☐ HVAC Electric Systems
- ☐☐ Piping Systems
- ☐☐ Split Systems
- ☐☐ Winterizing Systems
- ☐☐ Cooling Systems
- ☐☐ Drainage Systems
- ☐☐ Gas Systems
- ☐☐ Heating Systems
- ☐☐ HVAC Systems
- ☐☐ Plumbing Systems
- ☐☐ Refrigeration Systems
- ☐☐ Sprinkler Systems
- ☐☐ Other: ______

☐ WELDING / STEAMFITTING SYSTEM TYPES

- ☐☐ Boilers (Gas / Electric / Open Flame)
- ☐☐ Cooling Systems
- ☐☐ Drainage Systems
- ☐☐ Energy Related Equipment & Control Systems
- ☐☐ Heating Systems
- ☐☐ HVAC Electric Systems
- ☐☐ Piping Systems
- ☐☐ Residential Plumbing Systems
- ☐☐ Water Systems
- ☐☐ Building Management Systems
- ☐☐ Distribution Systems & Controls
- ☐☐ Energy Management Control System
- ☐☐ Gas & Electric Heating Systems
- ☐☐ Heating, Cooling & Ventilation Systems
- ☐☐ In-Door Plumbing Systems
- ☐☐ Plumbing Systems
- ☐☐ Split Systems
- ☐☐ Winterizing Systems
- ☐☐ Commercial Plumbing Systems
- ☐☐ Domestic Plumbing Systems
- ☐☐ Fire Sprinkler Systems
- ☐☐ Gas Systems
- ☐☐ HVAC Systems
- ☐☐ Industrial Plumbing Systems
- ☐☐ Refrigeration Systems
- ☐☐ Sprinkler Systems
- ☐☐ Other: ______

Welding / Steamfitting

☐ WELDING / STEAMFITTING

- ☐☐ Atlas Machines
- ☐☐ All Phases of Building Trades
- ☐☐ Blueprint Reading
- ☐☐ CNC Machines
- ☐☐ Compressed Air Systems
- ☐☐ Core Drilling
- ☐☐ Cutting & Threading Pipe
- ☐☐ Drill Presses
- ☐☐ Domestic Water Systems
- ☐☐ Gear Cutting Machines
- ☐☐ Hydraulic Pistons & Seals
- ☐☐ Hydraulic Oil Pressure
- ☐☐ Hydraulic Systems
- ☐☐ Industrial Welding
- ☐☐ Lathes
- ☐☐ Milling Machines
- ☐☐ Industrial Plumbing
- ☐☐ Modified Torch Down Systems
- ☐☐ Rigging
- ☐☐ Pipefitting
- ☐☐ Soldering
- ☐☐ Torch Cutting
- ☐☐ Welding & Arc Welding
- ☐☐ Air Handling Units (Motors, Pneumatic Controls & Coil Units)
- ☐☐ Air Compressor & Sanitary Piping
- ☐☐ Centrifugal Chiller & Steam Absorption Machines
- ☐☐ Cooling Tower Maintenance
- ☐☐ Connecting Water, Steam, Gas, Oxygen, Vacuum & Air Lines
- ☐☐ Computerized Energy Management Building System Program
- ☐☐ HVAC & Sterilization Equipment
- ☐☐ Exotic Metals: Carbon, Stainless, Aluminum, Tungsten & Cast Iron
- ☐☐ Gas Dangers & Safety Requirements
- ☐☐ Gases: Argon, Helium, Oxygen & Acetylene
- ☐☐ Fire Suppression Sprinkler Systems
- ☐☐ HVAC Piping, Equipment & Duct Work
- ☐☐ MIG, TIG, Plasma, Heliarc, Brazing
- ☐☐ Installation, Service & Repair
- ☐☐ Joint Welding: Groove, Bead, Edge, Plug, Slot, Fillet & Arc-Seam
- ☐☐ Medical Gas Piping: Oxygen, Nitrogen, Medical Air & Vacuum Piping
- ☐☐ Low Pressure & High Pressure Boilers / Steam Lines
- ☐☐ Service, Repair & Maintenance
- ☐☐ Precision-measuring Instruments
- ☐☐ Roto Rooter, Jetter & Lift Operator
- ☐☐ Sterilization & Sanitation Equipment
- ☐☐ Wet, Dry & Deluge Sprinkler Systems
- ☐☐ Other: ______

☐ SYSTEM TYPES

☐☐ Boilers (Gas/Electric/Open Flame)
☐☐ Cooling Systems
☐☐ Drainage Systems
☐☐ Energy Related Equipment & Control Systems
☐☐ Heating, Cooling & Ventilation Systems
☐☐ HVAC Electric Systems
☐☐ Piping Systems
☐☐ Residential Plumbing Systems
☐☐ Water Systems
☐☐ Building Management Systems
☐☐ Distribution Systems & Controls
☐☐ Energy Management Control System
☐☐ Gas & Electric Heating Systems
☐☐ Heating Systems
☐☐ In-Door Plumbing Systems
☐☐ Plumbing Systems
☐☐ Split Systems
☐☐ Winterizing Systems
☐☐ Commercial Plumbing Systems
☐☐ Domestic Plumbing Systems
☐☐ Fire Sprinkler Systems
☐☐ Gas Systems
☐☐ HVAC Systems
☐☐ Industrial Plumbing Systems
☐☐ Refrigeration Systems
☐☐ Sprinkler Systems
☐☐ Other: ______

Technical Skills

☐ TECHNICAL SKILLS

☐☐ The Internet
☐☐ Email
☐☐ Microsoft Word
☐☐ CAD: ______
☐☐ Microsoft Excel
☐☐ Other: ______
☐☐ Microsoft Outlook

Next: Check off your Personal Attributes and Capabilities.

STEP 3
CHECK OFF YOUR PERSONAL ATTRIBUTES & CAPABILITIES

CONTENTS OF STEP 3

PERSONAL ATTRIBUTES & CAPABILITIES

INTRODUCTION

In this step you will be identifying your personal attributes (your assets / features) and honing in on your top 10 to 15 attributes that match your prospective employers' needs. Those would be your unique qualities, characteristics, attributes, capabilities, and/or skills that can be valuable to an employer. You will use these attributes in ***Step 4: Develop Your Personal Brand and Professional Summary***.

Below are the primary attributes, capabilities, and skills employers seek in candidates in this profession as obtained from actual job postings. You will want to be sure to include in your resume the primary ones that are applicable to you. Place one **"X"** before the attributes you feel you own. Then, review the ones you checked off, and double check (**"XX"**) those that are most important to your specific targeted position.

Personal Attributes & Capabilities for Trade Positions

- ☐☐ Ability to adjust the eye to bring an object into sharp focus
- ☐☐ Ability to balance to structures
- ☐☐ Ability to communicate effectively
- ☐☐ Ability to interpret a variety of complex instructions
- ☐☐ Ability to manage change efficiently and responsibly
- ☐☐ Ability to observe critically and obtain accurate data
- ☐☐ Ability to perform strenuous daily activities
- ☐☐ Ability to read blueprints and drawings
- ☐☐ Ability to stay calm in stressful situations
- ☐☐ Ability to train and instruct others in related work
- ☐☐ Ability to sit, kneel, and stand for extended periods
- ☐☐ Ability to work without supervision
- ☐☐ Current driver's license and acceptable driving record
- ☐☐ Active Listening
- ☐☐ Attention to Detail
- ☐☐ Control Precision
- ☐☐ Critical Thinking
- ☐☐ Depth Perception
- ☐☐ Hard Working
- ☐☐ Initiative
- ☐☐ Math Skills
- ☐☐ Multitasker
- ☐☐ Persistence
- ☐☐ Rate Control
- ☐☐ Responsible
- ☐☐ Teamworker
- ☐☐ Adaptable / Flexible
- ☐☐ Attention to Detail
- ☐☐ Cooperation
- ☐☐ Customer Focused
- ☐☐ Detail-oriented
- ☐☐ High Degree of Concentration
- ☐☐ Innovation
- ☐☐ Mathematical Reasoning
- ☐☐ Near & Far Vision
- ☐☐ Problem Sensitivity
- ☐☐ Reaction Time
- ☐☐ Self Control
- ☐☐ Ability to apply knowledge of codes and regulations
- ☐☐ Ability to climb scaffolds and ladders
- ☐☐ Ability to drive a vehicle safely
- ☐☐ Ability to lift and/or move up to 50 to 100 pounds
- ☐☐ Ability to manage multiple projects simultaneously
- ☐☐ Ability to organize and coordinate work of a unit or laborers
- ☐☐ Ability to read and interpret plans and specifications
- ☐☐ Ability to solve practical problems
- ☐☐ Ability to stoop, twist, turn, crouch, and reach
- ☐☐ Ability to walk, crawl, and bend for extended periods
- ☐☐ Ability to work in inclement weather conditions
- ☐☐ Basic Computer Skills
- ☐☐ Good balance and physical strength
- ☐☐ Analytical
- ☐☐ Auditory Attention
- ☐☐ Coordination
- ☐☐ Decision Making
- ☐☐ Dynamic Strength
- ☐☐ Information Processing
- ☐☐ Judgment
- ☐☐ Mechanical Aptitude
- ☐☐ Oral Expression
- ☐☐ Problem Solver
- ☐☐ Reasoning Ability
- ☐☐ Self-Management
- ☐☐ Arm-Hand Steadiness
- ☐☐ Communication skills
- ☐☐ Deductive Reasoning
- ☐☐ Dependable
- ☐☐ Independent
- ☐☐ Initiative
- ☐☐ Manual Dexterity
- ☐☐ Multilimb Coordination
- ☐☐ Organized
- ☐☐ Quality Control Analysis
- ☐☐ Resourceful
- ☐☐ Service Orientation

INSTRUCTIONS FOR ADDITIONAL PERSONAL ATTRIBUTES

Below are comprehensive lists of attributes people in general may have. Not all attributes are applicable to all jobseekers or positions. Even though attributes are categorized by executives and managers, professionals, and social and general attributes, review each list as a number of attributes cross over into other categories and may be applicable to your targeted position. Again, place one **"X"** before those attributes you feel come closest to who you are and two **"Xs"** for those assets that are most important in your position.

Personal Attributes & Capabilities for Managers *(if applicable)*

- ☐☐ Action-Driven Leadership
- ☐☐ Brainstormer
- ☐☐ Change Agent / Manager
- ☐☐ Commitment to Quality & Safety
- ☐☐ Conceptualizer
- ☐☐ Critical Thinker
- ☐☐ Customer Intimacy
- ☐☐ Approachable / Nonthreatening
- ☐☐ Budget Conscious
- ☐☐ Collaborative
- ☐☐ Commitment to Team Success
- ☐☐ Conflict Manager
- ☐☐ Cultivator
- ☐☐ Decisive
- ☐☐ Authoritative
- ☐☐ Career Developer
- ☐☐ Command Presence
- ☐☐ Concept Formulator
- ☐☐ Continuous Improvement Skills
- ☐☐ Cultivator
- ☐☐ Deductive Reasoning

- ☐☐ Delegator
- ☐☐ Direction Provider
- ☐☐ Drive for Value-Added Results
- ☐☐ Exercise Good Judgment
- ☐☐ Handling People with Diplomacy
- ☐☐ Influential
- ☐☐ Inspirational
- ☐☐ Long-Term Success Minded
- ☐☐ Morale Builder
- ☐☐ Organizational Developer
- ☐☐ Overcoming Adversity
- ☐☐ People Manager
- ☐☐ Proactive Problem-Solver
- ☐☐ Project Leadership
- ☐☐ Regrouping Skills
- ☐☐ Responsive
- ☐☐ Solutions Developer
- ☐☐ Strategic Agility & Thinking
- ☐☐ Talent Leader
- ☐☐ Thirst for Innovation
- ☐☐ Visionary Mindset
- ☐☐ Developing Loyalty in Staff
- ☐☐ Director of High Producing Teams
- ☐☐ Effective Communicator
- ☐☐ Exercise Insightful Judgment
- ☐☐ Idea Incubator
- ☐☐ Initiator
- ☐☐ Leadership Developer
- ☐☐ Mediator
- ☐☐ Motivator / Motivational
- ☐☐ Outcome Focused
- ☐☐ Overcoming Boundaries
- ☐☐ Planner & Conceptualizer
- ☐☐ Profitability-Conscious
- ☐☐ Rapport Builder
- ☐☐ Relationship Builder
- ☐☐ Risk Taker
- ☐☐ Sound Decision-Maker
- ☐☐ Tackling Challenges & Obstacles
- ☐☐ Team Approach to Solving Problems
- ☐☐ Top Performer
- ☐☐ Other: ______
- ☐☐ Directing High Producing Teams
- ☐☐ Diversity Management
- ☐☐ Effective Presenter
- ☐☐ Forward-Thinker
- ☐☐ Improvement-oriented
- ☐☐ Innovative
- ☐☐ Leadership Skills
- ☐☐ Mentor
- ☐☐ Negotiator / Mediator
- ☐☐ Outside-the-Box Thinker
- ☐☐ People Development Skills
- ☐☐ Presenter
- ☐☐ Profitability-Conscious
- ☐☐ Recruiting
- ☐☐ Resourceful
- ☐☐ Role Model
- ☐☐ Straight Forward
- ☐☐ Tactical Action Planner
- ☐☐ Team Builder & Leader
- ☐☐ Transformational

Personal Attributes & Capabilities for Professionals

- ☐☐ Ability to Handle Pressure
- ☐☐ Accepting of Responsibility
- ☐☐ Aesthetic Sensibility
- ☐☐ Attentive to Detail
- ☐☐ Big Picture Thinker
- ☐☐ Changeable
- ☐☐ Commitment to Excellence
- ☐☐ Communicator
- ☐☐ Conflict Handler
- ☐☐ Conviction, person of
- ☐☐ Cost Conscious
- ☐☐ Deal well with Ambiguity
- ☐☐ Diplomatic / Tactful
- ☐☐ Employee Retainer
- ☐☐ Exhibits Conviction
- ☐☐ Expert
- ☐☐ Follow-up Oriented
- ☐☐ Hypothesizer
- ☐☐ Integrity
- ☐☐ Learning-oriented
- ☐☐ Mathematical Reasoning
- ☐☐ Open Thinker
- ☐☐ People-oriented
- ☐☐ Political
- ☐☐ Priority Setter
- ☐☐ Progressive
- ☐☐ Quality-oriented
- ☐☐ Sales-oriented
- ☐☐ Service Oriented
- ☐☐ Strong Work Ethic
- ☐☐ Team Player
- ☐☐ Time Manager
- ☐☐ Troubleshooter
- ☐☐ Visualizer
- ☐☐ Academic-oriented
- ☐☐ Accurate
- ☐☐ Affiliated
- ☐☐ Autocratic as needed
- ☐☐ Broad Thinker
- ☐☐ Child-focused
- ☐☐ Commitment to Quality
- ☐☐ Community-oriented
- ☐☐ Conjecturing
- ☐☐ Coordinator
- ☐☐ Criteria Evaluator
- ☐☐ Deductive
- ☐☐ Educated / Degreed
- ☐☐ Entrepreneurial
- ☐☐ Expansive
- ☐☐ Facilitator
- ☐☐ Fundraiser
- ☐☐ Inclusive
- ☐☐ Interpersonal Skills
- ☐☐ Left- & Right-brained Thinker
- ☐☐ Multicultural
- ☐☐ Open to Change
- ☐☐ Perceptive / Perceptual
- ☐☐ Powerful
- ☐☐ Proactive
- ☐☐ Project-Oriented
- ☐☐ Quantitative
- ☐☐ Scientific-minded
- ☐☐ Simplistic in Complex Ideas
- ☐☐ Synergetic
- ☐☐ Technically Competent
- ☐☐ Time-conscious
- ☐☐ Urgency-oriented
- ☐☐ Willing to Try New Things
- ☐☐ Accepting of Criticism
- ☐☐ Active Listener
- ☐☐ Altruistic
- ☐☐ Awareness
- ☐☐ Bureaucratic
- ☐☐ Client Focused
- ☐☐ Commitment to Safety
- ☐☐ Computer Literate
- ☐☐ Connected
- ☐☐ Coping Ability
- ☐☐ Customer-focused
- ☐☐ Detail-oriented
- ☐☐ Educational Leader
- ☐☐ Error Conscious
- ☐☐ Expeditor
- ☐☐ Fact Finder
- ☐☐ Goal-oriented
- ☐☐ Independent Judgment
- ☐☐ Interpreter
- ☐☐ Logical Thinker
- ☐☐ Negotiator
- ☐☐ Originator
- ☐☐ Persistent / Sustaining
- ☐☐ Predictor
- ☐☐ Problem Recognizer
- ☐☐ Psychological Well-being
- ☐☐ Researcher
- ☐☐ Sense of Proportion
- ☐☐ Social Networker
- ☐☐ Tackle Obstacles
- ☐☐ Technologically Literate
- ☐☐ Tolerance for Uncertainty
- ☐☐ Value Analyzer
- ☐☐ Work-oriented
- ☐☐ Accepting of Others
- ☐☐ Adaptable to Change
- ☐☐ Analytical
- ☐☐ Bias Detector
- ☐☐ Challenger
- ☐☐ Client Service-Oriented
- ☐☐ Common Sense Thinker
- ☐☐ Conciliator
- ☐☐ Connector
- ☐☐ Correlation Reasoning
- ☐☐ Deadline-conscious
- ☐☐ Differentiator
- ☐☐ Efficiency-oriented
- ☐☐ Evaluator
- ☐☐ Experimentally-inclined
- ☐☐ Flexible / Adaptable
- ☐☐ Goodwill Oriented
- ☐☐ Inductive Reasoning
- ☐☐ Knowledgeable
- ☐☐ Mastermind
- ☐☐ Networker
- ☐☐ Outcome Focused
- ☐☐ Personal Presentation
- ☐☐ Presenter
- ☐☐ Problem-solver
- ☐☐ Qualitative
- ☐☐ Results Driven
- ☐☐ Sense of Urgency
- ☐☐ Statistical Thinker
- ☐☐ Task-oriented
- ☐☐ Tech-savvy
- ☐☐ Tolerance of Ambiguity
- ☐☐ Value-oriented
- ☐☐ Other: ______

Social & General Attributes

The following attributes generally answer the question, *"What kind of a person are you?"* Think about how you view yourself as well as how others view you. Different attributes are applicable to different positions. For example, being aggressive, diligent, determined, and methodical would be applicable for an Internal Revenue Services Manager, but definitely not for a Social Worker who would need to be caring, compassionate, empathetic, inspiring, and concerned for others.

Accommodating	Accomplished	Accountable	Adventurous
Advocate	Aggressive	Alert	Ambitious
Animated	Approachable	Articulate	Artistic
Aspiring	Assertive	Attentive	Authoritative
Autonomous	Balanced	Bold	Bright
Calm / Level-headed	Candid	Careful / Cautious	Caring
Challenge Seeker	Charismatic	Cheerful	Clear Thinker
Coachable	Collaborative	Colorful	Committed
Compassionate	Competent	Competitive	Composed
Comprehensive	Conceptual	Concerned for Others	Concise
Confident	Congenial	Conscientious	Conservative
Considerate / Thoughtful	Consistent	Constructive	Contemporary
Convincing	Cooperative	Courageous	Courteous
Creative	Credible	Critical Thinker	Curious
Decisive	Dedicated	Delegator	Democratic
Dependable	Determined	Devoted	Diligent
Discerning	Disciplined	Discoverer	Discreet
Dramatic	Driven	Dynamic	Earnest
Easygoing	Eclectic	Efficient	Elaborative
Eloquent	Emotionally Stable	Empathetic	Empowered
Empowering	Encouraging	Engaging	Enterprising
Enthusiastic	Ethical	Exciting	Expressive
Extroverted	Exuberant	Fair / Impartial	Faithful
Fast Learner	Focused	Foresighted	Forgiving
Friendly	Frugal	Generous	Gentle
Genuine	Giving	Good Judgment	Good Listener
Grateful	Gregarious	Harmonious	Healthy Perspective
Helpful	Honest / Trustworthy	Humble	Humorous
Imaginative	Independent	Industrious	Influential
Initiator	Inquisitive	Insightful	Intellectual
Interactive	Interested	Interesting	Introspective
Intuitive	Inventive	Judgment, Good	Judicious
Kind	Life-long Student	Likable	Literate
Loyal	Mature	Methodical	Meticulous
Mindful	Modest	Moral Minded	Motivated
Multitasker	Nondiscriminatory	Nonjudgmental	Objective
Observant	Open	Open-minded	Optimistic
Organized	Original	Outgoing	Participative
Particular	Passionate	Patient	Perfectionist
Perseverant	Personable	Persuasive	Philosophical
Pioneer	Planner	Poised	Positive
Practical	Pragmatic	Precise	Prestigious
Productive	Professional	Prolific	Promise Keeper
Promotable	Punctual / Prompt	Quick Learner	Quick-Witted
Rational	Realistic	Reasonable	Refined
Reflective Thinker	Relate well with others	Reliable	Resilient
Resourceful	Respected by Others	Respectful	Responsible
Responsive	Sassy	Savvy	Self-assessor
Self-assured	Self-confident	Self-controlled	Self-correcting
Self-directed	Self-disciplined	Self-esteem	Selfless
Self-manager	Self-motivated	Self-reliant	Self-sacrificing
Self-starter	Sense of Humor	Sensible	Sensitive

☐☐ Sincere	☐☐ Sociable	☐☐ Sophisticated	☐☐ Spirited
☐☐ Spiritual Values	☐☐ Stamina	☐☐ Story Teller	☐☐ Striving
☐☐ Strong Willed	☐☐ Success-Driven	☐☐ Successful	☐☐ Supportive
☐☐ Sympathetic	☐☐ Systematic	☐☐ Tactful	☐☐ Talented
☐☐ Tenacious	☐☐ Thorough	☐☐ Thoughtful	☐☐ Tolerant
☐☐ Traditional	☐☐ Traveler	☐☐ Trusted by others	☐☐ Trusting
☐☐ Truthful / Truth Teller	☐☐ Unconventional	☐☐ Understanding	☐☐ Unintimidating
☐☐ Unique	☐☐ Unpretentious	☐☐ Values, Person of	☐☐ Versatile
☐☐ Well-rounded	☐☐ Willing to Learn	☐☐ Willpower	☐☐ Wise
☐☐ Worldly	☐☐ Zen-like	☐☐ Other: ______	

LIST YOUR TOP 10-15 PERSONAL ATTRIBUTES

INSTRUCTIONS

Select from above and list *in order of importance* your ***top 10 to 15 assets / features*** you possess that help you in your profession. Those would be your unique qualities, characteristics, attributes, capabilities, or skills that can be valuable to an employer and/or its clients. (Check these against the positions you Googled in ***Step 1: Start Your Resume*** to see which attributes your targeted employers seek.)

These attributes will be used in ***Step 4: Develop Your Personal Brand & Professional Summary.***

YOUR TOP 10-15 ASSETS / FEATURES

Asset #1:

Asset #2:

Asset #3:

Asset #4:

Asset #5:

Asset #6:

Asset #7:

Asset #8:

Asset #9:

Asset #10:

Asset #11:

Asset #12:

Asset #13:

Asset #14:

Asset #15:

STEP 4

DEVELOP YOUR PERSONAL BRAND & PROFESSIONAL SUMMARY

CONTENTS OF STEP 4

BRANDING FOREVER CHANGES YOU

ONCE YOU IDENTIFY AND DEFINE YOUR BRAND, IT BECOMES A CATHARSIS!

Your ***Personal Brand*** plays a strategic role in managing your career much the same way as a brand does for a business. Knowing what your unique brand is and how it helps you in your profession is critical to your career success. The good news is that everyone already has a Personal Brand whether they are aware of it or not. The secret is to discover what it is and use it to your advantage. This chapter will show you how to identify and define your own unique brand.

Personal Branding is an essential career marketing tool that creates a credible identity so hiring managers who view your brand know your value proposition and are compelled to seek you out over your competition. A well-defined brand will capture the interest of hiring managers, set you apart from other candidates, and help position you in the top percentage in your area of expertise. The five critical components of successful branding include your ***Assets / Features, Benefits, Competitive Edge, Value Proposition,*** and ***Return on Investment*** and are explained in this section.

INSTRUCTIONS

The information you compile in the ***Personal Branding Worksheet*** that follows will help you develop your ***Personal Brand Message*** in four formats: ***(1) Personal Brand Biography, (2) LinkedIn Profile, (3) Elevator Pitch,*** and ***(4) Slogan*** so you can incorporate it into all of your career marketing materials and use it in your networking and interviews. Use the supplied foundations and samples as a guide to spur the development of your brand.

You will then ***Create Your Professional Summary*** for the top portion of your resume. That section also contains foundations where you can input your unique information along with sample completed summaries for various professions. Finally, at the end of this chapter, you will find a guide to help you ***Establish and Evolve Your Brand*** going forward.

10 REASONS WHY PERSONAL BRANDING IS ESSENTIAL

Personal branding is essential to your personal growth and career success. Here are ten reasons why effective Personal Branding is important and why you should be sure to develop your unique brand:

1. ***Personal Branding*** *helps position you in the Top 2 Percent of candidates in your field of expertise!*
2. ***Personal Branding*** *empowers you with confidence and selling power to sell yourself because you will feel the full value of your worth.*
3. ***Personal Branding*** *invites readers in to want to read your career marketing materials and learn more about you.*
4. ***Personal Branding*** *allows you to significantly stand out from the competition and receive many more interview calls.*
5. ***Personal Branding*** *compels prospective employers to seek you out and call you ahead of other applicants.*
6. ***Personal Branding*** *helps you network successfully.*
7. ***Personal Branding*** *establishes you as an expert in your niche and helps you build a solid reputation.*
8. ***Personal Branding*** *takes less time to fulfill your goals.*
9. ***Personal Branding*** *provides for higher earnings potential.*
10. ***Personal Branding*** *allows you to become successful more quickly and earn much more!*

SOMETHING MAGICAL HAPPENS WHEN YOU DISCOVER AND DEFINE YOUR BRAND!

Something magical truly does happen when you discover and define your brand. For those who have, they call it a *"catharsis,"* an *"epiphany,"* and a *"revelation."* It provides you with self-empowerment, confidence, and selling power to go after and achieve your goals because you know the value of your full worth and what you bring to the table. Hiring managers will seek you out, and it provides high earnings potential.

Identifying and defining your unique brand puts you on the road to unlimited success!

Stand out from your competition. Discover and define ***your*** *unique brand.*

THE 5 CRITICAL COMPONENTS OF SUCCESSFUL BRANDING

INTRODUCTION

The five critical components of successful business and personal branding that are essential for any brand to be effective include your: **(1) Assets / Features, (2) Benefits, (3) Competitive Edge, (4) Value Proposition,** and **(5) Return on Investment** along with your matching achievements. Keep in mind that you are the product / brand you are selling. All successful brands use this strategy.

Following are definitions and examples of each:

DEFINITIONS AND EXAMPLES

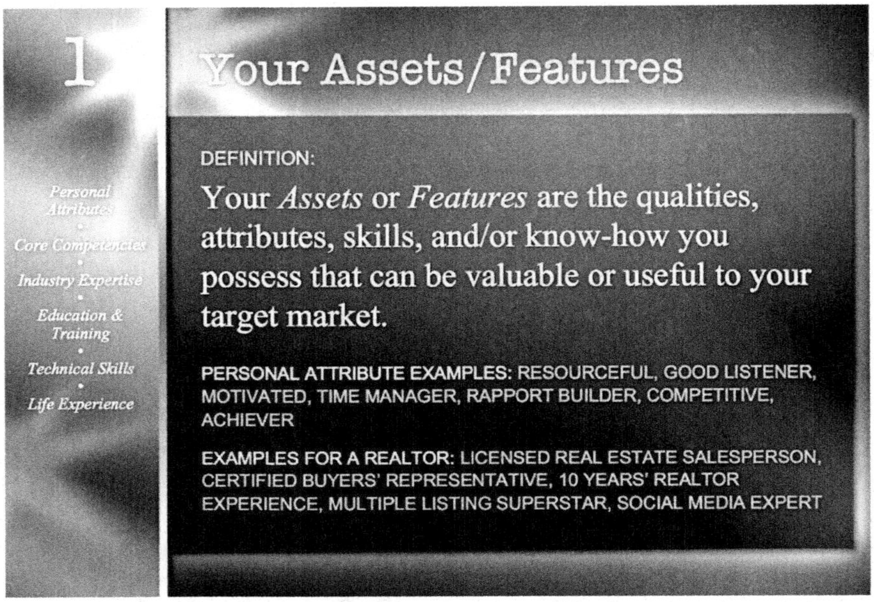

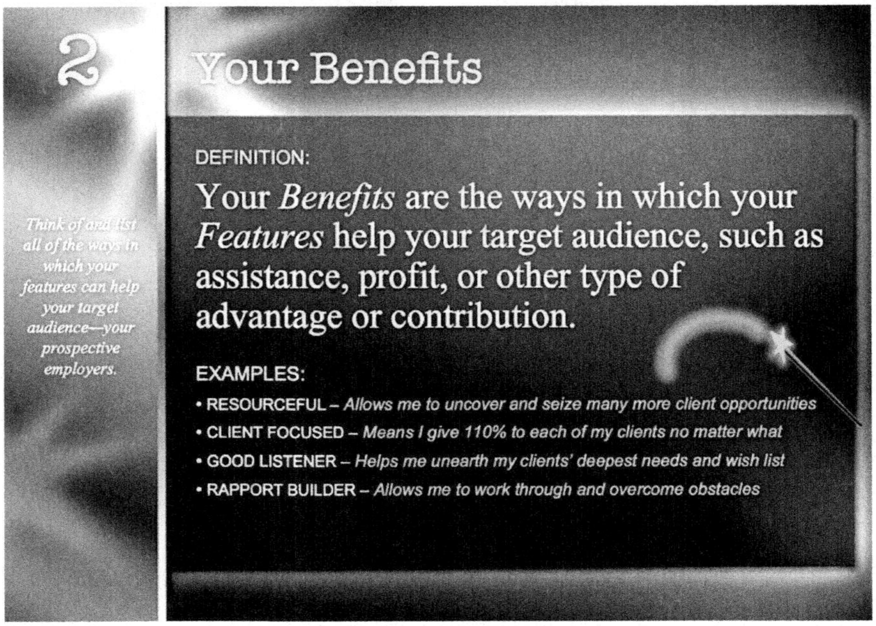

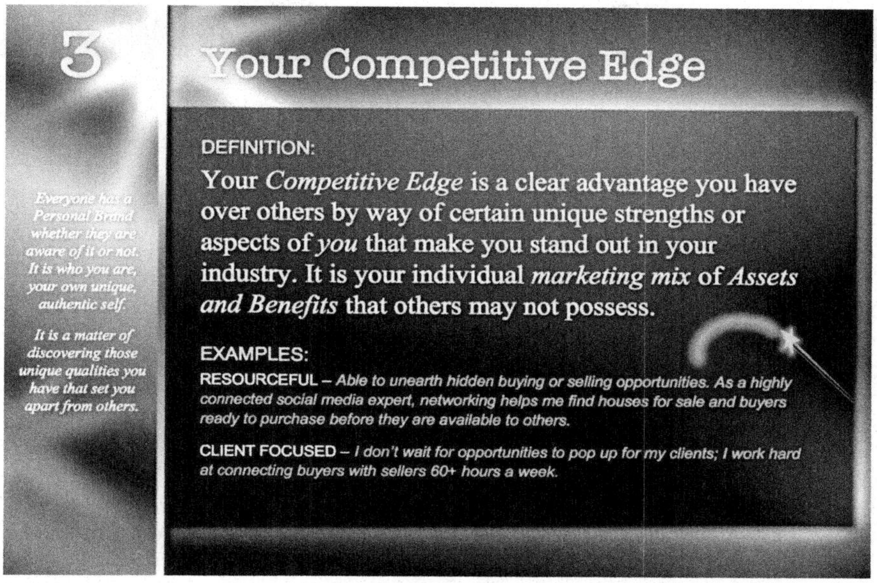
3
Your Competitive Edge
Everyone has a Personal Brand whether they are aware of it or not. It is who you are, your own unique, authentic self.
It is a matter of discovering those unique qualities you have that set you apart from others.
DEFINITION:
Your *Competitive Edge* is a clear advantage you have over others by way of certain unique strengths or aspects of *you* that make you stand out in your industry. It is your individual *marketing mix* of *Assets and Benefits* that others may not possess.
EXAMPLES:
RESOURCEFUL – *Able to unearth hidden buying or selling opportunities. As a highly connected social media expert, networking helps me find houses for sale and buyers ready to purchase before they are available to others.*
CLIENT FOCUSED – *I don't wait for opportunities to pop up for my clients; I work hard at connecting buyers with sellers 60+ hours a week.*

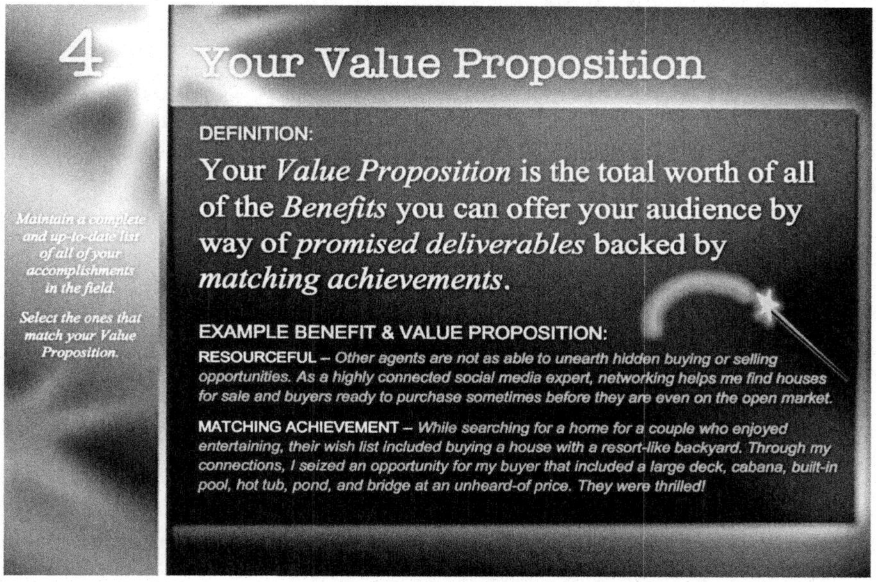
4
Your Value Proposition
Maintain a complete and up-to-date list of all of your accomplishments in the field.
Select the ones that match your Value Proposition.
DEFINITION:
Your *Value Proposition* is the total worth of all of the *Benefits* you can offer your audience by way of *promised deliverables* backed by *matching achievements*.
EXAMPLE BENEFIT & VALUE PROPOSITION:
RESOURCEFUL – *Other agents are not as able to unearth hidden buying or selling opportunities. As a highly connected social media expert, networking helps me find houses for sale and buyers ready to purchase sometimes before they are even on the open market.*
MATCHING ACHIEVEMENT – *While searching for a home for a couple who enjoyed entertaining, their wish list included buying a house with a resort-like backyard. Through my connections, I seized an opportunity for my buyer that included a large deck, cabana, built-in pool, hot tub, pond, and bridge at an unheard-of price. They were thrilled!*

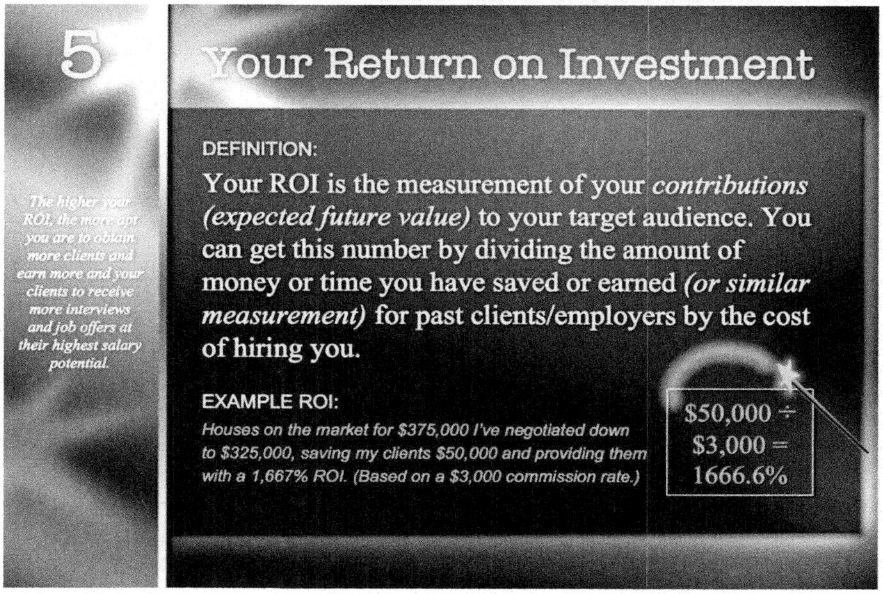
5
Your Return on Investment
The higher your ROI, the more apt you are to obtain more clients and earn more and your clients to receive more interviews and job offers at their highest salary potential.
DEFINITION:
Your ROI is the measurement of your *contributions (expected future value)* to your target audience. You can get this number by dividing the amount of money or time you have saved or earned *(or similar measurement)* for past clients/employers by the cost of hiring you.
EXAMPLE ROI:
Houses on the market for $375,000 I've negotiated down to $325,000, saving my clients $50,000 and providing them with a 1,667% ROI. (Based on a $3,000 commission rate.)
$50,000 ÷
$3,000 =
1666.6%

COMPLETE THE PERSONAL BRAND WORKSHEET

1. DESCRIBE YOUR CAREER GOALS AND DREAM JOB.

What are your long-term career goals?

What position title(s) are you seeking now?

In what industry do you prefer to work?

Are there any specific (types of) firms where you would like to work?

What type of work do you prefer to handle?

What activities would you prefer not to do?

(Keep these essential requirements in mind when targeting your resume and pursuing your next position. Other than the position title(s), this information will not become a part of your resume.)

2. RESEARCH JOB DESCRIPTIONS IN YOUR PROFESSION.

Conduct an Internet search of job descriptions for your most sought-after position(s). *[Google "Job Descriptions for (Position Title)."]* List the job functions and requirements from the top three job postings that interest you in order of your preference. **"X"** each listed function in which you have the experience and qualifications. In compiling your resume later, be sure you include those functions under the position(s) where you actually performed them and include how well you did.

JOB DESCRIPTION #1

POSITION TITLE:

- ☐
- ☐
- ☐
- ☐
- ☐
- ☐
- ☐
- ☐
- ☐
- ☐
- ☐
- ☐
- ☐
- ☐
- ☐

JOB DESCRIPTION #2

POSITION TITLE:

- ☐
- ☐
- ☐
- ☐
- ☐
- ☐
- ☐
- ☐
- ☐
- ☐
- ☐
- ☐
- ☐

JOB DESCRIPTION #3

POSITION TITLE:

- ☐
- ☐
- ☐
- ☐
- ☐
- ☐
- ☐
- ☐
- ☐
- ☐
- ☐
- ☐
- ☐
- ☐

3. LIST YOUR PRIMARY ASSETS / FEATURES.

From the attributes you selected in ***Step 3: Check Off Your Personal Attributes***, list below your top 10 to 15 assets that are of most importance to your targeted profession.

EXAMPLES: *a good listener, resourceful, strategic, innovative, organized, customer-service oriented, and so on.*

YOUR TOP 10-15 ASSETS

ASSET #1:	**ASSET #9:**
ASSET #2:	**ASSET #10:**
ASSET #3:	**ASSET #11:** *(Optional)*
ASSET #4:	**ASSET #12:** *(Optional)*
ASSET #5:	**ASSET #13:** *(Optional)*
ASSET #6:	**ASSET #14:** *(Optional)*
ASSET #15: *(Optional)*	

4. DETERMINE YOUR BENEFITS.

Describe the benefits of your top 10 to 15 assets. In what ways do each of your assets help you to conduct your work, solve problems on the job, help employers save money, or otherwise benefit a company or its clients?

EXAMPLES: *Being a* ***good listener*** *helps me to unearth my clients' deepest needs and sell to match those needs.*
Being ***resourceful*** *allows me to uncover and seize many more client opportunities that my peers may not be aware of.*

THE BENEFITS OF YOUR ASSETS

BENEFIT OF ASSET #1:

BENEFIT OF ASSET #2:

BENEFIT OF ASSET #3:

BENEFIT OF ASSET #4:

BENEFIT OF ASSET #5:

BENEFIT OF ASSET #6:

BENEFIT OF ASSET #7:

BENEFIT OF ASSET #8:

BENEFIT OF ASSET #9:

BENEFIT OF ASSET #10:

BENEFIT OF ASSET #11: *(Optional)*

BENEFIT OF ASSET #12: *(Optional)*

BENEFIT OF ASSET #13: *(Optional)*

BENEFIT OF ASSET #14: *(Optional)*

BENEFIT OF ASSET #15: *(Optional)*

5. FIGURE OUT YOUR VALUE PROPOSITION.

Explain the deliverables a prospective employer can expect to obtain from hiring you by indicating below the results your top benefits obtain. For each benefit listed in No. 4 above, ask yourself, *"How does that help?"* Keep asking that question and documenting your answers until there are no more answers left for each. This becomes your value proposition.

EXAMPLE for a ***good listener****: After unearthing my clients' deepest needs, I apply in-depth product knowledge coupled with my industry experience to provide matching solutions to their challenges.* ***How does that help?*** *They see value in the product as it solves their problems and meets their needs.* ***How does that help?*** *Prospects are more apt to purchase.* ***How does that help?*** *It increases sales and referrals for my employer.*

THE VALUE OF YOUR BENEFITS

VALUE OF BENEFIT #1:

VALUE OF BENEFIT #2:

VALUE OF BENEFIT #3:

VALUE OF BENEFIT #4:

VALUE OF BENEFIT #5:

VALUE OF BENEFIT #6:

VALUE OF BENEFIT #7:

VALUE OF BENEFIT #8:

VALUE OF BENEFIT #9:

VALUE OF BENEFIT #10:

VALUE OF BENEFIT #11: *(Optional)*

VALUE OF BENEFIT #12: *(Optional)*

VALUE OF BENEFIT #13: *(Optional)*

VALUE OF BENEFIT #14: *(Optional)*

VALUE OF BENEFIT #15: *(Optional)*

6. INCLUDE YOUR MATCHING ACHIEVEMENTS.

What have you accomplished in your career that proves your value? Check the Achievements you included under your employers in ***Step 1: Start Your Resume.*** If these match your value, skip to the next section. Otherwise…

For each achievement, document what your original CHALLENGE was, the problem-solving ACTIONS you took to meet the challenge, and the end RESULTS and BENEFITS your efforts derived. Use numbers (amounts, dollars, percentages, and so on) wherever possible. Then put that information into a sentence that starts with your achievement to create your resume bullets.

EXAMPLE *for a* ***Good Listener:***

Your Challenge: *To sell customized IT solutions to Fortune 500 firms.*

Your Actions: *Met with, assessed, and determined a Fortune 100 prospect's greatest needs by listening carefully to their goals and challenges, brainstorming all possible scenarios, providing options, and customizing solutions that solved their problems.*

Your Results / Benefits: *Saved the client $250,000 annually while bringing in $.5 million in sales for my employer. Also increased my employer's competitive edge in the marketplace by adding a high-profile firm to their client market list.*

Your Resume Bullet: *Saved a Fortune 100 client $250,000 while bringing in $.5 million in sales for employer and increasing the firm's competitive edge in the marketplace by assessing the client's greatest needs, listening carefully to their goals and challenges, providing options, and selling customized IT solutions that met their goals.*

ACHIEVEMENT THAT PROVES VALUE #1:

YOUR CHALLENGE:

YOUR ACTIONS:

YOUR RESULTS:

ACHIEVEMENT THAT PROVES VALUE #2:

YOUR CHALLENGE:

YOUR ACTIONS:

YOUR RESULTS:

ACHIEVEMENT THAT PROVES VALUE #3:

YOUR CHALLENGE:

YOUR ACTIONS:

YOUR RESULTS:

ACHIEVEMENT THAT PROVES VALUE #4:

YOUR CHALLENGE:

YOUR ACTIONS:

YOUR RESULTS:

ACHIEVEMENT THAT PROVES VALUE #5:

YOUR CHALLENGE:

YOUR ACTIONS:

YOUR RESULTS:

ACHIEVEMENT THAT PROVES VALUE #6:

YOUR CHALLENGE:

YOUR ACTIONS:

YOUR RESULTS:

ACHIEVEMENT THAT PROVES VALUE #7:

YOUR CHALLENGE:

YOUR ACTIONS:

YOUR RESULTS:

ACHIEVEMENT THAT PROVES VALUE #8:

YOUR CHALLENGE:

YOUR ACTIONS:

YOUR RESULTS:

ACHIEVEMENT THAT PROVES VALUE #9:

YOUR CHALLENGE:

YOUR ACTIONS:

YOUR RESULTS:

ACHIEVEMENT THAT PROVES VALUE #10:

YOUR CHALLENGE:

YOUR ACTIONS:

YOUR RESULTS:

OTHER ACHIEVEMENTS:

7. IDENTIFY YOUR COMPETITIVE EDGE.

What unique qualities do you possess that differentiates you from others in your field and what advantage does this provide a prospective employer? Consider and list all areas you excel over your counterparts.

FOR EXAMPLE: *What do you do better, faster, bigger, or more strategically, creatively, productively, or other in your profession than others in your profession? Think about what your superiors have praised you for, what is documented in your performance evaluations, and/or what others have stated that sets you apart from your peers.*

YOUR COMPETITIVE EDGE

DIFFERENTIATOR #1:

DIFFERENTIATOR #2:

DIFFERENTIATOR #3:

DIFFERENTIATOR #4:

DIFFERENTIATOR #5:

8. DETERMINE YOUR RETURN ON INVESTMENT (ROI).

Employers have a "what's in it for me" approach. Explain why a hiring manager should hire you. What measurement of your contributions *(expected future value)* do you bring to the table? What promise can you make based on what you have accomplished in the past? Think about how your contributions equate to being able to help an employer, such as by increasing sales, cutting costs, streamlining operations, elevating productivity, increasing customer service levels, and the like. Use dollars, numbers, and percentages.

EXAMPLE for a Real Estate Salesperson: *Say that due to your excellent negotiation and interpersonal skills, you show more houses to more buyers and/or bring in more leads to more sellers, on average you (1) save buyers $35,000-$50,000 on houses they purchase, (2) are able to obtain a sellers' asking price 85% of the time, (3) sell houses 6 to 9 months sooner in a market where the norm is 1.5 years, (4) have a 65% faster turnaround time. These numbers become your ROI (expected future value) and will attract your target audience.*

YOUR RETURN ON INVESTMENT

9. INCLUDE YOUR TESTIMONIALS.

Testimonials are optional but extremely helpful in catching the attention of hiring managers as they add credence to your resume content and showcase qualities others have found in you and your work. Include below any positive comments you have received from others which speaks to how well you perform(ed) your job. Try to include a variety of endorsements that address the brand components you included above. *(If you do not have these now, don't hesitate to ask others to provide them.)*

EXAMPLE: *Include comments obtained from letters of recommendation, LinkedIn endorsements, customer thank you letters, performance evaluations, and other means received from superiors, customers, vendors, peers, and others.*

TESTIMONIAL #1

TESTIMONIAL #2

TESTIMONIAL #3

10. NEXT, YOU WILL DEVELOP YOUR PERSONAL BRAND MESSAGE IN 5 FORMATS.

In the next section, you will be applying the information you compiled above to create your ***Personal Brand Message*** in five formats for use in your resume, career marketing materials, networking, social media, and interviews. Each serves its own purpose, as follows:

- **Personal Brand Biography** for use as your Sell Sheet in your Networking and as a leave-behind for your interviews
- **LinkedIn Profile** for your LinkedIn account and other Social Media
- **Elevator Pitch** for use in all of your Networking and Interviews (can also be included in your Cover Letter)
- **Slogan / Tag Line** for your Resume, Cover Letter, Business Cards, and other Career Marketing Materials
- **Professional Summary** for the top portion of your Resume

Foundations are included for each Brand Message format for you to fill in with your brand components and related information, along with sample completed messages in various professions.

When I develop Personal Brands for clients, I start off with their full Biography, then condense it for the LinkedIn Profile, further condense it for an Elevator Pitch, and lastly create the Slogan and Professional Summary. Using this method in the sequence in this chapter will help with that process.

DEVELOP YOUR PERSONAL BRAND BIOGRAPHY:

TO USE AS YOUR SELL SHEET FOR NETWORKING & INTERVIEWS

INTRODUCTION

Here is where you will create your ***Personal Brand Biography (Sell Sheet)*** to use in all of your networking and as an interview leave-behind. Your Sell Sheet will become an important part of your career marketing repertoire. Circulating it to all those with whom you network can help put your brand in the hands of influential professionals and ultimately hiring managers.

You can use the following foundations as a guide to develop your own unique Biography. Mix and match the paragraphs in the various foundations as they pertain to you. Then expand upon the content as it is applicable to your profession, expertise, knowledge, achievements, education, professional affiliations, publications, and/or other pertinent career information. Be sure to incorporate all of your brand elements you developed in this chapter: your features, benefits, competitive edge, value proposition, and return on investment. Tell your story in your biography.

BRING OVER YOUR PERSONAL BRAND COMPONENTS

Start out by opening a blank document and keying in all of your primary Features *(from #3 above)*, Benefits *(from #4)*, Value Proposition *(from #5)*, Competitive Edge *(from #7)*, and Return on Investment *(from #8)*. Having all of your relevant branding information in front of you will help you start the process of creating your ***Personal Brand*** in its various formats. You can use the Foundations that follow or you can create sentences on your own. Just be sure your brand message includes all five of your personal branding components.

BIOGRAPHY FOUNDATION #1

Biography of: ______ (Name)

______ *[your full name]* **is a** ______ *[title]* **and the/a** [☐ world's | ☐ nation's | ☐ region's | ☐ other: ______] [☐ leading | ☐ multiaward-winning | ☐ highly knowledgeable | ☐ creative | ☐ strategic | ☐ responsive | ☐ other attributes: ______] ______ *[your profession]* [☐ executive | ☐ professional | ☐ other: ______] **who has** ______, ______, **and** ______ *[include your value proposition and matching achievements]*.

As a credentialed ______ *[what title or field?]* [☐ expert | ☐ thought leader | ☐ other: ______], ______ *[your first name]* **is one of the top** ______ *[your field of expertise]*. **He/She is a** ______, ______, **and** ______ *[noteworthy professional affiliation positions you hold]* **and author of** ______, ______, **and** ______ *[publication titles]*.

______ *[first name]* **is the founder of** ______ *[business name]*, **a** ______ *[type of]* **firm in** ______ *[town]*, ______ *[state]* **where he/she** ______ *[does what?]* **for** ______ *[what purpose?]*. **He/She** [☐ spearheads | ☐ develops | ☐ facilitates | ☐ performs | ☐ creates | ☐ conducts | ☐ other: ______] ______ *[what?]* **for** ______ *[whom?]*. ______ *[first name]* **has been** ______, ______, **and** ______ *[doing what?]* **by** ______ *[how you do it well]*. **His/Her services include** ______, ______, **and** ______ *[services]*, **and he/she also provides** ______, ______, **and** ______ *[other services]*.

His/Her ______ *[type of]* **work in the** ______ *[which?]* **field has been referred to as** "______," "______," **and** "______" **by her** [☐ superiors | ☐ peers | ☐ clients | ☐ others: ______] **and** ______ *[who?]* **refers to her** ______ *[what work?]* **as** "______," **and** "______" *[testimonial excerpts]*.

______ *[name]* [☐ attended | ☐ obtained his/her (☐ master's / ☐ bachelor's / ☐ associate's) degree(s) at] ______ *[college]* **and started his/her career in** ______ *[which?]* **field where he/she progressed to** ______ *[title]*, **after which** ______ *[name]* ______ *[did what type of work?]* **prior to** [☐ starting his/her business | ☐ other: ______].

Write a paragraph or two concerning your own unique value proposition and competitive edge: ______.

He/She is a member of ______, ______, **and** ______ *[professional affiliations]*. **His/Her talents encompass** ______, ______, **and** ______ *[what areas?]*.

______ *[name]* **Web Portfolio and resume are viewable at** ______.com).

Sample Biography #1 For a Career Management Industry Leader

(The Author's biography at the beginning of the book is a sample of how this foundation can be applied.)

BIOGRAPHY FOUNDATION #2

______ (Name) ***Biography***

Your Slogan / Tagline

______ *[your full name]* **balances** ______ *[type of]* **experience with** ______, ______, **and** ______ *[type of]* [☐ knowledge | ☐ expertise | ☐ abilities | ☐ skills | ☐ other:______] **to** [☐ develop | ☐ execute | ☐ perform | ☐ other: ______] **successful** ______ *[type of]* [☐ strategies | ☐ programs | ☐ solutions | ☐ projects | ☐ processes | ☐ other: ______] **that** ______, ______, **and** ______ *[do what?]*.

Coupled with ______' *[first name]* [☐ Master's | ☐ Bachelor's | ☐ Associate's | ☐ other: ______] **Degree(s) in** ______ *[what?]*, **his/her** ______ *[type of]* **experience and** ______ *[which?]* **abilities allow him/her to** ______ *[do what?]* **that helps** ______ *[accomplish what?]* **for** ______ *[type of]* [☐ firms | ☐ clients | ☐ customers | ☐ patrons | ☐ others: ______].

______' *[first name]* ______ *[type of]* **areas of expertise include** ______, ______, **and** ______ *[what areas?]* **with additional proficiencies in** ______, ______, **and** ______ *[what areas?]*.

With a proven track record of [☐ exceeding goals and expectations | ☐ increasing sales ______% *(percentage)* | ☐ catapulting profits $______ *(amount)* | ☐ maximizing revenues $______ *(amount)* | ☐ elevating productivity ______% *(percentage)* | ☐ expanding market share | ☐ increasing customer service levels | ☐ other: ______] **for his/her** [☐ employers | ☐ clients], **notable achievements** ______, **and** ______ *[your top matching achievements]*.

As a [☐ results-oriented | ☐ client-focused | ☐ solutions-oriented | ☐ revenue-focused | ☐ detail-oriented | ☐ other: ______] *[your primary attributes]* ______ *[type of]* **professional, he/she believes that** ______, ______, **and** ______ *[your profession-related beliefs or mission statement]*.

Write a paragraph or two concerning your own unique value proposition and competitive edge: ______.

______ *[name]* **is proficient in** ______, ______, **and** ______ *[computer programs]*, **which allows him/her to** ______ *[do what?]*. **He/She has participated in** ______, ______, **and** ______ *[what other functions?]* **and brings** [☐ experience | ☐ enthusiasm | ☐ drive ☐ other: ______] **to all of his/her** [☐ projects | ☐ functions | ☐ other: ______].

Sample Biography #2 for a Marketing Specialist

The following up-and-coming Marketing Specialist with dual Bachelor's Degrees in Marketing and Business Administration had experience in sales, publishing, and graphic design, but not so much in marketing—yet. There was no question he was going to succeed in his career endeavors because he is smart, marketing savvy, technically inclined, a quick learner, and has in-depth Internet marketing knowledge.

The following sample also depicts how you can turn a "negative" situation into a "positive" asset. I developed his slogan into a "true statement" by coupling it with a silhouette of a business person on a balancing beam: ***"Balancing Marketing Experience with Sales, Graphic Design, and Publishing Expertise to Develop Successful Marketing Campaigns."*** The client received a number of job opportunities, landed his first noninternship position as a Marketing Specialist, and further progressed to a more challenging position at a larger firm where he handles more of the Internet Marketing analytics functions he enjoys.

His bio was designed into a Sell Sheet that was also used as his Web Portfolio home page.

Kenshin Friedman
BIOGRAPHY

KENSHIN FRIEDMAN balances marketing experience with sales, graphic design, and publishing expertise to develop successful online and print marketing campaign strategies and programs that generate leads, procure new target markets, and maximize return on investment for companies and clients alike.

Coupled with Kenshin's dual Bachelor's Degrees in Marketing and Business Administration, his nine years' successful marketing and sales experience and creative abilities allow him to develop innovative marketing programs that help establish brand recognition, product visibility, and consumer awareness for small to large businesses within highly competitive business markets.

Kenshin's Internet Marketing and online advertising areas of expertise include SEO, SEM, PPC management, and digital content management with additional proficiencies in brand management, social media management, multiplatform advertising, and the publishing market.

With a proven track record of exceeding goals and expectations for his employers and clients, notable achievements include developing effective marketing collateral, creating strategic PowerPoint virtualization presentations, and coordinating lead-generating events.

As a client-focused and solutions-oriented marketing professional, Kenshin believes that unearthing target audience needs, presenting product options that meet those needs, and delivering to exceed expectation is the key to success. And that networking, building strong client relationships and key account leadership solidifies long-term connections that maximize that success!

He is proficient in Adobe Photoshop, Illustrator, and InDesign; Microsoft PowerPoint and Excel; as well as SharePoint, which allows him to creatively conceptualize and design unique marketing collateral that meet client needs. He has participated in trend research, analysis, tracking, and forecasting in the launch of new services.

Kenshin brings experience, enthusiasm, and drive to all of his projects.

"I had the pleasure of collaborating with Kenshin through our company's interest in his internet knowledge. Through our growth, Kenshin gave us excellent feedback on markets to target, helping to grow each company's internet presence, which helped us to focus on areas with the highest ROI for our market. His marketing knowledge was able to find us new avenues to target larger companies, which were monumental in growing our business, and track our marketing campaigns for success."

JOHN GELBERG, Account Manager
EFGH Internet Marketing

Kenshin was one of our brightest young account managers at ABCD Print Solutions. He is a great self starter and is driven to succeed. I was impressed with Kenshin's intellect and his inquisitive nature as he learned about our business and sought to develop his territory. I believe Kenshin is mature beyond his years and handles himself very well in business and professional settings.

MARGE JONES, Executive Vice President, CFO
Treasurer, ABCD Print Solutions

CONTACT KENSHIN AT:

Phone: (000) 000-0000
Email: KFriedman@xxxxx.com
Mail: 1234 Any Road
Any Town, State 00000

CONNECT WITH KENSHIN ON:

Balancing Marketing Experience with Sales, Graphic Design, and Publishing Expertise to Develop Successful Marketing Campaigns

Personal Brand Marketing by CareerCatapult.com

BIOGRAPHY FOUNDATION #3

______ (Name)
Your Slogan / Tagline

As a(n) ______ and ______ *[your primary attributes]* ______ *[your title or profession]*, ______ *[your full name]* ______ *[does what?]*. **He/She works hard to ______** *[achieve what?]*.

With his/her expert knowledge of [☐ the market place | ☐ ______ *(type of)* products | ☐ competitive pricing | ☐ technology | ☐ other expertise: ______] **coupled with exceptional** [☐ relationship-building | ☐ negotiation | ☐ diversity management | ☐ people development | ☐ other: ______] *[your primary skills]* **skills,** ______ *[your first name]* **is able to** [☐ negotiate better prices | ☐ develop cost-effective solutions | ☐ successfully manage ______ *(type of)* projects | ☐ other: ______] **and as a result** ______ *[what you accomplish / the end result]*.

______ *[Name]* **is** ______ *[your competitive edge]*. **Unlike most ______s** *[your title]*, **he/she** ______ *[does what?]*.

As a ______, ______, and ______ *[your secondary attributes]* ______ *[title]*, **he/she always ______, ______, and ______** *[does what?]*. ______ *[explanation of how you do this well]*. ______ **and** ______ *[additional attributes]*, ______ *[name]* **is** [☐ trusted | ☐ well-respected | ☐ well-liked | ☐ other: ______] **in the industry and** ______ *[does what?]*.

Being [☐ positive | ☐ unbiased | ☐ optimistic | ☐ other: ______] **and** [☐ having a sense of humor | ☐ other: ______], **helps ______, ______, and ______** *[with what?]*.

______ *[Name]* **constantly keeps abreast of current** [☐ market conditions | ☐ updated technology | ☐ other: ______] **that can affect** ______ *[what?]* **which helps him/her** ______ *[do what?]*.

Write a paragraph or two concerning your own unique value proposition and competitive edge: ______.

______ *[Name]* **is** [☐ accessible | ☐ approachable | ☐ reliable | ☐ accountable | ☐ other (your secondary) attributes: ______] **to/for** ______ *[what?]*. **As a** [☐ friendly | ☐ genuine | ☐ impartial | ☐ other: ______] **person, he/she is** ______ *[attributes]* **and helps his/her** [☐ firm | ☐ clients | ☐ other: ______] **achieve their goals by way of** ______ *[doing what?]*.

Take Your First Step: Contact ______ *[name]* at **000.000.0000 or email him/her at ______@______**.

Sample Biography #3 for a Realtor

Following is an example of a branded bio for a Realtor using Biography Foundation #3 that includes all five elements of personal branding as well as resume keywords. *(Her positive attributes are shown in italics.)* See if you don't agree that you would select *this* realtor over any others if you were buying or selling your home.

When preparing your bio, be sure to include any additional pertinent information relative to you, as was done in the following biography sample. It is important to include matching achievements in your resume, and you can also add them to your bio. In this example, the achievements were included in the client's biography.

Jane Murphy

LICENSED REAL ESTATE SALESPERSON & CERTIFIED BUYERS' REPRESENTATIVE

House turnaround expert who accelerates results, gets the best prices for her clients in competitive real estate markets, ensures the process goes smoothly, and makes the overall experience enjoyable.

Most people think they should find a house they like and then go with whichever agent advertised that home. Truth is, most agents have access to the same homes for sale. The better method is to first interview and select the realtor who you feel will work hard for you at buying or selling your home, and then go forward with your search for a home or a buyer.

Since 10% of all agents sell 80% of the houses on the market and 90% sell the remainder, as a ***Top Real Estate Producer*** *who is often in the* ***Top 10*** *of the* ***No. 1*** *producing real estate firm on Long Island, Jane Murphy is more able to help you buy or sell your home than 90% of other agents.*

With 7 years in the field, she has built a solid reputation of honesty, fairness, and professionalism. With hundreds of homes for sale, her geographic area covers all of Suffolk County.

As both a Licensed Real Estate Salesperson and a Certified Buyers' Rep, Jane Murphy lists, markets, and sells more houses and finds more homes for buyers that match their needs than her average counterpart. She works hard to turn around your sale or purchase more quickly and smoothly in the shortest timeframe using all resources available to achieve your goals.

With her expert knowledge of the market place and competitive pricing coupled with exceptional negotiation skills, Jane is able to negotiate better prices for buyers and sellers and as a result has saved her clients *tens of thousands of dollars,* getting the process done quickly and with less issues and stress.

> **FOR EXAMPLE:** *A recent buyer selected a home priced at $250,000. Jane put in an offer of $225,000 which was more appropriate for the market in that area, and the seller came back with an offer of $248,000. Though the back-and-forth negotiations didn't prove easy, she got the price down to $230,000 plus concessions saving her client $22,000, which represented a 1100% return on the buyer's investment of $2000.*

As a *fair, honest, and reputable* realtor, she always keeps you current, in the loop, and feeling safe by telling you exactly how it is. If a deal looks like it is falling apart and her clients get discouraged, she doesn't give up. Her *resiliency* keeps everything moving forward by trying out different approaches and solutions, *using fortitude, staying positive,* and *bouncing back.* Whether you are a seller or buyer, she helps you feel comfortable and stay positive even when obstacles occur.

> **FOR EXAMPLE:** *When working with a bi-polar client, Jane helped appease her frustration when an issue with permits arose by refocusing her and working very closely with the attorney on her behalf. The house closed and the client was very thankful.*

Outcome-focused and *hardworking*, Jane is always there for her clients. Because she is *trusted, well-respected, and well-liked* in the industry, she "plays well" with other realtors who are more apt to do the things she needs them to do to help her clients, making the process go a lot *easier, quicker, and more smoothly.*

While other agents work primarily with sellers using a one-sided process, as a designated agent for both buyers and sellers, Janet's entire focus is on you. Being *positive and unbiased with a sense of humor,* she helps make the whole process *more pleasant, less stressful,* and the *fun and exciting experience* it should be.

> **FOR EXAMPLE:** *When working with a divorced couple, she gained the confidence and trust of both parties, and neither felt she favored one over the other which resulted in a smooth process for both in the sale of their house.*

Jane is available to her clients on and off business hours and will return your calls the same day. And unlike most agents, she makes herself available during *every stage of the process* to look out for your best interests.

> **FOR EXAMPLE:** *She doesn't just send the engineer out to appraise your home which is common practice, she is present to be sure the home is appraised correctly, understands problem areas that may require fixing, ensures that any required price adjustments are fair, and can generally save an additional 10% of the market value for her clients. Not many agents can or will do that.*

Having obtained *more training, certifications,* and *expertise* than most agents, Jane constantly keeps abreast of current market conditions that can affect her clients by taking real estate training classes and reading related books and articles on topics such as short sales, foreclosures, mortgages, and the like which helps her find more ways to help and benefit her clients.

With a high referral base from satisfied clients, Jane finds and sells single-family residential properties, condominiums, land, foreclosures, short sales, and apartment rentals.

She puts her real estate knowledge, resources, and connectivity to work for you which spans everything from client needs assessment, market value analysis, competitive pricing, and appraisals—to prequalifying buyers for mortgages and educating you on current real estate market conditions, certificates of title, real estate taxes, underwriters insurance, PITI, mortgage types, contract negotiations, and more.

She invites you to call her. You don't have to commit to anything up front as she doesn't sign on clients until she's walked you through a house or two and you first feel comfortable with her and the process. So there is no risk to you and you have everything to gain.

FOR EXAMPLE: *When working with short sales (that is when the bank agrees to take less than what was originally paid for the house in lieu of the seller having to go into foreclosure), she works with attorneys who are very familiar with all the banks and highly skilled in getting approvals a lot quicker rather than having to wait 6 months to a year stalemating your entire house searching process.*

Today's market conditions represent extreme challenges for not only clients but for realtors as well. Many drop out of the field while others get disgruntled. But because Jane is an *optimistic* person who doesn't get discouraged, she will keep your process moving forward while communicating with you, the attorneys, appraisers, inspectors, engineers, mortgage brokers, and/or builders regularly to ensure everything is moving along smoothly.

Jane doesn't wait for opportunities to pop up for her clients; she works hard at connecting buyers with sellers and unearthing hidden buying or selling opportunities for them.

FOR EXAMPLE: *She found an unlisted property for one of her clients within 2 months and sold their 2 homes within 6 months as opposed to the norm of 1 to 1.5 years in today's market.*

Jane is accessible, approachable, reliable, and accountable to each and every one of her clients. When times get rough, she will help empower, motivate, and inspire you to go forward and will put a smile on your face through her outgoing, entertaining, and playful nature. As a friendly, genuine, and impartial person, she is a good listener, and will try to help you achieve your goals in the very best way possible giving you the unbiased facts in a straightforward manner.

TAKE YOUR FIRST STEP: CONTACT JANE MURPHY at **000-000-000**
or email her at **Xxxxxxx@Xxxxxxxxx.com**.

BIOGRAPHY FOUNDATION #4

______ (Name)

Your Slogan / Tagline

______ *[Your full name]* **is a** ______, ______, **and** ______ *[your primary attributes]* [☐ leader | ☐ executive | ☐ manager | ☐ professional | ☐ other: ______] **who** ______ *[does what?]*. **This includes** ______, ______, **and** ______ *[your primary core competencies / keywords]*.

______ *[Your first name]* **has** ______ *[#]* **years'** [☐ progressive | ☐ tenured | ☐ other: ______] **experience and** [☐ extensive | ☐ in-depth | ☐ proficient | ☐ working] **knowledge of** ______, ______, **and** ______ *[your secondary keywords]*. **Expert in** ______, ______, **and** ______ *[your remaining keywords]*. ______ *[name]* **is also proficient in/at** ______, ______, **and** ______ *[other functions]*. **He/She is a(n)** ______, ______, **and** ______ *[other personal attributes]*.

In his/her most current position as ______ *[title]* **at** ______ *[company]*, **he/she was recruited to** ______ *[do what?]*. **At the time of hire, the** [☐ firm | ☐ company | ☐ organization | ☐ institution | ☐ other: ______] **had/was** ______ *[original situation]*; **it is now at** ______ *[current situation]*. ______' *[Name]* **notable achievements include** ______, ______, **and** ______ *[your primary achievements that match your value proposition]*.

At ______ *[previous employer]*, ______ *[name]* ______ *[accomplished what?]*. **There he/she served on the** ______ *[which?]* **Committee and** ______ *[accomplished what?]*. ______ *[name]* [☐ developed | ☐ conducted | ☐ performed | ☐ other: ______] **the** [☐ Company's | ☐ Region's | ☐ Division's | ☐ Department's | ☐ other: ______] **first** ______ *[which?]* **Program for** ______ *[what purpose?]* **and** ______ *[what else?]*.

Previously, ______ *[name]* **was** ______ *[title]* **at** ______ *[company]*, **where he/she** [☐ developed | ☐ conducted | ☐ performed | ☐ other: ______] ______ *[what functions?]*. **While serving on the** ______ *[which?]* **Committee, he/she created and implemented** ______ *[what?]*. ______ *[Name]* **was selected as** ______ *[acting title]* **to perform** ______ *[what functions?]*. **His/Her earlier career development involved** ______ *[what?]* **where he/she** ______ *[performed what?]*.

Write a paragraph or two concerning your own unique value proposition and competitive edge: ______.

______ *[Name]* **obtained his/her** ______ *[degree]* **Degree in** ______ *[major]* **from** ______ *[college or university]*. **He/She is a member of** ______, ______, **and** ______ *[professional affiliations]*.

______ *[Name]* **can be reached at** ______ *[email]* ______ *[phone number]* [☐ or visit his/her Web Portfolio at ______ *(URL)*].

Sample Biography #4 for a Higher Education Leader

Marianne Jones **is a** strategic, innovative, **and** energetic higher-education leader **who** promotes continuous improvement to the quality of instruction at universities and colleges. **This includes** higher education specialist degree plan development, online program architecture, curriculum design, student assessment program creation, learning resource management, **and** student success coordination.

Marianne **has** 14 **years'** tenured **experience with** extensive **knowledge of** academic culture in multicultural instruction where she has served as Faculty Lead, Head of Academic Advising, and as subject matter expert to instructional staff, advisory committees, **and** students. **Expert in** on-site and online undergraduate and graduate program development, adult education, and Customer Relationship Management administration, Marianne **is also proficient at** time management, budget development, **and** planning. She is a resourceful, adaptable life-long learner **and** team builder.

In her most current position as Mentor **at** ABC University, **she was recruited to** help create and facilitate the University's learning communities. **At the time of hire,** the University had 5000 students; the student body **is now at** 30,000+. Marianne consummated a 98% student graduation success rate by performing ongoing audits that align students' learning needs with assessments; achieved a high retention rate of the student body; helped increase the faculty team's Key Performance Indicators; significantly improved student learning outcomes and pass scores; and achieved "very satisfied" metrics and interdepartmental recognition.

At DEF College, Marianne **served on the** Curriculum Design and Assessment **Committee. She** developed assessment measures and outcomes for each course taught that ensured alignment between performance metrics and learning outcomes. Marianne teaches Business, International Business, Consumer Behavior, and Marketing Research.

Previously, Marianne **was** Lead Faculty and/or Adjunct Faculty **at** GHI Institute, JKL School, and MNO Community College **where she** developed curriculum and taught Business, Finance, Management, and Marketing classes. **While serving on the Committee** for Accreditation, **she created and implemented** a Student Support Center. Her **earlier career development involved** store management **where she** managed the daily operations, customer service, human resources, budgeting, job scheduling, **and** training and development.

Marianne **attained her** MBA **in** General Management and Finance **from** PQR College, and her BA in Economics at STU University. **She is a member of** the Association of International Business.

ADDITIONAL BIOGRAPHY PARAGRAPHS

______ *[Your full name]* **is a** ______ *[title]* **who** [☐ spearheads | ☐ champions | ☐ develops | ☐ establishes | ☐ performs | ☐ executes | ☐ other: ______] ______ *[type of]* [☐ services | ☐ solutions | ☐ other: ______] **for his/her** [☐ firm | ☐ clients | ☐ other: ______]. **He/She represents** [☐ small | ☐ medium | ☐ large] [☐ firms | ☐ businesses | ☐ individuals | ☐ other: ______] **in the** ______, ______, **and** ______ *[which?]* [☐ industries | ☐ markets | ☐ professions | ☐ other: ______] **by providing** ______ *[type of]* **services including** ______, ______, **and** ______ *[services]*.

______ *[First name]* **is a recognized expert in** ______, ______, **and** ______ *[primary areas of expertise]*. **With** ______ *[#]* **years of demonstrated experience in** ______, ______, **and** ______ *[additional areas of expertise]* **and proven success at** ______, ______, **and** ______ *[doing what well?]* **is a highly** [☐ knowledgeable | ☐ responsive | ☐ creative | ☐ other: ______] ______ *[title]* **with** [☐ vision | ☐ integrity | ☐ strategic insight | ☐ other attribute: ______].

______ *[Name]* **is a** [☐ innovative | ☐ strategic | ☐ energetic | ☐ other: ______] ______ *[title]* **who promotes continuous improvement in** ______ *[what?]*. **This includes** ______, ______, **and** ______ *[areas of expertise]*. **He/She is proficient in** ______, ______, **and** ______ *[programs or projects]* **to develop** ______ *[what?]* **that** [☐ generates sales | ☐ procures new markets | ☐ maximizes profits | ☐ slashes costs | ☐ maximizes productivity | ☐ other benefit(s): ______]. ______ *[name]* **is expert in** ______ *[what areas?]* **from the ground up and is also proficient in** ______, ______, **and** ______ *[what areas?]*.

_____ *[Name]* **balances** ______ *[type of]* **experience with** ______, ______, **and** ______ *[type of]* [☐ expertise | ☐ knowledge | ☐ other: _____] **to develop successful** _____ *[type of]* [☐ programs | ☐ projects | ☐ products | ☐ solutions | ☐ other: ______] **that result in** ______ *[what benefits?]*. **His/Her** ______, ______, **and** ______ *[type of]* **abilities allow him/her to** ______ *[do what?]* **that help** ______ *[do what?]* **for** ______ *[whom or what?]*.

In his/her most current position as ______ *[title]* **at** ______ *[employer]*, **he/she was recruited to** ______ *[do what?]*. ______ *[Name]* **consummated a** ______**%** *[percentage]* **success rate by** ______ *[doing what?]*. **Previously, he/she was** ______ *[title]* **at** ______ *[employer]* **where he/she** ______ *[did what?]*. **And at** ______ *[where?]*, **he/she was selected as** ______ *[function]* **where he/she** ______ *[accomplished what?]*. ______**'s** *[Name]* **earlier career development involved** ______, ______, **and** ______ *[type of work]* **where he/she** ______, ______, **and** ______ *[did what?]*.

______ *[Name]* **obtained his/her** ______ *[which?]* **Degree in** ______ *[major]* **from** ______ *[college or university]*, **and his/her** ______ *[which?]* **Degree in** ______ *[major]* **from** ______ *[college or university]*.

CREATE YOUR LINKED-IN PROFILE:
FOR USE IN YOUR SOCIAL MEDIA

INTRODUCTION

LinkedIn is hiring managers' social network of choice as most firms seek candidates to fill their open positions primarily through LinkedIn. All careerists and jobseekers should have a LinkedIn account. It can be written in the first person or third person. *(The LinkedIn Profile Samples below are written in the third person.)*

As in your Biography, your *LinkedIn Profile* should include your brand components. LinkedIn allows 2000 characters *(including spaces)* for your profile. The best way to create your LinkedIn profile is to start off with the *Personal Brand Biography* you just created and keep condensing down it until it is within the 2000-character limit. Or you can apply one of the Foundations below.

Here are four foundations and samples you can use to create your profile. Samples follow each Foundation.

LINKED-IN PROFILE FOUNDATION #1

______ *[Name]* **is the founder of** ______ *[Business Name]*, **a** ______ *[type of]* **firm.** ______ *[Name]* ______ *[does what?]* **to meet the** ______ *[type of]* **needs of** ______ *[whom or what?]*. **A(n)** ______ **and** ______ *[your attributes]*, **he/she has** ______ *[accomplished what?]*.

______ *[Name]* **strategically** ______ *[does what?]* **by** ______, ______, **and** ______ *[doing what well?]*.

He/She [☐ performs | ☐ creates | ☐ develops | ☐ strategizes | ☐ other: ______] ______ *[what?]* **by** ______ *[doing what?]*. **His/Her** [☐ industry-leading | ☐ expert | ☐ other: ______] ______ *[type of]* [☐ expertise | ☐ knowledge | ☐ other: ______] **spans** ______, ______, ______, **and** ______ *[what areas?]*.

Sample LinkedIn Profile #1 for the Career Management Industry Leader *(See LinkedIn image at end of this section.)*

Evelyn Salvador **is the founder of** Creative Image Builders, **a** Business and Personal Branding Strategy and Marketing **firm.** Evelyn fosters a comprehensive, innovative approach to meeting the business-building needs of companies and the career-development needs of the 21st century job seeker—both through successful branding. **A** visionary thought leader, **she has** championed the success of hundreds of businesses and thousands of job seekers since 1990.

Evelyn **strategically** markets businesses and individuals **by** identifying their benefits, defining their (business or personal) brand, creating their brand message, determining their value proposition, **and** capitalizing on their return on investment to their target audience (consumers and prospective employers, respectively) through innovative marketing communications.

She brands companies **by** creating successful websites, logos, brochures, direct mail pieces, and so on. **Her** industry-leading career development **expertise spans** resume writing, career coaching, job searching, web portfolio development, **and** positive online identity building.

LINKED-IN PROFILE FOUNDATION #2

______ *[Name]* **balances** ______ *[type of]* **experience with** ______ *[what?]* [☐ expertise | ☐ knowledge | ☐ education | ☐ other: ______] **to develop successful** ______ *[type of]* [☐ products | ☐ campaigns | ☐ projects | ☐ other: ______] **that** [☐ generate leads | ☐ increase sales | ☐ procure new target markets | ☐ maximize return on investment | ☐ catapult revenues | ☐ elevate productivity | ☐ decrease costs | ☐ other: ______]. **Coupled with his/her** [☐ Master's | ☐ Bachelor's | ☐ Associate's] **Degrees in** ______ *[what?]*, ______ *[#]* **years of successful** ______ *[type of]* **experience and** ______ **as well as** ______ *[what?]* **abilities allow him/her to help** ______ *[whom or what?]*.

______**'s** *[Name]* ______ *[which?]* **areas of expertise include** ______, ______, **and** ______ *[what areas?]*. **Notable achievements include** ______, ______, **and** ______ *[state matching achievements]*. [☐ Client-focused | ☐ Solutions-oriented | ☐ Profitability-conscious | ☐ other attributes: ______], ______ *[name]* **believes that** ______ *[your beliefs]* **is the key to success. And that** ______, ______, **and** ______ *[what?]* **maximizes success.**

He/She is proficient in ______, ______, **and** ______ *[what programs?]* **that allows him/her to** ______ *[do what?]*. ______ *[Name]* **has participated in** ______, ______, **and** ______ *[what areas?]* **and brings** [☐ experience | ☐ enthusiasm | ☐ drive | ☐ other: ______] **to all of his/her** [☐ projects | ☐ other: ______].

Sample LinkedIn Profile #2 for the Marketing Specialist

Kenshin Friedman **balances** marketing **experience with** sales, graphic design, and publishing expertise **to develop successful** online and print marketing campaigns **that** generate leads, procure new target markets, and maximize return on investment. **Coupled with his** dual Bachelor's **Degrees in** Marketing and Business Administration, nine **years of successful** marketing and sales **experience as well as** creative **abilities allow him to help** establish brand recognition, product visibility, and consumer awareness within highly competitive markets.

Kenshin's marketing and online advertising **areas of expertise include** SEO, SEM, PPC management, digital content management, brand management, social media management, **and** multiplatform advertising. **Notable achievements include** developing effective marketing collateral, creating strategic PowerPoint presentations, coordinating lead-generating events, and exceeding goals and expectations.

Client-focused and solutions-oriented, Kenshin **believes that** unearthing target audience needs and presenting product options that meet those needs **is the key to success. And that** networking, building strong client relatic connections that **maximize that success!**

He is proficient in Adobe Photoshop, Illustrator, and InDesign, Microsoft Power **that allows him to** creatively conceptualize Kenshin **has participated in** trend research, analysis, tracking, and forecasting in the launch of new services **and brings** experience and enthusiasm **to all of his** projects.

LINKED-IN PROFILE FOUNDATION #3

As a _______ *[title],* _______ *[name]* _______ *[does what?].* **He/She works hard to** _______ *[do what?]* **in order to achieve his/her** [ ] employers' | [ ] clients' | [ ] others: _______] **goals.**

With his/her expert knowledge of _____ *[what?]* **coupled with exceptional** _______, _______, **and** _______ *[your primary abilities]* **skills,** _______ *[name]* **is able to** _______ *[do what?]* **and as a result has** _______, _______, **and** _______ *[accomplished what?].* **He/She keeps abreast of current** _____ *[type of]* **conditions that can affect his/her** [ ] firm | [ ] clients | [ ] other: _______] **and stays on top of** _______ *[what areas?],* **which helps him/her** _______ *[do what?].*

Write a few sentences or paragraph concerning your own unique value proposition and competitive edge: _______. **Because** _______ *[name]* **is a(n)** _______ *[type of]* **person who** _______ *[does what?],* **he/she will** _______ *[do what well?].* _______ *[Name]* **doesn't wait for opportunities to present themselves; he/she** _______ *[does what well?].*

_______ *[Name]* **is** [ ] accessible | [ ] approachable | [ ] reliable | [ ] accountable | [ ] other attributes: _______] **to/for** _______ *[what?].* **As a** [ ] friendly | [ ] genuine | [ ] impartial | [ ] other attributes: _______] **person, he/she is** _______ *[attributes]* **and helps his/her** [ ] firm | [ ] clients | [ ] other: _______] **achieve their goals by way of** _______ *[doing what?].*

Sample LinkedIn Profile #3 for the Realtor

As a Licensed Real Estate Salesperson and a Certified Buyers' Rep, Jane Murphy lists, markets, and sells more houses and finds more homes for buyers that match their needs than her average counterpart. **She works hard to** turn around sales or purchases more quickly and smoothly in the shortest timeframe using all resources available **in order to achieve her** clients' **goals.**

With her expert knowledge of the market place and competitive pricing **coupled with exceptional** negotiation **skills,** Jane **is able to** negotiate better prices for buyers and sellers **and as a result has** saved her clients tens of thousands of dollars, getting the process done quickly and with less issues and stress. **She keeps abreast of** current market **conditions that can affect her** clients **and stays on top of** short sales, foreclosures, and mortgage rates, **which helps her find more ways to benefit her clients.**

Today's market conditions represent extreme challenges for not only clients but for realtors as well. Many drop out of the field while others get disgruntled. **Because** Jane **is an** optimistic **person who** doesn't get discouraged, **she** will keep the process moving forward while communicating with her clients, the attorneys, appraisers, inspectors, engineers, mortgage brokers, and/or builders regularly to ensure everything is moving along smoothly. Jane **doesn't wait for opportunities** to pop up for her clients; **she** works hard at connecting buyers with sellers and unearthing hidden buying or selling opportunities for them.

Jane **is** accessible, approachable, reliable, and accountable **to** each and every one of her clients. When times get rough, she will help empower, motivate, and inspire you to go forward and will put a smile on your face through her outgoing, entertaining, and playful nature. **As a** friendly, genuine, and impartial **person, she is** a good listener **and helps her** clients **achieve their goals** in the very best way possible giving them the unbiased facts in a straight-forward manner.

LINKED-IN PROFILE FOUNDATION #4

I am a(n) ______, ______, **and** ______ *[your primary attributes]* [☐ leader | ☐ executive | ☐ professional | ☐ other: ______] **who** ______ *[does what?]*. **Including** ______, ______, ______, ______, **and** ______ *[your primary keywords / core competencies]*.

With ______ *[#]* **years' experience in** ______, ______, **and** ______ *[your secondary keywords]*, **I have served as** ______, ______, **and** ______ *[your various titles]*. **I am expert in** ______, ______, **and** ______ *[what key areas?]*.

As ______ *[your title or function]* **at** ______ *[company or organization]*, **I was recruited to** ______ *[do what?]* **where I** ______, ______, **and** ______ *[accomplished what?]* **and achieved** ______ *[what?]*.

At ______ *[company or organization]*, **I** ______ *[performed what?]*. **As** ______ *[title]*, **I** ______, ______, **and** ______ *[accomplished what?]*. **Serving on the** ______ *[which?]* **Committee, I developed** ______ *[what?]*. **Previously, as** ______ *[title]*, **I** ______, ______, **and** ______ *[accomplished what?]*.

Sample LinkedIn Profile #4 for the Higher Education Leader

I am a strategic, innovative, and energetic higher-education leader **who** promotes continuous improvement to the quality of instruction at universities and colleges. **Including** degree plan development, online program architecture, curriculum design, student assessment program creation, academic and international student advisement, learning resource management, and student success coordination.

With 14 **years' experience in** academic culture **and** multicultural instruction, **I have served as** Faculty Lead, Head of Academic Advising, Adjunct Faculty, **and** subject matter expert. **I am expert in** on-site and online undergraduate and graduate program development, adult education, and Customer Relationship Management administration.

As Mentor at ABC University, **I was recruited to** help create and facilitate the University's learning communities **where I** consummated a 98% student graduation success rate, helped increase the faculty team's Key Performance Indicators, significantly improved student learning outcomes, **and achieved** "very satisfied" metrics.

Serving on the Curriculum Design and Assessment **Committee**, **I** developed course assessment measures and co-championed the Department's Master of Science in Business plan. **Previously, as** Lead Faculty and Adjunct Faculty **at** various colleges, I devised curriculum and taught business, economics, and marketing courses and served on the Committee for Accreditation.

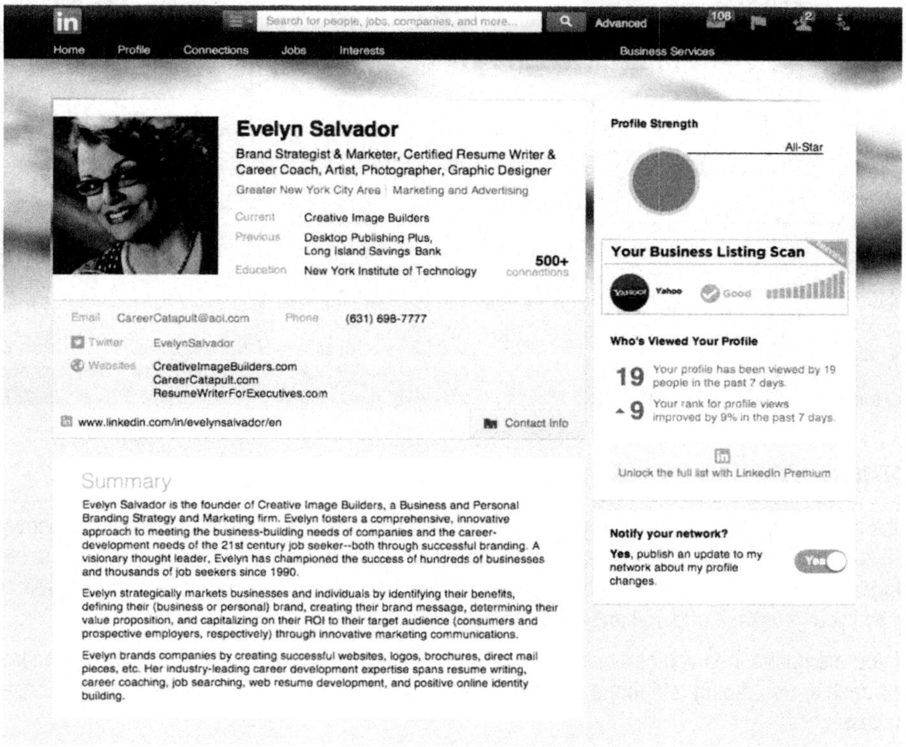

DEVELOP YOUR ELEVATOR PITCH:
FOR USE IN ALL OF YOUR NETWORKING & INTERVIEWS

INTRODUCTION

Your ***Personal Brand Message*** written in the form of an ***Elevator Pitch*** is what you will convey when you introduce yourself to others while networking and—most importantly—conducting your interviews. It serves as your standard response to the question, ***"What do you do?"*** or ***"What can you tell me about yourself?"*** and is best kept to within 30 to 60 seconds to catch your listener's attention and make it easier for you to memorize it. There is no "one size fits all" foundation suitable for everyone concerning the development of a brand message. However, guidelines, foundations, and samples follow that you can use as a guide to develop your own unique message.

PERSONAL BRAND "BEFORE AND AFTER" EXAMPLE

In the graphic that follows, take note of the **"KEY"** and where the five personal branding components are included in the brand message.

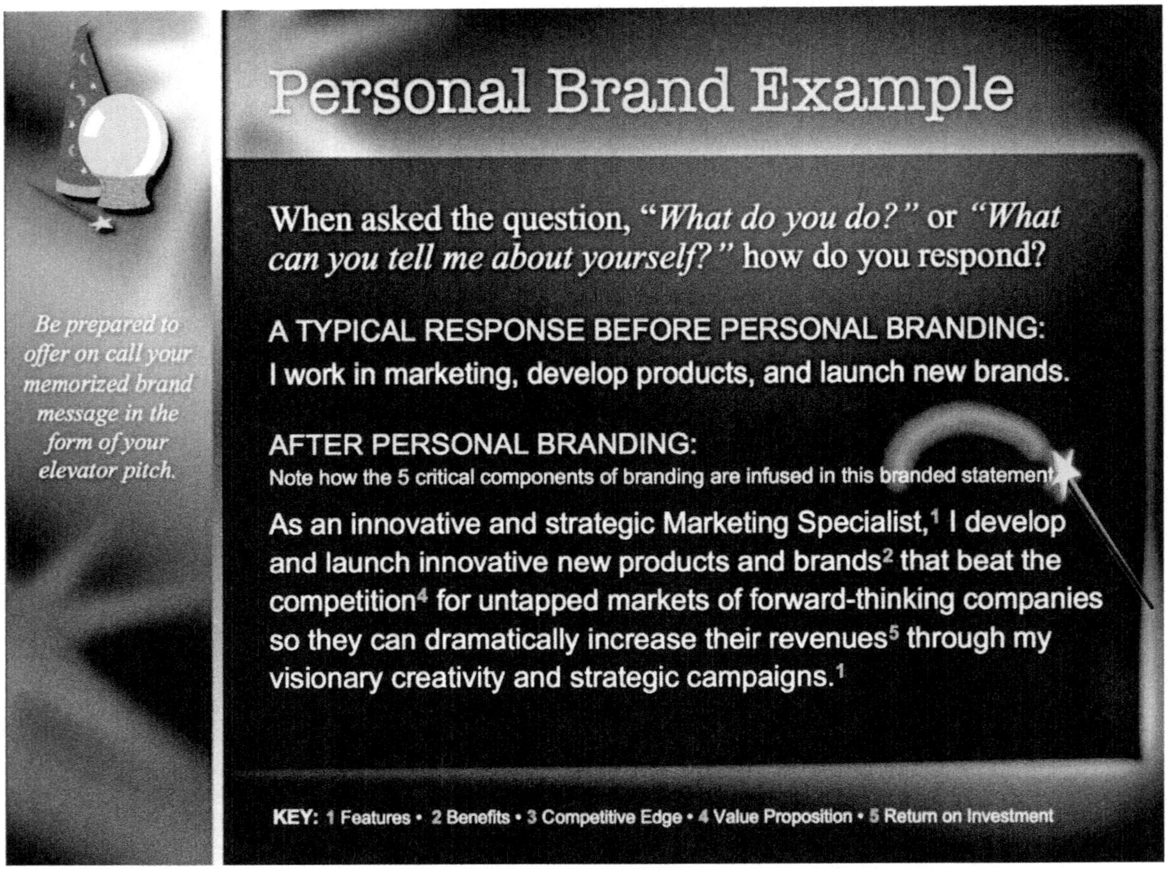

START DEVELOPING YOUR ELEVATOR PITCH

Now that you have all of the ingredients you need to write your Elevator Pitch, brainstorm all possible solutions that convey your brand; edit it until you are comfortable that it is accurate, ensure it includes all of your brand components, and presents you in the best of light. You can start with your ***Personal Brand Biography*** or ***LinkedIn Profile*** and condense it further, or take the lists you developed and sentences you wrote and join them, recreate them, and edit your message until you are satisfied. Make it memorable!

Then repeat it daily until you memorize it so you can use it over and over again whenever you network and go on interviews. Keep it handy on your person or at your desk to use during telephone conversations so you can read it until you start to memorize and own it. It will help empower you to your success!

ELEVATOR PITCH FOUNDATION #1

As a(n) ______ **and** ______ *[your primary attributes]* ______ *[job title]*, **I** ______ *[what you do, your features and benefits]* **for** ______ *[type of firms you provide benefits to]* **so they can** ______ *[what you help them achieve through your value proposition and ROI]* **through my** ______, ______, **and** ______ *[your competitive edge and/or attributes / features]*.

Sample Elevator Pitch #1 for a Vice President of New Business Development

As an innovative and strategic New Business Development Executive, **I** develop visionary products, increase market share, drive sales and revenues, and elevate product profitability **for** forward-thinking technology firms **so they can** deliver profits to shareholders **through my** strategic planning leadership and direction, new program creation, and business development initiatives.

Sample Elevator Pitch #1 for a Customer Service Manager

As an experienced Customer Service Manager, **I** direct and oversee sales, customer service, merchandising, front end, and warehouse areas **for** Fortune 500 grocery chains **so they can** improve staff performance, increase service levels, streamline supply flow, elevate customer loyalty, and increase sales **through my** consumer-needs awareness and value-added approach.

Sample Elevator Pitch #1 for a Compliance Officer

As a proactive, quality-oriented Compliance Officer, **I** am an objective reviewer and evaluator **for** various departments of large corporations **so they can** be sure that all business activities are in compliance with regulatory requirements and company policies and procedures **through my** ability to identify potential risk areas and immediately resolve compliance issues.

Sample Elevator Pitch #1 for a Purchasing Agent

As a detail-oriented Purchasing Agent, **I** perform all facets of buying, merchandising, inventory control, and order processing **for** all departments of small to midsize businesses **so they can** successfully delivery products on time, increase purchasing service levels, and slash costs **through my** skillful contract negotiations and ability to manage and control inventory to meet the firms' needs.

ELEVATOR PITCH FOUNDATION #2

I am a ______ *[job title]*, **who** ______ *[does what?]* **with a** ______ *[type of]* **success rate of** ______**%** *[percentage]*. **I do this by** ______ *[how accomplished]* **that includes** ______, ______, **and** ______ *[what areas?]*. **I am expert in/at** ______, ______, **and** ______ *[what areas?]*.

Sample Elevator Pitch #2 for the Career Management Industry Leader

I am a Business and Personal Brand Strategist, author, and award-winning career management industry leader **who** positions people in the top 2 percent in their industry. As such, they succeed a lot quicker and earn a lot more than their average counterpart. **I do this by** discovering and building their Personal Brand and leveraging it across marketing platforms in all of their print and online communications through creative design and marketing-savvy wordsmithing that compels hiring managers to seek them out.

Sample Elevator Pitch #2 for the Realtor

I am a Real Estate Turnaround Expert **who** accelerates results, gets the best prices for my buyers and sellers, and ensures the whole process runs smoothly—while making your house buying or selling experience enjoyable. **I have a** turnaround **success rate of** 95% for both my buyers and sellers.

Sample Elevator Pitch #2 for the Higher Education Leader

I am a higher-education leader **who** promotes continuous improvement to the quality of instruction at colleges and universities **with a** student graduation **success rate of** 98%. **I do this by** spearheading and launching new programs, plans, and curriculum design. **I am expert in** on-site and online undergraduate and graduate program development, adult education, affiliation agreements, and Customer Relationship Management.

ELEVATOR PITCH FOUNDATION #3

I balance ______ *[type of]* [☐ experience | ☐ knowledge] **with** ______, ______, **and** ______ *[what?]* **expertise to develop successful** ______ *[what?]* [☐ strategies | ☐ programs | ☐ products | ☐ plans | ☐ solutions | ☐ campaigns | ☐ other: ______] **that** ______, ______, **and** ______ *[does what?]*.

Sample Elevator Pitch #3 for the Marketing Specialist

I balance marketing **experience with** sales, graphic design, **and** publishing **expertise to develop successful** online and print marketing campaign strategies and programs **that** generate leads, procure new target markets **and** maximize return on investment for companies and clients alike.

ELEVATOR PITCH FOUNDATION #4

As a(n) ______ **and** ______ *[your primary attributes]* ______ *[job title]*, **I** [☐ analyze | ☐ build | ☐ champion | ☐ conduct | ☐ conceptualize | ☐ configure | ☐ develop | ☐ design | ☐ direct | ☐ establish | ☐ implement | ☐ improve | ☐ launch | ☐ manage | ☐ maximize | ☐ oversee | ☐ perform | ☐ spearhead | ☐ strategize | ☐ structure | ☐ validate | ☐ other: ______] ______ *[what?]* **for** ______ *[whom or what?]* **that** ______ *[does what?]*, **thereby** ______ *[accomplishing what through your benefits and competitive edge?]* **and resulting in** ______ *[your value proposition]*.

Sample Elevator Pitch #3 for an Architect / Construction Manager

As an innovative, detail-oriented Architect, **I** design and build highly complex multimillion-dollar commercial buildings and restoration sites **for** a leading national construction management firm **that** involves supervising up to 12 trades simultaneously, meeting all budgets, and coming in ahead of schedule **thereby** satisfying clients **and resulting in** obtaining referrals and escalating profits for my employer.

CREATE YOUR UNIQUE ELEVATOR PITCH

As mentioned earlier, developing your Personal Brand is the most thought-provoking part of all of the content contained in this Book; and since your brand message is critical to help position you in the top percentage of candidates in your field of expertise, take the time it needs to get it right. Your Elevator Pitch will be the first thing you say when meeting new contacts while networking and conducting your interviews, so you will want to ensure it is just the right message for you. It can also be included in your career marketing materials.

Answer the question, ***"What do you do?"*** or ***"Tell me about yourself"*** by brainstorming many different ways you can infuse your brand components into marketing-savvy sentences that sell your unique value. Jot down the first things that come to mind. Nothing is "wrong" at this stage. Construct a number of sentences or paragraphs as possible Elevator Pitches. Review each and combine and/or edit them to ensure it includes all of your brand components.

Write out several possible brand messages, and perfect it until you feel you "own" it. Come back to it several times to edit it until you feel it is "right." In fact, as I often do when I craft resumes, circle back to it again after you complete the ***Step-by-Step Resumes*** process. Once you finalize it, double-check that it includes all of your brand components and start to memorize it. Keep it near your phone and/or computer at all times so you can use it as a script until you have memorized it.

Try Out Several Brand Messages for Your Elevator Pitch:

WRITE YOUR SLOGAN / TAG LINE

FOR USE IN ALL OF YOUR CAREER MARKETING MATERIALS

INTRODUCTION

A ***Slogan***—or ***Tag Line***—is a memorable, succinct phrase or motto that best sells you apart from your competition. Although optional, a Slogan is very beneficial to include in your resume as it states what you are good at and what you have to offer a prospective employer as soon as they view your resume. Your slogan should provide an idea of who you are or what you do in as few words as possible.

Add your Slogan to all of your career marketing materials including on your Resume, Cover Letter, Web Portfolio, LinkedIn Profile, all email and online messages, business cards, letterhead, blog, Career Portfolio, Interview Thank You Letters, and any other professional communications. In your resume, it is typically placed under your resume header centered in large italics.

Here you will create ***Your Slogan / Tag Line.*** It can be a condensed version of your Elevator Pitch or other catchy words that include your value proposition. The more catchy your Slogan, the easier it will be to remember. Using a well-defined, short Slogan can sell your value proposition to hiring managers right up front...before even reading your resume.

SAMPLE SLOGANS

- **FOR THE CAREER MANAGEMENT INDUSTRY LEADER:** *"Positioning Candidates in the Top 2 Percent in their Field of Expertise"*
- **FOR THE MARKETING SPECIALIST:** *"Balancing Marketing Experience with Sales, Graphic Design, and Publishing Expertise to Develop Successful Marketing Campaigns"*
- **FOR THE REALTOR:** *"House turnaround expert who accelerates results, gets the best prices for her clients in competitive real estate markets, ensures the process goes smoothly, and makes the overall experience enjoyable"*
- **FOR THE HIGHER EDUCATION EXECUTIVE:** *"Higher Education Leader Promoting Continuous Improvement to the Quality of Instruction with a 98% Student Graduation Success Rate."*
- **FOR A CONSTRUCTION MANAGER:** *"Bringing Projects in On Time and Within Budget...Every Time!"*
- **FOR A CREATIVE DIRECTOR:** *"Helping You Brand Your Clients Ahead of Their Competition"*
- **FOR A SALES MANAGER:** *"Meeting Challenges, Overcoming Obstacles, Selling Solutions, and Closing Sales"*
- **FOR AN EXECUTIVE CHEF:** *"From Gourmet Appetizers to Fine Desserts"*
- **FOR A CHARTER PILOT:** *"Flying from the Caribbean to Mexico and Everywhere in Between"*
- **FOR A REGISTERED NURSE:** *"Providing Caring, Professional Medical Care to All Patients...from Infants to Geriatrics"*
- **FOR AN ELEMENTARY TEACHER:** *"Creating a Trusting and Nurturing Learning Environment for All Students"*
- **FOR A HIGH SCHOOL TEACHER:** *"Helping Students Take Positive Steps Toward their Future"*
- **FOR AN INFORMATION TECHNOLOGY PROFESSIONAL:** *"Providing complete IT solutions with dedication to service."*

WRITE YOUR SLOGAN

To write your own unique Slogan, start by culling out the critical keywords and phrases from your *Elevator Pitch* by moving around and editing the words until you come up with an impactful Slogan that exemplifies what you have to offer. Brainstorm a host of other short phrases that include your value proposition and/or some of your branding words. Edit and refine them. Try out a number of different phrases, condensing it to as few words as possible, until you feel your Slogan is just right for you.

CREATE YOUR PROFESSIONAL SUMMARY
FOR YOUR RESUME

INTRODUCTION

Your ***Professional Summary / Executive Profile***—the first section of your resume—differs somewhat from the ***Elevator Pitch*** and other personal branding formats you completed above, however, uses the same branding components you identified in the ***Personal Brand Worksheet*** you completed. Since your ***Professional Summary*** is an all-important encapsulated summary of your professional self and can determine whether or not your resume will be read, it should whet the appetite of the reader by showcasing the value you have to offer an employer.

Professional Summary Foundations (and corresponding samples) are provided below for you to include your unique information in order to construct a summary that showcase(s) your primary keywords, primary personal attributes, and brand components. Adjust sentences as they are applicable to your unique experience. Go back to ***Step 3: Check Off Your Personal Attributes & Capabilities*** and infuse some of the attributes you checked off under *"Skill Sets."*

Note how each sample below and throughout this section that uses the same foundation is entirely different, and it is impossible to recognize that the same foundation was used to construct the *Professional Summary.*

PROFESSIONAL SUMMARY FOUNDATION #1

______ *[#]* **years of** [☐ progressive | ☐ tenured] ______ *[type of]* **experience in the** ______ *[which?]* **field** ______ *[doing what?]* **including** ______, ______, ______, **and** ______ *[your primary keywords].* **Proven proficiency in** ______, ______, ______, **and** ______ *[what areas?]* [☐ with additional knowledge of ______ and ______ *(additional skill sets)*]. [☐ Clientele have included ______, ______, and ______ *(whom?)* | ☐ Interface directly with ______ *[whom?]* regarding ______ *[primary areas of expertise]*.] **A(n)** ______ *[industry]* **professional with excellent** ______, ______, **and** ______ *[type of]* **skills** [☐ and the ability to ______ *[do what well?]* | ☐ who delivers ______ *(your value proposition)*.]

SAMPLE FOR A CREATIVE DIRECTOR / GRAPHIC DESIGNER

Three **years of** creative direction and graphic design **experience in the** advertising **field** designing successful advertising campaigns **including** client needs assessment, solutions strategizing, layout and design conceptualization, illustration, **and** photo retouching. **Proven proficiency in** creating logos, ads, brochures, **and** publications **with additional knowledge of** Website design and development. **Interface directly with** key advertising agencies and public relations firms **regarding** marketing, press coverage, publicity, and visual communications. **Clientele have included** Fortune 500 firms, industrial manufacturers, **and** small businesses. **An** advertising **professional with excellent** client relations, design, **and** problem-solving **skills who delivers** revenue-generating solutions for employers and clients alike.

SAMPLE FOR AN EXECUTIVE CHEF

Fourteen **years of** progressive **experience in** restaurant and hotel management in an Executive or Head Chef position **in the** culinary arts **field including** hiring and training sous chefs and cooks, menu planning and cooking, buying, catering, maintaining inventory, controlling and negotiating food costs, **and** delegating tasks. **Proven proficiency in** Continental and Italian culinary arts, butchering, **and** food decoration. **A** culinary management **professional with excellent** creativity and staff development **skills and the ability to** motivate staff to achieve the highest quality of culinary arts standards encompassing appetizers, entrees, and desserts resulting in high revenue returns.

SAMPLE FOR A SOCIAL WORKER

Eight **years of** tenured social work **experience** counseling adolescents at various cognitive and emotional levels in various settings including group homes, schools, **and** mental-health facilities. **Proven proficiency in** advocacy and linkage, casework, client needs assessments, goal planning, **and** life skills training **with knowledge of** housing coordination **and** referral servicing. **Clientele have included** emotionally disturbed, learning disabled, developmentally delayed, and depressed adolescents as well as those diagnosed with ADHD, bipolar disorder, schizophrenia, autism, cerebral palsy, **and** mental retardation. **A** mental health **professional with excellent** communications, advocacy, **and** troubleshooting **skills and the ability to** establish and build positive, solid relationships with clients, their families, associates, and all mental health professionals.

PROFESSIONAL SUMMARY FOUNDATION #2

A(n) ______ **and** ______ *[primary personal attributes]* ______ *[type of]* [☐ professional | ☐ executive | ☐ manager] **experienced in** ______, ______, ______, **and** ______ *[primary skill areas]*. [☐ Fully versed in ______, ______, **and** ______ *(secondary skill areas)* | ☐ Background encompasses the ability to ______ *(do what?)*]. **High degree of responsibility in** ______ *[what area?]*. [☐ Demonstrated | ☐ Proven] **ability to work effectively both independently and as an integral part of a team effort to achieve** ______ *[what?]* **goals. A strong** ______ *[title / function]* **with a high degree of responsibility** [☐ in ______ *[what?)* | ☐ who works well with ______ and ______ alike]. **Adept at handling** ______ *[what?)* **and developing proactive** ______ *[type of strategies, methods, procedures]*. [☐ Computer experience includes ______, ______, and ______ *(programs)*.]

SAMPLE FOR A DATABASE MANAGER

A results-oriented Information Technology **professional experienced in** database installation, implementation, troubleshooting, and management, as well as office management and customer relations. **Fully versed in** tracking customer information, report generation, account management, estimate development, **and** project scheduling. **Demonstrated ability to work effectively both independently and as an integral part of a team effort to achieve** business **goals. A strong** problem-solver **with a high degree of responsibility** in tacking challenges with automated solutions.

SAMPLE FOR AN ACCOUNTING VICE PRESIDENT

A seasoned upper-level financial **executive with extensive experience in** accounting management. **Background encompasses the ability to** reduce overall costs while increasing levels of productivity and profitability. **Proven ability to** train and develop staff to exceed goals while raising morale. **Fully versed in** addressing and resolving client concerns and maintaining a positive rapport with all levels of internal and external clients. Analytically inclined problem-solver with leadership and management development skills. **Computer experience includes** Microsoft Word and Excel, Simply Accounting, Filemaker Pro, **and** ACCPAC.

SAMPLE FOR A SCHOOL PSYCHOLOGIST

A caring **and** patient mental-health **professional experienced in** psychology, early childhood intervention and evaluation, **and** testing gifted to multihandicapped children. **Fully versed in** psychological assessments, designing IEP goals, identifying and interpreting situations, counseling, running parent workshops, representing the school district at impartial hearings, **and** working with various clientele. **High degree of responsibility in** problem-solving with resolution follow up, client relations, **and** crisis intervention. **A strong** advocate who works well with staff, clients, and resource personnel alike. **Adept at handling** crises **and developing proactive** counseling plans to assist students in realizing their fullest potential.

PROFESSIONAL SUMMARY FOUNDATION #3

A(n) ______ *[attribute]* ______ *[title]* **with a** [☐ distinctive | ☐ progressive] **career in** ______ **and** ______ *[primary targeted areas]* **management including** ______, ______, **and** ______ *[primary skill areas]* **with full responsibility for** ______ **and** ______ *[what?]*. **Diverse business spheres include** ______, ______, **and** ______ *[what environments?]*. **Broad-based experience encompasses** ______, ______, ______, **and** ______ *[primary keywords]*. **Recognized for the ability to** ______ *[do what well?]*. **A(n)** [☐ effective | ☐ self-directed | ☐ motivated | ☐ other: ______] [☐ leader | ☐ team builder | ☐ professional | ☐ executive | ☐ manager | ☐ other: ______] **with the ability to consistently achieve objectives. Computer experience includes** ______, ______, **and** ______ ***(programs)***.

SAMPLE FOR A CHIEF FINANCIAL OFFICER

A results-oriented senior financial officer **with a distinctive career in** general and financial management **including** the direction and streamlining of corporate financial operations **with full responsibility for** financial reporting and cost reduction. **Diverse business spheres include** manufacturing, distribution, and entrepreneurial business startup. **Broad-based experience encompasses** business restructuring and reengineering, strategic planning, and cost containment. **Recognized for the ability to** coach and develop staff. **A self-directed and motivated executive with the ability to consistently achieve objectives. Computer experience includes** Microsoft Access, Excel, Word, Outlook, and Explorer; ACTI; Visual Manufacturing; Crystal Report Writer; **and** UNIX.

SAMPLE FOR AN IT SALES & MARKETING EXECUTIVE

A proactive information technology **executive with a progressive career in** the high-tech industry and the electronic communications field **with full responsibility for** sales, marketing, advertising, **and** public relations functions. **Diverse business spheres include** the systems integration market place interfacing with distribution and manufacturing channels. **Broad-based experience encompasses** systems analysis, LAN-to-host connectivity, system component design, heterogeneous network solutions, **and** software customization. **Recognized for the ability to** stay on top of the high-tech industry and consistently increase profits. An effective problem-solver and staff motivator.

SAMPLE FOR A QUALITY ASSURANCE MANAGER

A seasoned Quality Assurance Manager **with a distinctive career in** quality assurance, operations, and front-line management **including** customer service, research and analysis, quality control, auditing, **and** personnel management. **Recognized for the ability to** manage multicounter operations, service agent productivity, **and** increase revenues. **An effective leader and team builder skilled in** training, developing, coaching, and motivating others **with the ability to consistently achieve objectives.**

PROFESSIONAL SUMMARY FOUNDATION #4

A(n) ______, ______ *[your primary attributes]* ______ *[title]* **with** ______ *[#]* **years of experience spanning all aspects of** ______, ______, **and** ______ *[your main core competencies].* **Extensive background in** [☐ managing | ☐ executing | ☐ performing | ☐ other: ______] ______ *[what?]* **for this** ______ *[type of]* **firm including** [☐ commercial | ☐ residential | ☐ industrial | ☐ civil | ☐ municipal | ☐ other: ______] [☐ design | ☐ design-and-build | ☐ construction | ☐ carpentry | ☐ installation | ☐ remodeling | ☐ repair | ☐ other: ______] **projects including** ______, ______, **and** ______ *[project types]*. **Adept at** ______ *[what functions?]* **including** ______, ______, **and** ______ *[what?]*. **A solid knowledge of** ______, ______, **and** ______ *[what?]* **with exceptional** [☐ mechanical | ☐ mathematical | ☐ analytical | ☐ problem-solving | ☐ other: ______] **skills. Consistent record of completing projects on time and within budget, while providing superior** [☐ workmanship | ☐ productivity | ☐ customer service | ☐ other: ______].

SAMPLE FOR A PROJECT MANAGER

A results-oriented, profitability-conscious Project Manager **with** more than 12 **years of experience spanning all aspects of** project lifecycle management, trades coordination, labor relations management, **and** structural problem solving via action-driven leadership, direction, and support. **Extensive background in managing** major commercial construction **projects for this construction management firm** including high-rise buildings, universities, industrial plants, and retail malls. **Adept at** coordinating multiple subcontractors simultaneously and in developing tactical action plans that direct high-producing teams to overcome boundaries and successfully meet all challenges and goals

SAMPLE FOR AN ELECTRICIAN

A Licensed Electrician **with** 10 **years of experience spanning all aspects of** electrical installations, repairs, and maintenance **for** major civil and industrial **projects. Adept at** installing, testing, troubleshooting, and resolving all types of electrical **systems with a solid knowledge of** high-voltage electrical systems, high-tension distribution systems, above-ground conduits, **and** underground electrical services **with exceptional** mechanical and problem-solving **skills. Consistent record of completing projects on time and within budget, while providing superior** workmanship and customer service.

SAMPLE FOR A CONSTRUCTION LABORER

A trusted and dedicated Construction Laborer **with** seven **years of experience spanning all aspects of** carpentry, framing, floor-to-floor build-outs, steel reinforcement, drywall, tiling, trim work, roofing, **and** decking **for** residential construction **projects. Solid knowledge of** the use of all carpentry equipment, tools, **and** materials **with** high quality workmanship.

PROFESSIONAL SUMMARY FOUNDATION #5

______ *[#]* **years of professional** ______ **and** ______ *[type of]* **experience in the** ______ *[which field or industry?]* **working for various** ______ *[type of]* [☐ facilities | ☐ firms | ☐ organizations | ☐ agencies | ☐ other: ______]. **Full knowledge of** ______, ______, **and** ______ *[primary skill areas].* **Proven ability to** ______, ______, ______, **and** ______ *[do what?]*. **Highly skilled in** ______ **and** ______ *[additional skill areas].* [☐ Multiskilled ______ *[type of]* professional who is ______, ______, and ______ *(primary attributes)*. | ☐ Attributes include ______, ______, and ______ *(primary attributes)*.] **Proficient in** ______ **with knowledge of** ______ *[additional knowledge areas].*

SAMPLE FOR A MEDICAL BILLING & COLLECTIONS SPECIALIST

Twelve **years of professional** billing, collection, and supervisory **experience in the** medical **field working for various** multimodality **facilities. Full knowledge of** medical terminology and insurance laws as well as policies of Medicare, No-Fault, Workers' Compensation, HMOs, **and** third-party payers. **Highly skilled in** productivity improvement, quality assurance, research and analysis, bookkeeping, **and** general accounting. **Multiskilled** medical **professional who is** honest, hard working, **and** detail-oriented with ability to work in a fast-paced environment, establish effective relationships, and work as a team player with patients, staff, and management. **Proficient in** Versyss, AccuMed, and Medic Vision systems **with knowledge of** ADS and Microsoft Word.

SAMPLE FOR A SECURITY DIRECTOR

Ten **years of experience in the** security and investigations **field. Full knowledge of** security investigations, employee and premises security, building integrity, product security, transporting of valuable items, bomb threat investigations, **and** handling volatile situations. **Proven ability in** managing personnel functions including scheduling, evaluations, **and** training. **Highly skilled in** making cost-effective recommendations regarding surveillance **and** detection equipment technology. **Attributes include** integrity, honesty, and ability to interact with all levels of management.

SAMPLE FOR A MOVIE SCREENING COORDINATOR

Three **years of professional** communications **experience in the** entertainment **industry. Full knowledge of** public relations, public speaking, and speech preparation. **Proven ability to** handle national and international special events coordination and movie screenings. **Highly skilled in** interpersonal communication and effective listening. **Attributes include** creativity, strong organization and conflict resolution skills, **and** outstanding public speaking abilities. **Ability to** take on difficult challenges and get things done in an impeccable manner while being deadline-conscious. **Proficient in** Excel, Kedit, SPSS, and SAS.

ADDITIONAL PROFESSIONAL SUMMARY SENTENCES

You can infuse or swap out some of these additional sentences, as relative, into your *"Professional Summary."*

☐ **A seasoned ______** *[type of]* [☐ executive | ☐ professional | ☐ other: ______] **with extensive expertise in ______** *[what field?]*. **Background encompasses the ability to ______** *[do what?]*.

SAMPLE FOR A FINANCE EXECUTIVE

A seasoned upper-level financial executive **with extensive expertise in** accounting management**. Background encompasses the ability to** reduce overall costs while increasing levels of productivity and profitability.

☐ **Strong ______** *[type of]* **ability, ______** *[type of]* **knowledge, ______** *[which?]* **skills, and ______** *[features]* **with a good understanding of the ______** *[field]* **business and company success goals.**

SAMPLE FOR A SALES ASSOCIATE

Strong sales **ability,** operational **knowledge,** merchandising **skills, and** work ethic **with a good understanding of the** retail business **and company success goals.**

☐ **Seasoned, ______ and ______** *[attributes]* **______** *[job title]* **specializing in ______** *[areas]*.

SAMPLE FOR A TEACHER

Seasoned, energetic, **and** enthusiastic teacher **specializing in** developing innovative, interactive lesson plans utilizing the integration of technology and basic math principles.

☐ **A(n) ______, ______, and ______** *[primary attributes]* **professional ______** *[job title]* **offering substantial experience in ______, ______, and ______** *[type of]* **settings.**

SAMPLE FOR A NURSE

A dedicated, compassionate, results-oriented **professional** Nurse **offering substantial experience in** shift management and patient care in acute-care **settings.**

☐ **Possess** [☐ excellent | ☐ in-depth | ☐ working] **______, ______, and ______** *[type of]* [☐ skills | ☐ knowledge | ☐ expertise] **coupled with the ability to ______** *[do what?]*. **Proven ______ and ______** *[type of skills]* **adeptness and the ability to maintain superior levels of ______** *[what?]* **under all types of circumstances.**

SAMPLE FOR A HEALTHCARE PROFESSIONAL

Possess excellent interpersonal, critical thinking, **and** assessment **skills coupled with the ability to** put individuals at ease. **Proven** planning **and** organizational **adeptness and the ability to maintain superior levels of** quality care **under all types of circumstances.**

CONTINUE TO EVOLVE, BUILD & ENHANCE YOUR BRAND

MANAGE YOUR BRAND

Managing your brand much the same way as a firm manages theirs is key to your success. And applying marketing techniques to help brand you in your field allows you to promote it successfully. (Your ***Marketing Campaign*** is addressed in ***Step 7: Market Yourself!***)

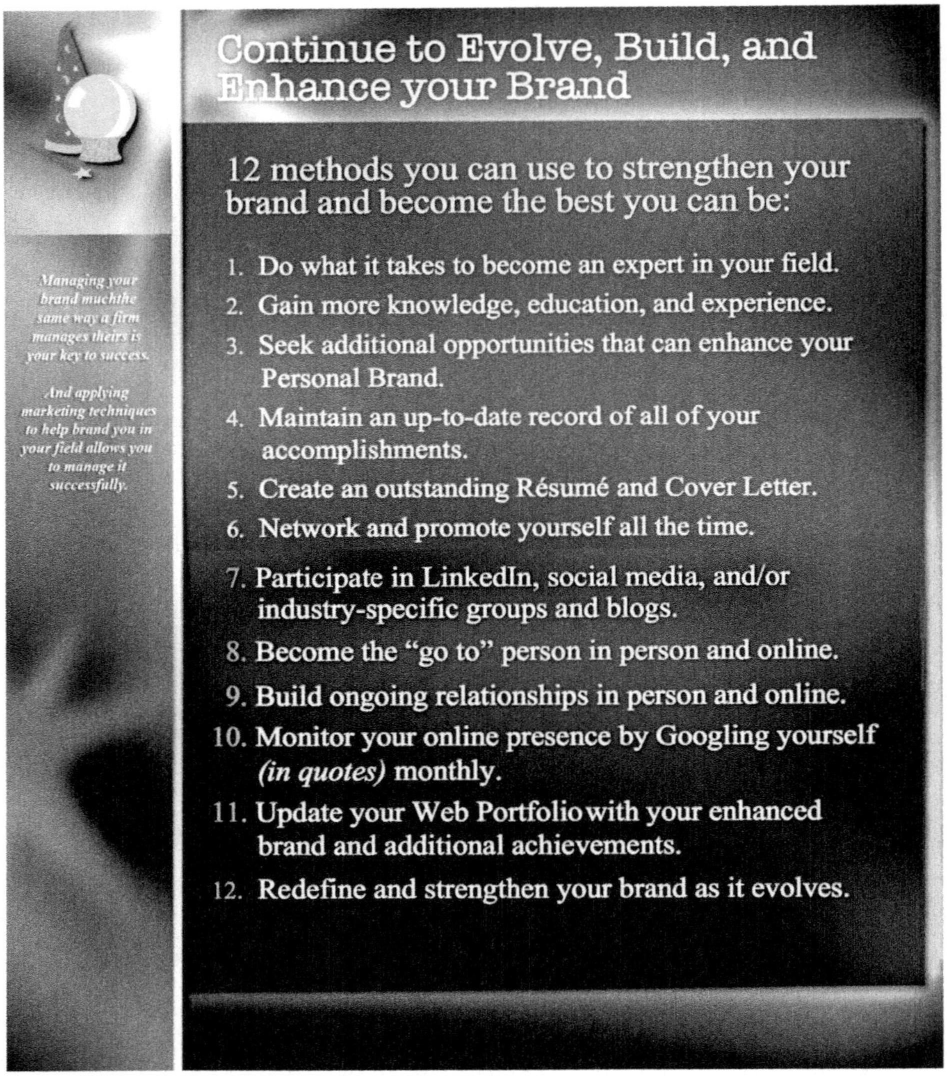

PICK YOUR BRAND COLORS

Another way to build and enhance your brand is by selecting suitable colors that, to you, exemplify your personal brand. Pretty much any color or combination of (two or three) colors can be used to depict your brand. Professional colors, for example, are deep colors, such as navy, burgundy, dark green, and even deep purple. You can either select to use one of these colors for your brand colors or choose one of your own.

Think about colors you would create a logo or your marketing materials in (to use for your Web Portfolio or Twitter background, for example), would wear on your person (in the form of overall attire, a scarf, eyeglasses, a belt, tie, shoes, or even a hat), colors you would feel comfortable with surrounding yourself in, such as a purse or an attaché, your office accessories, or executive pen. If you select "loud" colors, such as chartreuse or bright orange, for example, suggest keeping them to a minimum in your attire, just enough to make a professional brand statement.

Then infuse your chosen brand colors into all of your career marketing materials. For example, you can make your resume header and headings in your brand color(s). The number one rule is to ensure consistency in your overall brand, so that when people see you or your branded materials, it will denote your brand for image recall.

STEP 5

SELECT YOUR RESUME CLIPBULLETS™

FOR USE IN YOUR "PROFESSIONAL EXPERIENCE" SECTION

CONTENTS OF STEP 5

- ☐ Introduction
- ☐ Resume ClipBullet Instructions and Samples
- ☐ Select Your Resume ClipBullets™ *(from the Table of Contents)*

INTRODUCTION & INSTRUCTIONS

INTRODUCTION

Resume ClipBullets™ are prewritten, completely customizable bullet foundations you can place right into the *"Professional Experience"* section of your resume as job function and achievement bullets under your specific employers / job positions.

If you have not already done so, refer to the ***Table of Contents*** and check off all those functions you have handled**.** Then locate them in this chapter and select the bullet(s) under each category that best describes what you performed. Each bullet includes all of the necessary information required to complete it. Since all sentences (bullet foundations) are already written for you, simply find the most suitable bullet(s) within each section, select options, fill in the blanks, and put them directly into your resume. It's that easy!

Resume ClipBullet categories contains different types and levels of experience, possible achievements relative to that function, and a variety of ways to write similar information so you can use different bullets for various positions in your resume. Also, providing you with many possibilities also ensures no two resumes using this ***Step-by-Step Resumes*** process will ever be alike.

Bullets are written as **CAR** statements to include your **Challenge**, **Action**, and **Results**, wherever possible. If you have a specific achievement not mentioned, be sure to include it in your resume. The most important thing to keep in mind when compiling your resume is:

Don't just say what you did, state the challenge you were faced with, the actions you took to resolve it, how well you accomplished it, and the end results / benefits derived from your efforts.

INSTRUCTIONS

Resume ClipBullet categories are listed alphabetically. From the categories you identified under the ***Table of Contents,*** select functional and achievement options relative to your work, fill in the blanks, and change as appropriate to make all bullets true statements as to your own experience. When you complete this section, chances are you will have more bullets than you need. That's okay, as you will be editing them down in ***Step 6: Pull Your Resume Together***. It's always better to have more than enough information to start with than to try to determine what else to include, such as in a standard template.

Each resume bullet contains a foundation **(in bold text)** and many applicable options from which to select. Bracketed *italics (in red, if you purchased the e-book version)* signifies instructional information. Since achievements are the most important part of your resume and everyone has different accomplishments, if you see a function that you performed well, be sure to include the benefits derived from your efforts.

SAMPLE BULLETS

Some Resume ClipBullets contain quite a number of options from which you can select to ensure all bases are covered. Here is such an example followed by various different bullets you can create with just this one foundation. When completing your bullets, if you find you have checked off a number of applicable options and the bullet is long, it is best to break it into two and slightly reword, as needed. Try not to exceed four lines per bullet wherever possible.

☐ [☐ Manage and oversee | ☐ Supervise] **all aspects of construction work including** [☐ reviewing project plans | ☐ preparing job estimates | ☐ estimating material and labor costs | ☐ securing competitive bids | ☐ selecting contractors and subcontractors | ☐ developing crew assignments and work schedules | ☐ coordinating projects with contractors | ☐ preparing work orders | ☐ ordering and setting up equipment | ☐ purchasing materials and supplies | ☐ directing and coordinating building construction | ☐ supervising a crew of ______ *(#)* | ☐ evaluating staff performance | ☐ inspecting work area | ☐ obtaining permits | ☐ mediating and resolving disputes | ☐ ensuring debris removal | ☐ providing technical construction assistance | ☐ preparing punch lists | ☐ overseeing inspection deadlines | ☐ negotiating and processing change orders | ☐ ensuring punch list item completion and customer satisfaction | ☐ coordinating concrete trucks | ☐ recommending land purchases to management | ☐ monitoring inventory and supply requests | ☐ ensuring safety practices | ☐ preparing accident reports | ☐ other: ______] **ensuring all jobs are completed in compliance with specifications and codes.**

SAMPLE COMPLETED BULLETS:

FOR A CONSTRUCTION PROJECT MANAGER:

- **Manage and oversee all aspects of construction work including** reviewing project plans, preparing job estimates, securing competitive bids, selecting subcontractors, coordinating construction, inspecting work, obtaining permits, preparing punch lists, and negotiating change orders, **ensuring all jobs are completed in compliance with specifications and codes.**

FOR A SUPERINTENDENT:

- **Supervise all aspects of construction work including** estimating material and labor costs, ordering and setting up equipment, developing work schedules, supervising a crew of 15, inspecting work area, ensuring debris removal, providing technical construction assistance, **ensuring all jobs are completed in compliance with specifications and codes.**

SELECT YOUR RESUME CLIPBULLETS™

Achievement Samples – Construction Trades

*See also **"Construction Projects"** and Achievements under specific areas of expertise.*

ACHIEVEMENT SAMPLES:

☐ **Established a reputation for quality workmanship at competitive prices by** [☐ maintaining superior levels of craftsmanship | ☐ providing excellent customer service | ☐ other: ______].

☐ **Assisted in** ______ *[type of]* **installations and repairs of this** [______ *[#]*-square foot ______ *[#]*-story] **building to ensure compliance with all** [☐ building | ☐ electrical | ☐ plumbing | ☐ fire safety | ☐ other: ______] codes.

☐ **Facilitated hands-on installation, maintenance, and/or repair of** [☐ commercial | ☐ domestic | ☐ industrial | ☐ other: ______] [☐ indoor | ☐ outdoor] ______ *[type of]* **systems including** ______, ______, **and** ______ *[what?].*

☐ **Guided a** [☐ major | ☐ highly complex | ☐ technical | ☐ other: ______] ______ *[type of]* **project through to completion in accordance with the schedule and budget by** ______ *[doing what well?].*

☐ **Mastered the use of** ______ *[what tools or methods?]* **including** ______, ______, **and** ______ *[what?]* **to accomplish** ______ *[what?].*

☐ **Managed the completion of** ______ *[#]* ______ *[type of]* **jobs** [☐ monthly | ☐ annually] [☐ averaging $______ to $______ *(amounts)* | ☐ totaling $______] **including** [☐ estimating job times, materials, and costs | ☐ selecting materials and hardware | ☐ preparing materials estimates | ☐ reviewing bids | ☐ ordering required job-related materials | ☐ scheduling jobs | ☐ inspecting completed jobs for code compliance | ☐ other: ______].

☐ **Working with minimal supervision under tight deadlines on a** ______ *[type of]* **project, accomplished** ______ *[what?].*

☐ **Handled on-site** ______ *[what functions?]* **while** [☐ company remained open for business | (☐ homeowners / ☐ employees) remained on premises | ☐ other: ______] **by** ______ *[doing what?],* **which minimized the work impact so** [☐ business | ☐ home | ☐ facility | ☐ other: ______] **operations remained functional.**

☐ **Recommended and implemented** ______ *[type of]* **improvements to** ______ *[what?],* **which helped facilitate** ______ *[what functions?]* **and resulted in** ______ *[what benefits?].*

☐ **Participated in client consultations and overseeing** [☐ construction | ☐ design-and-build | ☐ development | ☐ other: ______] **of a** ______ *[project type]*. **Received commendations from** [☐ client | ☐ employer | ☐ other: ______] **for** [☐ professional expertise | ☐ dedication to job | ☐ a job well done | ☐ other: ______]. ***(See "Testimonials.")*** *[Note: Include a "Testimonials" section in resume.]*

☐ **Involved in** [☐ managing | ☐ performing | ☐ coordinating | ☐ facilitating | ☐ other: ______] ______ *[what?]* **efforts that required** ______ *[what actions?]* **to meet** ______ *[what challenges?]* **and resulted in** ______ *[benefits].*

☐ **Successfully turned around** ______ *[what challenge?]* **by** ______ *[doing what?],* **which resulted in** ______ *[what benefits?].*

☐ **Managed and coordinated** [☐ continuous | ☐ frequent] ______ *[type of]* **office space planning to accommodate** ______**%** *[percentage]* **employee growth in** ______ *[#]* **years. Required** [☐ locating | ☐ building | ☐ leasing | ☐ renovating | ☐ furnishing | other: ______] **offices within** ______ *[#]* **months of notice, including** [☐ telephone systems | ☐ equipment | ☐ furniture | ☐ other: ______].

☐ **Initiated and implemented** ______ *[type of]* **new programs that served to** ______ *[do what?]* **and resulted in** ______ *[what benefits?].* **Program was executed company-wide and saved the firm $**______ *[amount]* **annually.**

☐ **Organized company's move from a** ______ *[#]***-square foot building in** ______ *[what town?]* **to a** ______ [#]**- square foot building** [☐ in the business section] **of** ______ *[what town?],* **allowing the firm to** [☐ construct a front office | ☐ increase staff size | ☐ stock more supplies and materials | ☐ other: ______].

☐ [☐ Developed and established | ☐ Recommended and implemented] ______ *[type of]* [☐ management] [☐ plans | ☐ standards | ☐ guidelines | ☐ policies | ☐ procedures | ☐ methods | ☐ other: ______] **that maximized the effective use of** ______ *[what?]* **and supported the continuing improvement of** ______ *[which?]* **standards.**

☐ **Successfully met difficult challenges faced by** ______ *[what obstacles?]* **by** ______ *[doing what?],* **which resulted in** ______ *[what benefits?].*

☐ [☐ Developed | ☐ established | ☐ performed] **a "company first" in the area of** ______ *[what area?]* **by** ______ *[doing what?],* **which resulted in** ______ *[what benefits?].*

☐ **Gained extensive experience in** ______, ______, **and** ______ *[what areas or functions?]* **that helped facilitate** ______ *[what?].*

Administrative Functions – General

☐ **Coordinate and facilitate daily office administration activities for this** ______ *[type of]* **firm including** [☐ office management | ☐ general administration | ☐ account servicing | ☐ customer service | ☐ human resources | ☐ general accounting | ☐ bookkeeping | ☐ payroll processing | ☐ purchasing | ☐ benefits administration | ☐ other: ______] **for an office staff of** ______ *[#].*

☐ **Handle various office administrative activities including** [☐ developing material and equipment lists | ☐ preparing cost estimates | ☐ costing materials | ☐ purchasing supplies | ☐ ordering parts | ☐ writing contract specifications | ☐ coordinating materials shipping | ☐ matching invoices to purchase orders and packing slips | ☐ issuing and evaluating contractor bids | ☐ scheduling jobs | ☐ coordinating jobs with ______ *(whom)* | ☐ processing payroll | ☐ answering phones | ☐ handling insurance needs | ☐ generating ______ *(type of)* reports | ☐ entering Accounts Payable data | ☐ recording cash receipts | ☐ preparing deposits | ☐ updating budget databases | ☐ preparing contract records and reports | ☐ handling data entry | ☐ filing and copying | ☐ other: ______].

☐ [☐ Manage | ☐ Supervise | ☐ Prepare | ☐ Coordinate] [☐ payroll | ☐ bookkeeping | ☐ billing | ☐ accounts payable | ☐ accounts receivable | ☐ general ledger | ☐ inventory | ☐ purchasing | ☐ other: ______] **for a** [☐ staff | ☐ customer base] **of** ______ *[#]*, **keeping all records current and ensuring accuracy.**

☐ **Collaborate at all levels of the firm to** [☐ clarify scope | ☐ overcome obstacles | ☐ identify issues | ☐ solve problems | ☐ reach decisions | ☐ obtain solutions acceptance | ☐ other: ______] **during the development and implementation of** ______ *[type of]* **projects.**

☐ **Prepare and review budgets and forecasts for** [☐ support service departments | ☐ construction projects | ☐ other: ______].

☐ **Review and approve requisitions of all** [☐ national | ☐ regional | ☐ local | ☐ other: ______] **purchasing of** [☐ office equipment | ☐ telephone systems | ☐ office furniture | ☐ work stations | ☐ other: ______].

☐ **Ensure the firm's** ______ *[type of]* [☐ computer databases | ☐ documents | ☐ work schedules | ☐ payroll | ☐ files | ☐ reports | ☐ other: ______] **are accurately updated and maintained and in accordance with** [☐ all legal requirements | ☐ the firm's policies and procedures | ☐ other: ______].

☐ [☐ Develop | ☐ Coordinate | ☐ Manage | ☐ Implement] **the firm's corporate** [☐ domestic | ☐ international] **travel policy, resulting in annual cost reductions of $**______ *[amount]* **in** [☐ air travel | ☐ hotel rental | ☐ car rental | ☐ meal expenses | ☐ other: ______].

☐ **Supervise all** ______ *[type of]* **office administration activities including** [☐ budget preparation | ☐ the direction of trades work | ☐ assignment of jobs | ☐ verification and approval of material requisitions | ☐ approval of time cards | ☐ other: ______].

☐ **Develop and maintain all** ______ *[type of]* [☐ systems | ☐ records | ☐ data | ☐ information | ☐ other: ______]; **and provide accurate periodic** [☐ progress | ☐ revenue | ☐ other: ______] **reports for** ______ *[whom?].*

☐ **Perform office and administrative functions including** [☐ switchboard operations | ☐ word processing | ☐ data entry | ☐ client correspondence | ☐ document processing | ☐ opening and sorting mail | ☐ filing | ☐ basic bookkeeping | ☐ making bank deposits | ☐ other: ______] **for this** ______ *[type of]* **firm.**

☐ **Plan, develop, and write** ______ *[type of]* **policy and procedure manuals containing** ______ *[what?].*

☐ **Handle** [☐ general office administration | ☐ account servicing | ☐ daily customer service matters | ☐ payroll issues | ☐ health insurance | ☐ 401K matters | ☐ other: ______] **for an office staff of** ______ *[#].*

☐ **Interpret and translate laws, regulations, and policies; and document** ______ *[type of]* [☐ operating | ☐ legal | ☐ technical | ☐ other: ______] **procedures required for** ______ *[purpose].*

☐ **Coordinate the development and review process of** ______ *[type of]* **policies and procedures for** ______ *[what or whom?].*

ACHIEVEMENT SAMPLES: *See Achievement Samples under **"Administrative Management & Leadership."***

Administrative Functions – Project Specific

*See also **"Project Management."***

☐ **Oversee administrative support to the project management team in the areas of** ______, ______, **and** ______ *[which areas?]* **in setting project strategies and priorities.**

☐ **Perform quality control of reports prepared by** [☐ Architects | ☐ Engineers | ☐ Project Managers | ☐ others: ______] **including** ______, ______, **and** ______ *[type of reports]* **by** ______ *[doing what well?].*

☐ **Manage and oversee all aspects of** ______ *[type of]* **projects including project** [☐ scope | ☐ initiation | ☐ planning | ☐ scheduling | ☐ budgeting | ☐ team selection | ☐ resource allocation | ☐ cost control | ☐ other: ______] **as well as** [☐quality control | ☐ change management | ☐ system integration | ☐ other: ______] **keeping in line with all business objectives.**

☐ **Facilitate business management of this** ______ *[type of]* **firm including** [☐ leading and overseeing projects | ☐ prioritizing projects and balancing competing demands | ☐ reviewing contracts to verify legal requirements | ☐ translating requirements into effective legal solutions | ☐ establishing quality control procedures | ☐ developing revenue contracts | ☐ preparing specifications | ☐ performing inspections to facilitate quality assurance | ☐ identifying contractual problems or errors | ☐ quality testing materials | ☐ researching and writing legal and/or technical procedures | ☐ setting up and maintaining contract database | ☐ developing budgets and monitoring expenses | ☐ preparing inspection deficiency reports | ☐ recommending corrective actions | ☐ reviewing and approving cost estimates | ☐ approving contracting changes | ☐ holding meetings to discuss project progress processing documents | ☐ other: ______].

☐ **Initiate and implement** ______ *[type of]* [☐ policy formulation | ☐ procedure development | ☐ improvement methods] **in the areas of** [☐ safety | ☐ emergency measures | ☐ other: ______] **which served to improve** ______ *[what process?].*

☐ **Review** [☐ construction schedules | ☐ job cost reports | ☐ payment requisitions | ☐ other: ______] **for** ______ *[purpose]* **and prepare and generate** [☐ monthly | ☐ weekly | ☐ periodic] **cost reports on** ______ *[type of projects]* **to** [☐ senior technical staff | ☐ senior management | ☐ project engineers | ☐ others: ______].

☐ **Apply expertise in** [☐ specifications preparation | ☐ bid evaluations | ☐ bid awards | ☐ standard price and purchasing reference sources | ☐ modern purchasing methods and practices | ☐ government polices | ☐ other: ______] **in the procurement of** ______ *[what?]* **resulting in** ______ *[benefits].*

☐ [☐ Compose and update | ☐ Draft and edit] ______ *[type of]* [☐ contracts | ☐ agreements | ☐ technical material | (☐ company / ☐ department) policies and procedures | ☐ other: ______] **for** ______ *[purpose].*

☐ **Perform** [☐ materials costing | ☐ job estimating | ☐ contract negotiations | ☐ other: ______] **with** [☐ contractors | ☐ suppliers | ☐ other: ______] **of** ______ *[type of]* **jobs ranging $______ to $______** *[amounts].*

☐ **Define, plan, and implement** ______ *[type of]* **projects including the** [☐ design | ☐ development | ☐ implementation | ☐ tracking | ☐ other: ______] **of those projects in support of the firm's business objectives.**

☐ **Accurately maintain up-to-date** [☐ job file records | ☐ project database information | ☐ project invoices | ☐ contractor's shop drawings | ☐ product data | ☐ field reports | ☐ other: ______] **and other records ensuring** ______ *[what?].*

☐ **Accurately update and maintain** ______ *[type of]* [☐ documents | ☐ files | ☐ reports | ☐ other: ______] **according to** [☐ legal requirements | ☐ the firm's policies and procedures | ☐ other: ______].

☐ **Develop and maintain all** ______ *[type of]* [☐ systems | ☐ records | ☐ data | ☐ information | ☐ other: ______]; **and provide accurate periodic** [☐ progress | ☐ revenue | ☐ campaign | ☐ other: ______] **reports to** ______ *[whom?].*

☐ **Review, approve, and implement** ☐ [legal | ☐ technical | ☐ other: ______] **documents to** [☐ ensure they conform to current standards and regulations | ☐ incorporate new developments | ☐ maintain optimal production | ☐ other purpose: ______].

☐ **Research, coordinate, document, edit, and periodically update the publication of** [☐ legal | ☐ policy and procedure | ☐ training | ☐ other: ______] **manuals and related** [☐ legal | ☐ technical | ☐ public information | ☐ user | ☐ other: ______] materials.

☐ **Document, implement, and monitor** ______ *[type of]* **quality assurance procedures ensuring their implementation on all projects including** [☐ client relationship management | ☐ contract drafting | ☐ legal document management | ☐ rights and clearances documentation | ☐ financial data verification | ☐ database updating | ☐ vendor compliance | ☐ project tracking | ☐ executive approval process | ☐ other: ______].

☐ **Process** [☐ customer invoices | ☐ correspondence | ☐ payments | ☐ other: ______] **in a timely manner.**

☐ **Coordinate new practices with** [☐ research and development | ☐ manufacturing | ☐ auditing | ☐ marketing | ☐ regulatory affairs | ☐ legal | ☐ other: ______] **personnel to** [☐ research existing practices | ☐ analyze auditing requirements | ☐ ensure compliance with all regulations | ☐ other: ______].

☐ **Work with the firm's** [☐ internal counsel | ☐ outside attorney] **to resolve** ______ *[type of]* **legal matters.**

ACHIEVEMENT SAMPLES: *See Achievement Samples under **"Administrative Management & Leadership."***

Administrative Management & Leadership

*See also **"Business Management & Leadership," "Office Management & Supervision"** and **"Staff Management & Supervision."***

☐ **Provide leadership and support to the** ______ *[which?]* **department(s) overseeing various** [☐ operational aspects of | ☐ administrative support services for] **this $______** *[revenues]* ______ *[type of firm],* **covering** [☐ cost management | ☐ records management | ☐ research and analysis | ☐ procedures development | ☐ materials distribution | ☐ other: ______].

☐ **Oversee the administrative and office support services including** [☐ budget preparation | ☐ evaluation and reporting | ☐ contract negotiations | ☐ assignment of jobs | ☐ appointment scheduling | ☐ approval of time cards | ☐ supplies purchasing | ☐ material requisitions | ☐ recordkeeping | ☐ data entry | ☐ reception area | ☐ other: ______].

☐ **Direct office management and administrative activities that include** [☐ pricing strategies development | ☐ contract negotiations | ☐ claims avoidance | ☐ claims and litigations research | ☐ risk management | ☐ quality assurance methods development | ☐ research and analysis | ☐ ______ *(type of)* proposals and estimates | ☐ contractual initiatives | ☐ dispute resolution | ☐ grant applications submittal | ☐ employee interface | ☐ other: ______].

☐ **Manage and direct the firm's office and administrative functions, including** [☐ general office administration | ☐ payroll issues | ☐ data entry | ☐ document processing | ☐ inventory | ☐ purchasing | ☐ other: ______] **for an office staff of** ______ *[#].*

☐ **Plan, set, and establish** ______ *[type of]* **administrative** [☐ goals | ☐ policies and procedures | ☐ objectives | ☐ budget projections | ☐ expense planning | ☐ other: ______].

☐ **Direct the day-to-day** ______ *[which?]* **administrative functions of this** [☐ multibillion-dollar | ☐ multimillion-dollar | ☐ $______ *(revenues)*] ______ *[type of]* **firm including** ______, ______, **and** ______ *[which areas?].*

☐ **Manage and oversee various** [☐ operational aspects of | ☐ administrative support services for] **this $**______ *[revenues]* ______ *[type of firm],* **including** [☐ payroll | ☐ word processing | ☐ records management | ☐ data processing | ☐ materials distribution | ☐ security | ☐ computer troubleshooting | ☐ other: ______].

☐ **Serve on** ______ *[which?]* **Committee that** [☐ formulates | ☐ improves | ☐ recommends | ☐ prioritizes | ☐ coordinates | ☐ implements | ☐ establishes | ☐ tests | ☐ approves | ☐ monitors] ______ *[what?]* **for the purpose of** *[what outcome or benefits?].*

☐ **Manage the coordination and facilitation of** [☐ office management | ☐ general administration | ☐ human resources | ☐ payroll processing | ☐ benefits administration | ☐ purchasing | ☐ inventory management and control | ☐ other: ______] **functions for this** ______ *[type of]* **firm.**

☐ **Supervise all** ______ *[type of]* **office administration activities including** [☐ budget preparation | ☐ the direction of trades work | ☐ assignment of jobs | ☐ verification and approval of material requisitions | ☐ approval of time cards | ☐ other: ______].

☐ [☐ Direct and oversee | ☐ Supervise] **all administrative support services, including** [☐ payroll | ☐ inventory | ☐ purchasing | ☐ other: ______] **for** ______ *[#]* [☐ departments | ☐ offices | ☐ other: ______] **requiring** [☐ accurate data entry of all information | ☐ determining ordering needs | ☐ other: ______].

☐ **Manage** [☐ office operations | ☐ administrative services | ☐ other: ______] **including** [☐ office space planning | ☐ procedures development | ☐ other: ______].

ACHIEVEMENT SAMPLES:

☐ **Assisted the** [☐ Executive Director | ☐ President | ☐ other title: ______] **in** [☐ evaluating | ☐ prioritizing | ☐ coordinating | ☐ developing | ☐ establishing | ☐ other: ______] **long-range** ______ *[type of]* **plans including** [☐ system-wide policies and standards | ☐ technology enhancements | ☐ other: ______].

☐ **Designed and executed** ______ *[type of]* [☐ administrative | ☐ operational | ☐ other: ______] **solutions that effectively addressed and adhered to the firm's requirements** [☐ in accordance with all project timelines and budget | ☐ verifying quality project standards | ☐ ensuring a smooth transition | ☐ other: ______].

☐ **Built a strong, supportive administrative team environment by exhibiting and modeling leadership skills in** [☐ communication | ☐ negotiation | ☐ problem-solving | ☐ obstacle tackling | ☐ other: ______].

☐ **Spearheaded and implemented a** ______ *[type of]* [☐ program | ☐ policy | ☐ procedure] **that** ______ *[did what?].*

☐ **Championed** [☐ large-scale | ☐ complex | ☐ cross-organizational | ☐ other: ______] ______ *[type of]* [☐ administrative | ☐ operational] [☐ program | ☐ system | ☐ policy | ☐ procedures | ☐ solutions | ☐ implementation projects | ☐ other: ______] **involving** ______ *[what?]* **that** ______ *[accomplished what?]* **by** ______ *[doing what?].*

☐ **Converted the firm's manual processing** ______ *[type of]* **office system to a functional** [☐ peer-to-peer] ______ *[type of]* **computerized** [☐ account database | ☐ billing | ☐ payroll | ☐ accounting | ☐ other: ______] [☐ system | ☐ environment] **increasing overall** [☐ productivity | ☐ efficiency | ☐ sales | ☐ other: ______] **increasing overall** [☐ productivity | ☐ efficiency | ☐ sales | ☐ other: ______].

☐ **Conceptualized, developed, and managed a $**______ *[revenues]* ______ *[type of]* [☐ network | ☐ division | ☐ other: ______] **by** ______ *[doing what?],* **resulting in it becoming the backbone of the company's growth from** ______ *[what size or measure?]* **to** ______ *[what size or measure?].*

☐ **Assisted the** [☐ Executive Director | ☐ President | ☐ other title: ______] **in** [☐ evaluating | ☐ prioritizing | ☐ coordinating | ☐ developing | ☐ establishing | ☐ other: ______] **long-range** ______ *[type of]* **plans including** [☐ repair and improvement projects | ☐ building renewal plans | ☐ system-wide policies and standards | ☐ technology enhancements | ☐ other: ______].

☐ **Managed and implemented the firm's corporate** [☐ domestic | ☐ international] **travel policy, resulting in annual cost reductions of $**______ *[amount]* **in** [☐ air travel | ☐ hotel rental | ☐ car rental | ☐ meal expenses | ☐ other: ______].

☐ **Organized company's move from a** ______ *[#]***-square foot building in** ______ *[what town?]* **to a** ______ *[#]***- square foot building** [☐ in the business section] **of** ______ *[what town?],* **allowing the firm to** [☐ construct a front office | ☐ increase staff size | ☐ stock more supplies and materials | ☐ other: ______].

☐ **Managed and coordinated** [☐ continuous | ☐ frequent] ______ *[type of]* **office space planning to accommodate** ______**%** *[percentage]* **employee growth in** ______ *[#]* **years. Required** [☐ locating | ☐ building | ☐ leasing | ☐ renovating | ☐ furnishing

| ☐ other: ______] **offices within** ______ [#] **months of notice, including** [☐ telephone systems | ☐ equipment | ☐ furniture | ☐ other: ______].

☐ **Designed and executed** ______ *[type of]* [☐ administrative | ☐ operational | ☐ other: ______] **solutions that effectively addressed and adhered to** [☐ firm's | ☐ clients'] **requirements** [☐ in accordance with all project timelines and budget | ☐ verifying quality project standards | ☐ ensuring a smooth transition | ☐ other: ______].

☐ [☐ Developed and established | ☐ Recommended and implemented] ______ *[type of]* [☐ management] [☐ plans | ☐ standards | ☐ guidelines | ☐ policies | ☐ procedures | ☐ methods | ☐ other: ______] **that maximized the effective use of** ______ *[what?]* **and supported the continuing improvement of** ______ *[which?]* **standards.**

☐ **Recruited as right hand to** ______ *[title]* **to save a once-profitable company from a then-floundering situation ($**______ *[amount]* **loss on $**______ *[amount]* **in sales) through effective** [☐ strategic and tactical efforts | ☐ other: ______] **resulting in its turnaround to $**______ *[amount]* **profit on $**______ *[amount]* **sales.**

☐ **Developed and implemented a** ______ *[type of]* **change involving** ______ *[what?]* **that resulted in** [☐ better inventory control | ☐ improved workflow | ☐ increased productivity | ☐ streamlined operations | ☐ other: ______] **in the areas of** ______, ______, **and** ______ *[what areas?].*

☐ **Built a strong, supportive administrative team environment by exhibiting and modeling leadership skills in** [☐ communication | ☐ negotiation | ☐ problem-solving | ☐ obstacle tackling | ☐ other: ______].

☐ **Spearheaded and implemented a** ______ *[type of]* [☐ program | ☐ policy | ☐ procedures] **that** [☐ maximized service and equipment utilization | ☐ other: ______] **by** ______ *[doing what?].*

☐ **Managed the completion of** ______ *[#]*______ *[type of]* **jobs** [☐ monthly | ☐ annually] [☐ averaging $______ to $______ *(amounts)* | ☐ totaling $______ *(amount)*] **including** [☐ estimating job times, materials, and costs | ☐ selecting materials and hardware | ☐ preparing materials estimates | ☐ reviewing bids | ☐ ordering required job-related materials | ☐ scheduling jobs | ☐ inspecting completed jobs for code compliance | ☐ other: ______].

☐ **Involved in** [☐ managing | ☐ performing | ☐ coordinating | ☐ facilitating | ☐ other: ______] ______ *[what?]* **efforts that required** ______ *[what actions?]* **to meet** ______ *[what challenges?]* **and resulted in** ______ *[benefits].*

Awards & Recognition – Construction Trades

ACHIEVEMENT SAMPLES:

☐ **Starting as** [☐ Apprentice | ☐ Laborer | ☐ Carpenter | ☐ Superintendent | ☐ other: ______], **received promotions to** [☐ Labor Foreman | ☐ Lead Carpenter | ☐ General Foreman | ☐ Construction Superintendent | ☐ Project Manager | ☐ other: ______] **by learning the tools of the trade and exceeding expectations in the performance of** ______ *[list functions].*

☐ **Selected amongst** ______ *[#]* **other laborers to perform** ______, ______, **and** ______ *[which activities?]* **for** ______ *[purpose].*

☐ **Commended by** [☐ Project Manager | ☐ Site Foreman | ☐ Facility Manager | ☐ Building Operations Manager | ☐ Project Superintendent | ☐ ______ *(type of)* client | ☐ other: ______] **for** [☐ performance in the areas of ______, ______, and ______ *(which areas?)* | ☐ contributing to a safe workplace environment | ☐ other: ______] **by**[☐ providing strategic insights in the ______ *(what project or function?)* | ☐ identifying and reporting safety hazards | ☐ successfully completing ______ *(what?)* | ☐ other: ______].

☐ **Recipient of the "**______**"** *[name of award]* **by** ______ *[whom?]* **for outstanding contributions in the areas of** ______, ______, **and** ______ *[which areas?].*

☐ **Commended by** ______ *[whom?]* **for** [☐ performance in the areas of ______, ______, and ______ *(which areas?)* | ☐ contributing to a safe workplace environment | ☐ other: ______] **by successfully completing** ______ *[what?].*

☐ **Selected amongst** ______ *[#]* [☐ other laborers | ☐ peers] **to** [☐ oversee | ☐ perform | ☐ facilitate | ☐ other: ______] ______, ______, **and** ______ *[which activities?]* **for** ______ *[what purpose?].*

☐ **Received** [(☐ excellent | ☐ high performing) evaluations from superiors | ☐ commendations from clients | ☐ congratulatory letters | ☐ recommendations | ☐ testimonials | ☐ other: ______] **for** [☐ precise workmanship | ☐ dependability | ☐ professional expertise | ☐ other: ______] **in the performance of** ______ *[what?].*

☐ **Selected to travel to** ______ *[where?]* **with company to** [☐ train crew | ☐ construct ______ *(what?)* | ☐ set up a repair facility | ☐ other: ______] **that involved** ______ *[what functions?]* **and resulted in** ______ *[what benefits?].*

☐ **Earned an outstanding reputation for knowledge and expertise** [☐ in the areas of ______, ______, and ______ *(which areas?)* | ☐ as trusted advisor to senior management | ☐ other: ______].

☐ **Received commendations from** [☐ client | ☐ employer | ☐ other: ______] **for** [☐ professional expertise | ☐ dedication to job | ☐ other: ______]. ***(See "Testimonials.")*** *[Note: Include a "Testimonials" section in resume.]*

☐ **Recruited as ______** *[job title]*, **received promotions to ______** *[job title]* **and ______** *[job title]*, **by exceeding expectations in the performance of ______, ______, and ______** *[list functions]*.

☐ **Originally assigned as ______** *[title]* **for ______** *[type of work]*, **and within ______** *[time period]* **received promotion to ______** *[title]*.

Bids & Proposals

*See also **"Purchasing," "Contract Negotiations," "Contracts Administration,"** and **"Contracts Development & Review."***

☐ **Direct and lead the review and evaluation of vendor** [☐ proposals | ☐ bids | ☐ specifications] **and selection of vendors with awards issued based on product** [☐ quality | ☐ value | ☐ source | ☐ usefulness | ☐ unique features and benefits | ☐ broad target market | ☐ copyrights | ☐ pricing | ☐ payment terms | ☐ delivery dates | ☐ shipping charges | ☐ packaging | ☐ final cost | ☐ other: ______] **for this ______** *[type of]* **firm which services the ______** *[which?]* **market.**

☐ **Review and evaluate bids and issue awards using** [☐ value analysis | ☐ lifecycle costing | ☐ weighted value procedures | ☐ value analysis | ☐ other: ______] **for ______** *[what?]*.

☐ **Obtain, review, and verify ______** *[type of]* [☐ bids | ☐ plans | ☐ specifications | ☐ cost estimates | ☐ contracts | ☐ other: ______] **checking for compliance with** [☐ the firm's | ☐ clients' | ☐ department's] **requirements and** [☐ the Environmental Quality Act | ☐ Occupational Safety and Health Act | ☐ other: ______].

☐ **Determine all** [☐ product requirements | ☐ methods of acquisition | ☐ material costs | ☐ other: ______], **prepare bid specifications, select vendors, and obtain written** [☐ bids | ☐ quotes | ☐ estimates] **on all ______** *[type of]* **purchases.**

☐ **Conduct** [☐ vendor bids | ☐ comparative cost analyses | ☐ other: ______], **and make sound selections based on** [☐ build quality | ☐ vendor reliability | ☐ ability to meet required deadlines | ☐ other: ______] **for ______** *[what?]*.

☐ **In ordering ______** *[type of]* [☐ merchandise | ☐ services | ☐ materials | ☐ supplies | ☐ equipment | ☐ tools | ☐ other: ______], **monitor and evaluate** [☐ vendor performance | ☐ price changes | ☐ back orders | ☐ other: ______], **correspond with vendors regarding** [☐ product | ☐ consumer | ☐ contract | ☐ other: ______] **problems, resolving any product delivery problems.**

☐ **Monitor and evaluate** [☐ vendor performance | ☐ price changes | ☐ back orders | ☐ other: ______]; **and correspond with vendors regarding any** [☐ product | ☐ consumer | ☐ contract | ☐ other: ______] **problems to work out solutions to the customers' satisfaction.**

☐ **Evaluate and interpret ______** *[type of]* **product information, identify purchasing alternatives, prepare specifications, develop contracts, and initiate ______** *[type of]* **purchasing transactions.**

☐ **Review and evaluate all vendor** [☐ proposals | ☐ bids | ☐ specifications]; **select appropriate vendors; and issue awards based on** [☐ quality | ☐ value | ☐ source | ☐ usefulness | ☐ features | ☐ benefits | ☐ pricing | ☐ payment terms | (☐ availability / ☐ delivery) dates | ☐ shipping charges | ☐ final costs | ☐ other: ______] **factors.**

☐ **Perform detailed reviews of** [☐ purchase orders | ☐ invoices | ☐ requisitions | ☐ job estimates | ☐ other: ______] **to ensure conformance with all policies and procedures and ______** *[other requirements]*.

☐ **Resolve** [☐ product delivery problems | ☐ vendor conflicts | ☐ other: ______] **regarding** [☐ undelivered shipments | ☐ shipment shortages | ☐ product defects | ☐ other: ______].

ACHIEVEMENT SAMPLES:

☐ **Increased margins ______%** *[percentage]* **by conducting** [☐ contractor | ☐ subcontractor] **searches for best quality and costs procuring ______** *[which trades?]* **to ______** *[do what?]* **for ______** *[type of]* **projects.**

☐ **Prepared** [☐ commercial | ☐ residential | ☐ industrial | ☐ public works | ☐ other: ______] **construction cost estimates; interpreted commercial plans, contract drawings, and specifications; and obtained construction bids, selected contractors, and negotiated construction contracts on all ______** *[type of]* **projects resulting in a savings of $______** *[amount]*.

Billing / Invoicing

See *"Client Billing."*

Blueprint Reading, Interpreting & Updating

☐ **Read, interpret, and evaluate** ______ *[type of]* [☐ engineering | ☐ architectural] [☐ drawings | ☐ blueprints | ☐ diagrams | ☐ renderings | ☐ schematics | ☐ plans | ☐ specifications | ☐ other: ______] **for compliance with** ______ *[which?]* codes.

☐ **Review schematic drawings and construction details for** ______ *[type of]* **projects, make recommendations to modify as needed, and discuss** ______ *[type of]* **changes with clients before implementation.**

☐ **Interpret, review, and evaluate** ______ *[type of]* [☐ plans | ☐ specifications | ☐ drawings] **to** [☐ determine compatibility and adaptability with existing systems | ☐ ensure compliance with all codes | ☐ advise (☐ Project Engineer / ☐ Foreman / ☐ other: ______) on code requirements | ☐ other: ______]; **and modify blueprints to meet as-built specifications and dimensions.**

☐ **Interpret and update** [☐ blueprints | ☐ architectural drawings | ☐ plans | ☐ specifications | ☐ other: ______] **to reflect required changes made to** ______ *[type of]* **systems.**

☐ **Read** ______ *[type of]* **blueprints to unload the correct amount of** [☐ steel | ☐ wood | ☐ other materials: ______] **for various projects, arrange and lay out materials according to daily project needs, and** [☐ perform | ☐ oversee] **the construction of** ______ *[type of work]* **on schedule and within budget.**

☐ **Read and interpret** ______ *[type of]* [☐ blueprints | ☐ plans ☐ scale drawings | ☐ architectural details | ☐ other: ______] **regarding** [☐ design | ☐ specifications | ☐ materials | ☐ color | ☐ equipment | ☐ other: ______] **for the building of** ______ *[what?]*, **and discuss changes with clients before implementing.**

☐ **Suggested design improvements to** ______ *[what?]*, **which helped facilitate** ______ *[what?]* **and resulted in** ______ *[what benefits?]*.

Building Inspections

See *"Inspection & Compliance – Buildings & Structures."*

Building Maintenance – General

See also *"Building Maintenance & Repair," "Preventive & Seasonal Maintenance,"* and *"Carpentry / Construction Work."*

☐ **Manage** [☐ a facility | ☐ a corporate | ☐ an industrial | ☐ other: ______] **maintenance team of** ______ *[#]* [☐ superintendents | ☐ foremen | ☐ electricians | ☐ carpenters | ☐ maintenance workers | ☐ custodians | ☐ other: ______] **covering** [☐ two | ☐ three] **shifts of operation.**

☐ **Perform** [☐ building | ☐ facilities | ☐ grounds | ☐ other: ______] **maintenance functions for this** ______ *[type of]* **firm including** [☐ construction | ☐ renovation | ☐ repair | ☐ remodel | ☐ other: ______] **projects ensuring they meet all** [☐ government | ☐ environmental | ☐ health | ☐ safety | ☐ security | ☐ other: ______] **standards.**

☐ **Conduct** [☐ facilities | ☐ building maintenance | ☐ grounds upkeep | ☐ space planning | ☐ remodel | ☐ other: ______] **projects for this** ______ *[#]*-**square foot building with ground acreage of** ______ *[#]* **and** ______ *[#]* [☐ employees | ☐ work stations | ☐ offices | ☐ facilities | ☐ other: ______].

☐ **Maintain** [☐ buildings | ☐ facilities | ☐ grounds | ☐ other: ______] **in good repair including** [☐ heating | ☐ air conditioning | ☐ plumbing | ☐ electrical | ☐ wood | ☐ drywall | ☐ wall coverings | ☐ insulation | ☐ drop ceilings | ☐ painting | ☐ grading | ☐ underground utilities | ☐ drains | ☐ gutters | ☐ paving | ☐ other: ______].

☐ **Handle various** [☐ buildings | ☐ facilities | ☐ grounds | ☐ other: ______] **maintenance functions including** [☐ building maintenance and repair | ☐ office relocations | ☐ renovations | ☐ remodeling | ☐ roofing repairs | ☐ machinery maintenance and repair | ☐ regular and preventive maintenance | ☐ carpentry | ☐ electrical wiring | ☐ plumbing | ☐ HVAC systems | ☐ painting | ☐ custodial services | ☐ janitorial maintenance | ☐ groundskeeping | ☐ security systems | ☐ sprinkler systems | ☐ fire extinguisher and smoke alarm inspections | ☐ safety checks | ☐ boiler system | ☐ water system | ☐ heating system | ☐ cooling system | ☐ machinery maintenance and repair | ☐ other: ______].

☐ **Conduct the repair and maintenance of all** [☐ plumbing | ☐ electrical | ☐ HVAC | ☐ motors | ☐ appliances | ☐ fixtures | ☐ lights | ☐ ballasts | ☐ receptacles | ☐ switches | ☐ other: ______] **to** [☐ help improve the work environment | ☐ maintain proper operation of all equipment | ☐ maintain compliance with all OSHA and environmental regulations | ☐ other: ______].

☐ **Perform the** [☐ structural | ☐ mechanical | ☐ electrical | ☐ plumbing | ☐ other: ______] **aspects of** ______ *[type of]* **building** [☐ design | ☐ utilization | ☐ space planning | ☐ construction | ☐ operation | ☐ maintenance | ☐ repair | ☐ remodel | ☐ other: ______] **projects ensuring that all work is performed in compliance with building codes, laws, and regulations.**

☐ **Apply** [☐ expert | ☐ proficient | ☐ working] knowledge of [☐ general principles and practices of building construction | ☐ building maintenance | ☐ physical plant operations | ☐ technical systems | ☐ building codes | ☐ ordinances | ☐ fire regulations | ☐ safety precautions | ☐ health and safety regulations | ☐ automated building control | ☐ indoor air quality | ☐ energy management systems | ☐ record-keeping techniques | ☐ other: ______] **to all aspects of building maintenance.**

☐ **Operate and maintain the company's fleet of** ______ *[#]* [☐ lift trucks | ☐ pickup trucks | ☐ forklifts | ☐ hydraulic boom lifts | ☐ boom trucks | ☐ digger derricks | ☐ bucket trucks | ☐ other: ______].

ACHIEVEMENT SAMPLES: *See **"Building Operations Projects," "Construction Projects,"** and various trades achievements.*

Building Maintenance & Repair

☐ **Coordinate all aspects of the physical workplace ensuring** [☐ the integration and coordination of business practices | ☐ work and people requirements | ☐ fulfilling maintenance and repairs | ☐ other: ______].

☐ **Assist the** [☐ Building Superintendent | ☐ Facilities Manager | ☐ other: ______] **in** [☐ evaluating | ☐ prioritizing | ☐ coordinating | ☐ developing | ☐ establishing] **long-range facility plans including** [☐ office relocations | ☐ repair and improvement projects | ☐ building renewal plans | ☐ system-wide policies and standards | ☐ regular, preventive, and seasonal maintenance | ☐ technical requirements | ☐ other: ______].

☐ **Perform skilled maintenance and repair of** ______ *[type of]* [☐ buildings | ☐ complexes | ☐ facilities] **in the areas of** ______ *[which areas?].*

☐ **Handle** [☐ new construction | ☐ remodeling | ☐ repair | ☐ maintenance | ☐ leasing | ☐ space planning | ☐ other: ______] **projects of** ______ *[what?]* **that require** ______ *[what actions?].*

☐ **Provide building** [☐ maintenance | ☐ space planning | ☐ renovations | ☐ repairs | ☐ other: ______] **ensuring the physical, mechanical, and electrical aspects of the facility run smoothly including** [☐ examining facility for damage and leaks | ☐ maintaining building heating system and boilers | ☐ performing cooling system maintenance and repair | ☐ repairing water heaters | ☐ maintaining emergency generator | ☐ maintaining plumbing, electrical, and HVAC systems | ☐ performing carpentry work | ☐ maintaining sprinkler systems | ☐ checking security systems | ☐ performing groundskeeping | ☐ painting (☐ walls / ☐ furniture) | ☐ setting up sound systems | ☐ using specialized tools and equipment | ☐ replacing outlets and switches | ☐ ensuring vehicles are in safe operating condition | ☐ responding to emergency repair situations | ☐ installing lighting circuits | ☐ upgrading electrical wiring | ☐ repairing faucets and toilets | ☐ cutting, threading, and soldering piping | ☐ performing safety checks | ☐ repairing pumps | ☐ replacing seals, bearings, and couplings | ☐ other: ______].

☐ **Assist the** [☐ Foreman | ☐ Assistant Foreman | ☐ General Maintenance Foreman | ☐ other: ______] **in various administrative activities including** [☐ budget preparation | ☐ work direction | ☐ job assignments | ☐ material requisitions verification | ☐ time cards review | ☐ research and analysis | ☐ feasibility studies | ☐ other: ______].

☐ **On call 24 hours per day seven days a week, respond to emergency repair situations such as** ______ *[what?]* **by** ______ *[doing what?]* **resulting in** ______ *[what benefits?].*

☐ **Prepare recommendations to** ______ *[whom?]* **regarding** [☐ contractual defaults | ☐ time extensions | ☐ liquidated damages | ☐ other: ______].

☐ **Provide support and feedback to** [☐ Building Superintendent | ☐ Facilities Manager | ☐ other: ______] **regarding** [☐ maintenance | ☐ structural | ☐ mechanical | ☐ environmental | ☐ other: ______] **issues at the site.**

☐ **Helped improve the workplace and work environment by** ______ *[doing what?],* **which has resulted in** ______ *[what benefits?].*

☐ **Assisted Licensed Electrician in electrical installations and repairs of this** ______ *[#]*-**square foot building to ensure plant is in compliance with all electrical codes.**

ACHIEVEMENT SAMPLES: *See **"Building Operations Projects"** and **"Facility Management."***

Business / Department Goals Setting

*See also **"Executive Functions"** and **"Cost Reductions,"** as applicable*

☐ [☐ Establish | ☐ Assist in establishing] **the** [☐ division's | ☐ department's] ______ *[type of]* [☐ goals | ☐ action plans | ☐ project priorities | ☐ policies | ☐ procedures | ☐ guidelines | ☐ other: ______] **in** ______ *[what?]* **to support the firm's mission and objectives.**

☐ **Develop** [☐ short-term | ☐ long-range | ☐ short- and long-term] _______ *[type of]* [☐ plans | ☐ goals and objectives | ☐ other: ______] **encompassing** ______ *[type of]* [☐ research and analysis | ☐ program enhancements | ☐ operational effectiveness monitoring | ☐ budgetary requirements | ☐ financial support | ☐ resource generating | ☐ improvement changes | ☐ other: ______].

☐ **Devise and implement** [☐ one-year | ☐ multi-year | ☐ three-year | ☐ five-year | ☐ other: ______] **roadmap(s) for** ______ *[type of]* **initiatives encompassing** [☐ engaging stakeholders | ☐ cross-functional collaboration and support | ☐ relationship building | ☐ project execution | ☐ other: ______] **focusing on** ______ *[what areas?]*.

☐ **Ensure company and programs remain reputable, economically viable, and current by** [☐ providing a clear vision | ☐ proactive leadership | ☐ other: ______] **through strategically sound** [☐ mission statements | ☐ business plans | ☐ ongoing planning and implementation | ☐ other: ______] **that result in** [☐ sales increases of $______ *(amount)* | ☐ other benefits: ______].

☐ **Develop and execute short- and long-term** [☐ company | ☐ division | ☐ departmental | ☐ other: ______] [☐ plans | ☐ objectives | ☐ projects | ☐ programs] **as well as its** ______ *[which?]* **operating policies and procedures.**

☐ **Develop and implement** ______ *[type of]* **business plans and set goals and objectives that support the firm's overall strategic vision by collaborating with** ______ *[whom?]* **in the** [☐ brainstorming of ideas | ☐ identifying of problems | ☐ evaluating of alternatives | ☐ implementing of effective solutions | ☐ evaluation of risk | ☐ other: ______].

☐ **Assist the** [☐ Chief Executive Officer | ☐ President | ☐ Board | ☐ Executive Vice President | ☐ Executive Director | ☐ Senior Vice President | ☐ Vice President of ______ *(type of)* | ☐ other: ______] **in** [☐ establishing | ☐ evaluating | ☐ prioritizing | ☐ coordinating | ☐ developing | ☐ other: ______] [☐ short-term plans | ☐ long-range goals | ☐ operating strategies | ☐ the firm's overall strategic vision | ☐ departmental goals | ☐ ______ *(which?)* action plans | ☐ other: ______] **to support business vision and corporate objectives**.

☐ **Co-develop the firm's overall strategy for** [☐ competitive | ☐ quality | ☐ cost-effective | ☐ visionary | ☐ other: ______] ______ *[type of]* [☐ projects | ☐ procedures | ☐ goals | ☐ products | ☐ services | ☐ other: ______].

☐ **Successfully support the business mission and goals of the firm by leading and managing the development and implementation of** ______ *[what initiatives?]* **to accomplish** ______ *[what?]*.

☐ **Assist in the preparation of** [☐ the firm's financial objectives | ☐ the annual budget | ☐ expenditure scheduling | ☐ variance analysis | ☐ corrective actions | ☐ other: ______] **for** ______ *[what?]*.

☐ **Lead and direct the** [☐ planning | ☐ setting | ☐ establishment] **of** ______ *[what?]* [☐ goals | ☐ policies | ☐ procedures | ☐ objectives | ☐ projections | ☐ strategies | ☐ other: ______].

☐ [☐ Establish | ☐ Lead the development of] **one-year tactical plans and** | [☐ five-year | ☐ three-year | ☐ multi-year | ☐ other: ______] [☐ enterprise | ☐ corporate | ☐ division | ☐ department | ☐ other: ______]**-level strategic plans** [☐ for supported ______ *(type of)* programs] **with alignment between the firm's strategic priorities** [☐ and learning] **investments.**

☐ [☐ Set | ☐ Partake in setting] **the firm's strategic goals and priorities, and establish** [☐ department standards and procedures | ☐ project management practices | ☐ other: ______] **that meet the organization's strategy including** ______, ______, **and** ______ *[what?]*.

☐ **Formulate and establish the** [☐ firm's | ☐ division's | ☐ department's] ______ *[which?]* [☐ goals and objectives | ☐ strategies and plans | ☐ standards and processes | ☐ policies and procedures | ☐ systems and guidelines | ☐ other: ______] **ensuring the highest standard of accuracy and efficiency.**

☐ **Working with** ______ *[whom?]*, **develop, implement, and maintain** [☐ long-term | ☐ short-range] [☐ company | ☐ division | ☐ departmental | ☐ other: ______] [☐ plans | ☐ goals | ☐ objectives | ☐ projects | ☐ programs] **as well as operating policies and procedures.**

☐ **Serve on** ______ *[which?]* **committee that** [☐ strategizes | ☐ formulates | ☐ plans | ☐ improves | ☐ recommends | ☐ prioritizes | ☐ coordinates | ☐ implements | ☐ establishes | ☐ tests | ☐ approves | ☐ monitors] ______ *[what?]*.

☐ [☐ Plan and set | ☐ Establish and Implement] ______ *[which?]* [☐ goals | ☐ policies | ☐ procedures | ☐ objectives | ☐ budget projections | ☐ expense planning | ☐ other: ______].

ACHIEVEMENT SAMPLES:

☐ **Assisted the** [☐ Executive Director | ☐ President | ☐ other title: ______] **in** [☐ evaluating | ☐ prioritizing | ☐ coordinating | ☐ developing | ☐ establishing | ☐ other: ______] **long-range** ______ *[type of]* **plans including** [☐ process improvements | ☐ building renewal plans | ☐ repair and improvement projects | ☐ system-wide policies and standards | ☐ technical requirements | ☐ other: ______].

Business Management & Leadership

*See also "**Administrative Management & Leadership**" and "**Office Management & Supervision.**"*

☐ **Facilitate business management of this** ______ *[type of]* **firm including** [☐ leading and overseeing projects | ☐ prioritizing and balancing competing demands | ☐ reviewing contracts to verify legal requirements | ☐ establishing quality control procedures | ☐ developing revenue contracts | ☐ preparing specifications | ☐ performing inspections to facilitate quality assurance | ☐ quality testing materials | ☐ researching and writing (☐ legal / ☐ technical) procedures | ☐ setting up and maintaining contract database | ☐ developing budgets and monitoring expenses | ☐ preparing inspection deficiency reports | ☐ recommending corrective actions | ☐ reviewing and approving cost estimates | ☐ holding meetings to discuss project progress ☐ other: ______].

☐ **Provide leadership and support to the** ______ *[which?]* **departments overseeing various** [☐ operational aspects of | ☐ administrative support services for] **this $**______ *[revenues]* ______ *[type of firm],* **including** [☐ payroll | ☐ data processing | ☐ materials distribution | ☐ records management | ☐ security | ☐ telecommunications | ☐ other: ______].

☐ **Lead and direct the administrative and office support services for this $**______ *[revenues]* ______ *[type of]* **firm specializing in** ______ *[what?]* **including** [☐ budget preparation | ☐ inventory management and control | ☐ receivables monitoring and reporting | ☐ stock level control | ☐ evaluation and reporting | ☐ contract negotiations | ☐ assignment of jobs | ☐ maintenance activities | ☐ appointment scheduling | ☐ material requisitions | ☐ approval of time cards | ☐ supplies purchasing | ☐ accounting | ☐ invoicing ☐ recordkeeping | ☐ data entry | ☐ reception area | ☐ mailroom | ☐ other: ______].

☐ **Direct the day-to-day operations of this** [☐ multibillion-dollar | ☐ multimillion-dollar | ☐ $______ *(revenues)*] ______ *[type of]* **firm including** ______, ______, **and** ______ *[areas of primary responsibility].*

☐ **Manage the coordination and facilitation of** [☐ office management | ☐ general administration | ☐ facility management | ☐ human resources | ☐ general accounting | ☐ payroll processing | ☐ benefits administration | ☐ purchasing | ☐ inventory management and control | ☐ other: ______] **functions for this** ______ *[type of]* **firm.**

☐ **Lead and oversee the** [☐ Office Manager | ☐ Administrator | ☐ others: ______] **in their interactions and negotiations with** [☐ clients | ☐ customers | ☐ vendors | ☐ others: ______] **facilitating** [☐ purchasing | ☐ customer service | ☐ troubleshooting | ☐ other: ______].

☐ **Plan, set, and establish** ______ *[type of]* **administrative** [☐ goals | ☐ policies and procedures | ☐ objectives | ☐ budget projections | ☐ expense planning | ☐ other: ______].

☐ [☐ Direct and oversee | ☐ Supervise] **all administrative support services, including** [☐ inventory | ☐ purchasing | ☐ payroll | ☐ invoicing | ☐ other: ______] **for all** ______ *[#]* [☐ departments | ☐ offices | ☐ stores | ☐ other: ______] **requiring** [☐ calculating current stock | ☐ determining ordering needs | ☐ accurate data entry of all information | ☐ other: ______].

☐ **Oversee administrative support to the project management team in the areas of** ______, ______, **and** ______ *[which areas?]* **in setting project strategies and priorities**.

☐ **Manage** [☐ the office building | ☐ office operations | ☐ administrative services | ☐ other: ______] **including** [☐ office space planning | ☐ procedures development | ☐ account servicing | ☐ customer service | ☐ other: ______] **for this** [☐ leading | ☐ established | ☐ other: ______] ______ *[type of]* **firm.**

☐ [☐ Compose and update | ☐ Draft and edit] ______ *[type of]* [☐ contracts | ☐ agreements | ☐ technical material | (☐ company / ☐ department) policies and procedures | ☐ other: ______] **for** ______ *[purpose].*

☐ **Research, coordinate, document, edit, and periodically update the publication of** [☐ legal | ☐ policy and procedure | ☐ training | ☐ other: ______] **manuals and related** [☐ legal | ☐ technical | ☐ public information | ☐ user | ☐ other: ______] **materials.**

☐ **Coordinate new practices with** [☐ research and development | ☐ manufacturing | ☐ auditing | ☐ marketing | ☐ regulatory affairs | ☐ legal | ☐ other: ______] **personnel to** [☐ research existing practices | ☐ analyze auditing requirements | ☐ ensure compliance with all regulations | ☐ other: ______].

☐ **Define, plan, and implement** ______ *[type of]* **projects including the** [☐ design | ☐ development | ☐ implementation | ☐ tracking | ☐ other: ______] **of those projects in support of the firm's business objectives.**

ACHIEVEMENT SAMPLES:

☐ **Championed** [☐ large-scale | ☐ complex | ☐ cross-organizational | ☐ other: ______] ______ *[type of]* [☐ administrative | ☐ operational] [☐ program | ☐ system | ☐ policy | ☐ procedures | ☐ solutions | ☐ implementation projects | ☐ other: ______] **involving** ______ *[what?]* **that** ______ *[accomplished what?]* **by** ______ *[doing what?].*

☐ **Conceptualized, developed, and managed a $**______ *[revenues]* ______ *[type of]* [☐ network | ☐ division | ☐ other: ______] **by** ______ *[doing what?],* **resulting in it becoming the backbone of the company's growth from** ______ *[what size or measure?]* **to** ______ *[what size or measure?].*

☐ **Converted the firm's manual processing** ______ *[type of]* **office system to a functional** [☐ peer-to-peer] ______ *[type of]* **computerized** [☐ account database | ☐ billing | ☐ payroll | ☐ accounting | ☐ other: ______] [☐ system | ☐ environment] **increasing overall** [☐ productivity | ☐ efficiency | ☐ sales | ☐ other: ______] **increasing overall** [☐ productivity | ☐ efficiency | ☐ sales | ☐ other: ______].

- ☐ **Assisted the** [☐ Executive Director | ☐ President | ☐ other title: ______] **in** [☐ evaluating | ☐ prioritizing | ☐ coordinating | ☐ developing | ☐ establishing | ☐ other: ______] **long-range** ______ *[type of]* **plans including** [☐ repair and improvement projects | ☐ building renewal plans | ☐ system-wide policies and standards | ☐ technology enhancements | ☐ other: ______].
- ☐ **Managed and coordinated** [☐ continuous | ☐ frequent] ______ *[type of]* **office space planning to accommodate** ______**%** *[percentage]* **employee growth in** ______ *[#]* **years. Required** [☐ locating | ☐ building | ☐ leasing | ☐ renovating | ☐ furnishing | ☐ other: ______] **offices within** ______ *[#]* **months of notice, including** [☐ telephone systems | ☐ equipment | ☐ furniture | ☐ other: ______].
- ☐ **Manage and implement the firm's corporate** [☐ domestic | ☐ international] **travel policy, resulting in annual cost reductions of $**______ *[amount]* **in** [☐ air travel | ☐ hotel rental | ☐ car rental | ☐ meal expenses | ☐ other: ______].
- ☐ **Organized company's move from a** ______ *[#]*-**square foot building in** ______ *[what town?]* **to a** ______ *[#]*-**square foot building** [☐ in the business section] **of** ______ *[what town?],* **allowing the firm to** [☐ construct a front office | ☐ increase staff size | ☐ stock more supplies and materials | ☐ other: ______].
- ☐ [☐ Developed and established | ☐ Recommended and implemented] ______ *[type of]* [☐ management] [☐ plans | ☐ standards | ☐ guidelines | ☐ policies | ☐ procedures | ☐ methods | ☐ other: ______] **that maximized the effective use of** ______ *[what?]* **and supported the continuing improvement of** ______ *[which?]* **standards.**
- ☐ **Recruited as right hand to** ______ *[title]* **to save a once-profitable company from a then-floundering situation ($**______ *[amount]* **loss on $**______ *[amount]* **in sales) through effective** [☐ strategic and tactical efforts | ☐ other: ______] **resulting in its turnaround to $**______ *[amount]* **profit on $**______ *[amount]* **sales.**
- ☐ **Spearheaded and implemented a** ______ *[type of]* [☐ program | ☐ policy | ☐ procedures] **that** [☐ maximized service and equipment utilization | ☐ other: ______] **by** ______ *[doing what?].*
- ☐ **Involved in** [☐ managing | ☐ performing | ☐ coordinating | ☐ facilitating | ☐ other: ______] ______ *[what?]* **efforts that required** ______ *[what actions?]* **to meet** ______ *[what challenges?]* **and resulted in** ______ *[benefits].*

CAD Drafting – General

*For all types of **CAD Drafting,** refer to the **ARCHITECTURE & ENGINEERING BOOK**.*

- ☐ **Plan, design, and draft** ______ *[type of]* **client projects applying** [☐ expert | ☐ in-depth] **knowledge of** [☐ drafting | ☐ CAD programs | ☐ drafting devices | ☐ mathematics | ☐ zoning and building codes | ☐ building materials | ☐ other: ______].
- ☐ **Develop detailed visual guidelines that depict the technical details of** ______ *[type of]* [☐ structures | ☐ buildings | ☐ products | ☐ other: ______] **and include** [☐ specific dimensions | ☐ required materials | ☐ procedures and processes to be followed | ☐ other: ______] **for this $**______ *[revenues]* [☐ drafting | ☐ engineering | ☐ architecture | ☐ construction management | ☐ other: ______] **firm**.
- ☐ **Draft to scale the technical details of** ______ *[what?]* **from** ______ *[type of]* [☐ architectural | ☐ engineering | ☐ surveyor | ☐ scientific | ☐ other: ______] [☐ drawings | ☐ rough sketches | ☐ specifications | ☐ codes | ☐ calculations | ☐ other: ______] **for** ______ *[whom or what?].*
- ☐ **Create detailed** [☐ technical drawings | ☐ visual guidelines | ☐ plans] for [☐ construction workers | ☐ assemblers | ☐ others: ______] **to build** ______ *[type of]* [☐ structures | ☐ buildings | ☐ water systems | ☐ manufactured products | ☐ industrial machinery | ☐ machine parts | ☐ tools | ☐ pipelines | ☐ other: ______] **applying sound architectural standards for this $**______ *[revenues]* ______ *[type of]* **firm**.
- ☐ **Draft** [☐ various | ☐ multiple | ☐ numerous] [☐ large-scale | ☐ moderate-size | ☐ highly complex | ☐ moderately complex | ☐ multisite | ☐ cross-organizational | ☐ other: ______] **projects for this** ______ *[type of]* **firm that** ______ *[does what?]* **for** ______ *[whom or what?].*
- ☐ **Prepare** ______ *[type of]* [☐ scale drawings | ☐ architectural renderings] **using** ______ *[which software?]* **computer-aided design and drafting that incorporate** [(☐ interior | ☐ exterior) elevations | ☐ design | ☐ specifications | ☐ materials | ☐ color | ☐ equipment | ☐ other: ______] **and discuss specifications with interior designers to ensure all objectives are accomplished within established time frames.**
- ☐ **Produce** [☐ working plans | ☐ profile drawings | ☐ base drawings | ☐ perspective drawings | ☐ overlays | ☐ maps | ☐ illustrations | ☐ other: ______] **of** ______ *[what?];* **and prepare quantities and cost estimates using** [☐ AutoCAD | ☐ Land Development Desktop | ☐ WaterCAD | ☐ other: ______].
- ☐ **Draft CAD specifications for** ______ *[type of]* [☐ buildings | ☐ structures | ☐ other: ______] **to meet the** [☐ aesthetic | ☐ functional | ☐ safety | ☐ budgetary | ☐ project-timeline | ☐ other: ______] **goals of** [☐ commercial | ☐ residential | ☐ public works | ☐ other: ______] **clients ensuring compliance with all** [☐ building codes | ☐ zoning laws | ☐ fire regulations | ☐ OSHA | ☐ other: ______] **for this** ______ *[type of]* **firm.**

☐ **Create and design all aspects of** [☐ commercial sites | ☐ residential masterplan communities | ☐ other: ______] **applying an expert knowledge of** [☐ LDD (Land Development Desktop) | ☐ AutoCAD | ☐ MicroStation | ☐ other: ______] **software**.

☐ **Draft to scale the technical details of** ______ *[what?]* **from** [☐ drawings | ☐ rough sketches | ☐ specifications | ☐ codes | ☐ calculations | ☐ other: ______] **for** ______ *[what]*.

☐ **Provide hands-on CAD design of** ______ *[type of]* [☐ construction | ☐ renovation | ☐ new addition | ☐ restoration | ☐ grounds design | ☐ other: ______] **drawings for this** ______ *[type of]* **firm successfully meeting** ______ *[what?]* **drafting challenges**.

☐ **Apply extensive experience in AutoCAD and drafting standards in the preparation of** ______ *[type of]* **drawings consisting of** [☐ layouts | ☐ flow sheets | ☐ assemblies | ☐ isometrics | ☐ other: ______] **from** [☐ rough sketches | ☐ engineering and design information | ☐ other: ______].

ACHIEVEMENT SAMPLES: *See "Design-and-Build Projects."*

Carpentry Labor Management & Supervision

See "Trades / Crew Supervision" and "Trades Coordination & Oversight."

Carpentry Projects – General

Refer also to "Construction Projects" and individual trades positions, as applicable.

☐ **Perform a multitude of** ______ *[type of]* **carpentry work including** [☐ rough and finish carpentry | ☐ concrete forms setting | ☐ scaffolding erecting | ☐ tile installation | ☐ roof building and patching | ☐ flooring installations | ☐ stair building | ☐ insulation and weather stripping | ☐ siding installations | ☐ cabinet repair | ☐ partition installation | ☐ custom framing | ☐ wood and vinyl siding | ☐ conventional roofs | ☐ window replacements | ☐ door installations | ☐ other: ______] **according to blue print specifications**.

☐ **Ensure** [☐ trucks arrive on time to pour concrete | ☐ laborers meet each day's scheduled workload | ☐ all materials are stored at the end of each day | ☐ all debris is cleared up | ☐ customer is satisfied with work | ☐ other: ______].

☐ **Conduct hands-on** [☐ carpentry | ☐ masonry | ☐ concrete pouring | ☐ other: ______] **work in the areas of** ______, ______, **and** ______ *[type of work]*, **order materials, estimate projects, and lay out jobs for** ______ *[type of]* **projects ensuring all safety practices are followed on carpentry job sites.**

☐ **Construct, replace, repair, and/or install** [☐ windows | ☐ flooring | ☐ doors | ☐ walls | ☐ ceilings | ☐ door locks and closures | ☐ door jambs | ☐ drywall | ☐ railings | ☐ stair treads | ☐ partitions | ☐ ramps | ☐ fences | ☐ insulation | ☐ weather stripping | ☐ wall coverings | ceilings | ☐ plastic laminates | ☐ other: ______] **for this** ______ *[type of]* **firm**.

☐ **Set up prefabricated components including** [☐ frames | ☐ stairs | ☐ wall panels | ☐ other: ______] **to construct and build** ______, ______, **and** ______ *[what?]*.

☐ **Assemble, build, and/or install** [☐ foundations | ☐ ceilings | ☐ flooring | ☐ carpeting | ☐ sheetrock | ☐ walls, partitions, and panels | ☐ cabinets | ☐ wall coverings | ☐ stairs | ☐ roofs | ☐ tiling | ☐ insulation and weather stripping | ☐ windows | ☐ door jambs and doors | ☐ retainer walls | ☐ trim work | ☐ platforms and podiums | ☐ railings, stair treads, nosings, and gratings | ☐ baseboard heating | ☐ garage doors | ☐ other: ______].

☐ **Fit and install prefabricated** [☐ window frames | ☐ doorframes and doors | ☐ weather stripping | ☐ trim work | ☐ hardware | ☐ other: ______] **applying** [☐ sound-deadening | ☐ shock-absorbing | ☐ insulated | ☐ decorative | ☐ other: ______] **paneling to ceilings and walls resulting in successful** ______ *[type of]* **jobs**.

☐ **Handle various carpentry job functions including** [☐ interpreting project blueprints and schematics | ☐ preparing job site | ☐ performing rough and finish carpentry | ☐ ensuring debris removal | ☐ maintaining machinery, tools, and equipment | ☐ ensuring safety practices | ☐ unloading trucks with heavy equipment | ☐ ensuring customer satisfaction | ☐ operating (☐ forklifts / ☐ payloaders / ☐ cranes / ☐ bulldozers / ☐ other: ______) | ☐ preparing punch lists and ensuring item completion | ☐ other: ______] **ensuring compliance with all codes and regulations and meeting required deadlines**.

☐ **Read blueprints to unload correct amounts of** [☐ steel | ☐ wood | ☐ other materials: ______] **for each project; arrange and lay out materials according to daily project needs; and oversee the construction of** [☐ window replacement | ☐ door layouts | ☐ walls | ☐ decks | ☐ roofing | ☐ other: ______] **on schedule, within budget**.

☐ **Working as a team**, [☐ unload trucks with heavy equipment and cranes | ☐ transport tools to job sites | ☐ set up daily materials and equipment | ☐ operate (☐ forklifts / ☐ payloaders / ☐ bulldozers) | ☐ tear down old construction | ☐ handle steel and concrete construction work | ☐ guide machinery to dig, clear, and backfill land | ☐ set up windows and doors for replacement | ☐ take accurate measurements for new construction | ☐ cut and connect PVC pipes from buildings to cesspool | ☐ other: ______] **ensuring customer satisfaction on all jobs.**

- ☐ **Cut, shape, and assemble** [☐ wood | ☐ steel | ☐ drywall | ☐ tiles | ☐ glass | ☐ plastic | ☐ fiberglass | ☐ other: ______], **and other materials for the construction of** [☐ buildings | ☐ highways | ☐ bridges | ☐ marinas | ☐ boats | ☐ other: ______], **and modify as needed to fit properly.**
- ☐ **Work with** ______ *[which?]* **teams supporting** [☐ project managers | ☐ superintendents | ☐ plumbers | ☐ electricians | ☐ roofers | ☐ framers | ☐ finish carpenters | ☐ others: ______] [☐ in the preparation of building sites | ☐ throughout all project lifecycle phases | ☐ other: ______].
- ☐ **Develop** [☐ complex | ☐ extensive | ☐ detailed] ______ *[type of]* **building plan specifications to support the overall design and construction of** ______ *[what?]*.
- ☐ **Prepare recommendations to** ______ *[whom?]* **regarding** [☐ contractual defaults | ☐ time extensions | ☐ liquidated damages | ☐ other: ______].
- ☐ **Apply a thorough knowledge of** [☐ construction methods | ☐ building codes | ☐ finish carpentry | ☐ tools, equipment, and materials | ☐ safety practices | ☐ building techniques | ☐ other: ______] in all [☐ wood and metal framing | ☐ shingle and plywood roofing | ☐ wood and vinyl siding | ☐ masonry work | ☐ window and garage door replacement | ☐ home renovations | ☐ railroad ties | ☐ retainer walls | ☐ other: ______] **carpentry activities and ensure safety practices are followed.**
- ☐ **Provide support and feedback to** ______ *[whom?]* **regarding** [☐ structural | ☐ renovation | ☐ mechanical | ☐ environmental | ☐ other: ______] **issues at the site.**

ACHIEVEMENT SAMPLES: *See "Construction Projects."*

Carpentry Projects – Supervision

Refer also to "Construction Projects" and individual trades positions, as applicable.

- ☐ **Supervise rough and finish carpentry work in all phases of construction including** [☐ pouring foundations | ☐ framing and sheetrocking | ☐ taping and spackling | ☐ other: ______] **and installing** [☐ windows | ☐ doors | ☐ flooring | ☐ tiling | ☐ ceilings | ☐ roofing | ☐ wall coverings | ☐ trim work | ☐ platforms | ☐ hardware | ☐ partitions | ☐ fences | ☐ ramps | ☐ insulation | ☐ other: ______].
- ☐ **Plan, coordinate, and oversee** [☐ rough | ☐ finish] **carpentry in the construction and** [☐ demolition | ☐ remodeling | ☐ renovation | ☐ assembly | ☐ repair | ☐ restoration | ☐ other: ______] **of** ______ *[type of]* **projects for this** ______ *[type of]* **firm.**
- ☐ **Manage multiple** [☐ large-scale | ☐ moderate-size | ☐ highly complex | ☐ moderately complex | ☐ multisite | ☐ cross-organizational | ☐ multiyear-timeline | ☐ multimonth-timeline | ☐ simultaneous | ☐ other: ______] **project rollouts from inception to successful completion for this** ______ *[type of]* **firm that** ______ *[does what?]* **for** ______ *[whom?]*.
- ☐ **Supervise** [☐ remodeling | ☐ renovations | ☐ finish carpentry | ☐ other: ______] **including installation of** [☐ custom framing | ☐ wood and vinyl siding | ☐ conventional roofs | ☐ window replacements | ☐ doors | ☐ tiling | ☐ countertops | ☐ other: ______] **according to blueprint specifications.**
- ☐ **Direct the construction and/or installation of** [☐ concrete forms | ☐ walls | ☐ doors | ☐ door jambs | ☐ roofs | ☐ floors | ☐ wall coverings | ☐ ceilings | ☐ paneling | ☐ plastic laminates | ☐ cabinets | ☐ platforms | ☐ partitions | ☐ hardware | ☐ podiums | ☐ partitions | ☐ fences | ☐ ramps | ☐ insulation | ☐ weather stripping | ☐ other: ______] **on** ______ *[type of]* **construction projects for this** ______ *[type of]* **firm.**
- ☐ **Supervise landscape installation functions including** [☐ grading | ☐ retainer walls | ☐ landscape borders | ☐ walkways | ☐ sprinkler systems | ☐ concrete masonry walls | ☐ soil thatching | ☐ tree and shrub plantings | ☐ others: ______].
- ☐ **Oversee maintenance and repair work including** [☐ windows | ☐ doors | ☐ walls | ☐ ceilings | ☐ furniture | ☐ railings / hand railings | ☐ stair treads | ☐ other: ______].
- ☐ **Direct the construction, replacement, repair, and/ or installation of** [☐ windows | ☐ flooring | ☐ doors | ☐ walls | ☐ ceilings | ☐ door locks and closures | ☐ door jambs | ☐ drywall | ☐ gratings | ☐ railings | ☐ stair treads | ☐ partitions | ☐ ramps | ☐ fences | ☐ insulation | ☐ weather stripping | ☐ other: ______].
- ☐ **Supervise** [☐ home construction | ☐ home improvement | ☐ interior renovation | ☐ room additions | ☐ finished attics and basements | ☐ other: ______] **including** [☐ framing | ☐ insulation | ☐ sheetrocking | ☐ taping and spackling | ☐ painting | ☐ flooring | ☐ tiling | ☐ roofing | ☐ landscaping | ☐ other: ______] **for individual clients.**
- ☐ **Oversee the concrete and steel reinforcement of** ______ *[type of]* **construction projects and the finishing of walls with** [☐ wood | ☐ structural metal | ☐ lath | ☐ plaster | ☐ other: ______] **materials meeting all project budgets and deadlines.**

☐ **Manage** [☐ home remodeling and renovations | ☐ various types of carpentry work | ☐ finish carpentry | ☐ other: ______] **including installation of** ______, ______, **and** ______ *[what?]* **according to blue print specifications.**

☐ **Prepare** [☐ job estimates | ☐ budgeting | ☐ other: ______] **with fair financial arrangements for customers and at good profits for company.**

☐ **Supervise the application of textured surfaces to** [☐ walls | ☐ ceilings | ☐ flooring | ☐ other: ______] **on** ______ [type of] **construction projects.**

ACHIEVEMENT SAMPLES: *See "Construction Projects."*

Carpentry Supervision – General

See also "Carpentry Projects," "Construction Supervision," "Construction Project Management," "Trades / Crew Supervision," "Trades Coordination & Oversight," and various Carpentry and Construction categories.

☐ **Supervise and oversee** ______ *[#]* **laborers in all phases of carpentry projects including** [☐ demolition | ☐ foundations | ☐ wall framing and partitions | ☐ insulation | ☐ sheet-rock installation| ☐ building and installing (☐ stairs / ☐ windows / ☐ doors / ☐ brattices) | ☐ taping and spackling | ☐ painting | ☐ trim work | ☐ flooring | ☐ tiling | ☐ ceilings | ☐ roofing | ☐ cabinet installations | ☐ masonry | ☐ welding | ☐ plumbing | ☐ electrical | ☐ HVAC | ☐ landscaping | ☐ other: ______].

☐ **Plan, coordinate, and supervise** [☐ rough | ☐ finish] **carpentry in the construction and** [☐ demolition | ☐ remodeling | ☐ renovation | ☐ assembly | ☐ repair | ☐ maintenance] of [☐ buildings | ☐ cabinets | ☐ roofs | ☐ furnishings | ☐ vinyl siding | ☐ other: ______] **for this $**______ *[revenues]* ______ *[type of]* **firm.**

☐ **Supervise the daily carpentry operations for this $**______ *[revenues]* ______ *[type of]* **firm including** [☐ blueprint reading | ☐ work scheduling | ☐ job site preparation | ☐ project management | ☐ building inspections | ☐ other: ______].

☐ **Lead all aspects of** [☐ carpentry | ☐ construction] **project lifecycles including** [☐ project scope | ☐ initiation | ☐ planning | ☐ scheduling | ☐ budgeting | ☐ contractor selection | ☐ resource allocation | ☐ risk assessment | ☐ quality control | ☐ change orders | ☐ cost control | ☐ punch lists | ☐ close-out billing | ☐ other: ______].

☐ **Oversee all aspects of carpentry work including** [☐ reviewing project plans | ☐ reading and interpreting blueprints | ☐ estimating time | ☐ preparing job estimates | ☐ estimating material and labor costs | ☐ securing competitive bids | ☐ selecting contractors and subcontractors | ☐ preparing work orders | ☐ developing crew assignments and work schedules | ☐ coordinating projects with contractors | ☐ preparing job sites | ☐ ordering and setting up equipment | ☐ purchasing materials and supplies | ☐ directing and coordinating building construction | ☐ supervising a crew of ______ *(#)* | ☐ performing rough and finish carpentry | ☐ evaluating staff performance | ☐ inspecting work area | ☐ obtaining permits | ☐ mediating and resolving disputes | ☐ ensuring debris removal | ☐ providing technical construction assistance | ☐ preparing punch lists | ☐ overseeing inspection deadlines | ☐ negotiating and processing change orders | ☐ ensuring punch list item completion and customer satisfaction | ☐ coordinating concrete trucks | ☐ recommending land purchases to management | ☐ monitoring inventory and supply requests | ☐ ensuring safety practices | ☐ preparing accident reports | ☐ other: ______] **ensuring all jobs are completed in compliance with specifications and codes.**

☐ **Supervise** [☐ home | ☐ office | ☐ commercial | ☐ industrial | ☐ public | ☐ other: ______] [☐ carpentry | ☐ construction | ☐ renovation] **for this** [☐ $______ *(revenues)* | ☐ leading | ☐ established] ______ *[type of]* **general contractor, overseeing a** ______ *[#]*-**man crew and bringing jobs in on time and within budget.**

☐ **Manage a multitude of carpentry work including** [☐ setting concrete forms | ☐ erecting scaffolding | ☐ installing ceiling tiles | ☐ repairing cabinets | ☐ installing partitions | ☐ other: ______] **and perform finishing work for** ______ *[type of]* **projects.**

☐ **Review schematic drawings and construction details for** ______ *[type of]* **projects, interpret specifications, make recommendations to modify as needed, discuss changes with clients before implementation, and make field inspections.**

☐ **Plan and coordinate all activities of** [☐ small- | ☐ moderate- | ☐ large-] **scale** ______ *[type of]* **carpentry projects in collaboration with** [☐ client reps | ☐ contractors | ☐ subcontractors] **for this** ______ *[type of]* **firm that generates fiscal-year revenues of $**______ *[revenues].*

☐ **Coordinate and oversee** [☐ rough | ☐ finish] **carpentry in the construction and** [☐ demolition | ☐ remodeling | ☐ renovation | ☐ assembly | ☐ repair | ☐ restoration | ☐ other: ______] **of** ______ *[type of]* **projects.**

☐ **Conceive, sketch, and design** ______ *[type of]* **carpentry projects for** ______ *[whom or what?]* **and prepare job estimates with fair financial arrangements for customers and at good profits for company.**

☐ **Prepare** [☐ site plans | ☐ planning applications | ☐ specifications | ☐ cost estimates | ☐ other: ______] **for land development of** ______ *[what?]*; **and coordinate proposed land features and structures.**

☐ **Order materials, estimate projects, and lay out jobs for this** [☐ residential | ☐ commercial | ☐ other: ______] **contractor specializing in** ______ *[what?]* **ensuring** [☐ trucks arrive on time to pour concrete | ☐ laborers meet each day's scheduled workload |

☐ safety practices are followed on job sites | ☐ all materials are stored at the end of each day | ☐ all debris is cleared | ☐ customer satisfaction with work | ☐ other: ______].

☐ **Oversee rough and finish carpentry in the construction and/or installation of** [☐ buildings | ☐ houses | ☐ remodels | ☐ roofing | ☐ siding | ☐ cabinets | ☐ fencing | ☐ other: ______].

☐ **Obtain permits, estimate jobs, and hire and schedule trades acting as liaison with** [☐ building managers | ☐ inspectors | ☐ architects | ☐ engineers | ☐ others: ______].

☐ **Ensure all** ______ *[type of]* **carpentry** [☐ machinery | ☐ tools | ☐ equipment | ☐ vehicles] **used by the trade are repaired and maintained.**

ACHIEVEMENT SAMPLES: *See "Construction Projects."*

Carpentry Work – General

Refer also to other related trades positions.

☐ **Handle** [☐ carpentry | ☐ construction] **projects from project start through completion including** [☐ client relations | ☐ construction drawings review | ☐ project initiation | ☐ trades coordination | ☐ change orders | ☐ cost control | ☐ punch lists | ☐ inspection | ☐ other: ______] **within the parameters of project cost, time, and quality**.

☐ **Work on several** [☐ demolition | ☐ construction | ☐ remodeling | ☐ renovation | ☐ restoration | ☐ repair | ☐ other: ______] **projects** [☐ some simultaneously] **with projects ranging from $______ to $______** *[amounts]* **including** [☐ commercial buildings | ☐ shopping malls | ☐ stores | ☐ restaurants | ☐ manufacturing plants | ☐ schools | ☐ colleges and universities | ☐ corporate offices | ☐ building lobbies | ☐ government agencies | ☐ houses | ☐ condominiums | ☐ apartment buildings | ☐ hospitals | ☐ laboratories | ☐ clean rooms | ☐ landmark restorations | ☐ highways | ☐ other: ______] **completing all projects on time and within budget.**

☐ **As** [☐ Lead Carpenter | ☐ General Contractor] perform [☐ home construction | ☐ home improvement | ☐ interior renovation | ☐ room additions | ☐ finished attics and basements | ☐ other: ______] **for individual clients including** [☐ framing | ☐ insulation | ☐ sheetrocking | ☐ taping and spackling | ☐ painting | ☐ flooring | ☐ tiling | ☐ roofing | ☐ other: ______] that result in ______ *[benefits].*

☐ **Specializing in** [☐ demolition | ☐ carpentry | ☐ framing | ☐ sheetrocking | ☐ taping and spackling | ☐ flooring | ☐ painting | ☐ insulation | ☐ electrical | ☐ plumbing | ☐ tiling | ☐ trim work | ☐ ceilings | ☐ welding | ☐ roofing | ☐ masonry | ☐ other: ______] **perform** ______ *[type of]* [☐ large-scale | ☐ mid-size | ☐ highly complex | ☐ moderately complex | ☐ multisite | ☐ other: ______] **construction projects for** ______ *[whom?]* **resulting in** ______ *[what benefits?].*

☐ **Handle all aspects of remodeling** [☐ residential homes | ☐ commercial buildings | ☐ civil projects | ☐ other: ______] **including** ______, ______, **and** ______ *[type of renovations].*

☐ **Facilitate** [☐ home | ☐ office | ☐ commercial | ☐ industrial | ☐ public | ☐ other: ______] **carpentry projects for this** [☐ leading | ☐ established | ☐ other: ______] **general contractor, bringing all jobs in on time and within budget**.

☐ **Perform** [☐ residential | ☐ commercial | ☐ industrial | ☐ other: ______] [☐ new construction | ☐ remodeling | ☐ carpentry work | ☐ finish carpentry | ☐ other: ______] including installation of [☐ custom framing | ☐ wood/vinyl siding | ☐ conventional roofs | ☐ window replacements | ☐ doors | ☐ ceramic tile | ☐ other: ______] **according to blue print specifications**.

☐ **Involved in all aspects of** [☐ construction | ☐ carpentry] **including** [☐ reviewing project plans | ☐ reading and interpreting blueprints | ☐ estimating time | ☐ developing work schedules | ☐ preparing work orders | ☐ ordering and setting up equipment | ☐ purchasing supplies | ☐ preparing job sites | ☐ performing rough and finish carpentry | ☐ inspecting work areas | ☐ other: ______] **ensuring jobs are completed in compliance with all specifications and building codes.**

☐ **Work as a team with** ______ *[#]* **laborers in the construction and installation of** [☐ walls | ☐ doors | ☐ door jambs | ☐ roofs | ☐ floors | ☐ wall coverings | ☐ ceilings | ☐ partitions | ☐ fences | ☐ ramps | ☐ insulation | ☐ weather stripping | ☐ other: ______] **for this** ______ *[type of]* **firm**.

☐ **Perform hands-on rough and finish carpentry work including** [☐ pouring foundations | ☐ framing and sheet-rocking walls and partitions | ☐ taping and spackling | ☐ building stairs | ☐ installing windows | ☐ replacing doors | ☐ flooring | ☐ tiling | ☐ ceilings | ☐ painting | ☐ siding | ☐ roofs | ☐ ceilings | ☐ kitchen and bathroom cabinets | ☐ other: ______].

ACHIEVEMENT SAMPLES: *See "Construction Projects."*

Ceiling, Lathing, Insulation & Drywall Installation

*See also **"Carpentry / Construction Work"** and other Carpentry / Construction Projects (specific).*

☐ **Mount** [☐ drywall sheets | ☐ acoustical tiles | ☐ shock-absorbing materials | ☐ other: _____] **that reduce / reflect sound to ceilings and walls for _____, _____, and _____** *[type of projects or companies].*

☐ **Prepare for** [☐ ceiling | ☐ drywall | ☐ other: _____] **installation jobs by first inspecting areas for** [☐ electrical wire | ☐ ductwork | ☐ piping | ☐ other: _____] **obstructions and** [☐ removing existing plaster, drywall, or paneling | ☐ measuring and marketing surfaces according to specifications | ☐ determining materials and installation methods | ☐ hanging dry lines to wall moldings to guide main runners | ☐ installing furring strips to framing to create flat, even surfaces | ☐ marking wall studs, light fixtures, and electrical boxes for ceiling joist locations | ☐ building and using T-braces for leverage and support to raise drywall panels | ☐ hanging and affixing drywall sheets | ☐ abutting tapered edges | ☐ taping and spackling | ☐ other: _____].

☐ **Fasten** [☐ metal | ☐ rockboard | ☐ wood | ☐ other: _____] **laths to inside framing of** [☐ walls | ☐ ceilings | ☐ partitions | ☐ other: _____] **of _____** *[type of]* [☐ commercial | ☐ residential | ☐ other: _____] **buildings working with** [☐ wire | ☐ metal mesh | ☐ rockboard lath | (☐ decorative / ☐ functional) tiling | ☐ other: _____] **using hand and power tools to** [☐ nail | ☐ screw | ☐ staple | ☐ wire-tie | ☐ other: _____] **lath directly to structural framework.**

☐ **Perform various** [☐ ceiling | ☐ lathing | ☐ drywall] **installation functions including** [☐ cutting and/or bending lath to fit openings and corners | ☐ fastening (☐ metal / ☐ rockboard) lath to (☐ framework / ☐ ceiling joists / ☐ partitions / ☐ concrete surfaces) | ☐ welding metal frame supports | ☐ fitting and fastening wallboards | ☐ cutting openings for outlets, plumbing, vents, and windows | ☐ adding decorative trim to doorways and windows | ☐ inspecting (☐ furrings / ☐ masonry) surfaces | ☐ installing tiling | ☐ sealing joints between tiles and walls | ☐ coordinating work with drywall finishers | ☐ installing insulation | ☐ filling cracks with sealing compound | ☐ installing metal casings around openings | ☐ other: _____]

☐ **Properly insulate** [☐ buildings | ☐ attics | ☐ exterior walls | ☐ ceilings | ☐ boilers | ☐ steam and hot water pipes | ☐ other: _____] **with** [☐ fiberglass | ☐ foam | ☐ cellulose | ☐ rock wool batt | ☐ other: _____] **insulation and** [☐ use wire meshes to spray foam insulation | ☐ wrap it with (☐ aluminum / ☐ plastic / ☐ canvas / ☐ other: _____) | ☐ screw sheet metal around insulated pipes | ☐ apply drywall and plaster | ☐ other: _____].

☐ **Apply _____** *[type of]* **insulation to _____** *[what?]* **using** [☐ stapling guns | ☐ power saws | ☐ compressor hose | ☐ trowels | ☐ brushes | ☐ knives | ☐ saws | ☐ pliers | ☐ tape | ☐ other: _____] **to keep seasonal air conditioning and heat in and vice versa, following all safety guidelines.**

☐ **Use** [☐ power saws to cut insulating materials | ☐ welding machines to join sheet metal and secure clamps | ☐ compressors to spray insulation | ☐ other: _____] **and** [☐ saws | ☐ compressor hose | ☐ trowels | ☐ brushes | ☐ knives | ☐ pliers | ☐ tape | ☐ stapling guns | ☐ other: _____] **to cut and secure insulation.**

☐ [☐ Oversee | ☐ Conduct] **drywall panel fastening to the framework of _____** *[type of]* **buildings and prepare panels for painting by filling, taping, troweling, and finishing joints for _____** *[what?].*

☐ **Specializing in drywall installations, perform _____** *[type of]* **projects for _____** *[whom?]* **including** [☐ fastening drywall panels to framework | ☐ taping and spackling | ☐ painting, filling, taping, troweling, and finishing joints | ☐ measuring, cutting, fitting, gluing, and screwing wallboard panels to framework | ☐ applying textured surfaces | ☐ other: _____].

☐ **Measure, cut, fit, glue and/or screw wallboard panels to wood and metal framework, cutting holes in panels for** [☐ windows | ☐ doors | ☐ electrical outlets | ☐ air-conditioning units | ☐ plumbing | ☐ other: _____] **and applying textured surfaces to** [☐ walls | ☐ ceilings | ☐ floors | ☐ other: _____] **using** [☐ trowels | ☐ brushes | ☐ spray guns | ☐ other: _____].

☐ **Use automatic taping tools and sand all treated areas on** [☐ large | ☐ midsize | ☐ variable] **_____** *[type of]* **projects, ensuring smoothness perfection to match remaining wall surfaces.**

ACHIEVEMENT SAMPLES: *See also "**Construction Projects.**"*

☐ **Increased productivity _____%** *[percentage],* **slashed _____** *[type of]* **project times, and decreased man hours from _____** *[#]* [☐ hours | ☐ days] **to _____** [☐ hours | ☐ days] **by using** [☐ ratcheting cargo jacks and telescopic paint roller handles to attach to beams and ladder treads to support sheetrock | ☐ other methods: _____] **allowing for one-person drywall ceiling installations.**

☐ **Reduced energy consumption _____%** *[percentage]* **on _____** *[type of]* **project by properly insulating** [☐ buildings | ☐ attics | ☐ exterior walls | ☐ ceilings | ☐ plaster walls | ☐ paneling | ☐ boilers | ☐ steam and hot water pipes | ☐ storage rooms | ☐ vats | ☐ tanks | ☐ other: _____] **with** [☐ fiberglass | ☐ foam | ☐ cellulose | ☐ rock wool | ☐ other: _____] **insulation protecting from weather conditions and damage.**

☐ **Completed drywall installation on various _____** *[#]* [☐ room | ☐ square footage | ☐ other: _____] _____ *[type of]* [☐ demolition | ☐ construction | ☐ renovation | ☐ restoration | ☐ repair | ☐ other: _____] **projects ranging from $_____ to $_____** *[amounts],* **completing all projects on time and within budget.**

Client Billing / Invoicing

See also "Project Tracking and Reporting" and "Database Setup & Data Entry."

- ☐ [☐ Manage | ☐ Supervise | ☐ Prepare | ☐ Coordinate] **billing for a customer base of** ______ *[#]*, **keeping all records current and ensuring accuracy.**
- ☐ **Supervise computer entry of daily** [☐ billing | ☐ payments | ☐ recordkeeping | ☐ client communiqué | ☐ other: ______], **ensuring accurate data entry at all times.**
- ☐ **Accurately bill clients on all time and labor charges associated with** ______ *[what?]* [☐ projects | ☐ services | ☐ other: ______] **within** ______ *[what time frame?]* **from completion to delivery, securing $**______ **in annual receipts**.
- ☐ **Oversee data entry of** [☐ customer | ☐ contractual | ☐ sales | ☐ other: ______] **information, including** ______, ______, **and** ______ *[areas]* **on** ______ *[name of]* **system**.
- ☐ **Accurately complete and verify data entry of** ______ *[#]* [☐ daily | ☐ weekly | ☐ monthly] invoices using [☐ Quick Books | ☐ Quicken | ☐ Excel | ☐ other: ______] **ensuring project management team consistency**.
- ☐ **Created a** ______ *[type of]* [☐ filing | ☐ data entry | ☐ other: ______] [☐ system | ☐ procedure | ☐ program | ☐ other: ______] **that provided** ______ *[benefits]*.
- ☐ **Keep track of all client billable hours and types of jobs performed, and calculate client fees based on dollar amounts to charge for each task for this** ______ *[type of]* **firm**.
- ☐ **Compile accurate records of all** [☐ services rendered | ☐ goods sold | ☐ other: ______], **calculate amounts due, and post entries to client accounts.**
- ☐ **Prepare, verify and send client itemized** [☐ statements | ☐ invoices] containing [☐ dates of services provided | ☐ types and codes of services performed | ☐ credit terms | ☐ completion dates | ☐ shipment dates | ☐ other: ______] **and total amounts due.**
- ☐ **Process approximately** ______ *[#]* [☐ invoice pages | ☐ sales contracts | ☐ letters of credit | ☐ other: ______] [☐ daily | ☐ weekly | ☐ monthly] **compared to a norm of** ______ *[#]* **completing a five-day workload in only** ______ *[#]* **days**.
- ☐ **Create accurate** [☐ invoices | ☐ job estimates | ☐ other: ______] **by consulting rate books to determine** [☐ product | ☐ shipping | ☐ other: ______] **costs and using** [☐ Quick Books | ☐ Quicken | ☐ Excel | ☐ other: ______] **to** [☐ post entries | ☐ calculate charges | ☐ prepare customer invoices | ☐ update client files | ☐ other: ______].
- ☐ **Review** [☐ purchase orders | ☐ sales tickets | ☐ charge slips | ☐ change orders | ☐ other: ______] **to calculate customer amounts due taking into account any** [☐ discounts | ☐ special rates | ☐ credit terms | ☐ other: ______].
- ☐ **Respond to customer questions and resolve all concerns relative to** [☐ invoice entries | ☐ billing errors | ☐ discrepancies | ☐ other: ______] **resulting in** [☐ customer satisfaction | ☐ decreased accounts receivables | ☐ customers paying their bills on time | ☐ other: ______].
- ☐ **Prepare, verify, and send client itemized** [☐ statements | ☐ invoices] **containing** [☐ dates of services provided | ☐ types and codes of services performed | ☐ credit terms | ☐ completion dates | ☐ shipment dates | ☐ other: ______] **and total amounts due.**
- ☐ **Handle monthly billing for** ______ *[#]* **accounts with recordkeeping of all** ______ *[type of]* **purchases and supplies per account.**

Client Meeting & Strategizing – General

See also "Client Relations," "Client Presentations & Proposals," and "Customer Service,"

- ☐ **Strategize and collaborate with** ______ *[type of]* **clients to** [☐ determine the scope of their projects | ☐ assess their needs | ☐ understand their goals | ☐ identify options | ☐ define challenges | ☐ generate ideas | ☐ strategize solutions | ☐ provide alternative methods | ☐ ascertain budget | ☐ define project scope | ☐ identify challenges | ☐ generate ideas | ☐ present proposals | ☐ set project time frames | ☐ determine options | ☐ provide alternative methods | ☐ present proposals | ☐ communicate tradeoffs | ☐ prepare job estimates | ☐ provide technical advice | ☐ resolve challenges | ☐ solicit feedback | ☐ establish a high level of trust | ☐ deliver client expectations | ☐ sell high-dollar projects | ☐ other: ______].
- ☐ **Assess** [☐ business | ☐ client] **needs and translate** ______ *[type of]* **challenges into successful** ______ *[type of]* **projects that reflect** [☐ clients' | ☐ firm's] **goals and objectives.**
- ☐ **Meet with potential** ______ *[type of]* **clients to** [☐ determine their needs | ☐ provide cost estimates | ☐ define requirements | ☐ demonstrate benefits of ______ *(what?)*] **in** ______ *[what projects?]*.
- ☐ **Meet with customers to determine their** ______ *[type of]* **requirements and develop automated solutions that take into account** [☐ safety | ☐ time | ☐ cost | ☐ project management | ☐ other: ______] **factors**.

☐ **As the Company's primary client contact, evaluate the strengths and weaknesses of ______** *[type of]* **initiatives, determine whether clients' needs are adequately being met, and offer alternative solutions.**

☐ **Meet with customers to determine their** [☐ product | ☐ project | ☐ service | ☐ other: ______] **requirements and develop ______** *[type of]* **solutions that take into account** [☐ safety | ☐ time | ☐ cost | ☐ project management | ☐ other: ______] **factors**.

☐ **Consult with clients to discuss project** [☐ objectives | ☐ scope | ☐ requirements | ☐ budget | ☐ other: ______] **required for proposed ______** *[type of]* **projects; determine ______** *[type of]* **requirements; and provide clients with various options.**

☐ **Meet and strategize with clients to assess their ______** *[type of]* **needs, define their goals, and provide workable solutions in the development of ______** *[what?]* **complying with ______** *[what?]*.

☐ **Identify, define, and document client priorities and translate those requirements into effective ______** *[type of]* **strategies and ______** *[type of]* **projects.**

☐ **Meet with customers to determine their product requirements and develop automated solutions that take into account** [☐ safety | ☐ time | ☐ cost | ☐ project management | ☐ other: ______] **factors**.

☐ **Represent ______** *[type of]* **clients in** [☐ industry meetings | ☐ public hearings | ☐ other: ______] **and interactions with** [☐ federal | ☐ state | ☐ local] **environmental agencies including ______, ______, and ______** *[which agencies?]* **on ______** *[type of]* **issues**.

Client Meeting & Strategizing – Architecture & Construction

*See also **"Client Relations"** and **"Client Presentations & Proposals,"** and **"Customer Service & Problem Resolution,"***

☐ **Meet and strategize with ______** *[type of]* **clients to determine the scope of their projects and related architectural design services required to build those projects including** [☐ assessing needs | ☐ identifying options | ☐ defining challenges | ☐ generating ideas | ☐ strategizing solutions | ☐ ascertaining budget | ☐ selling high-dollar projects | ☐ providing alternative methods | ☐ preparing job estimates | ☐ determining design direction | ☐ defining project scope | ☐ setting project timeframes | ☐ presenting proposals | ☐ providing technical advice | ☐ resolving challenges | ☐ delivering architectural drawings | ☐ other: ______].

☐ **Consult with clients to assess their** [☐ architectural | ☐ carpentry | ☐ electrical | ☐ plumbing | ☐ HVAC-R | ☐ other: ______] **needs, define their goals, and provide workable solutions for the** [☐ design | ☐ installation | ☐ construction | ☐ other: ______] **of ______** *[what?]*.

☐ **Assess** [☐ business | ☐ client] **needs and translate ______** *[type of]* **design and functional challenges into successful ______** *[type of]* [☐ buildings | ☐ complexes | ☐ structures | ☐ systems | ☐ products | ☐ services | ☐ equipment | ☐ other: ______] **that reflects** [☐ clients' | ☐ firm's] **goals and objectives.**

☐ **Meet with potential ______** *[type of]* **clients to** [☐ determine their design and construction needs | ☐ provide cost estimates | ☐ define requirements | ☐ demonstrate benefits of ______ *(what?)*] **in the design and build of ______** *[what?]*.

☐ **Consult with client representatives to discuss ______** *[type of]* [☐ design | ☐ construction | ☐ design-and-build] **project** [☐ objectives | ☐ scope | ☐ requirements | ☐ budget | ☐ other: ______] **required for proposed ______** *[type of]* [☐ engineering | ☐ architectural | ☐ other: ______] **projects for the design and build of ______** *[what?]*; **determine ______** *[type of]* **requirements; and provide clients with various options.**

☐ **Meet and strategize with clients to assess their ______** *[type of]* [☐ engineering | ☐ architectural | ☐ other: ______] **needs, define their goals, and provide workable solutions in the development of ______** *[what?]* **complying with all** [☐ client goals and challenges | ☐ electrical codes | ☐ building codes | ☐ zoning laws | ☐ fire regulations | ☐ other: ______].

☐ **Identify, define, and document client priorities and translate those requirements into effective ______** *[type of]* **design strategies and construction projects.**

☐ **Consult with clients on** [☐ the selection of building sites | ☐ the preparation of land-use studies | ☐ land development planning | ☐ energy saving measures | ☐ other: ______]; [☐ and conduct feasibility and/or environmental impact studies as needed].

Client Presentations & Proposals

*See also **"Client Meeting & Strategizing," "Client Relations,"** and **"Customer Service."***

☐ [☐ Create and generate | ☐ Review and approve] **detailed ______** *[type of]* **client** [☐ presentations | ☐ proposals | ☐ cost estimates | ☐ project plans | ☐ contracts | ☐ other: ______] **based on clients' understanding and expectations so desired ______** *[type of]* **solutions can be successfully implemented on time and within budget**.

☐ **Determine** [☐ internal | ☐ external] **client** ______ *[type of]* **goals and develop detailed** ______ *[type of]* [☐ project plans | ☐ proposals | ☐ presentations | ☐ other: ______] **for** ______ *[what?]* **that include all project** [☐ objectives | ☐ specifications | ☐ time frames | ☐ costs | ☐ budget | ☐ resource allocation | ☐ quality assurance | ☐ other: ______] **to ensure needs of all parties are met.**

☐ **Interface and work closely with** ______ *[whom?]* **in the** [☐ development of project strategies | ☐ identification of project scope | ☐ executing of project plans | ☐ determination of required materials and resources | ☐ coordination of resources | ☐ other: ______].

☐ **Define and document client priorities and translate those requirements into effective** ______ *[type of]* **solutions and strategies.**

☐ **Identify and define project scope and objectives with all** [☐ internal | ☐ external] **clients; and provide** [☐ project management | ☐ other: ______] **expertise in the development of** ______ *[type of]* [☐ project plans | ☐ proposals | ☐ presentations | ☐ other: ______].

☐ **Create and generate** ______ *[type of]* **client** [☐ presentations | ☐ publications | ☐ other: ______], **including** ______ *[type of]* [☐ newsletters | ☐ financials | ☐ manuals | ☐ reports | ☐ other: ______] **using** [☐ Microsoft (☐ PowerPoint / ☐ Publisher / ☐ Word) | ☐ Adobe InDesign | ☐QuarkXpress | ☐other: ______].

☐ **Use advanced word-processing functions such as** [☐ calculating tables | ☐ style galleries | ☐ columns | ☐ charts and graphs | ☐ headers and footers | ☐ mail merges | ☐ cross-referencing | ☐ borders and shading | ☐ other: ______] **to prepare** [☐ presentations | ☐ newsletters | ☐ brochures | ☐ sales materials | ☐ procedure manuals | ☐ training manuals | ☐ other: ______].

☐ **Use** ______ *[type of]* **software to create attractive** ______ *[type of]* [☐ presentations | (☐ company / ☐ product) brochures | ☐ flyers | ☐ direct mail pieces | ☐ other: ______] **for** [☐ prospective customers | ☐ management meetings | ☐ special events | ☐ other: ______].

☐ **Lay out, design, and produce** ______ *[what?]* **for** ______ *[whom?]* **that** [☐ creates a positive impression | ☐ increases value | ☐ achieves ______ *[what?]* | ☐ other: ______] **for company's high-end client projects.**

☐ **Deliver highly effective oral and visual sales presentations to a variety of** ______ *[type of]* **customers and attend industry trade shows to promote** ______ *[type of]* **company, products, and services resulting in** ______ *[benefits].*

☐ **Handle** ______ *[what processes?]* **in the** [☐ creation | ☐ design | ☐ development | ☐ production | ☐ other: ______] **of various** ______ *[type of]* **projects, managing all phases—from concept to completion.**

Client Relations

*See also "**Client Meeting & Strategizing,**" "**Client Presentations & Proposals,**" "**Customer Service,**" and "**Client Billing / Invoicing.**"*

☐ **Work with** [☐ Fortune ☐ 100 | ☐ 500 | ☐ 1000 | ☐ other: ______] **clients including** ______, ______, **and** ______ *[clients]* **to** [☐ understand their goals | ☐ identify their needs | ☐ conduct presentations | ☐ present proposals | ☐ help define strategy | ☐ provide technical advice | ☐ resolve challenges | ☐ solicit feedback | ☐ provide alternative solutions | ☐ communicate tradeoffs | ☐ establish a high level of trust | ☐ deliver client expectations | ☐ other: ______].

☐ **Collaborate with owners to maintain customer satisfaction by** [☐ listening to and interpreting their needs | ☐ paying careful attention to detail | ☐ making changes as needed | ☐ ensuring a 100% positive experience for all clients | ☐ other: ______].

☐ **Maintain direct client relationships and interact with** [☐ engineers | ☐ architects | ☐ contractors | ☐ subcontractors | ☐ urban planners | ☐ interior designers | ☐ landscape architects | ☐ zoning officials | ☐ inspectors | ☐ the town | ☐ other: ______] **and other professionals during the design and** [☐ construction | ☐ development | ☐ production] **process.**

☐ **Work with clients to maintain customer satisfaction by** [☐ listening to and interpreting their needs | ☐ paying careful attention to detail | ☐ making changes as needed | ☐ ensuring a 100% positive experience for all clients | ☐ other: ______].

☐ **Act as liaison with customer and project staff to ensure positive customer relationships, job satisfaction, and service quality and to** [☐ properly identify and process scope changes | ☐ address and resolve any issues | ☐ communicate regarding project milestones | ☐ other: ______].

☐ **Earned client respect and corporate recognition for providing exemplary care and ongoing support, service, and follow-up throughout all phases of** ______ *[type of]* **construction projects.**

☐ **As firm's primary client contact, evaluate the strengths and weaknesses of client** ______ *[which?]* **initiatives, determine whether they are adequately meeting clients' needs, and offer alternative creative solutions.**

☐ **Build long-term client relationships, maximizing** ______ *[what?]* **dollars, receiving repeat business and referrals by** ______ *[doing what?].*

ACHIEVEMENT SAMPLES:

☐ **Built strong, trusting, long-term client relationships, maximizing dollars and receiving repeat business and referrals by** [☐ ensuring customer needs are acknowledged, and addressed | ☐ promoting a partnership atmosphere | ☐ problem-solving challenges to the clients' satisfaction| ☐ demonstrating flexibility | ☐ clearly defining expectations | ☐ presenting alternative budget-friendly solutions | ☐ other: ______] **which resulted in** ______ *[what additional business or other benefits?].*

☐ **Earned client respect and corporate recognition for providing exemplary care and ongoing support, service, and follow-up throughout all phases of** ______ *[type of]* **projects.**

☐ **Actively maintained positive customer relationships to ensure satisfaction and service quality on all** [☐ service calls | ☐ projects | ☐ installations | ☐ repairs | ☐ other: ______] **by** [☐ relating to them in a professional and courteous manner | ☐ listening carefully to their concerns | ☐ responding to their questions or complaints | ☐ making satisfactory adjustments | ☐ escalating their requests to ______ *(whom?)* | ☐ other: ______].

☐ **Cultivated excellent client relations, resulting in a strong base of referral business and** ______ *[#]* **new accounts.**

Closeout Processing & Post Construction Services

*See also **"Inspections & Compliance"** (various categories), as applicable.*

☐ **Successfully complete and close out all** ______ *[type of]* [☐ design and] **construction projects, ensuring** [☐ verification of estimates | ☐ completion of all change orders and punch list items | ☐ all specifications and expected deliverables are met | ☐ client satisfaction with completed projects | ☐ receipt of client payment | ☐ all contractor disbursements are paid | ☐ other: ______].

☐ **Perform final project reviews for the construction close-out process, approve payment requests, and conduct building site inspections to ensure compliance with plans, specifications, and building codes.**

☐ **Conduct** [☐ post construction reviews | ☐ customer satisfaction surveys | ☐ project close-out documentation | ☐ approval of contractor invoices | ☐ records archival | ☐ other: ______] **for the administrative processing of all design-and-build project close-outs.**

☐ **Review contractors' close-out administration ensuring all contractual requirements have been met, administer the completion and closeout process on all** ______ *[type of]* **projects, and review change orders** [☐ with (☐ Architects / ☐ Engineers / ☐ Project Managers / ☐ other: ______) | ☐ in accordance with the client's approval process | ☐ other: ______] **to ensure accuracy and job completion.**

☐ **Provide** _______ *[type of]* **postconstruction services and advice to clients to determine how well** [☐ architectural | ☐ engineering] [☐ design | ☐ construction] **is adapting to their needs, and make needed improvements.**

Communications – Architecture & Construction

*See also **"Interdisciplinary / Project Team Member"** and **"Work Collaboration."***

☐ **Conduct** ______ *[type of]* [☐ weekly | ☐ regular | ☐ intermittent | ☐ other: ______] [☐ preconstruction conferences | ☐ project meetings ☐ strategy sessions | ☐ teleconferences | ☐ other: ______] **to review** [☐ project progress | ☐ approval processes | ☐ lines of authority | ☐ other: ______] **ensuring** [☐ communication among all involved parties | ☐ projects remain on schedule and within budget | ☐ change orders are effected | ☐ disputes are amicably resolved | ☐ compliance with all building codes | ☐ other: ______].

☐ **Effectively facilitate across-the-board communication regarding** ______ *[type of]* **project scope, expected deliverables, and major milestones with** ______ *[whom?]* **and other involved parties** [☐ during all phases of the project lifecycle | ☐ from concept to completion | ☐ other: ______].

☐ **Communicate with and regularly keep** [☐ Project Manager | ☐ Superintendent | ☐ Maintenance Manager | ☐ crew | ☐ District Administrators | ☐ field representatives | ☐ general contractors | ☐ architects | ☐ engineers | ☐ vendors | ☐ inspectors | ☐ others: ______] **informed of** [☐ production schedule | ☐ material and labor management | ☐ work production status | ☐ scope changes | ☐ back charges | ☐ other: ______].

☐ **Effectively communicate with** [☐ all project team members | ☐ management | ☐ clients | ☐ others: ______] **and other involved parties regarding** ______ *[type of]* **project objectives, scope, expected deliverables, and milestones** [☐ during all project phases | ☐ from concept to completion | ☐ other: ______] **by** ______ *[doing what?].*

☐ **Communicate with management staff, Architects, Engineers, subcontractors, and other involved parties regarding project scope, expected deliverables, and major milestones—from concept to completion.**

☐ **Determine appropriate recipient communication methods to ensure clear, effective, and up-to-date communications via** [☐ typed procedures | ☐ the firm's Intranet | ☐ formal memoranda | ☐ written reports | ☐ status meetings | ☐ continual direction | ☐ other: ______].

ACHIEVEMENT SAMPLES: *See also Achievements under **"Project Management – General."***

☐ **Optimized communication between** [☐ engineers | ☐ architects | ☐ project management | ☐ other: ______], **and management staffs to more closely meet client needs by** ______ *[doing what?]*, **resulting in** [☐ projects that meet client needs 100% on target | ☐ fewer client changes | ☐ increased productivity | ☐ other benefits: ______].

☐ **Persuasively and clearly present information, respond to** ______ *[type of]* **questions, and facilitate across-the-board communication regarding** ______ *[type of]* **status on all** ______ *[which?]* **projects with** ______ *[whom?]*.

☐ **Optimized communication between** ______ *[whom?]* **and management staffs to more closely meet client needs by** ______ *[doing what?]*, **resulting in** [☐ projects that meet client needs | ☐ fewer client changes | ☐ increased productivity | ☐ other benefits: ______].

Compliance Investigations & Inspections

See "Inspections & Compliance."

Concrete Pouring, Setting & Finishing – Labor

☐ **Set up** [☐ wood | ☐ plastic] **concrete forms, and spread, level, and finish poured concrete in segments at** ______ *[type of]* **construction sites, ensuring concrete is level and corners are finished off.**

☐ [☐ Construct | ☐ Fabricate | ☐ Install | ☐ Repair] [☐ concrete beams | ☐ columns | ☐ panels | ☐ structures | ☐ masonry | ☐ framework | ☐ roadways | ☐ driveways | ☐ sidewalks | ☐ bridges | ☐ parking lots | ☐ other: ______] **according to specifications for** ______ *[type of]* **jobs, conforming to all building codes.**

☐ **Set and align concrete forms to specified pitch and depth, direct the concrete casting, and check forms to ensure they are properly constructed for this** ______ *[type of]* **company.**

☐ **Install** [☐ steel plates | ☐ anchor bolts | ☐ door sills | ☐ ______ *(type of)* fixtures] **in poured concrete and** [☐ polish | ☐ stain | ☐ stamp | ☐ pattern | ☐ sprinkle colored (☐ marble / ☐ stone chips / ☐ powdered steel) to | ☐ other: ______] **surface to render an embedded** ______ *[type of]* **decorative finish.**

☐ **Spread, level, smooth, and finish concrete, using** [☐ pneumatic tampers | ☐ hand trowels | ☐ power trowels | ☐ edgers | ☐ jointers | ☐ hand screeds | ☐ power screeds | ☐ power vibrators | ☐ groovers | ☐ floats | ☐ bull floats | ☐ concrete saws | ☐ power tools | ☐ finishing spades | ☐ hoes | ☐ edging tools | ☐ polishing machines | ☐ surfacing machines | ☐ picks | ☐ shovels | ☐ brooms | ☐ rakes | ☐ levels | ☐ routers | ☐ sanders | ☐ calipers | ☐ other: ______] **applying hardening and sealing compounds to cure and waterproof surface.**

☐ **Perform general labor including** [☐ cleaning and preparing work sites | ☐ controlling passing traffic around work zones | ☐ measuring and marking layout areas | ☐ eliminating possible hazards | ☐ signaling construction equipment operators | ☐ compacting and leveling earth to grade specifications | ☐ safely operating concrete truck | ☐ facilitating concrete pouring | ☐ mixing cement | ☐ molding expansion joints and edges | ☐ identifying hazards | ☐ other: ______] **following all company policies and OSHA regulations.**

☐ **Assist** [☐ paving | ☐ construction] **crew with various activities including** [☐ loading and unloading materials | ☐ digging ditches or trenches | ☐ dumping trucks | ☐ backfilling excavations | ☐ building and clamping molds | ☐ spreading and leveling materials | ☐ shoveling and raking | ☐ running wheelbarrow | ☐ tearing down and cleaning forms when concrete is cured | ☐ other: ______].

☐ **Safely operate a concrete truck and deliver ready-mix concrete to** ______ *[type of]* **construction sites, recording sales and delivery information, keeping operator logs up to date in accordance with Department of Transportation (DOT) regulations, and maintaining delivery communication with Dispatcher.**

☐ **Apply** [☐ advanced | ☐ working] **knowledge of and experience in** [☐ blueprint reading | ☐ interpretation of plans and specifications | ☐ determining measurements and sizes | ☐ concrete formwork | ☐ concrete finishing | ☐ construction methods | ☐ concrete installation standards and procedures | ☐ concrete mixing procedures | ☐ surface finishing | ☐ concrete pile caps | ☐ heavy concrete columns | ☐ decorative concrete finishing | ☐ latex and epoxy applications | ☐ muriatic acid applications | ☐ chemical additives to speed up drying | ☐ concrete beams, columns, and panels fabrication | ☐ vertical face | ☐ pavement thickness | ☐ surface grout depth | ☐ safety policies and procedures | ☐ problem-solving | ☐ other: ______] **in performance of** ______ *[type of]* **jobs.**

☐ **Waterproof and/or restore** ______ *[type of]* **concrete surfaces using** ______ *[what?]* **applications and compounds.**

Concrete Pouring, Setting & Finishing – Supervision

☐ **Oversee the concrete and steel reinforcement of** [☐ residential | ☐ commercial | ☐ highway | ☐ other: ______] **construction projects and the finishing of** ______ *[type of]* **walls with** [☐ wood | ☐ structural metal | ☐ lath | ☐ plaster | ☐ other: ______] **materials meeting all project budgets and deadlines on or ahead of schedule.**

☐ **Plan, coordinate, and supervise the functions of** ______ *[#]* **concrete installers, finishers, and laborers for** ______ *[type of]* **jobs for this** ______ *[type of]* **firm.**

☐ **Supervise diverse ______** *[type of]* **concrete projects including** [☐ foundation inspection and testing | ☐ structural fills / backfills | ☐ precise and cast-in-place concrete, grout, and mortar | ☐ reinforcing and structural steel | ☐ roofing | ☐ fireproofing | ☐ asphalt | ☐ other: ______].

☐ **Coordinate and direct project team crew activities in the areas of** [☐ scheduling | ☐ concrete preparation and pouring | ☐ building to specifications | ☐ concrete measurements | ☐ formwork | ☐ mixing | ☐ installation | ☐ application of chemical additives | ☐ surface finishing | ☐ problem troubleshooting | ☐ other: ______] **ensuring accurate measurements, quality of finished concrete projects, and compliance with all safety policies, practices, and procedures.**

☐ **Supervise and direct ______** *[#]* **Concrete** [☐ Masons | ☐ Installers | ☐ Form Setters | ☐ Layers | ☐ Finishers | ☐ Smoothers | ☐ Laborers | ☐ Carpenters | ☐ Patchers | ☐ Grinder Operators | ☐ Curb Builders | ☐ Joint Setters | ☐ Joint Finishers | ☐ Stone Finishers | ☐ Material Testers | ☐ Floaters | ☐ Terrazzo Finishers | ☐ other: ______] [☐ as well as field supervisors and other contractors] **to ensure** [☐ efficient use of equipment and materials | ☐ correct elevation | ☐ all project objectives are met with quality | ☐ project is constructed in accordance with design, budget, and schedule | ☐ contractual performance of projects are met | ☐ other: ______].

☐ **Manage concrete operations including** [☐ quality control | ☐ monitoring labor budget | ☐ interpreting plans and specifications | ☐ ordering and maintaining sufficient supplies | ☐ inventory management and control | ☐ interviewing, hiring, and training (☐ employees / ☐ laborers) | ☐ equipment scheduling | ☐ identifying potential design or construction problems | ☐ clarifying discrepancies | ☐ administering Safety Program | ☐ scheduling equipment | ☐ monitoring how the weather affects the curing process | ☐ completing ______ *(type of)* paperwork | ☐ other: ______].

☐ **Collaborate with other on-site labor teams including ______** *[which?]* [☐ contractors | ☐ subcontractors | ☐ others: ______], **to resolve problems and ensure quality, safety, and support of ______** *[type of]* **project objectives.**

Concrete Pouring, Setting & Finishing – Project Oversight

☐ **Oversee trades in the concrete and steel reinforcement of** [☐ residential | ☐ commercial | ☐ highway | ☐ other: ______] **construction projects and the finishing of ______** *[type of]* **walls with** [☐ wood | ☐ structural metal | ☐ lath | ☐ plaster | ☐ other: ______] **materials meeting all project budgets and deadlines on or ahead of schedule.**

☐ **Manage and oversee project team crew activities in the areas of** [☐ scheduling | ☐ concrete preparation and pouring | ☐ building to specifications | ☐ concrete measurements | ☐ formwork | ☐ mixing | ☐ installation | ☐ application of chemical additives | ☐ surface finishing | ☐ problem troubleshooting | ☐ other: ______] **ensuring accurate measurements, quality of finished concrete projects, and compliance with all safety policies, practices, and procedures.**

☐ **Supervise and direct ______** *[#]* **Concrete** [☐ Masons | ☐ Installers | ☐ Form Setters | ☐ Layers | ☐ Finishers | ☐ Smoothers | ☐ Laborers | ☐ Carpenters | ☐ Patchers | ☐ Grinder Operators | ☐ Curb Builders | ☐ Joint Setters | ☐ Joint Finishers | ☐ Stone Finishers | ☐ Material Testers | ☐ Floaters | ☐ Terrazzo Finishers | ☐ other: ______] [☐ as well as field supervisors and other contractors] **to ensure** [☐ efficient use of equipment and materials | ☐ correct elevation | ☐ all project objectives are met with quality | ☐ project is constructed in accordance with design, budget, and schedule | ☐ contractual performance of projects are met | ☐ other: ______].

☐ **Provide project management oversight in concrete operations including** [☐ quality control | ☐ monitoring labor budget | ☐ interpreting plans and specifications | ☐ ordering and maintaining sufficient supplies | ☐ inventory management and control | ☐ interviewing, hiring, and training (☐ employees / ☐ laborers) | ☐ equipment scheduling | ☐ identifying potential design or construction problems | ☐ clarifying discrepancies | ☐ administering Safety Program | ☐ scheduling equipment | ☐ monitoring how the weather affects the curing process | ☐ completing ______ *(type of)* paperwork | ☐ other: ______].

☐ **Collaborate with other on-site labor teams including ______** *[which?]* [☐ contractors | ☐ subcontractors | ☐ others: ______], **to resolve problems and ensure quality, safety, and support of ______** *[type of]* **project objectives.**

Construction Management Projects

*See also **"Construction Projects"** and **"Construction Project Management."***
*For in-depth Project Management information, refer to the **ARCHITECTURE & ENGINEERING** book.*

☐ **Lead and direct all aspects of ______** *[type of]* [☐ design | ☐ construction | ☐ design-and-build | ☐ other: ______] **projects to successful conclusion within tight time frames including** [☐ reviewing architectural plans | ☐ modifying construction drawings | ☐ negotiating contracts | ☐ determining staffing needs | ☐ selecting contractors and subcontractors | ☐ scheduling and coordinating all trades | ☐ purchasing materials | ☐ monitoring construction schedules | ☐ evaluating work progress | ☐ mediating and resolving disputes | ☐ negotiating and processing change orders | ☐ conducting on-site inspections | ☐ other: ______].

☐ **Effectively plan, manage, and lead ______** *[type of]* **construction projects; and direct the activities of trades to ensure all projects are completed with high quality on time and within budget.**

☐ **Perform on-site construction supervision in all phases of construction—from demolition through completion—for various types of construction firms including** [☐ design-and-build | ☐ construction management | ☐ general contracting | ☐ commercial firms | ☐ the government | ☐ other: ______].

☐ **Oversee management of** [☐ residential | ☐ commercial | ☐ public works | ☐ other: ______] **construction projects including** [☐ commercial buildings | ☐ shopping malls | ☐ stores | ☐ restaurants | ☐ manufacturing plants | ☐ schools | ☐ colleges | ☐ corporate offices | ☐ building lobbies | ☐ state or government agencies | ☐ houses | ☐ condominiums | ☐ apartment buildings | ☐ hospitals | ☐ laboratories | ☐ clean rooms | ☐ landmark restorations | ☐ roads and highways | ☐ other: ______].

☐ **Provide** [☐ engineering | ☐ construction] **management leadership and direction in the design and build of** ______ *[type of]* **projects for this $**______ *[revenues]* [☐ construction management | ☐ engineering | ☐ architectural | ☐ contracting | ☐ other: ______] **firm.**

☐ **Direct the construction of all** ______ *[type of]* **projects including the** [☐ review and/or modification of construction drawings | ☐ development of job estimates and budgets | ☐ securing of competitive bids | ☐ handling of contract negotiations | ☐ maintaining of client relationships | ☐ scheduling and coordination of trades | ☐ performing of on-site construction supervision | ☐ negotiation and processing of change orders | ☐ other: ______], **completing all projects on time and within budget.**

☐ **Provide leadership and direction in the** [☐ concept | ☐ schematic design | ☐ site planning | ☐ construction | ☐ cost management | ☐ quantity control | ☐ other: ______] **of** [☐ interior spaces | ☐ exterior spaces | ☐ physical environments] **of** ______ *[type of]* **projects**.

☐ **Manage the construction of** [☐ structural | ☐ architectural | ☐ civil | ☐ other: ______] **construction projects including** ______, ______, **and** ______ *[type of]* **projects for this** [☐ architectural | ☐ design-and-build | ☐ construction management | ☐ engineering | ☐ other: ______] [☐ firm | ☐ government agency].

☐ **Draft** [☐ working plans | ☐ profile drawings | ☐ base drawings | ☐ perspective drawings | ☐ overlays | ☐ maps | ☐ illustrations | ☐ other: ______] **of** ______ *[what?]*; **and prepare quantities and cost estimates using** ______ [software].

☐ **Conceptualize design, and manage the construction of a wide variety of** [☐ buildings | ☐ complexes | ☐ structures] **including** [☐ commercial buildings | ☐ private and public buildings | ☐ residential houses | ☐ corporate offices | ☐ office space planning | ☐ shopping malls | ☐ stores | ☐ apartment complexes | ☐ condominiums | ☐ public schools | ☐ colleges and universities | ☐ manufacturing plants | ☐ hospitals | ☐ landmark restorations | ☐ building lobbies | ☐ clean rooms | ☐ other: ______] **with projects ranging from $**______ **to $**______ *[amounts]*.

☐ **Perform professional** [☐ architectural | ☐ project management | ☐ construction supervision | ☐ administrative | ☐ other: ______] **work involving the research, design, and construction of** ______ *[type of]* **projects ranging from $**______ **to $**______ *[amounts]* **per project ensuring quality control, structural stability, and** ______ *[other?]*.

☐ **Research and perform** ______ *[type of]* **studies to determine** [☐ the most effective use of space | ☐ functional and spatial requirements | ☐ required structural support | ☐ other: ______] **of** [☐ new structures | ☐ renovations | ☐ other: ______] **and** [☐ advise | ☐ consult with] **clients accordingly**.

☐ **Plan and oversee the design and construction of** ______ *[type of]* **client projects, applying knowledge of and expertise in** [☐ design | ☐ construction procedures | ☐ zoning and building codes | ☐ building materials | ☐ other: ______].

ACHIEVEMENT SAMPLES:

☐ **Spearheaded the construction of a** [☐______ *(#)*-square foot | ☐ ______ *(#)*-story | ☐ $______ *(amount)*] ______ *[type of]* **project designed to** ______ *[do what?]* **for** ______ *[whom?]* **with a design challenge of** ______ *[what?]* **resulting in** ______ *[what?]*.

☐ **Planned, managed, and led** ______ *[type of]* **construction projects with varying requirements; and directed all trade activities to ensure all projects were completed with high quality on time and within budget.**

☐ **Managed $**______ *[project cost]* ______ *[type of]* **project accommodating** ______ *[#]* [☐ employees | ☐ patrons | ☐ patients | ☐ other: ______] **within an aggressive** ______**-***[#]* **month timeframe, completing projects** [☐ $______ *(amount)* under budget | ☐ ______ *(#)* (☐ days / ☐ weeks) ahead of schedule | ☐ other achievement: ______].

☐ **Took over a $**______ *[project cost]* **problem-ridden** ______ *[type of]* **construction project that had** [☐ fallen behind schedule | ☐ exceeded cost estimates | ☐ other: ______] **by successfully spearheading the completion of** ______ *[which functions?]* **and passing all inspections.**

☐ **Oversaw the construction of** [☐ commercial buildings | ☐ private and public buildings | ☐ residential houses | ☐ corporate offices | ☐ office space planning | ☐ bridges | ☐ dams | ☐ shopping malls | ☐ stores | ☐ apartment complexes | ☐ condominiums | ☐ public schools | ☐ colleges and universities | ☐ manufacturing plants | ☐ hospitals | ☐ landmark restorations | ☐ building lobbies | ☐ clean rooms | ☐ other: ______] **with projects ranging from $**______ **to $**______ *[amounts]*.

☐ **Renovated this** ______ *[type of]* [☐ building | ☐ facility | ☐ other: ______] **involving coordination with** [☐ client | ☐ user group | ☐ engineer | ☐ trades | ☐ other: ______] **resulting in** ______ *[what benefits?]*.

☐ **Championed the completion of** [☐ multiple | ☐ highly complex | ☐ simultaneous | ☐ other: ______] ______ *[type of]* **construction**

projects within aggressive timeframes by [☐ applying business intelligence strategy and technical solutions | ☐ establishing clear guidelines | ☐ performing frequent field inspections | ☐ immediately resolving and repairing inspection issues | ☐ addressing (☐ structural / ☐ environmental / ☐ other: ______) **challenges** | ☐ maintaining exceptional quality and safety standards | ☐ ensuring adherence to specifications | ☐ influencing trades to perform | ☐ strictly enforcing codes | ☐ other: ______].

☐ **Directed and oversaw** [☐ partial demolition | ☐ renovation | ☐ restoration | ☐ remodeling | ☐ construction] **of this** ______ *[type of]* **project while** [☐ company | ☐ stores | ☐ other: ______] **remained open for business acting as liaison with** [☐ client representative | ☐ store tenants | ☐ other: ______] **toward a successful completion** [☐ meeting | ☐ exceeding] [☐ business | ☐ mall management's | ☐ store owners' | ☐ others: ______] **and employer's expectations.**

☐ **Managed** [☐ new store construction | ☐ mall renovation while stores remained open for business | ☐ other: ______] **through to completion—meeting mall management's, store owners', and company's expectations and bringing project in** [☐ on time | ☐ ______ *(time frame)* ahead of schedule | ☐ within budget | ☐ $______ *(amount)* under budget | ☐ other: ______].

☐ **Led the** [☐ demolition | ☐ new construction | ☐ renovation] **of the following** ______ *[type of]* **sites**: ______ *[name]*, ______ *[town]*, ______ *[state]*; ______ *[name]*, ______ *[town]*, ______ *[state]*; **and** ______ *[name]*, ______ *[town]*, ______ *[state]* **to their successful completion.**

☐ **Formulated, implemented, and delivered successful** ______ *[type of]* **project execution processes that** [☐ achieved total project excellence | ☐ other: ______] **including** [☐ Construction Safety Management Systems | ☐ Behavioral Modification Processes | ☐ Contractor Evaluation Processes | ☐ other: ______].

☐ **Managed new construction and renovation of** ______ *[type of]* **sites, some simultaneously, with major construction and renovations successfully completed within** ______ *[time period]* **by** ______ *[doing what well?]*.

☐ **Managed construction of** ______ *[project name]*, **taking over this $**______ *[amount]* **project when Senior Project Manager became ill. Required delicate negotiations working closely with client rep through to successful completion. Received commendations for a job well done.** ***(See "Testimonials.")*** ***Note:*** *Add a "Testimonials" section to the end of your resume.*

☐ **Directed and oversaw mall** [☐ partial demolition | ☐ renovation | ☐ restoration | ☐ remodeling | ☐ construction] **while stores remained open for business acting as liaison with store tenants for a successful completion and** [☐ meeting | ☐ exceeding] **mall management's, store owners', and employer's expectations.**

☐ **Spearheaded the design and construction of a** [☐______ *(#)*-square foot | ☐ ______ *(#)*-story | ☐ $______ *(amount)*] ______ *[type of]* **project designed to** ______ *[do what?]* **for** ______ *[whom?]* **with a design challenge of** ______ *[what?]* **resulting in** ______ *[what?]*.

☐ **Managed the** [☐ design | ☐ construction | ☐ trades supervision | ☐ administrative work | ☐ other: ______] **of** ______/ $______ *[project name and cost]*, ______/ $______ *[project name and cost]*, **and** ______/ $______ *[project name and cost]* **with varying requirements ensuring all objectives were accomplished with high quality and within established time frames and budget.**

Construction Project Management

*See **"Project Management," "Construction Superintendent Functions," "Facility Management,"** and/or **"General Contracting."***
*For in-depth Project Management information, refer to the **ARCHITECTURE & ENGINEERING** book.*

Construction Projects

*See also **"Design-and-Build Projects"** and **"Construction Management Projects."***

ACHIEVEMENT SAMPLES:

☐ **Handled on-site** ______ *[type of]* [☐ building | ☐ construction | ☐ installation | ☐ other: ______] **while** [☐ company remained open for business | ☐ homeowners remained on premises | ☐ other: ______] **by** ______ *[doing what?]*, **which minimized the work impact so** [☐ business operations remained functional | ☐ home remained livable].

☐ **Completed** ______ *[name of]* **project in record time and ahead of schedule; achieved by** [☐ organizing and planning daily workloads | ☐ getting the most productivity out of laborers | ☐ other: ______] **resulting in** [☐ company being awarded state bonuses | ☐ other achievement: ______].

☐ **Participated in a broad range of** ______ *[type of]* **construction projects involving** [☐ demolition | ☐ framing | ☐ sheetrocking | ☐ roofing | ☐ siding installation | ☐ site maintenance | ☐ materials transport | ☐ other: ______] **and general support of all phases of construction.**

☐ **Delivered all** ______ *[type of]* **projects on time and within budget by** [☐ performing quality workmanship | ☐ exceeding expectations | ☐ assuming additional responsibilities | ☐ working extended hours to meet project deadlines | other: ______].

☐ **Developed a** ______ *[#]*-**acre site for** ______ *[#]* **commercial buildings that encompassed** ______, ______, **and** ______ *[what processes?]*.

☐ **Selected by ______** *[whom?]* **to take over ______** *[type of]* **project to smooth out conflicts. Accomplished** [☐ through firm negotiations and teamwork with client rep and all trades to put project back on track | ☐ by successfully completing project without compromising each other's responsibilities | ☐ by maintaining an excellent rapport with all | ☐ other: ______] **and receiving commendations from client and employer.**

☐ **Remodeled several** [☐ commercial | ☐ office space | ☐ residential | ☐ condominium | ☐ other: _______] **projects with project costs ranging $______ to $______** *[amounts]*, **performing all** [☐ estimating | ☐ negotiating | ☐ buyout | ☐ operations supervision | ☐ other: ______].

☐ **Built a ______** *[#]*-**story, ______** *[#]*-**acre ______** *[type of]* **project with site work and construction cost at** $______ *[amount].*

☐ [☐ Performed | ☐ Coordinated and directed] **the** [☐ demolition | ☐ construction | ☐ remodeling | ☐ renovation | ☐ restoration | ☐ other: ______] **of ______** *[type of]* **building projects ranging from $______ to $______** *[amounts]* **for this** [☐ multimillion-dollar | ☐ $______] ______ *[type of]* **firm.**

☐ **Completed ______** *[type of]* **job** [☐ $______ *(amount)* under budget | ☐ ______ *[#]* (☐ days / ☐ weeks) ahead of schedule | ☐ other: ______] **by ______** *[doing what well?].*

☐ **Performed design and construction administration of a ______** *[#]*-[☐ floor | ☐ room | ☐ square foot | ☐ other: ______] ______ *[type of]* **project for ______** *[whom?]* [☐ with a design challenge of ______ *(what?)* resulting in ______ *(what?)* | ☐ meeting clients' and company's expectations | ☐ other achievement: ______].

☐ **Renovated this ______** *[type of]* **facility involving coordination with** [☐ client | ☐ user group | ☐ engineer | ☐ trades | ☐ other: ______] **resulting in a new design, which created ______** *[what?].*

☐ [☐ Completed | ☐ Assisted in the completion] **of ______** *[#]*______ *[type of]* [☐ new construction | ☐ remodel | ☐ home improvement | ☐ HVAC | ☐ electrical | ☐ plumbing | ☐ landscaping | ☐ other: ______] **projects with budgets up to $______** *[amount].* **Projects ranged from ______** *[type of small jobs]* **to ______** *[type of large projects].*

☐ **Built ______** *[type of]* [☐ homes | ☐ buildings | ☐ structures | ☐ other: ______] **valued at more than $______** *[amount]* **each, completing work on time and within budget while providing superior customer service.**

☐ **Saved ______%** *[percentage]* **on labor costs by completing a $______** *[project amount]* ______ *[type of]* **construction project** ______ *[time frame]* **ahead of schedule.**

☐ **Supervised all phases of ______** *[type of]* **construction of ______** *[type of]* **projects with varying requirements ensuring all objectives were accomplished with high quality and within established time frames and budget.**

☐ **Applying expertise in ______** *[what?]*, **led a** [☐ construction | ☐ carpentry | ☐ other: ______] **team of ______** *[#]*______ *[titles]* **in** [☐ building | ☐ installing | ☐ repairing | ☐ other: ______] ______ *[what?]* **for ______** *[whom?]* **which resulted in _______** *[what deliverables?].*

☐ **Built ______** *[type of]* [☐ homes | ☐ buildings | ☐ structures | ☐ other: ______] **valued at $______** *[amount]* **each.**

☐ **Simultaneously managed ______** *[#]*______ *[type of]* [☐ design-and-build | ☐ construction | ☐ other: ______] **projects each averaging $______** *[amount]*, **with project values totaling $______ to $______** *[amount].*

☐ **Utilize expertise in** [☐ all aspects of structural, mechanical, and electrical construction | ☐ state and local building codes | ☐ commercial roofing specifications | ☐ asbestos abatement procedures | ☐ construction contract administration | ☐ other: ______] **to successfully** [☐ design and] **build ______** *[what?].*

☐ **Coordinated and directed the** [☐ demolition | ☐ construction | ☐ remodeling | ☐ renovation | ☐ restoration | ☐ installation | ☐ repair | ☐ other: ______] **of ______** *[type of]* **building projects ranging from $______ to $______** *[amounts].*

☐ **Handled all aspects of remodeling** [☐ residential homes | ☐ commercial buildings | ☐ civil projects | ☐ other: ______] **including ______, ______, and ______** *[type of renovations].*

☐ **Supervised new construction and renovation of _______** *[type of]* **sites with major construction and renovations successfully completed on or ahead of schedule and within budget.**

☐ **Constructed ______** *[type of]* **specialized** [☐ structures | ☐ buildings | ☐ projects | ☐ other: ______] **that ______** *[did what?]* **while benefiting the** [☐ client | ☐ firm | ☐ other: ______] **by way of ______** *[benefits].*

☐ **Gained valuable experience in** [☐ performance of carpentry functions | ☐ building industry operations and processes | ☐ other: ______] **as construction worker for full-service residential developer.**

Construction Supervision – General

See also ***"Carpentry Supervision," "Project Management," "Construction Supervision Functions,"*** *and* ***"General Contracting."***

☐ **Provide construction supervision and direction for this $______** *[revenues]* [☐ construction management | ☐ contracting | ☐ other: ______] firm including [☐ reviewing plans | ☐ scheduling jobs | ☐ subbing out work | ☐ estimating projects | ☐ coordinating trades | ☐ purchasing materials | ☐ other: ______] **in all phases of construction**.

☐ **Supervise and oversee** [☐ home | ☐ office | ☐ other: ______] [☐ construction | ☐ renovation | ☐ carpentry] **activities for this** [$______ *(revenues)* | ☐ multimillion-dollar | ☐ leading] **general contractor overseeing from one- to ______** *[#]*-**man crews, bringing jobs in on time and within budget.**

☐ **Manage** [☐ residential | ☐ commercial | ☐ public works | ☐ other: ______] **construction projects including** [☐ single-family homes | ☐ multiple-family dwellings | ☐ condominiums | ☐ commercial buildings | ☐ shopping malls | ☐ stores | ☐ restaurants | ☐ manufacturing plants | ☐ schools | ☐ colleges | ☐ corporate offices | ☐ building lobbies | ☐ state or government agencies | ☐ hospitals | ☐ laboratories | ☐ clean rooms | ☐ landmark restorations | ☐ roads and highways | ☐ other: ______].

☐ **Plan, coordinate, and supervise the construction and** [☐ demolition | ☐ remodeling | ☐ renovation | ☐ assembly | ☐ repair | ☐ maintenance] **of** [☐ buildings | ☐ cabinets | ☐ roofs | ☐ furnishings | ☐ vinyl siding | ☐ other: ______] **for this $______** *[revenues]* ______ *[type of]* **firm**.

☐ **Coordinate and direct the** [☐ demolition | ☐ construction | ☐ remodeling | ☐ renovation | ☐ restoration | ☐ other: ______] **of** ______ *[type of]* **building projects ranging from $______ to $______** *[amounts]* **for this ______** *[type of]* **firm**.

☐ **Supervise all phases of construction from project start through completion including** [☐ reviewing construction drawings | ☐ developing job estimates and budgets | ☐ securing competitive bids | ☐ handling contract negotiations | ☐ maintaining direct client relationships | ☐ scheduling and coordinating all trades | ☐ performing on-site supervision | ☐ negotiating and processing change orders | ☐ other: ______] **completing all projects on time and within budget.**

☐ **Plan and coordinate all activities of** [☐ small- | ☐ medium- | ☐ large-] **scale client projects in collaboration with** [☐ client reps | ☐ architects | ☐ contractors | ☐ subcontractors | ☐ other: ______] **for this ______** *[type of]* **firm with ______** *[#]* [☐ locations | ☐ employees | ☐ other: ______] **that generates fiscal-year revenues of $______** *[revenues]*.

☐ **Lead and direct the daily construction operations for this $______** *[revenues]* **______** *[type of]* **firm including** [☐ blueprint reading | ☐ work scheduling | ☐ job site preparation | ☐ project management | ☐ building inspections | ☐ client close-out processing | ☐ other: ______].

☐ **Act as Superintendent on ______** *[type of]* **construction projects including the** [☐ planning | ☐ directing | ☐ coordinating | ☐ supervising | ☐ other: ______] **of building construction.**

☐ **Supervise all aspects of project management—from planning to completion—**[☐ using standardized project management methodology | ☐ for multiple implementation projects | ☐ for projects that vary in scope and size | ☐ in support of firm's strategic visions | ☐ to support client objectives | ☐ in accordance with all project timelines and budget | ☐ other: ______].

☐ **Supervise rough and finish carpentry work including** [☐ setting concrete forms | ☐ pouring foundations | ☐ framing and sheetrocking walls and partitions | ☐ taping and spackling | ☐ building stairs | ☐ installing (☐ windows / ☐ doors / ☐ flooring / ☐ tiling / ☐ ceilings / ☐ roofs / ☐ wall coverings / ☐ trim work / ☐ platforms / ☐ podiums / ☐ partitions / ☐ fences / ☐ ramps / ☐ insulation / ☐ weather stripping / ☐ cabinets / ☐ baseboard heating / ☐ retainer walls / ☐ other: ______) | ☐ other: ______].

☐ **Oversee the concrete and steel reinforcement of** [☐ residential | ☐ commercial | ☐ other: ______] **construction projects and the finishing of walls with** [☐ wood | ☐ structural metal | ☐ lath | ☐ plaster | ☐ other: ______] **materials meeting all project budgets and deadlines usually ahead of schedule.**

☐ **Supervise** [☐ home construction | ☐ home improvement | ☐ interior renovation | ☐ room additions | ☐ finished attics and basements | ☐ other: ______] **for individual clients including** [☐ framing | ☐ insulation | ☐ sheetrocking | ☐ taping and spackling | ☐ painting | ☐ flooring | ☐ tiling | ☐ roofing | ☐ landscaping | ☐ other: ______].

☐ **Coordinate and supervise construction and** [☐ demolition | ☐ remodeling | ☐ renovation | ☐ assembly | ☐ repair | ☐ maintenance] **for** [☐ residential | ☐ commercial] **construction projects for this $______** *[revenues]* [☐ general contractor | ☐ construction management | ☐ other: ______] **firm**.

☐ **Supervise the construction of all ______** *[type of]* **projects including the** [☐ review of construction drawings | ☐ development of job estimates and budgets | ☐ securing of competitive bids | ☐ handling of contract negotiations | ☐ maintaining of client relationships | ☐ scheduling and coordination of trades | ☐ performing of on-site construction supervision | ☐ negotiation and processing of change orders | ☐ other: ______], **completing all projects on time and within budget**.

☐ **Oversee** [☐ remodeling | ☐ renovations | ☐ carpentry work | ☐ finish carpentry | ☐ other: ______] **of the ______** *[what project(s)?]* including installation of [☐ custom framing | ☐ siding | ☐ conventional roofs | ☐ window replacements | ☐ doors | ☐ ceramic tile | ☐ other: ______] **according to blueprint specifications**.

ACHIEVEMENT SAMPLES: *See "Construction Projects" and "General Contracting."*

Construction Supervision – Functions

See also "Construction Supervision – General," "Inspections & Compliance," and "Carpentry / Construction Work."

- ☐ **Provide project management** [☐ coordination | ☐ consultation | ☐ supervision | ☐ review | ☐ other: ______] **during the construction phase of all projects.**
- ☐ **Involved in all phases of development, from initial client consultation through the entire construction process including** [☐ design | ☐ site selection | ☐ engineering | ☐ bidding process | ☐ field inspections | ☐ construction management | ☐ other: ______].
- ☐ **Supervise rough and finish carpentry in the construction and/or installation of** [☐ buildings | ☐ houses | ☐ remodels | ☐ roofing | ☐ siding | ☐ cabinets | ☐ fencing | ☐ other: ______].
- ☐ **Manage a multitude of carpentry work including** [☐ setting concrete forms | ☐ erecting scaffolding | ☐ installing ceiling tile | ☐ repairing cabinets | ☐ installing partitions | ☐ other: ______] **and perform finishing work for** ______ *[type of]* **projects**.
- ☐ **Obtain permits, estimate jobs, and hire and schedule trades acting as liaison with** [☐ building managers | ☐ inspectors | ☐ architects | ☐ others: ______].
- ☐ **Successfully plan and manage projects to achieve business objectives and fully use resource capabilities within the project parameters of cost, time, and quality which has resulted in** ______ *[what benefits?]*.
- ☐ **Oversee job operations and personnel management including** [☐ coordinating steel and concrete trades | ☐ scheduling laborers | ☐ managing construction | ☐ overseeing site materials and equipment set-up | ☐ other: ______].
- ☐ **Provide project management** [☐ coordination | ☐ consultation | ☐ supervision | ☐ review] **during construction phase of all projects.**
- ☐ **Prepare job estimates with fair financial arrangements for customers and at good profits for company**.
- ☐ **Apply a thorough knowledge of** [☐ construction methods | ☐ building codes | ☐ finish carpentry | ☐ tools, equipment, and materials | ☐ safety practices | ☐ building techniques | ☐ other: ______] **in all** [☐ wood and metal framing | ☐ shingle and plywood roofing | ☐ wood and vinyl siding | ☐ masonry work | ☐ window and garage door replacement | ☐ home renovations | ☐ girder manufacturing and installation | ☐ building decks | ☐ railroad ties | ☐ retainer walls | ☐ other: ______] **carpentry activities.**
- ☐ **Conduct hands-on carpentry and construction in the areas of** ______ *[type of work]*.
- ☐ **Provide technical assistance to laborers** [☐ in the areas of (☐ electrical / ☐ plumbing / ☐ carpentry / ☐ concrete construction / ☐ masonry / ☐ other: ______) | ☐ on projects involving ______ *(what?)* | ☐ other: ______].
- ☐ **Order materials, estimate projects, and lay out jobs for this** [☐ residential | ☐ commercial] **contractor specializing in** ______ *[what?]*.
- ☐ **Ensure** [☐ trucks arrive on time to pour concrete | ☐ laborers meet each day's scheduled workload | ☐ all materials are stored at the end of each day | ☐ all debris is cleared up | ☐ customer satisfaction with work | ☐ other: ______].
- ☐ **Ensure all safety practices are followed on carpentry job sites by** ______ *[doing what?]*.
- ☐ **Oversee the concrete and steel reinforcement of** ______ *[type of]* **construction projects and the finishing of walls with** [☐ wood | ☐ structural metal | ☐ lath | ☐ plaster | ☐ other: ______] **materials meeting all project budgets and deadlines.**
- ☐ **Manage the installation of** ______, ______, **and** ______ *[what?]* **according to blueprint specifications**.
- ☐ **Plan and coordinate** [☐ rough | ☐ finish] **carpentry in the construction and** [☐ demolition | ☐ remodeling | ☐ renovation | ☐ assembly | ☐ repair | ☐ maintenance] **of** [☐ buildings | ☐ cabinets | ☐ roofs | ☐ furnishings | ☐ siding | ☐ other: ______].
- ☐ **Conceive, sketch, and design** ______ *[type of]* **carpentry projects for** ______ *[whom or what?]*.
- ☐ **Meet with** [☐ Building | ☐ Department of Transportation (DOT) | ☐ other: ______] **Inspectors to ensure all work is performed satisfactorily.**

Construction Work / Labor

See "Carpentry / Construction Work."

Contract Administration

See also "Contracting Management" and "Policies & Procedures Development – Legal & Technical."

☐ **Facilitate various proposal development activities including** [☐ handling client interface | ☐ developing pricing strategies | ☐ preparing bids | ☐ preparing proposal terms | ☐ interpreting contract terms and conditions | ☐ identifying risks and risk mitigation strategies | ☐ negotiating contracts | ☐ monitoring contract status | ☐ processing contract closeouts | ☐ other: ______].

☐ **Provide support to** [☐ Project Managers | ☐ Engineers | ☐ Architects | ☐ Senior Contracts Manager | ☐ Director of Contracts | ☐ other: ______] **by** [☐ developing proposals | ☐ assisting with risk mitigation | ☐ preparing contracts | ☐ other: ______] **in a timely and professional fashion.**

☐ **Support the** ______ *[which?]* **contract of** ______ *[what?]* **by performing a** [☐ full range | ☐ wide variety] of [☐ commercial | ☐ governmental | ☐ other: ______] **contract administration functions—from proposal to contract completion.**

☐ **Perform various contract administrative functions including** [☐ assisting with contractual initiatives | ☐ developing pricing strategies | ☐ conducting research and analysis | ☐ preparing bids | ☐ performing contract negotiations | ☐ handling claims avoidance | ☐ researching contractor claims and litigations | ☐ responding to staff inquiries relating to contracts | ☐ performing risk management | ☐ incorporating quality assurance methods | ☐ developing client proposals and estimates | ☐ handling dispute resolution | ☐ developing and submitting grant applications | ☐ updating budget databases | ☐ preparing contract records and reports | ☐ handling data entry, filing, and copying | ☐ maintaining legal obligations records | ☐ interfacing with clients | ☐ document processing | ☐ other: ______].

☐ **Review, analyze, and approve** ______ *[type of]* [☐ contractor | ☐ subcontractor | ☐ other: ______] [☐ proposals | ☐ estimates | ☐ agreements | ☐ contractual documents | ☐ other: ______] **and monitor performance to ensure conformance to** [☐ original proposals | ☐ contracts | ☐ legal requirements | ☐ regulations | ☐ customer specifications | ☐ other: ______].

☐ **Prepare recommendations to** ______ *[whom?]* **regarding** [☐ contractual defaults | ☐ time extensions | ☐ liquidated damages | ☐ other: ______].

☐ **Facilitate contract administrative functions including** [☐ document processing | ☐ account servicing | ☐ data entry | ☐ client correspondence | ☐ customer questions | ☐ contract filing | ☐ other: ______] for an office staff of ______ *[#]*.

☐ **Support the** ______ *[which?]* **contract of** ______ *[what?]* **by performing a** [☐ full range | ☐ wide variety] **of** [☐ commercial | ☐ governmental | ☐ other: ______] **contract administration functions—from proposal to contract completion.**

Contract Development & Review

See also other Contracting categories.

☐ **Draft, review, and administer** ______ *[type of]* [☐ contractual documents | ☐ agreements | ☐ proposals | ☐ nondisclosure agreements | ☐ estimates | ☐ grant requests | ☐ service agreements | ☐ technical documents | ☐ license agreements | ☐ warrantees | ☐ guarantees ☐ teaming agreements | ☐ memoranda of understanding | ☐ government contracts | ☐ subcontractor agreements | ☐ amendments | ☐ provider agreements | ☐ real estate contracts | ☐ revenue contracts | ☐ estimates | ☐ amendments | ☐ other: ______] **with contracts ranging from $______to $______** *[amounts]*.

☐ **Write and execute** _______ *[type of]* **contracts for** ______ *[what?]* **that ensures compliance with all** [☐ corporate policies | ☐ client specifications | ☐ business requirements | ☐ legal requirements | ☐ codes and regulations | ☐ best practices | ☐ contract guidelines | ☐ bidding process procedures | ☐ Federal contract law | ☐ Service Contract Act | ☐ departmental practices | ☐ other: ______] **for this** ______ *[type of]* **firm.**

☐ **Draft, review, and edit** ______ *[type of]* [☐ contracts | ☐ agreements | ☐ legal documents | ☐ other: ______] **in conformance with** [☐ company policies | ☐ standard contract templates | ☐ other: ______] **to include** [☐ customer | ☐ product | ☐ services | ☐ terms | ☐ cost | ☐ product | ☐ other: ______] **information using** ______ *[what?]*.

☐ **Document and execute** ______ *[type of]* [☐ contractual documents | ☐ license agreements | ☐ proposals | ☐ agreements | ☐ provider agreements | ☐ nondisclosure agreements | ☐ service agreements | ☐ government contracts | ☐ subcontractor agreements | ☐ real estate contracts | ☐ revenue contracts | ☐ estimates | ☐ amendments | ☐ guarantees | ☐ warrantees | ☐ other: ______] **for** ______ *[what?]* **in compliance with all** [☐ corporate policies | ☐ client specifications | ☐ business requirements | ☐ legal requirements | ☐ codes and regulations | ☐ best practices | ☐ contract guidelines | ☐ Federal contract law | ☐ Service Contract Act | ☐ other: ______].

☐ **Develop and negotiate** ______ *[type of]* **legal documents that include** [☐ services | ☐ terms | ☐ cost | ☐ materials | ☐ other: ______] **information in conformance with company policies and in support of major business initiatives.**

☐ **Prepare** [☐ client | ☐ architect | ☐ engineer | ☐ contractor | ☐ other: ______] **contracts ranging from $______ to $______** *[amount]* **for** [☐ architectural plans for | ☐ design and build of | ☐ construction of] ______ *[what?]*.

☐ **Review, approve, and execute** [☐ a wide range of] ______ *[type of]* [☐ contracts | ☐ contractual agreements | ☐ legal documents | ☐ agreements] of [☐ a complex nature | ☐ varying scope and complexity], and document related [☐ policies | ☐ procedures | ☐ processes | ☐ other: ______] **for** ______ *[what?]*.

☐ **Document** ______ *[type of]* **agreements that meet** [☐ business | ☐ client | ☐ building code | ☐ legal | ☐ regulatory | ☐ audit | ☐ other: ______] **requirements with contracts ranging from $______ to $______** *[amounts]* **for this** ______ *[type of]* **firm servicing** ______ *[which?]* **clientele base.**

☐ **Develop** ______ *[type of]* **revenue contracts for** ______ *[name of]* [☐ protocols | ☐ amendments] **from all** ______ *[type of]* **areas, making use of benchmarking cost data from the** ______ *[which?]* **database** [☐ provided | ☐ developed] **by** ______ *[whom?]*.

ACHIEVEMENT SAMPLES: *See also Achievements under* ***"Contract Negotiations."***

☐ **Reviewed and evaluated** [☐ monthly | ☐ quarterly | ☐ periodic | ☐ annual] ______ *[type of]* **compliance status reports insofar as compliance** [☐ planning | ☐ activity | ☐ efforts | ☐ investigations | ☐ assessments | ☐ risks | ☐ audits | ☐ actions taken | ☐ effectiveness | ☐ other: ______], **and determined** ______ *[type of]* **changes to improve compliance in the area of** ______ *[what?]*.

☐ **Designed and implemented** ______ *[type of]* **solutions that effectively addressed and adhered to** [☐ the firm's | ☐ clients'] **requirements in the area(s) of** ______ *[area(s)]* [☐ in accordance with all project timelines and budget | ☐ ensuring quality project standards | ☐ ensuring a smooth transition | ☐ other: ______].

☐ **Secured** [☐ preferred provider agreements | ☐ wholesale distribution agreements | ☐ other: ______] **with** ______, ______, **and** ______ *[companies]*, **by developing** ______ *[what?]*, **positioning firm as the recognized leader in the sales of** ______ *[what?]*.

☐ **Developed new** ______ *[type of]* **program to secure preferred and exclusive provider contracts with** ______ *[whom?]* **resulting in increased sales of $______**.

☐ **Successfully coordinated and implemented** ______ *[type of]* **contracting projects with varying requirements completing all project phases with high quality and within established time frames and budget.**

☐ **Established win-win** ______ *[type of]* **contracts with** ______ *[whom?]* **and developed** ______ *[type of]* **project plans involving coordinating, scheduling, and managing jobs from start through completion.**

☐ **Effectively** [☐ planned | ☐ directed | ☐ coordinated | ☐ implemented] ______ *[type of]* **projects** [☐ and direct the activities of resources] **ensuring all objectives were accomplished with high quality and within established time frames and budget.**

Contract Development – Technical Proposals & Service Contracts

See also ***"Contract Development & Review."***

☐ **Write** ______ *[type of]* **technical proposals and service contracts consisting of** ______ *[what?]* **ranging from $______ to $______** *[amounts]*.

☐ **Negotiate** ______ *[type of]* **service contracts with** ______ *[type of]* [☐ clients | ☐ vendors | ☐ others: ______], **ensuring** [☐ competitive pricing | ☐ quality work | ☐ all deadlines are met | ☐ other: ______].

☐ [☐ Develop and negotiate | ☐ Review and approve] ______ *[type of]* [☐ service contracts | ☐ technical proposals | ☐ legal agreements | ☐ amendments | ☐ nondisclosure agreements | ☐ license agreements | ☐ technical documents | ☐ other: ______] **for** ______ *[what?]* **in support of major business initiatives.**

☐ **Write and execute** [☐ service contracts | ☐ technical proposals | ☐ license agreements | ☐ other: ______] **for** ______ *[type of]* [☐ software | ☐ hardware | ☐ technology services | ☐ equipment | ☐ maintenance services | ☐ other: ______] **in compliance with** [☐ company policies | ☐ client specifications | ☐ business requirements | ☐ legal requirements | ☐ other: ______].

☐ **Negotiate** ______ *[type of]* [☐ contracts | ☐ agreements] **that meet** [☐ business | ☐ client | ☐ legal | ☐ regulatory | ☐ audit | ☐ other: ______] [☐ requirements | ☐ needs] **with contracts ranging from $______ to $______** *[amounts]* **for this** ______ *[type of]* **firm servicing** ______ *[which?]***clientele base**.

☐ **Draft, review, and edit** ______ *[type of]* [☐ contracts | ☐ agreements | ☐ legal documents | ☐ other: ______] **in conformance with** [☐ company policies | ☐ standard contract templates | ☐ other: ______] **to include** [☐ client | ☐ customer | ☐ product | ☐ services | ☐ terms | ☐ cost | ☐ product | ☐ other: ______] **information using** ______ *[what?]*.

☐ **Prepare, negotiate, and administer** [☐ a wide range of] ______ *[type of]* [☐ contracts | ☐ contractual agreements | ☐ legal documents | ☐ agreements] **of** [☐ a complex nature | ☐ varying scope and complexity], **and document related** [☐ policies | ☐ procedures | ☐ processes | ☐ instructions | ☐ other: ______] **for** [☐ same | ☐ ______ *(what?)*].

☐ **Played an integral role in obtaining a $______** *[amount]* **contract from** ______ *[whom?]* **to replace its current** ______ *[type of]* [☐ technology | ☐ methodology | ☐ products | ☐ other: ______] **with** ______ *[what?]*.

☐ **Led negotiations with** ______ *[whom?]* **for long-term** ______ *[type of]* **agreements with forecasted savings of $______** *[amount]* **over a** ______ *[#]***-year period.**

☐ **Negotiated a $______** *[amount]* **contract with ______** *[whom?]*, **which served to ______** *[purpose]* **and resulted in ______** *[what win/win for firm and client?].*

Contract Development – Translating Requirements Into Legal Solutions

*See also **"Contracts Administration"** and other Contracting categories as well as **"Policies & Procedures Development,"** as applicable.*

☐ **Translate** [☐ client | ☐ firm | ☐ legal | ☐ technical | ☐ other: ______] **strategies, goals, deliverables, and requirements into specific project plans and tasks incorporating** [☐ industry knowledge | ☐ delivery methodology | ☐ other: ______] **resulting in** [☐ effective business solutions | ☐ successful project completions | ☐ clearly defined milestones and deliverables | ☐ other: ______].

☐ **Structure and develop client project plans following client-specific project management methodology translating requirements into effective legal solutions by ______** *[doing what?]* **resulting in ______** *[what benefits?].*

☐ **Formulate and define ______** *[type of]* **project plans which consider project** [☐ strategy | ☐ scope | ☐ goals | ☐ objectives | ☐ deliverables | ☐ need identification | ☐ costs | ☐ required skill sets | ☐ task requirements | ☐ resource allocations | ☐ work assignments | ☐ scope of authority | ☐ scheduling | ☐ project tracking and monitoring | ☐ identification of risks | ☐ contingency planning | ☐ technical scope | ☐ timeline check points | ☐ other: ______] **using project management planning and scheduling techniques.**

☐ **Ensure project plans are developed to deliver implementation within realistic** [☐ scope | ☐ schedule | ☐ cost | ☐ quality | ☐ other: ______] **by ______** *[doing what?].*

☐ **Develop detailed** [☐ project schedules | ☐ resource plans | ☐ budgets | ☐ status reports | ☐ other: ______] **for** [☐ business | ☐ client] ______ *[type of]* **projects averaging $______ with an annual return on investment of $______.**

ACHIEVEMENT SAMPLES: *See **"Contract Development & Review"** and **"Contract Negotiations."***

Contract Functions – General

See also other Contracting categories.

☐ **As the firm's primary** [☐ contractual | ☐ technical | ☐ legal | ☐ other: ______] **resource hub, provide** [☐ expertise | ☐ advice | ☐ guidance | ☐ assistance | ☐ consultation] **to** [☐ project managers | ☐ staff | ☐ contractors | ☐ others: ______] **in the areas of** [☐ contractual guidelines | ☐ recommendations | ☐ appropriations | ☐ budgets | ☐ schedules | ☐ other: ______] **regarding** [☐ contract development | ☐ interpretation of contract documents | ☐ ______ *(type of)* procedures | ☐ related regulations | ☐ litigation of claims | ☐ other: ______].

☐ **Develop and establish** [☐ proposals | ☐ contract templates | ☐ legal standards | ☐ best practices | ☐ contract guidelines | ☐ subcontracting procedures | ☐ the contract review process | ☐ formal bidding process review procedures | ☐ other: ______]; **and ensure contracts consistency with all established terms and conditions.**

☐ **Handle various contract functions including** [☐ leading and overseeing contract projects | ☐ prioritizing projects and balancing competing demands | ☐ reviewing contracts to verify legal requirements | ☐ translating requirements into effective legal solutions | ☐ developing revenue contracts | ☐ preparing specifications | ☐ performing inspections to facilitate quality assurance | ☐ identifying contractual problems or errors | ☐ researching and writing legal procedures | ☐ setting up and maintaining contract database | ☐ developing budgets and monitoring expenses | ☐ preparing inspection deficiency reports | ☐ recommending corrective actions | ☐ reviewing and approving cost estimates | ☐ approving contracting changes | ☐ holding meetings to discuss project progress processing documents | ☐ other: ______].

☐ [☐ Prepare and execute | ☐ Assist in the preparation of] [☐ contract documents | ☐ prenegotiation objectives | ☐ source selection reports | ☐ price negotiation memoranda | ☐ draft briefings | ☐ draft correspondence | ☐ contract modifications | ☐ contract closeouts | ☐ other: ______] **for review and approval by** [☐ Contracting Officer | ☐ other: ______].

☐ **Facilitate** [☐ legal | ☐ administrative | ☐ logistical | ☐ other: ______] **support and guidance to ______** *[whom?]* **in the areas of** [☐ contractual issues | ☐ past performance factors | ☐ cost evaluations | ☐ proposal evaluations | ☐ preproposal conferences | ☐ other: ______] **of ______** *[what?].*

☐ **Regularly review ______** *[type of]* **contracts in the area(s) of ______** *[what?]*, **make recommendations to senior management regarding** [☐ risks | ☐ issues | ☐ improvements | ☐ other: ______], **and implement ______** *[what?].*

☐ **Exercise** [☐ an in-depth | ☐ a proficient | ☐ a working] knowledge of contractual [☐ documents | ☐ language | ☐ types | ☐ terms | ☐ laws | ☐ regulations | ☐ practices | ☐ procedures | ☐ administration | ☐ other: ______] **in the preparation of** [☐ Subcontractor Agreements | ☐ Memoranda of Understanding | ☐ Nondisclosure Agreements | ☐ Teaming Agreements | ☐ government contracts | ☐ other: ______] **ensuring compliance with all** [☐ Federal Acquisition Regulations | ☐ Service Contract Act | ☐ zoning regulations | ☐ corporate policies | ☐ departmental practices | ☐ accounting principles | ☐ other: ______].

☐ **Apply expertise in and knowledge of** [☐ federal contracting law | ☐ contract terms | ☐ state and local building codes | ☐ Uniform Building Code | ☐ construction law | ☐ electrical and plumbing codes | ☐ fire and life safety codes | ☐ facility service contracts | ☐ license agreements | ☐ real estate leases | ☐ contract preparation and administration | ☐ contract negotiations | ☐ dispute resolution methods | ☐ architectural principles | ☐ construction requirements | ☐ other: ______] **in the** [☐ negotiation | ☐ documentation | ☐ evaluation | ☐ awarding | ☐ review | ☐ administration | ☐ other: ______] **of** [☐ construction] **contracts.**

☐ **Successfully** [☐ negotiate and manage | ☐ research, review, and process] ______ [type of] **revenue business contracts for** ______ *[what?]* **by** ______ *[doing what?].*

☐ **Determine contract terms and conditions of all proposed product purchases and** ______ *[do what?]* **achieving** ______ *[what results?].*

☐ **Calculate contractual** [☐ rental payment amounts | ☐ leasing options | ☐ one-time fees | ☐ other: ______] **to process payment vouchers for** ______ *[what?].*

ACHIEVEMENT SAMPLES: *See also "**Contract Development & Review**" and "**Contract Negotiations.**"*

☐ [☐ Prepare and execute | ☐ Assist in the preparation of] [☐ contract documents | ☐ prenegotiation objectives | ☐ source selection reports | ☐ price negotiation memoranda | ☐ draft briefings | ☐ draft correspondence | ☐ contract modifications | ☐ contract closeouts | ☐ other: ______] **for review and approval by** [☐ Contracting Officer | ☐ other: ______].

☐ **Facilitate** [☐ legal | ☐ administrative | ☐ logistical | ☐ other: ______] **support and guidance to** ______ *[whom?]* **in the areas of** [☐ contractual issues | ☐ past performance factors | ☐ cost evaluations | ☐ proposal evaluations | ☐ preproposal conferences | ☐ other: ______] **of** ______ *[what?].*

☐ **Exercise** [☐ an in-depth | ☐ a proficient | ☐ a working] knowledge of contractual [☐ documents | ☐ language | ☐ types | ☐ terms | ☐ laws | ☐ regulations | ☐ practices | ☐ procedures | ☐ administration | ☐ other: ______] **in the preparation of** [☐ Subcontractor Agreements | ☐ Memoranda of Understanding | ☐ Nondisclosure Agreements | ☐ Teaming Agreements | ☐ government contracts | ☐ other: ______] **ensuring compliance with all** [☐ Federal Acquisition Regulations | ☐ Service Contract Act | ☐ zoning regulations | ☐ corporate policies | ☐ departmental practices | ☐ accounting principles | ☐ other: ______].

☐ **Regularly review** ______ *[type of]* **contracts in the area(s) of** ______ *[what?],* **make recommendations to senior management regarding** [☐ risks | ☐ issues | ☐ improvements | ☐ other: ______], **and implement** ______ *[what?].*

☐ **Successfully** [☐ negotiate and manage | ☐ research, review, and process] ______ [type of] **revenue business contracts for** ______ *[what?]* **by** ______ *[doing what?].*

☐ **Determine contract terms and conditions of all proposed product purchases and** ______ *[do what?]* **achieving** ______ *[what results?].*

☐ **Calculate contractual** [☐ rental payment amounts | ☐ leasing options | ☐ one-time fees | ☐ other: ______] **to process payment vouchers for** ______ *[what?].*

Contract Management

See also other Contracting categories.

☐ **Provide leadership, vision, and direction to a team of** ______ *[#]* **to initiate, plan, and execute** ______ *[type of]* [☐ contracts | ☐ projects] **ranging from $**______ **to $**______ *[amounts]* **and resulting in** [☐ delivering bottom-line business value | ☐ business transformation | ☐ new product offerings | ☐ the translation of enterprise strategies into projects | ☐ increased productivity | ☐ other benefits: ______].

☐ **Define, plan, and implement** ______ *[type of]* **projects; and direct and oversee the** [☐ design | ☐ development | ☐ testing | ☐ implementation | ☐ tracking | ☐ reporting | ☐ other: ______] **of those projects in support of** [☐ the firm's | ☐ clients'] **business objectives.**

☐ **Provide support to the** [☐ Senior Contracts Manager | ☐ Director of Contracts | ☐ ______ *(which?)* **departments** | ☐ other: ______] **in all contractual matters including** [☐ proposals development | ☐ pricing strategies | ☐ risk management | ☐ negotiations | ☐ contract management | ☐ other: ______] **in a timely and professional fashion.**

☐ **Review, analyze, and approve** ______ *[type of]* [☐ proposals | ☐ estimates | ☐ agreements |☐ contractual documents | ☐ other: ______] **and monitor performance to ensure conformance to** [☐ original proposals | ☐ contracts | ☐ legal requirements | ☐ regulations | ☐ customer specifications | ☐ other: ______].

☐ **Direct and guide** ______ *[#]* **Contract Specialists and facilitate all office management functions including** [☐ financial records management | ☐ accounts payable and accounts receivable | ☐ quarterly taxes for accountant | ☐ client relationship management | ☐ estimating | ☐ contractor bids review | ☐ contract negotiations | ☐ project coordination | ☐ jobs scheduling | ☐ materials shipping | ☐ equipment purchasing (☐ and leasing) | ☐ payroll processing | ☐ equipment checks | ☐ company taxes | ☐ advertising campaigns to increase exposure | ☐ staff recruitment | ☐ payroll processing | ☐ other: ______].

☐ **Plan and coordinate all activities of ______** *[type of]* **contracting projects for a wide range of clients in collaboration with** [☐ clients | ☐vendors | ☐senior management | ☐other: ______].

ACHIEVEMENT SAMPLES: *See "Contract Development & Review" and "Contract Negotiations."*

Contract Negotiations

See also other Contracting categories.

☐ **Negotiate and document ______** *[type of]* [☐ contracts | ☐ agreements] **that meet** [☐ business | ☐ client | ☐ legal | ☐ regulatory | ☐ audit | ☐ other: ______] [☐ requirements | ☐ needs] **with contracts ranging from $______ to $______** *[amounts]* **for this $______** *[revenues]* **______** *[type of]* **firm servicing ______** *[which?]* **clientele base.**

☐ [☐ Prepare, negotiate, and administer | ☐ Review, approve, and execute] [☐ a wide range of] ______ *[type of]* **Construction** [☐ contracts | ☐ contractual agreements | ☐ legal documents | ☐ agreements] **of** [☐ a complex nature | ☐ varying scope and complexity], **and document related** [☐ policies | ☐ procedures | ☐ processes | ☐ instructions | ☐ other: ______] **for same.**

☐ **Prepare and negotiate ______** *[type of]* **contracts with ______** *[whom?]* **and determine contract terms and conditions.**

☐ **Successfully** [☐ negotiate and manage | ☐ research, review, and process] ______ *[type of]* **revenue business contracts for ______** *[what?]* by ______ *[doing what?].*

☐ [☐ Develop and negotiate | ☐ Review and approve] ______ *[type of]* [☐ contracts | ☐ contractual documents | ☐ agreements | ☐ proposals | ☐ amendments | ☐ legal documents | ☐ nondisclosure agreements | ☐ grant requests | ☐ license agreements | ☐ service agreements | ☐ technical documents | ☐ other: ______] **for ______** *[what?]* **in support of major business initiatives.**

☐ **Negotiate fees and develop ______** *[type of]* [☐ design | ☐ construction | ☐ repair | ☐ other: ______] **contracts with** [☐ architects | ☐ engineers | ☐ contractors | ☐ subcontractors | ☐ others: ______] **for ______** *[what?]* **commensurate with project scope and budget.**

ACHIEVEMENT SAMPLES: *See also "Contract Development & Review."*

☐ **Led negotiations with ______** *[whom?]* [☐ and investment bankers] **in acquiring company's most profitable** [☐ facility | ☐ plant | ☐ distribution center | ☐ branch | ☐ other: ______]. **With an appraised value versus purchase price of ______** *[#]* **to one, profits exceeded acquisition costs in less than ______** *[what time period?].*

☐ **Negotiated a $______** *[amount]* **contract with ______** *[whom?],* **which served to ______** *[purpose]* **and resulted in ______** *[what was the win/win for the firm and the client?].*

☐ **Led negotiations with ______** *[whom?]* **for long-term ______** *[type of]* **agreements with forecasted savings of $______** *[amount]* **over a ______** *[#]***-year period.**

☐ **Saved the firm $______** *[amount]* **in the** [☐ negotiation | ☐ litigation] **of** [☐ contractor | ☐ subcontractor | ☐ engineer | ☐ architect | ☐ other: ______] **claims ranging from $______ to $______** *[amounts]* **which involved** [☐ interpreting legal documents | ☐ handling unforeseen conditions | ☐ other: ______] **and resulted in ______** *[other benefits?].*

☐ **Negotiated and ratified ______** *[#]* ______ *[type of]* **agreements with various ______** *[type of]* **firms** [☐ nationwide | ☐ overseas | ☐ abroad], **resulting in ______** *[benefits].*

☐ [☐ Managed | ☐ Performed] ______ *[type of]* **contract project rollouts from inception to successful implementation for this $______** *[revenues]* **______** *[type of]* **firm that ______** *[does what?]* **for ______** *[whom?].*

☐ **Played an integral role in obtaining a $______ contract from ______** *[whom?]* **to replace its current ______** *[type of]* [☐ methodology | ☐ technology | ☐ products | ☐ other: ______] **with ______** *[what?].*

☐ **Negotiated and wrote** [☐ client | ☐ architect | ☐ engineer | ☐ contractor | ☐ other: ______] ______ *[type of]* **contracts ranging from $______ to $______** *[amounts]* **for** [☐ architectural plans for | ☐ the design and build of | ☐construction of] ______ *[what?].*

Contractor / Subcontractor Influence & Collaboration

See also "Trades/Crew Supervision – All Trades" and "Trades Coordination & Oversight."

ACHIEVEMENT SAMPLES:

- ☐ **Built a strong, supportive contractor/subcontractor team environment by exhibiting and modeling leadership skills in** [☐ communication | ☐ negotiation | ☐ problem-solving | ☐ obstacle tackling | ☐ other: ______] **and** ______ *[doing what?].*
- ☐ **Challenge contractors in all trades to perform quality work on schedule and within budget by** ______ [doing what well?].
- ☐ **Influence all contractors to develop and maintain positive working relationships with all levels of** [☐ internal | ☐ external | ☐ internal and external] **management by** ______ *[doing what?].*
- ☐ **Collaborate with contractors and at all levels of the firm to** [☐ clarify scope | ☐ overcome obstacles | ☐ identify issues | ☐ solve problems | ☐ reach decisions | ☐ obtain solutions acceptance | ☐ guide projects to their successful completion | ☐ other: ______] **during the development and implementation of all projects**.
- ☐ **Influence, energize, and motivate contractors to bring projects to a successful delivery by** ______ *[doing what?].*
- ☐ **Gain contractor/subcontractor cooperation and commitment by** [☐ providing clear direction | ☐ soliciting feedback | ☐ serving as the primary resource hub | ☐ insisting on mutual support | ☐ sharing information | ☐ modeling professional behavior | ☐ building a collaborative environment | ☐ removing all obstacles to project success | ☐ other: ______].
- ☐ **Persuaded crew to perform a clean job, ensuring all job site debris was removed before finishing. Accomplished through** [☐ peer pressure of others who were on task | ☐ other method: ______].
- ☐ **Successfully produce results through others by** ______ *[doing what?].*

Cost Estimating – Architecture & Construction

- ☐ **Provide advice and input to** [☐ Architects | ☐ Engineers | ☐ CAD Designers | ☐ subcontractors | ☐ others: ______] **from project inception to completion on the financial feasibility of the design and construction of** ______ *[type of]* **projects ranging $**______ **to $**______ *[amounts].*
- ☐ **Work with this** ______ *[type of]* **firm's** ______ *[which?]* **team to establish and/or confirm project budgets, prepare cost estimates, and serve as technical advisor to determine the financial success of** ______ *[type of]* **projects ranging $**______ **to $**______ *[amounts].*
- ☐ **Determine the financial feasibility and return on investment of** ______ *[type of]* **projects along with** [☐ the image it will create | ☐ if it is responsive to the needs of (☐ its users / ☐ the community) | ☐ how well they will serve its intended purpose | ☐ other: ______] **for this** ______ *[type of]* **firm**.
- ☐ **Establish realistic construction capital costs on** ______ *[type of]* **projects by detailing cost planning and control to ensure projects are bid, documented, and completed in the most economical manner considering** [☐ quality | ☐ aesthetics | ☐ cost | ☐ location | ☐ image | ☐ practicality | ☐ functionality | ☐ timeliness | ☐ reliability | ☐ climate | ☐ user ability | ☐ future growth | ☐ other: ______].
- ☐ **By combining the functions of an economist, estimator, and accountant, use** [☐ engineering judgment | ☐ application of scientific principles and techniques | ☐ cost management principles | ☐ other: ______] **to focus on the feasibility and management of construction project costs and values.**
- ☐ **Accurately forecast project costs on** ______ *[type of]* **projects for this** [☐ multimillion-dollar | ☐ $______] [☐ construction management | ☐ design-and-build | ☐ contracting | ☐ other: ______] **firm based on** ______ *[what factors or resources?].*
- ☐ **Develop project cost information for** [☐ Project Engineers | ☐ Architects | ☐ Construction Managers | ☐ Facility Managers | ☐ Building Operations Managers | ☐ general contractors | ☐ business owners | ☐ corporate managers | ☐ others: ______] **required to** [☐ make bids for contracts | ☐ determine if a proposed project will be profitably feasible | ☐ other: ______], **considering all factors that influence costs including** [☐ materials | ☐ labor | ☐ equipment | ☐ location | ☐ special machinery | ☐ computer hardware and software | ☐ subcontracts | ☐ overhead | ☐ taxes | ☐ insurance | ☐ mark-up | ☐ other: ______].
- ☐ **Financially manage and control all** ______ *[type of]* **construction projects by reviewing project costs from inception through completion including** [☐ cost estimating | ☐ establishing realistic construction budgets | ☐ monitoring and managing costs from planning through completion | ☐ other: ______].
- ☐ **Monitor actual costs as the project develops against bid specifications including** [☐ plumbing | ☐ electrical work | ☐ excavation | ☐ concrete | ☐ masonry | ☐ other: ______] **to ensure project stays financially on track**.

- ☐ **Conduct preliminary cost estimation work including** [☐ reviewing preliminary drawings and specifications | ☐ making site visits of proposed projects | ☐ gathering information on availability of (☐ electricity / ☐ water / ☐ drainage / ☐ surface topography / ☐ other: ______) | ☐ determining seasonal weather conditions | ☐ recording all related information | ☐ other: ______].
- ☐ **Prepare quantity surveys and total project-cost summaries using** ______ *[type of software]* **detailing material costs, equipment needs, required crew size and labor costs, and sequence of operations; and submit bid proposals to** [☐ owner | ☐ architect | ☐ engineer | ☐ other: ______].
- ☐ **Attend** [☐ weekly | ☐ bi-monthly | ☐ periodic] **cost meetings to review** [☐ procurement | ☐ project | ☐ change orders | ☐ other: ______] **status with** [☐ contractors | ☐ project managers | ☐ engineering teams | ☐ management | ☐ others: ______].
- ☐ **Chair** [☐ weekly | ☐ bi-monthly | ☐ monthly] **schedule management meetings with** [☐ Project Managers | ☐ owner's representatives | ☐ contractors | ☐ others: ______] **to coordinate and report on project progress, address problem areas, and determine remedies to bring schedule progress back on track.**
- ☐ **Develop and monitor the $**______ *[amount]* **construction budget including all project costs.** *(See **"Budget Development and Expenditure Control"** for additional bullets.)*
- ☐ **Review Construction Manager reports of total predicted costs, schedules, and variations to** [☐ proactively manage financial and physical aspects of all projects | ☐ accurately predict construction outcomes | ☐ assess risk | ☐ establish realistic capital costs of construction projects | ☐ assist project managers with handling changes and variations | ☐ other: ______].
- ☐ **Using an objective, unbiased approach, review and analyze** ______ *[what?]* **to determine the best course(s) of action regarding project cost estimations, cost control, profitability, and return on investment of** ______ *[type of]* **projects. Ensure all projects are completed within budget and meet all** [☐ performance | ☐ quality | ☐ other: ______] **standards.**
- ☐ **Maximize and protect the firm's interest in the planning and completion of** ______ *[type of]* **projects enhancing the value of each project by** ______ *[doing what?].*
- ☐ **Coordinate** [☐ monthly | ☐ quarterly | ☐ year-end] **close requirements and prepare standard cost and gross margin variance analysis, reconciliation, and reporting.**
- ☐ **Use** ______ *[type of]* **control estimate and control schedules to** [☐ establish baselines | ☐ measure progress | ☐ track changes | ☐ predict cost overruns and schedule delays | ☐ provide information for management should intervention be required | ☐ other: ______] **on** ______ *[type of]* **projects.**
- ☐ **Collaborate with** ______ *[whom?]* **to optimize project planning, delivery, and operations.**
- ☐ **Establish project budgets ranging $**______ **to $**______ *[amounts]* **and baseline schedules for all** ______ *[type of]* **projects encompassing** ______ *[what?].*
- ☐ **Structure estimates and schedules based on** ______ *[type of]* **project** [☐ execution strategy | ☐ budget | ☐ other: ______], **test competitiveness of bids, and determine risk guidelines before authorizing project start.**
- ☐ **Predict final project costs and scheduling and identify possible variations from authorized baseline estimates and schedules by** ______ *[doing what?].*

ACHIEVEMENT SAMPLES: *See Achievements under **"Cost Management."***

Cost Management – Architecture & Construction

*See also **"Cost Estimating," "Cost Reductions & Savings," "Increased Sales,"** and **"Increased Revenues & Profits."***

- ☐ **Provide detailed cost management services to/for** ______ *[whom or what?]* **involving** [☐ cost forecasting and reporting | ☐ invoice validation | ☐ change management | ☐ procurement management | ☐ project earned value analyses | ☐ other: ______].
- ☐ **Conduct analytical costing studies and provide** ______ *[#]* **alternative** ______ *[type of]* **solutions and/or selections based on proposed** ______ *[type of]* **projects to better utilize** ______ *[what?].*
- ☐ **Provide cost advice to** ______ *[whom?]* **on their proposed** ______ *[type of]* **projects during the early stages of development to assist in** [☐ determining project viability prior to design | ☐ preparing cost estimates | ☐ assessing the feasibility of undertaking the project | ☐ establishing a tentative budget | other: ______].
- ☐ **Use schematic drawings to conduct analytical costing studies and provide** ______ *[#]* **alternative design solutions / selections based on proposed** ______ *[type of]* **projects to better utilize** [☐ building size and shape | ☐ construction materials | ☐ other: ______].
- ☐ **Develop** ______ *[type of]* **cost estimates based on preliminary drawings supplied by** [☐ Architect | ☐ Engineer | ☐ CAD Drafter | ☐ outsourced firm | ☐ other: ______] **breaking down the cost of each functional construction element in its relationship to the whole to judge the economic viability of the entire project and make any needed changes.**

- ☐ **Undertake feasibility studies on the budget requirements of** ______ *[type of]* **construction projects to include** [☐ construction costs | ☐ operating and maintenance costs | ☐ site servicing | ☐ cash flows | ☐ other: ______] **by evaluating** [☐ market analysis | ☐ commercial returns | ☐ profitability | ☐ financing arrangements | ☐ land acquisition | ☐ revenue forecasts | ☐ other: ______].
- ☐ **Review all project costs to** [☐ analyze work progress | ☐ factor in amounts spent | ☐ determine reimbursable costs | ☐ track changes | ☐ summarize individual costs | ☐ predict total construction cost | ☐ other: ______].
- ☐ **Provide construction cost advice to** [☐ Architects | ☐ Engineers | ☐ CAD Drafters | ☐ other: ______] **on their proposed** ______ *[type of]* **projects during early stages of development to assist in determining project viability prior to design. Prepare cost estimates to assist in assessing the feasibility of undertaking the project and in establishing a tentative budget.**
- ☐ **Provide procurement services for** ______ *[type of]* [☐ construction | ☐ engineering | ☐ architectural | ☐ project management | ☐ other: ______] **services, including preparing Requests for Proposals (RFPs) and bid analysis.**
- ☐ **Conduct and prepare** [☐ Reserve Fund Studies | ☐ Cost-to-Complete Reports | ☐ Property Condition Reports | ☐ Insurance Replacement Cost Assessments | ☐ Risk Analysis | ☐ Bills of Quantities and Materials | ☐ Cost Control Estimates | ☐ Functional Cost Analysis | ☐ other: ______] **that include all costs related to** [☐ project management | ☐ project scheduling | ☐ construction management | ☐ related cash flows | ☐ mediation and arbitration | ☐ materials | ☐ other: ______].

ACHIEVEMENT SAMPLES:

- ☐ **Spearheaded a** ______ *[type of]* ***Cost Estimate System*** **whereby direct comparisons can be made between contractor price breakdowns and** ______ *[what else?]*.
- ☐ **Established and implemented a *Project Controls System (PCS)* for all capital projects based on their** [☐ size | ☐ complexity | ☐ execution strategy | ☐ other: ______] **that encompassed** [☐ cost | ☐ planning | ☐ scheduling | ☐ change | ☐ other: ______] **management processes. The PCS** [☐ estimates project costs | ☐ monitors activities completion | ☐ reports schedule status | ☐ estimates change impact | ☐ predicts project outcomes | ☐ allows for corrective action | ☐ other: ______].
- ☐ **Established and implemented the firm's *Project Change Management System* that identifies and reports on all variations from contract drawings and specifications and provides** ______ *[what?]*.
- ☐ **Monitored and suggested changes to the** ______ *[which?]* **accounting** [☐ policies | ☐ practices | ☐ systems] **that drove improved analysis in the form of** ______ *[what?]*.
- ☐ **Championed a** ______ *[type of]* ***Cost Estimate System*** **whereby direct comparisons can be made between contractor price breakdowns and** ______ *[what else?]*.
- ☐ **Developed a** ______ *[type of]* **plan that manages project execution costs, schedules, and changes** and ______ *[benefited how?]*.
- ☐ **Established and implemented the firm's *Project Change Management System* that identifies and reports on all variations from contract drawings and specifications and provides** ______ *[what?]*.
- ☐ **Planned, organized, and defined the policies and procedures for all cost accounting activities including** ______, ______, **and** ______ *[which activities?]*.
- ☐ **Drove** ______ *[type of]* **profit improvement activities that** ______ *[did what?]*.
- ☐ **Established and implemented a *Project Controls System (PCS)* for all capital projects based on their** [☐ size | ☐ complexity | ☐ execution strategy | ☐ other: ______] **that encompassed** [☐ cost | ☐ planning | ☐ scheduling | ☐ change | ☐ other: ______] **management processes. The PCS** [☐ estimates project costs | ☐ monitors activities completion | ☐ reports schedule status | ☐ estimates change impact | ☐ predicts project outcomes | ☐ allows for corrective action | ☐ other: ______].
- ☐ **Established and implemented the firm's *Project Change Management System* that identifies and reports on** ______ *[what?]* **and provides** ______ *[what?]*.
- ☐ [☐ Established and implemented | ☐ Monitored and suggested changes to] **the firm's Human Resource** ______ *[which?]* [☐ policies | ☐ practices | ☐ systems] **that drove improved analysis in the form of** ______ *[what?]*.
- ☐ **Developed a** ______ *[type of]* **plan that manages project execution costs, schedules, and changes** and ______ *[benefited how?]*.
- ☐ **Planned, organized, and defined the policies and procedures for all cost accounting activities including** ______, ______, **and** ______ *[which activities?]*.

Cost Reductions & Savings – General

*See also "**Cost Management,**" "**Purchasing,**" and various Cost Reductions & Savings categories, applicable.*

ACHIEVEMENT SAMPLES:

☐ **Developed and implemented a cost-effective method to** ______ *[do what?]* **that improved** ______ *[what process?]* **and reduced** ______ *[which?]* [☐ payroll | ☐ compensation | ☐ overtime | ☐ employee benefits | ☐ operating | ☐ overhead | ☐ other: ______] **expenses by $**______ *[amount]* **/** ______**%** *[percentage].*

☐ **Created and implemented a successful** ______ *[type of]* **program to** [☐ cut down the workload | ☐ reduce overtime | ☐ increase productivity | ☐ streamline operations | ☐ reduce expenses | ☐ other: ______], **resulting in a savings of $**______ *[amount].*

☐ **Generated a cost savings of $**______ *[amount]* **in** ______ *[what?]* **by** [☐ spearheading | ☐ developing and implementing | ☐ recommending | ☐ other: ______] **a** ______ *[type of]* **business** [☐ forecasting | ☐ analysis | ☐ other: ______] **model that** ______ *[does what?]* **by way of** ______ *[what?].*

☐ **Reduced total** [☐ operating expenses | ☐ overhead costs] [☐ by ______% *(percentage)* | ☐ in excess of $______ *(amount)*] **annually by establishing a(n)** ______ *[type of]* **initiative to** ______ *[do what?].*

☐ **Decreased** ______ *[which?]* **costs $**______ *[amount]* **/** ______**%** *[percentage]* [☐ annually] **by** [☐ spearheading cost-reduction methods in ______ *(what?)* | ☐ establishing ______ *(what?)* standards | ☐ coming in under budget in ______ *(what area?)* | ☐ training all employees on ______ *(what?)* | ☐ implementing cutting-edge solutions in ______ *(what?)* | ☐ anticipating and proactively meeting (☐ clients' / ☐ the firm's) needs | ☐ using state-of-the-art technology to ______ *(accomplish what?)* | ☐ bringing payroll in line with budget | ☐ developing a more efficient ______ *(what?)* process | ☐ eliminating the need for ______ *(what process?)* | ☐ selecting more cost-effective vendors | ☐ other: ______].

☐ **Successfully cut** ______ *[which?]* **costs $**______ *[amount]* **and increased revenues $**______ *[amount]* **annually by** [☐ introducing | ☐ implementing] **a new** ______ *[type of]* [☐ concept | ☐ cost-reduction method | ☐ other: ______] **to** ______ *[do what?]* **in** ______ *[#]* [☐ offices | ☐ locations | ☐ departments].

☐ **Cut company** ______ *[which?]* **costs $**______ *[amount]* / ______**%** *[percentage]* **and increased revenues $**______ *[amount]* **annually by introducing the** ______ *[what?]* [☐ concept | ☐ program | ☐ procedure] **and** [☐ eliminating the need for ______ *(what process?)* | ☐ demonstrating how information technology can be used as a competitive edge | ☐ other: ______], **which resulted in** ______ *[additional benefits?].*

☐ **Spearheaded a** ______ *[type of]* **cost-reduction program that** ______ *[does what?]* **by** [☐ evaluating business bottlenecks and turning them into assets | ☐ other method: ______], **which involved** ______ *[what actions?].*

☐ **Designed and executed business forecasting and analysis models that generated a cost savings of** ______**%** *[percentage]* **/ $**______ *[amount]* **after executing a new** ______ *[type of]* [☐ training | ☐ production | ☐ other: ______] **program that** ______ *[does what?].*

☐ **Saved $**______ *[amount]* **annually by implementing a cost-effective** ______ *[type of]* [☐ policy | ☐ procedure | ☐ program | ☐ campaign | ☐ method | ☐ other: ______] **that improved** ______ *[what?].*

Cost Reductions & Savings – Construction

*See also "**Cost Reductions & Savings – General.**"*

ACHIEVEMENT SAMPLES:

☐ **Saved $**______ *[amount]* **by** [☐ coming in under budget on ______ *(project)* | ☐ reconfiguring ______ *(type of)* space without reconstruction | ☐ resolving a complex ______ (type of) problem quickly | ☐ implementing a cost-effective ______ *(type of)* method to ______ *(do what?)* | ☐ other: ______] **resulting in** ______ *[what benefits?].*

☐ **Cut lost tools costs down to a minimum by assigning the job of "Tool Counter" to a different person every week, saving company $**______ *[amount]* **annually**.

☐ **Decreased** ______ *[which?]* **costs $**______ [☐ through selection of more cost-effective vendors | ☐ training all employees on product features and benefits | ☐ other: ______].

☐ **Reduced labor costs $**______ *[amount]* **and increased profitability $**______ *[amount]* [☐ using direct field labor in lieu of subcontractors on smaller projects | ☐ hiring more effective crews for specific assignments | ☐ assigning laborers to handle simple tasks and freeing up mechanics to work on more technical issues | ☐ purchasing company-owned equipment in lieu of rentals | ☐ other achievement: ______].

☐ **Reduced** ______ *[which?]* **fees by $**______ *[amount]* **annually by spearheading the construction of a** ______ *[type of]* **facility for** ______ *[purpose],* **which resulted in** ______ *[what benefit?].*

Cost Reductions & Savings – Overhead / Operations

*See also "**Cost Reductions & Savings – General**" and "**Cost Management.**"*

ACHIEVEMENT SAMPLES:

☐ **Reduced overhead costs $______** *[amount]* **annually by** [☐ purchasing company-owned equipment | ☐ keeping operations running smoothly | ☐ giving 100% to the job | ☐ implementing a bidding process | ☐ successfully negotiating down costs | ☐ focusing on a commitment to excellence | ☐ other: ______].

☐ **Spearheaded a ______** *[type of]* **cost-reduction program that ______** *[does what?]* **by** [☐ evaluating business bottlenecks and turning them into assets | ☐ other method: ______] **which saved $______** *[amount]* **annually**.

☐ **Slashed ______** *[type of]* **overhead costs $______** *[amount]* | ______% *[percentage]* **annually by** [☐ anticipating and proactively meeting the firm's needs | ☐ implementing employee bonus programs with salaries based on their production | ☐ acquiring newer technology to meet the facility's needs | ☐ updating computers | ☐ implementing a more efficient network | ☐ evaluating and enhancing the operational effectiveness of ______ *(which?)* (☐ systems | ☐ hardware | ☐ software) | ☐ other: ______] **resulting in** [☐ workers exhibiting a genuine mental sharpness | ☐ fewer job-related errors | ☐ better attendance | ☐ higher team spirit | ☐decreased turnover | ☐ increased production | ☐ other: ______].

☐ **Reduced total** [☐ operating expenses | ☐ overhead costs] [☐ by ______% *(percentage)* | ☐ in excess of $______ *(amount)]* **annually by establishing a ______** *[type of]* **initiative to ______** *[do what?]*.

☐ **Successfully cut** [☐ operating expenses | ☐ overhead costs | ☐ other: ______] **$______** *[amount]* **by** [☐ introducing a new ______ *(type of)* concept | ☐ establishing a ______ *(type of)* initiative that ______ *[does what?]* | ☐ implementing cost-reduction methods | ☐ improving employee morale | ☐ reducing turnover and training costs | ☐ other achievement: ______].

☐ **Lowered total** [☐ operating expenses | ☐ overhead costs | ☐ controllable expenses | ☐ other: ______] **$______ / ______%** *[amount]* [☐ annually | ☐ over previous year] **by** [establishing a ______ *(type of)* initiative to ______ *(do what?)* | ☐ implementing improved (☐ security | ☐ safety awareness programs) | ☐ other: ______].

☐ **Implemented a cost-effective method to ______** *[do what?]*, **which improved ______** *[what process?]* **and reduced operating expenses by $______ | ______%** *[dollars and percentage]*.

Cost Reductions & Savings – Payroll & Overtime

*See also "**Cost Reductions & Savings – General.**"*

ACHIEVEMENT SAMPLES:

☐ **Decreased** [☐ overtime | ☐ payroll costs | ☐ contractor expenses | ☐ other: ______] **$______ by** [☐ scheduling employees to match their skills | ☐ developing troubleshooting programs to address quality issues | ☐ developing a scheduling program with a limited staff that met both the Company's and employees' needs | ☐ implementing vendor checks | ☐ structuring daily work schedules | ☐ other: ______] **resulting in** [☐ less absenteeism | ☐ decreased turnover | ☐ better customer servicing | ☐ other: ______].

☐ **Created and implemented a successful ______** *[type of]* **program that** [☐ reduced (☐ workload / ☐ overtime) $______ *(amount)* | ☐ increased productivity ______% *(amount)* | ☐ streamlined operations | ☐ cut expenses | ☐ other: ______].

☐ **Eliminated** $______ *[amount]* **in extraneous payroll costs by** [☐ reviewing employees' performance on a(n) (☐ weekly / ☐ monthly / ☐ annual) basis | ☐ terminating employees who were not meeting established performance levels | ☐ other: ______].

☐ **Slashed** [☐ payroll | ☐ overtime] **expenses $______** *[amount]* **annually by** [☐ improving employee morale | ☐ reducing turnover rate | ☐ decreasing training costs | ☐ bringing payroll in line with budget | ☐ introducing a new ______ *(type of)* concept | ☐ implementing cost-reduction methods | ☐ evaluating business bottlenecks and turning them into assets | ☐ implementing a comprehensive scheduling program with a limited staff which met both the Company's and employees' needs, resulting in (☐ less absenteeism / ☐ better customer servicing) | ☐ other method: ______].

☐ **Cut** [☐ payroll | ☐ benefits | ☐ other: ______] **costs ______%** *[percentage]* **while maintaining** [☐ personnel | ☐ store | ☐ employee benefit | ☐ other: ______] **coverage by** [☐ splitting full-time positions amongst ______ *(#)* other stores in district | ☐ hiring part-time help in lieu of filling open full-time positions | ☐ other method(s): ______].

☐ **Saved $______** *[amount]* **annually to the bottom line by reducing payroll expenses while simultaneously increasing productivity levels ______%** *[percentage]* **from an already low ______%** *[percentage]* **the prior year** [☐ despite union raises during this period].

Cost Reductions & Savings – Technology Upgrades

*See also "**Technology Upgrades & Enhancements**" and "**Cost Reductions & Savings – General.**"*

☐ **Cut costs $______** *[amount]* **and increased revenues $______** *[amount]* **annually by** [☐ updating ______ *(type of)* (☐ hardware / ☐ software) | ☐ using information technology as a competitive edge | ☐ other: ______], **which resulted in ______** *[what other benefits?].*

☐ **Decreased ______** *[type of]* **costs ______%** *[percentage]* **by** [☐ anticipating clients' needs | ☐ using state-of-the-art technology | ☐ implementing cutting-edge solutions | ☐ other achievement: ______].

☐ **Achieved an annual savings of $______** *[amount]* **in ______** *[which?]* **costs and dramatically improved ______** *[what?]* **by** [☐ upgrading | ☐ purchasing | ☐ installing | ☐ other: ______] ______ *[type of]* **equipment.**

☐ **Saved $______** *[amount]* **annually by** [☐ evaluating and enhancing the operational effectiveness of ______ *(type of)* (☐ systems / ☐ hardware / ☐ software) | ☐ acquiring newer technology to meet the organization's needs | ☐ other method: ______], **which resulted in ______** *[what benefits?].*

☐ **Reduced ______** *[type of]* **overhead costs $______** *[amount]* **/ ______%** *[percentage]* **annually by** [☐ anticipating and proactively meeting the firm's needs | ☐ updating computers | ☐ implementing a more efficient network | ☐ establishing (☐ high-speed network capability / ☐ ISDN teleconferencing / ☐ effective cost-reduction methods) | ☐ reducing turnover | ☐ other: ______].

☐ **Wrote** [☐ support documentation for computer requisitions | ☐ recommendations for (☐ hardware / ☐ software) purchases | ☐ other: ______] **to link together multiple areas with similar needs, translating end user needs into system requirements, and saving the** [☐ firm | ☐ department | ☐ division | ☐ other: ______] **$______** *[amount]* **in ______** *[what areas?].*

☐ **Dramatically improved ______** *[what?]* **by** [☐ upgrading | ☐ purchasing | ☐ other: ______] ______ *[type of]* **equipment, which resulted in an annual savings of $______** *[amount]* **in production costs.**

Crew Supervision

*See "**Trades Coordination & Oversight**" and/or "**Staff Management & Supervision.**"*

Customer Complaints & Problem Resolution

☐ **Successfully handle and resolve customer problems through effective** [☐ customer service | ☐ teamwork | ☐ troubleshooting | ☐ patience | ☐ other: ______] **and by implementing a ______** *[type of]* **philosophy.**

☐ **Research, evaluate, and resolve customer complaints to their satisfaction by applying effective** [☐ listening skills | ☐ problem-solving techniques | ☐ mediating skills | ☐ other: ______] [☐ via an ear for understanding their point of view | ☐ by balancing customer satisfaction without "giving away the store" | ☐ other: ______].

☐ **Working with a wide range of clientele, resolve difficult problems and/or discrepancies in a** [☐ diplomatic | ☐ patient | ☐ calm | ☐ friendly | ☐ courteous | ☐ positive | ☐ knowledgeable | ☐ professional | ☐ caring] **manner and by keeping composure during peak periods by** [☐ tackling each situation as it arises | ☐ remaining calm | ☐ soliciting and obtaining help from peers making short-staff situations transparent to customers | ☐ other methods: ______].

☐ **Obtain customer satisfaction through** [☐ quick resolution of customer issues regarding (☐ pricing / ☐ signing / ☐ company policies / ☐ returns) | ☐ other: ______] **ensuring the quality of customer service delivered meets high standards of excellence by** [☐ monitoring and evaluating staff's progress | ☐ other means: ______].

☐ **Troubleshoot, research, evaluate, and resolve customer inquiries and complaints to their satisfaction by using effective** [☐ listening skills | ☐ problem-solving techniques | ☐ mediating skills | ☐ understanding | ☐ other: ______].

☐ **Handle and resolve all customer complaints, resolving time-sensitive issues in an expedient manner by using effective** [☐ listening skills | ☐ problem-solving techniques | ☐ mediating skills | ☐ other: ______] **and** [☐ lending an ear for understanding their point of view | ☐ troubleshooting the problem | ☐ balancing customer satisfaction without "giving away the store" | ☐ other means: ______].

☐ **Keep composure during peak times by** [☐ tackling each situation as it arises | ☐ remaining calm | ☐ soliciting and obtaining help from peers to make short-staff situations transparent to customers | ☐ other methods: ______].

☐ **Appease dissatisfied customers and turn them into satisfied consumers through** [☐ effective listening | ☐ patience | ☐ a caring manner | ☐ understanding | ☐ other methods: ______].

ACHIEVEMENT SAMPLES:

☐ **Tackled and resolved customer** [☐ problems | ☐ complaints | ☐ account discrepancies | ☐ other: ______] **through** [☐ effective customer service | ☐ teamwork | ☐ troubleshooting | ☐ patience | ☐ a caring manner | ☐ other methods: ______] **and** [☐ an ear for understanding their point of view | ☐ balancing customer satisfaction with not "giving away the store" | ☐ by implementing a ______ *(type of)* philosophy | ☐ other: ______], **thereby appeasing dissatisfied customers and turning them into satisfied clients.**

☐ **Received** [☐ many | ☐ ______ *(#)*] [☐ client | ☐ customer] **commendations** [☐ regarding staff performance | ☐ due to (☐ having a positive attitude / ☐ being efficient / ☐ a quest for excellence / ☐ going beyond the expected / ☐ other trait: ______], **resulting in** [☐ more satisfied customers | ☐ an increased account base | ☐ repeat business | ☐ referrals | ☐ other: ______] **for company.**

☐ **Successfully** [☐ developed | ☐ resurrected | ☐ implemented] **a $______** *[amount]* **project bringing it to fruition through** [☐ field research | ☐ tactical marketing | ☐ market, competition, product, and pricing awareness | ☐ other: ______]. **Company profited $______** *[revenues]*—**earmarking this as the first of the high budget projects it would undertake.**

Customer Service

See also ***"Customer Service Management," "Customer Complaints & Problem Resolution," "Client Meeting & Strategizing," "Client Presentations & Proposals,"*** *and* ***"Client Relations."***

☐ [☐ Manage and oversee | ☐ Supervise | ☐ Facilitate] **customer service—from handling inquiries and assisting customers with their buying decisions to resolving problems using effective problem-solving techniques—resulting in superior customer service to ______** *[type of]* **consumers.**

☐ **Identify, define, and document client needs and priorities as well as** [☐ options | ☐ risks | ☐ costs | ☐ benefits | ☐ alternative solutions | ☐ other: ______] **and translate requirements into effective ______** *[type of]* **solutions.**

☐ **Oversee customer service operations of this ______** *[type of]* **firm that provides ______** *[type of]* **services to the ______** *[which?]* **market including providing customers with** [☐ advice | ☐ professional help | ☐ consultation | ☐ follow up | ☐ other: ______] **in** ______ *[what functions?]*.

☐ **Provide** [☐ pre- | ☐ post-] **construction support to** [☐ customers | ☐ clients | ☐ other: ______] **in the areas of ______, ______, and** ______ *[what areas?]*.

☐ **Interface with and assist ______** *[type of]* **customers by** [☐ providing information | ☐ answering all project-related questions | ☐ offering solutions that meet their needs | ☐ processing and expediting their requests | ☐ solving credit problems | ☐ resolving customer complaints | ☐ handling client billing | ☐ checking project scheduling | ☐ providing follow-up and advisement | ☐ other: ______].

☐ **Provide customers with** [☐ advice | ☐ professional help | ☐ consultation | ☐ other: ______] **in ______** *[what functions?]* **for this** $______ *[revenues]* ______ *[type of]* **firm with ______** *[#]* [☐ locations | ☐ employees | ☐ accounts].

☐ **Handle various customer service functions including** [☐ preparing purchase orders | ☐ facilitating customer orders | ☐ answering inquiries | ☐ solving credit problems | ☐ resolving customer complaints | ☐ handling client billing | ☐ other: ______].

☐ **Regularly interact with** [☐ consumers | ☐ customers | ☐ clientele | ☐ owners] **to maintain high levels of customer satisfaction by** [☐ listening to and interpreting their needs | ☐ giving careful attention to detail | ☐ providing solution selling | ☐ offering alternative options | ☐ upselling higher-end services | ☐ other: ______].

☐ **Convert customer desires into needs by ______** *[doing what?]*, **achieving** [☐ increased sales | ☐ repeat business | ☐ referrals | ☐ other achievement: ______] **for company**.

☐ **Handle** [☐ heavy | ☐ moderate] **telephone contact with** [☐ clients | ☐ suppliers | ☐ contractors | ☐ other: ______] **in a professional manner, always ensuring appropriate follow-through within a ______** *[#]*-[☐ hour | ☐ minute] **timeframe.**

☐ **Assist customers with service inquiries both in person and via** [☐ phone | ☐ e-mail | ☐ fax] **by ______** *[how accomplished]*.

☐ **Greet and direct all customers in a professional manner, assisting them with ______, ______, and ______ while promoting company and going above and beyond to fulfill customer needs.**

☐ **Ensure all greetings leave a positive first impression by being** [☐ courteous | ☐ professional | ☐ helpful | ☐ businesslike | ☐ other: ______] **to all company visitors and callers.**

☐ **Screen and service all** [☐ internal | ☐ external | ☐ internal and outside] **calls in a professional manner, ensuring all callers get the help they need with** [☐ confidentiality | ☐ courtesy | ☐ follow-up | ☐ other: ______].

ACHIEVEMENT SAMPLES:

☐ **Through direct, consumer-sensitive approach and ______** *[other method]*, **increased** [☐ customer loyalty | ☐ repeat business | ☐ referrals | ☐ sales | ☐ other: ______].

☐ **Spearheaded cost-effective, high quality ______** *[type of]* [☐customer service | ☐ sales support] **program(s) that resulted in increased** [☐ annual sales of $______ *(amount)* | ☐ customer satisfaction levels of ______% *(percentage)* | ☐ other: ______].

☐ **Identified and implemented** [☐ cross-sell | ☐ upsell | ☐ add-on | ☐ other: ______] **opportunities, including ______ and ______ by** [☐ providing employee incentives | ☐ other method: ______], **resulting in ______** *[what benefit?]*.

☐ **Regularly obtain customer satisfaction through** [☐ quick resolution of customer issues regarding (☐ pricing / ☐ signing / ☐ company policies / ☐ returns) | ☐ other: ______] **ensuring the quality of customer service delivered meets high standards of excellence by** [☐ monitoring and evaluating staff's progress | ☐ other means: ______].

☐ **Convert customer desires into needs by ______** *[doing what?]*, **achieving** [☐ increased sales | ☐ repeat business | ☐ referrals | ☐ other achievement: ______] **for company**.

☐ **Developed and implemented a new ______** *[name of]* **Customer Service Program that ______** *[program purpose]* **resulting in $______** *[amount]* **in new business.**

Customer Service Management

☐ [☐ Manage and oversee | ☐ Facilitate] **all facets of customer service—from handling inquiries and assisting customers with their buying decisions to resolving problems with difficult customers using effective problem-solving techniques—resulting in superior customer service for this $______** *[revenues]* **______** *[type of]* **company with ______** *[#]* [☐ stores | ☐ locations | ☐ employees | ☐ accounts] **that sells ______** *[what?]* **to ______** *[type of]* **consumers.**

☐ [☐ Manage and oversee | ☐ Supervise] [☐ customer service operations | ☐ the distribution center | ☐ purchasing | ☐ other: ______] **of this ______** *[type of]* **firm that provides ______** *[type of]* [☐ products | ☐ services] **to the ______** *[which?]* **market.**

☐ **Manage and oversee all** [☐ customer service | ☐ order processing | ☐ merchandising | ☐ other: ______] **functions including** [☐ encoding products | ☐ preparing purchase orders | ☐ processing, tracing, and expediting all sales orders | ☐ taking phone orders | ☐ providing product research | ☐ answering customer inquiries about products and services | ☐ solving credit problems | ☐ facilitating data entry | ☐ resolving customer complaints | ☐ preparing monthly statements | ☐ handling client billing | ☐ checking customer orders on computer | ☐ resolving shipment delays | ☐ other: ______].

☐ **Lead and direct daily and long-range operations and ______** *[type of]* **project management for this $______** *[revenues]* **______** *[type of]* **firm.**

☐ **Direct and oversee** [☐ sales | ☐ customer service operations | ☐ warehouse | ☐ purchasing | ☐ stock level control | ☐ evaluation and reporting | ☐ contract negotiations | ☐ other: ______] **areas with operational budget responsibilities of $______** *[amount]*.

☐ **Oversee customer service operations of this ______** *[type of]* **firm that provides ______** *[type of]* **services to the ______** *[which?]* **market including providing customers with** [☐ advice | ☐ professional help | ☐ consultation | ☐ other: ______] **in ______** *[what functions?]*.

☐ **Plan and organize ______** *[whose?]* **work schedules to ensure** [☐ excellent customer service | ☐ availability of staff | ☐ optimum personnel utilization | ☐ successful completion of work activities | ☐ other benefits: ______].

☐ **Monitor, track, and review** [☐ service | ☐ productivity | ☐ product promotions | ☐ cash control | ☐ inventory control | ☐ auditing | ☐ training | ☐ other: ______] **ensuring compliance with all policies, procedures, and standards.**

☐ **Lead and direct** [☐ customer service | ☐ inventory management | ☐ receivables monitoring and reporting | ☐ stock level control | ☐ contract negotiations | ☐ purchasing | ☐ other: ______].

☐ **Work closely with ______** *[whom?]* **to address** [☐ business needs | ☐ client solutions] **in the development of ______** *[type of]* **project plans to meet those needs.**

ACHIEVEMENT SAMPLES: *See "Customer Service – General" and "Customer Complaints & Problem Resolution."*

Customer Service & Satisfaction Levels Improvement

See also "Customer Service Management," "Customer Complaints & Problem Resolution," and "Increased Account Base."

ACHIEVEMENT SAMPLES:

☐ **Fostered good business relationships with all** [☐ clients | ☐ customers | ☐ referral sources | ☐ other: ______] **by** [☐ successfully meeting their needs | ☐ being above board with all communications | ☐ other: ______], **which increased ______** *[which?]* **service levels from ______% to ______%** *[percentages]*.

☐ **Successfully achieved a** [☐ 100% | ☐ other: ______%] *[percentage]* **customer satisfaction rate by** [☐ providing superior customer service | ☐ completing all projects on time and within budget | ☐ answering all project-related questions | ☐ offering solutions | ☐

rectifying customer complaints and problems as they arose | ☐ resolving time-sensitive issues in an expedient manner | ☐ using effective problem-solving techniques | ☐ successfully appeasing dissatisfied customers and turning them into satisfied clients | ☐ using effective listening skills | ☐ accomplishing goal to turn every customer into a satisfied customer | ☐ other: ______].

☐ **Increased safety and customer satisfaction by** [☐ providing professional services | ☐ ensuring end-of-day clean up and debris removal from all work areas and sites | ☐ other: ______].

☐ **Spearheaded a successful customer service program that resulted in high customer satisfaction levels of ______%** *[percentage]* **and ______** *[other benefits?].*

☐ **Elevated levels of client satisfaction by ______%** *[percentage]* **by** [☐ providing knowledgeable service in a friendly manner | ☐ researching and resolving customer complaints in a timely fashion | ☐ other: ______].

☐ **Successfully achieved a** [☐ 100% | ☐ other: ______%] *[percentage]* **customer satisfaction rate by** [☐ providing superior customer service | ☐ answering all project-related questions | ☐ offering solutions | ☐ rectifying customer complaints and problems as they arose | ☐ resolving time-sensitive issues in an expedient manner | ☐ using effective problem-solving techniques | ☐ successfully appeasing dissatisfied customers and turning them into satisfied clients | ☐ using effective listening skills | ☐ accomplishing goal to turn every customer into a satisfied customer | ☐ other: ______].

☐ **Recommended and oversaw ______** *[what?]* **resulting in increased customer service levels of ______%** *[percentage]* **and profitability of $______** *[amount].*

☐ **Increased customer satisfaction level from ______% to ______%** *[percentages]* **at a value of $______** *[amount]* **annually by ______** *[doing what?].*

☐ **Through direct, consumer-sensitive approach and ______** *[other method],* **increased** [☐ customer loyalty | ☐ repeat business | ☐ referrals | ☐ sales | ☐ other: ______].

☐ **Reduced customer-service delivery time from ______** *[time]* **to ______** *[time]* **by ______** *[doing what?].*

☐ **Increased customer loyalty and satisfaction levels ______%** *[percentage]* **by** [☐ providing a direct consumer-sensitive approach | ☐ other methods: ______].

☐ **Conceptualized and developed seamless, cost-effective customer service strategies, such as ______, ______, and ______** *[type of strategies],* **resulting in ______** *[what benefits?].*

Drywall Installation

See **"Ceiling, Lathing, Insulation & Drywall Installation"** and **"Carpentry Work."**

Electrical – General

See also other Electrical and Electrician categories as well as **"Equipment, Tools & Testing Devices – Electrician," "Inspections & Compliance – Electrical,"** and **"Maintenance & Repair Projects."**

☐ **Install, maintain, service, and repair ______** *[type of]* **electrical** [☐ systems | ☐ equipment | ☐ components | ☐ instruments | ☐ apparatus | ☐ accessories | ☐ other: ______] **including** [☐ electrical equipment | ☐ electronic controllers | ☐ motors | ☐ starters | ☐ switches | ☐ fixtures | ☐ fuse boxes | ☐ coax cables | ☐ wiring | ☐ circuit breakers | ☐ lighting fixtures | ☐ electrical panels | ☐ cables | ☐ outlets | ☐ switches | ☐ pumps | ☐ fans | ☐ transformers | ☐ generators | ☐ other: ______] **for this ______** *[type of]* **firm.**

☐ **Install, maintain, repair, and/or replace** [☐ air compressors | ☐ steam boilers | ☐ pump seals, bearings, and couplings | ☐ gas boilers | ☐ electric boilers | ☐ water heaters | ☐ steam lines | ☐ heat return lines | ☐ main water lines | ☐ roof drains | ☐ motors | ☐ blower cages | ☐ electrical outlets | ☐ switches | ☐ lighting circuits | ☐ power lines | ☐ fan motors | ☐ plant lighting | ☐ windows | ☐ doors | ☐ walls | ☐ ceilings | ☐ furniture | ☐ railings | ☐ stair treads | ☐ gratings | ☐ faucets | ☐ toilets | ☐ urinals | ☐ other: ______] **of** [☐ heating | ☐ cooling | ☐ ventilating | ☐ refrigeration | ☐ other: ______] **systems for ______** *[what or whom?].*

☐ **Perform** [☐ installation | ☐ servicing | ☐ repair | ☐ rewiring | ☐ testing | ☐ inspection | ☐ troubleshooting | ☐ diagnosis | ☐ replacement | ☐ maintenance] **of** [☐ electrical | ☐ lighting | ☐ climate control | ☐ conduit | ☐ motor control | ☐ security | ☐ communications | ☐ intercom | ☐ signaling | ☐ bus bar | ☐ computer | ☐ fire alarm | ☐ industrial | ☐ digital | ☐ pneumatic tube | ☐ energy management | ☐ public address | ☐ other: ______] **systems for this $______** *[revenues]* [☐ electrician firm | ☐ general contractor | ☐ other: ______].

☐ **Serve as** [☐ journeyman electrician | ☐ apprentice | ☐ electrician | ☐ master electrician | ☐ lead electrician | ☐ other: ______] **on ______** *[#]* [☐ new home construction | ☐ commercial | ☐ other: ______] **projects.**

☐ **Perform** [☐ highly skilled | ☐ journeyman-level | ☐ apprentice-level | ☐ Master Electrician level] installation, repair, and trouble–shooting work of [☐ domestic | ☐ industrial | ☐ commercial] [☐ electrical | ☐ lighting | ☐ climate control | ☐ conduit | ☐ security |

☐ communications | ☐ signaling | ☐ computer | ☐ fire alarm | ☐ other: ______] [☐ systems | ☐ equipment | ☐ componentry | ☐ devices | ☐ other: ______] **for** ______ *[type of]* [☐ buildings | ☐ grounds | ☐ equipment | ☐ other: ______].

☐ **Install and repair** [☐ electrical equipment | ☐ electronic controls | ☐ other: ______] **used for** [☐ light | ☐ power circuits | ☐ automatically controlled circuits | ☐ elevators | ☐ conveyors | ☐ other: ______] **including** [☐ generators | ☐ conduits | ☐ transformers | ☐ programmable controllers | ☐ motor controllers | ☐ AC & DC motors | ☐ circuit breakers | ☐ heating units | ☐ pull boxes | ☐ switches | ☐ switchboards | ☐ transmission equipment | ☐ other: ______].

☐ **Inspect, service, troubleshoot, and repair** ______ *[type of]* **electrical systems for** ______ *[what?]* **ensuring compliance with all electrical and building codes, safety regulations, and customer specifications.**

☐ **Conduct** [☐ high-voltage | ☐ low-voltage | ☐ fiber optic | ☐ specialized | ☐ other: ______] **electrical work involved in the** [☐ installation | ☐ construction | ☐ remodeling | ☐ alteration | ☐ service | ☐ repair | ☐ other: ______] **of** [☐ public works | ☐ residential | ☐ industrial | ☐ commercial] [☐ electrical | ☐ climate control | ☐ security | ☐ communications | ☐ computer | ☐ fire alarm | ☐ other: ______] [☐ systems | ☐ equipment | ☐ components | ☐ instruments | ☐ devices | ☐ apparatus].

☐ **Install, repair, overhaul, and/or reconfigure** ______ *[type of]* [☐ alternating | ☐ direct current | ☐ other: ______] **electrical equipment, and maintain up-to-date documentation.**

ACHIEVEMENT SAMPLES:

☐ **Facilitated electrical wiring and installation for** ______ *[type of]* [☐ commercial | ☐ residential | ☐ other: ______] **construction projects, including** [☐ new construction | ☐ retrofits | ☐ remodels | ☐ reconfigurations | ☐ plant expansions | ☐ other: ______].

☐ [☐ Performed | ☐ Assisted in] **the complete** [☐ wiring | ☐ rewiring | ☐ reconfiguration | ☐ other: ______] **of** ______ *[what building, plant, or project?],* **which included** [☐ estimating job costs | ☐ scheduling electrical work | ☐ ordering parts and materials | ☐ overseeing the installation process | ☐ managing a staff of ______ *(#)* (☐ apprentices / ☐ electricians) | ☐ supervising quality control | ☐ ensuring electrical code compliance | ☐ billing clients | ☐ other: ______].

☐ **Completely re-wired a** ______ *[#]***-year-old,** ______ *[#]***-story** ______ *[type of]* **house, including** [☐ removing (☐ insulation / ☐ copper fittings) | ☐ installing ______ *(#)* ground faults | ☐ adding ______ *(#)* outlets | ☐ other: ______] **resulting in** ______ *[what benefits?].*

☐ **Developed specifications for the installation of** [☐ voltage transformers | ☐ overhead cables | ☐ underground cables | ☐ ______ *(type of)* electrical equipment | ☐ other: ______] **for conducting electrical energy from high-voltage distribution lines to consumers.**

☐ **Saved** [☐ the facility | ☐ clients] **$**______ *[amount]* **annually by implementing** ______ *[type of]* **energy-efficient solutions that** ______ *[did what?].*

☐ **Reviewed and upgraded** ______ *[type of]* **electrical systems including** ______ *[what?]* **by performing** ______ *[what functions?]* **ensuring electrical compatibility and compliance with all electrical codes, resulting in** ______ *[benefits].*

☐ **Installed, tested, and repaired** ______ *[type of]* [☐ electrical systems | ☐ electronic controllers | ☐ public works electrical equipment, overhead lines, and poles | ☐ telecommunications wiring and cable | ☐ lighting systems | ☐ intercom systems | ☐ climate control systems | ☐ fire alarm systems | ☐ low-voltage switching systems | ☐ high-voltage building panels | ☐ computer coax cables | ☐ conduit, conductors, and junction boxes | ☐ fuse boxes and circuit breakers | ☐ receptacles and switches | ☐ motors, transformers, and generators | ☐ security systems | ☐ signaling systems | ☐ bus bar | ☐ outlet boxes | ☐ receptacles | ☐ lighting systems | ☐ connectors | ☐ equipment | ☐ other: ______] **on** ______ *[type of]* **projects and hook up** [☐ primary | ☐ secondary] **power lines for** ______ *[purpose].*

☐ **Performed the upgrade of electrical wiring of** ______ *[#]*______ *[type of]* **workstations, which required** ______ *[what?]* **and resulted in** ______ *[what benefits?].*

☐ **Gained extensive experience in** [☐ electrical installations, repairs, and overhauls | ☐ complex troubleshooting and problem resolution | ☐ interpreting and following schematic diagrams, blueprints, and specifications | ☐ mastering the use of testing instruments | ☐ other: ______].

☐ **Designed and developed** ______ *[type of]* **electrical equipment that** ______ *[does what?],* **resulting in** ______ *[what benefits?].*

Electrical – Installations

See also other Electrical and Electrician categories as well as ***"Equipment, Tools & Testing Devices – Electrician," "Inspections & Compliance – Electrical,"*** *and* ***"Maintenance & Repair Projects."***

☐ **Read, interpret, and lay out** ______ *[type of]* **electrical work from** [☐ complex] [☐ electrical blueprints | ☐ schematic drawings | ☐ circuit diagrams | ☐ plans | ☐ specifications | ☐ manuals | ☐ written instructions | ☐ verbal instructions | ☐ other: ______] **following safety regulations, customer specifications, and company policies to** [☐ plan installation procedures | ☐ determine installation locations | ☐ install electrical equipment | ☐ other: ______].

☐ **Lay** [☐ inside | ☐ outside | ☐ underground | ☐ above-ground] [☐ conduit | ☐ electrical services | ☐ specialized electrical (☐ equipment / ☐ machinery) | ☐ conductors | (☐ single- / ☐ double- / ☐ triple-) phase electric cables | ☐ primary power lines | ☐ secondary service laterals | ☐ other: ______] **for** ______ *[what?]*.

☐ **Install complete electrical service on** [☐ new | ☐ existing] **construction in** [☐ upscale residential homes | ☐ apartment complexes | ☐ commercial buildings | ☐ public works projects | ☐ other: ______].

☐ **Facilitate installation of electrical** [☐ conduit | ☐ circuit breakers | ☐ switches | ☐ outlet boxes | ☐ cables | ☐ transformers | ☐ other: ______], **ensuring compliance with electrical code and OSHA practices**.

☐ **Install and maintain public works** [☐ electrical equipment | ☐ overhead lines | ☐ poles | ☐ other: ______] **used for the operation and control of** [☐ street lights | ☐ traffic signals | ☐ pumps | ☐ other: ______].

☐ **Conduct** [☐ high-voltage | ☐ low-voltage | ☐ fiber optic | ☐ specialized | ☐ other: ______] **electrical work involved in the** [☐ installation | ☐ construction | ☐ remodeling | ☐ alteration | ☐ maintenance | ☐ service | ☐ repair | ☐ other: ______] **of** [☐ public works | ☐ residential | ☐ industrial | ☐ commercial] [☐ electrical | ☐ electronic | ☐ climate control | ☐ security | ☐ communications | ☐ computer | ☐ fire alarm | ☐ other: ______] [☐ systems | ☐ equipment | ☐ componentry | ☐ instruments | ☐ devices | ☐ apparatus].

☐ **Assemble, install, and check** [☐ electrical | ☐ plumbing | ☐ mechanical | ☐ structural | ☐ other: ______] [☐ equipment | ☐ components | ☐ accessories | ☐ other: ______] **using hand and power tools.**

☐ **Install and test** ______, ______, **and** ______ *[what?]* **used for** ______ *[type of]* [☐ generators | ☐ conduits | ☐ transformers | ☐ controllers | ☐ motors | ☐ equipment | ☐ other: ______].

☐ **Install, operate, and test** [☐ commercial | ☐ industrial | ☐ residential | ☐ public works] **electrical** [☐ systems | ☐ equipment | ☐ components | ☐ other: ______] **ensuring correct** [☐ loads | ☐ amps | ☐ voltage | ☐ other: ______].

☐ **Install low-voltage wiring for** [☐ security systems | ☐ fire alarms | ☐ video systems | ☐ telephones | ☐ other: ______].

ACHIEVEMENT SAMPLES: *See Achievements under* ***"Electrical – General."***

Electrical – Maintenance & Repair Work

See also other Electrical and Electrician categories as well as ***"Equipment, Tools & Testing Devices – Electrician," "Inspections & Compliance – Electrical,"*** *and* ***"Maintenance & Repair Projects."***

☐ **Troubleshoot, diagnose, repair, and/or replace defective** [☐ parts | ☐ wiring | ☐ componentry | ☐ other: ______] **associated with** [☐ motors | ☐ starters | ☐ switches | ☐ pumps | ☐ fans | ☐ controls | ☐ fuse boxes | ☐ circuit breakers | ☐ electronic controllers | ☐ transformers | ☐ generators | ☐ other: ______] **for** ______ *[type of]* [☐ high-voltage | ☐ low-voltage ☐ variable frequency | ☐ wiring | ☐ other: ______] [☐ systems | ☐ electrical equipment | ☐ machinery | ☐ other: ______].

☐ **Monitor, troubleshoot, and repair** [☐ electrical | ☐ electronic] **control circuits, identify any safety or operational problems, and immediately resolve them.**

☐ **Perform maintenance and repair work on** ______ *[type of]* **electrical** [☐ wiring | ☐ equipment | ☐ motor controls | ☐ instruments | ☐ other: ______] **including** [☐ servicing | ☐ testing | ☐ inspecting | ☐ calibrating | ☐ replacing | ☐ lubricating | ☐ regulating | ☐ fine-tuning | ☐ other: ______] **for** ______ *[what?]*.

☐ **Conduct electrical maintenance and repair work and regular and preventive maintenance checks on** ______ *[what?]* **in compliance with all electrical codes and regulations.**

☐ **Service and maintain all types of** [☐ electrical | ☐ electronic] [☐ systems | ☐ equipment | ☐ components | ☐ instruments | ☐ apparatus | ☐ accessories | ☐ other: ______] **for** ______ *[what?]* **including** [☐ electronic controls | ☐ motors | ☐ starters | ☐ switches | ☐ fixtures | ☐ pumps | ☐ fans | ☐ controls | ☐ fuse boxes | ☐ circuit breakers | ☐ transformers | ☐ other: ______].

☐ **Troubleshoot, diagnose, repair, and test electrical problems in the facility's** [☐ power distribution | ☐ electrical equipment | ☐ instrument and control wiring | ☐ lighting systems | ☐ other: ______].

☐ **Facilitate** [☐ electrical | ☐ electronic] **repair of** ______ *[type of]* [☐ generators | ☐ air conditioning units | ☐ air compressors | ☐ water pumps | ☐ water heaters | ☐ motors | ☐ elevators | ☐ other: ______] **in compliance with all codes.**

☐ **Conduct troubleshooting and diagnostic work on** ______ *[type of]* [☐ electrical | ☐ electronic] **equipment including** [☐ lighting | ☐ climate control | ☐ conduit | ☐ motor control | ☐ security | ☐ communications | ☐ intercom | ☐ signaling | ☐ bus bar | ☐ computer | ☐ fire alarm | ☐ industrial | ☐ digital | ☐ pneumatic tube | ☐ energy management | ☐ public address | ☐ other: ______] **systems**.

☐ **Troubleshoot, maintain, and repair** [☐ electrical | ☐ electronic] [☐ equipment | ☐ motor controls | ☐ other: ______] **ensuring all** ______ *[type of]* **systems and equipment operate efficiently and all repairs are performed in a timely, professional manner.**

☐ **Use various methods and techniques to troubleshoot, isolate, diagnose, and repair defects and/or malfunctions in** [☐ high-voltage circuits | ☐ distribution systems | ☐ electrical controls | ☐ programmable logic controllers | ☐ motor control centers | ☐ cable runs | ☐ motors | ☐ ______ *(type of)* electrical equipment | ☐ wiring | ☐ switches | ☐ other: ______].

ACHIEVEMENT SAMPLES: *See Achievements under* ***"Electrical – General."***

Electrical – Projects & Functions

See also other Electrical and Electrician categories as well as ***"Equipment, Tools & Testing Devices – Electrician," "Inspections & Compliance – Electrical,"*** *and* ***"Maintenance & Repair Projects."***

☐ **Maintain emergency** [☐ lighting system | ☐ generator | ☐ other: ______] **and the proper operation of all equipment through regular scheduled** [☐ maintenance checks | ☐ safety inspections] **to ensure the** [☐ physical | ☐ mechanical | ☐ electrical | ☐ other: ______] **aspects of the facility run smoothly**.

☐ **Facilitate various electrical functions for** ______ *[type of]* **public works projects including** [☐ repairing underground conduits | ☐ trimming trees for wire clearance | ☐ operating underground cable locators to find, and updating maps to include, cable locations and underground faults | ☐ operating (☐ pickup trucks / ☐ digger derricks / ☐ bucket trucks / ☐ other: ______].

☐ **Operate and maintain a** ______ *[#]***-volt** [☐ high-tension | ☐ other: ______] **distribution systems including** ______ *[what functions?].*

☐ **Ensure that** [☐ buildings | ☐ facilities | ☐ grounds | ☐ employees | ☐ customers and others] **are safe and secure by** [☐ following safe work procedures | ☐ exercising a high degree of awareness | ☐ complying with all safety codes | ☐ other: ______] **and applying** [☐ an expert | ☐ a proficient | ☐ a working] **knowledge of** [☐ National Electric Code | ☐ electrical standards and practices | ☐ materials and tools of the electrical trade | ☐ occupational hazards | ☐ safety precautions | ☐ other: ______] **in performing all electrician functions.**

☐ **Handle administrative functions including** [☐ responding to emergency customer callbacks | ☐ completing work orders | ☐ preparing maintenance logs | ☐ ensuring quality control standards are met | ☐ keeping abreast of equipment improvements | ☐ training other Electricians in the installation and repair of electrical systems | ☐ other: ______].

☐ **Follow electrical** [☐ blueprints | ☐ schematic drawings | ☐ circuit diagrams | ☐ plans | ☐ other: ______] **to determine** [☐ circuit locations | ☐ outlets | ☐ load centers | ☐ panel boards | ☐ other: ______] in the installation and repair of ______ *[what?].*

☐ **Perform** [☐ highly-specialized | ☐ complex | ☐ routine] **electrical work for** ______ *[#]* [☐ clients | ☐ departments | ☐ buildings | ☐ other: ______] **in the areas of** [☐ heating | ☐ refrigeration | ☐ generators | ☐ motors | ☐ fire alarms | ☐ other: ______].

☐ **Facilitate** [☐ large-scale | ☐ complex] ______ *[type of]* **electrical projects for** [☐ commercial | ☐ residential | ☐ industrial | ☐ other: ______] **clients.**

☐ **Perform** ______ *[type of]* [☐ control wiring | ☐ welding | ☐ fabrication | ☐ other: ______] **of** ______ *[what?]* **facility electrical systems and other electrical and mechanical work.**

ACHIEVEMENT SAMPLES: *See Achievements under* ***"Electrical – General."***

Electrical – Testing

See ***"Inspections & Compliance – Electrical."***

Electrical – Tools & Equipment Usage

See ***"Equipment, Tools & Testing Devices – Electrical."***

Electrician Management – General

See also other Electrical and Electrician categories as well as ***"Equipment, Tools & Testing Devices – Electrician," "Inspections & Compliance – Electrical,"*** *and* ***"Maintenance & Repair Projects."***

☐ **Plan and supervise all phases of** ______ *[type of]* **electrical wiring projects in** [☐ commercial | ☐ residential | ☐ industrial | ☐ public works | ☐ other: ______] **settings including repairing and maintaining** [☐ electrical | ☐ electronic] [☐ systems | ☐ motors | ☐ devices | ☐ control panels | ☐ conduit | ☐ switches | ☐ other: ______] **for this** ______ *[type of]* **firm.**

☐ **Provide electrician oversight in the installation, maintenance, and servicing of** ______ *[type of]* **electrical** [☐ systems | ☐ equipment | ☐ components | ☐ instruments | ☐ apparatus | ☐ accessories | ☐ other: ______] **including** [☐ electronic controls | ☐ motors | ☐ starters | ☐ switches | ☐ fixtures | ☐ fuses | ☐ other: ______].

☐ **Provide decisive leadership and clear direction in all phases of** [☐ large-scale | ☐ complex] ______ *[type of]* **electrical projects for** [☐ commercial | ☐ residential | ☐ industrial | ☐ other: ______] **clients overseeing a top-performing team of** ______ *[#]*

electricians.

☐ **Manage and oversee the** [☐ installation | ☐ repair | ☐ rewiring | ☐ testing | ☐ inspection | ☐ troubleshooting | ☐ diagnosis | ☐ replacement | ☐ maintenance | ☐ servicing | ☐ other: ______] **of** [☐ electrical | ☐ lighting | ☐ climate control | ☐ conduit | ☐ motor control | ☐ telecommunications | ☐ security | ☐ intercom | ☐ signaling | ☐ computer | ☐ fire alarm | ☐ industrial | ☐ digital | ☐ pneumatic tube | ☐ energy management | ☐ public address | ☐ other: ______] **systems for this** [☐ multimillion-dollar | ☐ $______] [☐ electrical contractor | ☐ industrial plant | ☐ public services company | ☐ other: ______].

☐ **Lead and direct the installation, maintenance, and repair of** [☐ electrical equipment | ☐ electronic controls | ☐ other: ______] **used for** [☐ lighting | ☐ power circuits | ☐ automatically controlled circuits | ☐ elevators | ☐ conveyors | ☐ other: ______] **including** [☐ generators | ☐ conduits | ☐ transformers | ☐ programmable controllers | ☐ motor controllers | ☐ AC & DC motors | ☐ circuit breakers | ☐ heating units | ☐ pull boxes | ☐ switches | ☐ transmission equipment | ☐ other: ______].

☐ **Monitor and oversee** [☐ electrical installations | ☐ instrument and control wiring | ☐ control center wiring | ☐ other: ______], **ensuring all equipment and installations meet electrical code.**

☐ **Provide** [☐ highly skilled | ☐ Master Electrician level] installation, repair, and troubleshooting oversight of [☐ domestic | ☐ industrial | ☐ commercial] [☐ electrical | ☐ lighting | ☐ climate control | ☐ conduit | ☐ security | ☐ communications | ☐ signaling | ☐ computer | ☐ fire alarm | ☐ other: ______] [☐ systems | ☐ equipment | ☐ componentry | ☐ devices] **for** ______ *[type of]* [☐ buildings | ☐ grounds | ☐ equipment | ☐ other: ______].

☐ **Supervise all electrical work involved in the** [☐ installation | ☐ construction | ☐ remodeling | ☐ alteration | ☐ maintenance | ☐ service | ☐ repair | ☐ other: ______] **of** [☐ public works | ☐ residential | ☐ industrial | ☐ commercial] [☐ electrical | ☐ electronic | ☐ climate control | ☐ security | ☐ communications | ☐ computer | ☐ fire alarm | ☐ other: ______] [☐ systems | ☐ equipment | ☐ components | ☐ instruments | ☐ devices | ☐ apparatus].

☐ **Oversee and direct the installation, maintenance, and repair of** [☐ electrical equipment | ☐ electronic controls | ☐ other: ______] **used for** [☐ light | ☐ power circuits | ☐ automatically controlled circuits | ☐ elevators | ☐ conveyors | ☐ other: ______] including [☐ generators | ☐ conduits | ☐ transformers | ☐ programmable controllers | ☐ motor controllers | ☐ AC & DC motors | ☐ circuit breakers | ☐ heating units | ☐ pull boxes | ☐ switches | ☐ switchboards | ☐ transmission equipment | ☐ other: ______].

ACHIEVEMENT SAMPLES: *See Achievements under **"Electrical – General."***

Electrician Management – Functions

*See also other Electrical and Electrician categories as well as **"Equipment, Tools & Testing Devices – Electrical," "Inspections & Compliance – Electrical,"** and **"Maintenance & Repair Projects."***

☐ **Oversee the installation and repair of various** [☐ domestic | ☐ industrial | ☐ commercial] systems including [☐ electrical | ☐ lighting | ☐ climate control | ☐ conduit | ☐ security | ☐ communications | ☐ signaling | ☐ computer | ☐ fire alarm | ☐ other: ______] **for** ______ *[type of]* [☐ buildings |☐ grounds | ☐ equipment | ☐ other: ______].

☐ **Supervise and coordinate electrical work involved in the** [☐ installation | ☐ construction | ☐ remodeling | ☐ alteration | ☐ maintenance | ☐ service | ☐ repair | ☐ other: ______] **of** [☐ public works | ☐ residential | ☐ industrial | ☐ commercial] [☐ electrical | ☐ electronic | ☐ climate control | ☐ security | ☐ communications | ☐ computer | ☐ fire alarm | ☐ other: ______] [☐ systems | ☐ equipment | ☐ componentry | ☐ instruments | ☐ devices | ☐ apparatus].

☐ **Assist Electricians with the installation, testing, and repair of** ______ *[type of]* [☐ electrical systems | ☐ electronic controllers | ☐ public works electrical equipment, overhead lines, and poles | ☐ telecommunications wiring and cable | ☐ lighting systems | ☐ intercom systems | ☐ climate control systems | ☐ fire alarm systems | ☐ low-voltage switching systems | ☐ high-voltage building panels | ☐ computer coax cables | ☐ conduit, conductors, and junction boxes | ☐ fuse boxes and circuit breakers | ☐ motors, transformers, and generators | ☐ security systems | ☐ signaling systems | ☐ lighting systems | ☐ equipment | ☐ other: ______] **on** ______ *[type of]* **projects.**

☐ **Lead and direct electrical functions for** ______ *[type of]* **public works projects including** [☐ repairing underground conduits | ☐ trimming trees for wire clearance | ☐ operating underground cable locators to find, and updating maps to include, cable locations and underground faults | ☐ operating (☐ pickup trucks / ☐ digger derricks / ☐ bucket trucks / ☐ other: ______)].

☐ **Manage the inspection, servicing, and repair of** ______ *[type of]* **electrical systems for** ______ *[what?]* **ensuring compliance with all electrical codes, safety regulations, customer specifications, and company policies.**

☐ **Inspect Electrician work to evaluate and ensure compliance with electrical codes, quality work performance, and** [☐ electrical compatibility | ☐ component safety | ☐ operating problems are resolved | ☐ performance criteria | ☐ other: ______].

☐ **Inspect, test, and calibrate** ______ *[type of]* [☐ electrical devices | ☐ equipment | ☐ structures | ☐ materials | ☐ other: ______] **to identify and solve** ______ *[type of]* **problems or defects using specialized electrical testing equipment.**

☐ **Manage and oversee electrical and administrative functions including** [☐ responding to emergency customer callbacks | ☐ completing work orders | ☐ developing maintenance schedules | ☐ estimating job time and materials | ☐ preparing cost estimates

| ☐ handling subcontractor contract negotiations | ☐ meeting with clients | ☐ calculating electrical equipment requirements | ☐ ordering electrical parts and supplies | ☐ coordinating materials shipping | ☐ documenting maintenance logs | ☐ ensuring quality control standards are met | ☐ keeping abreast of equipment improvements | ☐ training Electricians in the installation and repair of electrical systems | ☐ documenting performance standards | ☐ interpreting electrical circuit diagrams | ☐ evaluating performance criteria | ☐ ensuring component safety | ☐ inspecting and testing electrical equipment | ☐ developing specifications | ☐ handling inventory management and control | ☐ other: ______].

☐ **Maintain emergency** [☐ lighting system | ☐ generator | ☐ other: ______] **and the proper operation of all equipment to ensure the** [☐ physical | ☐ mechanical | ☐ electrical | ☐ other: ______] **aspects of the facility run smoothly.**

☐ **Test, troubleshoot, and diagnose electrical** [☐ circuits | ☐ equipment | ☐ installations | ☐ machinery | ☐ components | ☐ devices | ☐ other: ______] **of** [☐ safety equipment | ☐ emergency lighting | ☐ generators | ☐ other: ______] **to locate and correct** ______ *[type of]* **problems and ensure compliance with all electrical codes.**

☐ **Direct and manage the installation and repair of** [☐ domestic | ☐ industrial | ☐ commercial] [☐ electrical | ☐ lighting | ☐ climate control | ☐ conduit | ☐ security | ☐ communications | ☐ signaling | ☐ computer | ☐ fire alarm | ☐ other: ______] [☐ systems | ☐ equipment | ☐ components | ☐ devices] **for** ______ *[type of]* [☐ buildings | ☐ grounds | ☐ equipment | ☐ other: ______].

☐ **Manage and oversee electrical maintenance and repair work and regular and preventive maintenance checks on** ______ *[what?]* **to ensure compliance with all electrical codes and regulations.**

ACHIEVEMENT SAMPLES: *See Achievements under **"Electrical – General."***

Electrician Supervision

*See also **"Staff Management & Supervision," "Team Leadership & Direction,"** and/or **"Trades/Crew Supervision,"** as applicable.*

☐ **Supervise the day-to-day activities of** ______ *[#]* [☐ Electricians | ☐ Mechanics | ☐ Apprentices | ☐ other: ______] **in their performance of** ______, ______, **and** ______ *[what functions?].*

☐ **Lead, guide, and train** ______ *[#]* **Electricians in the installation and maintenance of electronic controls for** [☐ construction | ☐ maintenance | ☐ other: ______] **business equipment applying and meeting all electrical principles and codes.**

☐ **Schedule and supervise** ______ *[#]* **Electricians in the inspection, maintenance, troubleshooting, and repair of** ______ *[type of]* **electrical systems for** ______ *[what?]* **ensuring compliance with all codes and specifications.**

☐ **Guide and support Electricians in their troubleshooting and diagnosing of** ______ *[type of]* [☐ electrical | ☐ lighting | ☐ climate control | ☐ conduit | ☐ motor control | ☐ security | ☐ communications | ☐ intercom | ☐ signaling | ☐ bus bar | ☐ computer | ☐ fire alarm | ☐ industrial | ☐ digital | ☐ pneumatic tube | ☐ energy management | ☐ public address | ☐ other: ______] **systems.**

☐ **Oversee** ______ *[#]* **electricians and coordinate trades work in the installation of** [☐ electrical equipment | ☐ electronic controls | ☐ electrical outlets and switches | ☐ other: ______] **for** [☐ lighting systems | ☐ power circuits | ☐ automatically controlled circuits | ☐ elevators | ☐ conveyors | ☐ other: ______] **including** [☐ generators | ☐ conduits | ☐ transformers | ☐ programmable controllers | ☐ motor controllers | ☐ AC & DC motors | ☐ circuit breakers | ☐ heating units | ☐ pull boxes | ☐ switches | ☐ switchboards | ☐ transmission equipment | ☐ lighting circuits | ☐ new equipment power lines | ☐ fan motors | ☐ plant lighting | ☐ other: ______] **to ensure all electrical codes and principles are followed.**

☐ **Supervise and oversee Electrician performance of** [☐ highly-specialized | ☐ complex | ☐ routine | ☐ other: ______] **electrical work for** ______ *[#]* [☐ clients | ☐ departments | ☐ buildings | ☐ other: ______] in the areas of [☐ heating | ☐ refrigeration | ☐ generator equipment | ☐ motors | ☐ fire alarms | ☐ other: ______] **ensuring quality control.**

☐ **Facilitate electrician oversight in the** [☐ installation | ☐ repair | ☐ rewiring | ☐ testing | ☐ inspection | ☐ troubleshooting | ☐ diagnosis | ☐ replacement | ☐ maintenance | ☐ servicing] **of** [☐ electrical | ☐ lighting | ☐ climate control | ☐ conduit | ☐ motor control | ☐ security | ☐ communications | ☐ intercom | ☐ signaling | ☐ bus bar | ☐ computer | ☐ fire alarm | ☐ industrial | ☐ digital | ☐ pneumatic tube | ☐ energy management | ☐ public address | ☐ other: ______] **systems covering** [☐ electronic controls | ☐ motors | ☐ starters | ☐ switches | ☐ fixtures | ☐ fuses | ☐ coax cables | ☐ wiring | ☐ lighting fixtures | ☐ electrical panels | ☐ cables | ☐ outlets | ☐ other: ______].

☐ **Oversee** ______ *[#]* **electricians in the installation, maintenance, and servicing of** ______ *[type of]* **electrical** [☐ systems | ☐ equipment | ☐ components | ☐ instruments | ☐ apparatus | ☐ accessories | ☐ other: ______] **including** [☐ electronic controls | ☐ motors | ☐ starters | ☐ switches | ☐ fixtures | ☐ fuses | ☐ other: ______].

☐ **Oversee electricians in the installation and maintenance of electronic controls for** [☐ construction | ☐ maintenance | ☐ other: ______] **business equipment and machinery applying all electrical principles and meeting codes.**

ACHIEVEMENT SAMPLES: *See Achievements under **"Electrical – General."***

Electrician Tools & Testing Devices

See "Equipment Tools & Testing Devices – Electrical."

Employee Retention & Decreased Turnover

ACHIEVEMENT SAMPLES:

☐ **Improved** [☐ executive | ☐ management | ☐ employee | ☐ labor] **retention by** [☐ recruiting top talent | ☐ building loyal employee-employer relationships | ☐ allowing for job flexibility | ☐ improving overall communications | ☐ fostering strong internal relationships | ☐ offering recognition and appreciation | ☐ following through on promises | ☐ increasing decision-making authority and accountability | ☐ empowering subordinates to succeed | ☐ adding meaning to employee career challenges | ☐ other: ________]* **through the development and execution of** [☐ a formal employee retention program | ☐ direct report surveys | ☐ other program: ______] **company-wide.** **Ideas generated from Hornberger Management Company human resource surveys.*

☐ **Increased morale and minimized turnover through** [☐ mutual respect | ☐ honesty | ☐ effective two-way communication | ☐ other: ______], **which provided a healthy and positive environment that allowed employees to succeed and the company to grow.**

☐ **Minimized turnover ______%** *[percentage]* [☐ achieving the lowest employee turnover rate in the (☐ firm's | ☐ department's) history] **by** [☐ implementing proactive hiring policies | ☐ facilitating ongoing training and development programs | ☐ improving employee morale and staff loyalty | ☐ creating a positive and proactive atmosphere | ☐ developing reachable but challenging goals | ☐ elevating employee satisfaction with their jobs | ☐ treating all employees fairly | ☐ providing equal opportunity for promotion | ☐ other: ______].

☐ **Decreased employee turnover ______% (from ______% to ______%)** *[percentages]* **by** ______ *[doing what?],* **which resulted in** ______ *[what additional benefits?].*

☐ **Retained ______%** *[percentage]* **of recruited** [☐ employees | ☐ management staff] **and minimized turnover ______%** *[percentage]* [☐ achieving the lowest employee turnover rate in the (☐ firm's / ☐ department's) history] **by** [☐ implementing proactive (☐ recruitment policies / ☐ succession planning programs / ☐ other: ______) | ☐ facilitating ongoing training and development programs | ☐ improving employee morale and staff loyalty | ☐ creating a positive and proactive atmosphere | ☐ developing reachable but challenging goals | ☐ elevating employee satisfaction with their jobs | ☐ allowing all employees to feel they have a stake in the firm | ☐ promoting top-notch staff | ☐ other: ______].

☐ **Maximized** [☐ employee morale | ☐ productivity | ☐ other: ______] **and improved job turnover rate by** [☐ effectively using employee skills and talents | ☐ providing training opportunities to enhance employees' skills | ☐ elevating employee satisfaction with their jobs | ☐ other: ______].

☐ **Achieved the lowest employee turnover rate in the firm's history by implementing** [☐ proactive hiring policies | ☐ ongoing training and development programs | ☐ other achievement: ______].

☐ **Maintain one of the lowest employee turnover ratios of ______%** *[percentage]* **in the** [☐ district | ☐ region | ☐ department | ☐ company | ☐ other: ______] **due to the implementation of** [☐ proactive hiring and training policies | ☐ ongoing training and development | ☐ effective mentoring | ☐ productivity monitoring | ☐ other achievement: ______].

☐ **Through effective use of** _______ *[what initiatives?],* **increased employee morale and minimized turnover, which resulted in** [☐ an extremely low turnover rate for the industry | ☐ an employee turnover ratio of ______% *(percentage)* | ☐ an annual cost savings of $______ *(amount)* | ☐ other benefits: ______].

☐ **Improved** [☐ employee morale | ☐ productivity | ☐ job turnover rate | ☐ other: ______] **by** [☐ effectively using employee skills and talents | ☐ providing training opportunities to enhance employees' skills | ☐ elevating employee satisfaction with their jobs | ☐ other: ______].

☐ **Minimized turnover ______%** *[percentage]* **by increasing** [☐ employee morale | ☐ staff loyalty | ☐ other: ______] **by** [☐ using morale-building techniques | ☐ creating a positive and proactive atmosphere | ☐ developing reachable but challenging goals | ☐ treating all employees fairly | ☐ providing equal opportunity for promotion | ☐ enforcing company guidelines | ☐ other: ______].

Environmental, Safety & Health Management Compliance

See also "Safety & Responsibility for Others."

☐ **Research, evaluate, and develop methods, plans, and specifications that ensure** [☐ quality air | ☐ clean water | ☐ solid waste removal | ☐ hazardous materials pollution control | ☐ other: ______], **addressing all environmental, safety, and health concerns.**

☐ **Determine pollution levels in** ______ *[what?]* **and recommend required actions to ensure compliance with all environmental control legislation and regulations.**

- ☐ **Manage and oversee the firm's environmental, safety, and health activities including ______, ______, and ______** *[which activities?]* **to ensure compliance with the** [☐ Occupational Safety and Health Act (OSHA) | ☐ Environmental, Safety, and Health Management Policy (ES&HMP) | ☐ Environmental Management System (EMS) | ☐ Resource Conservation and Recovery Act (RCRA) | ☐ Environmental Protection Act (EPA) | ☐ Clean Air Act (CAA) | ☐ Clean Water Act (CWA) | ☐ Safe Drinking Water Act (SDWA) | ☐ Superfund Amendments and Reauthorization Act (SARA) | ☐ National Ambient Air Quality Standard (NAAQS) | ☐ Toxic Substances Control Act (TSCA) | ☐ Comprehensive Environmental Response, Compensation, and Liability Act (CERCLA) | ☐ Code of Federal Regulations (CFR) | ☐ National Emission Standards for Hazardous Air Pollutants (NESHAP) | ☐ other: ______].
- ☐ [☐ Develop | ☐ Administer] **the firm's Health and Safety Program by** [☐ updating the Employee Safety Manual | ☐ ensuring compliance with current OSHA requirements | ☐ preparing health and safety staff bulletins | ☐ serving on the firm's Health and Safety Committee | ☐ scheduling and planning employee Wellness Training Programs | ☐ conducting safety meetings | ☐ other: ______].
- ☐ **Coordinate and oversee field investigations that review and evaluate ______** *[type of]* **activities related to** [☐ department buildings | ☐ equipment operations | ☐ work procedures | ☐ other: ______] **to ensure compliance with all safety practices and standards.**
- ☐ [☐ Administer | ☐ Co-administer] **the firm's Health and Safety Program by** [☐ writing and updating the Employee Safety Manual | ☐ ensuring compliance with current OSHA requirements | ☐ preparing health and safety staff bulletins | ☐ serving on the firm's Health and Safety Committee | ☐ scheduling and planning employee Wellness Training Programs | ☐ other: ______].
- ☐ **Manage daily environmental compliance issues, interpret applicable regulations, and provide regulatory support to ______** *[whom?]* **ensuring** [☐ plant | ☐ site | ☐ process | ☐ operational | ☐ other: ______] **compliance with state, local, and federal requirements.**
- ☐ **Promote** [☐ environmental | ☐ health | ☐ project | ☐ worksite | ☐ other: ______] **safety and health by ______** *[doing or applying what?].*
- ☐ **Review, evaluate, and interpret** [☐ proposed] [☐ air- | ☐ water- | ☐ soil- | ☐ other: ______] **related environmental** [☐ regulations | ☐ EPA documentation | ☐ compliance requirements | ☐ other: ______] **for** [☐ environmental | ☐ industrial | ☐ financial | ☐ public | ☐ other: ______] **impact on ______** *[what?]* **and interact with** [☐ federal | ☐ state | ☐ local] **regulators to resolve compliance issues.**
- ☐ **Implement and maintain Title V compliance for ______** *[what?]* **by way of ______** *[doing what?].*
- ☐ [☐ Establish | ☐ Update] **the firm's** [☐ compliance | ☐ operational] **processes, report questionable activities, investigate complaints, resolve incidents, and audit the performance of its** [☐ Compliance Program | ☐ Environmental, Safety, and Health Management Policy | ☐ other: ______].
- ☐ **Review and interpret ______** *[type of]* **environmental regulations, anticipate new regulations, and apply environmental principles to ______** *[type of]* **operations to minimize their impact on operations and ensure compliance with all regulations.**
- ☐ **Manage this ______** *[type of]* **firm's environmental compliance issues in the areas of ______, ______, and ______** *[areas].*
- ☐ **Notify** [☐ senior management | ☐ Corporate Compliance | ☐ Compliance Officer | ☐ other: ______] **of** [☐ audit findings | ☐ areas of compliance vulnerability | ☐ associated risk | ☐ unresolved compliance issues | ☐ status of compliance efforts | ☐ other: ______] **involving potential** [☐ regulatory issues | ☐ safety hazards | ☐ environmental concerns | ☐ ______ *(type of)* exposures | ☐ job-related accidents | ☐ personal injuries | ☐ potential work-related illnesses | ☐ other: ______].
- ☐ **Compile, set up, and review ______** *[type of]* **databases for tracking** [☐ permit compliance | ☐ record keeping requirements | ☐ other: ______].

ACHIEVEMENT SAMPLES:

- ☐ **Developed and administered he firm's Health and Safety Program by** [☐ ensuring compliance with current OSHA requirements | ☐ preparing health and safety staff bulletins | ☐ serving on the firm's Health and Safety Committee | ☐ updating the Employee Safety Manual | ☐ scheduling and planning employee Wellness Training Programs | ☐ conducting safety meetings | ☐ other: ______].
- ☐ **Maintain optimum** [☐ company | ☐ facility | ☐ building] **safety and security by** [☐ overseeing supply orders | ☐ ensuring accounting reconciliation | ☐ minimizing materials theft | ☐ filing theft reports | ☐ other: ______] **and implementing safety procedures in accordance with** [☐ OSHA | ☐ other: ______] **regulations.**
- ☐ **Developed and delivered Safety Management Systems for major ______** *[type of]* [☐ construction projects | ☐ turnaround ventures | ☐ other: ______] **ensuring all client requirements, governmental regulations, and company procedures were met.**
- ☐ **Achieved safety performance levels to ______** *[what level?]* **from previous incident rate of ______** *[what level?]* **by ______** *[doing what?],* **ensuring overall business and personnel safety and security.**
- ☐ **Decreased controllable expenses by $______** *[amount]* **over previous year by implementing improved ______** *[type of]* [☐ safety programs | ☐ security programs | ☐ safety awareness | ☐ other: ______] **that ______** *[does what?],* **resulting in ______** *[what benefits?].*
- ☐ **Recommended and implemented ______** *[type of]* **safety features that reduced ______** *[whose?]* **exposure to**

[☐ chemical | ☐ physical | ☐ biological | ☐ other: ______] **hazards in support of the firm's environmental goals.**

☐ **Performed environmental compliance in the areas of** [☐ wastewater treatment operations and testing | ☐ storm-water testing and permitting | ☐ well testing monitoring | ☐ yearly stack testing | ☐ hazardous waste removal | ☐ solid waste storage | ☐ materials recycling program | ☐ dust collector performance evaluations | ☐ continuous emissions monitoring | ☐ other: ______], **resolving** ______ *[type of]* **issues by** ______ *[doing what?].*

☐ **Evaluated hazardous conditions in** ______ *[what?]* **and developed** ______ *[type of]* **hazard control methods that ensure compliance with all environmental, health, and safety regulations in the design and development of** ______ *[what?].*

☐ **Designed and developed** ______ *[what?]* **projects that considered the impact on the environment by** ______ *[doing what?].*

☐ **Developed, implemented, and provided training on** [☐ environmental | ☐ health | ☐ safety | ☐ other: ______] **procedures insofar as tracking the compliance status of** ______ *[what?].*

☐ **Performed environmental compliance management and oversight at** ______ *[#]* ______ *[type of]* **facilities including the** [☐ review of federal, state, and local (☐ regulations | ☐ submittals) | ☐ involvement with ______ *(type of)* systems design | ☐ other: ______].

☐ **Coordinated and oversaw field investigations that review and evaluate** ______ *[type of]* **activities related to** [☐ department buildings | ☐ equipment operations | ☐ work procedures | ☐ other: ______] **to ensure compliance with all safety practices and standards.**

Equipment, Tools & Testing Devices – General

*See also **"Heavy Equipment Operations"** and other **"Equipment, Tools & Testing Devices"** categories.*

☐ **Operate and maintain all** ______ *[trade]* **equipment, machinery, and tools including** ______, ______, **and** ______ *[equipment]* **to ensure safe operating condition, abiding by all safety rules and precautions.**

☐ **Provide production management oversight to a staff of** ______ *[#]* **in the set-up and operation of** ______ *[type of]* **equipment to produce** ______ *[what?].*

☐ **Lead and direct the operation of** ______ *[type of]* [☐ heavy] **equipment used to** [☐ produce | ☐ develop | ☐ manufacture | ☐ test | ☐ other: ______] ______ *[what?].*

☐ [☐ Manage and oversee | ☐ Set up and operate] ______ *[type of]* **equipment for the** [☐ construction | ☐ production | ☐ installation | ☐ other: ______] **of** ______ *[what?].*

☐ **Follow safety precautions using protective equipment around exposure to** [☐ extreme temperatures | ☐ toxic chemicals | ☐ biohazardous materials | ☐ smoke and fumes | ☐ other: ______].

☐ **Ensure all equipment is maintained in optimum running condition including** ______, ______, **and** ______ *[types of equipment].*

☐ **Safely use and maintain various** [☐ electrical | ☐ plumbing | ☐ welding | ☐ other: ______] [☐ hand and power tools | ☐ testing instruments | ☐ measuring devices | ☐ conduit bending and threading equipment | ☐ drills | ☐ hoists | ☐ other: ______] **associated with the trade.**

☐ **Troubleshoot, diagnose, repair, adjust, and maintain all** ______ *[type of]* **equipment to ensure optimum running condition; and troubleshoot and repair** ______ *[type of]* **computer malfunctions.**

☐ **Operate** ______ *[type of]*-**related equipment including** [☐ hand and power tools | ☐ measurement tools | ☐ wire and cable winches | ☐ knock-out punches | ☐ PVC benders | ☐ hydraulic pipe benders | ☐ pipe cutters | ☐ pipe threaders | ☐ grinders | ☐ sand blasters | ☐ bead blasters | ☐ drill presses | ☐ cement cutters | ☐ cutting torches | ☐ jackhammers | ☐ electric drills and hacksaws | ☐ skill saws | ☐ portable generators | ☐ portable compressors | ☐ other: ______], **conforming to all safety codes.**

☐ **Use various instruments, equipment, and devices during the inspection process including** [☐ survey instruments | ☐ metering devices | ☐ test equipment | ☐ tape measures | ☐ concrete strength measurers | ☐ other: ______].

☐ **Perform** [☐ preventive | ☐ routine | ☐ periodic | ☐ other: ______] **cleaning and maintenance of** ______ *[type of]* **equipment on** ______, ______, **and** ______ *[what?].*

☐ **Ensure all** ______ *[type of]* [☐ machinery | ☐ tools | ☐ equipment | ☐ vehicles | ☐ other: ______] **used in the** ______ *[which?]* **trade are repaired and maintained.**

☐ **Operate all tools and equipment following safety methods and precautions; and maintain equipment to ensure safe operating condition.**

☐ **Maintain all office equipment, including** [☐ multiline telephone systems | ☐ computers | ☐ photocopiers | ☐ postal stamp machines | ☐ telex machines | ☐ fax machines | ☐ others: ______].

☐ [☐ Oversee | ☐ Perform] **minor maintenance and repair on** [☐ construction vehicles | ☐ equipment | ☐ power tools | ☐ trucks | ☐ bulldozers | ☐ graders | ☐ cement mixers | ☐ welders | ☐ other: ______].

☐ **Maintain the proper operation of all** ______ *[type of]* **equipment to ensure the physical, mechanical, and electrical aspects of the facility run smoothly**.

ACHIEVEMENT SAMPLES:

☐ **Due to clear focusing and quick decoding abilities, learned to operate** ______ *[type of]* **machines after one time on-the-job instruction.**

☐ **Brought** ______ *[type of]* [☐ equipment | ☐ machinery] **downtime to** ______**%** *[percentage]* **by ensuring** [☐ all workers had parts available when needed | ☐ other achievement: ______].

☐ **Mastered the use of testing devices and measuring instruments including** [☐ voltmeters | ☐ thermometers | ☐ manometers | ☐ pressure gauges | ☐ ammeters | ☐ ohmmeters | ☐ testing lamps | ☐ other: ______] **to check** [☐ airflow | ☐ refrigerant pressure | ☐ electrical circuits | ☐ burners | ☐ other: ______] **and various tools** [☐ metal snips | ☐ electric drills | ☐ pipe cutters and benders | ☐ measurement gauges | ☐ acetylene torches | ☐ other: ______] **to service** [☐ refrigerant lines | ☐ air ducts | ☐ other: ______].

☐ **By purchasing and using a variety of** ______ *[type of]* **machines including** ______, ______, **and** ______ *[which?]*, **able to serve a wide variety of customers handling their** __________ *[type of]* **needs**.

☐ **Configured, troubleshot, and resolved** ______ *[type of]* **equipment problems and provided technical assistance and troubleshooting on** ______ *[what?]*.

☐ **Developed a preventive maintenance schedule for all** ______ *[type of]* **equipment that encompasses** ______ *[what?]*.

☐ **Purchased and implemented** ______ *[type of]* **equipment that** [☐ allows the integration of various ______ *(type of)* technologies | ☐ helped the firm service all ______ *(type of)* markets | ☐ other: ______].

Equipment, Tools & Testing Devices – Carpentry / Construction

See also other ***"Equipment, Tools & Testing Devices"*** *categories.*

☐ **Safely operate and maintain various types of heavy equipment including** [☐ 18-wheel semi-trucks | ☐ A-frame mowers | ☐ backhoes | ☐ backup trucks | ☐ bulldozers | ☐ bush hogs | ☐ catch basin cleaners | ☐ concrete mixers | ☐ concrete pavers | ☐ cranes | ☐ distributors | ☐ draglines | ☐ dump trucks | ☐ electric dollies ☐ excavators | ☐ forklifts | ☐ front-end loaders | ☐ grinders | ☐ heavy dump trucks (with ☐ plows / ☐ wings / ☐ spreaders) | ☐ hoists | ☐ hydraulic equipment | ☐ lane closure trucks | ☐ large rollers | ☐ loaders | ☐ motor graders | ☐ orange peelers | ☐ patch rollers | ☐ payloaders | ☐ pilot cars | ☐ planers | ☐ plow trucks | ☐ pneumatic asphalt tampers | ☐ post pounders | ☐ power shovels | ☐ scaffolding | ☐ seeders | ☐ sewer cleaners | (☐ single-blade / ☐ wing) plows | ☐ semi-truck trailers | ☐ sprayers | ☐ snowplows | ☐ stump grinders | ☐ sweepers | ☐ tractor mowers | ☐ tractors | ☐ trench diggers | ☐ wideners | ☐ wrecking balls | ☐ other: ______] **with an excellent safety record**.

☐ **Operate various hand and power tools including** [☐ air compressors | ☐ axes | ☐ brush hooks | ☐ bush axes | ☐ chainsaws | ☐ compressor hose | ☐ hammers | ☐ hand shovels | ☐ mattocks | ☐ mechanical soil compactors | ☐ picks | ☐ power saws | ☐ post hole diggers | ☐ rakes | ☐ sledge hammers | ☐ stapling guns | ☐ trowels | ☐ welding machines | ☐ other: ______] **in accordance with workplace safety practices**.

☐ **Use** [☐ glass cutters | ☐ glazing knives | ☐ power saws | ☐ suction cups | ☐ drills | ☐ grinders | ☐ other: ______] **to lay out, cut, install, and weatherproof** ______ *[type of]* [☐ windows | ☐ glass doors | ☐ tempered glass | ☐ laminated glass panels | ☐ skylights | ☐ sun rooms | ☐ bath and shower enclosures | ☐ table tops | ☐ room dividers | ☐ metal framework extrusions | ☐ windshields | ☐ other: ______] **for various** ______ *[type of]* **projects ranging $**______ **to $**______ *[amounts]*.

☐ **Perform** [☐ carpentry | ☐ masonry | ☐ concrete pouring | ☐ other: ______] **using** ______, ______, **and** ______ *[type of]* **tools and equipment ensuring all safety practices are followed on job sites**.

☐ **Operate heavy plow truck to keep major arteries of** ______ *[territory]* **open and passable for traffic flow during snow and ice conditions and inclement weather ensuring caution around electrical wires, gas lines, and cable lines.**

☐ **Operate all** ______ *[type of]* **equipment including** [☐ hand and power tools | ☐ measurement tools | ☐ grinders | ☐ sand blasters | ☐ drill presses | ☐ cement cutters | ☐ cutting torches | ☐ jackhammers | ☐ electric drills | ☐ hacksaws | ☐ skill saws | ☐ other: ______], **conforming to all safety codes**.

☐ **Use** [☐ knee kickers | ☐ carpet shears | ☐ loop pile cutters | ☐ heat irons | ☐ hammers | ☐ staple guns | ☐ carpet knives | ☐ drills | ☐ rubber mallets | ☐ wall trimmers | ☐ power stretchers | ☐ rollers | ☐ trowels | ☐ sanding machines | ☐ machine saw | ☐ power wet saw | ☐ other: ______] **to install** ______ *[type of]* **floor coverings**.

☐ **Measure, cut, fit, glue and/or screw wallboard panels to wood and metal framework, cutting holes in panels for** [☐ windows | ☐ doors | ☐ electrical outlets | ☐ air-conditioning units | ☐ plumbing | ☐ other: ______] **and applying textured surfaces to** [☐ walls | ☐ ceilings | ☐ floors | ☐ other: ______] **using** [☐ trowels | ☐ brushes | ☐ spray guns | ☐ other: ______].

ACHIEVEMENT SAMPLES:

☐ **Reduced equipment downtime ______%** *[percentage].* **by** [☐ cleaning and maintaining all equipment after each use | ☐ repairing machinery | ☐ following preventive maintenance schedules | ☐ meeting scheduled timeframes | ☐ being alert and operating all machinery properly | ☐ other: ______] **thereby** [☐ extending equipment life | ☐ reducing company costs | ☐ minimizing property damage | ☐ keeping the public safe | ☐ other: ______].

Equipment, Tools & Testing Devices – Electrical

*See also other "**Equipment, Tools & Testing Devices**" categories.*

☐ **Safely use and maintain all** [☐ electrical | ☐ electronics | ☐ Electrician's] [☐ hand and power tools | ☐ testing instruments | ☐ drills | ☐ measuring devices | ☐ conduit bending and threading equipment | ☐ hoists | ☐ other: ______] **associated with the trade.**

☐ **Use all electrician-related equipment including** [☐ hand and power tools | ☐ measurement tools | ☐ wire and cable winches | ☐ knock-out punches | ☐ PVC benders | ☐ hydraulic pipe benders | ☐ pipe cutters | ☐ pipe threaders | ☐ grinders | ☐ sand blasters | ☐ bead blasters | ☐ drill presses | ☐ cement cutters | ☐ cutting torches | ☐ jackhammers | ☐ electric drills and hacksaws | ☐ skill saws | ☐ other: ______], **conforming to all safety codes.**

☐ **Operate and use all** [☐ electrical | ☐ electrical | ☐ other: ______] **machinery and equipment including** [☐ hand and power tools | ☐ pipe benders | ☐ propane torches | ☐ welding equipment | ☐ sewer rooters | ☐ other: ______] **in a safe manner according to established safety precautions.**

☐ **Troubleshoot, diagnose, repair, adjust, and maintain all electrical equipment and machinery to ensure optimum running condition and safety including** [☐ hand and power tools | ☐ pipe benders | ☐ propane torches | ☐ welding equipment | ☐ forklifts | ☐ other: ______].

☐ **Operate and maintain the company's fleet of ______** *[#]* [☐ lift trucks | ☐ pickup trucks | ☐ forklifts | ☐ hydraulic boom lifts | ☐ boom trucks | ☐ digger derricks | ☐ bucket trucks | ☐ other: ______].

☐ **Use specialized testing equipment and measurement tools to test, install, and/or repair electrical circuits and equipment including** [☐ ampmeters | ☐ ohmmeters | ☐ oscilloscopes | ☐ voltmeters | ☐ volt-ohm meters | ☐ test lamps | ☐ cable locating meters | ☐ fault locators | ☐ Megger meters | ☐ other: ______] **to check** [☐ circuits | ☐ other: ______] **for** [☐ proper connections | ☐ electrical compatibility | ☐ component safety | ☐ functionality | ☐ proper operation | ☐ other: ______].

☐ **Operate all** [☐ electrical | ☐ electrical | ☐ other: ______] **tools and equipment following safety techniques and precautions, and maintain equipment to ensure safe operating condition by abiding by all safety rules.**

☐ **Handle various electrical functions for ______** *[type of]* **public works projects including** [☐ repairing underground conduits | ☐ trimming trees for wire clearance | ☐ operating underground cable locators to find, and updating maps to include, cable locations and underground faults | ☐ operating (☐ pickup trucks / ☐ digger derricks | ☐ bucket trucks | ☐ other: ______].

☐ **Operate and maintain ______** *[#]*-**volt** [☐ high-tension | ☐ other: ______] **distribution systems including ______** *[what functions?].*

Equipment, Tools & Testing Devices – HVAC / HVAC-R

*See also other "**Equipment, Tools & Testing Devices**" categories.*

☐ **Service** [☐ refrigerant lines | ☐ air ducts | ☐ other: ______] **using various hand and power tools of the trade including** [☐ pipe cutters and benders | ☐ measurement gauges | ☐ acetylene torches | ☐ metal snips | ☐ electric drills | ☐ other: ______].

☐ **Use a variety of testing devices including** [☐ voltmeters | ☐ thermometers | ☐ manometers | ☐ pressure gauges | ☐ other: ______] **to check** [☐ airflow | ☐ refrigerant pressure | ☐ electrical circuits | ☐ burners | ☐ other: ______]; **and various tools including** [☐ metal snips | ☐ electric drills | ☐ pipe cutters and benders | ☐ measurement gauges | ☐ acetylene torches | ☐ other: ______] **to service refrigerant lines and air ducts**.

☐ **Ensure proper** [☐ furnace | ☐ heating equipment | ☐ other: ______] **system functioning using combustion test equipment including** [☐ carbon dioxide testers | ☐ oxygen testers | ☐ other: ______] **and ______** *[other methods]* **resulting in ______** *[what benefits?].*

☐ **Operate and use all HVAC machinery and equipment including** [☐ hand and power tools | ☐ pipe benders | ☐ propane torches | ☐ welding equipment | ☐ sewer rooters | ☐ other: ______] **in a safe manner according to established safety precautions.**

☐ **Troubleshoot, diagnose, repair, adjust, and maintain all HVAC equipment to ensure optimal running condition and safety**

including [☐ hand and power tools | ☐ pipe benders | ☐ propane torches | ☐ welding equipment | ☐ sewer rooters | ☐ forklifts | ☐ trenchers | ☐ backhoes | ☐ other: ______].

☐ **Operate all** [☐ HVAC | ☐ plumbing | ☐ other: ______] [☐ tools | ☐ machinery | ☐ equipment] **following safety techniques and precautions, and maintain equipment to ensure safe operating condition.**

☐ **Perform** [☐ preventive | ☐ routine | ☐ periodic | ☐ other: ______] **cleaning and maintenance of all plumbing equipment including** [☐ hand and power tools | ☐ pipe benders | ☐ propane torches | ☐ welding equipment | ☐ sewer rooters | ☐ other: ______].

Equipment, Tools & Testing Devices – Landscaping & Masonry

See also other ***"Equipment, Tools & Testing Devices"*** *categories.*

☐ **Set up, operate, repair, and/or maintain all** [☐ landscaping | ☐ groundskeeping | ☐ masonry] **equipment** [☐ and vehicles] including [☐ backhoes | ☐ boom trucks | ☐ bulldozers | ☐ cement mixers | ☐ compressors | ☐ cranes | ☐ crawlers | ☐ dozers | ☐ dump bodies | ☐ force-feed loaders | ☐ forklifts | ☐ front loaders | ☐ gear cutting machines | ☐ graders | ☐ heavy dump trucks | ☐ hoists | ☐ hook lift hoists | ☐ hook lifts | ☐ hydraulic excavators | ☐ mowers | ☐ municipal dump bodies | ☐ orange peelers | ☐ paving equipment | ☐ payloaders | ☐ pick-up trucks | ☐ piggy-back forklifts | ☐ platforms | ☐ plow trucks | | ☐ rear loaders | ☐ road milling machines | ☐ roadrangers | ☐ roll-offs | ☐ roof mowers | ☐ sewer jets | ☐ side loaders | ☐ snow plows | ☐ spreaders | ☐ steam rollers | ☐ street sweepers | ☐ tiger mowers | ☐ tractors | ☐ trenchers | ☐ truck loaders | ☐ other: ______].

☐ **Use hand tools and power equipment including** [☐ shovels | ☐ rakes | ☐ electric clippers | ☐ sod cutters | ☐ saws | ☐ pruning saws | ☐ chain saws | ☐ hedge and brush trimmers | ☐ axes | ☐ snow blowers | ☐ other: ______] **to ensure the proper upkeep and repair of** ______ *[what?]*.

☐ **Ensure all employees use correct operational procedures for all groundskeeping** [☐ tools | ☐ machinery | ☐ equipment | ☐ vehicles | ☐ other: ______] **and that all safety practices are followed**.

☐ **Use** [☐ chisels | ☐ diamond blade saws | ☐ mallets | ☐ trowels | ☐ crowbars | ☐ other: ______] **to form masonry materials and build** ______ *[type of]* **projects**.

☐ **Follow safety practices in** [☐ operating equipment and power tools | ☐ mixing and using landscape chemicals | ☐ other: ______].

☐ **Use** [☐ truck-mounted lifts | ☐ power pruners | ☐ handsaws | ☐ shears | ☐ pruning hooks | ☐ clippers | ☐ other: ______] **to trim trees and shrubs; and fill tree cavities to promote healing and prevent deterioration**.

☐ **Working closely with related trades to create** ______ *[type of]* **structures, precisely align all** [☐ stones | ☐ bricks | ☐ pavers | ☐ edgers | ☐ other: ______] **with wedges, plumblines, levels, and brackets to ensure a precision fit and attractive finish using chisels, diamond blade saws, mallets, trowels, and crowbars.**

Equipment, Tools & Testing Devices – Plumbing

See also other ***"Equipment, Tools & Testing Devices"*** *categories.*

☐ **Service** ______ *[what?]* **using various hand and power tools of the trade including** [☐ pipe cutters and benders | ☐ measurement gauges | ☐ acetylene torches | ☐ metal snips | ☐ electric drills | ☐ other: ______].

☐ **Ensure proper** [☐ furnace | ☐ heating equipment | ☐ other: ______] **system functioning using combustion test equipment including** [☐ carbon dioxide testers | ☐ oxygen testers | ☐ other: ______] **and** ______ *[other methods]* **resulting in** ______ *[what benefits?]*.

☐ **Repair and maintain** ______ *[type of]* **plumbing** [☐ tools | ☐ equipment | ☐ other: ______] **used in the trade including** ______ *[what?]*.

☐ **Troubleshoot, diagnose, repair, adjust, and maintain all plumbing equipment and machinery to ensure optimum running condition and safety including** [☐ hand and power tools | ☐ pipe benders | ☐ propane torches | ☐ welding equipment | ☐ sewer rooters | ☐ forklifts | ☐ trenchers | ☐ backhoes | ☐ other: ______].

☐ **Safely operate and use various plumbing machinery and equipment including** [☐ hand and power tools | ☐ pipe benders | ☐ propane torches | ☐ welding equipment | ☐ sewer rooters | ☐ other: ______].

☐ **Operate all plumbing tools and equipment following safety techniques and precautions, and maintain equipment to ensure safe operating condition by abiding by all safety rules.**

Equipment, Tools & Testing Devices – Welding / Steamfitting

*See also other **"Equipment, Tools & Testing Devices"** categories.*

☐ **Operate and maintain various steamfitting machinery and equipment including** [☐ metal forming equipment | ☐ centrifugal chiller and steam absorption machines | ☐ drill presses | ☐ metal-removing machines | ☐ milling machines | ☐ gear cutting machines | ☐ CNC machines | ☐ Atlas machines | ☐ other: ______] **and other heavy equipment a safe manner and according to established safety precautions.**

☐ **Use** ______ *[type of]* **precision instruments and operate** [☐ metal-removing machines | ☐ metal-forming equipment | ☐ drill presses | ☐ ______ *(type of)* welding devices | ☐ other: ______] **and** [☐ milling | ☐ gear cutting | ☐ CNC | ☐ Atlas | ☐ centrifugal chiller | ☐ steam absorption | ☐ other: ______] **to** [☐ fabricate | ☐ fit | ☐ assemble | ☐ manufacture | ☐ repair | ☐ other: ______] ______ *[type of]* [☐ parts | ☐ equipment | ☐ other: ______] **working from** [☐ blueprints | ☐ plans | ☐ diagrams | ☐ specifications] **to determine dimensions, tolerances, and work layout.**

☐ **Handle all aspects of torch cutting using precision-measuring instruments including** [☐ protractors | ☐ micrometers | ☐ vernier calipers | ☐ other: ______] **welding in various positions including** [☐ flat | ☐ horizontal | ☐ vertical | ☐ overhead | ☐ other: ______].

☐ **Keep fleet of trucks in running condition by ensuring** [☐ hydraulics pistons and seals and hopper blades are all in excellent working order | ☐ hydraulic oil and pressure is at right levels at all times | ☐ other: ______].

☐ **Perform** [☐ torch cutting | ☐ joint welding | ☐ other: ______] **for** ______ *[what?]* **including** [☐ groove | ☐ bead | ☐ edge | ☐ plug | ☐ slot | ☐ fillet | ☐ arc-seam | ☐ other: ______] **using precision-measuring instruments including** [☐ protractors | ☐ micrometers | ☐ venire calipers | ☐ other: ______].

☐ **Operate and** [☐ troubleshoot | ☐ diagnose | ☐ repair | ☐ adjust | ☐ maintain] **all** [☐ electrical | ☐ plumbing | ☐ other: ______] **equipment and machinery to ensure optimum running condition and safety including** [☐ hand and power tools | ☐ pipe benders | ☐ propane torches | ☐ welding equipment | ☐ sewer rooters | ☐ forklifts | ☐ other: ______].

☐ **Ensure proper** ______ *[type of]* **system functioning using combustion test equipment including** [☐ carbon dioxide testers | ☐ oxygen testers | ☐ other: ______] **and** ______ *[other methods]* **for** ______ *[what?].*

☐ **Service** ______ *[what?]* **using hand and power tools of the trade including** [☐ pipe cutters | ☐ benders | ☐ measurement gauges | ☐ acetylene torches | ☐ metal snips | ☐ electric drills | ☐ other: ______].

☐ **Troubleshoot, diagnose, repair, adjust, and maintain all welding equipment and machinery to ensure optimum running condition and safety including** ______, ______, **and** ______ *[which equipment or what functions?].*

☐ **Follow safety precautions using protective equipment around exposure to** [☐ extreme temperatures | ☐ toxic chemicals | ☐ explosive gases | ☐ biohazardous materials | ☐ helium | ☐ oxygen | ☐ acetylene | ☐ smoke and fumes | ☐ grease | ☐ other: ______].

Estimating

*See **"Cost Estimating."***

Facility Management – General

*See also **"Facility Management Functions," "Building Operations Management," "Inspections & Compliance – Facilities & Plants"** and **"Inspections & Compliance – General."***

☐ **Manage** ______ *[#]* **buildings and** ______ *[#]***-acre grounds for this** ______ *[type of]* **firm including overseeing** [☐ construction | ☐ renovation | ☐ repair | ☐ remodel | ☐ maintenance | ☐ other: ______] **projects to ensure they meet** [☐ government | ☐ environmental | ☐ health | ☐ safety | ☐ security | ☐ environmental | ☐ other: ______] **standards.**

☐ **Direct and oversee the** [☐ facilities | ☐ building maintenance | ☐ grounds upkeep | ☐ space planning | ☐ remodel projects | ☐ other: ______] **of this** ______ *[#]***-square foot building with ground acreage of** ______ *[#]* **and** ______ *[#]* [☐ employees | ☐ work stations | ☐ offices | ☐ facilities].

☐ **Direct architectural** [☐ design | ☐ planning | ☐ review | ☐ management] **of** [☐ construction | ☐ remodeling | ☐ maintenance] **projects for** [☐ commercial | ☐ department | ☐ other: ______] **buildings and facilities of this** ______ *[type of]* **firm.**

☐ **Manage and oversee this** ______ *[type of]* **plant's facilities handling all aspects of** [☐ office administration | ☐ facilities management | ☐ construction oversight | ☐ purchasing | ☐ lease negotiations | ☐ space planning | ☐ budget preparation | ☐ executive expense analysis | ☐ other: ______].

☐ **Direct the day-to-day operations of this** ______ *[type of]* **facility including** [☐ client meeting | ☐ needs assessment | ☐ estimating | ☐ proposal development | ☐ bidding | ☐ work orders | ☐ budgeting | ☐ project prioritizing | ☐ timelines | ☐ scheduling

| ☐ site inspections | ☐ equipment and supplies purchasing | ☐ sales and marketing | ☐ payroll processing | ☐ company taxes | ☐ preventive maintenance | ☐ trades coordination | ☐ other: ______] **ensuring all projects are completed on time and professionally and job sites are left clean of debris to increase safety and customer satisfaction.**

☐ **Check and evaluate the** [☐ physical | ☐ mechanical | ☐ structural | ☐ other: ______] **aspects of facilities to ensure everything is operating in a safe, functional, and proper manner.**

☐ **Manage and maintain Executive Office facilities consisting of** ______ *[#]* **floors and** ______ *[#]* **square feet, with responsibility for Executive Office Facility budget of $**______ *[amount]*.

☐ **Manage, coordinate, and oversee all aspects of** [☐ building maintenance | ☐ project planning | ☐ facility function | ☐ environmental factors | ☐ lease management | ☐ architectural planning and design | ☐ real estate purchases and sales | ☐ space planning | ☐ renovations | ☐ other: ______] **for this** ______ *[type of]* **company**.

☐ **Oversee the** [☐ structural | ☐ mechanical | ☐ electrical | ☐ plumbing | ☐ other: ______] **aspects of** ______ *[type of]* **building** [☐ design | ☐ utilization | ☐ space planning | ☐ construction | ☐ operation | ☐ maintenance | ☐ repair | ☐ remodel | ☐ other: ______] **projects ensuring that all work is performed in compliance with building codes, laws, and regulations.**

☐ **Direct and review** [☐ grounds | ☐ facilities | ☐ other: ______] **improvement projects including the** [☐ development of building plan specifications | ☐ inspection of facilities under construction or renovation | ☐ review of contractors' progress schedules | ☐ other: ______].

☐ [☐ As an independent subcontractor,] **work as a team to assist and support management in directing all building** [☐ construction | ☐ maintenance | ☐ improvement | ☐ repair | ☐ remodel | ☐ other: ______] **work; and monitor facilities to ensure they are safe, secure, and well maintained.**

☐ **Successfully balance managing facility operations and coordinating all aspects of the physical workplace with** [☐ overseeing | ☐ performing] [☐ carpentry | ☐ maintenance and repair | ☐ groundskeeping | ☐ other: ______] **functions by** ______ *[doing what?]*.

☐ **Manage various** [☐ building | ☐ facility | ☐ grounds] **maintenance functions including** [☐ building maintenance and repair | ☐ office relocations | ☐ renovations | ☐ remodeling | ☐ roofing repairs | ☐ machinery maintenance and repair | ☐ regular and preventive maintenance | ☐ carpentry | ☐ electrical wiring | ☐ plumbing | ☐ HVAC systems | ☐ painting | ☐ custodial services | ☐ janitorial maintenance | ☐ groundskeeping | ☐ security systems | ☐ sprinkler systems | ☐ fire extinguisher and smoke alarm inspections | ☐ safety checks | ☐ boiler system | ☐ water system | ☐ heating system | ☐ cooling system | ☐ other: ______].

☐ **Direct all aspects of** [☐ multiple | ☐ simultaneous] ______ *[type of]* [☐ construction | ☐ facility | ☐ other: ______] **management projects including** [☐ budgeting | ☐ subcontractor selection | ☐ trades scheduling | ☐ materials acquisition | ☐ design revisions | ☐ client satisfaction | ☐ inspections | ☐ other: ______].

ACHIEVEMENT SAMPLES:

See also "Achievement Examples – General," "Building Operations Projects," "Construction Projects," "Cost Reductions & Savings," "Overcoming Obstacles," and "Productivity Improvement."

☐ **Significantly improved operating conditions of the building's** ______ *[what machinery?]* **by implementing and rigidly following a regular maintenance schedule which proved critical to the successful and continuous operation of Company's production equipment.**

☐ **Involved in** [☐ managing | ☐ performing] ______ *[which?]* **relocation efforts that required** ______ *[what actions?]* **to meet** ______ *[what challenges?]* **and resulted in** ______ *[what benefits?]*.

☐ **Improved operating conditions of** [☐ buildings | ☐ plants | ☐ structures | ☐ machinery | ☐ equipment | ☐ other: ______] **by** [☐ championing a ______ *(type of)* program that ______ *(does what?)* | ☐ implementing and rigidly following a preventive maintenance schedule | ☐ modifying machinery to run more efficiently | ☐ other: ______], **which resulted in** [☐ eliminating shutdowns by maintaining all equipment in optimum operating condition | ☐ other: ______].

☐ **Made recommendations for the** [☐ maintenance | ☐ upgrade | ☐ remodel | ☐ other: ______] **of** ______ *[which?]* **physical facilities; and prepared comprehensive** ______ *[type of]* **reports to support these recommendations, which resulted in** ______ *[what benefits?]*.

☐ **Totally eliminated need for equipment shutdowns by** [☐ maintaining air compressors and boilers in optimum operating condition at all times | ☐ performing regularly scheduled maintenance checks | ☐ changing oil and filters as needed | ☐ other: ______].

☐ **Reduced air compressor downtime from an average of** ______ *[#]* **machine(s) per** [☐ day | ☐ week | ☐ other: ______] **to once every** ______ *[#]* [☐ weeks | ☐ months] **by** [☐ contributing to a new air piping layout | ☐ setting up and maintaining a Preventative Maintenance Program | ☐ other: ______].

☐ **Improved operating conditions of** ______ *[type of]* **machinery by paying close attention to detail in performing and planning** ______ *[type of]* **jobs.**

☐ **Converted building heat from steam to hot water, installing heat exchangers and blower units, resulting in lowering the company's fuel bills by $**______ *[amount]* **annually**.

☐ **Modified ______** *[type of]* [☐ equipment | ☐ machinery | ☐ other: ______] **to run more efficiently through a team effort approach.**

☐ **Reorganized and inventoried machine and repair parts, saving ______** *[#]* **hours in prep time by ______** *[doing what?].*

☐ **Helped improve the workplace and work environment by ______** *[doing what?],* **which has resulted in ______** *[benefits].*

Facility Management – Functions

*See also **"Facility Management – General," "Building Operations Management,"** and **"Inspections & Compliance – Facilities & Plants."***

☐ **Maintain** [☐ buildings | ☐ facilities | ☐ grounds | ☐ machinery | ☐ other: ______] **in good repair including** [☐ heating | ☐ air conditioning | ☐ plumbing | ☐ electrical | ☐ drywall | ☐ wall coverings | ☐ insulation | ☐ drop ceilings | ☐ painting | ☐ grading | ☐ underground utilities | ☐ drains | ☐ gutters | ☐ paving | ☐ other: ______].

☐ **Evaluate, prioritize, and coordinate short- and long-range facility plans including** [☐ repair and improvement projects | ☐ building renewal plans | ☐ system-wide policies and standards | ☐ technical requirements | ☐ other: ______].

☐ **Apply** [☐ expert | ☐ proficient | ☐ working] **knowledge of** [☐ general principles and practices of building construction | ☐ building maintenance | ☐ physical plant operations | ☐ technical systems | ☐ bid specification | ☐ inspection methods | ☐ building codes | ☐ ordinances | ☐ fire regulations | ☐ safety precautions | ☐ health and safety regulations | ☐ principles of contract law | ☐ automated building control | ☐ indoor air quality requirements | ☐ energy management systems | ☐ recordkeeping techniques | ☐ other: ______] **to all aspects of facility management.**

☐ **Successfully balance managing facility operations and coordinating all aspects of the physical workplace with overseeing carpentry, maintenance, groundskeeping, and ______** *[other?]* **functions in an exemplary manner by ______** *[doing what well?].*

☐ **Handle** [☐ new construction | ☐ remodeling | ☐ repair | ☐ maintenance | ☐ leasing | ☐ space planning | ☐ other: ______] **projects of ______** *[what?]* **that require ______** *[what actions?].*

☐ **Perform various business-related facility management functions including** [☐ managing and overseeing all aspects of facilities projects | ☐ coordinating department proposals | ☐ directing architectural design and planning | ☐ handling lease negotiations and management | ☐ overseeing construction and remodeling | ☐ coordinating janitorial maintenance and custodial services | ☐ maintaining compliance with all OSHA and environmental regulations | ☐ ensuring facility is safe, secure, and well maintained | ☐ coordinating all aspects of the physical workplace | ☐ analyzing and overseeing the physical and mechanical aspects of the facility | ☐ ensuring facility runs smoothly at all times | ☐ examining facility for damage and overseeing repairs | ☐ developing project plans and overseeing planning | ☐ setting up preventive maintenance schedules | ☐ developing budgets and monitoring expenses | ☐ conducting feasibility studies | ☐ developing safety and security solutions | ☐ conducting research and analysis | ☐ approving cost estimates | ☐ writing maintenance and administrative reports | ☐ following up on security reports | ☐ other: ______]. *(See also **"Administrative Management"** and **"Office Management."**)*

☐ **Plan and direct skilled maintenance and repair of ______** *[type of]* [☐ buildings | ☐ complexes | ☐ facilities] **in the areas of ______** *[which areas?].*

☐ **Prepare recommendations to ______** *[whom?]* **regarding** [☐ contractual defaults | ☐ time extensions | ☐ liquidated damages | ☐ other: ______].

☐ **Manage a multitude of facility** [☐ installation | ☐ construction | ☐ maintenance | ☐ repair | ☐ other: ______] **functions including** [☐ ensure proper operation of boiler, water heater, furnace, and refrigeration | ☐ maintain plumbing, electrical, and HVAC systems | ☐ maintain the facility and grounds | ☐ maintain sprinkler systems | ☐ supervise machinery maintenance and repair | ☐ evaluate equipment life expectancy | ☐ replace equipment when needed | ☐ handle environmental factors | ☐ plan and design office spaces | ☐ direct architectural design and planning | ☐ project manage all renovations | ☐ determine project deadlines | ☐ spearhead corporate office relocations | ☐ initiate and implement policies and procedures | ☐ purchase furniture and equipment | ☐ serve as technical advisor | ☐ negotiate contracts | ☐ review and approve space requests | ☐ inspect proposed space leasing sites and direct space planning | ☐ determine critical maintenance priorities | ☐ conduct facility surveys | ☐ procure contracting services | ☐ review contractor work and inspect for compliance | ☐ project future needs | ☐ estimate material needs | ☐ supervise skilled trades staff | ☐ ensure vehicles are in safe operating condition | ☐ monitor security systems | ☐ handle real estate (☐ purchases / ☐ sales) | ☐ evacuate staff in emergencies | ☐ manage energy conservation programs | ☐ other: ______].

☐ **Coordinate all aspects of the physical workplace ensuring** [☐ the integration and coordination of business practices | ☐ work and people requirements | ☐ architecture | ☐ other: ______].

☐ **Conduct ______** *[type of]* [☐ research and analysis | ☐ feasibility studies | ☐ other: ______] **for ______** *[purpose]* **resulting in ______** *[what benefits?].*

☐ **Provide** [☐ building maintenance | ☐ space planning | ☐ renovations | ☐ other: ______] **for ______** *[type of]* **projects.**

☐ **Oversee and inspect** [☐ new construction | ☐ remodeling | ☐ repair | ☐ maintenance | ☐ leasing | ☐ space planning | ☐ other: ______] **projects of ______** *[what?]* **that require ______** *[what actions?].*

ACHIEVEMENT SAMPLES: *See "**Facility Management,**" Achievements under "**Building Operations Projects,**" "**General Contracting Projects & Functions,**" and "**Construction Projects.**"*

Flooring Projects & Functions

*See also "**Carpentry/Construction Work Functions**" and all Carpentry/Construction Projects (specific).*

☐ **Lay** [☐ wood | ☐ tile | ☐ carpet | ☐ other: ______] **floor coverings according to blueprints in** [☐ homes | ☐ corporate offices | ☐ building lobbies | ☐ schools | ☐ colleges | ☐ apartment buildings | ☐ hospitals | ☐ manufacturing plants | ☐ shopping malls | ☐ stores | ☐ restaurants | ☐ other: ______] **with professional results.**

☐ **Install ______** *[type of]* **floor covering materials for** [☐ decorative | ☐ sound deadening | ☐ shock absorbing | | ☐ air-tight | ☐ heat insulating | ☐ other: ______] **purposes to meet client needs**.

☐ **Closely inspect all floor surfaces prior to installation and correct ______** *[type of]* **imperfections to ensure a smooth foundation before installing ______** *[type of]* **floor coverings**.

☐ **Prepare for floor installations by** [☐ measuring floor areas | ☐ planning layouts and seam placements around traffic patterns and stairs | ☐ installing tackless strips and padded cushions | ☐ other: ______] **ensuring all seams are joined evenly for best appearance, maximum wear, and a professional job. Finish with moldings that match client's décor**.

☐ **Accurately cut, trim, apply, and set** [☐ marble tile | ☐ slabs | ☐ other: ______] **to floors, walls, and ceilings ensuring all tiles are laid evenly and polished to a high luster according to specified designs for a uniform appearance.**

☐ **Use** [☐ knee kickers | ☐ carpet shears | ☐ loop pile cutters | ☐ heat irons | ☐ hammers | ☐ staple guns | ☐ carpet knives | ☐ drills | ☐ rubber mallets | ☐ wall trimmers | ☐ power stretchers | ☐ rollers | ☐ trowels | ☐ sanding machines | ☐ machine saw | ☐ power wet saw | ☐ tile cutters | ☐ other: ______] **to install ______** *[type of]* **floor coverings**.

ACHIEVEMENT SAMPLES: *See "**Construction Projects.**"*

General Contracting

*See also "**Construction Projects.**"*

☐ **Direct day-to-day operations of this general contracting firm providing a full array of construction services including** [☐ demolition | ☐ floor-to-floor buildouts | ☐ metal stud framing | ☐ bathroom, kitchen, and tile installations | ☐ drywall | ☐ HVAC | ☐ plumbing | ☐ electrical | ☐ acoustical ceilings | ☐ millwork | ☐ masonry | ☐ other: ______] **and other general contracting work to ______** *[type of]* **clients**.

☐ **Manage and oversee all facets of operations for this general contracting firm with ______** *[#]* [☐ employees | ☐ clients | ☐ locations] **and annual revenues in excess of $______** *[amount]*.

☐ **Manage the day-to-day operations of this ______** *[type of]* **firm including** [☐ client meeting | ☐ needs assessment | ☐ estimating | ☐ proposal development | ☐ bidding | ☐ work orders | ☐ budgeting | ☐ project prioritizing | ☐ timelines | ☐ scheduling | ☐ site inspections | ☐ equipment and supplies purchasing | ☐ sales and marketing | ☐ payroll processing | ☐ company taxes | ☐ preventive maintenance | ☐ trades coordination | ☐ other: ______] **ensuring all projects are completed on time and professionally and job sites are left clean of debris to increase safety and customer satisfaction**.

☐ **Direct all facets of operations including** [☐ sales and marketing | ☐ estimating | ☐ budgeting | ☐ design | ☐ construction | ☐ other: ______] **efforts for this** [☐ commercial and residential | ☐ roofing | ☐ painting | ☐ other: ______] **general contracting firm.**

☐ **Oversee the daily operations of ______** *[type of]* **job sites including** [☐ reviewing project schedules | ☐ coordinating resources and materials | ☐ managing and scheduling crew | ☐ generating task tools and material lists | ☐ ordering materials | ☐ supervising installations | ☐ collaborating with other trades | ☐ identifying issues | ☐ troubleshooting and resolving problems | ☐ adherence to contract scope, specifications, and code | ☐ managing materials and inventory levels | ☐ facilitating technical and milestone communication | (☐ coordinating / ☐ developing) electrical maintenance programs | ☐ accurately completing all assignment-related paperwork | ☐ other: ______].

☐ **Assess each project's needs, provide clients with proposals and estimates, work out accurate timelines, sub out and supervise construction, set up and coordinate crews for all trades, perform site inspections, and complete all ______** *[type of]* **customer projects in a timely and efficient manner.**

☐ **Plan, direct, and supervise all ______** *[type of]* [☐ design | ☐ construction | ☐ fabrication | ☐ installation | ☐ repair | ☐ other: ______] **tasks required for ______** *[what?]*.

☐ **Oversee job site protection and safety during all construction projects by** [☐ protecting all (☐ furniture / ☐ decks / ☐ windows / ☐ driveways / ☐ bushes / ☐ other: ______) | ☐ ensuring no damage to site | ☐ keeping jobs neat and clean of debris on an ongoing basis | ☐ other: ______].

☐ **Effectively negotiate and manage ______** *[type of]* **contract services and ensure that services are provided by all trades in accordance with contract specifications, codes, and company standards.** *(See also **"Contract Negotiations."**)*

☐ **Facilitate ______** *[which trade?]* **management functions including** [☐ reviewing and evaluating specifications | ☐ coordinating bid selections | ☐ estimating project time, materials, and costs | ☐ preparing estimates | ☐ negotiating contracts | ☐ writing purchase requests | ☐ evaluating subcontractor bids | ☐ prioritizing work assignments | ☐ scheduling jobs | ☐ supervising various trades | ☐ setting up projects with materials | ☐ determining safety requirements | ☐ coordinating materials shipping | ☐ purchasing or leasing equipment | ☐ preparing cost estimates | ☐ ensuring safety practices | ☐ maintaining tools and equipment | ☐ ordering equipment | ☐ obtaining required permits | ☐ making on-site visits | ☐ inspecting work for compliance with codes | ☐ training staff | ☐ handling inventory control | ☐ coordinating projects with (☐ engineers / ☐ architects) | ☐ monitoring equipment | ☐ other: ______].

☐ **Perform computer layout and design services using ______** *[software program]* **to meet ______** *[type of]* **client needs on ______** *[kind of]* **projects.**

☐ **Document reports and maintain up-to-date records of** [☐ individual's time | ☐ man hours expended on job orders | ☐ accidents and injuries | ☐ work progress | ☐ other: ______].

☐ **Actively maintain positive customer relationships to ensure satisfaction and service quality on all** [☐ service calls | ☐ projects | ☐ installations | ☐ repairs | ☐ other: ______] **by** [☐ relating to them in a professional and courteous manner | ☐ listening carefully to their concerns | ☐ responding to their questions or complaints | ☐ making satisfactory adjustments | ☐ escalating their requests to ______ *(whom?)* | ☐ other: ______].

☐ **Maintain the upkeep of all ______** *[type of]* **equipment and tools including ______, ______, and ______** *[equipment].*

ACHIEVEMENT SAMPLES: *See also **"Achievement Examples – General," "Construction Projects," "Increased Sales & Profitability,"** and all other achievement categories.*

☐ **Working with other subcontractors, built ______** *[#]* [☐ new homes | ☐ extensions | ☐ finished basements | ☐ attics | ☐ custom-built kitchens | ☐ remodeled bathrooms | ☐ other: ______] **including ______, ______, and ______** *[projects]* **ranging $______ to $______** *[amounts].*

☐ **Established a reputation for quality workmanship at competitive prices by** [☐ maintaining superior levels of craftsmanship | ☐ ensuring excellent customer service | ☐ providing after job follow-up | ☐ other: ______].

Glazier Projects & Functions

*See also **"Carpentry / Construction Work."***

☐ [☐ Direct and manage | ☐ Supervise | ☐ Handle] [☐ small to large | ☐ multiple | ☐ complex | ☐ other: ______] ______ *[type of]* [☐ residential | ☐ commercial | ☐ other: ______] **glazing projects, handling the full project scope—from contract award through closeout for this** [☐ commercial glazing company | ☐ contractor | ☐ other: ______].

☐ **Supervise and oversee the work of ______** *[#]* **commercial glaziers upholding a high quality of work standards and ensuring the completion of successful projects on time and within budget.**

☐ **Lay out, cut, install, and weatherproof ______** *[type of]* [☐ windows | ☐ glass doors | ☐ tempered glass | ☐ glass panels | ☐ blast resistant windows | ☐ skylights | ☐ doors | ☐entrance enclosures | ☐ sun rooms | ☐ storefronts | ☐ shower enclosures | ☐ aluminum curtain walls | ☐ backsplashes | ☐ display cases | ☐ table tops | ☐ decorative room dividers | ☐ security windows | ☐ metal framework extrusions | ☐ windshields | ☐ aluminum storefronts | ☐ glass railing systems | ☐ mirrors | ☐ other: ______] **using** [☐ glass cutters | ☐ glazing knives | ☐ power saws | ☐ suction cups | ☐ drills | ☐ grinders | ☐ other: ______] **for various ______** *[type of]* **projects ranging $______ to $______** *[amounts].*

☐ **Coordinate and collaborate with ______** *[which?]* **trades in the installation of ______** *[type of]* **glass projects for** [☐ commercial | ☐ residential | ☐ automotive | ☐ other: ______] **clients** [☐ using precision-cutting methods | ☐ cutting glass panes manually | ☐ spreading glazing compound around molding edges | ☐ trimming excess material | ☐ other: ______] **for a perfect fit and polished, professional look.**

☐ **Work closely with** [☐ plastics | ☐ granite | ☐ marble | ☐ steel | ☐ aluminum | ☐ other: ______] **laborers to** [☐ install | ☐ replace] **glass and** [☐ mount sashes | ☐ install frames | ☐ attach locks, hinges, rubber gaskets, and moldings | ☐ other: ______] **resulting in a** [☐ professional look | ☐ unique design | ☐ decorative finish | ☐ other: ______].

☐ **Inspect and monitor work to ensure quality installation, compliance, and customer satisfaction according to** [☐ contractual obligations | ☐ manufacturer's installation instructions | ☐ industry standards | ☐ estimated manhours and benchmarks | ☐ safety program | ☐ other: ______].

☐ **Communicate with** [☐ customers | ☐ Project Manager | ☐ Superintendent | ☐ Shop Foreman | ☐ Estimator | ☐ Glaziers |

☐ draftsmen | ☐ vendors | ☐ Architects | ☐ General Contractor | ☐ co-workers | ☐ others: ______] **regarding** [☐ project scope and requirements | ☐ setting and managing expectations | ☐ project specifications | ☐ project scheduling | ☐ daily work schedules | ☐ materials lead time | ☐ equipment requirements | ☐ material deliveries | ☐ project progress | ☐ labor coordination with other contractors | ☐ scope changes | ☐ risks and liabilities | ☐ quality | ☐ production | ☐ other: ______] **throughout project stages—taking project from inception through completion.**

☐ **Handle various project-related administrative functions including** [☐ reviewing and verifying project drawings | ☐ interpreting specifications | ☐ securing material quotes | ☐ negotiating vendor pricing | ☐ estimating project costs | ☐ preparing bid proposals | ☐ issuing purchase orders | ☐ determining equipment costs | ☐ reviewing and approving project contracts | ☐ ordering and scheduling materials | ☐ documenting project progress and conditions | ☐ maintaining accurate progress records | ☐ photographing progress and results | ☐ approving invoices for payment | ☐ managing shop drawing process | ☐ closeout processing | ☐ processing change orders | ☐ closeout processing | ☐ records management | ☐ other: ______].

☐ **Apply** [☐ working | ☐ proficient] **knowledge and experience in** [☐ the glass industry | ☐ reading and interpreting blueprints and instructions | ☐ calculating figures including area, circumference, and volume | ☐ measuring and cutting glass to size or pattern | ☐ installing frames | ☐ insulating glass | ☐ using (☐ sanding / ☐ beveling / ☐ polishing) machines | ☐ other: ______].

ACHIEVEMENT SAMPLES: *See "Construction Projects."*

Grievance Investigations & Dispute Resolution

See also "Equal Employment Opportunity Compliance," "Union Leadership," and "Union Functions."

☐ **Investigate and resolve** [☐ discrimination complaints | ☐ Equal Employment Opportunity (EEO) matters | ☐ Affirmative Action grievances | ☐ civil rights infractions | ☐ staff disputes | ☐ staff misconduct | ☐ policy infractions | ☐ violations of corporate practices | ☐ other: ____________], **perform statistical analyses** [☐ reports of findings | ☐ EEO statistical reports | ☐ other: ______], **and/or negotiate settlements.**

☐ **Advise and counsel** [☐ employees | ☐ labor] **and management to prevent and/or resolve disputes over** [☐ employee | ☐ labor] **relation's issues including** [☐ contractual agreements | ☐ labor agreements | ☐ other: ______] **to avoid costly litigation, strikes, or other disruptions.**

☐ **Coordinate and oversee field investigations that review and evaluate** ______ *[type of]* **activities related to** [☐ department buildings | ☐ equipment operations | ☐ work procedures | ☐ other: ______] **to ensure compliance with all safety practices and standards.**

☐ **Confer with** [☐ employees | ☐ employee representatives | ☐ union representatives | ☐ management | ☐ ______ *(which?)* government agencies | ☐ others: ______] **to resolve** ______ *[type of]* [☐ problems | ☐ grievances | ☐ discipline issues | ☐ other: ______] **and negotiate solutions and/or settlements.**

☐ **Conduct** [☐ confidential fact-finding investigations | ☐ grievance management | ☐ other: ______] **on** ______ *[what matters or issues?],* **examine corporate practices to determine violations, prepare reports of findings, and provide** [☐ mediation | ☐ guidance | ☐ advice] **as warranted**.

☐ **Arbitrate and decide disputes that bind both** [☐ employees | ☐ labor] **and management to specific terms and conditions of** [☐ employees | ☐ labor] **contracts.**

☐ [☐ Research and analyze | ☐ Investigate] **Human Resource** [☐ management | ☐ organization] [☐ problems | ☐ issues | ☐ grievances | ☐ other: ______] **and formulate** ______ *[type of]* [☐ reports | ☐ recommendations | ☐ settlements | ☐ other: ______], **which have produced** ______ *[what results?].*

☐ **For all complaints and violations that warrant a grievance, attempt to resolve disputes prior to pursuing them under the grievance process by speaking with all involved parties, management, and any witnesses and** ______ *[doing what?].*

☐ **Process all stages of grievances, arbitrations, and appeals including** [☐ investigations | ☐ witness preparation | ☐ exhibits | ☐ position papers | ☐ filing | ☐ other: ______].

☐ **Investigate and resolve any and all reported violations of the firm's compliance program and work with** ______ *[whom?]* **to handle violations promptly, accurately, and consistently.**

☐ **Thoroughly investigate all problems carefully, calmly resolve disputes, and advise members as to their rights in** ______ *[type of]* **matters to ensure** [☐ members are properly represented | ☐ management gives serious consideration to legitimate complaints | ☐ other: ______].

☐ **Present** ______ *[type of]* [☐ employee | ☐ labor] **grievances to the** [☐ management team | ☐ designated labor relations staff member | ☐ other: ______] **meeting all** [☐ grievance filing | ☐ bargain requests | ☐ Unfair Labor Practice filings | ☐ other: ______] **deadlines**.

☐ **Review all involved** [☐ jobs and classifications | ☐ job descriptions | ☐ work area and equipment | ☐ pay rates and computation methods | ☐ seniority list and names and addresses of all involved | ☐ previous settlement and arbitration history | ☐ past practice information | ☐ government acts and laws | ☐ safety codes | ☐ workers' compensation regulations | ☐ collective agreement | ☐ company rules and policies | ☐ other: ______].

ACHIEVEMENT SAMPLES:

☐ [☐ Settled | ☐ Closed out] ______ *[#]* **potentially significant lawsuits involving** ______ *[what?]* **and amounting to $**______ *[amount]* **for under $**______ *[amount]* [☐ by offering buy-out packages | ☐ through effective attorney negotiations | ☐ other: ______].

☐ **Disengaged teamsters' organization effort of the** ______ *[which?]* [☐ union | ☐ center | ☐ division | ☐ department | ☐ unit | ☐ other: ______] **by** ______ *[doing what?].*

Heavy Equipment Operations

☐ **Coordinate and direct crews in the execution of all** [☐ construction | ☐ road-building | ☐ earth moving | ☐asphalt batching and paving | ☐ concrete batch plant operations | ☐ concrete paving | ☐ transit mixer operation | ☐ quarrying | ☐ water well | ☐ other: ______] **assignments and operations.**

☐ **Operate and maintain** ______ *[type of]* **heavy construction equipment to** [☐ demolish and rebuild | ☐ build | ☐ construct | ☐ pave] ______ *[type of]* [☐ structures | ☐ foundations | ☐ highways | ☐ roads | ☐ bridges | ☐ buildings | ☐ retaining walls | ☐ outdoor areas | ☐ piers | ☐ streets | ☐ other: ______] **requiring** [☐ rebuilding | ☐ restructuring | ☐ other: ______] **for this** [☐ construction company | ☐ heavy equipment contractor | ☐ public works department | ☐ other: ______].

☐ **As a(n)** [☐ Equipment Operator | ☐ Heavy Equipment Operator | ☐ Operating Engineer | ☐ Back Hoe Operator | ☐ Loader Operator | ☐ Motor Grader Operator | ☐ Track Hoe Operator | ☐ Excavator Operator | ☐ Grader Operator | ☐ other: ______], **safely operate various types of heavy construction equipment including** [☐ bulldozers | ☐ compressors | ☐ crawler tractors | ☐ derricks | ☐ dump trucks | ☐ front-end loaders | ☐ graders | ☐ motor graders | ☐ pile drivers | ☐ power cranes | ☐ pumps | ☐ road graders | ☐ scrapers | ☐ tracked loaders | ☐ trench excavator | ☐ tractors | ☐ truck loaders | ☐ trucks | ☐ other: ______] **to** [☐ excavate, backfill, and grade earth | ☐ compact soil | ☐ grade curves and shoulders | ☐ locate underground services | ☐ erect structures | ☐ pour concrete | ☐ clear brush and tree stumps | ☐ load and move (☐ dirt / ☐ sand / ☐ boulders / ☐ rocks / ☐ coal / ☐ cargo / ☐ refuse) | ☐ other: ______] **to specifications, complying with all safety protocols.**

☐ **Spread, level, and compact** [☐ asphalt | ☐ concrete | ☐ other: ______] **for** [☐ highway construction | ☐ community roads | ☐ parking lots | ☐ driveways | ☐ other: ______] **using** [☐ asphalt spreaders | ☐ concrete paving machines | ☐ tamping equipment | ☐ other: ______].

☐ **Conduct preoperational checks on** ______ *[type of]* [☐ mobile | ☐ stationary] [☐ equipment | ☐ machinery] **prior to use and clean and lubricate equipment and maintain** ______ *[type of]* [☐ records | ☐ reports].

☐ **Handle various labor functions to prepare for** ______ *[type of]* [☐ building | ☐ demolition | ☐ excavation | ☐ heavy construction | ☐ highway | ☐ other: ______] **projects including** [☐ reviewing plans and specifications | ☐ cleaning and preparing sites | ☐ clearing up debris | ☐ erecting scaffolding | ☐ digging trenches | ☐ setting up braces | ☐ removing hazardous materials | ☐ eliminating obstacles and hazards | ☐ loading and unloading building materials and machinery | ☐ positioning and dismantling concrete forms | ☐ positioning and aligning structural components | ☐ digging trenches | ☐ leveling and compacting earth to grade specifications | ☐ signaling equipment operators | ☐ other: ______].

☐ **Apply** [☐ basic | ☐ in-depth] **knowledge of** [☐ soil composition and conformation | ☐ terrain features | ☐ equipment attachments | ☐ other: ______] **to determine proper approaches and attachments according to surface and subsurface conditions.**

☐ **Operate heavy dredging equipment to** [☐ reclaim earth fill | ☐ determine excavation depth | ☐ excavate waterways | ☐ remove sand, rock, and gravel | ☐ deepen waterways | ☐ other: ______] **from** [☐ harbors | ☐ lakes | ☐ rivers | ☐ streams] **to** [☐ restore wetlands | ☐ reclaim land | (☐ create / ☐ maintain) beaches | ☐ other: ______].

☐ **Apply** [☐ hands-on | ☐ working | ☐ proficient] **knowledge of** ______ *[type of]* [☐ equipment | ☐ machines | ☐ controls | ☐ attachments | ☐ materials | ☐ methods | ☐ tools | ☐ other: ______] **involved in the** [☐ demolition | ☐ construction | ☐ repair | ☐ other: ______] **of** [☐ buildings | ☐ houses | ☐ structures | ☐ other: ______].

☐ **Deploy and operate heavy equipment including** [☐ boom trucks | ☐ boom / digger trucks | ☐ cranes | ☐ bucket trucks | ☐ 5th wheel tractors | ☐ 2-ton line trucks | ☐ other: ______] **for work on** [☐ high-voltage transmissions | ☐ low-voltage lighting systems | ☐ distribution powerlines | ☐ other: ______] **for** [☐ highways and streets | ☐ traffic signal systems | ☐ airport runways | ☐ taxiways | ☐ athletic field lighting | ☐ conducting energy between generating stations, substations, and consumers | ☐ other: ______].

Highway & Bridge Maintenance – General

See also "Highway & Bridge Maintenance Work."

☐ [☐ Manage and oversee | ☐ Perform] **various highway maintenance activities including** [☐ traffic control | ☐ highway inspection and repair | ☐ preventative maintenance | ☐ herbicide and pesticide application | ☐ roadway right of way maintenance during emergencies | ☐ excessive foliage removal in right-of-way areas | ☐ following up on road complaints | ☐ other: ______] **for the** ______ *[state]* **Department of Transportation (DOT).**

☐ [☐ Perform | ☐ Supervise] **inspections and repairs on damaged bridge** [☐ components | ☐ guardrails | ☐ pavement | ☐ barrier walls | ☐ overpass structures | ☐ drainage structures | ☐ signs | ☐ delineators | ☐ lighting | ☐ fencing | ☐ other: ______].

☐ [☐ Perform | ☐ Supervise] **maintenance crew work including** [☐ flagging motorists | ☐ diverting traffic around work areas | ☐ removing debris and litter from roadways | ☐ controlling snow and ice | ☐ spreading (☐ sand / ☐ salt / ☐ gravel) | ☐ erecting guardrails | ☐ installing sign and warning signals | repairing highway lighting | ☐ mowing grass | ☐ operating heavy machinery | ☐ driving trucks to transport crews and equipment to work sites | ☐ preventive maintenance of heavy equipment | ☐ other: ______] **and other physical maintenance work.**

☐ [☐ Perform | ☐ Supervise a crew of ______ *(#)* in] **bridge maintenance work including the** [☐ repair | ☐ construction] **of** ______ *[type of]* **bridge-building structures and** [☐ bridge opening machinery | ☐ engine generator sets | ☐ routine maintenance | ☐ other: ______] **to ensure efficient and dependable bridge operations including all electrical and mechanical systems.**

☐ **Work on a wide range of highway projects including** [☐ picking up roadside litter | ☐ repairing ditches and other drainage structures | ☐ repairing highway signs | ☐ cleaning roadway signs and markers | ☐ acting as flag person | ☐ closing lanes | ☐ sealing road patches and cracks | ☐ removing undergrowth from highway rights of ways | ☐ working on traffic control using traffic cones and flares | ☐ sweeping, shoveling, and raking asphalt | ☐ plowing snow | ☐ hauling garbage | ☐ other: ______].

☐ [☐ Oversee | ☐ Perform] [☐ bridge and work zone inspections | ☐ repair functions | ☐ bridge cleaning | ☐ traffic control functions | ☐ preventive maintenance and repairs | ☐ concrete repairs | ☐ vegetative activities | ☐ debris cleaning around structures | ☐ snow removal | ☐ other: ______] **to ensure bridge safety, proper traffic control, and compliance with all safety and environmental regulations as well as** [☐ proper methods | ☐ quality control | ☐ timely project completion | ☐ other: ______].

ACHIEVEMENT SAMPLES: *See "Highway & Bridge Maintenance Management," "Completed Projects – General" and "Completed Construction Projects."*

Highway & Bridge Maintenance – Management

See also other Highway & Bridge categories, as applicable.

☐ **Plan, direct, and supervise** [☐ a crew of ______ *(#)* | ☐ multiple crews] **engaged in** [☐ new | ☐ reconstruction] **highway work including** [☐ clearing | ☐ filling | ☐ grading | ☐ laying | ☐ other: ______] **of new surfaces.**

☐ **Supervise a** [☐ district-wide | ☐ maintenance patrol | ☐ other: ______] [☐ highway | ☐ bridge | ☐ other: ______] **maintenance crew of** ______ *[#]* **in their performance of** ______, ______, **and** ______ *[what functions?].*

☐ **Supervise and oversee** [☐ pavement care | ☐ roadside shoulder restoration and repairs | ☐ equipment deliveries | ☐ snow removal operations | ☐ other: ______] **ensuring environmental compliance in all areas.**

☐ **Maintain** [☐ local | ☐ interstate | ☐ country | ☐ township] **highways and adjacent right-of-way properties including** [☐ roadways | ☐ municipal roads | ☐ rural roads | ☐ airport runways | ☐ other: ______] **through** [☐ road repair | ☐ brush removal | ☐ tree trimming and pruning | ☐ litter removal | ☐ snow and ice containment | ☐ fence and guard rail repair | ☐ other: ______].

☐ **Work closely with the** [☐ Department of Transportation (DOT) | ☐ State Police | ☐ Traffic Management Center | ☐ government officials | ☐ private entities | ☐ the public | ☐ others: ______] **in the areas of** ______, ______, **and** ______ *[which areas?]* **to minimize traffic flow interruptions and ensure public safety is maintained.**

☐ **Oversee the** ______ *[which?]* **maintenance section to provide for safe driving thoroughfare within** ______ [what?] **area(s) covering** ______ *[#]* **miles of highways and roadways by ensuring the maintenance of all roads, structures, and rights-of-way.**

☐ **Ensure all incident responses to highway emergencies are handled timely and professionally.**

☐ **Inspect** [☐ construction | ☐ maintenance | ☐ repair] **of** ______ *[type of]* [☐ highway | ☐ bridge | ☐ other: ______] **projects to determine and order the materials and equipment needed for** ______ *[what?]* **in order to maximize production and ensure highest standards of performance.**

☐ **Supervise and coordinate maintenance crew activities in the installation and repair of** [☐ traffic signals | ☐ signs | ☐ traffic islands | ☐ barriers | ☐ other: ______].

ACHIEVEMENT SAMPLES: *See also "Completed Projects – General" and "Completed Construction Projects."*

- ☐ **Facilitated restoration and repair of** ______ *[which?]* **roadway surfaces which helped maintain the integrity of state** [☐ highways | ☐ bridges | ☐ other: ______]. **Performed roadway, roadside, and structural maintenance activities keeping** [☐ pavement surfaces | ☐ shoulders | ☐ clear zones | ☐ roadways | ☐ other: ______] **in good repair.**
- ☐ **By promoting and practicing a culture of safety**, [(☐ reduced / ☐ eliminated) accidents and injuries | ☐ other achievements: ______].
- ☐ **Recipient of** [☐ "Highway Safety" | ☐ "Snow Fighter" | ☐ other: "______"] **Award** ______ *[#]* **consecutive years for** [☐ having no accidents | ☐ reducing company liability | ☐ work at Ground Zero | ☐ other: ______].
- ☐ **As part of the** ______ *[which?]* **Committee, evaluated the *Safety and Accident Prevention Program* and recommended** ______ *[what?]*, **which helped improve the state's DOTs safety rating from** ______ *[previous rating]* **to** ______ *[current rating]* **by** ______ *[doing what?]* **and reduced risk in the area(s) of** ______ *[which area(s)?]*.
- ☐ **Often requested by** ______ *[whom?]* **to** ______ *[perform what?]* **due to** [☐ my safety precautions | ☐ diligent highway work oversight | ☐ other: ______].
- ☐ **Received** [☐ excellent | ☐ above average] **performance evaluations for** [☐ safety measures | ☐ damage control methods | ☐ machinery knowledge | ☐ diligence in completing ______ *(what?)* | ☐ other achievements: ______].

Highway & Bridge Maintenance – Work

See also "Highway & Bridge Maintenance Scope."

- ☐ **Certified on** ______ *[what?]*, **operate highway maintenance equipment and machinery including** ______ *[which machinery?]* **for** ______ *[purpose]*.
- ☐ **Haul, dump, and/or spread** [☐ sand | ☐ salt | ☐ gravel | ☐ asphalt | ☐ clay | ☐ chlorides | ☐ other: ______] **to** [☐ abate ice | ☐ fill washouts | ☐ repair road shoulders | ☐ repair joints | ☐ patch broken pavement | ☐ other: ______].
- ☐ [☐ Maintain | ☐ Improve | ☐ Construct | ☐ Repair | ☐ Clean | ☐ other: ______] [☐ highways | ☐ roadways | ☐ right-of-ways | ☐ bridges | ☐ other: ______] **including** [☐ cutting brush and grass | ☐ excavating and grading ditches | ☐ digging channels | ☐ applying chemicals to vegetation | ☐ performing traffic control | ☐ patching and sealing pavement | ☐ handling drainage work | ☐ hauling trash | ☐ performing emergency response | ☐ conducting snow and ice control | ☐ assisting stranded motorists | ☐ inspecting and repairing drainage systems | ☐ making minor equipment repairs | ☐ loading and unloading freight | ☐ emptying litter barrels | ☐ controlling graffiti | ☐ other: ______].
- ☐ **Help maintain the integrity of state highways by performing various roadway, roadside, and structural maintenance activities including** ______, ______, **and** ______ *[what functions?]*.
- ☐ **Under the direction of the** [☐ Zone Manager | ☐ Project Manager | ☐ other: ______], **manage and direct a team of** ______ *[#]* **bridge crew members in their bridge maintenance and repair functions.**
- ☐ **Stripe roadways throughout the** ______ *[state, county, township, or region]* **operating center, edge-line, and automatic-skip-line controls and ensuring correct longitude and transverse pavement markings are first measured and tested in order to provide proper traffic control and safety.**
- ☐ **Erect, install, or/or repair** [☐ guardrails | ☐ road shoulders | ☐ highway lighting | ☐ highway markers | ☐ warning signals | ☐ berms | ☐ other: ______] **using** ______ *[type of hand and power tools]*.
- ☐ [☐ Install and repair | ☐ Supervise the installation and repair of] **highway and roadway** [☐ signs | ☐ fences | ☐ guardrails | ☐ drainage structures | ☐ other: ______].
- ☐ **Remove debris and litter from** [☐ paved surfaces | ☐ roadways | ☐ catch basins | ☐ drain structures | ☐ rock and mud slides | ☐ culverts | ☐ drop inlets | ☐ ditches | ☐ other: ______].
- ☐ **Conduct physically demanding labor in the areas of** [☐ cleaning and reshaping ditches | ☐ erecting signs | ☐ performing landscaping activities | ☐ other: ______].
- ☐ **Respond to 24/7 emergency callouts within** [☐ 30 minutes | ☐ one hour | ☐ other: ______] **to perform emergency clean-up of** [☐ snow and ice removal | ☐ downed trees | ☐ storm debris clean-up | ☐ other: ______].
- ☐ **Perform snow and ice clearance using** [☐ single-blade | ☐ wing] **plows and applying** [☐ chlorides | ☐ salt | ☐ other: ______] **in** ______ *[what areas?]*.

ACHIEVEMENT SAMPLES: *See "Highway & Bridge Maintenance Management" and "Construction Projects."*

HVAC / HVAC-R – General

See also other HVAC/HVAC-R categories, as applicable.

- ☐ **Conduct** [☐ journey- | ☐ apprentice- | ☐ masters- | ☐ other: ______] **level** [☐ installation | ☐ maintenance | ☐ servicing | ☐ repair] **of HVAC systems for this $______** *[revenues]* ______ *[type of]* **firm that services** ______ *[type of]* **clientele**.
- ☐ **Install, repair, and service** [☐ heating and air conditioning systems | ☐ industrial and commercial refrigerant systems | ☐ other: ______] **to ensure control of temperature, humidity, and air quality in** ______ *[type of]* **buildings for this** [☐ HVAC firm | ☐ contracting company | ☐ manufacturer | ☐ wholesaler | ☐ school district | ☐ other: ______].
- ☐ **Service and repair climate-control equipment in** [☐ residential homes | ☐ office buildings | ☐ stores | ☐ malls | ☐ schools | ☐ hospitals | ☐ restaurants | ☐ factories | ☐ other: ______].
- ☐ **Handle air conditioning installations and repair for** [☐ commercial | ☐ industrial | ☐ residential] **customers including** [☐ roof-top installations | ☐ attic duct work | ☐ condenser connections | ☐ charging systems with Freon | ☐ other: ______] **for this $______** *[revenues]* ______ *[type of]* **firm**.
- ☐ [☐ Conduct | ☐ Supervise] **all** [☐ HVAC | ☐ HVAC-R | ☐ mechanical systems | ☐ other: ______] **related activities including** [☐ preventive maintenance | ☐ heating and cooling equipment inspections | ☐ duct airflow readings | ☐ HVAC systems balancing | ☐ fuel system components maintenance | ☐ building and automation systems monitoring | ☐ production and injection systems repair | ☐ water treatment tests | ☐ firing and fuel ratio controls upkeep | ☐ other: ______].
- ☐ **Troubleshoot, diagnose, repair, and/or adjust** [☐ oil burner | ☐ gas burner | ☐ hot water | ☐ refrigeration | ☐ other: ______] **systems to ensure they are operating efficiently by checking and testing** [☐ thermostats | ☐ blowers | ☐ burners | ☐ nozzles | ☐ controls | ☐ other: ______], **and other components**.
- ☐ **Install, service, replace, and/or repair** [☐ air conditioning units | ☐ HVAC control systems | ☐ air conditioning compressors | ☐ chillers | ☐ air distribution equipment | ☐ variable speed equipment | ☐ air handlers | ☐ forced air systems | ☐ furnaces | ☐ boilers | ☐ water heaters | ☐ heat pumps | ☐ split systems | ☐ rooftop units | ☐ electrical circuits | ☐ air movement equipment | ☐ electric motors | ☐ evaporative coolers | ☐ cooling towers | ☐ fire control systems | ☐ exhaust systems | ☐ pneumatic controls | ☐ air filters | ☐ pumps | ☐ duct work | ☐ grills | ☐ piping | ☐ blowers | ☐ shafts | ☐ bearings | ☐ coils | ☐ dampers | ☐ diffusers | ☐ package units | ☐ other: ______] **of various makes and models including** [☐ American Standard | ☐ Bryant | ☐ Carrier | ☐ Coleman | ☐ Frigidaire | ☐ Honeywell | ☐ Johnson Controls | ☐ Liebert | ______☐ Lennox | ☐ Luxaire | ☐ Maytag | ☐ McQuay | ☐ Rheem | ☐ Ruud | ☐ Seibe | ☐ Siemens | ☐ Tappan | ☐ Thermo King | ☐ Toshiba | ☐ Trane | ☐ Westinghouse | ☐ York | ☐ others: ______] **consisting of** [☐ one to five | ☐ 5 to 20 | ☐ 20 to 50 | ☐ other: ______] **tons**.
- ☐ **Handle approximately** ______ *[#]* **HVAC jobs** [☐ weekly | ☐ monthly | ☐ annually] [☐ averaging $______ to $______ | ☐ totaling $______] **including** [☐ estimating job times and costs | ☐ selecting materials | ☐ preparing materials estimates | ☐ reviewing bids | ☐ ordering job-related materials | ☐ scheduling jobs | ☐ performing HVAC functions | ☐ inspecting completed jobs | ☐ other: ______].
- ☐ **Working as apprentice with** [☐ owner of (☐ small / ☐ large) proprietorship | ☐ Plumbing Foreman | ☐ other: ______], **acquired skills necessary to perform** [☐ oil burner | ☐ gas burner | ☐ air conditioning refrigeration | ☐ other: ______] [☐ installation | ☐ servicing] **within** ______ *[timeframe]*.
- ☐ **Install, service, and repair** [☐ industrial | ☐ commercial] **refrigeration systems and equipment including** [☐ motors | ☐ condensing units | ☐ compressors | ☐ evaporators | ☐ piping | ☐ other: ______] **following** [☐ design specifications | ☐ blueprints | ☐ manufacturers' instructions | ☐ other: ______].

ACHIEVEMENT SAMPLES: *See **"HVAC / HVAC-R Projects & Functions"** and **"Construction Projects."***

HVAC / HVAC-R – Installations

See also other HVAC / HVAC-R categories, as applicable.

- ☐ **Install and service** [☐ HVAC | ☐ HVAC-R control | ☐ central air conditioning | (☐ gas / ☐ electric / ☐ solid fuel) heating systems | ☐ solar panels | ☐ commercial refrigerant | ☐ pneumatic HVAC control | ☐ digital HVAC | ☐ natural gas and water piping | ☐ production and injection | ☐ pneumatic piping | ☐ water supply | ☐ air distribution and balance | ☐ auxiliary control | ☐ forced air | ☐ other: ______] **systems for** ______ *[what?]* **in accordance with blueprint specifications.**
- ☐ **Handle air conditioning installations and repair for** [☐ commercial | ☐ industrial | ☐ residential] **customers including** [☐ roof-top installations | ☐ attic duct work | ☐ connecting condensers | ☐ charging systems with Freon | ☐ other: ______], **testing all units for proper installation and operation.**
- ☐ [☐ Coordinate HVAC jobs with | ☐ Perform the functions of] [☐ Sheet Metal Workers | ☐ Electricians | ☐ Plumbers | ☐ Pipe Fitters | ☐ Pipe Layers | ☐ Steamfitters | ☐ Boilermakers | ☐ other: ______] **in the installation and servicing of** ______ *[type of]* [☐ cooling | ☐ heating | ☐ other: ______] **systems including** ______ *[what functions?]*.

☐ **Oversee the installation and replacement of heating and cooling systems including** [☐ air conditioning units | ☐ HVAC control systems | ☐ air conditioning compressors | ☐ chillers | ☐ air distribution equipment | ☐ variable speed equipment | ☐ air handlers | ☐ forced air systems | ☐ furnaces | ☐ boilers | ☐ water heaters | ☐ heat pumps | ☐ split systems | ☐ rooftop units | ☐ electrical circuits | ☐ air movement equipment | ☐ electric motors | ☐ evaporative coolers | ☐ cooling towers | ☐ fire control systems | ☐ exhaust systems | ☐ pneumatic controls | ☐ air filters | ☐ pumps | ☐ duct work | ☐ grills | ☐ piping | ☐ blowers | ☐ shafts | ☐ bearings | ☐ coils | ☐ dampers | ☐ diffusers | ☐ package units | ☐ other: ______] **of various makes and models.**

☐ **Facilitate the installation and servicing of** [☐ central air-conditioning systems | ☐ fuel and water supply lines | ☐ air ducts | ☐ vents | ☐ pumps | ☐ fuel lines | ☐ water supply lines | ☐ air compressors | ☐ steam boilers | ☐ pump seals, bearings, and couplings | ☐ solar panels | ☐ other: ______], **connect wiring and controls to** [☐ ductwork | ☐ refrigerant lines | ☐ electrical wiring | ☐ other: ______]; **charge systems with refrigerant;, and test for proper operation.**

ACHIEVEMENT SAMPLES: *See "HVAC/HVAC-R Projects & Functions" and "Construction Projects."*

HVAC / HVAC-R – Maintenance & Repair Work

See also "Maintenance & Repair Projects," "Equipment, Tools & Testing Devices – HVAC / HVAC-R," and other HVAC categories.

☐ **Diagnose, repair, and test the performance of** [☐ mechanical | ☐ electrical] **components throughout HVAC systems, including** [☐ motors | ☐ compressors | ☐ condensing units | ☐ evaporators | ☐ piping | ☐ metal and fiberglass ducts | ☐ pumps | ☐ fans | ☐ thermostats | ☐ other: ______] **and other components**.

☐ **Working as apprentice with** [☐ owner of small proprietorship | ☐ Plumbing Foreman | ☐ other: ______], **acquired skills to perform** [☐ oil burner | ☐ gas burner | ☐ air conditioning | ☐ other: ______] **servicing within** ______ *[#]* **months**.

☐ **Repair and service** [☐ heating and air conditioning systems | ☐ industrial and commercial refrigerant systems | ☐ other: ______] **to ensure control of temperature, humidity, and air quality in** [☐ residential | ☐ commercial | ☐ industrial | ☐ manufacturing | ☐ other: ______] **buildings for this** [☐ HVAC firm | ☐ contracting company | ☐ manufacturer | ☐ wholesaler | ☐ school district | ☐ other: ______].

☐ **Monitor and maintain** [☐ firing and fuel ratio controls | ☐ fuel system components | ☐ heat exchangers and sand traps | ☐ heat exchange equipment | ☐ feed and return water pumps | ☐ other: ______].

☐ **Service and repair climate-control equipment in** [☐ residential homes | ☐ office buildings | ☐ stores | ☐ schools | ☐ hospitals | ☐ restaurants | ☐ factories | ☐ other: ______].

☐ **Identify and correct** ______ *[type of]* **problems of** ______ *[type of]* **systems through the use of** ______ *[what methods, tools, or equipment?].*

☐ **Troubleshoot, dismantle, optimize, and repair** [☐ heating | ☐ cooling | ☐ ventilating | ☐ refrigeration | ☐ other: ______] **systems including** [☐ oil burners | ☐ gas boilers | ☐ electric boilers | ☐ water heaters | ☐ steam lines | ☐ heat return lines | ☐ main water lines | ☐ roof drains | ☐ electromechanical equipment | ☐ chillers | ☐ vacuum pumps | ☐ water pumps | ☐ air compressors | ☐ fans | ☐ other: ______] **to ensure they are operating efficiently by checking and testing** [☐ thermostats | ☐ blowers | ☐ burners | ☐ nozzles | ☐ controls | ☐ other: ______] **and other components**.

☐ **Perform cooling system maintenance and repair including** [☐ replacing burned out motors | ☐ cleaning blower cages | ☐ other: ______].

☐ **Complete inspection and maintenance work by** [☐ overhauling compressors | ☐ replacing filters and ducts | ☐ other: ______] **to ensure its efficient** [☐ HVAC | ☐ HVAC-R] **operation**.

☐ **Successfully complete all** ______ *[type of]* **HVAC repair work orders consisting of** ______ *[type of]* **work** [☐ ahead of schedule | ☐ within required timeframes] **by** ______ [doing what well?].

☐ **Maintain plant's heating system boilers including cleaning** [☐ heads | ☐ flame sensor | ☐ igniter | ☐ other: ______] **and repair as needed all** [☐ leaks | ☐ broken pipes | ☐ other: ______], **maintaining accurate records of all** [☐ labor hours | ☐ materials used | ☐ other: ______].

☐ **Diagnose, service, and adjust oil burner systems to ensure they are operating efficiently by checking and testing** [☐ thermostats | ☐ blowers | ☐ burners | ☐ nozzles | ☐ controls | ☐ other: ______], **and other components**.

☐ **Prevent the release of chlorofluorocarbon and hydro chlorofluorocarbon refrigerants in air-conditioning and refrigeration systems from entering the ozone layer by** [☐ ensuring there are no system leaks | ☐ venting refrigerant into cylinders | ☐ other manner: ______].

☐ **Apply an expert working knowledge of** [☐ electrical | ☐ electronic | ☐ mechanical] [☐ heating | ☐ ventilation | ☐ air conditioning | ☐ refrigeration] [☐ theory | ☐ methods | ☐ practices | ☐ other: ______] **in the** [☐ troubleshooting and repair of electrical control systems | ☐ design of (☐ centrifugal / ☐ reciprocal) compressors | ☐ operation of pneumatic control systems | ☐ maintenance of steam condensate return traps, pumps, and compressors | ☐ other: ____________] **to operate, maintain, and repair HVAC systems.**

☐ **Maintain and repair all kitchen appliances including** [☐ gas and electric stoves and ovens | ☐ refrigerators | ☐ freezers | ☐ dishwashers | ☐ garbage disposals | ☐ microwaves | ☐ steam cookers | ☐ sinks | ☐ faucets | ☐ valves | ☐ other: ______].

☐ **Complete inspection and maintenance work by** [☐ overhauling compressors | ☐ replacing filters and ducts | ☐ other: ______] **to ensure its efficient** [☐ HVAC | ☐ HVAC-R] **operation**.

ACHIEVEMENT SAMPLES: *See "HVAC/HVAC-R Projects & Functions" and "Construction Projects."*

HVAC / HVAC-R – Management

See also "HVAC / HVAC-R Work," "Plumbing Management Scope," "Trades/Crew Supervision – All Trades," "Inspections & Compliance – Trades," "Contractor/Subcontractor Influence & Collaboration," "Work Collaboration," and other HVAC categories.

☐ **Manage and lead the installation and servicing of** [☐ heating and air conditioning systems | ☐ refrigeration systems | ☐ industrial and commercial refrigerant systems | ☐ fuel supply lines | ☐ water supply and drain lines | ☐ steam lines | ☐ water heaters | (☐ gas / ☐ electric / ☐ open flame) boilers | ☐ pipes, faucets, and valves | ☐ specialty items | ☐ other: ______] **and test units to ensure proper control of temperature, humidity, and air quality in** [☐ residential | ☐ commercial | ☐ industrial | ☐ other: ______] **buildings**.

☐ **Provide a full array of** [☐ plumbing | ☐ HVAC | ☐ refrigeration | ☐ steamfitting | ☐ welding | ☐ carpentry | ☐ other: ______] **services including** [(☐ plumbing / ☐ electrical / ☐ general contracting) work | (☐ bathroom / ☐ kitchen / ☐ tile) installations | ☐ other: ______] **for this** [☐ HVAC | ☐ general contracting | ☐ construction | ☐ other: ______] **firm**.

☐ **Oversee and supervise air conditioning installations and repair for** [☐ commercial | ☐ industrial | ☐ residential] **customers including** ______ *[what functions?]* **for this $**______ *[revenues]* ______ *[type of]* **firm**.

☐ **Direct day-to-day operations of this** [☐ HVAC | ☐ plumbing | ☐ general contracting | ☐ construction | ☐ other: ______] **firm providing a full array of** [☐ HVAC | ☐ plumbing | ☐ steamfitting | ☐ carpentry | ☐ other: ______] **services including** [☐ bathroom and kitchen installation | ☐ plumbing, electrical, and general contracting work | ☐ other: ______].

☐ **Supervise and perform the installation, maintenance, repair, and/or replacement of all required HVAC** [☐ equipment | ☐ systems | ☐ pipes | ☐ fixtures | ☐ valves | ☐ pumps | ☐ other: ______] **to** [☐ set up | ☐ operate | ☐ maintain] **the** [☐ water distribution | ☐ heating and cooling | ☐ other: ______] **system(s) and related equipment of** ______ *[what?]*.

☐ **Lead and direct approximately** ______ *[#]* **HVAC jobs** [☐ weekly | ☐ monthly | ☐ annually] [☐ averaging $______ to $______ *(amounts)* | ☐ totaling $______ *(amount)*] **including** [☐ estimating job times and costs | ☐ selecting materials | ☐ preparing materials estimates | ☐ reviewing bids | ☐ ordering required job-related materials | ☐ scheduling jobs | ☐ performing HVAC functions | ☐ inspecting completed jobs | ☐ other: ______].

☐ **Supervise all** [☐ HVAC | ☐ HVAC-R | ☐ mechanical systems | ☐ other: ______] **related activities including** [☐ preventive maintenance | ☐ heating and cooling equipment inspections | ☐ duct airflow readings | ☐ HVAC systems balancing | ☐ fuel system components maintenance | ☐ building and automation systems monitoring | ☐ production and injection systems repair | ☐ water treatment tests | ☐ firing and fuel ratio controls upkeep | ☐ other: ______].

☐ **Supervise and oversee** ______ *[#]* **HVAC Technicians in the service and repair of climate-control equipment in** [☐ residential homes | ☐ office buildings | ☐ stores | ☐ schools | ☐ hospitals | ☐ restaurants | ☐ factories | ☐ hotels ☐ other: ______].

☐ **Provide leadership and direction to** ______ *[#]* **HVAC Technicians in the installation and maintenance of** [☐ central air conditioning systems | ☐ fuel and water supply lines | ☐ gas | ☐ oil | ☐ electric | (☐ solid-fuel / ☐ multiple-fuel) heating | ☐ other: ______]; **and test units for proper installation and operation ensuring compliance with** [☐ blueprints | ☐ specifications].

☐ **Supervise** [☐ journey- | ☐ apprentice- | ☐ masters-] **level** [☐ installation | ☐ maintenance | ☐ servicing | ☐ repair] **of HVAC systems for this $**______ *[revenues]* ______ *[type of]* **firm that services** ______ *[type of]* **clientele**.

☐ **Direct the HVAC** [☐ installation | ☐ replacement | ☐ maintenance | ☐ repair | ☐ administrative | ☐ other: ______] **operations including all aspects of plumbing required in** [☐ new construction | ☐ remodel | ☐ maintenance | ☐ repair | ☐ other: ______] **jobs for this $**______ *[revenues]* ______ *[type of]* **firm**.

☐ **Supervise HVAC** [☐ installation | ☐ replacement | ☐ repair | ☐ other: ______] **functions including all aspects of plumbing required in** [☐ new construction | ☐ remodel | ☐ maintenance | ☐ other: ______] **jobs on** ______ *[type of]* **projects**.

☐ [☐ Lead and direct] [☐ Supervise and perform] **the installation, maintenance, repair, and/or replacement of all required HVAC** [☐ equipment | ☐ systems | ☐ pipes | ☐ fixtures | ☐ valves | ☐ pumps | ☐ other: ______] **to** [☐ set up | ☐ operate | ☐ maintain] **the** [☐ water distribution | ☐ heating and cooling | ☐ other: ______] **system(s) and related equipment of** ______ *[what?]*.

☐ **Oversee the installation, maintenance, and servicing of** [☐ heating and air conditioning systems | ☐ industrial and commercial refrigerant systems | ☐ other: ______] **to ensure control of temperature, humidity, and air quality in** [☐ residential | ☐ commercial | ☐ industrial | ☐ manufacturing | ☐ other: ______] **buildings for this** ______ *[type of]* **firm**.

☐ **Review and evaluate HVAC** [☐ plans | ☐ specifications | ☐ drawings] **and other** [☐ blueprints | ☐ diagrams | ☐ schematics | ☐ specifications] **to** [☐ determine compatibility and adaptability with existing systems | ☐ ensure compliance with all codes | ☐ advise (☐ Project Engineer / ☐ HVAC Foreman / ☐ Lead Plumber / ☐ other: ______) on code requirements | ☐ other: ______]; **and modify blueprints to meet as-built specifications and dimensions.**

ACHIEVEMENT SAMPLES: *See "HVAC/HVAC-R Projects & Functions" and "Construction Projects."*

HVAC / HVAC-R – Monitoring & Testing

See "Inspections & Compliance – HVAC / HVAC-R" and "Equipment, Tools & Testing Devices – HVAC/HVAC-R."

HVAC / HVAC-R – Projects & Functions, Other

See "Maintenance & Repair Projects" as well as other HVAC / HVAC-R categories.

☐ **Specializing in the** [☐ installation | ☐ maintenance | ☐ service | ☐ repair] **of** [☐ heating | ☐ cooling | ☐ refrigeration | ☐ other: ______] **equipment, perform** ______, ______, **and** ______ *[which?]* **functions required for** ______ *[what?].*

☐ [☐ On call 24 hours a day, seven days a week | ☐ ______ *(#)* days a week] **to respond to customer emergency callbacks within a** ______ *[#]*-**mile radius and** ______ *[#]*-**hour turnaround.**

☐ **Prepare for all HVAC jobs by** [☐ prioritizing work assignments | ☐ ordering required materials | ☐ determining equipment needed | ☐ setting up each project with the correct tools, materials, and supplies | ☐ coordinating contracting vendors/trades | ☐ determining conditions and safety requirements | ☐ identifying required repairs and/or replacements | ☐ other: ______].

☐ **Apply** [☐ expert | ☐ proficient | ☐ basic] **working knowledge of** [☐ electrical | ☐ electronic | ☐ mechanical] [☐ heating | ☐ ventilation | ☐ air conditioning | ☐ refrigeration] [☐ theory | ☐ methods | ☐ practices | ☐ other: ______] **in the** [☐ troubleshooting and repair of electrical control systems | ☐ design of (☐ centrifugal / ☐ reciprocal) compressors | ☐ operation of pneumatic control systems | ☐ maintenance of steam condensate return traps, pumps, and compressors | ☐ other: ______] **to install, maintain, and repair HVAC systems.**

☐ **Handle various HVAC-related plumbing functions including** [☐ cutting and threading pipe | ☐ soldering copper | ☐ installing PVC pipe | ☐ other: ______] **for** [☐ compressed air | ☐ potable water | ☐ cooling water | ☐ other: ______] **maintaining proper operation of all equipment.**

☐ **Interpret and update** [☐ blueprints | ☐ architectural drawings | ☐ plans | ☐ specifications | ☐ other: ______] **to reflect required changes made to HVAC systems.**

☐ **Connect refrigeration equipment to** [☐ refrigerant lines | ☐ ductwork | ☐ electrical power source | ☐ other: ______], **charge with refrigerant, test systems, and program controls.**

☐ **Prevent release of chlorofluorocarbon and hydro chlorofluorocarbon refrigerants in** [☐ air conditioning | ☐ refrigeration] **systems from depleting the ozone layer and protect against ultraviolet radiation by** [☐ ensuring there are no system leaks | ☐ using care to recover and conserve refrigerants | ☐ venting refrigerant into cylinders | ☐ recycling it for reuse | ☐ other methods: ______].

☐ **Perform a number of additional HVAC activities including** [☐ inspecting heating and cooling equipment | ☐ conducting water treatment tests | ☐ operating high-pressure steam boilers | ☐ replacing filters and ducts | ☐ testing and maintaining generators | ☐ troubleshooting chiller operations | ☐ running wire and installing outlet boxes | ☐ checking fans, piping, gauges, and indicator lights | ☐ welding and repairing brazing pipes | ☐ diagnosing and repairing heating and hot water problems | ☐ overhauling compressors | ☐ operating microprocessor fan controls | ☐ performing attic duct work | ☐ charging refrigerant systems with Freon | ☐ performing roof-top installations | ☐ programming energy management equipment | ☐ analyzing water treatment and adjusting chemicals for chill water and heating systems | ☐ monitoring building and automation systems for HVAC and fire hazards | ☐ other: ______].

☐ **Coordinate all aspects of HVAC projects with** [☐ clients | ☐ engineers | ☐ architects | ☐ municipal officials | ☐ county officials | ☐ code officers | ☐ others: ______] **ensuring compliance with all** [☐ plumbing codes | ☐ quality standards | ☐ work schedules | ☐ other: ______].

ACHIEVEMENT SAMPLES:

☐ **Significantly increased production and efficiency** ______% *[percentage]* **by renovating a** ______ [#]-**foot-long** ______ *[type of]* **furnace with new** [☐ control room | ☐ structural work | ☐ refractory | ☐ burners | ☐ blowers | ☐ ductwork | ☐ gas trains | ☐ other: ______].

☐ **Installed** ______ *[type of]* [☐ HVAC | ☐ HVAC-R] **systems including** ______, ______, **and** ______ *[which systems?]* **to provide** [☐ gas heaters for freeze protection | ☐ fresh-air supply for control rooms | ☐ furnace waste heat for pipe drying | ☐ infrared tube heaters for curing rooms | ☐ other: ______].

Increased Account Base

See also "Increased Sales" and "Increased Revenue & Profitability."

ACHIEVEMENT SAMPLES:

- ☐ **Elevated** [☐ customer base | ☐ new business | ☐ referrals] **by** ______ *[#]* **/** ______**%** *[percentage]* **over previous year(s) by** [☐ developing (☐ dynamic presentations / ☐ unique concepts / ☐ innovative ideas) | ☐ providing clients with superior service and opportunities | ☐ developing a strong rapport with satisfied clients | ☐ concentrating on higher-end sales | ☐ increasing loyalty of existing customer base | ☐ gaining increased referrals | ☐ problem-solving customer problems | ☐ customer needs awareness | ☐ other means: ______].
- ☐ **Successfully persuaded new clients to make an investment in the future by** [☐ selling high-end projects | ☐ presenting value proposition | ☐ demonstrating the return on their investment | ☐ educating consumers on ______ *(what?)* | ☐ other: ______].
- ☐ **Expanded firm's account base by** [☐ delivering (☐ fresh / ☐ unique) design concepts | ☐ finding new talent to help develop those concepts | ☐ creating innovative client proposals | ☐ developing dynamic presentation layouts | ☐ concentrating on higher-end sales | ☐ increasing loyalty of existing client base | ☐ problem-solving customer challenges | ☐ creating a work environment that offered excitement and challenge | ☐ other methods: ______]
- ☐ **Brought in multiple, high-volume** ______ *[type of]* **clients generating $**______ **in new business by** ______ *[how you accomplished this].*
- ☐ **Instrumental in reviving** ______ *[what account?]* **via** [☐ strong customer rapport | ☐ follow-up techniques | ☐ diligent service | ☐ other: ______].
- ☐ **Procured the nation's** ______ *[#]* **largest** ______ *[type of]* **company as a client via** [☐ thorough research | ☐ professional persistence | ☐ dedication to my goal | ☐ persuasive marketing materials | ☐ convincing phone campaign | ☐ other: ______] **resulting in increased annual income of** ______**%** *[percentage]* **/ $**______ *[amount].*
- ☐ **Configured, proposed, and closed sale of** ______ *[what?]* **for** ______ *[what or whom?],* **resulting in $**______ **in increased sales.**
- ☐ **Increased account base** ______ *[#]* / ______**%** *[percentage]*—**from** ______ *[#]* **to** ______ *[#]* **accounts—by** [☐ concentrating on higher-end sales | ☐ increasing loyalty of existing client base | ☐ obtaining repeat customers | ☐ problem-solving customer challenges | ☐ other: ______].
- ☐ **Increased profitability of account base from** ______**% to** ______**%** *[percentages]* **by** ______ *[what methods?].*
- ☐ **Through** [☐ client trust | ☐ relationship building | ☐ other method: ______] [☐ received many referrals | ☐ maintained loyal, enduring customer relationships | ☐ increased account base | ☐ other benefit: ______].
- ☐ **Successfully solicit and obtain new business through** [☐ networking with ______ *(whom?)* | ☐ client referrals | ☐ advertising in ______ *(what publication?)* | ☐ canvassing | ☐ other means: ______].
- ☐ **Created large-dollar projects bringing return on investment for clients and higher sales for firm, resulting in** [☐ higher per-project sales | ☐ repeat business | ☐ referrals | ☐ other: ______].
- ☐ **Through** [☐ client trust | ☐ relationship building | ☐ creative initiatives | ☐ other method: ______] [☐ received many referrals | ☐ maintained loyal, enduring customer relationships | ☐ increased profitability of account base by ______% | ☐ other benefit: ______]
- ☐ **Increased existing business by** [☐ assessing and servicing client needs | ☐ working within their budgets | ☐ meeting all deadlines | ☐ other methods: ______].
- ☐ **Brought in multiple, high-volume** ______ *[type of]* **clients generating $**______ *[amount]* **in new business by** ______ *[how you accomplished this].*
- ☐ **Generated annual sales of** $______ **through** [☐ attractive visual presentations | ☐ attaining referrals through word of mouth from satisfied clients | ☐ other: ______].

Increased Customer Service Levels

See "Customer Service & Satisfaction Levels Improvement."

Increased Market Share

ACHIEVEMENT SAMPLES:

☐ **Drove market share ______%** *[percentage]* **/ $______** *[amount]* **in ______** *[which?]* **product line by** [☐ performing feasibility studies | ☐ researching and analyzing historic activities | ☐ determining new markets in the ______ *[which?]* region | ☐ adding new ______ *[type of]* (☐ products / ☐ services) | ☐ creating a ______ *[type of]* program designed to ______ *(do what?)* | ☐ promoting (☐ coordinating products / ☐ add-on sales) | ☐ brainstorming with long-time (☐ employees / ☐ customers / ☐ distributors) | ☐ strategizing successful marketing plans | ☐ maintaining an open line of communication with planners, merchandisers and buyers | ☐ remerchandising items based upon demographic expectations | ☐ presenting in-depth performance reports | ☐ structuring profitable but user-friendly pricing | ☐ other methods: ______].

☐ **Grew the ______** *[which?]* **market in the ______** *[which?]* **area, increasing sales of ______** *[what products]* **by $______** *[amount]* **annually by developing a previously untapped market.**

☐ **Increased market share ______%** *[percentage]* **/ $______** *[amount]* **in the ______** *[which?]* **market, bringing annual sales to $______ by** [☐ recruiting a talented staff | ☐ providing product training | ☐ other: ______], **allowing company to be more** [☐ service- | ☐ product- | ☐ other: ______] **oriented.**

☐ **Prospected and developed untouched new territory including ______, ______, and ______** [☐ Fortune (☐ 100 / ☐ 500) companies] **by** [☐ setting up trade shows | ☐ hiring and training a winning sales management staff | ☐ other: ______].

☐ **Successfully managed and fulfilled mission to develop company into a major full-service ______** *[type of]* **firm by penetrating the ______** *[type of]* **marketplaces and ______** *[doing what?].*

☐ [☐ Researched and studied ______ *(what?)* | ☐ Visited various ______ *(what?)*] **in major markets throughout the** [☐ U.S. | ☐ region | ☐ district | ☐ other: ______] **to** [☐ gain new product development ideas | ☐ participate in international trade shows | ☐ other: ______] **promoting company's ______** *[type of]* **products to ______** *[which?]* **consumers.**

☐ **Spearheaded Company's entrance into the ______** *[which?]* **market environment by ______** *[doing what?].*

☐ **By creating a ______** *[type of]* **program that enabled ______** *[what?],* **increased annual sales in the ______** *[which?]* **marketplace by ______% (from $______ to $______** *(amounts)*) **and profits from $______ to $______** *[amounts].*

☐ **Grew a previously untapped ______** *[type of]* **market in the ______** *[which?]* **area, resulting in increased annual sales of $______** *[amount].*

Increased Revenue & Profitability

See also ***"Cost Reductions & Savings."***

ACHIEVEMENT SAMPLES:

☐ **Drove profitability $______** *[amount]* **/ ______%** *[percentage]* **by** [☐ analyzing and costing proposals | ☐ determining profitability ratios | ☐ working with more creditworthy clientele | ☐ analyzing and troubleshooting customer complaints | ☐ resolving problems quickly | ☐ providing product ability analyses | ☐ acquiring a niche market for ______ *(type of)* | ☐ other methods: ______].

☐ **Drove revenues ______%** *[percentage]* [☐ annually] **through the acquisition of a** [☐ contract from ______ *(where?)* | ☐ foreclosed development and turning it into a profitable venture in less than ______ *(timeframe)* | ☐ other: ______].

☐ **Raised overall business from $______ to $______** *[amounts]* **in revenue in a ______** *[#]*-**year period by implementing a ______** *[type of]* **program involving** [☐ all aspects of quality production | ☐ other: ______].

☐ **Increased profits $______** *[amount]* **and improved customer service ______%** *[percentage]* **by effectively** [☐ leading continuous improvement | ☐ planning production activities | ☐ establishing production priorities | ☐ managing cost performance | ☐ forecasting demand / soliciting and welcoming customer feedback | ☐ building a positive production team environment | ☐ meeting commitments | ☐ shortening life cycles | ☐ integrating leaner business processes | ☐ forecasting budgets | ☐ executing distribution | ☐ improving customer satisfaction | ☐ meeting operation targets | ☐ minimizing risk and errors | ☐ improving product quality | ☐ meeting daily productivity and quality requirements | ☐ maintaining profit loss control | ☐ other: ______].

☐ **Planned, developed, and implemented resource-generating strategies that resulted in identifying and securing ______** *[type of]* [☐ revenue sources | ☐ funding in the amount of $______] **from ______** *[whom?]* **for the firm, which resulted in** [☐ building | ☐ developing | ☐ other: ______] ______ *[what?].*

☐ **Increased revenues ______%** *[percentage]* **by** [☐ obtaining a solid referral business with a reputation for excellent work | ☐ developing targeted advertising campaigns | ☐ creating a website | ☐ dropping off flyers in local communities | ☐ other: ______].

☐ **Drove ______** *[type of]* **profit improvement activities by ______** *[doing what?],* **which resulted in ______** *[benefits].*

☐ **Steadily increased revenues annually by** [☐ developing strong networking contacts in the real estate community | ☐ advertising in local print media | ☐ networking at local Chambers of Commerce | ☐ providing discounts on customer referrals | ☐ other: ______].

☐ **Contributed to increased company profits by $______** *[amount]* **by** [☐ purchasing | ☐ recommending the purchase of] ______ *[type* *of]* **state-of-the-art tools resulting in reduced** [☐ employee | ☐ labor | ☐ other: ______] **costs.**

☐ **Build revenue by** [☐ increasing sales and profits $______ *(amount)* | ☐ controlling expenses | ☐ ensuring a consistent, quality experience for customers | ☐ other: ______].

☐ **Elevated profitability $______** *[amount]* **and reduced labor costs by $______** *[amount]* **by purchasing ______** *[type of]* **state-of-the-art** [☐ equipment | ☐ tools | ☐ materials | ☐ other: ______].

☐ **Increased profitability and decreased costs by $______** *[amount]* **annually by seeking out high quality, and lower cost** [☐ contractor | ☐ subcontractor | ☐ vendor] **pricing for ______** *[what?].*

Increased Sales

*See also **"Increased Account Base"** and **"Cost Reductions & Savings."***

ACHIEVEMENT SAMPLES:

☐ **Established a reputation for quality workmanship at competitive prices by** [☐ maintaining superior levels of craftsmanship | ☐ providing excellent customer service | ☐ meeting or exceeding customer needs, challenges, and demands | ☐ other: ______] **which resulted in ______** *[what measurable benefits?].*

☐ **Increased sales $______** *[amount]* **by working with a network of ______** *[which?]* **trade professionals to increase exposure throughout the ______** *[which?]* **industry and keeping informed of current and future ______** *[type of]* **projects resulting in ______** *[what benefits?].*

☐ **Eliminated potential liability for client and increased contract amount by $______** *[amount]* **by recommending ______** *[what?]* **which resulted in ______** *[what client and firm benefits?].*

☐ **Spearheaded the ______** *[type of]* **initiative to ______** *[do what?]* **which realized increased** [☐ sales | ☐ profits | ☐ corporate gains | ☐ market share | ☐ other: ______] **of $______** *[amount]* **/ ______%** *[percentage]* **in ______** *[what areas?].*

☐ **Elevated** [☐ annual] **sales $______** *[amount]* **/ ______%** *[percentage]* **in ______** *[timeframe]* **by** [☐ designing and implementing successful ______ *(type of)* promotions | ☐ selling trust | ☐ educating consumers | ☐ changing management culture | ☐ creating a marketing portfolio containing photographs and letters of recommendation from previous clients | ☐ obtaining many repeat clients | ☐ elevating referral business by developing a strong rapport with satisfied clients | ☐ ensuring persistent follow-up | ☐ providing loyal customer service | ☐ promoting coordinating services ☐ presenting creative presentations | ☐ attending trade shows | ☐ networking | ☐ promoting a consumer-sensitive approach | ☐ promoting add-on | ☐ other method(s): ______].

☐ **Catapulted sales $______** *[amount]* **by ______** *[doing what?]* **which received** [☐ significant business for the firm | ☐ rave reviews from clients | ☐ other: ______] **and resulted in ______** *[what?].*

☐ **Brought company from an original staff of ______** *[#]* **to a staff of ______** *[#]*, **with sales increases of $______** *(amount)* **after ______** *[timeframe]*. **Accomplished through** [☐ increased marketing | ☐ added services | ☐ increased sales coverage | ☐ providing ancillary support departments with a turnkey approach | ☐ other: ______].

☐ **Contributed to the firm's increased sales and growth in the area(s) of ______** *[what areas?]* **by successfully ______** *[doing what?].*

☐ **Elevated sales with a ______** *[#]*-**year compounded annual growth of ______%** *[percentage]* **and net income with a ______** *[#]*-**year compounded annual growth of ______%** *[percentage]* **through effective use of ______** *[methods].*

Inspections & Compliance – General

*See also **"Inspections & Compliance"** in other areas.*

☐ **Make periodic visits during the** ______ *[type of]* [☐ construction | ☐ installation | ☐ repair | ☐ other: ______] **process to monitor compliance with codes, specifications, and regulations including** [☐ initial inspections before foundation is poured | ☐ completed foundations | ☐ first phase of construction | ☐ follow-up inspections during the construction phase | ☐ final comprehensive inspection upon project completion | ☐ other: ______] **conducting** ______ *[what?]* **during closeout processing.**

☐ **Provide guidance on applicable** ______ *[type of]* **codes and requirements to** [☐ architects | ☐ engineers | ☐ contractors | ☐ developers | ☐ owners | ☐ governmental officials | ☐ the general public | ☐ other: ______] **and other interested parties.**

☐ **Perform** ______ *[type of]* **inspection functions including** [☐ inspecting approved plans and specifications | ☐ testing (☐ new installations / ☐ alternations) of ______ *(what?)* | ☐ interpreting laws, regulations, and codes to particular situations | ☐ writing code violation notices | ☐ gathering code violation evidence | ☐ testifying at hearings | ☐ preparing reports | ☐ determining work priorities of lower-level Inspectors | ☐ performing accident investigations | ☐ evaluating complaints | ☐ other: ______].

☐ **Conduct various** ______ *[type of]* **inspection functions to ensure compliance in all areas including** [☐ reviewing plans to verify code requirements | ☐ identifying construction problems or design errors | ☐ quality testing construction materials | ☐ conducting energy audits | ☐ issuing stop-work orders | ☐ notifying contractors of defective work | ☐ recommending corrective action | ☐ resolving construction personnel disputes | ☐ conducting preventive maintenance | ☐ negotiating plan changes with architects | ☐ holding meetings to discuss project progress | ☐ maintaining work logs and reports | ☐ other: ______].

☐ **Monitor** ______ *[type of]* **the** [☐ construction | ☐ installation | ☐ repair | ☐ other: ______] **progress through on-site field inspections and review to ensure conformance to** [☐ design specifications | ☐ cost estimates | ☐ time schedules | ☐ other: ______] **and to** [☐ quality test materials | ☐ identify problems | ☐ recommend corrective actions | ☐ other: ______] **and immediately** [☐ resolve | ☐ refer] **any problems.**

☐ **Investigate and resolve any and all reported violations of the firm's compliance program and work with** ______ *[whom?]* **to handle violations promptly, accurately, and consistently.**

☐ **Assist** [☐ Plan Examiner | ☐ Foreman | ☐ Project Superintendent | ☐ Building Inspector | ☐ other: ______] **in conducting** ______ *[type of]* **site inspections to determine** [☐ building code and life-safety compliance | ☐ handicap accessibility | ☐ conformance with plans, specifications and state laws | ☐ other: ______].

☐ [☐ Prepare and submit | ☐ Review and approve] ______ *[type of]* **records and reports including** ______ *[type of]* [☐ plans | ☐ plan review documentation | ☐ inspection reports | ☐ permit forms | ☐ permits | ☐ other: ______].

☐ **Perform** [☐ initial | ☐ incremental | ☐ follow-up | ☐ final | ☐ periodic] **worksite inspections of the** [☐ construction | ☐ installation | ☐ remodeling | ☐ repair | ☐ maintenance | ☐ other: ______] **of** [☐ commercial | ☐ residential | ☐ civil | ☐ other: ______] ______ *[type of]* [☐ structures | ☐ buildings | ☐ projects] **through each phase of construction to ensure code and contract compliance.**

☐ **Interact and communicate with** [☐ inspectors | ☐ contractors | ☐ plumbers | ☐ electricians | ☐ HVAC contractors | ☐ owner representatives | ☐ architects | ☐ engineers | ☐ governmental officials | ☐ the general public | ☐ other: ______] **to discuss** ______ *[which?]* **code requirements.**

☐ **Perform final project inspections of all completed work during the construction close-out process, approve payment requests, conduct building site inspections, and** ______ *[other?]* **to ensure compliance with plans, specifications, and building codes.**

☐ **Check** [☐ plans | ☐ specifications | ☐ other: ______] **for compliance with** [☐ Building Code | ☐ other: ______] **and approve and issue consents on** ______ *[what?]*.

☐ **Track and monitor** ______ *[type of]* [☐ job | ☐ installation | ☐ construction | ☐ project | ☐ design-and-build | ☐ other: ______] **progress by conducting on-site inspections to ensure conformance to** [☐ design specifications | ☐ cost estimates | ☐ contracts | ☐ building codes | ☐ zoning regulations | ☐ time schedules | ☐ electrical codes | ☐ plumbing codes | ☐ other: ______] **and** [☐ resolve | ☐ refer] **any problems.**

☐ **Ensure quality compliance with all** [☐ engineering contracts | ☐ state and local regulations | ☐ electrical codes | ☐ building codes | ☐ zoning laws | ☐ fire regulations | ☐ plumbing codes | ☐ life-safety codes | other: ______] **and other ordinances.**

☐ **Inspect and monitor** [☐ new construction | ☐ installations | ☐ alternations | ☐ other: ______] **of** ______ *[type of]* [☐ private | ☐ public | ☐ other: ______] **construction sites to ensure adherence to and enforce all safety standards, building codes, and specifications.**

☐ **Perform compliance-related activities including building** [☐ inspections | ☐ consents | ☐ investigations | ☐ issues | ☐ resolutions | ☐ compliance schedules | ☐ other: ______] **that comply with all statutory obligations.**

☐ **Research, evaluate, and resolve** [☐ complex | ☐ sensitive] **customer** [☐ service issues | ☐ complaints] **as they relate to** [☐ commercial buildings | ☐ residential homes | ☐ building construction and code compliance | ☐ other: ______].

☐ **Track and monitor** ______ *[type of]* **compliance actions through** ______ *[type of]* **inspections, and review to ensure conformance to** ______ *[which?]* **regulations.**

Inspections & Compliance – Buildings & Structures

See also ***"Inspections & Compliance – General"*** *and* ***"Inspections & Compliance – Facilities & Plants."***

☐ **Inspect** [☐ new | ☐ existing] [☐ commercial | ☐ residential] **buildings including** _______ *[type of projects]* **during various stages of** [☐ construction | ☐ remodeling | ☐ repair] **recommend modifications, and enforce compliance with all applicable codes, ordinances, and regulations.**

☐ **Facilitate site inspections of** ______ *[type of]* **projects in collaboration with** [☐ Project Manager | ☐ Project Superintendent | ☐ Foreman | ☐ Building Inspector | ☐ other: ______] **to determine** [☐ building code and life-safety compliance | ☐ conformance with plans, design specifications, and state laws | ☐ handicap accessibility | ☐ other: ______] **and ensure quality compliance with all** [☐ construction contracts | ☐ Uniform Building Code (UBC) | ☐ Federal regulations | ☐ state and local building codes | ☐ International Code Council (ICC) | ☐ zoning laws | ☐ fire regulations | ☐ electrical codes | ☐ plumbing codes | ☐ life-safety codes | ☐ ANSI | ☐ handicap accessibility | ☐ asbestos removal requirements | ☐ other: ______].

☐ **Monitor building construction progress through on-site field inspection and review to ensure conformance to** [☐ design specifications | ☐ cost estimates | ☐ time schedules | ☐ building codes | ☐ other: ______].

☐ **Conduct on-site building inspections to ensure contractors and subcontractors are following design specs and codes, using specified materials, meeting quality work standards and deadlines, and** ______ *[other?]* **to determine** [☐ building code and life-safety compliance | ☐ handicap accessibility | ☐ conformance with state laws | ☐ compliance with client specifications | ☐ other: ______].

☐ **Check** [☐ plans | ☐ specifications | ☐ other: ______] **for compliance with** [☐ Building Code | ☐ other: ______] **and approve and issue consents on** ______ *[what?].*

☐ **Perform** [☐ initial | ☐ incremental | ☐ follow-up | ☐ final | ☐ periodic] **worksite inspections throughout the construction process to inspect the** [☐ soil conditions | ☐ excavation and fill operations | ☐ positioning and depth of footings | ☐ concrete forms and foundations | ☐ asphalt paving | ☐ grading operations | ☐ workmanship quality | ☐ structural safety | ☐ other: ______]; **and to monitor compliance with specifications and codes.**

☐ **Jointly with the Construction** [☐ Foreman | ☐ Superintendent | ☐ Project Manager | ☐ Engineer | ☐ other: ______], **facilitate on-site inspections of** ______ *[type of]* [☐ buildings | ☐ structures | ☐ grading | ☐ footings | ☐ other: ______] **while** [☐ construction | ☐ remodeling | ☐ maintenance] **work is in process to ensure compliance with approved specifications and enforce all applicable building codes, ordinances, and regulations.**

☐ **Inspect commercial** [☐ buildings | ☐ facilities | ☐ structures | ☐ other: ______] **to identify required** [☐ repairs | ☐ maintenance | ☐ improvement | ☐ disaster-related damage | ☐ other: ______] **to meet current** [☐ building and safety codes | ☐ zoning ordinances | ☐ land use permits | ☐ other: ______] **including** [☐ fire escapes | ☐ signage | ☐ equipment | ☐ other: ______].

☐ **Perform on-site building inspections to ensure contractors and subcontractors are following design specs and codes, using specified materials, meeting quality work standards and deadlines, and** ______ *[other?]* **to determine** [☐ building code and life-safety compliance | ☐ handicap accessibility | ☐ conformance with state laws | ☐ compliance with client specifications | ☐ other: ______].

☐ **Inspect the** [☐ construction | ☐ repair] **of** [☐ buildings | ☐ structures | ☐ highways | ☐ sewer systems | ☐ water systems | ☐ bridges | ☐ land development | ☐ other: ______] **and other structures to ensure compliance with** [☐ state and local building codes | ☐ zoning laws and regulations | ☐ contract specifications | ☐ fire regulations | ☐ electrical codes | ☐ plumbing codes | ☐ life-safety codes | ☐ OSHA standards | ☐ Environmental Health and Safety Standards | ☐ energy conservation requirements | ☐ asbestos abatement requirements | ☐ other: ______].

☐ **Apply an expert working knowledge of** [☐ construction methods and materials | ☐ building codes and standards | ☐ other: ______] **in the review and inspection of** ______ *[what?]* **using** ______ *[type of]* [☐ survey instruments | ☐ metering devices | ☐ test equipment | ☐ other: ______] **in the inspection process.**

☐ **Perform work-site inspections of building projects to determine** [☐ building code and life-safety compliance | ☐ handicap accessibility | ☐ conformance with plans, specifications, and state and county laws | ☐ correct asbestos removal | ☐ other: ______] **and to** [☐ quality test construction materials | ☐ identify construction problems | ☐ notify (☐ Construction Foreman / ☐ Project Manager / ☐ others: ______) of defective contractor work | ☐ recommend corrective action | ☐ other: ______].

Inspections & Compliance – Electrical

See also ***"Inspections & Compliance – General."***

☐ **Inspect Electrician work to evaluate and ensure compliance with electrical codes, quality work performance, and** [☐ electrical compatibility | ☐ component safety | ☐ operating problems are resolved | ☐ performance criteria | ☐ other: ______].

☐ **Inspect and troubleshoot** ______ *[type of]* **electrical** [☐ systems | ☐ structures | ☐ installations | ☐ components | ☐ wiring | ☐ equipment | ☐ materials | ☐ other: ______] **for** ______ *[what?]* **ensuring compliance with all** [☐ electrical codes | ☐ building codes | ☐ safety regulations | ☐ customer specifications | ☐ company policies | ☐ other: ______].

☐ **Inspect, maintain, troubleshoot, and repair** ______ *[type of]* **electrical systems for** ______ *[what?]* **ensuring compliance with all** [☐ electrical codes | ☐ building codes | ☐ safety regulations | ☐ customer specifications | ☐ company policies | ☐ other: ______].

☐ **Perform** [☐ first-piece inspections | ☐ in-process inspections | ☐ final inspections | ☐ inspections of all production phases | ☐ other: ______], **ensuring compliance with all regulations, state and federal laws, and manufacturing specs**.

☐ **Oversee** ______ *[type of]* **electrical installations and repairs to ensure all procedures are followed with quality control and deadlines in mind by** [☐ taking hourly production counts | ☐ handling mechanical difficulties | ☐ overseeing quality control personnel's functions | ☐ other: ______].

☐ **Visit worksites to examine** [☐ new | ☐ existing] ______ *[type of]* [☐ structures | ☐ electrical wiring | ☐ HVAC systems | ☐ mechanical equipment | ☐ other: ______] **and other** [☐ systems | ☐ components] **and recommend necessary repair.**

☐ **Conduct site inspections to determine** [☐ electrical, building code, and life-safety compliance | ☐ compliance with state laws | ☐ conformance to client specifications | ☐ other: ______].

☐ **Test, troubleshoot, and diagnose electrical** [☐ circuits | ☐ equipment | ☐ installations | ☐ machinery | ☐ components | ☐ devices | ☐ other: ______] **of** [☐ safety equipment | ☐ emergency lighting | ☐ generators | ☐ other: ______] **to locate and correct** ______ *[type of]* **problems and ensure compliance with all electrical codes.**

☐ **Check** ______ *[what?]* **for** [☐ accurate assembly and installation | ☐ proper operation | ☐ control | ☐ safety | ☐ faulty wires | ☐ defects | ☐ loose connections | ☐ other: ______] **to identify any required** [☐ repairs | ☐ maintenance | ☐ improvement | ☐ other: ______] **in order to meet current** [☐ electrical codes | ☐ building codes | ☐ safety regulations | ☐ OSHA and environmental regulations | ☐ other: ______].

☐ **Perform** [☐ initial | ☐ incremental | ☐ follow-up | ☐ final | ☐ periodic] **worksite inspections of all electrical engineering projects throughout the installation process to ensure contractors are following** [☐ design specs | ☐ electrical code | ☐ contract specifications | ☐ other: ______] **and** [☐ meeting quality work standards and deadlines | ☐ using specified materials | ☐ other: ______].

☐ **Ensure quality compliance with all** [☐ engineering contracts | ☐ electrical codes | ☐ building codes | ☐ zoning laws | ☐ fire regulations | ☐ plumbing codes | ☐ life-safety codes | ☐ other: ______].

☐ **Conduct** ______ *[type of]* **inspections of all** [☐ generators | ☐ conduits | ☐ transformers | ☐ programmable controllers | ☐ motor controllers | ☐ AC & DC motors | ☐ circuit breakers | ☐ heating units | ☐ pull boxes | ☐ switches | ☐ switchboards | ☐ transmission equipment | ☐ other: ______] **to ensure** [☐ all systems are running smoothly | ☐ compliance with all OSHA and environmental regulations | ☐ other: ______].

☐ **Inspect, test, and calibrate** ______ *[type of]* **electrical systems and components to identify and solve** ______ *[type of]* **problems or defects using specialized electrical testing equipment.**

☐ **Ensure proper safety precautions and regulations are observed during all electrical installations and repairs by** ______ *[doing what?]* **to prevent physical injury to self and others**.

☐ **Test and troubleshoot** ______ *[type of]* [☐ assemblies | ☐ systems | ☐ communication cables | ☐ hardware | ☐ software products | ☐ operating system | ☐ other: ______] **to** [☐ isolate faults | ☐ ensure the integration of design supports | ☐ other: ______] **and** [☐ resolve malfunctions using (☐ analogue | ☐ digital | ☐ video circuits | ☐ logic systems | ☐ other: ______) applications | ☐ replace parts as required to maintain optimum online condition of network | other: ______].

☐ **Monitor development progress through on-site field inspection and review to ensure conformance to** [☐ design specifications | ☐ cost estimates | ☐ time schedules | ☐ building codes | ☐ other: ______] **and immediately resolve any problems**.

☐ **Conduct** [☐ initial | ☐ incremental | ☐ follow-up | ☐ final | ☐ periodic] **worksite inspections throughout the development process to inspect** ______ *[what?]* **and to monitor compliance with all** [☐ contract specifications | ☐ electrical codes | ☐ other: ______].

☐ **Inspect the installation of all** ______ *[type of]* **electrical components of** ______ *[what?]* **including** ______ *[which components?]*.

☐ **Perform all aspects of** [☐ functional | ☐ operational | ☐ other: ______] **testing and troubleshooting including** [☐ calibration | ☐ alignments | ☐ acceptance | ☐ other: ______], **collect relevant data, write test and discrepancy reports, and prepare rework instructions as required.**

☐ [☐ Develop | ☐ Use] **various test documentation including** [☐ blueprints | ☐ block diagrams | ☐ schematics | ☐ specifications | ☐ other: ______] **to conform to established test procedures and provide direction on all rework or repair required**.

☐ **Operate** ______ *[type of]* **test equipment to perform functional and operational testing of** ______ *[what?]* **to ensure the highest quality of services at all times.**

☐ **Conduct testing, troubleshooting, and repair of** [☐ systems | ☐ electronic equipment | ☐ electromechanical components | ☐ assemblies | ☐ subassemblies | ☐ other: ______] **to ensure conformance to product specifications**.

ACHIEVEMENT SAMPLES:

☐ **Designed and implemented** ______ *[type of]* **testing** [☐ requirements | ☐ methods | ☐ programs | ☐ guides | ☐ other: ______] **that** ______ *[does what?]* **for new product development projects resulting in** ______ *[what benefits?]*.

☐ **Conducted testing of** ______ *[type of]* **boards and handled electronic parts with an acceptance rate of** ______**%** *[percentage]* **where a** ______**%** *[percentage]* **failure rate was accepted as the norm.**

☐ **Troubleshoot and pinpoint problems faster than the norm due to** [☐ math | ☐ electronics | ☐ other: ______] **expertise and ability to grasp concepts quickly.**

☐ **Investigated** ______ *[type of]* **technical problems on** ______ *[what?]* **and established** [☐ procedures | ☐ corrective actions | ☐ other: ______] **to avoid recurrences**.

Inspections & Compliance – Facilities & Plants

*See also **"Inspections & Compliance – General"** and **"Inspections & Compliance – Buildings & Structures."***

☐ **Inspect facilities for** [☐ maintenance and repair needs | ☐ fire, safety, and health hazards | ☐ safe and efficient operation | ☐ other: ______] **including** [☐ boilers | ☐ heaters | ☐ chillers | ☐ furnace | ☐ fans | ☐ filters | ☐ plumbing | ☐ electrical | ☐ HVAC | ☐ motors | ☐ appliances | ☐ fixtures | ☐ lights | ☐ ballasts | ☐ receptacles | ☐ switches | ☐ fire extinguishers | ☐ alarm systems | ☐ air compressors | ☐ steam boilers | ☐ pump seals | ☐ bearings | ☐ couplings | ☐ other: ______].

☐ **Conduct facility and grounds inspections of all** [☐ plumbing | ☐ electrical | ☐ HVAC | ☐ motors | ☐ appliances | ☐ fixtures | ☐ other: ______] **to ensure** [☐ all systems are running smoothly | ☐ compliance with all OSHA and environmental regulations | ☐ all facilities, grounds, and people are safe and secure | ☐ other: ______] **by** ______ *[doing what?]*.

☐ **Inspect and evaluate the** [☐ physical | ☐ mechanical | ☐ structural | ☐ other: ______] **aspects of facilities to ensure everything is operating in a safe, functional, and proper manner, checking for** ______, ______, **and** ______ *[what aspects?]*.

☐ **Check and evaluate the** [☐ physical | ☐ mechanical | ☐ structural | ☐ other: ______] **aspects of** ______ *[#]* [☐ buildings | ☐ facilities | ☐ offices | ☐ other: ______] **to identify required** [☐ repairs | ☐ maintenance | ☐ improvement | ☐ other: ______] **in order to meet current** [☐ building and safety codes | ☐ OSHA and environmental regulations | ☐ other: ______] **and ensure everything is operating in a safe, functional, and proper manner.**

☐ **Assist the** [☐ Foreman | ☐ Project Superintendent | ☐ Building Inspector | ☐ other: ______] **in conducting site inspections to determine** [☐ building code and life-safety compliance | ☐ handicap accessibility | ☐ conformance with plans, specifications, and state laws | ☐ compliance with specifications | ☐ other: ______].

☐ **Track and monitor** ______ *[type of]* [☐ installation | ☐ construction | ☐ manufacture | ☐ other: ______] **progress through** ______ *[type of]* **inspections, and review to ensure conformance to** [☐ specifications | ☐ cost estimates | ☐ time schedules | ☐ contracts | ☐ codes | ☐ other: ______] **and immediately** [☐ resolve | ☐ refer] **any problems**.

☐ **Inspect, maintain, troubleshoot, and repair** ______ *[type of]* **electrical systems for** ______ *[what?]* **ensuring compliance with all** [☐ electrical codes | ☐ building codes | ☐ plumbing codes | ☐ safety regulations | ☐ customer specifications | ☐ company policies | ☐ other: ______].

☐ **Examine building interior(s) and exterior(s) for any damage or operating difficulties and schedule necessary repairs as required to ensure** [☐ all systems are running smoothly | ☐ compliance with all OSHA and environmental regulations | ☐ other: ______].

☐ **Inspect water and steam systems for proper operation of** [☐ boiler | ☐ water heater | ☐ furnace | ☐ refrigeration | ☐ other: ______] **ensuring systems have no leaks and all machinery is functioning properly**.

☐ **Ensure that all** [☐ buildings | ☐ facilities | ☐ grounds | ☐ employees | ☐ customers and others | ☐ other: ______] **are safe and secure by inspecting** ______ *[doing what?]*.

☐ **Review and approve all** ______ *[type of]* **building plans to determine whether they** [☐ comply with building and electrical codes and standards | ☐ are suitable for the engineering demands of the site | ☐ are environmentally-friendly | ☐ do not pose any risk to adjoining buildings | ☐ other: ______].

☐ **Conduct** [☐ initial | ☐ incremental | ☐ follow-up | ☐ final | ☐ periodic] ______ *[type of]* **inspections throughout the project lifecycle process to inspect** ______ *[what?]* **and monitor compliance with** ______ *[what?]*.

☐ **Inspect** ______ *[type of]* [☐ systems | ☐ facilities | ☐ other: ______] **for** [☐ proper operation | ☐ any damage | ☐ malfunction | ☐ operating difficulties | ☐ leaks | ☐ other: ______] **and oversee needed repairs to ensure** [☐ quality compliance | ☐ everything is functioning a safe and proper manner | ☐ other: ______].

☐ **Review and approve facility and grounds inspection reports to ensure all** [☐ plumbing | ☐ electrical | ☐ HVAC | ☐ water | ☐ steam | ☐ heating | ☐ cooling | ☐ other: ______] **systems are** [☐ running smoothly | ☐ safe and secure | ☐ in proper operating condition | ☐ in compliance with all OSHA and environmental regulations | ☐ meet building codes | ☐ other: ______].

☐ **Check** ______ *[what?]* **to identify required** [☐ repairs | ☐ maintenance | ☐ improvement | ☐ other: ______] **to meet current codes, and ensure** ______ *[what?]* **is safe and secure by** ______ *[doing what?].*

Inspections & Compliance – HVAC / HVAC-R

*See also "**Inspections & Compliance – General.**"*

☐ **Inspect and test** [☐ mechanical | ☐ electrical | ☐ electronic | ☐ pneumatic | ☐ other: ______] **components of** [☐ heating | ☐ air conditioning | ☐ refrigeration | ☐ ventilation | ☐ other: ______] **systems including** [☐ motors | ☐ compressors | (☐ metal / ☐ fiberglass) ducts | ☐ pipes | ☐ pumps | ☐ fans | ☐ switches | ☐ thermostats | ☐ other: ______] **for** ______ *[type of]* **clients.**

☐ **Test the performance of** [☐ mechanical | ☐ electrical | ☐ other: ______] **components throughout HVAC systems, including** [☐ motors | ☐ compressors | ☐ condensing units | ☐ evaporators | ☐ piping | ☐ metal and fiberglass ducts | ☐ pumps | ☐ fans | ☐ thermostats | ☐ other: ______] **and other components, and make required repairs.**

☐ **Monitor, test, and maintain** [☐ emergency electrical equipment | ☐ generators | ☐ battery-operated lighting] **and appliances such as** [☐ coolers | ☐ freezers | ☐ refrigerators | ☐ washers | ☐ dryers | ☐ dishwashers | ☐ ice machines | ☐ other: ______].

☐ **Test and diagnose problems related to the repair of** ______ *[type of]* [☐ HVAC systems | ☐ control devices | ☐ other: ______] **including** ______ *[what?].*

☐ **Inspect and monitor** [☐ feed and return water pumps | ☐ internal and external boiler components | ☐ sump pumps | ☐ chemical pumps | ☐ water softeners | ☐ heat exchangers | (☐ pneumatic / ☐ automatic) piping systems | ☐ sand traps | ☐ check valves | ☐ related electrical systems | ☐ other: ______] **for proper operation and safety, and make necessary repairs as warranted.**

☐ **Test the performance of** [☐ mechanical | ☐ electrical] **components throughout HVAC systems, including** [☐ motors | ☐ compressors | ☐ condensing units | ☐ evaporators | ☐ piping | ☐ ducts | ☐ pumps | ☐ fans | ☐ thermostats | ☐ other: ______] **and other components, and make required repairs.**

☐ **Monitor and adjust** [☐ water heaters | ☐ boilers | ☐ heating pipes | ☐ pneumatic valves | ☐ mixing valves | ☐ pumps | ☐ pump seals | ☐ steam traps | ☐ bearing assembles | ☐ backflow devices | ☐ dampers | ☐ coils | ☐ fans | ☐ heat exchangers | ☐ air handlers | ☐ water softeners | ☐ sump and chemical pumps | ☐ geothermal pumps | ☐ thermostats | ☐ boiler components | ☐ thermostats | ☐ valves | ☐ faucets | ☐ flush valves | ☐ sinks | ☐ fountains | ☐ toilets | ☐ urinals | ☐ other: ______].

☐ **Complete inspection and maintenance work by** [☐ overhauling compressors | ☐ replacing filters and ducts | ☐ other: ______] **to ensure its efficient** [☐ HVAC | ☐ HVAC-R] **operation.**

☐ **Monitor, balance, and control the temperature, humidity, and air quality of** [☐ heating | ☐ air conditioning | ☐ other: ______] **systems in** [☐ residential | ☐ commercial | ☐ industrial | ☐ other: ______] **buildings by performing** ______ *[functions].*

☐ **Pressure test all** ______ *[type of]* **pipes, assess** [☐ leakage | ☐ breakage | ☐ rust | ☐ damage | ☐ other: ______] **problems, identify plumbing malfunction sources, and perform required** ______ *[type of]* **plumbing repairs within specified timeframes.**

☐ **Prevent the release of chlorofluorocarbon and hydro chlorofluorocarbon refrigerants in air-conditioning and refrigeration systems from entering the ozone layer by** [☐ ensuring there are no system leaks | ☐ venting refrigerant into cylinders | ☐ other manner: ______].

☐ **Apply an expert working knowledge of** [☐ electrical | ☐ electronic | ☐ mechanical] [☐ heating | ☐ ventilation | ☐ air conditioning | ☐ refrigeration] [☐ theory | ☐ methods | ☐ practices | ☐ other: ______] **in the** [☐ troubleshooting and repair of electrical control systems | ☐ design of (☐ centrifugal / ☐ reciprocal) compressors | ☐ operation of pneumatic control systems | ☐ maintenance of steam condensate return traps, pumps, and compressors | ☐ other: ______] **to operate, maintain, and repair HVAC systems.**

Inspections & Compliance – Landscape & Masonry

*See also "**Inspections & Compliance – General.**"*

☐ **Inspect excavation and fill operations including** [☐ grading operations | ☐ placement of forms for concrete | ☐ concrete mixing and pouring | ☐ poured foundations | ☐ asphalt paving | ☐ reinforced concrete structures | ☐ ditching and dredging operations | ☐ other: ______].

☐ **Conduct initial, incremental, follow-up, and final comprehensive worksite inspections throughout the construction process to inspect the** [☐ soil conditions | ☐ excavation and fill operations | ☐ positioning and depth of footings | ☐ concrete forms and foundations | ☐ asphalt paving | ☐ grading operations | ☐ workmanship quality | ☐ structural safety | ☐ other: ______] **and to monitor compliance with all contract specifications, building codes, and regulations.**

- ☐ **Perform on-site inspections of ______** *[what?]* **for compliance with regulations and enforce state and local mandates and zoning regulations, as required.**

Inspections & Compliance – Plumbing

*See also "**Inspections & Compliance – General.**"*

- ☐ **Reporting to** [☐ the Chief Plumbing Inspector | ☐ other title: ______], **examine and test** [☐ new | ☐ existing | ☐ new and existing] **plumbing systems of ______** *[type of]* **projects for this** [☐ city agency | ☐ county agency | ☐ plumbing firm | ☐ other: ______], **reporting and informing owners of any national, state, county, and/or city plumbing code violations.**

- ☐ **Inspect and test all phases of** [☐ plumbing | ☐ heating | ☐ ventilating | ☐ cooling | ☐ energy management | ☐ control | ☐ other: ______] **system installations** [☐ and repairs] **by** [☐ making frequent on-site visits | ☐ using ______ *(type of)* control software | ☐ verifying temperature controls | ☐ ensuring its efficiency | ☐ recommending the adjustment of (☐ mixed / ☐ return / ☐ discharge) air | ☐ performing combustion analyses | ☐ other methods: ______] **to ensure they are properly installed and comply with all national, state, county, and city codes.**

- ☐ **Inspect** [☐ plumbing | ☐ sewer line | ☐ gas | ☐ other: ______] **system and equipment installations in** [☐ new | ☐ existing | ☐ new and existing] ______ *[type of]* [☐ buildings | ☐ structures | ☐ businesses | ☐ homes | ☐ schools | ☐ retail stores | ☐ other: ______] **including** [☐ hot water systems | ☐ domestic water systems | ☐ sanitary plumbing systems | ☐ water heaters | ☐ gas piping | ☐ cesspools | ☐ septic tanks | ☐ sewer lines | ☐ wet and dry sandpipes | ☐ fire sprinkler systems | ☐ lawn sprinkler systems | ☐ other: ______] **for** [☐ quality | ☐ tank capacity | ☐ pressure | ☐ leakage | ☐ size and type of pipes and fittings | ☐ any hazardous conditions | ☐ other: ______] **to ensure compliance with plans and specifications, plumbing code, and safety and health standards.**

- ☐ **Review, verify, and approve applications for** [☐ plumbing | ☐ gas | ☐ sewage | ☐ other: ______] **installation permits to determine compliance with code requirements.**

- ☐ **Pressure test all ______** *[type of]* **pipes, assess** [☐ leakage | ☐ breakage | ☐ rust | ☐ damage | ☐ other: ______] **problems, identify plumbing malfunction sources, and perform required ______** *[type of]* **plumbing repairs within specified timeframes.**

- ☐ **Handle various plumbing inspection functions including** [☐ reviewing (☐ proposed) construction plans | ☐ conducting testing | ☐ evaluating (☐ buildings / ☐ construction sites) | ☐ issuing permits | ☐ writing reports | ☐ making recommendations | ☐ investigating complaints | ☐ other: ______] **to determine compliance with all plumbing laws, regulations, and codes.**

- ☐ **Perform ______** *[type of]* **plumbing** [☐ installations | ☐ repairs | ☐ alterations | ☐ inspections | ☐ other: ______] **ensuring all** [☐ new plumbing | ☐ plumbing alterations | ☐ drainage installations | ☐ other: ______] **in ______** *[type of]* [☐ public | ☐ private] **buildings are in compliance with all codes, laws, and regulations.**

- ☐ **Functioning as a** [☐ lead | ☐ senior] **inspector, perform a full range of plumbing inspection functions including** [☐ inspecting approved plans and specifications | ☐ testing (☐ new installations / ☐ alternations) of plumbing systems | ☐ interpreting laws, regulations, and codes to particular situations | ☐ checking (☐ piping size / ☐ connections / ☐ trap seals / ☐ cleanouts / ☐ use of materials, devices, fixtures, and equipment / ☐ other: ______) | ☐ verifying plumbers are properly licensed | ☐ writing code violation notices | ☐ gathering code violation evidence | ☐ testifying at hearings | ☐ preparing reports | ☐ determining work priorities of lower-level Plumbing Inspectors | ☐ performing accident investigations | ☐ evaluating complaints | ☐ other: ______].

- ☐ **Apply** [☐ in-depth | ☐ proficient | ☐ working] **knowledge of** [☐ the plumbing trade | ☐ plumbing codes, laws, rules, and regulations | ☐ plumbing practices and processes | ☐ investigative procedures and methods | ☐ plumbing inspection techniques | ☐ occupational hazards and safety precautions | ☐ plumbing tools, equipment, and materials | ☐ other: ______] **in performing plumbing inspections and testing.**

Inspections & Compliance – Public Works / Civil Projects

*See also "**Inspections & Compliance – General"** and all other categories for additional bullets.*

- ☐ **Ensure that** [☐ Federal | ☐ state | ☐ local] **government construction of** [☐ reinforced concrete | ☐ water systems | ☐ sewer systems | ☐ highways | ☐ streets | ☐ bridges | ☐ dams | ☐ ditches | ☐ dredging operations | ☐ other: ______] **conforms to detailed contract specifications.**

- ☐ **Inspect the** [☐ construction | ☐ repair] **of** [☐ buildings | ☐ structures | ☐ highways | ☐ sewer systems | ☐ water systems | ☐ bridges | ☐ land development | ☐ other: ______] **and other structures to ensure compliance with** [☐ state and local building codes | ☐ zoning laws and regulations | ☐ detailed contract specifications | ☐ fire regulations | ☐ electrical codes | ☐ plumbing codes | ☐ life-safety codes | ☐ OSHA standards | ☐ Environmental Health and Safety Standards | ☐ energy conservation requirements | ☐ asbestos abatement requirements | ☐ other: ______].

☐ **Facilitate engineering** [☐ building | ☐ structural | ☐ other: ______] **consultation and inspections of** [☐ elevators | ☐ escalators | ☐ fire sprinklers | ☐ alarms | ☐ smoke control systems | ☐ building contents | ☐ mechanical equipment | ☐ fire exits | ☐ conveying devices | ☐ handicap access | ☐ other: ______].

☐ **Perform on-site inspections of** [☐ highways | ☐ bridges | ☐ equipment | ☐ other: ______] **projects to** [☐ determine needed repairs | ☐ evaluate progress | ☐ comply with plans | ☐ ensure quality of construction | ☐ other: ______].

☐ **Examine** [☐ buildings | ☐ highways and streets | ☐ sewer and water systems | ☐ bridges | ☐ other: ______] **for their structural quality and safety to ensure** [☐ construction | ☐ repair | ☐ other: ______] **conforms to all contract specifications, building codes and ordinances, and zoning regulations.**

☐ **Manage daily environmental compliance issues, interpret applicable regulations, and provide regulatory support to** ______ *[whom?]* **ensuring** [☐ plant | ☐ site | ☐ process | ☐ operational | ☐ other: ______] **compliance with state, local, and federal requirements.**

☐ **Check and evaluate the** [☐ physical | ☐ mechanical | ☐ structural | ☐ other: ______] **aspects of facilities to ensure everything is operating in a safe, functional, and proper manner.**

Inspections & Compliance – Recordkeeping

☐ **Log, route, monitor, and process all incoming** ______ *[type of]* **plans and respond to** [☐ homeowners | ☐ owner's representatives | ☐ architects | ☐ contractors | ☐ builders | ☐ others: ______] **regarding any code or related questions, keeping track of all construction inspection activities and status.**

☐ **Accurately record all** [☐ project | ☐ inspection] **details; and prepare** ______ *[type of]* **reports using** ______ *[which?]* **program(s), to include** [☐ project progress | ☐ inspection deficiencies | ☐ construction conditions | ☐ detected violations | ☐ enforcement actions | ☐ court rulings | ☐ other: ______].

☐ **Maintain all** ______ *[type of]* **inspection activity files including** [☐ plans | ☐ blueprints | ☐ site layouts | ☐ specifications | ☐ construction methods | ☐ findings | ☐ compliance reports | ☐ photographs | ☐ testing data | ☐ hazardous conditions | ☐ abatement reports | ☐ corrections of violations | ☐ correspondence | ☐ other: ______] **on all active projects**.

☐ **Gather evidence and prepare** ______ *[type of]* **inspection reports on all** ______ *[type of]* **violations and assist local municipalities in the enforcement of building codes.**

Inspections & Compliance – Residential Projects

*See also **"Inspections & Compliance – General."***

☐ **Perform engineering inspections on all** [☐ newly built | ☐ previously owned | ☐ remodeled] home [☐ structures | ☐ systems | ☐ components | ☐ other: ______] **including their electrical, plumbing, heating, and/or cooling systems; and report findings to home** [☐ buyers | ☐ owners].

☐ **Examine building interior and exterior for** [☐ damage | ☐ malfunction | ☐ leaks | ☐ operating difficulties | ☐ other: ______], **and make necessary repairs as required, such as** ______ *[type of repairs]*.

☐ **Check** ______, ______, **and** ______, *[what?]* **to identify required** [☐ repairs | ☐ maintenance | ☐ improvement | ☐ other: ______] **to meet current** ______ *[what?]*.

☐ **Represent** [☐ building owners | ☐ insurance companies | ☐ financial institutions | ☐ others: ______] **to ensure that** ______ *[type of]* **residential work is performed and completed according to design specifications**.

☐ **Inspect previously occupied** ______ *[type of]* **homes for code compliance, verify legal data, and authorize** [☐ permits | ☐ Certificates of Occupancy | ☐ other: ______] **for approved areas**.

Inspections & Compliance – Trades Work (General)

*See also "**Inspections & Compliance – General.**"*

☐ **Facilitate** [☐ plumbing | ☐ electrical | ☐ HVAC | ☐ welding | ☐ carpentry | ☐ other: ______] **inspections to ensure compliance with all relevant** [☐ building | ☐ safety | ☐ plumbing | ☐ electrical | ☐ other: ______] **codes, standards, and** [☐ specifications | ☐ contracts | ☐ regulations | ☐ policies | ☐ standards | ☐ other: ______] **including relevant aspects of** [☐ OSHA | ☐ EPA | ☐ MSDS | ☐ ADA | ☐ other: ______].

☐ **Monitor installation of** ______ *[type of]* [☐ plumbing | ☐ electrical wiring | ☐ equipment | ☐ appliances | ☐ other: ______] **to ensure installation is performed in compliance with all applicable codes and regulations.**

☐ **Track and monitor** ______ *[type of]* **progress through** [☐ grounds | ☐ top-out | ☐ finish] [☐ phases of construction | ☐ plumbing inspections], **and review to ensure conformance to** [☐ specifications | ☐ cost estimates | ☐ time schedules | ☐ contracts | ☐ codes | ☐ other: ______] **and immediately** [☐ resolve | ☐ refer] **any problems.**

☐ **Examine the construction, installation, and functioning of all** [☐ concrete structures | ☐ framing | ☐ insulation | ☐ electrical wiring | ☐ plumbing fixtures, traps, and systems | ☐ water supply systems | ☐ water distribution systems | ☐ irrigation systems | ☐ drainage systems | ☐ waste and vent lines | ☐ HVAC equipment | ☐ security systems | ☐ smoke control systems | ☐ alarm systems | ☐ fire sprinklers | ☐ fire protection equipment | ☐ disposal systems | ☐ gas and oil piping | ☐ gasoline and butane tanks | ☐ escalators | ☐ elevators | ☐ asbestos abatement | ☐ roofing systems | ☐ fire exits | ☐ other: ______] **to ensure adherence to all related codes and standards.**

☐ **Inspect and monitor** [☐ new construction | ☐ installations | ☐ alternations | ☐ other: ______] **of** ______ *[type of]* [☐ private | ☐ public | ☐ other: ______] **construction sites to ensure adherence to and enforce all safety standards, building codes, and specifications.**

☐ **Manage and oversee inspection and compliance functions including** [☐ reviewing plans to verify code requirements | ☐ overseeing construction projects | ☐ performing on-site construction inspections | ☐ identifying construction problems | ☐ quality testing construction materials | ☐ notifying foremen and contractors of defective work | ☐ recommending corrective actions | ☐ resolving construction personnel disputes | ☐ conducting preventive maintenance | ☐ negotiating plan changes with architects | ☐ holding meetings to discuss project progress | ☐ other: ______].

☐ **Facilitate on-site inspections of** [☐ building | ☐ highway | ☐ bridge | ☐ equipment | ☐ other: ______] **projects to** [☐ determine needed repairs | ☐ evaluate progress | ☐ comply with plans | ☐ ensure quality of construction | ☐ other: ______].

☐ **Visit worksites to examine** [☐ new | ☐ existing | ☐ other: ______] ______ *[type of]* [☐ structures | ☐ electrical wiring | ☐ lighting | ☐ HVAC systems | ☐ mechanical equipment | ☐ plumbing systems | ☐ other: ______] **and other** [☐ systems | ☐ components] **and recommend any necessary repair.**

☐ **Conduct** [☐ initial | ☐ incremental | ☐ follow-up | ☐ periodic | ☐ final] ______ *[type of]* **inspections throughout the** [☐ plumbing | ☐ electrical | ☐ HVAC | ☐ other: ______] **installation and repair process to inspect** ______ *[what?]* **and monitor compliance with all related codes.**

☐ **Inspect the** [☐ demolition | ☐ carpentry | ☐ framing | ☐ sheetrocking | ☐ taping and spackling | ☐ flooring | ☐ painting | ☐ insulation | ☐ electrical | ☐ plumbing | ☐ HVAC | ☐ tiling | ☐ trim work | ☐ ceilings | ☐ welding | ☐ roofing | ☐ masonry | ☐ landscaping | ☐ other: ______] **perform** ______ *[type of]* [☐ large-scale | ☐ moderate-size | ☐ highly complex | ☐ moderately complex | ☐ multisite | ☐ other: ______] **construction projects for** ______ *[whom?]* **resulting in** ______ *[what benefits?].*

☐ **Inspect the installation of all** ______ *[type of]* **components of** ______ *[what?]* **including** ______, ______, **and** ______ *[which components?].*

☐ **Use various instruments, equipment, and devices during the inspection process including** [☐ survey instruments | ☐ metering devices | ☐ test equipment | ☐ tape measures | ☐ concrete strength measurers | ☐ other: ______].

☐ **Conduct on-site inspections of** [☐ buildings | ☐ structures | ☐ grading | ☐ footings | ☐ other: ______] **while** [☐ construction | ☐ remodeling | ☐ maintenance] **work is in process to ensure compliance with approved specifications; and enforce all applicable building codes, ordinances, and regulations.**

Insulation Functions & Projects

*See "**Ceiling, Lathing, Insulation & Drywall Installation**" as well as "**Carpentry / Construction Work.**"*

Interaction & Liaison – Strategic Level

*See also "**Work Coordination**" and "**Interdisciplinary/Project Team Member.**"*

☐ **Interact and liaise with** [☐ architects | ☐ engineers | ☐ contractors | ☐ subcontractors | ☐ project management staff | ☐ building officials | ☐ other: ______] **to ensure that** [☐ construction | ☐ demolition | ☐ remodel | ☐ alteration | ☐ other: ______] **work is within parameters identified by the firm and in compliance with** ______ *[what?]* **and all building codes**.

☐ **Oversee staff interactions with** [☐ building officials | ☐ contractors | ☐ contractor reimbursement agencies | ☐ Accounts Payable | ☐ departmental service coordinators | ☐ others:______] **to** [☐ maintain productive working relationships with ______ *(type of)* agencies | ☐ schedule construction | ☐ facilitate final inspections | ☐ ensure proper handling and receipt of payments | ☐ other: ______].

☐ **Serve as principal liaison with** [☐ architects | ☐ human resources | ☐ purchasing officers | ☐ legal | ☐ others: ______] **in** [☐ selecting contractors | ☐ handling documentation | ☐ executing legal actions | ☐ other: ______] **related to** [☐ design | ☐ new construction | ☐ project management | ☐ facility improvement issues | ☐ other: ______] **issues**.

☐ **Collaborate with** ______ *[whom?]* **to ensure that** ______ *[type of]* **work is within parameters identified by the firm and in compliance with all building codes and client specifications.**

☐ **Liaise with owners to maintain customer satisfaction by** [☐ listening to and interpreting their needs | ☐ giving careful attention to detail | ☐ other: ______].

☐ **Liaise and interface regularly with** [☐ architects | ☐ engineers | ☐ contractors | ☐ subcontractors | ☐ project management staff | ☐ departmental management | ☐ governmental regulators | ☐ outside agencies | ☐ vendors | ☐ other: ______] **to** [☐ determine project scope | ☐ develop project plans | ☐ review feedback on project goals and timelines | ☐ schedule projects | ☐ identify and problem solve issues | ☐ manage construction | ☐ track projects | ☐ other: ______] **in various project phases.**

Interdisciplinary / Project Team Member

*See also "**Work Coordination**" and "**Team Leadership & Direction.**"*

☐ **Participate in** [☐ interdisciplinary | ☐ multidisciplinary | ☐ interagency | ☐ other: ______] **team meetings with** ______, ______, **and** ______ *[whom?]* **working together** [☐ for the benefit of | ☐ to meet | ☐ to ensure] ______ *[what goals?]* **and communicate milestones, commitments, and achievements**.

☐ **Actively participate in meetings with the interdisciplinary team consisting of** ______, ______, **and** ______ *[whom?]* **in the development and monitoring of** ______ *[type of]* **goals and to provide progress update reports.**

☐ **Serve on a project team of** ______ *[#]* including ______ *[whom?]* **that defines, plans, and implements new** ______ *[type of]* **projects; and perform the** [☐ design | ☐ development | ☐ deployment | ☐ other: ______] **of those projects in support of the** [☐ firm's | ☐ clients'] **objectives.**

☐ **As a member of the** ______ *[which?]* [☐ interdisciplinary | ☐ multidisciplinary | ☐ interagency] **team** [☐ develop | ☐ implement | ☐ track | ☐ assess | ☐ modify | ☐ other: ______] ______ *[type of]* [☐ programs | ☐ plans] **to** [☐ resolve ______ *(type of)* problems and challenges | ☐ write ______ *(what?)* reports | ☐ other: ______] **concerning** ______ *[type of]* **complex projects**.

☐ **Work collaboratively in a team environment with** ______ *[whom?]* [☐ while leading multiple projects | ☐ adapting to frequently changing priorities | ☐ demonstrating a strong commitment to improvement | ☐ other: ______].

☐ **Participate as a member of a project team of** ______ *[#]* **to** [☐ prepare and distribute project schedules | ☐ provide support | ☐ communicate project status | ☐ resolve issues | ☐ other: ______] **that meet schedule requirements** .

☐ **In collaboration with the** ______ *[what team?]* [☐ create accurate project estimates | ☐ prepare schedules | ☐ allocate resources | ☐ other: ______] **that support company-wide projects and maintain project management practices.**

ACHIEVEMENT SAMPLES:

☐ **As a member of the** ______ *[which?]* **team, presented** ______ *[type of]* **ideas, made** ______ *[what?]* **recommendations, and developed** ______ *[type of]* **plans designed to** ______ [do what?].

Inventory Audits

*See also "**Inventory Management & Control,**" "**Purchasing,**" and "**Recordkeeping.**"*

☐ **Execute thorough, independent internal** [☐ appraisals | ☐ audits | ☐ investigations | ☐ quality assurance reviews] **of the firm's inventory management and control** [☐ policies | ☐ procedures | ☐ standards | ☐ systems] **effectiveness.**

☐ **Perform** [☐ daily | ☐ weekly | ☐ monthly] **inventory** [☐ counts | ☐ analysis | ☐ audits] **of** ______ *[type of]* [☐ products | ☐ merchandise | ☐ goods | ☐ supplies | ☐ materials | ☐ other: ______] **to determine any discrepancies, quickly resolve any inventory issues, and ensure sufficient in-house** [☐ stock | ☐ systems | ☐ programs | ☐ other: ______] **are adequate to meet** [☐ the firm's | ☐ the Division's | ☐ client | ☐ others: ______] **needs.**

- ☐ **Conduct** [☐ general | ☐ special | ☐ independent | ☐ other: ______] **inventory audits to evaluate the accuracy of all inventory records including** [☐ shipments | ☐ deliveries | ☐ warehousing | ☐ storekeeping | ☐ recordkeeping | ☐ fulfillment | ☐ replenishment | ☐ purchase orders | ☐ invoices | ☐ receipts | ☐ bills of lading | ☐ other: ______] **including performing** [☐ physical inventory inspections | ☐ procedures review | ☐ internal controls | ☐ shipping and receiving processes | ☐ security controls efficiency | ☐ irregularities investigations | ☐ other: ______] **to ensure** [☐ transaction accuracy | ☐ compliance with applicable laws and established policies and procedures | ☐ the safeguarding of assets | ☐ other: ______].
- ☐ **Verify the accuracy of the company's inventory records, checking for any** [☐ discrepancies | ☐ mismanagement | ☐ security breaches | ☐ system risks | ☐ fraud | ☐ illegal activities | ☐ other: ______] **which has resulted in** ______ *[findings].*
- ☐ **Audit the** [☐ firm's | ☐ Department's] **inventory records including** [☐ shipments | ☐ deliveries | ☐ warehousing | ☐ storekeeping | ☐ recordkeeping | ☐ purchase orders | ☐ invoices | ☐ receipts | ☐ logs | ☐ other: ______].
- ☐ **Conduct inventory audits covering all areas of inventory management and control including** [☐ conducting physical inventories | ☐ examining documents | ☐ analyzing and interpreting data | ☐ conducting transaction reviews | ☐ investigating questionable items | ☐ conducting cost analyses | ☐ identifying errors | ☐ preparing reports | ☐ communicate findings | ☐ making recommendations | ☐ following up on audits | ☐ other: ______].
- ☐ **Conduct comprehensive audits of inventory records including** [☐ performing physical inventory counts | ☐ developing audit findings | ☐ reviewing work papers | ☐ conducting negotiations | ☐ editing drafts | ☐ preparing final audit reports | ☐ other: ______].
- ☐ **Apply auditing principles and practices and sound decision-making in the** [☐ audit plans preparation | ☐ exposure assessment | ☐ risk identification | ☐ evidence gathering | ☐ conclusions documentation | ☐ other: ______].
- ☐ **Recommended** ______ *[type of]* **automated controls to ensure** [☐ data integrity | ☐ system reliability | ☐ other: ______] **which has brought about** [☐ positive changes in | ☐ a resultant savings of $______] **in** ______ *[what areas?].*
- ☐ **Make sound decisions regarding** [☐ establishment of audit objectives | ☐ scope of investigations needed | ☐ depth of audit testing required | ☐ significance of audit issues | ☐ corrective remedies required | ☐ recommended means to obtain compliance | ☐ disposition of audit results | ☐ other: ______].
- ☐ **Review and evaluate efficiency of the firm's inventory operations, effectiveness of policies, and compliance with procedures and regulations for this** ______ *[type of]* **firm with** ______ *[#]* [☐ locations | ☐ employees].
- ☐ **Formulate and document appropriate required actions and effectively complete all audit activities by** [☐ using a variety of data analysis techniques | ☐ incorporating the type and quantity of information and evidence needed | ☐ analyzing processes within the context of audit objectives | ☐ executing innovative approaches | ☐ identifying areas for improvement | ☐ performing subsequent audits | ☐ ensuring corrective measures have been taken | ☐ auditing financial statements | ☐ other: ______].

ACHIEVEMENT SAMPLES: *See "Inventory Achievement Samples."*

Inventory Management & Control

*See also **"Purchasing"** and **"Recordkeeping."***

- ☐ **Order sufficient** ______ *[type of]* [☐ materials | ☐ supplies | ☐ products | ☐ goods | ☐ other: ______] **in accordance with project needs and the firm's** [☐ inventory usage cycles | ☐ project requirements | ☐ quality initiatives | ☐ established procedures | ☐ other: ______] **while effectively balancing physical storage and usage demands.**
- ☐ **Manage and control inventory on a** [☐ daily | ☐ weekly | ☐ monthly] **basis including** [☐ purchasing, inspecting, and storing materials and supplies | ☐ managing and overseeing the purchase and distribution of tools and equipment | ☐ ordering sufficient products and supplies to meet demand | ☐ conducting audits to determine any discrepancies and resolving inventory issues | ☐ ensuring a continuous and adequate supply of materials, tools, and equipment at all times | ☐ other: ______].
- ☐ **Ensure the inventory of all** ______ *[type of]* [☐ equipment | ☐ tools | ☐ supplies | ☐ raw materials | ☐ merchandise | ☐ furniture | ☐ other: ______] **is sufficient to meet** [☐ the firm's | ☐ clients'] **needs for all** ______ *[type of]* **projects**.
- ☐ **Perform** [☐ daily | ☐ weekly | ☐ monthly] **inventory** [☐ counts | ☐ analysis | ☐ audits | ☐ other: ______] **to determine any discrepancies and resolve any inventory issues.**
- ☐ **Direct and lead the** [☐ acquisition | ☐ purchase | ☐ distribution | ☐ control | ☐ sale | ☐ transfer | ☐ disposition] **of** [☐ reusable | ☐ recyclable] [☐ property | ☐ furniture | ☐ equipment | ☐ supplies | ☐ goods | ☐ product | ☐ merchandise | ☐ materials | ☐ other: ______] **in compliance with** [☐ the firm's established policies and procedures | ☐ federal and state regulations | ☐ other: ______].
- ☐ **Manage and oversee the** [☐ purchase | ☐ distribution | ☐ control] **of** ______ *[type of]* [☐ supplies | ☐ materials | ☐ tools | ☐ equipment | ☐ other: ______] **to ensure a continuous and adequate supply is maintained to meet current and future usage requirements.**
- ☐ **Receive and inspect all** ______ *[type of]* [☐ equipment | ☐ supplies | ☐ materials | ☐ goods | ☐ merchandise | ☐ furniture | ☐

other: ______] **and evaluate their condition.**

- ☐ **Direct and lead the** [☐ inventory control | ☐ receiving | ☐ storage | ☐ other: ______] **staff responsible for inventory** [☐ planning | ☐ management | ☐ control | ☐ replenishment | ☐ distribution | ☐ scheduling | ☐ other: ______ **of tools, materials, and equipment totaling $**______ *[amount].*
- ☐ **Conduct physical inventories of** ______ *[what?]* **and other materials to ensure sufficient supply on hand to meet demand requirements.**
- ☐ **Maintain effective physical inventory control of** [☐ receiving | ☐ shipping | ☐ storage | ☐ warehousing | ☐ distribution | ☐ other: ______] **by** ______ *[doing what?];* **and ensure adequate product inventory to meet the firm's needs.**
- ☐ **Manage inventory control up to $**______ *[amount],* **and dispose of destroyed merchandise.**
- ☐ **Ensure a continuous and adequate supply of** ______ *[type of]* [☐ tools | ☐ equipment | ☐ supplies | ☐ materials | ☐ other: ______] **is maintained meet current and future usage requirements.**
- ☐ **Facilitate inventory control of all** ______ *[type of]* [☐ product | ☐ goods | ☐ supplies | ☐ materials | ☐ other: ______], **ensuring sufficient in-house stock to meet** [☐ the firm's | ☐ client] **needs.**
- ☐ **Maintain inventory control of all** ______ *[type of]* [☐ product | ☐ merchandise | ☐ goods | ☐ supplies | ☐ materials | ☐ other: ______], **ensuring sufficient in-house stock to meet** [☐ the firm's | ☐ client] **needs.**
- ☐ [☐ Receive and] **Inspect all** ______ *[type of]* [☐ furniture | ☐ equipment | ☐ supplies | ☐ goods | ☐ merchandise | ☐ materials | ☐ other: ______] **and evaluate their condition.**
- ☐ **Oversee inventory control for all aspects of this $**______ *[revenues]* **store inventory including** ______, ______, **and** ______ *[what major inventory or merchandise?].*
- ☐ **Perform** [☐ daily | ☐ weekly | ☐ monthly] **inventory** [☐ counts | ☐ analysis | ☐ audits] **to determine any discrepancies and quickly resolve any and all inventory issues.**
- ☐ **Update and maintain records of the** [☐ receipt | ☐ inspection | ☐ distribution | ☐ transporting | ☐ warehousing | ☐ other: ______] **of all** [☐ property | ☐ furniture | ☐ equipment | ☐ supplies | ☐ goods | ☐ product | ☐ merchandise | ☐ materials | ☐ other: ______] **acquisitions and dispositions.**

ACHIEVEMENT SAMPLES:

- ☐ **Spearheaded a/an** ______ *[type of]* **inventory control** [☐ program | ☐ management system | ☐ strategies | ☐ other: ______] **for improving the firm's** [☐ operating efficiency | ☐ service levels | ☐ storage capacity by $______ *(amount)* | ☐ waste management by ______% *(percentage)* | ☐ other: ______] **while reducing** [☐ inventory levels | ☐ operating costs | ☐ waste | ☐ other: ______].
- ☐ **Developed, implemented, and maintain an automated inventory control program utilizing** ______ *[name of]* **software, which provided real time information on** [☐ product costs | ☐ usage | ☐ transfers | ☐ monthly overages and shortages | ☐ previous month comparisons | ☐ balances | ☐ other: ______].
- ☐ **Increased inventory turns by** [☐ working with merchants to set the merchandise for pallet type quantities | ☐ other method: ______].
- ☐ **Developed, implemented, manage, and control the firm's annual inventory** [☐ control procedures | ☐ budget | ☐ business plan | ☐ other: ______].

Job Preparation

- ☐ **Prepare for all** ______ *[type of]* **jobs by** [☐ prioritizing work assignments | ☐ ordering required inventory | ☐ determining equipment needed | ☐ setting up each project with the correct tools, materials, and supplies | ☐ coordinating contracting trades | ☐ determining conditions and safety requirements | ☐ identifying required repairs and/or replacements | ☐ other: ______].
- ☐ [☐ Lay out | ☐ Draft | ☐ Evaluate] [☐ engineering proposals | ☐ shop drawings | ☐ technical devices | ☐ parts specifications | ☐ other: ______] **depicting the fabrication, construction, and assembly of** ______ *[what?]* **ensuring** [☐ sound electrical engineering practice | ☐ compliance with all electrical codes | ☐ conformance with established (☐ safety / ☐ design) criteria].
- ☐ **Handle** [☐ estimating | ☐ contract negotiations | ☐ other: ______] **with** [☐ contractors | ☐ subcontractors | ☐ suppliers | ☐ other: ______] **involving** ______ *[what?].*
- ☐ **Apply an adapt knowledge of** ______ *[which?]* **trade** [☐ tools, equipment, and materials | ☐ safety practices | ☐ building codes | ☐ electrical codes | ☐ plumbing codes | ☐ zoning regulations | ☐ other: ______] **related to the installation, maintenance, and repair of** ______ *[what?].*
- ☐ **Provide technical** [☐ assistance | ☐ support | ☐ guidance | ☐ expertise | ☐ consultation | ☐ resolution] **on** ______ *[type of]* **issues** [☐ before | ☐ during | ☐ after] **the construction process.**

☐ **Apply provisions of all** [☐ building codes | ☐ electrical codes | ☐ safety standards and regulations | ☐ fire codes | ☐ other: ______] **in the** ______ *[which?]* **trade to** ______ *[type of]* **projects.**

☐ **Coordinated all aspects of** ______ *[type of]* **projects with** [☐ clients | ☐ engineers | ☐ architects | ☐ municipal officials | ☐ county officials | ☐ code officers | ☐ others: ______] **ensuring compliance with all** [☐______ *(which?)* codes | ☐ quality standards | ☐ work schedules | ☐ other: ______].

ACHIEVEMENT SAMPLES:

☐ **Performed the complete** ______ *[what building, plant, or other project?]*, **which included** [☐ estimating job costs | ☐ scheduling ______ *(type of)* work | ☐ ordering parts and materials | ☐ overseeing the installation process | ☐ managing a staff of ______ *(#)*______ *(titles)* | ☐ supervising quality control | ☐ billing clients | ☐ other: ______] [☐ meeting | ☐ exceeding] **aggressive timeframes.**

☐ **Coordinated all aspects of** ______ *[type of]* **projects with** [☐ clients | ☐ engineers | ☐ architects | ☐ municipal officials | ☐ county officials | ☐ code officers | ☐ others: ______] **ensuring compliance with all** [☐______ *(which?)* codes | ☐ quality standards | ☐ work schedules | ☐ other: ______].

Labor Management & Supervision

*See **"Trades / Crew Supervision."***

Labor Relations

*See **"Union Functions"** and **"Union Leadership."***

Landscape Design

See also other Landscape categories, as applicable.

☐ **Manage and oversee all aspects of this landscape design firm including** [☐ sales | ☐ customer service | ☐ installations | ☐ contract negotiations | ☐ account servicing | ☐ administration | ☐ cash management | ☐ client and financial database | ☐ hiring, training, and scheduling employees | ☐ budgeting | ☐ other: ______].

☐ **Design and install attractive, functional landscape areas including building and/or installing** [☐ sidewalks | ☐ walkways | ☐ retainer walls | ☐ decks | ☐ porches | ☐ patios | ☐ terraces | ☐ arbors | ☐ gazebos | ☐ pools | ☐ cabanas | ☐ fountains | ☐ fences | ☐ planters | ☐ benches | ☐ parking lots | ☐ sprinkler systems | ☐ lighting | ☐ flower beds | ☐ borders | ☐ other: ______].

☐ **Provide full-service landscape design services to** [☐ commercial | ☐ residential | ☐ public] **clients for** [☐ residential buildings | ☐ custom homes | ☐ office buildings | ☐ shopping malls | ☐ hotels | ☐ stores | ☐ other: ______].

☐ **Manage daily activities of a landscaping design team of** ______ *[#]* **coordinating all functions for** ______ *[#]* ______ *[type of]* **accounts including** ______ [type of accounts] **ensuring all work is completed according to landscaping plans and schedules.**

☐ **Design** [☐ indoor | ☐ outdoor] [☐ garden areas | ☐ tree groves | ☐ other: ______] **in** [☐ commercial | ☐ public] **facilities including** [☐ botanical gardens | ☐ parks | ☐ shopping malls | ☐ hotels | ☐ other: ______].

☐ **Work with** ______ *[which?]* **trades to coordinate the design and installation of** [☐ walkways | ☐ terraces | ☐ patios | ☐ decks | ☐ other: ______] **to create** [☐ functional | ☐ aesthetic | ☐ homogenous | ☐ attractive | ☐ pleasant | ☐ other: ______] **environments for** ______ *[whom or what?]*.

☐ **Provide** [☐ large-scale | ☐ intricate | ☐ complex | ☐ other: ______] **landscape design services for** ______ *[#]* [☐ commercial | ☐ residential | ☐ public] **properties including** [☐ condominiums | ☐ apartment complexes | ☐ residential properties | ☐ commercial grounds | ☐ public facilities | ☐ parks | ☐ shopping centers | ☐ golf courses | ☐ botanical gardens | ☐ nurseries | ☐ garden centers | ☐ banks | ☐ factories | ☐ school grounds | ☐ public parking lots | ☐ train stations | ☐ club houses | ☐ hotels | ☐ athletic fields | ☐ college campuses | ☐ large estates | ☐ highways and roadways | ☐ communities | ☐ other: ______].

☐ **Use** ______ *[type of]* **landscaping methods to develop attractive, functional landscape designs including** [☐ ensuring required soil conditions | ☐ grading property | ☐ planting new gardens | ☐ constructing terraces | ☐ installing walkways | ☐ building cabanas | ☐ other: ______].

☐ **Plan, design, and direct the installation of** ______ *[#]* **acres of** ______ *[type of]* **landscapes for** ______ *[whom or what?]* **covering all aspects of** ______ *[what?]* **including** [☐ installing landscaped areas | ☐ building walkways, terraces, patios, decks | ☐ grading property | ☐ installing lighting | ☐ planting new gardens | ☐ maintaining swimming pools | ☐ controlling weeds, disease, and insect infestation | ☐ other: ______].

☐ **Create detailed specifications for multiple** [☐ large-scale | ☐ moderate-size | ☐ highly complex | ☐ moderately complex | ☐ other: ______] **landscape projects with varying requirements ensuring all objectives are accomplished within established time frames.**

ACHIEVEMENT SAMPLES: *See also "Completed Design-and-Build Projects," and "Completed Projects – General."*

- ☐ **Designed and installed** ______ *[type of]* **unique landscaped areas for** ______ *[whom or what?]* **by** ______ *[doing what?].*
- ☐ **Simultaneously drafted detailed landscaping plans and specifications for the following sites:** ______ *[name],* ______ *[town],* ______ *[state];* ______ *[name],* ______ *[town],* ______ *[state];* **and** ______ *[name],* ______ *[town],* ______ *[state],* **resulting in their successful completion.**
- ☐ **Apply an in-depth knowledge of** [☐ site environments | ☐ plant types | ☐ nutritional requirements | ☐ soil preparation | ☐ ground covers | ☐ other: ______] **in** [☐ identifying best planting methods | ☐ adjusting soil pH | ☐ determining fertilizer applications | ☐ other: ______].
- ☐ **Created and installed a detailed landscape plan of** ______ *[what?]* **that involved** ______ *[what?]* **with a design challenge of** ______ *[what?]* **resulting in** ______ *[what achievements?].*

Landscape Installation

See also "Landscaping/Groundskeeping Projects & Functions," "Masonry Projects & Functions," "Inspections & Compliance – Landscape & Masonry" and "Construction Projects," as applicable.

- ☐ **Supervise the installation of** [☐ retainer walls | ☐ flower beds | ☐ landscape borders | ☐ walkways | ☐ sprinkler systems | ☐ concrete masonry wall units | ☐ other: ______] **including** [☐ grading | ☐ planting | ☐ sod laying | ☐ transplanting | ☐ trimming | ☐ masonry | ☐ other: ______] **of** [☐ lawns | ☐ flowers | ☐ plants | ☐ shrubbery | ☐ shade and ornamental trees | ☐ annuals | ☐ perennials | ☐ other: ______] **taking into account** [☐ sun exposure | ☐ shading | ☐ existing soil | ☐ other: ______] **conditions.**
- ☐ **Handle landscaping components such as** [☐ property grading | ☐ masonry | ☐ walkway installations | ☐ new garden plantings | ☐ irrigation systems | ☐ testing soil composition | ☐ detaching and aerating lawns | ☐ mulching | ☐ other: ______].
- ☐ **Lay out, design, and install** ______ *[what?]* **to** [☐ achieve pleasant and functional outdoor environments | ☐ increase property values | ☐ create a positive first impression | ☐ establish a tranquil mood | ☐ other: ______] **of** ______ *[what?].*
- ☐ **Minimize landscape installation impact so** [☐ business | ☐ home] **operations can still be functional by** ______ *[doing what?].*
- ☐ **Manage and oversee all landscaping installations including** [☐ building retainer walls | ☐ constructing pathways | ☐ installing patios | ☐ other: ______].
- ☐ **Plan, organize, coordinate, and direct landscaping activities including** [☐ planting trees, shrubs, flowers | ☐ maintaining lawns | ☐ applying fertilizers and pesticides | ☐ other: ______] **to meet contract specifications.**
- ☐ **Handle** ______ *[type of]* **specialized landscaping work at this** ______ *[type of]* **firm including** [☐ planting new grass | ☐ pruning bushes | ☐ mulching gardens | ☐ other: ______].
- ☐ **Install and maintain sprinkler systems including** [☐ sprinkler system layout and design | ☐ installation | ☐ testing | ☐ other: ______] **ensuring complete customer satisfaction.**
- ☐ **Review client contracts to determine required services, equipment, methods, materials, and labor.**
- ☐ **Plant and transplant** [☐ trees | ☐ shrubs | ☐ sod | ☐ plants | ☐ flowers | ☐ bulbs | ☐ annuals | ☐ perennials | ☐ other: ______] **by** [☐ correcting soil conditions to allow proper drainage | ☐ using the appropriate grasses | ☐ other: ______] **to ensure proper growth and prevent disease and spoilage.**
- ☐ **Plan and install** ______ *[type of]* **irrigation systems, making efficient use of the system to cover all grounds by effectively** ______ *[doing what well?].*

Landscape Management

See also "Landscaping / Groundskeeping Projects & Functions," "Landscape Design," "Masonry Projects & Functions," "Inspections & Compliance – Landscape & Masonry," "Trades/Crew Supervision," "Trades Coordination & Oversight – Landscaping & Masonry," and "Construction Projects."

- ☐ **Manage and oversee all aspects of this** ______ *[type of]* **landscaping business including** [☐ sales | ☐ customer service | ☐ installations | ☐ maintenance | ☐ account servicing | ☐ administration | ☐ cash management | ☐ client and financial database | ☐ hiring, training, and scheduling employees | ☐ equipment maintenance | ☐ budgeting | ☐ other: ______].
- ☐ **Supervise the installation of** [☐ retainer walls | ☐ flower beds | ☐ landscape borders | ☐ walkways | ☐ sprinkler systems | ☐ concrete masonry wall units | ☐ other: ______] **including** [☐ grading | ☐ planting | ☐ sod laying | ☐ transplanting | ☐ trimming | ☐ masonry | ☐ other: ______] **of** [☐ lawns | ☐ flowers | ☐ plants | ☐ shrubbery | ☐ shade and ornamental trees | ☐ annuals | ☐ perennials | ☐ other: ______] **taking into account** [☐ sun exposure | ☐ shading | ☐ existing soil | ☐ other: ______] **conditions.**

- ☐ **Schedule and supervise the daily operations and landscaping activities of a crew of** ______ *[#]*; **and oversee the complete upkeep of the** ______ *[which?]* **grounds for this** ______ *[type of]* [☐ landscaping | ☐ groundskeeping | ☐ lawn maintenance | ☐ general contracting | ☐ public services | ☐ other: ______] **company**.
- ☐ **Supervise all** [☐ landscaping | ☐ grounds maintenance | ☐ other: ______] **activities including the installation of** [☐ structural wall panels | ☐retainer walls | ☐ pathways | ☐ patios | ☐ decks | ☐ firebrick linings | ☐ refractory tile | ☐ soaking pits | ☐ other: ______] **and the application of** [☐ marble | ☐ granite | ☐ limestone | ☐ concrete block | ☐ marble chips | ☐ brick veneer | ☐ tile | ☐ other: ______] **and other masonry projects**.
- ☐ **Direct the installation of** ______ *[#]* **acres of** ______ *[type of]* **landscapes for** ______ *[whom or what?]* **covering all aspects of** ______ *[what?]* **including** [☐ installing landscaped areas | ☐ building walkways, terraces, patios, decks | ☐ grading property | ☐ installing lighting | ☐ planting new gardens | ☐ maintaining swimming pools | ☐ controlling weeds, disease, and insect infestation | ☐ other: ______].
- ☐ **Manage all aspects of grounds maintenance services including** [☐ lawn mowing | ☐ leaf removal | ☐ tree trimming | ☐ weed control | ☐ fertilizing | ☐ insect control | ☐ pest elimination | ☐ flower gardening | ☐ shrub pruning | ☐ horticulture | ☐ grading | ☐ seeding | ☐ detaching | ☐ aerating | ☐ planting | ☐ plant damage care | ☐ snow removal | ☐ other: ______].
- ☐ **Manage a landscaping team of** ______ *[#]* **including hiring, training, scheduling, and evaluating crew; and supervise and coordinate daily crew operations for this** ______ *[type of]* **firm.**
- ☐ **Plan, organize, coordinate, and direct** [☐ landscaping | ☐ groundskeeping | ☐ lawn service] **activities including** ☐ planting trees, shrubs, flowers | ☐ maintaining lawns | ☐ applying fertilizers and pesticides | ☐ other: ______] **to meet contract specifications.**
- ☐ **Manage and oversee all** [☐ landscaping | ☐ landscaping installations | ☐ grounds maintenance] including [☐ lawn | ☐ shrub | ☐ flower] acreage care for ______ *[what?]* **including** [☐ building retainer walls | ☐ constructing pathways | ☐ installing patios | ☐ other: ______].
- ☐ **Provide decisive leadership and clear direction in all phases of** [☐ large-scale | ☐ complex] ______ *[type of]* **projects for** [☐ residential | ☐ commercial | ☐ industrial | ☐ other: ______] **clients overseeing a top-performing team of** ______ *[#]* **landscapers**.
- ☐ **Direct and schedule landscape crew's functions and oversee the complete upkeep of the** ______ *[which?]* **grounds for this** ______ *[type of]* **firm with** ______ *[#]* **clients to maximize property potential and aesthetics**.
- ☐ **Supervise and coordinate the activities of a crew of** ______ *[#]* [☐ skilled | ☐ semi-skilled | ☐ unskilled] [☐ Landscape Laborers | ☐ Greenhouse Workers | ☐ Park Caretakers | ☐ Nursery Workers | ☐ other: ______] **in the grounds upkeep of** ______ *[what?]*.
- ☐ **Oversee and supervise the** ______ *[type of]* **activities of a team of** ______ *[#]* **skilled** [☐ Landscape Architects | ☐ Ornamental Horticulturists | ☐ Park Naturalists | ☐ other: ______] **in the design and installation of** ______ *[what?]*.
- ☐ **Manage daily activities of a landscaping team of** ______ *[#]* **coordinating all** [☐ landscaping | ☐ grounds maintenance | ☐ horticulture | ☐ other: ______] **work functions for** ______ *[#]* [☐ commercial | ☐ residential | ☐ public] **accounts including** ______ *[type of accounts]* **ensuring all work is completed according to landscaping plans and schedules**.
- ☐ **Coordinate landscaping and masonry functions with other trades in the design and installation of** ______ *[what?]*.
- ☐ **Direct concrete casting and supervise** ______ *[#]* **laborers who spread, level, float, and smooth concrete, create joints, and trowel surfaces to ensure wedges, plumblines, levels, and brackets create a precision fit and attractive finish**.
- ☐ **Review client contracts to determine required services, equipment, methods, materials, and labor and make project determinations based on** ______ *[what?]*.
- ☐ **Plan, organize, and coordinate landscaping and masonry activities including** [☐ planting trees, shrubs, and flowers | ☐ installing lawns | ☐ applying fertilizers and pesticides | ☐ other: ______] **to meet** [☐ client needs | ☐ contract specifications].
- ☐ **Schedule and supervise the daily operations and all landscaping activities of a crew of** ______ *[#]*; **and oversee the complete upkeep of the** ______ *[which?]* **grounds**.

ACHIEVEMENT SAMPLES: *See "Construction Projects."*

Landscape Equipment Operation & Maintenance

*See "**Equipment, Machinery, Tools & Testing Devices – Landscaping & Masonry.**"*

Landscape Projects Oversight

*See also "**Landscaping/Groundskeeping Projects & Functions,**" "**Landscape Design,**" "**Masonry Projects & Functions,**" "**Inspections & Compliance – Landscape & Masonry,**" "**Trades/Crew Supervision,**" "**Trades Coordination & Oversight – Landscaping & Masonry,**" and "**Construction Projects.**"*

☐ **Oversee landscaping and masonry trades in their landscape work for** [☐ commercial | ☐ residential | ☐ public] ______ *[type of]* **properties including** [☐ condominiums | ☐ apartment complexes | ☐ residential properties | ☐ commercial grounds | ☐ public facilities | ☐ parks | ☐ shopping centers | ☐ golf courses | ☐ botanical gardens | ☐ nurseries | ☐ garden centers | ☐ banks | ☐ factories | ☐ school grounds | ☐ parking lots | ☐ train stations | ☐ club houses | ☐ hotels | ☐ athletic fields | ☐ cemeteries | ☐ college campuses | ☐ large estates | ☐ highways and roadways | ☐ communities | ☐ other: ______].

☐ **Inspect** [☐ lawns | ☐ trees | ☐ shrubs | ☐ plants | ☐ crops | ☐ other: ______] **for** [☐ disease | ☐ insect | ☐ pest | ☐ other: ______] **problems and apply** [☐ fertilizers | ☐ insecticides | ☐ pesticides | ☐ herbicides | ☐ fungicides | ☐ ______ *(type of)* chemicals] **to** [☐ eradicate weeds | ☐ stimulate growth | ☐ eliminate insect infestation | ☐ rid of pests | ☐ other: ______] **resulting in** ______ *[what outcome?]*.

☐ **Oversee the performance of various landscaping functions including installing** [☐ landscaped areas | ☐ sod | ☐ retainer walls | ☐ terraces | ☐ patios | ☐ decks and porches | ☐ flower beds | ☐ botanical crops | ☐ landscape borders | ☐ walkways | ☐ sprinkler systems | ☐ concrete masonry wall units | ☐ lighting | ☐ irrigation systems | ☐ shade and ornamental trees | ☐ annuals | ☐ perennials | ☐ other: ______] **and** [☐ grading | ☐ planting | ☐ transplanting | ☐ trimming | ☐ thatching | ☐ seeding | ☐ raking | ☐ masonry | ☐ other: ______] **lawns**.

☐ **Coordinate landscaping and masonry functions with other trades in the design and installation of** ______ *[what?]*.

ACHIEVEMENT SAMPLES: *See "**Construction Projects.**"*

Landscaping & Greenskeeping – General

*See also "**Landscape Management,**" "**Landscape Design,**" and "**Masonry Projects & Functions.**"*

☐ **Tend to the landscaping needs of** ______ *[type of]* **clients'** [☐ private homes | ☐ businesses | ☐ other: ______] **by maintaining** [☐ lawns | ☐ trees | ☐ shrubbery | ☐ gardens | ☐ leaf removal | ☐ weed control | ☐ other: ______].

☐ **Provide** [☐ all | ☐ various] **aspects of commercial** [☐ grounds | ☐ landscape | ☐ masonry | ☐ other: ______] **maintenance services for** ______ *[whom or what?]* **including** [☐ lawn mowing | ☐ leaf removal | ☐ tree trimming | ☐ weed control | ☐ fertilizing | ☐ insect control | ☐ pest elimination | ☐ flower gardening | ☐ shrub pruning | ☐ horticulture | ☐ grading | ☐ seeding | ☐ dethatching | ☐ aerating | ☐ planting | ☐ plant damage care | ☐ snow removal | ☐ other: ______].

☐ **Maintain** ______ *[what?]* **grounds including all** [☐ mowing | ☐ edging | ☐ trimming | ☐ fertilizing | ☐ gardening | ☐ pruning | ☐ grading | ☐ seeding | ☐ dethatching | ☐ aerating | ☐ planting | ☐ transplanting | ☐ irrigating | ☐ harvesting | ☐ raking | ☐ mulching | ☐ weeding | ☐ painting | ☐ troubleshooting | ☐ other: ______] **services and activities for** ______ *[what?]*.

☐ **Provided customer service for this** [☐ local nursery | ☐ garden center | ☐ other: ______] **with an in-house landscaping contractor.**

☐ **Handle specialized** ______ *[type of]* [☐ landscaping | ☐ grounds maintenance] **work at this** ______ *[type of]* **firm including** [☐ thatching soil | ☐ planting new grass | ☐ pruning bushes | ☐ mowing lawns | ☐ mulching gardens | ☐ pulling weeds | ☐ raking leaves | ☐ eliminating pests | ☐ watering acreage | ☐ other: ______].

☐ **Plan, design, install, and maintain** ______ *[type of]* **landscapes for** ______ *[whom or what?]* **covering all aspects of** ______ *[what?]*.

☐ **Provide full-service landscape maintenance services to** [☐ residential | ☐ commercial] **clients for** [☐ residential buildings | ☐ office buildings | ☐ shopping malls | ☐ hotels | ☐ other: ______].

☐ **Keep** [☐ natural | ☐ artificial] **turf fields in top condition by** [☐ correcting soil conditions to allow proper drainage | ☐ using the appropriate grasses | ☐ disinfecting synthetic turf after each use | ☐ other: ______] **to prevent** [☐ disease | ☐ bacteria | ☐ spoilage | ☐ other: ______] [☐ and ensure proper growth].

☐ **Provide** [☐ large-scale] **weekly** [☐ grounds | ☐ landscape | ☐ greenskeeping | ☐ other: ______] **maintenance services for** ______ *[#]* [☐ commercial | ☐ residential | ☐ public] **properties including** [☐ condominiums | ☐ apartment complexes | ☐ residential properties | ☐ commercial facilities | ☐ parks | ☐ shopping centers | ☐ golf courses | ☐ parks | ☐ picnic areas | ☐ botanical gardens | ☐ nurseries | ☐ garden centers | ☐ banks | ☐ factories | ☐ school grounds | ☐ public parking lots | ☐ train stations | ☐ club houses | ☐ hotels | ☐ public facilities | ☐ athletic fields | ☐ recreational facilities | ☐ cemeteries | ☐ colleges | ☐ university campuses | ☐ cemeteries | ☐ memorial gardens | ☐ large estates | ☐ highways | ☐ roadways | ☐ communities | ☐ country clubs | ☐ playgrounds | ☐ other public spaces | ☐ other: ______].

☐ **Install and maintain** ______ *[type of]* **landscapes for** ______ *[whom?]* **covering all aspects of** ______ *[what?]*.

☐ **Care for and maintain** [☐ indoor | ☐ outdoor] [☐ gardens | ☐ trees | ☐ plantings | ☐ other: ______] **in** [☐ commercial | ☐ public] **facilities including** ______, ______, **and** ______ *[type of facilities]*.

☐ **Identify and resolve** [☐ plant | ☐ crop | ☐ lawn | ☐ shrub | ☐ tree] **damage by successfully** ______ *[doing what well?]*.

ACHIEVEMENT SAMPLES: *See "Construction Projects."*

Landscaping & Greenskeeping – Projects & Functions

☐ **Review client contracts to determine required services, equipment, methods, materials, and labor and make project determinations based on** ______ *[what?]*.

☐ **Perform various landscaping functions including installing** [☐ landscaped areas | ☐ sod | ☐ retainer walls | ☐ terraces | ☐ patios | ☐ decks and porches | ☐ flower beds | ☐ botanical crops | ☐ landscape borders | ☐ walkways | ☐ sprinkler systems | ☐ concrete masonry wall units | ☐ lighting | ☐ irrigation systems | ☐ shade and ornamental trees | ☐ annuals | ☐ perennials | ☐ other: ______] **and** [☐ grading | ☐ planting | ☐ transplanting | ☐ trimming | ☐ thatching | ☐ seeding | ☐ raking | ☐ masonry | ☐ other: ______] **lawns**.

☐ **Handle** [☐ landscaping | ☐ landscaping installations | ☐ grounds maintenance] **including** [☐ lawn | ☐ shrub | ☐ flower | ☐ other: ______] **acreage care for** ______ *[what?]* **including** [☐ building retainer walls | ☐ constructing pathways | ☐ installing patios | ☐ other: ______] **taking into account** [☐ sun exposure | ☐ shading | ☐ existing soil | ☐ other: ______] **conditions**.

☐ **Plan, organize, and coordinate** [☐ landscaping | ☐ groundskeeping | ☐ lawn service | ☐ masonry | ☐ other: ______] **activities including** [☐ planting trees, shrubs, and flowers | ☐ maintaining lawns | ☐ applying fertilizers and pesticides | ☐ other: ______] **to meet** [☐ client needs | ☐ contract specifications].

☐ **Perform** [☐ landscaping | ☐ grounds maintenance | ☐ other: ______] **activities functions including** [☐ installations | ☐ maintenance | ☐ administration | ☐ hiring, training, and scheduling employees | ☐ equipment maintenance | ☐ budgeting | ☐ other: ______] **of** ______ *[what?]*.

☐ **Oversee the complete upkeep of the** ______ *[which?]* **grounds to maximize property potential and aesthetics including** [☐ dethatching and aerating (☐ lawns / ☐ fields / ☐ grounds) | ☐ transplanting trees and shrubs | ☐ pruning shrubs | ☐ trimming trees | ☐ mulching planting areas | ☐ cutting away dead branches | ☐ fertilizing flowering plants and lawns | ☐ identifying and resolving plant damage | ☐ mowing and edging lawns | ☐ repairing sidewalks and parking lots | ☐ applying pesticides, herbicides, fungicides, and insecticides | ☐ clearing snow from walkways and parking lots | ☐ raking and mulching leaves | ☐ ensuring required soil composition | ☐ disinfecting synthetic turf | ☐ recommending new plantings | ☐ painting outdoor furniture and structures | ☐ maintaining swimming pools | ☐ controlling weeds, disease, and insect infestation | ☐ other: ______].

☐ **Transport and plant** [☐ trees | ☐ shrubs | ☐ sod | ☐ plants | ☐ flowers | ☐ bulbs | ☐ other: ______]; **and water lawn and gardens to maintain the upkeep of** ______ *[what?]*.

☐ **Provide** [☐ large-scale] **weekly** [☐ grounds | ☐ landscape] **maintenance services for** ______ [#] **properties including** ______ *[properties]*.

☐ **Perform various greenskeeping functions for** ______ *[whom or what?]* **including** [☐ mowing lawns | ☐ pruning shrubs and trees | ☐ planting flowers | ☐ disinfecting synthetic turf | ☐ removing debris | ☐ applying fertilizers and pesticides | ☐ relocating putting green holes | ☐ covering ground with artificial turf | ☐ planting botanical gardens | ☐ painting outdoor structures and furniture | ☐ removing snow | ☐ other: ______] **to** [☐ eliminate uneven turf wear | ☐ add visual interest | ☐ make a positive aesthetic impression | ☐ other: ______].

☐ **Handle greenskeeping maintenance activities during the growing season for** ______ *[type of]* **clients on a regular basis including** [☐ mowing | ☐ edging | ☐ trimming | ☐ raking | ☐ fertilizing | ☐ dethatching | ☐ aerating | ☐ mulching | ☐ other: ______] [☐ fields | ☐ greens | ☐ grounds | ☐ acreage].

☐ **Schedule and supervise the daily operations and all landscaping activities of a crew of** ______ *[#]*; **and oversee the complete upkeep of the** ______ *[which?]* **grounds**.

- ☐ **Direct and schedule employees' functions and oversee the complete upkeep of the ______** *[which?]* **grounds to maximize property potential and aesthetics.**
- ☐ **Trim trees and shrubs to remove dead and excess branches in and around** [☐ parks | ☐ highways | ☐ roads | ☐ sidewalks | ☐ facilities | ☐ utilities | ☐ golf courses | ☐ private residences | ☐ other: ______] **to** [☐ improve the appearance and health of trees | ☐ maintain rights-of-way | ☐ clear power lines | ☐ other: ______].
- ☐ **Mix and apply** [☐ fertilizers | ☐ insecticides | ☐ pesticides | ☐ herbicides | ☐ fungicides | ☐ ______ *(type of)* chemicals] **to** [☐ lawns | ☐ trees | ☐ shrubs | ☐ flowering plants | ☐ crops | ☐ herb gardens | ☐ other: ______] **using** [☐ sprayers | ☐ applicators | ☐ handlers | ☐ other: ______] **on a** [☐ seasonal | ☐ bi-monthly | ☐ periodic | ☐ other: ______] **basis**.
- ☐ **Inspect** [☐ lawns | ☐ trees | ☐ shrubs | ☐ plants | ☐ crops | ☐ other: ______] **for** [☐ disease | ☐ insect | ☐ pest | ☐ other: ______] **problems and apply** [☐ fertilizers | ☐ insecticides | ☐ pesticides | ☐ herbicides | ☐ fungicides | ☐ ______ *(type of)* chemicals] **to** [☐ eradicate weeds | ☐ stimulate growth | ☐ eliminate insect infestation | ☐ rid of pests | ☐ other: ______] **resulting in** ______ *[what outcome?]*.

ACHIEVEMENT SAMPLES: *See **"Construction Projects."***

Maintenance & Repair Projects

*See **"Preventive & Seasonal Maintenance," "Facility Management,"** and position-related Maintenance and Repair Work of various trades (Electrical, HVAC, Plumbing, Welding, Landscaping, Masonry).*

Management – General

See areas of specialization for primary management functions and achievements.

- ☐ **Manage the daily operations of the ______** *[which?]* [☐ Department | ☐ Center | ☐ unit | ☐ office] **and all related services critical to ______** *[what?]* **including ______, ______, and ______** *[areas]*.
- ☐ [☐ Plan and develop | ☐ Coordinate and implement | ☐ Administer and quality control | ☐ other: ______] **day-to-day ______** *[which?]* **activities for this ______** *[type of]* **firm with ______** *[#]* **employees.**
- ☐ **Provide specialized ______** *[type of]* [☐ consultation | ☐ leadership and guidance | ☐ technical direction and support | ☐ other: ______] **to a ______** *[which?]* **staff of ______** *[#]* **in the areas of ______, ______, and ______** *[what areas?]*.
- ☐ **Partake in the development, implementation, and update of ______** *[what?]* [☐ short-and long-range planning | ☐ establishment of goals and objectives | ☐ policies and procedures development | ☐ new ______ *(type of)* program development | ☐ enhancement of integrated ______ *(type of)* services | ☐ records establishment and maintenance | ☐ other: ______].
- ☐ **Lead and direct a wide range of ______** *[which?]* **functions including the** [☐ planning | ☐ organizing | ☐ coordinating | ☐ developing | ☐ facilitating | ☐ other: ______] **of ______** *[what?]*.
- ☐ **Manage and oversee the ______** *[which?]* **operations and key functions including ______, ______, and ______** *[what areas?]* **to provide comprehensive ______** *[type of]* **services to ______** *[whom?]*.
- ☐ **Serve as a key member of the firm's ______** *[which?]* **management team accountable for developing ______** *[type of]* **strategies and plans that serve to ______, ______, and ______** *[do what?]*.
- ☐ **Direct and guide a ______** *[which?]* **staff of ______** *[#]* **in the development and maintenance of ______, ______, and ______** *[what?]*.
- ☐ **Direct and coordinate the organization's ______** *[which?]* [☐ Department | ☐ Center | ☐ unit | ☐ office] **including ______, ______, and ______** *[what functions or activities?]*.
- ☐ **Serving as ______** *[title]*, **perform management and administrative support to the ______** *[which?]* [☐ Department | ☐ Director | ☐ Manager] **in the areas of planning, coordinating, developing, and/or reviewing ______** *[what?]*.
- ☐ [☐ Manage and administer | ☐ Coordinate and oversee] **all facets of the firm's ______** *[which?]* **Department** [☐ services | ☐ support activities | ☐ operations] **including ______, ______, and ______** *[what areas?]*.
- ☐ **Implement and oversee the operation of ______** *[which?]* **Department's** [☐ systems | ☐ policies | ☐ procedures] **in ______, ______, and ______** *[what areas?]*.
- ☐ **Develop, administer, and update the firm's ______** *[which?]* [☐ policies and procedures | ☐ objectives | ☐ short- and long-range planning | ☐ five-year road map | ☐ other: ______].
- ☐ **Provide leadership, vision, and direction to a team of ______** *[#]* ______ *[which?]* **Specialists to initiate, plan, and implement ______** *[type of]* **projects that result in ______** *[what benefits?]*.

☐ **Manage and administer all facets of the firm's ______** *[which?]* [☐ services | ☐ support activities | ☐ operations | ☐ other: ______] **including ______, ______, and ______** *[what areas?]*.

☐ **Identify, define, and document ______** *[which?]* **priorities, as well as** [☐ options | ☐ costs | ☐ benefits | ☐ milestones | ☐ other: ______] **and translate requirements into effective ______** *[type of]* **solutions.**

ACHIEVEMENT SAMPLES:

☐ [☐ Co-developed | ☐ Designed and implemented] **the firm's ______** *[type of]* [☐ Policies and Procedures | ☐ initiatives | ☐ programs | ☐ work simplification methods | ☐ other: ______], **which benefited the firm by way of ______** *[how?]*.

☐ **Contributed to the success of this ______** *[type of]* **firm by ______** *[doing what?]*.

☐ **Recommended and implemented ______** *[type of]* **improvements to ______** *[what?]*, **which helped facilitate ______** *[what functions?]* **and resulted in ______** *[what benefits?]*.

☐ **Involved in managing and coordinating ______** *[what?]* **efforts that required ______** *[what actions?]* **to meet ______** *[what challenges?]* **and resulted in ______** *[benefits]*.

☐ **Run efficient ______** *[type of]* **business through** [☐ proper staffing and scheduling | ☐ improving staff morale and efficiency | ☐ ensuring quality work in all areas | ☐ other: ______].

Masonry Projects & Functions

*See also **"Landscape Installation," "Landscaping / Groundskeeping Projects & Functions," "Equipment, Tools & Testing Devices – Landscaping & Masonry,"** and **"Inspections & Compliance – Landscape & Masonry."***

☐ **Design and build attractive landscape designs including** [☐ walkways | ☐ sidewalks | ☐ patios | ☐ roadways | ☐ flooring | ☐ concrete surfaces | ☐ exposed aggregate walls | ☐ concrete beams | ☐ columns | ☐ panels | ☐ other: ______] **for this** [☐ masonry | ☐ landscaping | ☐ general contracting | ☐ other: ______] **firm that services** [☐ residential | ☐ commercial | ☐ other: ______] **clients**.

☐ **Use a variety of masonry techniques to build creative and functional projects, such as** [☐ colorizing concrete for a decorative finish | ☐ polishing and sealing masonry surfaces to prevent breakage, separation, and chipping | ☐ installing decorative interlocking pavers and edging materials | ☐ staggering blocks to create unique designs | ☐ creating ornate stone walls | ☐ designing and installing decorative patios and steps | ☐ embedding gravel chips for a pebble finish | ☐ brushing surfaces for a coarse, nonskid finish | ☐ creating unique finishes by applying ______ *(what?)* | ☐ using various masonry materials that create contrast and visual interest | ☐ other: ______].

☐ **Specialize in installing** [☐ structural wall panels | ☐ firebrick linings in industrial furnaces | ☐ refractory tile in boilers and furnaces | ☐ soaking pits in industrial establishments | ☐ other: ______] **using** [☐ marble | ☐ granite | ☐ limestone | ☐ concrete block | ☐ marble chips | ☐ brick veneer | ☐ tile | ☐ glass | ☐ other: ______] **and other masonry materials**.

☐ **Lay out, cut, and install a variety of interlocking pavers and edging materials to create decorative** [☐ landscape designs | ☐ walkways | ☐ paths | ☐ driveways | ☐ patios | ☐ panels | ☐ playgrounds | ☐ steps | ☐ other: ______] **for ______** *[whom or what?]*.

☐ **Design, cut, and lay out different masonry shapes and effects, such as ______** *[what?]* **for various ______** *[type of]* **projects, which result in ______** *[what client or employer benefits?]*.

☐ **Build ______** *[type of]* **structures with precision and uniformity by** [☐ aligning masonry materials with wedges, plumb lines, levels, and brackets for a precision fit | ☐ using the corner lead and corner pole methods | ☐ other technique: ______] **depending on job complexity and blueprint specifications.**

☐ **Install ______** *[type of]* [(☐ structural / ☐ insulated / ☐ other: ______) wall panels | ☐ exposed aggregate and retainer walls | ☐ roadways | ☐ driveways | ☐ walkways | ☐ paths | ☐ playgrounds | ☐ stone walls | ☐ ornate exteriors | ☐ concrete beams and columns | ☐ other: ______].

☐ **Working closely with related trades to create ______** *[type of]* **structures, ensure the precise alignment of all** [☐ stones | ☐ bricks | ☐ pavers | ☐ edgers | ☐ other: ______] **with wedges, plumblines, levels, and brackets for a precision fit and attractive finish using chisels, diamond blade saws, mallets, trowels, and crowbars.**

☐ **Create and install decorative, durable ______** *[type of]* **masonry** [☐ surfaces | ☐ structures | ☐ other: ______] **with varying complexity for ______** *[type of]* **clients including** [☐ stone walls | ☐ masonry walkways | ☐ structural wall panels | ☐ concrete foundations | ☐ ornate exteriors | ☐ roadways | ☐ driveways | ☐ other: ______] **on** [☐ high-rise buildings | ☐ office buildings | ☐ residential homes | ☐ lobbies | ☐ other: ______] **by ______** *[doing what?]*.

☐ **Perform concrete demolition, installation, and repair functions including** [☐ removing existing pavement | ☐ grading soil | ☐ installing and compacting base material | ☐ accurately setting and aligning concrete forms | ☐ casting concrete | ☐ spreading, leveling, floating, and smoothing concrete | ☐ building solid, level concrete foundations | ☐ using corner lead and corner pole methods | ☐ troweling surface and creating joints | ☐ monitoring how the wind, heat, and cold affect concrete curing to prevent defects | ☐ laying pavers | ☐ grinding terrazzo | ☐ filling spaces with sand | ☐ installing edging materials | ☐ cleaning, polishing, and sealing surfaces | ☐ repairing cracks | ☐ other: ______] **on** ______ *[type of]* **projects.**

☐ **Build solid, level concrete** [☐ foundations | ☐ panels | ☐ other: ______] **creating joints and** [☐ blending marble chip mixtures into cement | ☐ grinding terrazzo | ☐ embedding gravel chips for a pebble finish | ☐ using colored concrete for a decorative finish | ☐ laying pavers | ☐ installing edging materials | ☐ other: ______] **and** [☐ cleaning | ☐ polishing | ☐ sealing | ☐ brushing | ☐ other: ______] **surfaces, taking necessary preventive measures to prevent defects from occurring.**

☐ **Repair cracks and imperfections in** [☐ walls | ☐ walkways | ☐ flooring | ☐ partitions | ☐ fireplaces | ☐ chimneys | ☐ parking lots | ☐ other: ______].

☐ **Accurately set and align concrete forms; direct concrete casting; and supervise laborers to spread, level, float, and smooth concrete; create joints; and trowel surfaces.**

ACHIEVEMENT SAMPLES: *See "Construction Projects."*

Overcoming Obstacles

ACHIEVEMENT SAMPLES:

☐ **Assigned to take over the** ______ *[which?]* **project to smooth out conflicts. Handled through firm negotiations and teamwork with client rep and all trades to put project back on track.**

☐ **Turned around a mismanaged** ______ *[type of]* **project; accomplished** [☐ through firm negotiations and teamwork with client rep and all trades to put project back on track | ☐ by successfully completing project without compromising each other's responsibilities | ☐ by maintaining an excellent rapport | ☐ other: ______] **and receiving commendations from client and employer.**

☐ **Successfully turned around** ______ *[what challenge?]* **by** ______ *[doing what?]*, **which resulted in** ______ *[what benefit?]*.

☐ **Effectively met difficult** ______ *[type of]* **challenge(s)** [☐ faced by ______ *(what obstacles?)* | to ______ *(do what?)* | ☐ other: ______] **by** ______ *[doing what?]*, **which resulted in** ______ *[what benefits?]*.

☐ **Faced with the challenge of** ______ *[what?]*, **successfully turned around a** ______ *[type of]* **project; accomplished by** ______ *[what means?]* **and receiving commendations from** [☐ senior management | ☐ client | ☐ employer | ☐ other: ______].

☐ **Acquired skills to build** ______ *[#]* **clean rooms for** ______ *[whom?]* **within** ______ *[#]* [☐ weeks | ☐ months] **on the job—which was essential as** ______ *[#]* **clean rooms were needed for** [☐ the return of an in-orbit Space Shuttle Mission to continue experiments conducted in space | ☐ other: ______].

☐ **Consistently met** [☐ project quality | ☐ timeline | ☐ safety | ☐ code | ☐ client | ☐ other: ______] **requirements despite** ______ *[type of]* **challenges and obstacles including** ______, ______, **and** ______ *[type of challenges]* **by** ______ *[doing what well?]*.

☐ **Resolved** [☐______ *(type of)* problems | ☐ conflicts with employees | ☐ other: ______] **through effective** [☐ influential skills | ☐ customer service | ☐ teamwork | ☐ other: ______].

Painting Projects & Functions

See also "General Contracting," "Carpentry/Construction Functions & Projects," "Carpentry/Construction Work Scope," and "Equipment, Tools & Testing Devices," as applicable.

☐ [☐ Supervise | ☐ Perform] **approximately** ______ *[#]* **painting jobs per** [☐ week | ☐ month] **ranging from $______ to $______** *[amounts]* **for** ______ *[type of]* **clients.**

☐ **Plan, organize, and** [☐ supervise | ☐ facilitate] **surface preparation and application of** [☐ paint | ☐ stain | ☐ varnish | ☐ other: ______] **products on** [☐ interiors | ☐ exteriors] **of** [☐ residential homes | ☐ commercial buildings | ☐ other: ______] **for this** ______ *[type of]* [☐ contracting firm | ☐ agency | ☐ other: ______].

☐ **Meet with prospective clients requiring painting work to** [☐ define project parameters | ☐ advise on surface effect(s) | ☐ determine suitable paint and stain products | ☐ estimate project time | ☐ estimate material and labor costs | ☐ provide job estimates | ☐ other: ______].

☐ **Provide decisive leadership and clear direction in all phases of** [☐ large-scale | ☐ complex] ______ *[type of]* **painting and staining projects for** [☐ residential | ☐ commercial | ☐ industrial | ☐ other: ______] **clients overseeing a top-performing team of** ______ *[#]* **painters.**

☐ **Prepare the surfaces of all ______** *[type of]* **painting jobs by removing dirt, mold, and any peeling paint; patching cracks and holes; and protecting areas by taping trim and using drop cloths; and preventing damage to location to ensure a professional outcome.**

☐ **Apply an in-depth knowledge of all types of painting** [☐ equipment | ☐ materials | ☐ techniques | ☐ safety techniques | ☐ other: ______] **in the preparation, application, and completion of ______** *[type of]* **painting, staining, varnishing projects.**

☐ **Mix, match, and color coordinate various paints and stains using** [☐ tinting bases | ☐ liquid color | ☐ primers | ☐ other: ______] **for application on ______** *[type of]* **projects using** [☐ power sprayers | ☐ rollers | ☐ brushes | ☐ and ______ *(type of)* equipment].

☐ **Maintain brushes, rollers, trays, sprayers, compressors, and related equipment; store paints and stains and inventories for future use; complete work orders and logs.**

☐ **Supervise journey-level painters, monitor painting projects to ensure effective and productive work, and troubleshoot and problem-solve any project or customer concerns by** [☐ listening carefully to their needs | ☐ immediately rectifying problems | ☐ offering alternative solutions | ☐ other methods: ______].

☐ **Coordinate painting work with other contractors to ensure it is completed according to agreement and complies with standards.**

☐ **Handle a variety of painting and other projects including** [☐ hanging wallpaper | ☐ staining furniture | ☐ painting stripes in ______ *(which?)* (☐ parking lots / ☐ football fields / ☐ gym floors / ☐ other: ______) | ☐ other: ______] **completing all projects on time.**

ACHIEVEMENT SAMPLES:

☐ **Increased revenues ______%** *[percentage]* **by** [☐ obtaining a solid referral business with a reputation for excellent work | ☐ developing targeted advertising campaigns | ☐ creating a website | ☐ dropping off flyers in local communities | ☐ other: ______].

☐ **Successfully achieved a 100% customer satisfaction rate by** [☐ achieving company's number one goal to turn every customer into a satisfied customer | ☐ completing all projects on time and within budget | ☐ other method: ______].

☐ **Steadily increased revenues annually by** [☐ developing strong networking contacts in the real estate community | ☐ advertising in local print media | ☐ networking at local Chambers of Commerce | ☐ providing discounts on customer referrals | ☐ other: ______].

☐ **Established a reputation for quality workmanship at competitive prices by** [☐ maintaining superior levels of craftsmanship | ☐ providing excellent customer service | ☐ other: ______].

☐ **Increased safety and customer satisfaction by** [☐ providing professional painting services | ☐ ensuring end-of-day clean up and debris removal from all work areas and sites | ☐ other: ______].

Plumbing – General

*See also **"Plumbing Projects," "HVAC/HVAC-R Scope," "Welding/Steamfitting Functions,"** and **"Work Collaboration"***

☐ **Install, maintain, and/or repair ______** *[type of]* [☐ plumbing systems | ☐ heating and cooling systems | ☐ refrigeration systems | ☐ water supply and drain lines | ☐ steam lines | ☐ roof drains | ☐ water heaters | (☐ gas / ☐ electric / ☐ open flame) boilers | ☐ fire sprinkler systems | ☐ sewer lines | ☐ storm drains | ☐ cesspools | ☐ septic tanks | ☐ pipes, faucets, valves, fixtures, and fittings | ☐ specialty plumbing items | ☐ other: ______].

☐ **Perform** [☐ journeyman | ☐ apprentice | ☐ master] **-level plumbing installation, maintenance, and repair of ______, ______, and ______** *[what?]* **following all current plumbing practices and techniques for the trade and ensuring compliance with all plumbing codes for this $______** *[revenues]* **______** *[type of]* **firm.**

☐ **Handle approximately ______** *[#]* **plumbing jobs** [☐ daily | ☐ weekly | ☐ monthly | ☐ annually] [☐ averaging $______ to $______ *(amounts)* | ☐ totaling $______] **including** [☐ estimating job times, materials, and costs | ☐ selecting materials and hardware | ☐ preparing materials estimates | ☐ reviewing materials bids | ☐ ordering required job-related materials | ☐ scheduling jobs | ☐ performing plumbing functions | ☐ inspecting completed plumbing jobs for code compliance | ☐ other: ______].

☐ **Perform hands-on installation, maintenance, and/or repair of** [☐ commercial | ☐ domestic | ☐ industrial | ☐ other: ______] [☐ indoor | ☐ outdoor] **plumbing systems including ______, ______, and ______** *[what?].*

☐ **Assemble, install, and test ______** *[type of]* **plumbing** [☐ equipment | ☐ pipes | ☐ fittings | ☐ fixtures | ☐ pumps | ☐ motors | ☐ other: ______] **of** [☐ heating | ☐ cooling | ☐ ventilation ☐ drainage | ☐ sprinkler | ☐ gas | ☐ water supply | ☐ sewer | ☐ other: ______] **systems ensuring compliance with all plumbing codes, specifications, and timeframes.**

☐ **Supervise the installation and/or repair of ______** *[what?]* **and the cutting, threading, and/or soldering of** [☐ galvanized | ☐ copper | ☐ PVC] **pipe for ______, ______, and ______** *[types of jobs].*

☐ **Facilitate all plumbing activities required in the installation, maintenance, and/or repair of ______** *[what projects?]* **including ______, ______, and ______** *[which functions?].*

☐ **Install and maintain all** ______ *[type of]* [☐ plumbing | ☐ fittings | ☐ fixtures | ☐ other: ______] **in accordance with the Uniform Plumbing Code including** [☐ cutting | ☐ fitting | ☐ connecting | ☐ installing | ☐ maintaining | ☐ repairing] ______ *[type of]* **plumbing piping for** ______ *[what or whom?]*.

☐ **Install, repair, and service** [☐ heating and air conditioning systems | ☐ industrial and commercial refrigerant systems | ☐ other: ______] **to ensure control of temperature, humidity, and air quality in** [☐ residential | ☐ commercial | ☐ industrial | ☐ manufacturing | ☐ other: ______] **buildings for this** [☐ HVAC firm | ☐ plumbing contractor | ☐ general contractor | ☐ manufacturer | ☐ wholesaler | ☐ other: ______].

☐ **Following** [☐ isometric drawings | ☐ architectural plans | ☐ building code specifications | ☐ other: ______], **install appropriate** [☐ piping | ☐ valves | ☐ fittings | ☐ fixtures | ☐ pumps | ☐ other: ______] **on** [☐ gas | ☐ water | ☐ waste | ☐ other: ______] **piping within specified timeframes**.

☐ **Facilitate hands-on installation, maintenance, and repair of** [☐ commercial | ☐ domestic | ☐ industrial | ☐ other: ______] [☐ indoor | ☐ outdoor | ☐ indoor and outdoor] **plumbing systems including** ______, ______, **and** ______ *[what?]*.

☐ **Apply plumbing knowledge of** [☐ tools, materials, and equipment of the trade | ☐ National plumbing code | ☐ time and materials estimating | ☐ building plans and blueprint interpreting | ☐ other: ______] **in performing** ______ *[which?]* **plumbing jobs.**

☐ **Prepare for all plumbing jobs by** [☐ prioritizing work assignments | ☐ ordering required inventory | ☐ determining equipment needed | ☐ setting up each project with the correct tools, materials, and supplies | ☐ coordinating contracting trades | ☐ determining conditions and safety requirements | ☐ identifying required repairs and/or replacements | ☐ other: ______].

☐ **Assist** [☐ plumbing | ☐ electrical | ☐ maintenance | ☐ carpentry | ☐ crafts | ☐ other: ______] **staff(s) in performing the** [☐ assembly | ☐ installation | ☐ repair | ☐ maintenance | ☐ monitoring | ☐ testing | ☐ upkeep | ☐ other: ______] **of** ______ *[what?]*.

☐ **Conduct a variety of plumbing functions including** [☐ cutting and threading ______ *(type of)* pipes | ☐ winterizing piping (☐ and sprinkler) systems | ☐ installing (☐ waste / ☐ gas) pipes and pipe fittings | ☐ repairing drain systems | ☐ dismantling and repairing plumbing devices | ☐ plumbing kitchen facilities | ☐ inspecting piping systems | ☐ installing and servicing HVAC systems | ☐ inspecting piping systems | ☐ replacing steam lines and roof drains | ☐ winterizing (☐ piping / ☐ sprinkler) systems | ☐ dismantling and repairing plumbing devices | ☐ unclogging sewer and cesspool lines | ☐ responding to client emergency situations | ☐ other: ______] **for** ______ *[what or whom?]*.

☐ **Handle various plumbing functions including** [☐ cutting and threading pipe | ☐ soldering copper | ☐ installing PVC pipe | ☐ other: ______] **for** [☐ compressed air | ☐ potable water | ☐ cooling water | ☐ other: ______] **maintaining proper operation of all equipment.**

☐ **Maintain and repair as needed all** [☐ leaks | ☐ broken pipes | ☐ other: ______] **of** ______, ______, **and** ______ *[what?]*, **maintaining accurate records of all** [☐ labor hours | ☐ materials used | ☐ other: ______].

Plumbing – Management

*See also **"Plumbing Projects," "Plumbing Scope," "HVAC/HVAC-R Management Scope,"** and **"Inspections & Compliance,"** and **"Trades/Crew Supervision,"** as applicable.*

☐ **Direct day-to-day plumbing operations of this** [☐ plumbing | ☐ general contracting | ☐ construction | ☐ other: ______] **firm providing a full array of** [☐ plumbing | ☐ HVAC | ☐ steamfitting | ☐ other: ______] **services including the installation and repair of** [☐ water heaters | ☐ steam lines | ☐ roof drains | ☐ water distributors | ☐ sewer lines | ☐ storm drains | ☐ cesspools | ☐ septic tanks | ☐ specialty plumbing items | ☐ sprinkler lines | ☐ drainage | ☐ water supply and drain lines | ☐ gas, electric, open flame boilers | pipes, faucets, valves, fixtures, and fittings | ☐ other: ______].

☐ **Oversee the installation of all required plumbing** [☐ equipment | ☐ systems | ☐ pipes | ☐ fixtures | ☐ valves | ☐ pumps | ☐ other: ______] **to** [☐ set up | ☐ operate | ☐ maintain] **the** [☐ water distribution | ☐ drainage | ☐ heating and cooling | ☐ sewage collection | ☐ sprinkler | ☐ other: ______] **system(s) and related equipment of** ______ *[what?]*.

☐ **Provide a full array of** [☐ plumbing | ☐ HVAC | ☐ refrigeration | ☐ steamfitting | ☐ welding | ☐ carpentry | ☐ other: ______] **services including** [(☐ plumbing / ☐ electrical / ☐ general contracting) work | (☐ bathroom / ☐ kitchen / ☐ tile) installations | ☐ other: ______] **for this** [☐ plumbing | ☐ general contracting | ☐ other: ______] **company**.

☐ **Maintain plant's heating and cooling systems including cleaning boiler** [☐ heads | ☐ flame sensor | ☐ igniter | ☐ other: ______] **and** [☐ replacing burned out motors | ☐ cleaning blower cages | ☐ other: ______].

☐ **Direct and supervise the plumbing** [☐ installation | ☐ replacement | ☐ maintenance | ☐ repair] **work required in** [☐ new construction | ☐ remodel | ☐ other: ______] **jobs for this** [☐ plumbing | ☐ general contracting | ☐ construction | ☐ other: ______] **firm.**

☐ **Manage and oversee the installation, maintenance, and repair of** [☐ plumbing | ☐ heating | ☐ cooling | ☐ ventilating | ☐ refrigeration | ☐ water supply | ☐ sewer | ☐ fire | ☐ sprinkler | ☐ other: ______] **systems including** [☐ drain lines |

☐ steam lines | ☐ roof drains | ☐ water heaters | (☐ gas / ☐ electric / ☐ open flame) ☐ boilers | ☐ storm drains | ☐ cesspools | ☐ septic tanks | ☐ pipes, faucets, valves, fixtures, and fittings | ☐ specialty plumbing items | ☐ other: ______].

☐ **Manage the completion of approximately ______** *[#]* **plumbing jobs** [☐ daily | ☐ weekly | ☐ monthly | ☐ annually] **averaging $______ to $______** *[average job amount]* **and handle** [☐ estimating of job times, materials, and costs | ☐ reviewing materials bids | ☐ ordering materials and hardware | ☐ scheduling jobs | ☐ performing plumbing functions | ☐ inspecting completed jobs for code compliance | ☐ other: ______].

☐ **Control and maintain the** [☐ heating | ☐ ventilating | ☐ cooling | ☐ systems] **of ______** *[what?]* **by** [☐ monitoring equipment | ☐ inspecting energy management systems | ☐ using ______ *(type of)* control software | ☐ making frequent on-site visits to check computer programming | ☐ verifying temperature controls | ☐ adjusting temperatures | ☐ maximizing the efficiency of control systems | ☐ adjusting (☐ mixed / ☐ return / ☐ discharge) air | ☐ performing combustion analyses | ☐ other methods: ______].

☐ **Supervise all plumbing activities required in the installation, maintenance, and/or repair of ______** *[what?]* **including ______, ______, and ______** *[which functions?]*.

☐ **Oversee the repair and maintenance of all** [☐ plumbing | ☐ electrical | ☐ HVAC | ☐ motors | ☐ appliances | ☐ fixtures | ☐ lights | ☐ ballasts | ☐ receptacles | ☐ switches | ☐ other: ______] **to** [☐ help improve the work environment | ☐ maintain proper operation of all equipment | ☐ maintain compliance with all OSHA and environmental regulations | ☐ other: ______].

☐ **Lead and direct a variety of plumbing activities including** [☐ cutting and threading ______ *(type of)* pipes | ☐ winterizing piping (☐ and sprinkler) systems | ☐ soldering copper | ☐ installing PVC piping | ☐ installing (☐ waste / ☐ gas) pipes and pipe fittings | ☐ repairing drain systems | ☐ dismantling and repairing plumbing devices | ☐ plumbing kitchen facilities | ☐ inspecting piping systems | ☐ responding to client emergency situations | ☐ other: ______] **for ______** *[what or whom?]*.

☐ **Facilitate plumbing management functions including** [☐ reviewing and evaluating plumbing specifications | ☐ coordinating bid selections | ☐ estimating project time, materials, and costs | ☐ preparing estimates | ☐ negotiating contracts | ☐ writing purchase requests | ☐ evaluating subcontractor bids | ☐ prioritizing work assignments | ☐ scheduling jobs | ☐ supervising various trades | ☐ setting up projects with materials | ☐ determining safety requirements | ☐ coordinating materials shipping | ☐ purchasing or leasing equipment | ☐ preparing cost estimates | ☐ ensuring plumbing safety practices | ☐ maintaining plumbing tools and equipment | ☐ ordering and maintaining plumbing parts | ☐ obtaining required permits | ☐ making on-site visits | ☐ inspecting work for compliance with codes | ☐ maintaining plumbing tools and equipment | ☐ training staff in plumbing techniques | ☐ handling inventory management and control | ☐ coordinating projects with (☐ engineers / ☐ architects) | ☐ monitoring equipment | ☐ other: ______].

☐ **Lead and direct the installation, maintenance, repair, and/or replacement of all required plumbing** [☐ equipment | ☐ systems | ☐ pipes | ☐ fixtures | ☐ valves | ☐ pumps | ☐ other: ______] **to** [☐ set up | ☐ operate | ☐ maintain] **the** [☐ water distribution | ☐ drainage | ☐ heating and cooling | ☐ sewage collection | ☐ sprinkler | ☐ other: ______] **system(s) and related equipment.**

☐ **Perform** [☐ machining | ☐ rigging | ☐ industrial pipefitting | ☐ other: ______] **for ______** *[what?]*.

☐ **Coordinate and oversee the installation of** [☐ plumbing | ☐ heating | ☐ cooling | ☐ ventilating | ☐ refrigeration | ☐ water supply | ☐ sewer | ☐ fire | ☐ sprinkler | ☐ other: ______] **systems including** [☐ drain lines | ☐ steam lines | ☐ roof drains | ☐ water heaters | (☐ gas / ☐ electric / ☐ open flame) boilers | ☐ storm drains | ☐ cesspools | ☐ septic tanks | ☐ pipes, faucets, valves, fixtures, and fittings | ☐ specialty plumbing items | ☐ other: ______].

☐ **Coordinate with other trades and oversee plumbing installations in** [☐ new construction | ☐ remodel | ☐ restoration | ☐ other: ______] **of ______** *[type of]* **projects**.

Plumbing – Projects

*See also **"Plumbing Functions," "Plumbing Scope," "HVAC/HVAC-R Scope,"** and **"Welding/Steamfitting Functions & Projects."***

☐ **Perform the installation, maintenance, repair, and/or replacement of all required ______** [type of] **plumbing** [☐ equipment | ☐ systems | ☐ pipes | ☐ fixtures | ☐ valves | ☐ pumps | ☐ other: ______] **to** [☐ set up | ☐ operate | ☐ maintain] **the** [☐ water distribution | ☐ drainage | ☐ heating and cooling | ☐ sewage collection | ☐ sprinkler | ☐ other: ______] **system(s) and related equipment of ______** *[what?]*.

☐ **Install** [☐ industrial plumbing | ☐ PVC piping | ☐ pipes, fittings, valves and fixtures | ☐ sewer lines, septic tanks, and storm drains | ☐ gas lines | ☐ kitchen and bathroom plumbing | ☐ fire sprinkler systems | ☐ water supply and drain lines | ☐ gas and electric heaters, steam lines, and/or chlorine gas feeders | ☐ waste or gas pipes and pipe fittings | ☐ open flame boilers and water heaters | ☐ other: ______] **for ______** *[whom or what?]*.

☐ **Repair** [☐ industrial | ☐ residential | ☐ commercial | ☐ other: ______] **plumbing systems including** [☐ leaks and broken pipes | ☐ drain systems | ☐ plumbing, sprinkler, and/or drain systems | ☐ water heaters, boilers, and steam controls | ☐ faucets and valves | ☐ HVAC heat return and main water lines | ☐ industrial | ☐ residential plumbing systems | ☐ circulating pumps | ☐ swimming pool filtration pumps | ☐ soda ash and chlorine gas feeders | ☐ other: ______] **for ______** *[whom or what?]*.

☐ **Facilitate all plumbing activities required in the installation and maintenance of in-ground pools including installing and/or repairing swimming pool** [☐ circulation pumps | ☐ filtration pumps | ☐ mixing valves | ☐ pumps | ☐ filters | ☐ underwater lighting | ☐ chlorine gas feeders | ☐ soda ash feeders | ☐ other: ______].

☐ **Maintain plant's heating system boilers, including cleaning** [☐ heads | ☐ flame sensor | ☐ igniter | ☐ other: ______].

☐ **Control and maintain the** [☐ heating | ☐ ventilating | ☐ cooling | ☐ other: ______] **systems of** ______ *[what?]* **by** [☐ monitoring equipment | ☐ inspecting energy management systems | ☐ using ______ *(type of)* control software | ☐ making frequent on-site visits to ensure quality control | ☐ verifying temperature controls | ☐ adjusting temperatures | ☐ maximizing the efficiency of control systems | ☐ adjusting (☐ mixed / ☐ return / ☐ discharge) air | ☐ performing combustion analyses | ☐ other: ______].

☐ [☐ Assemble and install | ☐ Monitor and adjust | ☐ Repair, replace, and maintain] [☐ water heaters | ☐ boilers | ☐ heating pipes | ☐ pneumatic valves | ☐ mixing valves | ☐ pumps | ☐ pump seals | ☐ steam traps | ☐ bearing assembles | ☐ backflow devices | ☐ dampers | ☐ univents | ☐ coils | ☐ fans | ☐ heat exchangers | ☐ air handlers | ☐ thermostats | ☐ valves | ☐ faucets | ☐ flush valves | ☐ sinks | ☐ fountains | ☐ toilets | ☐ urinals | ☐ other: ______].

☐ **Ensure all appliances are properly maintained including** [☐ gas and electric stoves and ovens | ☐ refrigerators | ☐ freezers | ☐ dishwashers | ☐ garbage disposals | ☐ microwaves | ☐ steam cookers | ☐ other: ______].

Plumbing Tools, Equipment & Testing Devices

*See **"Equipment, Tools & Testing Devices – Plumbing."***

Preventive & Seasonal Maintenance

*See also **"Facility Management Functions"** as well as trades-related Maintenance and Repair Work (Electrical, HVAC, Plumbing, Welding / Steamfitting, Landscaping, Masonry).*

☐ **Facilitate** [☐ regular | ☐ routine | ☐ weekly | ☐ monthly | ☐ periodic | ☐ other: ______] **preventive maintenance schedules on all** ______ *[what?]*, **and handle required maintenance and repair, as needed.**

☐ **Conduct regular and preventive maintenance checks on** ______ *[what?]* **ensuring** [☐ buildings | ☐ systems | ☐ machinery | ☐ equipment | ☐ appliances | ☐ vehicles | ☐ other: ______] **are in safe operating condition at all times.**

☐ **Perform preventive maintenance on** ______ *[what?]* **and repair and/or replace** ______, ______, **and** ______ *[which?]* **components of** ______ *[type of]* [☐ equipment | ☐ systems | ☐ other: ______] **as required.**

☐ **Facilitate** [☐ preventive | ☐ routine | ☐ periodic | ☐ seasonal | ☐ other: ______] **cleaning and maintenance of all** ______ *[type of]* **equipment including** [☐ hand and power tools | ☐ pipe benders | ☐ propane torches | ☐ welding equipment | ☐ sewer rooters | ☐ other: ______].

☐ **Perform seasonal furnace maintenance and repair work including** [☐ inspecting the system | ☐ servicing and adjusting burners and blowers | ☐ replacing filters and ducts | ☐ overhauling compressors | ☐ checking thermostat, burner nozzles, and controls | ☐ other: ______].

☐ **Conduct** [☐ seasonal overhauls | ☐ seasonal transitions | ☐ winterizing | ☐ other: ______] **of** ______ *[type of]* **systems to and from heating and cooling, ensuring** [☐ a comfortable air and temperature balance | ☐ other: ______] **throughout the four seasons.**

☐ **Conduct** [☐ preventive | ☐ routine | ☐ periodic] **maintenance, adjustments, and repair work on all** [☐ pneumatically | ☐ digitally | ☐ other: ______] **controlled** [☐ HVAC | ☐ boiler | ☐ fire | ☐ air distribution equipment | ☐ hot and chilled water distribution | ☐ variable volume | ☐ other: ______] **systems to keep the system(s) operating efficiently.**

☐ **Assess and detect any and all** ______ *[type of]* **repairs required on** ______ *[type of]* [☐ systems | ☐ buildings | ☐ facilities | ☐ grounds | ☐ equipment | ☐ other: ______] **and repair as needed following standard inspection procedures.**

☐ **Successfully complete all** ______ *[type of]* **repair work orders consisting of** ______ *[type of]* **work** [☐ ahead of schedule | ☐ within required timeframes] **by** ______ *[doing what?].*

☐ **Oversee installation, operation, maintenance, and/or repair of** ______ *[type of]* [☐ machines | ☐ tools | ☐ engines | ☐ other: ______] **and other equipment including centralized** [☐ heat | ☐ gas | ☐ water | ☐ steam | ☐ other: ______] **systems.**

☐ **Maintain and repair as needed all** ______ *[what?]* of ______, ______, **and** ______ *[what?]*, **maintaining accurate records of all** [☐ labor hours | ☐ materials used | ☐ other: ______].

☐ **[☐ Manage and oversee | ☐ Perform] ______ *[type of]* maintenance and repair including ______, ______, and ______ *[functions].***

ACHIEVEMENT SAMPLES

☐ **Assisted in establishing ______ *[type of]* preventive maintenance programs for ______ *[what?]* that included ______ *[what requirements?].***

☐ **Significantly improved operating conditions of the building's ______, ______, and ______ *[what functions?]* by rigidly following a regular maintenance schedule, which proved critical to the successful and continuous operation of ______ *[what?].***

☐ **Developed and established ______ *[type of]* preventive maintenance programs for ______ *[what?]* that incorporated ______ *[what?]* and resulted in ______ *[what benefits?].***

Productivity Improvement

See also "Process Improvement."

ACHIEVEMENT SAMPLES:

☐ **Focusing on ______ *[#]* targeted areas of improvement per month, look for opportunities to improve performance, which resulted in ______ *[what benefits?].***

☐ **Spearheaded the corporate-wide initiative to ______ *[do what?],* which realized production gains of ______% *[percentage]* with no additional labor expenses by ______ *[how?].***

☐ **Drove overall improvements in ______ *[what?]* performance efficiency via effective** [☐ capacity planning | ☐ schedule management | ☐ operations streamlining in ______ *(what areas?)* | ☐ ______ *(type of)* cost-cutting process improvements | ☐ other: ______] **that ______ *[did what?].***

☐ **Catapulted ______ *[type of]* productivity ______% *[percentage]* and company profits $______ *[amount]* by** [☐ educating laborers on smart, productive work methods | ☐ expecting employees to work to their full potential | ☐ not accepting mediocrity | ☐ ensuring all staff fully understood their assigned jobs | ☐ resolving issues and concerns | ☐ upholding company standards | ☐ creating a fair and equitable environment | ☐ maintaining inventory control | ☐ effective time management | ☐ other: ______].

☐ **Increased daily production from ______ *[what level?]* to ______ *[what level?]* without raising overhead by ______ *[doing what?]* while monitoring project deliverables and maintaining compliance with all government regulations, engineering drawings, and customer requirements.**

☐ **Created forecasting and troubleshooting procedures in the areas of ______, ______, and ______ *[what areas?]* to identify and rectify ______ *[type of]* problem areas, which resulted in ______ *[benefit to company].***

☐ **Increased productivity ______% *[percentage]* and saved $______ *[amount]* in annual costs by initiating an outsourcing ______ *[type of]* concept for ______ *[which?]* operations that ______ *[accomplished what?].***

☐ **Significantly enhanced productivity by spearheading ______ *[what initiative?]* that resulted in ______ *[benefits].***

☐ **Developed and implemented ______ *[type of]* operational systems, which improved productivity ______% *[percentage]* and increased profitability ______% *[percentage]*. Accomplished by** [☐ streamlining operations | ☐ increased training and development | ☐ building a strong support system amongst staff | ☐ other: ______].

☐ **Increased ______ *[type of]* productivity ______% *[percentages]* (from ______% to ______%) *[percentages]* by** [☐ using smart, productive work methods | ☐ resolving ______ *(type of)* issues and concerns | ☐ upholding company standards | ☐ creating a fair and equitable environment | ☐ maintaining inventory control | ☐ effective time management | ☐ focusing on a commitment to excellence | ☐ giving 100% to the job | ☐ upgrading ______ *(type of)* (☐ systems | ☐ equipment) | ☐ initiating an outsourcing concept for ______ *(which?)* operations | ☐ other: ______], **which resulted in ______ *[benefits].***

☐ **Totally eliminated need for equipment shutdowns by** [☐ maintaining air compressors and boilers in optimum operating condition at all times | ☐ performing regularly scheduled maintenance checks | ☐ changing oil and filters as needed | ☐ other: ______].

☐ **Created and implemented a successful ______ *[type of]* program to** [☐ cut down the workload | ☐ increase sales | ☐ reduce overtime | ☐ increase productivity | ☐ streamline operations | ☐ cut expenses | ☐ other: ______], **which has resulted in ______ *[what benefits?].***

☐ **Utilize ______ *[type of]*** [☐ methods | ☐ techniques | ☐ skills | ☐ other: ______] **to maintain a productive, quality-producing staff, which has resulted in ______ *[what benefits?].***

☐ **Designed, developed, and implemented a ______ *[type of]*** [☐ product | ☐ process | ☐ device | ☐ other: ______] **from concept through the manufacturing, testing, and training stages which resulted in ______ *[benefit to company or users].***

- ☐ **After a major service disruption during a** [☐ heavy peak period | ☐ storm | ☐ snow emergency | ☐ other: ______], **got computers up and running within** ______ *[timeframe]* **by** ______ *[doing what?]*, **which resulted in** ______ *[benefits]*.
- ☐ **Increased productivity** ______**%** *[percentage]* **by** ______ *[doing what?]*, **which resulted in** ______ *[benefits to company]*.

Project Development & Initiation – General

*See also **"Product Development," "Project Planning & Coordination," "Project Prioritization & Demand Balancing,"** and **"Project Time Tracking,"** as applicable.*

- ☐ **Assess and identify** [☐ client needs | ☐ project resources | ☐ materials | ☐ contractor requirements | ☐ other: ______] **and translate business strategies and requirements into** [☐ functional | ☐ technical | ☐ other: ______] **specifications that reflect** [☐ client | ☐ firm's] **values, diversity, and vision and meet project objectives and deliverables.**
- ☐ **Determine best implementation strategy, approaches, and methodology to set projects in motion and obtain expected deliverables by** ______ *[doing what?]*.
- ☐ **Formulate and define project plans that consider project** [☐ strategy | ☐ scope | ☐ goals | ☐ objectives | ☐ deliverables | ☐ needs identification | ☐ costs | ☐ required skill sets | ☐ tasks | ☐ resource allocations | ☐ work assignments | ☐ scheduling | ☐ technical scope | ☐ timeline check points | ☐ other: ______] **using project management planning and scheduling techniques.**
- ☐ **Assess business needs and translate business strategies and requirements into** [☐ functional | ☐ technical] **specifications that reflect** [☐ client | ☐ firm's] **values, diversity, and vision.**
- ☐ **Translate new product development strategies and goals into specific project plans using** ______ *[what methods?]* **and resulting in** [☐ effective solutions | ☐ successful project completions | ☐ other: ______].
- ☐ **Identify, define, and document** ______ *[type of]* **priorities, as well as** [☐ options | ☐ risks | ☐ costs | ☐ benefits | ☐ milestones | ☐ solutions | ☐ other: ______] **and translate requirements into effective** ______ *[type of]* **projects.**
- ☐ **Assess and evaluate** ______ *[what?]* **in collaboration with** ______ *[whom?]* **to determine detailed business requirements in the design and implementation of** ______ *[what?]*.
- ☐ **Successfully plan and manage** ______ *[type of]* **projects to achieve business objectives; and utilize resource capabilities within project parameters of scope, cost, time, and quality.**
- ☐ **Organize, schedule and manage all** ______ *[type of]* **projects with sensitivity to client deadlines and project requirements.**
- ☐ **Determine client needs and ensure end products meet** [☐ client specifications | ☐ technical standards | ☐ regulatory compliance | ☐ other: ______].
- ☐ **Determine best implementation** [☐ strategy | ☐ approaches | ☐ methodology] **to set** ______ *[type of]* **projects in motion and obtain expected deliverables by** ______ *[doing what?]*.

ACHIEVEMENT SAMPLES: *See also Achievements under **"Project Management – General."***

- ☐ **Sourced, built, and directed the activities of a project team of** ______ *[#]* **with the necessary skill sets to take** ______ *[type of]* **projects from inception through completion.**
- ☐ **Developed new** ______ *[type of]* **approaches by** [☐ refining existing theories | ☐ blending creativity, problem-solving, and technical skills | ☐ employing benefits of leading edge technology | ☐ other: ______] **that resulted in** [☐ seizing new opportunities | ☐ achieving and sustaining business success | ☐ increasing productivity by ______% *(percentage)* | ☐ decreasing costs by $______ *(amount)* | ☐ other benefit: ______].
- ☐ **Organized various** ______ *[type of]* **projects including** [☐ coordinating schedules | ☐ organizing activities | ☐ ordering supplies and services | ☐ tracking progress and results | ☐ other: ______].
- ☐ **Addressed** ______ *[which?]* **business** [☐ strategies | ☐ goals | ☐ other: ______] **in the project** [☐ development | ☐ initiation | ☐ execution | ☐ other: ______] **stage(s) of** ______ *[what?]* **and determined the best implementation and execution approaches to set projects in motion and obtain expected deliverables.**
- ☐ **Identified and defined** ______ *[which?]* **priorities, as well as** [☐ options | ☐ risks | ☐ costs | ☐ benefits | ☐ milestones | ☐ alternative solutions | ☐ other: ______] **and translated requirements into effective** ______ *[type of]* **design-and-build projects.**
- ☐ **Defined, planned, and implemented** ______ *[type of]* **projects including the** [☐ design | ☐ development | ☐ implementation | ☐ tracking | ☐ other: ______] **of those projects in support of the firm's business objectives.**

Project Lifecycle Management – Construction & Engineering

*See also **"Project Development & Initiation," "Project Planning & Coordination," "Project Prioritization & Demand Balancing,"** and **"Project Time Tracking,"** as applicable.*

- ☐ **Lead all aspects of construction project management** [☐ for multiple construction projects | ☐ for projects that vary in scope and size | ☐ to support client objectives | ☐ in accordance with all project timelines and budget ☐ in support of firm's strategic vision | ☐ other: ______] **considering all key components of project lifecycle (scope, time, cost, quality, and resources) in the initiation and coordination of all design projects.**
- ☐ **Direct and oversee** [☐ design guidelines and specifications standards development | ☐ trades supervision | ☐ construction inspection | ☐ quality control | ☐ building and safety codes enforcement | ☐ other: ______].
- ☐ **Manage and oversee all aspects of design-and-build project lifecycles including** [☐ project scope | ☐ initiation | ☐ planning | ☐ scheduling | ☐ budgeting | ☐ contractor selection | ☐ resource allocation | ☐ risk assessment | ☐ quality control | ☐ change orders | ☐ cost control | ☐ other: ______].
- ☐ **Effectively plan, manage, and lead** ______ *[type of]* **construction projects; and direct the activities of trades to ensure all projects are completed with high quality on time and within budget.**
- ☐ **Manage and oversee all aspects of** ______ *[type of]* [☐ design-and-build] [☐ construction | ☐ engineering | ☐ other: ______] **project lifecycles including** [☐ project initiation | ☐ contractor selection | ☐ scheduling | ☐ budgeting | ☐ resource allocation | ☐ risk assessment | ☐ quality control | ☐ change orders | ☐ cost control | ☐ punch lists | ☐ close-out billing | ☐ other: ______].
- ☐ **Consider all key components of project management (scope, time, cost, quality, resources, communication, issues, risk, changes, integration) ensuring compliance with all standard project management methodologies in the** [☐ development of new | ☐ leveraging of existing] ______ *[type of]* **practices by** ______ *[doing what?].*
- ☐ **Direct and oversee all aspects of project management—from planning to completion—**[☐ using standardized project management methodology | ☐ for projects that vary in scope and size | ☐ in support of firm's strategic visions | ☐ for multiple implementation projects | ☐ to support client objectives | ☐ in accordance with all project timelines and budget].
- ☐ **Manage and direct all aspects of** ______ *[type of]* **project lifecycles including** [☐ project scope | ☐ initiation | ☐ planning | ☐ risk assessment | ☐ scheduling | ☐ budgeting | ☐ resource allocation | ☐ quality control | ☐ change orders | ☐ cost control | ☐ other: ______].
- ☐ **Formulate and define project plans that consider project** [☐ strategy | ☐ scope | ☐ goals | ☐ objectives | ☐ deliverables | ☐ needs identification | ☐ costs | ☐ required skill sets | ☐ tasks | ☐ resource allocations | ☐ work assignments | ☐ scheduling | ☐ technical scope | ☐ timeline check points | ☐ other: ______] **using project management planning and scheduling techniques.**
- ☐ **Manage and oversee all aspects of** ______ *[type of]* **projects including project** [☐ scope | ☐ initiation | ☐ planning | ☐ scheduling | ☐ budgeting | ☐ team selection | ☐ resource allocation | ☐ cost control | ☐ other: ______] **as well as** [☐quality control | ☐ change management | ☐ system integration | ☐ other: ______] **keeping in line with all business objectives.**
- ☐ **Provide project management** [☐ coordination | ☐ consultation | ☐ supervision | ☐ guidance] **during the** ______ *[which?]* **phase of all** ______ *[type of]* **projects.**
- ☐ **Manage and oversee** ______ *[type of]* **project lifecycles including** [☐ project scope | ☐ initiation | ☐ planning | ☐ scheduling | ☐ budgeting | ☐ resource allocation | ☐ risk assessment | ☐ quality control | ☐ change orders | ☐ cost control | ☐ other: ______].
- ☐ **Lead all aspects of project management** [☐ for multiple projects | ☐ for projects that vary in scope and size | ☐ in support of firm's strategic vision | ☐ to support client objectives | ☐ in accordance with all project timelines and budget | ☐ other: ______] **considering all key components of project management (scope, time, cost, quality, and resources) in the initiation and coordination of all** ______ *[type of]* **projects.**
- ☐ **Successfully plan and manage projects to achieve business objectives and utilize resource capabilities within the project parameters of cost, time, and quality which has resulted in** ______ *[what firm or client benefits?]*

ACHIEVEMENT SAMPLES:

- ☐ **Planned and coordinated all activities of** [☐ small- | ☐ medium- | ☐ large-] **scale client** ______ *[type of]* **projects for a wide range of** ______ *[type of]* **clients in collaboration with** [☐ client reps | ☐ contractors | ☐ subcontractors | ☐ other: ______] **for this** ______ *[type of]* **firm with** ______ *[#]* [☐ locations | ☐ employees | ☐ other: ______] **that generates fiscal-year revenues of $**______ *[revenues].*
- ☐ **Structured and developed** ______ *[type of]* **client project plans** [☐ following client-specific project management methodology | ☐ other methods: ______] **resulting in** ______ *[what benefits?].*
- ☐ **Oversaw close-out administration on a** [☐ large | ☐ complex | ☐ multisite | ☐ other: ______] ______ *[type of]* **project ensuring all contractual requirements were met, change orders were reviewed and approved, and closeout processing was completed, which involved meeting with** [☐ Architects | ☐ Engineers | ☐ Project Managers | ☐ others: ______] **to ensure accuracy and successful deliverables.**

Project Management – General

☐ **Oversee the management of ______** *[type of]* **projects to ensure cost-effective, functional completed projects that consider** [☐ fiscal | ☐ legal | ☐ technical | ☐ demographic | ☐ economic | ☐ safety | ☐ other: ______] **aspects**.

☐ **Proactively manage, lead, and guide** [☐ cross-functional | ☐ multilevel | ☐ other: ______] ______ *[which?]* **teams to ensure** ______, ______, **and** ______ *[what?]*.

☐ **Manage all phases of ______** *[type of]* **projects from project start through completion including** [☐ developing job estimates and budgets | ☐ securing competitive bids | ☐ handling contract negotiations | ☐ maintaining direct client relationships | ☐ other: ______] **completing all projects on time and within budget.**

☐ **Facilitate direct project management** [☐ coordination | ☐ consultation | ☐ supervision | ☐ review] **during development phase of all projects.**

☐ **Lead a team of ______** *[#]* ______ *[titles]* **providing support for project** [☐ management | ☐ execution | ☐ communication | ☐ logistics | ☐ other: ______] **of ______** *[type of]* **programs ensuring** [☐ team meets or exceeds all goals and objectives | ☐ the firm meets its stated growth objectives | ☐ other: ______].

☐ **Provide project management leadership and direction for this $______** *[revenues]* ______ *[type of]* **firm including** ______, ______, **and** ______ *[what areas?]* **and supervising all phases of ______** *[type of]* **projects.**

☐ **Design and implement various** [☐ large-scale] ______ *[type of]* [☐ solutions | ☐ implementation projects | ☐ other: ______] **that effectively address and adhere to** [☐ firm's | ☐ clients'] **requirements** [☐ in accordance with all project timelines and budget | ☐ ensuring quality project standards | ☐ ensuring a smooth transition | ☐ other: ______].

☐ **Manage the development and maintenance of project-related ______** *[type of]* **plans and operating strategies associated with the design and execution of ______** *[what?]*.

☐ **Prepare detailed and timely** [☐ project schedules | ☐ budgets | ☐ status reports | ☐ other: ______] **for all ______** *[type of]* **projects** [☐ averaging | ☐ up to] **$______** *[amount]* **with an annual return on investment of $______** *[amount]*.

☐ **Effectively** [☐ plan | ☐ direct | ☐ coordinate | ☐ implement] ______ *[type of]* **projects** [☐ and direct the activities of resources] **to ensure all objectives are accomplished with high quality and within established time frames and budget.**

☐ **Strategize, plan, and coordinate the activities of ______** *[type of]* **projects in collaboration with ______** *[whom?]* **for this ______** *[type of]* **firm with ______** *[#]* [☐ locations | ☐ employees | ☐ other: ______] **that generates fiscal-year revenues of** $______ *[revenues]*.

☐ **Plan, supervise, and lead ______** *[type of]* **projects with varying requirements to ensure all projects are completed with high quality and within established time frames and budget.**

☐ **Plan and coordinate all activities of ______** *[type of]* **projects for a wide range of clients in collaboration with** [☐ clients | ☐ vendors | ☐ senior management | ☐ other: ______].

☐ **Manage multiple** [☐ multimillion-dollar | ☐ large-scale | ☐ moderate-size | ☐ highly complex | ☐ moderately complex | ☐ multisite | ☐ cross-organizational | ☐ multiyear-timeline | ☐ multimonth timeline | ☐ simultaneous | ☐ other: ______] ______ *[type of]* **project rollouts from inception to successful completion.**

☐ **Manage and oversee all aspects of ______** *[type of]* **projects including** [☐ project scope | ☐ initiation | ☐ planning | ☐ scheduling | ☐ budgeting | ☐ team selection | ☐ resource allocation | ☐ quality control | ☐ change management | ☐ cost control | ☐ system integration | ☐ other: ______] **keeping in line with all business objectives**.

☐ **Define, plan, and implement ______** *[type of]* **projects; and perform the** [☐ design | ☐ development | ☐ testing | ☐ implementation | ☐ tracking | ☐ reporting | ☐ other: ______] **of those projects in support of the** [☐ firm's | ☐ clients'] **business objectives.**

☐ **Design and implement ______** *[type of]* **solutions that effectively address and adhere to** [☐ firm's | ☐ clients'] **requirements** [☐ in accordance with all project timelines and budget | ☐ ensuring quality project standards | ☐ and ensure a smooth transition | ☐ other: ______].

☐ **Effectively develop teamwork within** [☐ the department | ☐ other company departments | ☐ other: ______] **by successfully** ______ *[doing what?]*.

ACHIEVEMENT SAMPLES:

☐ **Designed and implemented ______** *[type of]* **structured resource management processes including** [☐ organizational charts | ☐ standardized roles | ☐ job description database | ☐ generic acquisition forms | ☐ tracking and reporting formats | ☐ skill set profiles | ☐ other: ______] **for all project resources that resulted in ______** *[what benefits?]*.

☐ **Determined best implementation strategy, approaches, and methodology of ______** *[what?]* **to set projects in motion and successfully obtain expected deliverables by ______** *[doing what?]*.

- ☐ **Formulated and defined project ______** *[type of]* **plans that consider project** [☐ design | ☐ scope | ☐ goals | ☐ costs | ☐ deliverables | ☐ task requirements | ☐ resource allocations | ☐ work assignments | ☐ scheduling | ☐ risk identification | ☐ timeline check points | ☐ project monitoring | ☐ other: ______] **using project management planning and scheduling techniques.**
- ☐ **Championed ______** *[type of]* **solutions that effectively addressed and adhered to** [☐ firm's | ☐ clients'] **requirements** [☐ in accordance with all project timelines and budget | ☐ ensuring quality project standards | ☐ allowing for a smooth transition | ☐ other: ______].
- ☐ **Developed a ______** *[type of]* **plan that manages project execution costs, schedules, and changes and ______** *[benefited how?].*
- ☐ **Directed and oversaw all aspects of** [☐ complex | ☐ multiple | ☐ large-scale | ☐ other: ______] ______ *[type of]* **projects including ______** *[what?]* **and consistently delivered all projects on time and within budget.**
- ☐ **Oversaw the management of ______** *[type of]* **projects ranging $______ to $______** *[project costs]* **and involving ______** *[what?].*
- ☐ **Significantly improved** [☐ cost efficiency | ☐ profitability | ☐ client satisfaction | ☐ other: ______] **and enhanced project outcomes by** [☐ by leveraging ______ *(type of)* experience | ☐ evaluating methods | ☐ implementing ______ *(type of)* quality control programs that ______ *(did what?)* | ☐ optimizing plans | ☐ other: ______].
- ☐ **Managed multiple** [☐ multimillion-dollar | ☐ large-scale | ☐ moderate-size | ☐ highly complex | ☐ moderately complex | ☐ multisite | ☐ cross-organizational | ☐ multiyear-timeline | ☐ multimonth-timeline | ☐ simultaneous | ☐ other: ______] **project rollouts from inception to successful completion.**
- ☐ **Successfully planned, managed, and led the development and implementation of ______** *[type of]* **projects with varying requirements ensuring all objectives were accomplished with high quality and within established time frames and budget.**
- ☐ **Helped improve the workplace and work environment by way of ______** *[doing what?],* **benefiting ______** *[whom?]* **through ______** *[what means?].*
- ☐ **Analyzed, interpreted, and met the unique ______** *[which?]* **needs of ______** *[type of]* **project and performed ______** *[what?],* **successfully applying ______** *[what?]* **expertise.**
- ☐ **Gained ______** *[type of]* **project cooperation and commitment from ______** *[whom?]* **by** [☐ providing clear direction | ☐ soliciting feedback | ☐ serving as the primary resource hub | ☐ insisting on mutual support | ☐ sharing information | ☐ modeling professional behavior | ☐ building a collaborative environment | ☐ removing all obstacles to project success | ☐ other: ______]
- ☐ **Supervised and oversaw ______** *[#]* ______ *[type of]* **projects averaging $______** *[amount]* **each, with** [☐ property values | ☐ other: ______] **totaling $______ to $______** *[amounts]* **annually.**
- ☐ **Championed the development and implementation of the ______** *[type of]* [☐ program | ☐ project | ☐ initiative | ☐ other: ______] **that ______** *[accomplished what?]* **and ______** *[benefited how?].*
- ☐ **Successfully completed ______** *[type of]* **projects within ______** *[time period]* **by ______** *[doing what well?].*
- ☐ **Effectively facilitate across-the-board communication regarding ______** *[type of]* **project scope, expected deliverables, and major milestones with ______** *[whom?]* **and other involved parties** [☐ during all phases of the project lifecycle | ☐ from concept to completion | ☐ other: ______].
- ☐ **Keep all ______** *[which?]* **team members informed about project scope, status, issues, and expected deliverables by** [☐ establishing effective means of communication | ☐ providing clear, concise, and complete written and verbal communication | ☐ adapting communication style to meet end user needs | ☐ other: ______].
- ☐ **Conduct ______** *[type of]* [☐ weekly | ☐ regular | ☐ intermittent | ☐ other: ______] [☐ project meetings ☐ strategy sessions | ☐ teleconferences | ☐ other: ______] **to review ______** *[type of]* **project progress ensuring** [☐ communication among all involved parties | ☐ projects remain on schedule and within budget | ☐ other: ______].
- ☐ **Ensure ______** *[which?]* [☐ department members | ☐ senior management | ☐ project team | ☐ others: ______] **and others are informed of projects' objectives, scope, tasks, milestones, and expected deliverables by ______** *[doing what?].*
- ☐ **Develop various ______** *[type of]* **project status formats for presentation to different audiences, such as** [☐ work session details | ☐ client status reports | ☐ executive report cards | ☐ budget reports | ☐ meeting minutes | ☐ other: ______].
- ☐ **Completed ______** *[name of]* **project in record time and ahead of schedule; achieved by** [☐ getting the most productivity out of laborers | ☐ organizing and planning daily workloads | ☐ other: ______] **resulting in** [☐ company being awarded state bonuses | ☐ other achievement: ______].

Project Management – Projects

*See also **"Construction Projects," "Construction Management Projects," "Project Management – General"** and various other Project Management categories, as applicable.*

- ☐ **Prepare detailed and timely** [☐ project schedules | ☐ budgets | ☐ status reports | ☐ other: ______] **for all client** ______ *[type of]* **projects** [☐ averaging | ☐ up to] **$**______ *[amount]* **with an annual return on investment of $**______ *[amount].*
- ☐ **Effectively plan, manage, and lead** ______ *[type of]* **construction projects; and direct the activities of trades to ensure all projects are completed with high quality on time and within budget.**
- ☐ **Provide** [☐ consultation | ☐ guidance | ☐ recommendations] **for** [☐ new building sites | ☐ building changes | ☐ other: ______] **for** ______ *[what?].*
- ☐ **Strategize, plan, and coordinate the activities of** [☐ small- | ☐ medium- | ☐ large-] **scale client projects for a wide range of** ______ *[type of]* **clients in collaboration with** [☐ client reps | ☐ contractors | ☐ subcontractors | ☐ other: ______] **for this** ______ *[type of]* **firm with** ______ *[#]* [☐ locations | ☐ employees | ☐ other: ______] **that generates fiscal-year revenues of $**______ *[revenues].*
- ☐ **Manage all construction activities including** [☐ client presentations | ☐ site logistics plans development and implementation | ☐ submittal review and approval | ☐ subcontractor coordination and scheduling | ☐ on-site quality assurance and quality control | ☐ on-site safety management | ☐ field conflicts resolution | ☐ project closeout processing | ☐ other: ______].
- ☐ **Plan, supervise, and lead the construction of** ______ *[type of]* **projects with varying requirements; and direct the activities of** ______ *[which?]* **trades to ensure all projects are completed with high quality and within established time frames and budget.**
- ☐ **Manage multiple** [☐ multimillion-dollar | ☐ large-scale | ☐ moderate-size | ☐ highly complex | ☐ moderately complex | ☐ multisite | ☐ cross-organizational | ☐ multiyear-timeline | ☐ multimonth timeline | ☐ simultaneous | ☐ other: ______] ______ *[type of]* **project rollouts from inception to successful completion.**
- ☐ **Oversee job operations and personnel management including** [☐ coordinating steel and concrete trades | ☐ scheduling laborers | ☐ managing construction | ☐ overseeing site materials and equipment set-up | ☐ other: ______].
- ☐ **Obtain permits, estimate jobs, and hire and schedule trades acting as liaison with** [☐ building managers | ☐ union delegates | ☐ architects | ☐ engineers | ☐ others: ______].
- ☐ **Direct the** ______ *[type of]* **projects of all** ______ *[type of]* **projects including the** [☐ review and/or modification of drawings | ☐ development of job estimates and budgets | ☐ securing of competitive bids | ☐ handling of contract negotiations | ☐ maintaining of client relationships | ☐ scheduling and coordination of trades | ☐ performing of on-site supervision | ☐ negotiation and processing of change orders | ☐ other: ______], **completing all projects on time and within budget**.
- ☐ **Oversee the management of** [☐ residential | ☐ commercial | ☐ public works | ☐ other: ______] **construction projects including** [☐ commercial buildings | ☐ shopping malls | ☐ stores | ☐ restaurants | ☐ manufacturing plants | ☐ schools | ☐ colleges | ☐ corporate offices | ☐ building lobbies | ☐ state or government agencies | ☐ houses | ☐ condominiums | ☐ apartment buildings | ☐ hospitals | ☐ laboratories | ☐ clean rooms | ☐ landmark restorations | ☐ roads and highways | ☐ other: ______].
- ☐ **Supervise the work of** [☐ Architects | ☐ Engineers | ☐ Drafters | ☐ others: ______] **in the preparation of** [☐ master plans | ☐ architectural renderings | ☐ cost estimates | ☐ specifications | ☐ construction drawings | ☐ other: ______] **in the completion of design projects**.
- ☐ **Manage and oversee** [☐ trades supervision | ☐ construction inspection | ☐ quality control | ☐ building and safety codes enforcement ☐ design guidelines and specifications standards development | ☐ other: ______] **to ensure quality compliance with all** [☐ construction contracts | ☐ state and local building codes | ☐ Uniform Building Code | ☐ zoning laws | ☐ fire regulations | ☐ electrical codes | ☐ plumbing codes | ☐ life-safety codes | ☐ other: ______] **and other ordinances.**
- ☐ **Monitor construction progress through on-site field inspection and review to ensure conformance to** [☐ design specifications | ☐ cost estimates | ☐ time schedules | ☐ building codes | ☐ other: ______] **and immediately resolve any problems**.
- ☐ **Supervise and oversee all aspects of** [☐ construction project | ☐ product development | ☐ other: ______] **project lifecycles including** [☐ project scope | ☐ initiation | ☐ planning | ☐ scheduling | ☐ budgeting | ☐ contractor selection | ☐ resource allocation | ☐ risk assessment | ☐ quality control | ☐ change orders | ☐ cost control | ☐ other: ______].
- ☐ **Manage and direct** [☐ trades supervision | ☐ construction | ☐ inspection | ☐ quality control | ☐ building and safety codes enforcement | ☐ design guidelines and specifications standards development | ☐ other: ______].

ACHIEVEMENT SAMPLES: *See also Achievements under **"Project Management – General."***

- ☐ **Successfully coordinated and supported various design-and-build projects with multiple interaction points and deadlines by** [☐ integrating effective communications | ☐ increasing productivity | ☐ other: ______].
- ☐ **Provided** ______ *[type of]* [☐ architectural design | ☐ project development services | ☐ environmental technical information | ☐ other: ______] **to** ______ *[whom?]* **in the development and implementation of long-range** ______ *[type of]* **development plans.**

Project Management Support

*See also **"Project Team Management Leadership"** and **"Interdisciplinary/Project Team Member."***

- ☐ **Support project management staff in the processing and tracking of** ______ *[type of]* **projects in the areas of** [☐ pay application processing | ☐ issues management | ☐ project auditing | ☐ meeting coordination | ☐ project filing | ☐ data entry | ☐ communications | ☐ other: ______] **for all** [☐ new construction | ☐ renovations | ☐ remodels | ☐ other: ______].

- ☐ **Provide technical support to** [☐ construction laborers | ☐ production workers | ☐ manufacturing staff | ☐ end users groups | ☐ client representatives | ☐ other: ______] **in the area(s) of** [☐ design | ☐ construction | ☐ installation | ☐ testing | ☐ maintenance | ☐ servicing | ☐ other: ______].

- ☐ **As the firm's Field representative on** ______ *[type of]* **projects, observe construction work for conformance with drawings and specifications and** ______ *[what else?]*.

- ☐ **Provide administrative support to the project management team in the areas of** ______, ______, **and** ______ *[areas]* **using** [☐ initiative | ☐ discretion | ☐ independent judgment | ☐ other: ______] **in setting priorities and carrying out assignments for this established** [☐ commercial construction | ☐ engineering and design | ☐ design-and-build | ☐ construction management | ☐ general contracting | ☐ other: ______] **firm.**

- ☐ [☐ Prepare and revise | ☐ Oversee the preparation and revisions of] [☐ construction contracts | ☐ subcontractor documents | ☐ bid comparisons | ☐ site visit field reports | ☐ owner change orders | ☐ cost reports | ☐ project correspondence | ☐ purchase orders | ☐ other: ______] **and other related documents for the project management team.**

- ☐ **Facilitate project-related administrative functions including** [☐ reviewing contract specifications | ☐ preparing cost estimates | ☐ compiling material lists | ☐ soliciting and evaluating contractor bids | (☐ making / ☐ recommending) bid selections | ☐ planning and coordinating projects | ☐ developing preventive maintenance schedules | ☐ recording work and materials | ☐ writing inspection deficiency reports | ☐ estimating repair and maintenance costs | ☐ preparing work orders | ☐ writing purchase requests | ☐ ordering parts | ☐ maintaining logs | ☐ preparing records and reports | ☐ other: ______] **for** ______ *[type of]* **projects.**

- ☐ **Review and approve all project-related** [☐ plans | ☐ specifications | ☐ cost estimates | ☐ change authorizations | ☐ pay requests | ☐ funds disbursements | ☐ other: ______].

- ☐ **In support of** ______ *[#]* **Project Managers, process and track** ______ *[type of]* **projects in the areas of** [☐ pay application processing | ☐ issues management | ☐ project auditing | ☐ meeting coordination | ☐ project filing | ☐ data entry | ☐ communications | ☐ other: ______] **for all** [☐ new construction | ☐ renovations | ☐ remodels | ☐ other: ______] **within the** ______ *[which?]* **industry.**

- ☐ **Expedite subcontractor documentation and reporting requirements and enter and maintain all** [☐ subcontractor data in ERP system | ☐ other: ______].

- ☐ **Coordinate and manage** [☐ drawings | ☐ submittals | ☐ Request for Quote (RFQ) process | ☐ Requests for Information (RFI) | ☐ purchase order tracking | ☐ job meetings | ☐ customer interactions | ☐ other: ______].

- ☐ **Perform a wide variety of administrative activities including** [☐ assisting with contractual initiatives | ☐ handling claims avoidance | ☐ updating budget databases | ☐ researching contractor claims and litigations | ☐ responding to staff inquiries relating to contract issues | ☐ handling data entry, filing, and copying | ☐ maintaining legal obligations records | ☐ other: ______].

- ☐ **Work closely with the firm's** [☐ Project Managers | ☐ Architects | ☐ Engineers | ☐ technical staff | ☐ others: ______] **in the coordination and performance of construction administration services, including** ______, ______, **and** ______ *[what functions?]* **on** ______ *[type of]* **projects.**

- ☐ **Track and review** ______ *[type of]* [☐ prequalification | ☐ contracts | ☐ authorizations | ☐ invoices | ☐ deliverables | ☐ correspondence | ☐ other: ______] **for Project Managers by** ______ *[doing what?]*.

- ☐ **Jointly with the** [☐ Project Manager | ☐ Site Manager | ☐ Construction Department | ☐ other: ______] **review and ensure the accuracy of all** [☐ project invoices | ☐ contractor requests for payment | ☐ change requests | ☐ subcontractor (☐ invoices / ☐ certificates / ☐ insurance requirements) | ☐ other: ______].

- ☐ **Administer** [☐ Change Order Management | ☐ Claim Management | ☐ other: ______] **and** [☐ review change orders | ☐ negotiate subcontractor closeout | ☐ finalize subcontract documents | ☐ identify risk and minimize consequences | ☐ coordinate approval process | ☐ maintain change order logs | ☐ other: ______] **on all** ______ *[type of]* **projects.**

ACHIEVEMENT SAMPLES: *See Achievements under **"Project Management – General."***

Project Planning & Coordination

*See also "**Project Development & Initiation,**" "**Project Lifecycle Management,**" "**Project Management Support,**" "**Project Prioritization & Demand Balancing.**"*

☐ **Identify, define, and document client needs and priorities, as well as** [☐ options | ☐ risks | ☐ costs | ☐ benefits | ☐ alternative solutions | ☐ other: ______] **and translate requirements into effective** ______ *[type of]* **system layouts and installations.**

☐ **Collaborated in the selection of** ______ *[type of]* **building sites including** [☐ directing site selection | ☐ preparing land-use studies | ☐ developing planning | ☐ considering environmental impact | ☐ infusing energy efficient methods | ☐ other: ______].

☐ **Plan and coordinate all activities of** [☐ small- | ☐ medium- | ☐ large-] **scale** [☐ client | ☐ in-house] **projects** ______ *[type of]* [☐ for a wide range of ______ *(type of)* clients] **in collaboration with** [☐ department representatives | ☐ architect | ☐ contractors | ☐ client reps | ☐ contractors | ☐ subcontractors | ☐ others: ______] **for this** ______ *[type of]* **firm.**

☐ **Partake in the project planning, development, and initiation stages by** [☐ collaborating and coordinating ______ *(what?)* with ______ *(whom?)* | ☐ applying project planning and scheduling methodology | ☐ formulating and defining project plans | ☐ performing ______ *(what activities?)* | ☐ other: ______].

☐ **Oversee the management of** ______ *[type of]* **projects to ensure cost-effective, functional completed projects that consider** [☐ fiscal | ☐ legal | ☐ technical | ☐ demographic | ☐ economic | ☐ safety | ☐ other: ______] **aspects.**

☐ [☐ Manage | ☐ Perform | ☐ Facilitate] **various** [☐ multimillion-dollar | ☐ large-scale | ☐ moderate-size | ☐ highly complex | ☐ moderately complex | ☐ multisite | ☐ simultaneous] **project types including** [☐ new construction | ☐ remodeling | ☐ renovation | ☐ restoration | ☐ maintenance and repair | ☐ demolition | ☐ installation | ☐ other: ______] **of** ______ *[what?].*

☐ **Read, review, and approve all** ______ *[type of]* **project plans and specifications to determine whether they** [☐ comply with building code requirements | ☐ conform to electrical codes and standards | ☐ are suitable for the engineering demands of the site | ☐ are environmentally-friendly | ☐ do not pose any risk to staff | ☐ are fire and life safe | ☐ other: ______].

☐ **Structure and develop client project plans following client-specific project management methodology resulting in** ______ *[what benefits?].*

☐ **Consult with** [☐ architect | ☐ department representatives | ☐ others: ______] **to discuss project** [☐ scope | ☐ objectives | ☐ requirements | ☐ budget | ☐ other: ______] **required for proposed** ______ *[type of]* **projects.**

☐ **Assess business needs and translate design and functional challenges into successful** ______ *[type of]* [☐ buildings | ☐ complexes | ☐ facilities | ☐ other: ______] **that reflect the firm's goals and objectives.**

☐ **Ensure project plans are developed to deliver implementation within realistic scope, schedule, cost, and quality by** ______ *[doing what?].*

☐ **Determine** [☐ best implementation strategy, approaches, and methodology | ☐ required staffing skill sets | ☐ other: ______]; **define project team roles and responsibilities; and develop project-specific job descriptions for** ______ *[#]* [☐ Project Managers | ☐ team members | ☐ others: ______] **to set engineering projects in motion and obtain expected deliverables**

☐ **Confer with** ______ *[whom?]* **on** [☐ proposed construction activities | ☐ land development planning | ☐ energy saving measures | ☐ the negotiation of plan changes to alleviate potential building problems | ☐ project progress | ☐ other: ______].

☐ **Assess and identify** [☐project resources | ☐staffing requirements | ☐system changes | ☐training needs | ☐ other: ______] **to meet project objectives and deliverables of** ______ *[type of]* **projects.**

☐ [☐ Manage and oversee | ☐ Perform] **approximately** ______ *[#]* **of** ______ *[type of]* **projects** [☐ weekly | ☐ monthly | ☐ annually] **ranging $**______ **to $**______ *[amounts].*

☐ **Source, build, and direct the activities of a project team of** ______ *[#]* **with the necessary skill sets to take** ______ *[type of]* **projects from inception through implementation and delivery.**

☐ **Formulate and define project plans that consider project** [☐ design | ☐ scope | ☐ goals | ☐ deliverables | ☐ costs | ☐ task requirements | ☐ resource allocations | ☐ work assignments | ☐ scheduling | ☐ risk identification | ☐ timeline check points | ☐ project monitoring | ☐ other: ______] **using project management planning and scheduling techniques.**

☐ **Prepare detailed and timely** [☐ project schedules | ☐ budgets | ☐ status reports | ☐ other: ______] **for all** ______ *[type of]* **projects averaging $**______ *[amount]* **with an annual return on investment of $**______ *[amount].*

ACHIEVEMENT SAMPLES: *See Achievements under "**Project Management – General.**"*

Project Prioritization & Demand Balancing

*See also "**Project Development & Initiation,**" "**Project Lifecycle Management,**" "**Project Planning & Coordination,**" and "**Project Resources & Staffing Requirements,**" as applicable.*

☐ **Review, prioritize, rank, and balance incoming project requests with competing demands and/or differing needs (relative to scope, time, cost, and quality) by** ______ *[doing what?].*

- ☐ **Prioritize and balance competing project demands of internal clients by** [☐ listening to and understanding departmental needs | ☐ weighing short- and long-term benefits against other groups' needs | ☐ building strong relationships with functional managers and understanding their priorities | ☐ identifying user requirements versus available time and resources | ☐ selecting projects with greatest organizational impact | ☐ designing cross-functional solutions with shared business vision | ☐ other: ______].
- ☐ **Rank and prioritize incoming project requests based on** ______ *[what criteria?]*.
- ☐ **Evaluate feasibility and rank proposals of all projects based on established criteria by** [☐ analyzing project requests | ☐ establishing project scope | ☐ determining required services | ☐ other: ______].
- ☐ **Balance project load between high-revenue projects and those that are** [☐ community-service oriented | ☐ smaller in scale | ☐ other: ______] **by** ______ *[doing what?]*.

ACHIEVEMENT SAMPLES:

- ☐ **Simultaneously managed and tackled dynamic** ______ *[type of]* **projects in varying stages by successfully** [☐ tackling change management | ☐ facilitating conflict resolution | ☐ increasing productivity and performance | ☐ other: ______].
- ☐ **Negotiated within and across business lines on** [☐ project strategy | ☐ functional impact | ☐ project deliverables | ☐ other: ______] **towards the successful implementation of** ______ *[type of]* **design-and-build projects**.
- ☐ **Successfully coordinated and supported various** ______ *[type of]* **projects with multiple interaction points and deadlines by** [☐ integrating effective communications | ☐ increasing productivity | ☐ other: ______].

Project Resources & Staffing Requirements

- ☐ **Assess and** [☐ identify | ☐ recommend] [☐ project resources | ☐ staffing requirements | ☐ system changes | ☐ training needs | ☐ other: ______] **to meet project objectives and deliverables of** ______ *[type of]* **projects.**
- ☐ **Determine required staffing skill sets, define project team roles and responsibilities, and develop project-specific job descriptions for** ______ *[#]* [☐ project managers | ☐ team members | ☐ others: ______].
- ☐ **Review and approve the resource acquisition plan identifying the required resource mix of** [☐ existing employees | ☐ new hires | ☐ outside consultants | ☐ outsourced resources | ☐ redeployments | ☐ vendors | ☐ other: ______] **to accomplish specific project objectives**.
- ☐ **Design and implement structured resource management processes including** [☐ organizational charts | ☐ standardized roles | ☐ job description database | ☐ generic acquisition forms | ☐ tracking and reporting formats | ☐ skill set profiles | ☐ other: ______] **for all project resources.**
- ☐ **Source, build, and direct the activities of a project team of** ______ *[#]* **with the necessary skill sets to take** ______ *[type of]* **projects from inception through launch**.
- ☐ [☐ Direct | ☐ Supervise] **the administrative processing for all new employees including** [☐ payroll | ☐ orientation | ☐ benefits | ☐ training | ☐ other: ______].

Project Tracking & Reporting

*See also **"Client Billing," "Recordkeeping,"** and **"Report Generation & Review."***

- ☐ **Track all time spent on each project, and detail project-time breakdowns achieving an average of ______%** *[percentage]* **billable capacity against project budgets for all projects.**
- ☐ **Regularly monitor and review** ______ *[type of]* **project reports and status including reporting of** [☐ budget variances | ☐ schedule compliance | (☐ firm / ☐ division / ☐ departmental) performance indicators | ☐ other: ______].
- ☐ **Use** [☐ Microsoft Project | ☐ Project Central | ☐ Primavera Project Management | ☐ SAP Project Management | ☐ other: ______] **software to establish project timelines, phases, activities, milestones, dependencies, and resource requirements in compliance with the** [☐ firm's | ☐ clients'] **strategic direction**.
- ☐ **Provide timely and accurate project status through effective** [☐ progress and variance tracking | ☐ risk and issues mitigation | ☐ other: ______] **throughout project lifecycles**.
- ☐ **Track projects and produce various status reports and documents including** [☐ project work plans | ☐ process documents | ☐ business requirements | ☐ budget analyses | ☐ functional documents | ☐ risk management plan | ☐ project deliverables | ☐ schedules | ☐ monthly management reports | ☐ meeting minutes | ☐ solution recommendations | ☐ test plans | ☐ reference guides | ☐ financial reports | ☐ other: ______].

☐ **Provide** [☐ daily | ☐ weekly | ☐ bi-weekly | ☐ monthly] **project tracking and reporting of all** [☐ tasks | ☐ activities | ☐ time | ☐ costs | ☐ controls | ☐ documentation | ☐ follow-up | ☐ other: ______] **in compliance with project methodology and standards for project reporting and documentation.**

☐ **Review and provide feedback and direction on status reports including** [☐ identifying and resolving potential time and cost slippages | ☐ actual work costs versus budgeted costs | ☐ issues resolution | ☐ task completion status | ☐ other: ______].

☐ **Track project success on a** [☐ daily | ☐ weekly | ☐ bi-monthly | ☐ monthly] **basis using project performance metrics; monitor project results against technical specifications; and produce detailed, intuitive project control reports including ______, ______, and ______** *[what reports?].*

☐ **Facilitate milestone management oversight and project control in all timeline areas to ensure all project management** [☐ phases | ☐ controls | ☐ progress] **are in compliance with project management methodology and expected deliverables.**

☐ **Use** [☐ Microsoft Project | ☐ Project Central | ☐ Primavera Project Management | ☐ SAP Project Management | ☐ other: ______] **software to establish project timelines, activities, milestones, dependencies, and resource requirements in compliance with** [☐ firm's / ☐ clients'] **strategic direction.**

☐ **Develop, produce, and deliver timely, clear reports on** [☐ project timelines | ☐ resource supply and demand | ☐ utilization analysis | ☐ cost tracking | ☐ work change orders | ☐ earned value | ☐ issues identification | ☐ test cases | ☐ project closures | ☐ other: ______] **which provide accurate, real-time project status.**

ACHIEVEMENT SAMPLES:

☐ **Prepared, initiated, and deliver accurate and detailed client** [☐ contract billing | ☐ support documentation | ☐ project hours logs | ☐ actual resource utilization | ☐ expense reports | ☐ actual versus projected budget records | ☐ overage justification | ☐ other: ______] **obtaining client payment for services and deliverables within a ______** *[what?]* **timeframe as opposed to ______** *[previous timeframe].*

Purchasing

*See also **"Inventory Management & Control"** and **"Recordkeeping."***

☐ **Purchase, inspect, and store all ______** *[type of]* [☐ materials | ☐ supplies | ☐ merchandise | ☐ goods | ☐ products | ☐ equipment | ☐ tools | ☐ machinery | ☐ other: ______] **at the best prices and quality ensuring** [☐ successful delivery to ______ *(where?)* | ☐ timely delivery schedules | ☐ all criteria are met | ☐ research value analysis criteria on all product purchases | ☐ correct storage | ☐ proper disposal of chemical waste and hazardous materials | ☐ other: ______].

☐ **Analyze and calculate all bids using various methods including** [☐ life-cycle costing | ☐ weighted value | ☐ value analysis | ☐ other methods: ______] **ensuring ______** *[what criteria?].*

☐ **Determine all** [☐ product requirements | ☐ methods of acquisition | ☐ other: ______], **prepare bid specifications, select vendors, and obtain written** [☐ bids | ☐ quotes | ☐ estimates] **on all purchases averaging $______ to $______** *[amounts].*

☐ **Perform various purchasing functions including** [☐ preparing specifications | ☐ determining bidding conditions and documents | ☐ preparing purchase orders | ☐ negotiating pricing | ☐ selecting vendors | ☐ awarding contracts | ☐ performing lifecycle costing | ☐ authorizing procurement | ☐ placing blanket orders | ☐ expediting open orders | ☐ handing high-volume buying | ☐ ensuring follow-up | ☐ troubleshooting delivery problems | ☐ processing internal stock numbers | ☐ maintaining up-to-date client and vendor records | ☐ preparing weekly inventory reports | ☐ updating the incoming shipment log | ☐ other: ______].

☐ **Research the cost and value of all ______** *[type of]* [☐ products | ☐ supplies | ☐ services | ☐ materials | ☐ equipment | ☐ other: ______] **for** [☐ department | ☐ company-wide | ☐ district | ☐ other: ______] **use; and negotiate and prepare vendor contracts.**

☐ **Monitor** [☐ production schedules | ☐ flow of merchandise and its components from vendor to company | ☐ inventory reports | ☐ other: ______].

☐ **Apply value-analysis criteria to ______** *[type of]* [☐ products | ☐ supplies | ☐ services | ☐ materials | ☐ equipment | ☐ other: ______] **analyzing the** [☐ quality | ☐ price | ☐ delivery | ☐ shipping charges | ☐ lifecycle costing | ☐ final costs | ☐ maintenance costs | ☐ other: ______].

☐ **Locate, select, and purchase ______** *[type of]* [☐ materials | ☐ equipment | ☐ tools | ☐ furniture | ☐ telephones | ☐ office equipment | ☐ other: ______] **for ______** *[what?]* **considering** [☐ least cost | ☐ most reliable sources | ☐ best quality | ☐ ability to meet deadlines | ☐ trade licensing requirements | ☐ other: ______].

☐ **Consult with manufacturers' representatives regarding** [☐ products | ☐ cost | ☐ quantities | ☐ trade policies | ☐ replacement policies | ☐ other: ______] **to select and approve the purchase of** [☐ construction materials | ☐ equipment | ☐ tools | ☐ furniture | ☐ telephones | ☐ office equipment | ☐ other: ______].

- ☐ **Order sufficient** [☐ product | ☐ supplies | ☐ goods | ☐ merchandise | ☐ materials | ☐ other: ______] **in accordance with the firm's** [☐ inventory usage cycles | ☐ quality initiatives | ☐ established procedures | ☐ other: ______] **while effectively balancing physical storage and usage demands.**
- ☐ **Directly interface with** [☐ vendors | ☐ clients | ☐ state and federal agencies | ☐ others: ______] **regarding the purchasing of products for best price and quality, maximizing the firm's return on investment.**
- ☐ **Coordinate the purchasing of all production materials including** ______ *[type of]* [☐ equipment | ☐ tooling | ☐ fixtures | ☐ components | ☐ parts | ☐ supplies | ☐ other: ______] **at the best prices and quality by** ______ *[doing what?].*
- ☐ **Negotiate, execute, and administer all purchase orders for** [☐ company and its various subsidiaries | ☐ materials required in the production of ______ *(what?)* | ☐ other: ______].
- ☐ **Conduct** [☐ vendor bids | ☐ comparative cost analyses | ☐ other: ______], **and make sound selections based on** [☐ product quality | ☐ vendor reliability | ☐ ability to meet required deadlines | ☐ other: ______] **for** ______ *[what?].*
- ☐ **Perform various purchasing functions for the** [☐ production | ☐ manufacturing | ☐ other: ______] **of** ______ *[what?]* **including** [☐ creating purchase orders | ☐ negotiating pricing | ☐ placing blanket orders | ☐ expediting open orders | ☐ handing high-volume buying | ☐ ensuring follow-up | ☐ troubleshooting delivery problems | ☐ maintaining up-to-date client and vendor records | ☐ preparing weekly inventory reports | ☐ other: ______].
- ☐ **Approve pricing of manufacturing components to ensure** [☐ best quality | ☐ pricing | ☐ delivery schedules | ☐ other: ______], **and ensure timely delivery of all** ______ *[type of]* [☐ parts | ☐ components | ☐ equipment | ☐ other: ______].
- ☐ **Purchase** ______ *[type of]* [☐ products | ☐ materials | ☐ supplies | ☐ equipment | ☐ other: ______] **from** ______ *[where purchased];* **ensuring successful delivery.**
- ☐ **Serve as liaison with vendors and** ______ *[other types of companies]* **handling** [☐ purchasing | ☐ merchandise buying and/or selling | ☐ customer service | ☐ delivery troubleshooting | ☐ other: ______].
- ☐ **Handle new and existing** ______ *[type of]* **customers** ______ *[type of]* **purchases averaging** ______ *[#]* | $______ *(amount)* [☐ weekly | ☐ monthly | ☐ annually].
- ☐ **By utilizing effective** [☐ inventory level monitoring | ☐ purchasing requirements |☐ other: ______], **created consistent** ______% **annual service levels, resulting in** [☐ enhanced company credibility | ☐ a following in the community | ☐ other benefits: ______].

ACHIEVEMENT SAMPLES:

- ☐ **Increased purchasing annual service levels from** ______% **to** ______% *[percentages]* **efficiency through various regimented disciplines including** [☐ inventory level monitoring | ☐ client and vendor interface and follow-up | ☐ enhanced computer purchasing programs to monitor inventory levels | ☐ frequent product line reviews | ☐ other: ______] **resulting in** ______ *[benefits].*
- ☐ **Conducted** ______ *[type of]* **research to identify best vendor selections by performing** [☐ value analysis | ☐ lifecycle costing] **on all** [☐ materials | ☐ equipment | ☐ products | ☐ supplies | ☐ services | ☐ other: ______] **for** ______ *[what?].*
- ☐ **Saved $______ in the negotiation and purchase of** ______ *[what]* **by obtaining product information from various sources and** [☐ reviewing literature | ☐ checking competitor pricing | ☐ consulting with sales reps | ☐ visiting trade shows | ☐ attending product demonstrations | ☐ other: ______].
- ☐ **Prepared $______ in purchase orders** [☐ monthly | ☐ quarterly | ☐ annually | ☐ other: ______] **for** ______ *[type of]* [☐ supplies | ☐ materials | ☐ machinery | ☐ equipment | ☐ tools | ☐ parts | ☐ accessories | ☐ other: ______] **for** ______ *[what?]* **ensuring** [☐ verification of all specifications | ☐ pricing and availability of merchandise | ☐ other: ______].
- ☐ **Process in excess of** ______ *[#]* [☐ pounds | ☐ pieces | ☐ packages | ☐ yards | ☐ other measure: ______] **per week, with yearly profits of $______,** *[amount]* **surpassing competitors by $______** *[amount].*
- ☐ **Saved the firm $______** *[amount]* **in extraneous costs by applying value-analysis criteria to** ______ *[type of]* [☐ supplies | ☐ services | ☐ materials | ☐ equipment | ☐ other: ______] **analyzing the** [☐ quality | ☐ price | ☐ delivery | ☐ shipping charges | ☐ lifecycle costing | ☐ final costs | ☐ maintenance costs | ☐ other: ______].
- ☐ **Slashed purchasing costs $______ by determining the best** [☐ acquisition | ☐ procurement | ☐ buying | ☐ other: ______] **methods in the purchase of** ______ *[type of]* **equipment and supplies, preparing specifications, selecting vendors, and awarding contracts for** ______ *[what?].*
- ☐ **As a persuasive negotiator, overcame** [☐ sales pitches | ☐ objections | ☐ other: ______] **to save on purchasing costs and meet the needs of company by way of** ______ *[what methods?]***.**
- ☐ **Working in a fast-paced, high-pressure environment, handle high-volume purchasing with effective follow-through ensuring all** [☐ governmental regulations | ☐ company policies | ☐ other: ______] **are met.**
- ☐ **Reduced purchasing costs in excess of $______ annually by establishing a** ______ *[what negotiation or initiative?]* **to** ______ *[do what?].*

Quality Assurance & Quality Control – Construction

☐ **Ensure compliance with all building codes, ordinances, laws, and regulations including** [☐ contract specifications | ☐ zoning regulations | ☐ Uniform Building Code (UBC) | ☐ International Code Council (ICC) | ☐ electrical codes | ☐ fire regulations | ☐ plumbing codes | ☐ life-safety codes | ☐ environmental safety codes | ☐ ANSI | ☐ Federal regulations | ☐ state and local building codes | ☐ Title I | ☐ Title II | ☐ Title III | ☐ Title IV | ☐ Title V | ☐ other: ______].

☐ **Oversee quality control and compliance of** ______ *[which?]* **trades in their installation of** [☐ commercial | ☐ industrial | ☐ residential | ☐ other: ______] ______ *[type of]* **systems.**

☐ **By** ______ *[doing what?]*, **ensured all contractors and subcontractors followed design specs, used specified materials, followed code, and met quality work standards and deadlines.**

☐ **Conduct** [☐ weekly | ☐ monthly | ☐ periodic] **meetings with** [☐ Project Managers | ☐ contractors | ☐ subcontractors | ☐ others: ______] **to identify ways to improve** [☐ workmanship | ☐ productivity | ☐ competitive edge | ☐ other: ______].

☐ **Ensure quality workmanship in all trade areas covering** [☐ project specifications | ☐ expected deliverables | ☐ timely completion | ☐ other: ______] **making sound decisions regarding** [☐ corrective actions required | ☐ recommended means to obtain compliance | ☐ other: ______].

☐ **Manage and oversee quality assurance activities including** [☐ project scheduling | ☐ milestone establishment | ☐ resource scheduling | ☐ project monitoring | ☐ progress reporting | ☐ regulatory requirements compliance | ☐ other: ______] **for** ______ *[what?]* **ensuring compliance with all codes and regulations.**

☐ **Facilitate project control in the areas of** ______, ______, **and** ______ *[which areas?]* **to ensure all project management phases and progress are in compliance with project management methodology and expected deliverables.**

☐ **Develop, coordinate, and execute** ______ *[type of]* **quality assurance** [☐ plans | ☐ procedures | ☐ programs] **and** [☐ corrective | ☐ preventive] **actions to support interdisciplinary project teams in the construction of** ______ *[what?]*.

☐ **Identify and resolve quality issues by** [☐ applying sound problem-solving methodologies | ☐ improving quality issues awareness | ☐ supporting quality (☐ goals / ☐ priorities / ☐ disciplines / ☐ practices) | ☐ other: ______].

☐ **Direct and lead a broad range of** ______ *[type of]* **activities including** [☐ strategy development | ☐ direction setting | ☐ project planning, coordination, scheduling, tracking, and reporting | ☐ quality assurance standards development | ☐ other: ______] **to attain business goals.**

Recordkeeping

*See also **"Client Billing/Invoicing," "Project Time Tracking,"** and **"Report Generation & Review."***

☐ **Perform computer entry of daily** [☐ billing | ☐ payments | ☐ recordkeeping | ☐ client communiqué | ☐ other: ______], **ensuring** [☐ accurate data entry | ☐ all client records are current and accurate | ☐ other: ______].

☐ **Document reports and maintain up-to-date records of** [☐ individual's time | ☐ man hours expended on job orders | ☐ accidents and injuries | ☐ work progress | ☐ other: ______].

☐ **Accurately complete and verify data entry of** ______ *[#]* **weekly invoices using** [☐ QuickBooks | ☐ Quicken | ☐ Excel | ☐ Microsoft Word | ☐ other: ______]

☐ **Update project records and generate reports that include** [☐ job history files | ☐ construction bids | ☐ cost breakdowns | ☐ material specifications | ☐ equipment specifications | ☐ preventive maintenance | ☐ maintenance history | ☐ work orders | ☐ material requisitions | ☐ project status | ☐ trade scheduling | ☐ inspection deficiencies | ☐ project time tracking | ☐ client billing | ☐ violations | ☐ other: ______].

☐ **Handle financial recordkeeping of all** [☐ purchases and supplies | ☐ monthly billing | ☐ budget monitoring | ☐ financial transaction processing | ☐ other process: ______] **for** ______ *[#]* **accounts.**

☐ **Accurately handle all monthly billing for** ______ *[#]* **accounts with recordkeeping of all purchases and supplies per account using** ______ *[what program or method?]*.

☐ **Record all** ______ *[type of]* **details and prepare** ______ *[which?]* **reports using** ______ *[which?]* **program(s) to include** ______ *[what?]*.

☐ **Update and maintain records of the** [☐ receipt | ☐ inspection | ☐ distribution | ☐ transporting | ☐ warehousing | ☐ other: ______] **of all** [☐ supplies | ☐ goods | ☐ product | ☐ merchandise | ☐ materials | ☐ property | ☐ furniture | ☐ equipment | ☐ other: ______] **acquisitions and dispositions.**

☐ **Maintain up-to-date client and vendor records of** ______ *[#]* **accounts using** ______ *[type of program]*.

☐ **Keep accurate, up-to-date** [☐ purchasing | ☐ merchandising | ☐ buying | ☐ inventory | ☐ other: ______] **records of all** ______ *[type of]* **items purchased including** [☐ costs | ☐ quantities | ☐ delivery | ☐ distribution | ☐ product performance | ☐ inventory levels | (☐ materials | ☐ supplies) usage | ☐ other: ______].

☐ **Update and maintain records of the** [☐ receipt | ☐ inspection | ☐ distribution | ☐ transporting | ☐ warehousing | ☐ other: ______] **of all** [☐ property | ☐ furniture | ☐ equipment | ☐ supplies | ☐ goods | ☐ merchandise | ☐ materials | ☐ other: ______] **acquisitions and dispositions.**

☐ **Handle all financial recordkeeping of the firm's** [☐ purchasing | ☐ merchandising | ☐ buying | ☐ billing | ☐ other: ______] **including** ______ *[what functions?].*

☐ **Review and approve all production records including** [☐ job orders | ☐ job tickets | ☐ customer invoices | ☐ production logs | ☐ meter reports | ☐ stock inventories | ☐ equipment time and supplies usage | ☐ inventory records | ☐ sales reports | ☐ budgets | ☐ financial reports | ☐ cash receipts | ☐ bank deposits | ☐ other: ______].

ACHIEVEMENT SAMPLES:

☐ **Set up and maintained** ______ *[type of]* [☐ preventive maintenance | ☐ history | ☐ work order | ☐ material requisition | ☐ scope of work | ☐ project status | ☐ other: ______] [☐ records | ☐ reports | ☐ documentation | ☐ schedules | ☐ manuals] **and submit to** ______ *[whom?]* **on a** [☐ weekly | ☐ monthly | ☐ other: ______] **basis.**

☐ **Developed the** ______ *[type of]* [☐ system | ☐ records | ☐ data | ☐ information | ☐ other: ______] **that provides accurate periodic** [☐ progress | ☐ revenue | ☐ campaign | ☐ other: ______] **reports to** ______ *[whom?].*

☐ **Assisted** ______ *[whom?]* **by preparing** ______ *[type of]* [☐ records | ☐ reports] **for** ______ *[type of]* [☐ bids | ☐ specifications | ☐ cost breakdowns | ☐ material and equipment inventory | ☐ orders | ☐ other: ______], **which benefited by way of** ______ *[what?].*

Recordkeeping Management

*See also **"Inventory – General."***

☐ **Manage the update and maintenance of inventory records including the** [☐ receipt | ☐ inspection | ☐ distribution | ☐ transporting | ☐ warehousing | ☐ other: ______] of all [☐ property | ☐ furniture | ☐ equipment | ☐ supplies | ☐ goods | ☐ product | ☐ merchandise | ☐ materials | ☐ other: ______] **acquisitions and dispositions.**

☐ **Manage the firm's financial recordkeeping of** [☐ inventory | ☐ purchasing | ☐ merchandising | ☐ buying | ☐ billing | ☐ other: ______] **including** ______ *[what functions?].*

☐ **Manage the firm's inventory recordkeeping to ensure accurate, up-to-date** [☐ inventory | ☐ purchasing | ☐ merchandising | ☐ buying | ☐ invoicing | ☐ other: ______] **records of all** ______ *[type of]* **items purchased including** [☐ costs | ☐ quantities | ☐ delivery | ☐ distribution | ☐ product performance | ☐ inventory levels | ☐ (materials/supplies) usage | ☐ other: ______].

☐ **Ensure all** [☐ property | ☐ supplies | ☐ goods | ☐ product | ☐ merchandise | ☐ materials | ☐ furniture | ☐ equipment | ☐ other: ______] **acquisition and disposition records are up to date, including** [☐ receipts | ☐ inspections | ☐ distribution | ☐ transporting | ☐ warehousing | ☐ other: ______].

☐ **Supervise and oversee computer entry of daily** [☐ receipts | ☐ billing | ☐ invoicing | ☐ payments | ☐ recordkeeping | ☐ client communiqué | ☐ other: ______], **ensuring** [☐ accurate data entry at all times | ☐ all client records are current and accurate | ☐ other: ______].

☐ **Review and verify data entry of** ______ *[#]* **weekly invoices using** [☐ QuickBooks | ☐ Quicken | ☐ Excel | ☐ Microsoft Word | ☐ other: ______].

☐ **Review and approve all construction records including** [☐ job orders | ☐ job tickets | ☐ customer invoices | ☐ stock inventories | ☐ equipment time and supplies usage | ☐ inventory records | ☐ sales reports | ☐ budgets | ☐ financial reports | ☐ cash receipts | ☐ bank deposits | ☐ other: ______].

☐ **Oversee all recordkeeping of** [☐ purchases and supplies | ☐ monthly billing | ☐ budget monitoring | ☐ financial transaction processing | ☐ other process: ______] **for** ______ *[#]* **accounts.**

☐ **Manage and oversee monthly billing for** ______ *[#]* **accounts with recordkeeping of all purchases and supplies per account using** ______ *[program or method].*

☐ **Prepare** ______ *[type of]* [☐ records | ☐ reports] **for** ______ *[type of]* [☐ bids | ☐ specifications | ☐ cost breakdowns | ☐ material and equipment inventory | ☐ orders | ☐ other: ______].

☐ **Prepare and maintain** ______ *[type of]* [☐ preventive maintenance | ☐ history | ☐ work order | ☐ material requisition | ☐ scope of work | ☐ project status | ☐ other: ______] [records | ☐ reports | ☐ documentation | ☐ schedules | ☐ manuals] and submit to ______ *[whom?]* **on a** [weekly | ☐ monthly | ☐ other: ______] **basis.**

Report Generation & Review

*See also "**Environmental Reporting,**" "**Client Billing/Invoicing**" and "**Project Time Tracking,**" as applicable.*

☐ **Prepare** ______ *[type of]* [☐ records | ☐ reports] **for** ______ *[type of]* [(☐ job | ☐ client) history files | ☐ construction bids | ☐ architectural drawings | ☐ specifications | ☐ cost breakdowns | ☐ material and equipment (☐ inventory | ☐ orders | ☐ specifications) | ☐ other: ______].

☐ **Perform quality control of reports prepared by** [☐ Architects | ☐ Engineers | ☐ Project Managers | ☐ others: ______] **including** ______, ______, **and** ______ *[type of reports]* **by** ______ *[doing what?].*

☐ **Accurately record all** [☐ project | ☐ inspection | ☐ other: ______] **details; and prepare** ______ *[type of]* **reports using** ______ *(which?)* **program(s), to include** [☐ project progress | ☐ inspection deficiencies | ☐ work conditions | ☐ detected violations | ☐ other: ______].

☐ **Maintain** ______ *[type of]* **reports, and follow up with** ______ *[which?]* [☐ departments | ☐ divisions | ☐ writers | ☐ other: ______] **to ensure timely submission of** ______ *[type of]* **items.**

☐ **Prepare** ______ *[type of]* [☐ records | ☐ reports] **for** ______ *[type of]* [☐ job files | ☐ client history files | ☐ bids | ☐ cost breakdowns | ☐ material and equipment | ☐ other: ______].

☐ **Accurately record all** ______ *[type of]* **details; and prepare** ______ *[type of]* **reports using** ______ *(which?)* **program(s), to include** ______ *[what?].*

☐ **Oversee the** [☐ preparation | ☐ analysis | ☐ negotiation | ☐ review] **of** [☐ contracts | ☐ invoices | ☐ estimates | ☐ billing | ☐ other: ______] **related to the** [☐ purchase | ☐ sale ☐ other: ______] **of** [☐ equipment | ☐ materials | ☐ supplies | ☐ products | ☐ services | ☐ other: ______].

☐ **Facilitate distribution of** [☐ financial statements | ☐ journal entries | ☐ articles | ☐ publications | ☐ other: ______] **and oversee the** [☐ compilation | ☐ coordination | ☐ accuracy | ☐ other: ______] **of all** ______ *[what data?].*

☐ **Regularly monitor and review** ______ *[type of]* **project reports and status including reporting of** [☐ budget variances | ☐ schedule compliance | (☐ firm / ☐ division / ☐ departmental) performance indicators | ☐ other: ______].

☐ **Prepare** ______ *[type of]* **reports detailing the progress of all** ______ *[type of]* **projects, addressing any related problems, and making sound recommendations to solve them.**

☐ **Interpret and evaluate** [☐ legal | ☐ contractual | ☐ practical | ☐ complex | ☐ engineering | ☐ other: ______] ______ *[type of]* [☐ data | ☐ problems | ☐ information], **and furnish** ______ *[type of]* **recommended solutions for** ______ *[what?]* **to** ______ *[whom?].*

ACHIEVEMENT SAMPLES:

☐ **Made recommendations for** ______ *[what?];* **and prepared comprehensive** ______ *[type of]* **reports to support these recommendations.**

☐ **Developed a(n)** ______ *[type of]* [☐ invoice | ☐ report | ☐ billing chart | ☐ template | ☐ form | ☐ other: ______] **to record** ______ *[what?]* **superceding the manual method and saving the company $**______ *[amount]* **in the area of** ______ *[what area?].*

☐ **Prepared and maintain** ______ *[type of]* [☐ history | ☐ work order | ☐ scope of work | ☐ compliance | ☐ project status | ☐ material requisition | ☐ preventive maintenance | ☐ other: ______] [☐ records | ☐ reports | ☐ documentation | ☐ schedules | ☐ manuals | ☐ other: ______] **and submit to** ______ [whom?] **on a** [☐ weekly | ☐ monthly | ☐ other: ______] **basis.**

☐ **Assessed compliance findings via** ______ *[type of]* **compliance reports, and followed up with** ______ *[which?]* [☐ departmental | ☐ divisional | ☐ other: ______] **managers to ensure compliance with** ______ *[what?].*

☐ **Developed a** ______ *[type of]* **compliance report that records** ______ *[what information?]* **and supplies** ______ *[what?]* **to** ______ *[whom?].*

Roofing Functions & Projects

*See also "**Carpentry/Construction Work Functions**" and all Carpentry/Construction Projects (specific).*

☐ [☐ Manage | ☐ Perform] ______ *[type of]* **roofing construction projects for** [☐ general commercial construction | ☐ residential homes | ☐ decks and porches | ☐ sunrooms | ☐ cabanas | ☐ other: ______] **according to company's established polices, procedures, and guidelines and in compliance with all codes.**

☐ **Plan and direct roofing surveys of** ______ *[what?]* **to determine** ______ *[type of]* **maintenance and new roof requirements.**

☐ **Apply** [☐ proficiency in | ☐ considerable knowledge of | ☐ other: ______] **various** [☐ commercial | ☐ residential | ☐ other: ______] **roofing systems, materials, and installation methods;** [☐ state and local building codes | ☐ Uniform Building Code | ☐ electrical codes | ☐ plumbing codes | ☐ other: ______]; **and** [☐ construction site development | ☐ commercial construction | ☐ demolition | ☐ other: ______] **procedures in the installation of** ______ *[type of]* **roofs.**

☐ [☐ Direct | ☐ Facilitate] [☐ large-scale | ☐ mid-size | ☐ other: ______] ______ *[type of]* **commercial roofing projects ensuring all quality standards are followed and all work is completed in accordance with standards, industry guidelines, and contracts.**

☐ **Prepare for roofing projects by** [☐ performing on-site reviews | ☐ reviewing surveys | ☐ taking dimensions | ☐ developing drawings | ☐ interpreting roofing plans, specifications, and standards | ☐ conducting roofing tests to provide architect with necessary information for contract completion | ☐ identifying and resolving project deficiencies | ☐ estimating materials, hours, and (replacement) costs | ☐ ordering required roofing materials | ☐ other: ______].

ACHIEVEMENT SAMPLES: *See "Completed Construction Projects" and "Completed Projects – General."*

Safety & Responsibility for Others

See also "Environment, Safety & Health Management Compliance."

☐ **Ensure that** [☐ employees | ☐ buildings | ☐ facilities | ☐ grounds | ☐ customers and others] **are safe and secure by** [☐ following safe work procedures | ☐ exercising a high degree of awareness | ☐ complying with all safety codes | ☐ other: ______].

☐ **Safeguard lives by** [☐ following safe work procedures | ☐ exercising a high degree of awareness | ☐ complying with all safety guidelines and precautions | ☐ other: ______].

☐ **Follow safety precautions using protective equipment around exposure to** [☐ extreme temperatures | ☐ toxic chemicals | ☐ biohazardous materials | ☐ smoke and fumes | ☐ other: ______].

☐ **Ensure proper safety precautions and regulations are observed during all** ______ *[type of]* [☐ installations | ☐ repairs | ☐ construction] **by** ______ *[doing what?]* **to prevent physical injury to self and others.**

ACHIEVEMENT SAMPLES:

☐ **Achieved safety performance levels to** ______ *[what level?]* **from previous incident rate of** ______ [what level?] **by** ______ *[doing what?]*, **ensuring overall business and personnel safety and security.**

☐ **Decreased controllable expenses $**______ *[amount]* **over previous year by implementing improved** ______ *[type of]* [☐ safety programs | ☐ security programs | ☐ safety awareness training | ☐ other: ______] **that** ______ *[did what?]*, **resulting in** ______ *[what benefits?]*.

☐ **Maintained optimum** [☐ company | ☐ plant | ☐ other: ______] **safety and security by** ______ *[doing what?]* **and implementing safety procedures in accordance with** [☐ OSHA | ☐ other: ______] **regulations.**

☐ **Achieved and maintained high levels of** [☐ employee | ☐ crew | ☐ customer | ☐ others: ______] **safety by** ______ *[doing what?]*.

Safety & Security Compliance

See "Environmental, Safety & Health Management Compliance."

Staff Management & Supervision – General

See also "Team Leadership & Direction" and "Work Collaboration," as applicable.

☐ **Provide strategic, comprehensive** [☐ leadership and direction | ☐ supervision and guidance | ☐ assistance and support] **to the** ______ *[which?]* **staff in the areas of** ______, ______, **and** ______ *[which areas?]* **that leads to** ______ *[what?]* **and the successful completion of all jobs.**

☐ **Supervise, coordinate, and oversee the day-to-day activities of the** ______ *[which?]* **Department team of** ______ *[#]* **including** ______, ______, **and** ______ *[titles or functions]* **including** [☐ prioritizing work assignments and project tasks | ☐ analyzing scope and importance of work | ☐ determining deadlines | ☐ strategizing best approach to meet commitments | ☐ delegating assignments | ☐ providing guidance and support | ☐ other: ______] **ensuring quality performance in all areas.**

☐ **Oversee the supervision of the** ______ *[which?]* **staff in the areas of** [☐ work prioritization | ☐ work allocation | ☐ job assignments | ☐ delegating | ☐ scheduling | ☐ employee development | ☐ performance evaluations | ☐ personnel actions | ☐ productivity and performance improvement | ☐ technical support | ☐ problem resolution | ☐ other: ______], **and motivate employees to achieve peak productivity and performance.**

- ☐ **Manage a(n)** ______ *[type of]* **team of** ______ *[#]* **ensuring** [☐ the highest quality work | ☐ fulfillment of all expected deliverables | ☐ timely development and completion of all projects | ☐ quality standards are adhered to | ☐ compliance with all company guidelines | ☐ measurable member participation and progress | ☐ other: ______].
- ☐ **Supervise and oversee the daily activities of the** ______ *[which?]* **staff including** [☐ assignment delegating | ☐ purchasing | ☐ payroll processing | ☐ administrative support | ☐ report generation | ☐ contract administration | ☐ other: ______] **ensuring quality performance in all areas.**
- ☐ **Monitor, fairly evaluate, and document subordinates' progress to ensure that** [☐ all required goals are met for the position | ☐ quality of work or customer service delivered meets firm's high standards of excellence | ☐ other requirements: ______].
- ☐ **Oversee personnel management functions including** [☐ new hire selections | ☐ training and development | ☐ performance ratings | ☐ commendatory and disciplinary actions | ☐ promotions | ☐ demotions | ☐ transfers | ☐ terminations | ☐ other: ______] **to** [☐ optimize staffing needs | ☐ maintain work force productivity | ☐ ensure quality workmanship ☐ other: ______].
- ☐ **Influence, energize, and motivate** ______ *[type of]* **staff to apply** ______ *[type of]* **skills to help them** [☐ solve dynamic challenges | ☐ overcome obstacles | ☐ other: ______] **to bring projects to a successful completion.**
- ☐ [☐ Manage | ☐ Supervise] **and oversee a team of** ______ *[#]* **in the initiation, planning, and development of** ______ *[type of]* **projects ranging from $______ to $______ and resulting in** [☐ delivering bottom-line business value | ☐ business transformation | ☐ new product offerings | ☐ the translation of enterprise strategies into projects | ☐ increased productivity | ☐ other benefits: ______].
- ☐ **Supervise and direct a staff of** ______ *[#]*______ *[titles]* **and oversee their daily activities ensuring** [☐ quality performance in all areas | ☐ all work is completed on time and to expectations | ☐ other: ______].
- ☐ **Guide and oversee a** ______ *[which?]* **staff of** ______ *[#]* **ensuring** [☐ the highest quality work | ☐ fulfillment of all expected deliverables | ☐ all functions are performed in a timely, cost-effective manner measurable member participation and progress | ☐ quality deliverables | ☐ other: ______] **which** [☐ meet customer needs | ☐ achieve business objectives].
- ☐ **Successfully delegate and follow up on** ______ *[what?]* **to ensure staff completes all assigned functions correctly and in accordance with** ______ *[what?]* [☐ policies and procedures | ☐ rules and regulations | ☐ other: ______], **resulting in** ______ *[what benefits?]*.
- ☐ **Manage and oversee** ______ *[#]*______ *[whom?]* **in a** ______ *[type of]* **environment including** [☐ recruiting staff | ☐ preparing work schedules | ☐ developing training programs | ☐ conducting performance appraisals | ☐ other: ______].
- ☐ **Hire, schedule, and supervise a** [☐ direct | ☐ indirect] **support staff of from** ______ *[#]* **to** ______ *[#]*.

ACHIEVEMENT SAMPLES:

- ☐ **Gained** ______ *[which?]* **team member cooperation, commitment, and buy-in by** [☐ providing clear direction | ☐ soliciting feedback | ☐ serving as primary resource hub | ☐ insisting on mutual support | ☐ sharing information | ☐ modeling professional behavior | ☐ building a collaborative environment | ☐ removing all obstacles to project success | ☐ other: ______].
- ☐ **Energized, inspired, and motivated the** ______ *[which?]* **Department staff of** ______ *[#]* **to** ______ *[perform what?]* **by** ______ *[doing what well?]*.
- ☐ **Provided strategic, comprehensive** [☐ leadership | ☐ direction | ☐ guidance | ☐ assistance | ☐ support] **to the** ______ *[which?]* **staff in the areas of** ______, ______, **and** ______ *[which areas?]* **that led to** ______ *[what?]* **and the successful completion of all jobs**.
- ☐ **Developed and maintain a** [☐ strong | ☐ knowledgeable | ☐ cooperative | ☐ supportive | ☐ high-energy | ☐ productive | ☐ creative | ☐ winning | ☐ other: ______] ______ *[which?]* **management team environment in the coordination and completion of all** ______ *[what?]* **activities by exhibiting and modeling influential leadership skills in** [☐ communication | ☐ problem-solving | ☐ obstacle tackling | ☐ negotiation | ☐ other: ______].
- ☐ **Developed and implemented a** ______ *[type of]* **employee incentive program to** ______ *[accomplish what?]*, **which resulted in** ______ *[what benefits?]*.
- ☐ **Instilled** ______ *[what?]* **in a project team of** ______ *[#]* **that resulted in attaining** [☐ the highest quality work | ☐ fulfillment of all expected deliverables regardless of obstacles | ☐ all projects staying on schedule and within budget | ☐ timely development and completion of all projects | ☐ meeting project success criteria | ☐ adherence to quality standards | ☐ lower turnover | ☐ compliance with all company guidelines and ordinances | ☐ other: ______].

- ☐ **Influenced, energized, and motivated team members to develop and maintain positive working relationships with all levels of management and to apply ______** *[type of]* **skills to help them** [☐ set realistic expectations | ☐ solve dynamic challenges | ☐ overcome obstacles | ☐ understand the impact of change | ☐ tackle political or bureaucratic obstacles | ☐ other: ______] **to bring ______** *[type of]* **projects to a successful completion.**
- ☐ **Tackled challenging ______** *[type of]* **employee situations through the means of ______** *[what?]* **methods, which has resulted in** [☐ a smooth workflow | ☐ less downtime | ☐ more productivity | ☐ more motivated employees | ☐ other: ______].
- ☐ **Developed effective relationships with ______** *[which?]* **staff by** [☐ fostering a cooperative team environment | ☐ promoting a cooperative working atmosphere | ☐ maximizing employee morale | ☐ other: ______].

Staff Management & Supervision – Carpentry / Labor

See also ***"Trades/Crew Supervision – All Trades"*** *and* ***"Trades Coordination & Oversight."***

- ☐ **Lead and direct a crew of ______** *[#]* [☐ carpenters | ☐ laborers] **involved in all aspects of** [☐ carpentry | ☐ construction] **including** [☐ reviewing project plans | ☐ reading and interpreting blueprints | ☐ estimating time | ☐ developing work schedules | ☐ assigning crews | ☐ delegating jobs | ☐ preparing work orders | ☐ ordering and setting up equipment | ☐ purchasing supplies | ☐ preparing job sites | ☐ performing rough and finish carpentry | ☐ inspecting work area | ☐ other: ______] **ensuring all jobs are completed in compliance with all specifications and building codes.**
- ☐ **Lead and supervise from ______** *[#]* **to ______** *[#]* **laborers in the construction and installation of** [☐ walls | ☐ doors | ☐ door jambs | ☐ roofs | ☐ floors | ☐ wall coverings | ☐ ceilings | ☐ paneling | ☐ plastic laminates | ☐ platforms | ☐ partitions | ☐ fences | ☐ ramps | ☐ insulation | ☐ weather stripping | ☐ other: ______] **for this ______** *[type of]* **firm.**
- ☐ **Oversee personnel management and job operations including** [☐ coordinating steel and concrete trades | ☐ scheduling laborers | ☐ managing construction | ☐ overseeing site materials and equipment set-up | ☐ other: ______].
- ☐ **Supervise and oversee laborers in all phases of construction projects including** [☐ pouring foundations | ☐ framing walls and partitions | ☐ installing sheetrock | ☐ building and installing (☐ stairs / ☐ windows / ☐ doors / ☐ brattices / ☐ roofing) | ☐ taping and spackling | ☐ painting | ☐ trim work | ☐ flooring | ☐ tiling | ☐ ceilings | ☐ cabinets | ☐ other: ______].
- ☐ **Provide construction support, feedback, and inspiration to a carpentry staff of ______** *[#]* ______ *[titles]* **in the development and coordination of major and minor ______** *[type of]* **projects.**
- ☐ **Oversee laborers in the set-up of prefabricated components including** [☐ frames | ☐ stairs | ☐ wall panels | ☐ other: ______] **to construct and build ______** *[what?]*.
- ☐ **Oversee the work of ______** *[#]* [☐ carpenters | ☐ laborers | ☐ contractors] **in the measuring, cutting, and fitting of wallboard panels to wood and metal framework, cutting holes in panels for** [☐ windows | ☐ doors | ☐ electrical outlets | ☐ air-conditioning units | ☐ plumbing | ☐ other: ______] and applying textured surfaces to [☐ walls | ☐ ceilings | ☐ floors | ☐ other: ______].
- ☐ **Supervise home** [☐ construction | ☐ improvement | ☐ renovation | ☐ additions | ☐ finished attics and basements | ☐ other: ______] **carpenters and other contractors for individual clients** [☐ on a consultant basis].
- ☐ **Oversee ______** *[#]* **laborers in fastening of drywall panels to framework of** [☐ residential houses | ☐ commercial buildings | ☐ other: ______]; **and prepare panels for painting by filling, taping, troweling, and finishing joints.**
- ☐ **Direct and oversee all** [☐ carpentry | ☐ plumbing | ☐ electrical | ☐ HVAC | ☐ welding | ☐ landscaping | ☐ other: ______] [☐ installation | ☐ replacement | ☐ maintenance | ☐ repair | ☐ other: ______] **work required in ______** *[type of]* **jobs for this $______** *[revenues]* ______ *[type of]* **firm.**
- ☐ **Monitor job progress through on-site field inspection and review to ensure conformance to** [☐ design specifications | ☐ cost estimates | ☐ time schedules | ☐ electrical codes | ☐ other: ______], **immediately resolving any problems.**

ACHIEVEMENT SAMPLES: *See Achievements under* ***"Staff Management & Supervision – General."***

Staff Management & Supervision – Office Support Staff

*See also **"Staff Management & Supervision – General."***

- ☐ **Manage and oversee the daily activities of an office support staff of______** *[#]* **including ______, ______, and ______** *[job titles]* **in the areas of** [☐ work scheduling | ☐ assignment delegating | ☐ administrative support | ☐ report generation | ☐ payroll processing | ☐ report generation | ☐ purchasing | ☐ contract administration | ☐ other: ______] **ensuring quality performance in all areas.**
- ☐ **Lead a team of ______** *[#]*______ *[titles]* **in the** [☐ development | ☐ implementation | ☐ sale | ☐ performance | ☐ other: ______] **of** [☐ high quality | ☐ cost-effective | ☐ other: ______] [☐ products | ☐ services | ☐ business solutions | ☐ other: ______] **that successfully ensure** [☐ quality standards are adhered to | ☐ compliance with all company guidelines | ☐ other: ______].
- ☐ **Prioritize work assignments and project tasks by** [☐ determining deadlines | ☐ analyzing scope and importance of work | ☐ strategizing best approach to meet commitments | ☐ other: ______].
- ☐ **Supervise a staff of ______** *[#]*______ *[what titles?]* **including accountability for their** [☐ customer service | ☐ client relations | ☐ sales support | ☐ other: ______], **ensuring prompt** [☐ sales | ☐ deliveries | ☐ order fulfillment | ☐ other: ______].
- ☐ **Supervise diversified office activities, including** [☐ correspondence | ☐ bookkeeping | ☐ billing | ☐ travel arrangements | ☐ insurance | ☐ dispatch | ☐ timekeeping | ☐ job inquiries | ☐ payroll reports | ☐ other: ______].
- ☐ **Manage an office-support staff of ______** *[#]*______ *[position titles]* **in the functions of** [☐ accounting | ☐ billing | ☐ filing | ☐ emailing | ☐ word processing | ☐ faxing | ☐ other: ______].
- ☐ **Oversee ______** *[#]* **first-line supervisors from ______** *[which?]* **departments, including the** [☐ administrative | ☐ secretarial | ☐ clerical | ☐ other: ______] **staff(s) that involves hiring and dismissing employees.**

ACHIEVEMENT SAMPLES: *See Achievements under **"Staff Management & Supervision – General."***

Staff Management & Supervision – Project Management Team

*See also **"Staff Management & Supervision – General."***

- ☐ **Guide a ______** *[job title]* **team of ______** *[#]* **to effectively** [☐ analyze project needs | ☐ establish strategy | ☐ determine project logistics | ☐ provide management consulting support | ☐ identify and mitigate risks | ☐ handle issue escalation and resolution | ☐ ensure quality deliverables | ☐ other: ______] **to meet client needs.**
- ☐ **Plan and coordinate all activities of** [☐ small- | ☐ medium- | ☐ large-] **scale ______** *[type of]* **projects for this ______** *[type of]* **firm with ______** *[#]* [☐ locations | ☐ employees | ☐ partners | ☐ other: ______] **that generates fiscal-year revenues of $______** *[amount].*
- ☐ **Provide leadership, vision, and direction to a ______** *[which?]* **team of ______** *[#]* **to initiate, plan, and implement ______** *[type of]* **projects ranging from $______ to $______ and resulting in** [☐ delivering bottom-line business value | ☐ business transformation | ☐ new product offerings | ☐ the translation of enterprise strategies into projects | ☐ increased productivity | ☐ other benefits: ______].
- ☐ **Lead the project team of ______** *[#]* **that defines, plans, and implements new ______** *[type of]* **projects; and oversee the development, execution, tracking, and reporting of those projects in support of the firm's business vision and objectives.**
- ☐ **Plan, schedule, and coordinate all ______** *[type of?]* [☐ projects | ☐ functions | ☐ activities | ☐ work] **by effectively prioritizing and delegating assignments and ensuring sufficient project manning to** [☐ meet client needs | ☐ perform required functions | ☐ facilitate job specifications | ☐ other: ______].
- ☐ **Lead the project team of ______** *[#]* **that defines, plans, and implements new ______** *[type of]* **projects; and oversee the development, execution, tracking, and reporting of those projects to support the business vision and objectives of the firm.**
- ☐ **Manage a(n) ______** *[which?]* **project team ensuring** [☐ the highest quality creative work | ☐ all projects stay on schedule and within budget | ☐ timely development and completion of all projects | ☐ quality standards | ☐ adherence to all objectives | ☐ other: ______].
- ☐ **Lead and direct a ______** *[type of]* **project implementation team of ______** *[#]* **in the development and execution of effective** [☐ marketing campaigns | ☐ Internet marketing programs | ☐ leads generation | ☐ market segmentation | ☐ website trafficking | ☐ data tracking methods | ☐ other: ______].
- ☐ **Provide strategic, comprehensive leadership to a ______** *[which?]* **team of ______** *[#]* **to initiate, and design complex ______** *[type of]* **projects ranging from $______ to $______** *[amounts]* **and resulting in resulting in** [☐ new product offerings | ☐ the translation of enterprise strategies into projects | ☐ delivering bottom-line business value | ☐ other benefits: ______].

☐ **Direct and oversee a project management of ______** *[#]*—**from design and coordination to implementation and delivery**—[☐ using standardized project management methodology | ☐ for multiple implementation projects | ☐ for projects that vary in scope and size | ☐ in support of firm's strategic visions | ☐ to support client objectives | ☐ in accordance with all project timelines and budget].

ACHIEVEMENT SAMPLES: *See Achievements under **"Staff Management & Supervision – General."***

Staff Recruitment

☐ **Interview, recruit,** [☐ schedule | ☐ train | ☐ develop] **a top-tier ______** *[type of]* **staff, selecting and assigning recruits based on their ability to ______** *[do what well?]* **and ensuring compliance with all Equal Employment Opportunity (EEO), affirmative action, Americans with Disabilities Act guidelines and laws, and the firm's human resources policies and procedures.**

☐ **Oversee all facets of staff hiring, training and development, scheduling and terminations for ______** *[#]* **employees.**

☐ **Run efficient ______** *[type of]* **business through** [☐ proper staffing and scheduling | ☐ improving staff morale and efficiency | ☐ ensuring quality work in all areas | ☐ other: ______].

☐ **Recruit, train, manage, and evaluate the performance of all ______** *[which?]* **staff, including ______, ______, and ______** *[job titles]*.

☐ **Investigate the backgrounds of potential employees by** [☐ researching applicant's resumes | ☐ interviewing references | ☐ other methods: ______] **resulting in** [☐ recruiting talented ______ (titles) employees | ☐ producing a high volume of quality work | ☐ other: ______].

☐ **Obtain ______** *[type of]* **qualitative background information from** [☐ educational | ☐ employment | ☐ military | ☐ other: ______] **references and sources to make informed hiring decisions.**

☐ **Hire, direct, train, and evaluate a supervisory staff of ______** *[#]* **and oversee a production team of ______** *[#]* **including** [☐ planning | ☐ scheduling | ☐ performance appraisals | ☐ employee incentives | ☐ disciplinary actions | ☐ problem resolution | ☐ other: ______].

☐ **Maintain employee records with** [☐ dates of hire | ☐ compensation | ☐ benefits | ☐ leave records | ☐ other: ______] **and other pertinent personnel data, and prepare and file employer reports to** [☐ government agencies | ☐ insurance companies | ☐ union | ☐ other: ______].

☐ **Direct field and office project management** [☐ recruiting | ☐ training and development | ☐ performance evaluations | ☐ compensation reviews | ☐ payroll administration | ☐ other: ______].

☐ **Recruit and hire the most qualified** [☐ laborers | ☐ professional staff | ☐ management team | ☐ other: ______] **to meet the firm's needs and develop trained** [☐ personnel | ☐ workers | ☐ staff] **by ______** *[methods used]*.

Team Leadership & Direction – Project Management Team

*See also **"Team Leadership & Direction – Project Management Team (General)"** and **"Team Leadership & Direction – Project Management Team (Engineering & Construction)."***

☐ **Direct and monitor the** [☐ architectural | ☐ engineering | ☐ other: ______] **project management team(s) in** [☐ support of (☐ major / ☐ complex / ☐ high-dollar / ☐ other: ______) projects and sound architectural standards | ☐ all related aspects of engineering applications for the (☐ design and) construction of ______ *(what?)* | ☐ the preparation of (☐ master plans / ☐ architectural renderings / ☐ cost estimates / ☐ specifications / ☐ construction drawings / ☐ other: ______].

☐ **Oversee ______** *[#]* [☐ Construction Project Managers | ☐ Project Engineers | ☐ Project Architects | ☐ others: ______] **in their daily functions including** [☐ review and/or modification of construction drawings | ☐ job estimates and proposals | ☐ securing competitive bids | ☐ contract negotiations | ☐ trades hiring, coordinating, and scheduling | ☐ permit obtainment | ☐ on-site supervision | ☐ maintaining direct client relationships | ☐ materials purchasing | ☐ expense monitoring and approval | ☐ change orders negotiations and processing | ☐ other: ______] **ensuring the completion of all projects on time, within budget, and at the clients' satisfaction.**

☐ **Provide proactive leadership, vision, and direction to a project management team of ______** *[#]* **______** *[titles]* **in the initiation, planning, design, and construction of ______** *[type of]* **projects ranging from $______ to $______** *[amounts]* **and resulting in** [☐ delivering bottom-line business value | ☐ business transformation | ☐ new product offerings | ☐ the translation of enterprise strategies into projects | ☐ increased productivity | ☐ other benefits: ______].

☐ **Direct and lead ______** *[#]* [☐ Engineers | ☐ Architects | ☐ Project Managers | ☐ other: ______] **in all project management phases—from concept development through the operational evaluation phases of ______** *[what?]* **considering** [☐ costs | ☐ resource requirements | ☐ scheduling | ☐ technical requirements | ☐ other: ______].

☐ **Lead a project team of ______** *[#]* [☐ Engineers | ☐ Architects | ☐ Project Managers | ☐ other: ______] **in the design and construction of high quality, cost-effective ______** *[type of]* **solutions that successfully address** [☐ the firm's | ☐ clients'] **requirements by** [☐ establishing clear guidelines | ☐ offering feedback on completed projects | ☐ providing methods to increase productivity | ☐ other: ______].

☐ **Provide leadership and direction to ______** *[which?]* **project staff in** [☐ project planning and coordination | ☐ determining costs | ☐ performing feasibility studies and estimates | ☐ developing specifications | ☐ preparing bills of materials | ☐ negotiating contracts | ☐ identifying resources | ☐ identifying materials | ☐ recordkeeping | ☐ other: ______] **to ensure timely and efficient completion of** ______ *[type of]* [☐ construction | ☐ renovation | ☐ remodel | ☐ extensions | ☐ ground improvement | ☐ other: ______] **projects.**

☐ **Supervise and support the work of ______** *[#]* [☐ Project Architects | ☐ Project Engineers | ☐ Project Managers | ☐ Foremen | ☐ Drafters | ☐ others: ______] **in the** [☐ design and build | ☐ management] **of ______** *[type of]* **projects and the preparation of** [☐ master plans | ☐ architectural renderings | ☐ cost estimates | ☐ specifications | ☐ construction drawings | ☐ other: ______].

☐ **Lead by example a project management staff of ______** *[#]* **in the** [☐ delegation of assignments | ☐ monitoring of work performance | ☐ development of performance evaluations | ☐ performance improvement coaching | ☐ other methods: ______].

☐ **Oversee and direct the daily activities of the project team** [☐ and contract staff] **including** [☐ assignment delegating | ☐ purchasing | ☐ payroll processing | ☐ administrative support | ☐ report generation | ☐ contract administration | ☐ other: ______] **ensuring quality performance in the successful completion of all projects.**

☐ **Provide** [☐ engineering | ☐ construction | ☐ other:______ **project team leadership and support in the development and coordination of major and minor projects in the areas of ______, ______, and ______** *[which areas?]*.

ACHIEVEMENT SAMPLES: *See "Staff Management & Supervision Achievement Samples."*

Testing & Inspections – Trades

See "Inspections & Compliance" and "Equipment, Tools & Testing Devices."

Tools & Testing Devices

See "Equipment, Tools & Testing Devices" (various categories).

Trades Coordination & Oversight

See also "Trades/Crew Supervision – All Trades," "Work Collaboration," "Contractor/Subcontractor Influence & Collaboration," "Inspections & Compliance – Trades," and "Job Preparation," as applicable.

☐ **Provide decisive leadership and clear direction in all phases of** [☐ large-scale | ☐ complex] **______** *[type of]* **projects for** [☐ commercial | ☐ residential | ☐ industrial | ☐ other: ______] **clients overseeing a top-performing team of ______** *[#]* ______ *[title(s)]*.

☐ **Coordinate and oversee trades including** [☐ demolition | ☐ framing | ☐ carpentry | ☐ electrical | ☐ plumbing | ☐ HVAC | ☐ roofing | ☐ insulation | ☐ sheetrock | ☐ tape and spackle | ☐ painting | ☐ tiling | ☐ flooring | ☐ ceilings | ☐ interior design | ☐ landscaping | ☐ masonry | ☐ other: ______] **in the** [☐ design and] **construction of ______** *[what?]*.

☐ **Provide a full array of** [☐ plumbing | ☐ HVAC | ☐ refrigeration | ☐ steamfitting | ☐ welding | ☐ carpentry | ☐ other: ______] **installation, maintenance, and repair services including** [(☐ plumbing / ☐ electrical / ☐ general contracting) work | (☐ bathroom / ☐ kitchen / ☐ tile) installations | ☐ other: ______] **for this** [☐ local] [☐ plumbing | ☐ general contracting | ☐ construction | ☐ other: ______] **firm.**

☐ **Exercise supervision over all trades including** [☐ Carpenters | ☐ Framers | ☐ Insulation Workers | ☐ Sheetrock Installers | ☐ Painters | ☐ Roofers | ☐ Electricians | ☐ Plumbers | ☐ HVAC Specialists | ☐ Carpet and Floor Installers | ☐ Tile Installers | ☐ Ceiling Installers | ☐ Space Planners | ☐ Interior Designers | ☐ Interior Decorators | ☐ Cabinet Makers | ☐ Landscape Technicians | ☐ Masons | ☐ Glaziers | ☐ other: ______].

☐ **Oversee** [☐ apprentice- | ☐ journeyman-] **level ______** *[type of]* **work related to the installation and/or repair of** [☐ air conditioning systems | ☐ boilers | ☐ refrigeration | ☐ hot and cold air ducts | ☐ heat exchangers | ☐ other: ______] **ensuring compliance with all codes.**

☐ **Coordinate, schedule, and supervise all trades including** [☐ demolition | ☐ concrete | ☐ welding | ☐ masonry | ☐ other: ______] **on ______** *[type of]* **projects.**

☐ **Ensure all jobs are completed in compliance with building codes, zoning laws, fire regulations, and ordinances by** [☐ proactively monitoring work performance | ☐ ensuring effective quality control | ☐ other methods: ______].

- ☐ **Supervise and inspect work performed by technicians and** [☐ contractors | ☐ subcontractors | ☐ contract service providers] **ensuring** [☐ safe working conditions | ☐ high quality | ☐ work completed properly and timely | ☐ compliance with all codes, OSHA, EPA, ADA, and MSDS | ☐ other: ______].
- ☐ **Obtain permits, estimate jobs, and hire and schedule trades acting as liaison with** [☐ building managers | ☐ client reps | ☐ inspectors | ☐ union delegates | ☐ architects | ☐ engineers | ☐ contractors | ☐ others: ______].
- ☐ **Coordinate, schedule, and supervise** ______ *[type of]* **projects including** [☐ building construction | ☐ asbestos abatement | ☐ roofing repairs | ☐ other: ______] **with sensitivity to client deadlines and project requirements, assigning projects based on staff's unique skills.**
- ☐ **Manage and oversee the work of** [☐ technical | ☐ construction | ☐ other: ______] [☐ contractors | ☐ subcontractors | ☐ staff] **involved in project activities including** ______, ______, **and** ______ *[which functions?].*
- ☐ **Work with** ______ *[which?]* **trades to coordinate the** [☐ design | ☐ construction | ☐ installation | ☐ repair | ☐ other: ______] **of** ______ *[what projects?]* **for** ______ *[whom or what?].*
- ☐ [☐ Oversee | ☐ Assist] [☐ HVAC | ☐ plumbing | ☐ electrical | ☐ maintenance | ☐ carpentry | ☐ crafts | ☐ other: ______] **staff(s) in performing the** [☐ construction | ☐ assembly | ☐ installation | ☐ repair | ☐ maintenance | ☐ monitoring | ☐ testing | ☐ upkeep | ☐ other: ______] **of** ______ *[what?].*
- ☐ **Coordinate various aspects of projects with** [☐ subcontractors | ☐ general contractors | ☐ architects | ☐ municipal officials | ☐ code officials | ☐ others: ______] **in the** ______ *[what phases of construction?].*
- ☐ **Oversee all** [☐ plumbing | ☐ HVAC | ☐ refrigeration | ☐ steamfitting | ☐ welding | ☐ carpentry | ☐ landscaping | ☐ masonry | ☐ painting | ☐ other: ______] **functions for this** [☐ general contracting | ☐ construction | ☐ other: ______] **firm.**
- ☐ **Supervise all** ______ *[type of]* **trade activities required in the installation, maintenance, and/or repair of** ______ *[what?]* **including** ______, ______, **and** ______ *[which functions?].*
- ☐ **Manage and oversee the building of** ______ *[type of]* **structures with precision and uniformity by** ______ *[doing what?]* **depending on job complexity and blueprint specifications.**
- ☐ **Working closely with related trades to create** ______ *[type of]* **structures to ensure** ______ *[what?].*
- ☐ **Oversee the planning, design, and** [☐ construction | ☐ installation | ☐ repair | ☐ other: ______] **of** ______ *[what?]* **including** ______, ______, **and** ______ *[which functions?]* **taking into account** ______ *[which?]* **conditions.**
- ☐ **Direct and oversee the completion of** ______ *[type of]* **services for** [☐ residential | ☐ commercial | ☐ industrial | ☐ other: ______] **clients for** ______ *[type of]* **projects.**
- ☐ **Review client contracts to determine required** ______ *[type of]* **services, equipment, methods, materials, and labor and make project determinations based on** ______ *[what?].*

ACHIEVEMENT SAMPLES:

- ☐ **Built a strong, supportive contractor / subcontractor team environment by exhibiting and modeling leadership skills in** [☐ communication | ☐ negotiation | ☐ problem-solving | ☐ obstacle tackling | ☐ other: ______].
- ☐ **Serving on a team of** ______ *[#]* **laborers, performed all** ______ *[type of]* **project** [☐ construction | ☐ remodels | ☐ repairs | ☐ other: ______] **to a successful completion in support of the** [☐ firm's | ☐ clients' | ☐ firm and clients'] **objectives and requirements.**
- ☐ **Influenced** [☐ contractors | ☐ subcontractors | ☐ vendors | ☐ others: ______] **to develop and maintain positive working relationships with all levels of** [☐ internal | ☐ external] **management by** ______ *[doing what well?].*

Trades / Crew Supervision – All Trades

*See also **"Inspections & Compliance – Trades Work" "Contractor / Subcontractor Influence & Collaboration," "Staff Management & Supervision," "Team Leadership & Direction," "Trades Coordination & Oversight,"** and **"Work Collaboration,"** as applicable.*

- ☐ **Supervise the day-to-day activities of** ______ *[#]* **laborers on** ______ *[type of]* **jobs ensuring quality control in all activities and that all work is performed according to job specs and code.**
- ☐ **Lead and oversee a team of** ______ *[#]* **laborers in the** [☐ installation | ☐ construction | ☐ maintenance | ☐ other: ______] **of** ______ *[what?]* **projects ranging from $**______ **to $**______ *[amounts]* **and resulting in** ______ *[what outcome?].*
- ☐ **Coordinate, lead, and train** ______ *[type of]* **crew(s) to complete** ______ *[type of]* [☐ commercial | ☐ industrial | ☐ residential | ☐ other: ______] **projects within established guidelines, timeframes, and budget with an emphasis on** [☐ quality | ☐ safety | ☐ attention to detail | ☐ regulatory compliance | ☐ other: ______].

☐ **Supervise and coordinate the activities of a crew of** ______ *[#]* **skilled** [☐ Plumbers | ☐ Electricians | ☐ HVAC Technicians | ☐ Carpenters | ☐ others: ______] [☐ in the design and installation of ______ *(what?)* | ☐ and oversee the complete upkeep of ______ *(what?)*] **for this** ______ *[type of]* **firm with** ______ *[#]* **clients** [☐ to maximize property potential].

☐ **Oversee an average of** ______ *[#]* **laborers on** ______ *[type of]* **jobs to ensure all work is performed according to job specs and code, on time and within budgets.**

☐ **Lead and direct a crew of** ______ *[#]*______ *[titles]* **involved in all aspects of** ______ *[which trade?]* **including** [☐ reviewing project plans | ☐ reading and interpreting blueprints | ☐ estimating time | ☐ developing work schedules | ☐ assigning crews | ☐ delegating jobs | ☐ preparing work orders | ☐ ordering and setting up equipment | ☐ purchasing supplies | ☐ preparing job sites | ☐ inspecting work area | ☐ other: ______] **ensuring all jobs are completed in compliance with specifications and codes.**

☐ **Provide decisive leadership and clear direction in all phases of** [☐ large-scale | ☐ complex] ______ *[type of]* **projects for** [☐ commercial | ☐ residential | ☐ industrial | ☐ other: ______] **clients overseeing a top-performing team of** ______ *[#]* ______ *[titles].*

☐ **Manage the daily activities of a team of** ______ *[#]*______ *[titles]* **coordinating all job functions for** [☐ commercial | ☐ residential | ☐ public | ☐ other: ______] **accounts including** ______ *[type of projects]* **ensuring all work is completed according to plans, specifications, and schedules.**

☐ **Schedule, coordinate, and supervise the daily operations and all** ______ *[which trade?]* **activities of a crew of** ______ *[#]* **including** ______, ______, **and** ______ *[what functions?]* **to ensure quality workmanship and compliance with all codes.**

☐ **Successfully lead a** ______ *[which?]* [☐ crew | ☐ project team] **of** ______ *[#]* **in the completion of** ______ *[type of]* **projects enforcing compliance with all safety, fire, and other regulations and ensuring** [☐ the highest quality work | ☐ fulfillment of all expected deliverables | ☐ timely completion of all work | ☐ quality standards are adhered to | ☐ measurable member participation and progress | ☐ all jobs are performed to code | ☐ other: ______].

☐ **Manage and oversee the day-to-day activities of a team of** ______ *[#]* **skilled** ______ *[titles]* **in the design and installation of** ______ *[what?]* **including** [☐ hiring, training, scheduling, and evaluating crew | ☐ supervising and coordinating daily crew operations and work functions | ☐ other: ______], **ensuring quality control in all activities.**

☐ **Direct and oversee all** [☐ carpentry | ☐ plumbing | ☐ electrical | ☐ HVAC-R | ☐ welding | ☐ landscaping | ☐ other: ______] [☐ installation | ☐ replacement | ☐ maintenance | ☐ repair | ☐ other: ______] **work required in** ______ *[type of]* **jobs.**

☐ **Coordinate, schedule, and supervise trades for** ______ *[type of]* **projects including** [☐ building construction | ☐ asbestos abatement | ☐ roofing repairs | ☐ other: ______] **with sensitivity to client deadlines and project requirements, assigning projects based on staff's unique skills.**

☐ **Manage a** ______ *[which trade?]* **team of** ______ *[#]* **including hiring, training, scheduling, and evaluating crew; and supervising and coordinating daily crew operations and work functions for this** ______ *[type of]* **firm.**

☐ **Schedule and supervise the daily activities of a team of** ______ *[#]*______ *[titles]* **coordinating all functions for** [☐ commercial | ☐ residential | ☐ public | ☐ other: ______] **accounts including** ______, ______, **and** ______ *[what functions?]* **ensuring all work is completed according to plans, specifications, codes, and schedules.**

☐ **Oversee and supervise a staff of** ______ *[#]*______ *[type of]* **technicians in their various functions including accountability for their** [☐ client relations | ☐ workmanship | ☐ other: ______] **and enforcing all codes.**

☐ **Provide** [☐ architectural | ☐ engineering | ☐ construction | ☐ other: ______] **support and inspiration to a staff of** ______ *[#]*______ [titles] **in the development and coordination of major and minor projects in the areas of** ______, ______, **and** ______ *[which areas?].*

☐ **Provide support and feedback to** ______ *[whom?]* **regarding** [☐ maintenance | ☐ structural | ☐ renovation | ☐ mechanical | ☐ environmental | ☐ other: ______] **issues at the site.**

Trades / Crew Supervision – Carpentry & Construction

- ☐ **Coordinate, schedule, and supervise** ______ *[type of]* **projects including** [☐ building construction | ☐ asbestos abatement | ☐ roofing repairs | ☐ other: ______] **with sensitivity to client deadlines and project requirements, assigning projects based on staff's unique skills.**
- ☐ **Lead and direct a crew of** ______ *[#]* [☐ carpenters | ☐ laborers] **involved in all aspects of** [☐ carpentry | ☐ construction] **including** [☐ reviewing project plans | ☐ reading and interpreting blueprints | ☐ estimating time | ☐ developing work schedules | ☐ assigning crews | ☐ delegating jobs | ☐ preparing work orders | ☐ ordering and setting up equipment | ☐ purchasing supplies | ☐ preparing job sites | ☐ performing rough and finish carpentry | ☐ inspecting work area | ☐ other: ______] **ensuring all jobs are completed in compliance with all specifications and building codes.**
- ☐ **Oversee personnel management and job operations including** [☐ coordinating steel and concrete trades | ☐ scheduling laborers | ☐ managing construction | ☐ overseeing site materials and equipment set-up | ☐ other: ______].
- ☐ **Lead and supervise from** ______ *[#]* **to** ______ *[#]* **laborers in the construction and installation of** [☐ walls | ☐ doors | ☐ door jambs | ☐ roofs | ☐ floors | ☐ wall coverings | ☐ ceilings | ☐ paneling | ☐ plastic laminates | ☐ platforms | ☐ partitions | ☐ fences | ☐ ramps | ☐ insulation | ☐ weather stripping | ☐ other: ______] **for this** ______ *[type of]* **firm.**
- ☐ **Provide construction support, feedback, and inspiration to a carpentry staff of** ______ *[#]*______ *[titles]* **in the development and coordination of major and minor** ______ *[type of]* **projects.**
- ☐ **Supervise and oversee laborers in all phases of construction projects including** [☐ pouring foundations | ☐ framing walls and partitions | ☐ installing sheetrock | ☐ building and installing (☐ stairs / ☐ windows / ☐ doors / ☐ brattices / ☐ roofing) | ☐ taping and spackling | ☐ painting | ☐ trim work | ☐ flooring | ☐ tiling | ☐ ceilings | ☐ cabinets | ☐ other: ______].
- ☐ **Oversee laborers in the set-up of prefabricated components including** [☐ frames | ☐ stairs | ☐ wall panels | ☐ other: ______] **to construct and build** ______ *[what?]*.
- ☐ **Oversee the work of** ______ *[#]* [☐ carpenters | ☐ laborers | ☐ contractors] **in the measuring, cutting, and fitting of wallboard panels to wood and metal framework, cutting holes in panels for** [☐ windows | ☐ doors | ☐ electrical outlets | ☐ air-conditioning units | ☐ plumbing | ☐ other: ______] and applying textured surfaces to [☐ walls | ☐ ceilings | ☐ floors | ☐ other: ______].
- ☐ **Supervise home** [☐ construction | ☐ improvement | ☐ renovation | ☐ additions | ☐ finished attics and basements | ☐ other: ______] **carpenters and other contractors for individual clients** [☐ on a consultant basis].
- ☐ **Oversee** ______ *[#]* **laborers in fastening of drywall panels to framework of** [☐ residential houses | ☐ commercial buildings | ☐ other: ______]; **and prepare panels for painting by filling, taping, troweling, and finishing joints.**
- ☐ **Direct and oversee all** [☐ carpentry | ☐ plumbing | ☐ electrical | ☐ HVAC | ☐ welding | ☐ landscaping | ☐ other: ______] [☐ installation | ☐ replacement | ☐ maintenance | ☐ repair | ☐ other: ______] **work required in** ______ *[type of]* **jobs for this $**______ *[revenues]* ______ *[type of]* **firm.**
- ☐ **Monitor job progress through on-site field inspection and review to ensure conformance to** [☐ design specifications | ☐ cost estimates | ☐ time schedules | ☐ electrical codes | ☐ other: ______], **immediately resolving any problems.**

Turnaround Times

ACHIEVEMENT SAMPLES:

- ☐ **Decreased a** ______ *[#]*-**week delivery delay to a** ______ *[#]*-**day waiting period by** [☐ negotiating with suppliers allowing for job to finish on time and under budget | ☐ other method(s): ______].
- ☐ **Completed** ______ *[name of]* **project in record time and ahead of schedule; achieved by** [☐ getting the most productivity out of laborers | ☐ organizing and planning daily workloads | ☐ other: ______] **resulting in** [☐ company being awarded state bonuses | ☐ other achievement: ______].
- ☐ **Complete all projects on time and within budget and at the client reps' and company's satisfaction by** ______ *[doing what well?]*.
- ☐ **Assigned to take over** ______ *[type of project]* **to smooth out conflicts; handled through firm negotiations and teamwork with client rep and all trades to put project back on track, successfully completing it on schedule and within budget.**

Union Functions

*See also "**Grievance Investigations,**" "**Union Leadership,**" and "**Compliance**" categories.*

☐ **Thoroughly investigate all employee complaints and disputes to determine if a violation of employee rights occurred by reviewing the circumstances and facts and researching** [☐ the Collective Agreement | ☐ Federal law | ☐ Workers Compensation Board regulations | ☐ Company safety policies and rules and regulations | ☐ established past practices | ☐ other: ______].

☐ **Make work site visits to monitor and enforce ______** *[which?]* **collective bargaining agreement provisions ensuring the firm and union workers are in compliance with all contractual terms such as ______, ______, and ______** *[what?].*

☐ **As the ______** *[which?]* **Union's primary advisor on** [☐ employee engagement | ☐ pro-employer campaigns | (☐ national | ☐ local) labor relations | ☐ other: ______], [☐ formulate and recommend program goals | ☐ participate in contract negotiations | ☐ administer labor agreements | ☐ implement grievance procedures | ☐ other: ______].

☐ **Apply expertise in** [☐ organizing | ☐ bargaining | ☐ representation | ☐ arbitration | ☐ coalition building | ☐ contract enforcement | ☐ grievance handling | ☐ political activity | ☐ analyzing and interpreting complex contract language | ☐ creating innovative problem-solving ideas | ☐ developing strategically sound contract campaigns | ☐ servicing large bargaining units | ☐ building effective union power and worker leadership | ☐ upholding union standards | ☐ other: ______] **in the development, negotiation, and/or ratification of contracts.**

☐ **Effectively negotiate with management on employee** [☐ hours | ☐ wages | ☐ benefits | ☐ grievances | ☐ other: ______] **and other work-related matters by ______** [doing what?].

☐ **Support administration of all** [☐ contract settlements | ☐ release agreements | ☐ Memorandum Agreements (MOA) | ☐ Side Letter Agreements (SLA) | ☐ other: ______] **between the company and Union including** [☐ negotiations with stakeholders | ☐ cost determinations | ☐ case-specific language | ☐ other: ______].

☐ **Studied and ensured familiarization with all** [☐ union policies and activities | ☐ jobs | ☐ rates of pay | ☐ member seniority | ☐ company rules | ☐ health and safety policy | ☐ departmental operations | ☐ other: ______] **in order to better represent members.**

☐ **Working in the spirit of cooperation and teamwork, ensure Collective Agreements include the rights and responsibilities of both employees and management including** [☐ work hours | ☐ overtime | ☐ wages | ☐ benefits | ☐ vacations | ☐ holidays | ☐ working conditions | ☐ seniority provisions | ☐ job security provisions | ☐ other: ______] **by presenting the facts and using effective listening and bargaining skills.**

☐ **Educate new Union Members on the Union and its role as well as** [☐ the collective agreement | ☐ ______ *(type of)* programs | ☐ the importance of the labor movement | ☐ attending rallies and sponsored events | ☐ assistance resources | ☐ counseling organizations | ☐ other: ______] **so they have an understanding about their rights and responsibilities, health and safety issues, and other workplace matters.**

☐ **As Union Representative,** [☐ enforce the union contract | ☐ ensure changes do not violate contract terms and conditions | ☐ orient new employees | ☐ identify and train new union activists | ☐ discuss members concerns | ☐ accompany employees to (☐ disciplinary | ☐ grievance | ☐ arbitration | ☐ administrative | ☐ formal dispute resolution) meetings and hearings | ☐ represent members in collective bargaining negotiations | ☐ meet with employer to find best possible solutions to workplace issues | ☐ develop health and safety procedures | ☐ develop campaign materials | ☐ hold training sessions | ☐ organize membership rallies | ☐ participate in organizing demonstrations | ☐ other: ______].

☐ **Interact with company management on behalf of union members and engage in collective bargaining regarding employee** [☐ hours | ☐ wages | ☐ grievances | ☐ other: ______] **and other work-related matters resulting in ______** *[benefits].*

☐ **As Organizer, handle various functions including** [☐ signing up members to ensure their job security, fair pay, and equal treatment | ☐ initiating contact with any employees dissatisfied with working conditions | ☐ scheduling union membership benefits meetings | ☐ providing employee opportunities to be active union leaders | ☐ other: ______].

☐ **As Contract Negotiator,** [☐ engage in collective bargaining on behalf of union members, working to achieve good wages and benefits that the entire employee base can live with | ☐ meet at the bargaining table with management and present what they believe are the best options for working conditions | ☐ to act in the best interest of the collective body | ☐ address ongoing work issues during collective bargaining season | ☐ other: ______].

☐ **Represent all workers fairly, completely, and free from bias and ensure compliance with the National Labor Relations Act by ______** *[doing what?].*

ACHIEVEMENT SAMPLES: *See Achievements under "**Union Leadership.**"*

Union Leadership

See also "Grievance Investigations," "Union Functions," and "Compliance" categories.

- ☐ **Manage and oversee all labor relations matters including** [☐ strategy | ☐ negotiations | ☐ interpretation | ☐ grievances | ☐ direction and advice | ☐ union relationship(s) | ☐ other: ______] **for this** ______ *[which?]* **Union representing** ______ *[#]* **employees in** ______ *[#]* **units throughout the state of** ______ *[state].*
- ☐ **Direct and coordinate the** ______ *[which?]* **labor organization functions including** [☐ promoting local membership | ☐ placing union members on jobs | ☐ maintaining labor organization and employer relations | ☐ developing safety and health measures | ☐ arranging local meetings | ☐ visiting work sites to ensure adherence to contractual specifications and labor codes | ☐ engaging in collective bargaining | ☐ acting as employee advocate | ☐ planning and implementing organizing campaigns | ☐ maintaining relations between union and employer's press representatives | ☐ other: ______].
- ☐ **Manage the business affairs of the** ______ *[which?]* **labor union including the coordination and direction of** [☐ local membership | ☐ job placement | ☐ work site visits | ☐ other: ______] **as well as strategic negotiations and the implementation of employee relations, employee engagement programs, and labor relations.**
- ☐ **Conduct** [☐ benefits orientations | ☐ job safety workshops | ☐ ______ *(type of)* meetings | ☐ other: ______] **that cover** [☐ rights and responsibilities | ☐ health and safety issues | ☐ workplace issues | ☐ other: ______] **and ensure compliance with OSHA standards.**
- ☐ **Act as** [☐ liaison between | ☐ subject matter expert to] **department managers, Union Representatives, and employees by** [☐ providing personnel policies and employment laws advice | ☐ responding to inquiries relating to ______ *(what?)* | ☐ interpreting labor agreements | ☐ participating in contract negotiations | ☐ providing labor relations support during negotiations | ☐ other: ______].
- ☐ **Play a leading role in union meetings and act as a conduit of information between workers and** [☐ the firm | ☐ management | ☐ union leadership] **by** ______ *[doing what?].*
- ☐ **Work with the firm's Human Resource Department to ensure all employee job descriptions are legally compliant in the areas of** [☐ job titles | ☐ job functions and responsibilities | ☐ education and experience required to perform jobs | ☐ reasoning abilities | ☐ physical demands | ☐ work environment | ☐ other: ______] **and other requirements for each job description**.
- ☐ **Interact with company representatives, assist local Union Stewards, and liaise with the National Labor Relations Board on matters concerning** ______ *[what?].*
- ☐ **Perform various union leadership functions including** [(☐ formulating | ☐ recommending) program goals and objectives | ☐ conducting risk assessments | ☐ creating risk mitigation solutions | ☐ monitoring program costs | ☐ conducting investigations and evaluating information | ☐ making policy change recommendations to the Human Resources Vice President | ☐ executing grievance procedures | ☐ researching and evaluating grievances and identifying effective solutions | ☐ reviewing liability reports | ☐ increasing employee engagement | ☐ act as Chief Spokesperson | ☐ developing budget and expense proposals | ☐ serving as Union Representative during arbitration hearings | ☐ other: ______].

ACHIEVEMENT SAMPLES:

- ☐ **Negotiated fair and equitable** ______ *[type of]* **contracts through** [☐ effective listening and understanding to both sides | ☐ thorough research and preparation | ☐ exhibiting honesty | ☐ providing information | ☐ other: ______], **resulting in** [☐ increased productivity for management | ☐ fair wages and benefits for employees | ☐ other: ______].
- ☐ **Significantly decreased arbitrations by** ______**%** *[percentage]* **by** [☐ setting up union/management meetings | ☐ resolving ______ *(type of)* problems | ☐ other: ______] **resulting in a cost savings of $**______ *[amount]..*
- ☐ **Build a united and involved membership in the workplace by** [☐ organizing the workplace | ☐ compiling research | ☐ handling grievances | ☐ solving problems | ☐ working out agreeable contracts | ☐ mitigating circumstances | ☐ negotiating with and providing solutions to management | ☐ educating workers on health and safety regulations and labor laws | ☐ other: ______] **for this** ______ *[type of company].*
- ☐ **Ratified** ______**%** *[percentage]* **of all** ______ *[type of]* **contracts without having a strike by** ______ *[doing what?].*
- ☐ **Established effective shop steward meetings that** [☐ better informed membership of ______ *(what?)* | ☐ resolved ______ *(type of)* potential problems before they became serious | ☐ helped ensure compliance with OSHA standards | ☐ other: ______], **which benefited by way of** ______ *[what results?].*
- ☐ **Selected out of** ______ *[#]* **union members to oversee regulatory compliance on all** ______ *[type of]* **projects in** ______ *[#]* [☐ counties | ☐ boroughs | ☐ regions | ☐ states | ☐ countries | ☐ other: ______].
- ☐ **Contributed to the strength of the Union by recruiting** ______ *[#]* **new Union members and growing its size from** ______ *[#]* **to** ______ *[#]* **by successfully** ______ *[doing what?].*

☐ **Reviewed and evaluated** ______ *[type of]* **documents in order to enhance union member job performance and workplace environment by** ______ *[doing what?]* **and ensured overall consistency, accuracy, and fairness by way of** ______ *[what measures?].*

☐ **Serviced over** ______ [#] **members, including** ______ [which?] **staffs, to investigate and resolve grievances in** ______ [which] [☐ public | ☐ private] **sector(s).**

☐ **Supported the** [☐ Human Resources Vice President | ☐ Union Officer | ☐ Labor Relations Director | ☐ other: ______] **in a major** ______ *[type of]* [☐ project | ☐ initiative] **that** ______ *[did what?],* **which ultimately benefited the firm and its employees by** ______ *[how?].*

☐ **While inspecting the worksite for health or safety issues, found and documented** ______ *[type of]* [☐ health | ☐ safety | ☐ other: ______] **OSHA (Occupational Safety and Health Administration) violations, resulting in** ______ *[what?].*

☐ **Established excellent communication networks throughout all organizational levels by** ______ [doing what well?].

☐ [☐ Developed and mentored | ☐ Motivated and empowered] ______ *[title of]* **leaders to act collectively and strategically in the** [☐ protection of their rights | ☐ improvement of the quality of union members' work lives | ☐ fight of unfairness | ☐ other: ______] **by** ______ *[doing what well?].*

☐ **Contributed to the** ______ *[which?]* **internal and external communications strategy and material by** ______ *[doing what?].*

☐ [☐ Developed and implemented | ☐ Assisted in developing] [☐ plant production | ☐ safety health | ☐ other: ______] **measures that** ______ *[did what?]* **and resulted in** ______ *[what benefits?].*

☐ **Formulated and delivered** ______ *[type of]* [☐ short-term | ☐ long-term] [☐ organizing plans | ☐ member development goals | ☐ capacity-building objectives | ☐ other: ______] **that** ______ *[did what?].*

☐ **Elected by union members as the** ______ *[which?]* **Union's Trade Union Representative and applied the National Occupational Standards for Trade Union Reps in the performance of** ______ *[what?].*

Vendor Bids & Proposals

*See "**Bids & Proposals.**"*

Welding / Steamfitting – General

*See also "**Welding / Steamfitting – Functions & Projects**" "**Trades / Crew Supervision – All Trades,**" "**Inspections & Compliance – Welding / Steamfitting,**" and "**Contractor / Subcontractor Influence & Collaboration.**"*

☐ **Provide decisive leadership and clear direction in all phases of** [☐ large-scale | ☐ complex] ______ *[type of]* **projects for** [☐ commercial | ☐ residential | ☐ industrial | ☐ other: ______] **clients overseeing a top-performing team of** ______ *[#]* [☐ welders | ☐ steamfitters | ☐ other: ______].

☐ **Handle various types of** [☐ welding | ☐ joint welding | ☐ steamfitting | ☐ soldering | ☐ arc welding | ☐ torch cutting | ☐ other: ______] **projects for this** ______ *[type of]* **firm including** [☐ industrial welding | ☐ industrial pipefitting | ☐ industrial plumbing | ☐ domestic water systems | ☐ sprinkler systems | ☐ HVAC piping | ☐ compressed air systems | ☐ fire sprinklers | ☐ truck bed body work | ☐ other: ______].

☐ **Perform** ______ *[#]* **welding projects** [☐ daily | ☐ weekly | ☐ monthly] **for this** [☐ industrial | ☐ mechanical | ☐ manufacturing | ☐ residential | ☐ commercial | ☐ public | ☐ other: ______] ______ *[type of]* **company**.

☐ **Handle approximately** ______ *[#]* **welding jobs** [☐ daily | ☐ weekly | ☐ monthly | ☐ annually] [☐ averaging $______ to $______ *(amounts)* | ☐ totaling $______ *(amount)*] **including** [☐ estimating job times, materials, and costs | ☐ selecting materials and hardware | ☐ preparing materials estimates | ☐ reviewing bids | ☐ ordering required job-related materials | scheduling jobs | ☐ inspecting completed jobs for quality and code compliance | ☐ other: ______].

☐ **Supervise the installation, servicing, and maintenance of new and existing domestic** [☐ water systems | ☐ sanitary piping | ☐ HVAC piping and equipment | ☐ other: ______].

☐ **Oversee** [☐ welding | ☐ arc welding | ☐ joint welding | ☐ soldering | ☐ steamfitting | ☐ torch cutting | ☐ industrial welding | ☐ other: ______] **trades in their installation of new and repair of existing domestic** [☐ water | ☐ steam | ☐ sanitary | ☐ HVAC | ☐ electrical | ☐ hydraulic | ☐ gas | ☐ vacuum | ☐ sprinkler | ☐ other: ______] **systems.**

☐ **Install and repair** ______ *[type of]* [(☐ electrical / ☐ hydraulic) systems | (☐ low / ☐ high) pressure steam piping | ☐ gas piping | ☐ air compressor piping | ☐ HVAC piping and equipment | (☐ gas / ☐ vacuum) piping | ☐ low- and high-pressure steam piping and equipment | ☐ truck beds | ☐ other: ______] **for** ______ *[what?].*

☐ **Maintain and service new and existing** [☐ domestic water systems | ☐ sanitary piping | ☐ HVAC piping and equipment | ☐ other: ______] **by** ______ *[doing what?].*

☐ [☐ Perform | ☐ Oversee] **all types of welding projects including** [☐ connecting water, steam, gas, oxygen, and air lines | ☐ performing fabrication of metals and alloys | ☐ heating, tempering, straightening, and shaping metals | ☐ working with (☐ water / ☐ steam / ☐ gas / ☐ oxygen / ☐ argon / ☐ helium / ☐ acetylene) | ☐ constructing specialized devices and structures | ☐ performing (☐ machining / ☐ rigging) | ☐ repairing (☐ electrical / ☐ hydraulic) systems | ☐ performing industrial pipefitting | ☐ welding exotic metals | ☐ installing (☐ low- and high-pressure steam / ☐ HVAC / ☐ gas / ☐ vacuum / ☐ air compressor) piping | ☐ maintaining and servicing steam boilers | ☐ constructing specialized devices and structures | ☐ designing, laying out, and cutting special parts | ☐ developing items from (☐ ferrous / ☐ nonferrous) metals | ☐ repairing (☐ electrical / ☐ hydraulic) systems | ☐ other: ______].

☐ **Install, service, and maintain fire suppression sprinkler systems, including** [☐ wet systems | ☐ dry systems | ☐ deluge systems | ☐ other: ______] **for** ______ *[what?].*

☐ **Weld** [☐ exotic metals | ☐ alloys | (☐ ferrous / ☐ nonferrous) metals | ☐ other: ______] **including** [☐ carbon | ☐ stainless steel | ☐ aluminum | ☐ tungsten | ☐ cast iron | ☐ other: ______] **in the steamfitting of** ______ *[what?]* **and ensure safety in use of all gases including** [☐ argon | ☐ helium | ☐ oxygen | ☐ acetylene | ☐ other: ______].

ACHIEVEMENT SAMPLES: *See **"Welding/Steamfitting Functions & Projects"** and **"Completed Projects – General."***

Welding / Steamfitting – Functions & Projects

*See also **"Welding / Steamfitting – General," "Equipment, Tools & Testing Devices – Welding / Steamfitting,"** and **"Inspections & Compliance – Trades,"** as applicable.*

☐ **Conduct various** [☐ welding | ☐ arc welding | ☐ joint welding | ☐ torch cutting | ☐ soldering | ☐ steamfitting | ☐ other: ______] **functions including** [☐ interpreting blueprints | ☐ preparing job sites | ☐ determining dimensions and tolerances | ☐ modifying, servicing, and repairing existing ______ *(type of)* systems | ☐ ensuring safety in use of all gases | ☐ maintaining supplies | ☐ designing, laying out and cutting special parts | ☐ fabricating and fitting equipment and parts | ☐ ensuring structural support | ☐ determining best welding methods and techniques | ☐ training staff on welding and machining equipment | ☐ determining project time and costs | ☐ cleaning, lubricating, and maintaining shop equipment | ☐ repairing heavy equipment | ☐ other: ______].

☐ **Perform all aspects of joint welding including** [☐ groove | ☐ bead | ☐ edge | ☐ plug | ☐ slot | ☐ fillet | ☐ arc-seam | ☐ other: ______] **in the welding of** ______ *[what?]* **for** ______ *[purpose].*

☐ **Prepare for** ______ *[type of]* **welding work by** [☐ reading and interpreting blueprints | ☐ determining dimensions and tolerances | ☐ estimating project time and costs | ☐ specifying best welding methods and techniques for the job | ☐ prioritizing work assignments | ☐ determining equipment needed | ☐ ordering required inventory | ☐ preparing job site for welding | ☐ setting up project with materials | ☐ coordinating vendors | ☐ determining safety requirements | ☐ identifying replacements and/or repairs | ☐ ensuring structural support where needed | ☐ maintaining inventory and supplies | ☐ other: ______].

☐ **Handle** [☐ welding | ☐ arc welding | ☐ joint welding | ☐ torch cutting | ☐ soldering | ☐ steamfitting | ☐ other: ______] **of** ______ *[what?]* **including** [☐ reading and interpreting blueprints | ☐ preparing job sites | ☐ using precision-measuring instruments | ☐ ensuring safety in use of all gases | ☐ modifying, repairing, and servicing existing systems | ☐ ensuring structural support | ☐ determining best welding methods and techniques for the job at hand | ☐ maintaining supplies and inventory | ☐ designing, laying out and cutting special parts | ☐ fabricating and fitting equipment and parts | ☐ determining dimensions and tolerances | ☐ training staff on welding and machining equipment | ☐ determining project time and costs | ☐ cleaning, lubricating, and maintaining shop equipment | ☐ operating metal forming equipment | ☐ repairing heavy equipment | ☐ operating (☐ drill presses / ☐ milling / ☐ gear-cutting / ☐ CNC / ☐ Atlas / ☐ metal-removing machines / ☐ other: ______) | ☐ operating centrifugal chiller and steam absorption machines | ☐ other: ______].

☐ **Construct** ______ *[type of]* [☐ specialized devices and structures | ☐ items from (☐ ferrous / ☐ nonferrous) metals | ☐ other: ______] **by** [☐ heating, tempering, straightening, and shaping metals | ☐ designing, laying out, and cutting special parts | ☐ other: ______] **and** ______ *[doing what?]* **for** ______ *[purpose].*

☐ [☐ Perform | ☐ Manage and oversee] **various** ______ *[type of]* **welding projects including** [☐ connecting and working with (☐ water / ☐ steam / ☐ gas / ☐ oxygen / ☐ air lines / ☐ argon / ☐ helium / ☐ acetylene / ☐ other: ______) | ☐ fabrication of metals and alloys | ☐ heating, tempering, straightening, and shaping metals | ☐ constructing specialized devices and structures | ☐ conducting (☐ machining / ☐ rigging) | ☐ repairing (☐ electrical / ☐ hydraulic) systems | ☐ performing industrial pipefitting | ☐ welding exotic metals | ☐ installing (☐ low and high pressure steam / ☐ air compressor / ☐ HVAC / ☐ gas / ☐ vacuum / ☐ other: ______) piping | ☐ maintaining and servicing steam boilers | ☐ constructing specialized devices and structures | ☐ designing, laying out, and cutting special parts | ☐ repairing (☐ electrical / ☐ hydraulic) systems | ☐ other: ______].

☐ **Work with** [☐ water | ☐ steam | ☐ gas | ☐ oxygen | ☐ argon | ☐ air lines | ☐ helium | ☐ acetylene | ☐ other: ______] **in the fabrication of** ______ *[what?]* **for** ______ *[purpose].*

☐ **Facilitate** [☐ machining | ☐ rigging | ☐ industrial pipefitting | ☐ fabrication of metals and alloys | ☐ other: ______] **for** ______ *[what?].*

ACHIEVEMENT SAMPLES: *See also "Completed Projects – General."*

☐ **Installed and repaired low- and high-pressure steam piping, including including** [☐ heating | ☐ ventilating | ☐ air condition | ☐ sterilization equipment | ☐ other: ______] **for a** ______ *[#]*-**floor,** ______ *[#]*-**room** [☐ plant | ☐ commercial building | ☐ facility | ☐ other: ______].

☐ **Constructed** ______ *[type of]* **specialized** [☐ structures | ☐ devices | ☐ programs | ☐ other: ______] **that** ______ *[did what?]* **while benefiting the** [☐ client | ☐ firm | ☐ other: ______] **by** ______ *[what means?]*.

☐ **Handled** [☐ welding | ☐ steamfitting | ☐ other: ______] **projects for** [☐ large office buildings | ☐ truck bed body work | ☐ industrial welding | ☐ industrial pipefitting | ☐ industrial plumbing | ☐ domestic water systems | ☐ sprinkler systems | ☐ HVAC piping | ☐ compressed air systems | ☐ other: ______] **for** ______ *[type of clients]*.

☐ **Installed medical gas piping, including** [☐ oxygen | ☐ nitrogen | ☐ medical air | ☐ vacuum | ☐ other: ______] **piping which required tying into existing systems while** [☐ clients | ☐ patrons | ☐ patients | ☐ other: ______] **were living off systems, ensuring proper safety and precautions at all times.**

☐ **Handled on-site** [☐ welding | ☐ steamfitting | ☐ other: ______] **while** [☐ company remained open for business | ☐ homeowners remained on premises | ☐ other: ______] **by** ______ *[doing what?]*, **which minimized the work impact so** [☐ business | ☐ home] **operations remained functional.**

Welding / Steamfitting Equipment Use

See "Equipment, Tools & Testing Devices – Welding / Steamfitting."

Welding / Steamfitting Projects Oversight

See also "Welding/Steamfitting Functions & Projects" "Trades/Crew Supervision – All Trades," "Inspections & Compliance – Welding/Steamfitting," and "Contractor/Subcontractor Influence & Collaboration."

☐ **Provide decisive leadership and clear direction in all phases of** [☐ large-scale | ☐ complex] ______ *[type of]* **projects for** [☐ commercial | ☐ residential | ☐ industrial | ☐ other: ______] **clients overseeing a top-performing team of** ______ *[#]* [☐ welders | ☐ steamfitters | ☐ other: ______].

☐ **Coordinate and oversee steamfitting trade functions for** [☐ large office buildings | ☐ industrial welding | ☐ industrial pipefitting | ☐ industrial plumbing | ☐ domestic water systems | ☐ sprinkler systems | ☐ HVAC piping | ☐ compressed air systems | ☐ fire sprinklers | ☐ other: ______] **on** ______ *[type of]* **projects to ensure quality control, regulation compliance, and machinery and equipment safety.**

☐ **Oversee various types of** [☐ welding | ☐ joint welding | ☐ steamfitting | ☐ soldering | ☐ arc welding | ☐ torch cutting | ☐ other: ______] **projects for this** ______ *[type of]* **firm including** [☐ industrial welding | ☐ industrial pipefitting | ☐ industrial plumbing | ☐ domestic water systems | ☐ sprinkler systems | ☐ HVAC piping | ☐ compressed air systems | ☐ fire sprinklers | ☐ truck bed body work | ☐ other: ______].

☐ **Manage and oversee welding jobs averaging** $______ **to** $______ *[amounts]* **including** [☐ estimating job times, materials, and costs | ☐ selecting materials and hardware | ☐ preparing materials estimates | ☐ reviewing bids | ☐ ordering required job-related materials | scheduling jobs | ☐ inspecting completed jobs for quality and code compliance | ☐ other: ______].

☐ **Oversee** [☐ welding | ☐ arc welding | ☐ joint welding | ☐ torch cutting | ☐ soldering | ☐ steamfitting | ☐ other: ______] **of** ______ *[what?]* **including** [☐ reading and interpreting blueprints | ☐ preparing job sites | ☐ using precision-measuring instruments | ☐ ensuring safety in use of all gases | ☐ modifying, repairing, and servicing existing systems | ☐ ensuring structural support | ☐ determining best welding methods and techniques for the job at hand | ☐ maintaining supplies and inventory | ☐ designing, laying out and cutting special parts | ☐ fabricating and fitting equipment and parts | ☐ determining dimensions and tolerances | ☐ training staff on welding and machining equipment | ☐ determining project time and costs | ☐ cleaning, lubricating, and maintaining shop equipment | ☐ operating metal forming equipment | ☐ repairing heavy equipment | ☐ operating (☐ drill presses / ☐ milling / ☐ gear-cutting / ☐ CNC / ☐ Atlas / ☐ metal-removing machines / ☐ other: ______) | ☐ operating centrifugal chiller and steam absorption machines | ☐ other: ______].

☐ **Supervise the installation and repair of** ______ *[type of]* [(☐ electrical / ☐ hydraulic) systems | (☐ low / ☐ high) pressure steam piping | ☐ gas piping | ☐ air compressor piping | ☐ HVAC piping and equipment | (☐ gas / ☐ vacuum) piping | ☐ low- and high-pressure steam piping and equipment | ☐ truck beds | ☐ other: ______] **for** ______ *[what?]*.

☐ **Oversee** [☐ welding | ☐ arc welding | ☐ joint welding | ☐ soldering | ☐ steamfitting | ☐ torch cutting | ☐ industrial welding | ☐ other: ______] **trades in their installation of new and repair of existing domestic** [☐ water | ☐ steam | ☐ sanitary | ☐ HVAC | ☐ electrical | ☐ hydraulic | ☐ gas | ☐ vacuum | ☐ sprinkler | ☐ other: ______] **systems.**

☐ **Ensure the safety in use of all gases including** [☐ argon | ☐ helium | ☐ oxygen | ☐ acetylene | ☐ other: ______].

☐ **Oversee all types of welding projects including** [☐ connecting water, steam, gas, oxygen, and air lines | ☐ performing fabrication of metals and alloys | ☐ heating, tempering, straightening, and shaping metals | ☐ working with (☐ water / ☐ steam / ☐ gas / ☐ oxygen / ☐ argon / ☐ helium / ☐ acetylene) | ☐ constructing specialized devices and structures | ☐ performing (☐ machining / ☐ rigging) | ☐ repairing (☐ electrical / ☐ hydraulic) systems | ☐ performing industrial pipefitting | ☐ welding exotic metals | ☐ installing (☐ low- and high-pressure steam / ☐ HVAC / ☐ gas / ☐ vacuum / ☐ air compressor) piping | ☐ maintaining and servicing steam boilers | ☐ constructing specialized devices and structures | ☐ designing, laying out, and cutting special parts | ☐ developing items from (☐ ferrous / ☐ nonferrous) metals | ☐ repairing (☐ electrical / ☐ hydraulic) systems | ☐ other: ______].

☐ **Supervise the installation, servicing, and maintenance of new and existing domestic** [☐ water systems | ☐ sanitary piping | ☐ HVAC piping and equipment | ☐ other: ______].

☐ **Oversee the construction of** ______ *[type of]* [☐ specialized devices and structures | ☐ items from (☐ ferrous / ☐ nonferrous) metals | ☐ other: ______] **through the** [☐ heating, tempering, straightening, and shaping metals | ☐ designing, laying out, and cutting special parts | ☐ other: ______] **and** ______ *[doing what?]* **for** ______ *[purpose].*

☐ **Manage and oversee various** ______ *[type of]* **welding projects including** [☐ connecting and working with (☐ water / ☐ steam / ☐ gas / ☐ oxygen / ☐ air lines / ☐ argon / ☐ helium / ☐ acetylene / ☐ other: ______) | ☐ fabrication of metals and alloys | ☐ heating, tempering, straightening, and shaping metals | ☐ constructing specialized devices and structures | ☐ conducting (☐ machining / ☐ rigging) | ☐ repairing (☐ electrical / ☐ hydraulic) systems | ☐ performing industrial pipefitting | ☐ welding exotic metals | ☐ installing (☐ low and high pressure steam / ☐ air compressor / ☐ HVAC / ☐ gas / ☐ vacuum / ☐ other: ______) piping | ☐ maintaining and servicing steam boilers | ☐ constructing specialized devices and structures | ☐ designing, laying out, and cutting special parts | ☐ repairing (☐ electrical / ☐ hydraulic) systems | ☐ other: ______].

ACHIEVEMENT SAMPLES: *See also "Construction Projects."*

☐ **Managed and oversaw the installation of low- and high-pressure steam piping, including** [☐ heating | ☐ ventilating | ☐ air condition | ☐ sterilization equipment | ☐ other: ______] **for a** ______ *[#]***-floor,** ______ *[#]***-room** [☐ plant | ☐ commercial building | ☐ facility | ☐ other: ______].

☐ **Oversaw the construction of** ______ *[type of]* **specialized** [☐ structures | ☐ devices | ☐ programs | ☐ other: ______] **that** ______ *[did what?]* **while benefiting the** [☐ client | ☐ firm | ☐ other: ______] **by** ______ *[what means?].*

☐ **Managed** [☐ welding | ☐ steamfitting | ☐ other: ______] **projects for** [☐ large office buildings | ☐ truck bed body work | ☐ industrial welding | ☐ industrial pipefitting | ☐ industrial plumbing | ☐ domestic water systems | ☐ sprinkler systems | ☐ HVAC piping | ☐ compressed air systems | ☐ other: ______] **for** ______ *[type of clients].*

☐ **Supervised medical gas piping, including** [☐ oxygen | ☐ nitrogen | ☐ medical air | ☐ vacuum | ☐ other: ______] **piping which required tying into existing systems while** [☐ clients | ☐ patrons | ☐ patients | ☐ other: ______] **were living off systems, ensuring proper safety and precautions at all times.**

☐ **Oversaw on-site** [☐ welding | ☐ steamfitting | ☐ other: ______] **while** [☐ company remained open for business | ☐ homeowners remained on premises | ☐ other: ______] **by** ______ *[doing what?],* **which minimized the work impact so** [☐ business | ☐ home] **operations remained functional**.

Work Collaboration – Construction

See also "Work Collaboration – General."

☐ **Conduct pre-construction meetings and confer with** [☐ architects | ☐ engineers | ☐ contractors | ☐ builders | ☐ project managers | ☐ superintendents | ☐ the general public | ☐ others: ______] **to review building requirements and restrictions**.

☐ **Coordinate all aspects of** [☐ drafting | ☐ construction | ☐ production | ☐ other: ______] **projects with** [☐ clients | ☐ engineers | ☐ architects | ☐ municipal officials | ☐ county officials | ☐ code officers | ☐ others: ______] **ensuring compliance with all codes and quality standards throughout project phases.**

☐ **Collaborate with various trades in the coordination of job functions including** [☐ plumbing | ☐ electrical | ☐ building maintenance | ☐ carpentry | ☐ HVAC | ☐ masonry | ☐ framing | ☐ landscaping | ☐ other: ______].

☐ **Interact with** [☐ clients | ☐ architects | ☐ engineers | ☐ general contractors | ☐ subcontractors | ☐ project managers | ☐ urban planners | ☐ interior designers | ☐ landscape architects | ☐ expeditors | ☐ zoning officials | ☐ inspectors | ☐ homeowners | ☐ (custom home) builders | ☐ electricians | ☐ plumbers | ☐ roofers | ☐ others: ______] **during the** [☐ design | ☐ design-and-build | ☐ construction | ☐ engineering | ☐ development] **process to** [☐ define project parameters | ☐ develop detailed project plans | ☐ schedule projects | ☐ identify and problem solve issues | ☐ manage construction | ☐ procure permits | ☐ other: ______].

☐ **Work with** ______ *[which?]* **trades to coordinate the** [☐ design and] **installation of** ______ *[what projects?]* **for** ______ *[whom or what?].*

☐ **Meet and coordinate jobs with** [☐ building managers | ☐ homeowners | ☐ subcontractors | ☐ zoning officials | ☐ architects | ☐ engineers | ☐ inspectors | ☐ union delegates | ☐ zoning officials | ☐ lumber yards | ☐ vendors | ☐ others: ______] **during the** ______ *[which trade(s)?]* **process.**

☐ **Work collaboratively in a team environment with** [☐ management | ☐ laborers | ☐ maintenance crew | ☐ subcontractors | ☐ others: ______] **while** [☐ leading | ☐ handling] **multiple projects and adapting to frequently changing priorities.**

☐ **Interface and work closely with** [☐ architects | ☐ designers | ☐ builders | ☐ general contractors | ☐ homeowners | ☐ project engineers | ☐ builders | ☐ electricians | ☐ plumbers | ☐ roofers | ☐ lumber yards | ☐ others: ______] [☐ on all relevant issues and project phases | ☐ to identify problems and recommend solutions | ☐ to modify plans as needed | ☐ other: ______].

☐ **Coordinate the implementation and monitoring of** ______ *[what?]* **with other departments, successfully producing results through others by** ______ *[doing what well?].*

☐ **Act as liaison with** ______ *[which?]* **staff to** [☐ ensure positive (☐ customer / ☐ internal / ☐ external) relationships | ☐ maintain service quality | ☐ address and resolve issues | ☐ communicate project milestones | ☐ properly identify and process scope changes | ☐ other: ______].

☐ **Establish and maintain effective working relations with** ______ *[whom?]* **for** ______ *[what purpose, process, or project?].*

☐ **Participate in work collaboration meetings with** ______ *[whom?]* **regarding** ______ *[what?].*

☐ **Collaborate with** [☐ state officials | ☐ state agencies | ☐ politicians | ☐ others: ______] **to improve conditions for** ______ *[what trade(s)?]* **regarding** [☐ licensing | ☐ safety | ☐ general welfare | ☐ other: ______].

ACHIEVEMENT SAMPLES:

☐ **Coordinated** ______ *[type of]* **projects with** [☐ subcontractors | ☐ general contractors | ☐ engineers | ☐ architects | ☐ municipal officials | ☐ code officials | ☐ county officials | ☐ clients | ☐ others: ______] **in all phases of construction, which enhanced compliance with codes and quality standards toward the successful completion of all jobs.**

☐ **Established and maintain** [☐ collaborative relationships | ☐ useful interfaces | ☐ effective working relations | ☐ other: ______] **with** [☐ clients | ☐ nternal staff | ☐ end users | ☐ management | ☐ other: ______] **as well as** ______ *[whom?]* **regarding all contractual issues and matters.**

☐ **In collaboration with the** ______ *[whom?]* [☐ created accurate project estimates | ☐ prepared schedules | ☐ allocated resources | ☐ other: ______] **that support company-wide projects and maintain project management practices.**

☐ **Developed a cooperative team effort with** ______ *[whom?]* **enhancing the coordination and successful completion of all** ______ *[type of]* **projects by** ______ *[doing what successfully?].*

Work Collaboration – Project Management

☐ **Collaborate at all levels of the firm on** ______ *[type of]* **projects using** [☐ tact | ☐ diplomacy | ☐ project management skills | ☐ other: ______] **to** [☐ define needs | ☐ clarify scope | ☐ identify issues | ☐ determine schedules | ☐ make changes | ☐ solve problems | ☐ overcome obstacles | ☐ recommend solutions | ☐ obtain solutions acceptance | ☐ keep projects running smoothly | ☐ reach ______ *(type of)* decisions | ☐ other: ______] **during the development and implementation of** ______ *[type of]* **projects.**

☐ **Oversee project management collaboration with** [☐ engineers | ☐ urban planners | ☐ interior designers | ☐ landscape architects | ☐ others: ______] **and other professionals during the** [☐ design and] **construction process.**

☐ **Liaise and interface regularly with** ______ *[whom?]* **to** [☐ determine project scope | ☐ develop strategies | ☐ gather data | ☐ define project parameters | ☐ create project plans | ☐ identify required materials and resources | ☐ execute plans | ☐ schedule projects | ☐ identify and problem solve issues | ☐ overcome obstacles | ☐ modify plans as needed | ☐ other: ______].

☐ **Interact and liaise with** _______ *[whom?]* **to ensure that** _______ *[type of]* **work is within parameters identified by the firm and in compliance with** _______ *[what?].*

☐ **Oversee staff interactions with** _______ *[whom?]* **to** [☐ maintain productive working relationships with _______ *(whom?)* | ☐ schedule projects | ☐ facilitate inspections | ☐ ensure proper handling and receipt of payments | ☐ other: _______].

☐ **Foster strong internal and external client relationships by** [☐ ensuring all client challenges are effectively viewed and solved | ☐ other: _______].

☐ **Interface and work closely with client representatives to** [☐ develop project strategies | ☐ determine project scope | ☐ execute project plans | ☐ determine required materials and resources | ☐ coordinate trades | ☐ apprise project management team of status | ☐ other: _______].

☐ **Serve as principal liaison with** [☐ human resources | ☐ purchasing officers | ☐ legal | ☐ others: _______] **in** [☐ handling documentation | ☐ executing legal actions | ☐ other: _______] **related to** _______ *[what?]* **issues.**

- ☐ **Liaise with ______** *[whom?]* **to maintain customer satisfaction by** [☐ listening to and interpreting their needs | ☐ giving careful attention to detail | ☐ other: ______].

ACHIEVEMENT SAMPLES:

- ☐ **In collaboration with the ______** *[whom?]* [☐ created accurate project estimates | ☐ prepared schedules | ☐ allocated resources | ☐ other: ______] **that support company-wide projects and maintain project management practices.**
- ☐ **Developed a cooperative team effort with ______** *[whom?]* **enhancing the coordination and successful completion of all ______** *[type of]* **projects by ______** *[doing what successfully?]*.

STEP 6

PULL YOUR RESUME TOGETHER

CONTENTS OF STEP 6

STEP-BY-STEP INSTRUCTIONS

INTRODUCTION

Everything you need to compile your resume you have completed within this Book. This chapter provides the instructions to pull the various components together to finalize your resume.

Take your time in completing these steps to ensure your resume is the best it can be and ready for distribution.

1. DECIDE ON YOUR RESUME DESIGN AND START YOUR RESUME.

Just as your resume content is important, so too is its layout and design to first get your resume noticed. In a pile of bland resumes, the ones that will get noticed first are those that attract the attention of hiring managers. And if after getting their attention, the content compels them to call, you have met your goal of getting yourself noticed above your competition.

Ensure your resume presentation is visually-appealing and professional by keeping the design clean and organized. Including bold headers, rules, and white space will make it easier to read and invite hiring managers in to want to read your resume. I generally set my resume margins at .5 at the top and bottom and .75 on the left and right sides. If you are savvy in MS Word, a two-column resume works well when you have a lot of information to include. Save your resume and entitle it, *"(Your Name) Resume.docx"* or *.doc.*

Use basic fonts such as Arial, Arial Narrow, Helvetica, Times, Times New Roman, Garamond, Trebuchet MS, or Verdana to ensure hiring managers have the fonts on their computer and your resume looks the same when they view it. Alternating serif and sans serif fonts for your headers and body copy organizes your content and creates visual interest. (More on font sizes in *"Determine Your Resume Length"* below.)

Consider adding a splash of color to your personal header and/or resume category headings. Deep blues, burgundies, and greens are professional and work well. If you selected brand colors in ***Step 4: Develop Your Personal Brand and Professional Summary,"*** you might consider infusing those colors instead.

At the end of this chapter you will find five resume design layouts you can use as a guide to lay out your resume. For actual layouts you can load onto your computer, my ***Step-by-Step Resumes: Build an Outstanding Resume in 10 Easy Steps!*** book *(published by JIST Publishing, $19.95)* includes a CD that contains 24 design templates in MS Word, which may make it easier for you to compile and customize your resume.

2. INPUT THE INFORMATION YOU COMPILED IN YOUR RESUME WORKSHEET.

From ***Step 1: Start Your Resume,*** start by including all of the information you completed in your *Resume Worksheet:*

- **ENTER YOUR PERSONAL INFORMATION.** Add your name, address, phone number(s), email address, and the URLs for your LinkedIn account and/or Web Portfolio at the top of your resume. You can also include your Twitter and/or Facebook URLs if your posts are professional. (More on that in ***Step 7: Market Yourself!***)
- **SET UP YOUR HEADINGS.** Key in all of the resume headings you identified in ***Step 1: Start Your Resume:*** *"Licenses & Certifications," "Professional Summary" / "Executive Profile," "Core Competencies" / "Areas of Expertise," "Key Accomplishments" / "Highlighted Achievements"* (addressed in #5 below), *"Professional Experience," "Education & Training," "Publications,"* and so on in that order. Make your headings in bold caps and add a rule under each. Leave space between each category so you can input your information from the remaining steps.
- **START YOUR "PROFESSIONAL EXPERIENCE" SECTION.** Chronologically set up your employment information by first keying in your current or most recent Job Title (in bold caps), your employers' Company Name (with Town and State) (in bold), and years of employment (months can be excluded) according to your chosen design layout. Include the responsibilities and achievements you listed in your ***Resume Worksheet*** under your applicable employers. You will go back and check, edit, and/or delete some content after you add your Resume ClipBullets *(in No. 6 below).*

  <u>NOTE:</u> Since hiring managers prefer the Reverse-Chronological Resume format, this Book addresses that format. If, however, your employment record shows a number of unexplained gaps, you are changing careers and cannot substantiate any experience in your targeted profession, you are re-entering the job market after a number of years, or otherwise require a nontraditional resume format, the four formats (Reverse Chronological, Combination, Functional, and Curriculum Vitae) are addressed in and contain templates for these on CD in my more generalized ***Step-by-Step Resumes: Build an Outstanding Resume in 10 Easy Steps!*** *book (JIST Publishing).*

- **ADD YOUR EDUCATION AND TRAINING.** If you are a recent grad, your *"Education & Training"* section belongs at the beginning of your resume. Include the year(s) you attended or obtained your degree. If you already have experience in your field, add your Education at the end of your resume. If you attended college more than ten years ago, you can omit the years. Leave off an Associate's degree if you obtained a Bachelor's degree. Be sure to include any related training in your field and where you obtained it. Again, if it is recent, include the years; if not, omit them.

3. TRANSFER OVER YOUR "PROFESSIONAL SUMMARY" AND SLOGAN.

Key in the personally branded *"Professional Summary" / "Executive Profile"* you developed in ***Step 4: Develop Your Personal Brand and Professional Summary*** onto the top portion of your resume under your main header (or under your *"Education"* section if you are a new grad). Make sure it contains all of your *"Primary Resume Keywords"* identified in ***Step 2: Check Off Your Resume Keywords.*** Check also that you have included your *"Primary Personal Attributes"* you listed in ***Step 3: Check Off Your Personal Attributes***. If not, infuse some of them within your Summary. If you created a slogan in ***Step 4,*** include it as well directly under your header.

4. LIST YOUR "CORE COMPETENCIES."

Input your "Secondary Resume Keywords" (from **Step 2: Check Off Your Resume Keywords**) into a "Core Competencies" or "Areas of Expertise" section positioned under your "Professional Summary." If you are laying out your resume in a two-column format, your core competencies work well in a left-hand column that consumes about one-fourth of the page.

Should you have expertise in several areas and/or have a long list of keywords, section them off under applicable headings, such as "Human Resource Management," "Employee Engagement," "Talent Acquisition," and so on. Those headings should generally be the same as your "Primary Keywords" you included above in #3. Alternatively, you can use the keyword categories listed in **Step 2.** Since this Book covers various levels of experience, you may have knowledge of lower-level functions / keywords that may not be as relevant to the position you are seeking. Those can be omitted unless hands-on knowledge is required in your targeted position.

5. CONSIDER INCLUDING A "KEY ACCOMPLISHMENTS" SECTION.

If you are an executive or manager or otherwise have quite a number of significant accomplishments that exhibit your value proposition, or if when developing your resume at least some of your primary accomplishments do not appear on its first page, consider adding a *"Key Accomplishments"* or *"Achievement Highlights"* section under your *"Professional Summary"* and *"Core Competencies"* sections to include them. Put your "heavy hitter" accomplishments at the top, such as where you made or saved the most amount of money for your employer, significantly increased percentages in productivity or customer service satisfaction levels, won a notable award for your employer, and so on. Hiring managers typically view the first page of prospective candidates' resumes during their first screening to decide which candidates to call. You will want to make sure they see your value with some of your matching achievements during their first screening.

6. ADD YOUR "PROFESSIONAL EXPERIENCE" BULLETS.

- **ENTER THE RESUME CLIPBULLETS** you checked off and completed throughout ***Step 5: Select Your Resume ClipBullets*** under your employers where they are applicable, adding them after the *"Responsibilities"* and *"Achievements"* you brought over from your *"Resume Foundation."* Omit the word "Responsibilities." At this time, do not worry about how long your resume draft will become. *(You will be editing these down in #11 below.)*

- **REVIEW AND PRIORITIZE YOUR BULLETS**. Verify that all of the functions your targeted position requires and you have performed have been included (from the *"Job Descriptions"* you Googled in ***Step 4: Develop Your Personal Brand & Professional Summary***). Include those at the top of your bullets under each employer. Then prioritize the bullets under each of your jobs in order of their importance to your targeted position.

- **CHECK THAT YOUR BULLETS ARE "CAR" STATEMENTS.** Always try to show how well you accomplished your responsibilities by including the **C**hallenge you were faced with, the **A**ctions you took to make it happen, and the **R**esults / Benefits your company or its clients derived from your efforts. Add if not already noted.

  Ensure quantifying information is included in your bullets by adding numbers *(dollars, percentages, measurements, and other statistics)* wherever you can to show *how well* you accomplished your functions. Ask yourself, *how large, how big, how much, how fast, how often?* Compare those numbers against the company or industry "norm." If better, include them.

- **IF YOU HAVE MANY BULLETS, CATEGORIZE THEM.** If you find you have a dozen or more bullets under your individual employers, separate out your accomplishments under an *"Achievements"* heading under those employers.

7. VERIFY THAT ALL OF YOUR CRITICAL KEYWORDS ARE INCLUDED IN YOUR RESUME.

Double-check that the resume keywords you identified in ***Step 2: Check Off Your Resume Keywords*** have all been included. That is, your ***Primary Keywords*** are contained within your *"Professional Summary"* and/or a slogan at the top of your resume under your header, your ***Secondary Keywords*** are listed under *"Core Competencies,"* and any ***remaining keywords*** have been included within the bullets in your *"Professional Experience"* section.

8. ENSURE YOUR RESUME BULLETS START WITH ACTION VERBS.

In essence, Action Verbs *(such as advocate, build, champion, approve, collaborate, and so on)* are the most basic form of a job function. All of your resume bullets in your *"Professional Experience"* section should start with an Action Verb. The exception to the rule is when you precede the Action Verb with an Adverb *(addressed next).* Never start your bullets with *"Responsible for…"* Instead, omit those words and jump right into the actions you perform(ed).

All of the *Resume ClipBullets* contained in this Book already contain Action Verbs, but a complete list is included in this chapter for you to ensure any bullets you created on your own include them and/or to check if there are any important "functions" you may have omitted and still require in your resume.

EXAMPLES BY POSITION TITLE

- **Executive** – spearhead, strategize, manage, oversee, direct, establish, forecast, increase, orchestrate
- **Social Worker** – assess, advocate, link, coordinate, counsel, evaluate, investigate, place
- **Attorney** – advise, consult, depose, examine, litigate, research, settle, summon
- **Graphic Designer** – conceptualize, create, design, render, strategize, synthesize
- **Programmer** – develop, configure, test, code, program, analyze, monitor, diagnose

9. INFUSE DESCRIPTIVE ADJECTIVES AND ADVERBS.

You can further show *how well* you performed a certain task, responsibility, or achievement by preceding the *Action Verb* with a *Descriptive Adverb* or by adding a *Descriptive Adjective* in front of a *Noun* within your bullets. (See examples.) Include some in your resume to help describe how well you accomplished your job functions or achievements.

Descriptive Adverb Examples: *Accurately invoice, Diplomatically negotiate, Efficiently conduct, Continuously improve, Virtually eliminated, Quickly intervene, Successfully spearhead, Regularly monitor, Dramatically reduced,* and so on.

Descriptive Adjective Examples: *Allocate appropriate resources, Conceptualize creative designs, Offer encouraging support, Facilitate timely negotiations, Develop effective solutions, Prepare accurate records,* and so on.

10. ADD COMPANY AND POSITION DESCRIPTORS UNDER YOUR EMPLOYERS.

At the end of this chapter, you will find foundations for ***Company and Position Descriptors*** to include under your employers in your *"Professional Experience"* Section. Although not mandatory, adding a short italicized paragraph under each of your jobs detailing the purpose for which you were hired, your primary responsibilities, and information about your firm is especially beneficial if you have a number of bullets where you can cull out some of this information to include in a Position Descriptor.

11. EDIT YOUR RESUME.

- **REVIEW AND EDIT ALL OF YOUR EMPLOYMENT BULLETS.** Because this Book contains so much relevant information for each position, when your first draft is complete, chances are good that you will have more bullets than you need to finalize your resume. Now is the time to edit down your information as much as possible *without* losing any important content. Review all of your bullets to check for redundancy. Join like bullets into one. Delete any less important bullets that are not as significant to or required in the position(s) you seek.
- **MAKE YOUR BULLETS CONCISE.** Condense everything down to the most concise sentences possible—what I call *"the lowest common denominator."* Always try to say the same thing in less words until you cannot edit down any further without losing substance. Omit words such as pronouns (I, me, my), "the," "that," and other nonessential words.
- **VARY YOUR BULLET LINE LENGTH.** To maintain the interest of your reader, vary your bullet line length alternating between one-, two-, three-, and four-line bulleted sentences (bearing in mind what you have already prioritized). Keep long bullets to a minimum. If you have a number of four- or five-line bullets, try condensing or splitting them.
- **MAKE SENSIBLE PAGE BREAKS.** If you can, end your resume pages with the completion of a particular position, starting the next position at the top of the following page. If you are off a bit, try to edit down further until it fits properly and/or adjust your spacing.
- **CHECK FOR CONSISTENCY.** To ensure your completed resume has a polished look, check for consistency in your fonts, verbiage, spacing, line breaks, rules, and other areas and that your margins are pretty much even all around.

- **SPELL-CHECK AND PROOFREAD YOUR RESUME.** Several times. It can take only one spelling error to disqualify you as an eligible candidate (in many positions). Be sure everything is accurate, there are no spelling errors, and all information is "true" before you consider it "done." If this is not your forte, have someone with good spelling, grammar, and punctuation skills do this for you.
- **EDIT EVERYTHING AGAIN AND AGAIN.** This is what professional resume writers do. Sleep on it and look it over again the next day and the following before considering it finished. There is usually always room for improvement—that is, more content you can edit down and perfect.

12. INCLUDE YOUR TESTIMONIALS.

Another way to add interest to your resume presentation is to include (three) *"Testimonials."* Testimonials from others in your industry add credence to your resume content by exhibiting what others say about you. Prospective employers generally ask for your references during an interview, but including testimonials in your resume can spark their interest in the first place and increase your interview odds. Testimonials can be added as call-outs in the scholar's margin of your resume, as a category at the end of your resume, or on a separate addendum page.

Include your *"Testimonials"* from ***Step 4: Develop Your Personal Brand and Professional Summary.*** Select testimonials and endorsements from LinkedIn, performance evaluations, letters of recommendation, client thank you letters, internship summaries, vendor satisfaction letters, and the like. If you don't have any reference letters, now is a good time to ask for them. Select comments that speak to your value and various abilities from a variety of sources, such as superiors, peers, subordinates, professors, clients, vendors, and others. If the testimonial is long, paraphrase it using an ellipse (...) to connect thoughts and indicate something was omitted.

13. CONSIDER ADDING "WOW" FACTORS TO YOUR RESUME.

Following are additional ways you can add interest to your resume presentation while showcasing your skills and abilities. Consider including a Mission Statement, Success Stories, Case Studies, Work Samples, Charts, and/or Graphs.

• A MISSION STATEMENT

A way to immediately capture a hiring manager's attention and show you are passionate about your profession is by creating a short mission statement (a promise or belief) that exhibits what you have to offer a prospective employer. You can include your mission statement in the margin of your resume and/or cover letter or at the bottom of your resume in a footer so it appears on each page.

EXAMPLES BY POSITION TITLE:

Executive Chef: *"An Executive Chef's talent lies in his ability to create innovative cuisine, instruct it masterfully, and wow his patrons."*

Service Manager: *"I believe the true quality of a good Service Manager is the ability to run an operation with an eye towards profitability while servicing the customer in a fair and honest way."*

Case Manager: *"An effective Case Manager takes time to listen, treats others the way she wants to be treated, inspires positive changes in people's lives, and is accountable for her actions and reactions."*

Teacher: *"Each step a child takes in his life has an effect on his future. I would like to help students take positive steps by creating an educational experience conducive to learning."*

Sales Associate: *"If the customer is happy and you are making a sale, it's a win/win."*

• CHARTS AND GRAPHS

Executives, managers, and others who have, for example, increased revenues, sales, productivity, or customer service satisfaction levels and/or decreased costs, labor, or employee turnover might consider putting this information in a chart or graph that depicts these numbers and include it in your resume. Doing so is a great way to showcase your achievements in a visual that readers will see first.

• SUCCESS STORIES OR CASE STUDIES

By including a "Success Stories" or "Case Studies" Addendum Page at the end of your resume, prospective employers can see first-hand how you have successfully performed your job and achieved your position goals. Always include the challenge you were faced with, the actions you took to solve it, and the end result to show the benefits of your work. Chances are your readers will flip through your resume and read this first.

EXAMPLES FOR A SOCIAL WORKER:

Success Story No. 1: An adoptive adolescent with a tough exterior and intimidating mannerisms was in the Mercy Residential Treatment Center because of her negative behaviors. Though Jane was intelligent, she was told she had to attend until her behaviors improved. She wanted to leave at the end of the year to be mainstreamed into her district public school; however, during the year her behavior fluctuated. Although several counselors had chosen not to work with her, I found that by working on her conflicts and offering my client a working relationship built on trust, it helped empower her to focus on her behavioral and academic goals. At the end of the school year, Jane was mainstreamed back into her district high school.

Success Story No. 2: A bi-polar patient felt very upset when her mom yelled at her. After inviting Mary's mom in for a meeting and discussing with her the impact it had on her daughter, while teaching Mary how to communicate with her mom, she learned to express her feelings when she was upset, and her mom became more understanding of the impact she had on her daughter. The relationship became more of a working one, and Mary responded better to treatment because she and her mom were talking things out.

Success Story No. 3: Derek, a 15-year-old client with impaired intelligence, was to receive a prison sentence of 15 years to life for sexual offenses. I built a relationship with his mother who found it very difficult to deal with the situation, was preoccupied with her own life, and resisted putting in time. Together, we worked on getting her son treatment instead of going to jail and I found a parent support group for her to attend. I followed through with appropriate agencies so he could receive psychiatric treatment and sent a detailed report to the District Attorney to present to the judge before trial. Now Derek is undergoing psychiatric care at the Children's Services Treatment Center with intense supervision.

Success Story No. 4: Jane, an alcoholic 17-year-old client who lived in a group home, had experienced difficulty living at home. Her mother was concerned with her living at home because she engaged herself in self-hazardous situations. My client didn't believe her mother listened to her side. By creating a neutral environment during sessions, building trust, and following up on issues, my client eventually disclosed her distrust for authoritative figures due to past experiences where she had been misled. The counseling helped Jane come to terms with her alcoholism that originated from her father and grandfather before her, and helped build a communicative relationship between mother and daughter.

- **WORK SAMPLES**

Especially helpful for Graphic Designers, Marketing professionals, Teachers, Architects, Construction Managers, Interior Decorators, Chefs, Artists, and Photographers, for example, ***Work Samples*** can show first-hand what you are capable of by including photos or illustrations of work you performed. You can include *Work Samples* under your specific employers where you performed this work, in the margin of your resume, or on an Addendum Page at the end of your resume.

Additional information regarding these and many other visual and verbal branding elements are contained in my more generalized book, ***Step-by-Step Resumes: Build an Outstanding Resume in 10 Easy Steps!*** *(JIST Publishing).*

14. DETERMINE YOUR RESUME LENGTH.

There is no "magical number" of pages a resume should be, though some may tell you otherwise. You want to enthral hiring managers to *want to* read your resume and *compel* them to call you. So if you hand them a four-page resume with just copy that is all in the same font and not organized or sectioned off in any way to invite your reader in, then it is too long and will likely not be read. View the resume design layouts at the end of this chapter as a guide, and ensure all of your information is organized and easy to read. Here are some guidelines:

- Your resume should be as long as it needs to be to include all of your critical content in its *most concise* form. Edit, edit, edit is the key.
- Executives and others with a lot of achievements will have longer resumes, such as three to five pages. If you are responsible for profit and loss, for example, your achievements will take up more space. A Project Engineer may also have many projects important to include. You can list the projects with their critical information under your employers and note *"See 'Completed Projects' for details on the addendum page,"* where you can provide more information, perhaps along with "before and after" photos.
- Your more recent position and/or those positions related to your targeted job should include more bullets, with successively less bullets for older positions as you go back chronologically. If you find your position content is longer than say two-thirds of a page, consider breaking out your achievements into a *"Key Accomplishments"* section *(see #5 above).* Try to keep your responsibility / function-related bullets to 8 to 12 in your more recent positions, depending upon how long your bullets are (again, not a "magical number").
- Font style and size makes a difference insofar as how long your resume is. Depending upon the font, it can actually be smaller or larger at the same size. Font examples in their indicated and recommended font sizes: Times New Roman at 11 point, Arial at 10 point, Verdana at 9.5 point. If your resume is long, I recommend using Arial Narrow at 10.5 point. If space allows, make your cover letter one-half to one point size larger.
- Your resume length could also depend upon the country you work in. In the United States for example, two to three pages is quite the norm. In Australia, if you submit a two-page resume, hiring managers will wonder where the "rest of the resume" is, and five to six pages is not unusual.

15. MAKE SURE YOUR RESUME IS TARGETED AND COMPELLING.

- **VERIFY THAT YOUR RESUME IS TARGETED.** Go back to when you Googled job descriptions in ***Step 4: Develop Your Personal Brand and Professional Summary.*** Check that everything required in the position(s) you seek in which you have accomplished during your career has been included. If not, add it. Also, double-check that all relative skills, keywords, and other requirements listed in the job descriptions are included as they are applicable to you.

- **IS YOUR FINAL RESUME COMPELLING?** When you feel your resume is done, take a look at it and ask yourself if it compels you to want to delve into and read it. When you read your resume, are you impressed with yourself? Does your resume contain your unique personal brand? Have you provided enough value that a hiring manager would feel compelled to want to call you in for an interview and hire you? If there is any question, go back to ***Step 4*** to make sure you have included all of your brand components.

16. ENSURE YOU HAVE LEFT NO STONE UNTURNED.

To ensure you have done absolutely everything you could possibly do to make your resume the best it can be, test yourself by reviewing my ***100 Components of an Exemplary Resume: How Does Your Resume Fare?*** article in this chapter by checking off what you feel you have included in your resume and revisiting any areas not taken care of.

17. CREATE AN ASCII (TEXT-ONLY) VERSION OF YOUR RESUME.

Some prospective employers and recruiters request a plain text version of your resume. Also, when you post your resume to job boards and attaching your resume does not automatically flow your information into their specific categories, you will need to copy and paste the sections in yourself. It is easier to use this plain resume version to do that.

Once you are 100% sure that your resume is complete, edited, and proofread, save an additional copy as "Text Only" within MS Word. Then close the document and reopen the ".txt" file. You will see that all font attributes and rules have been removed. Review the content for correct line breaks, any excess spacing between sections, and that everything is consistent. If you added headers for page breaks, delete them.

18. COMPOSE YOUR COVER LETTER.

Think of your Cover Letter as a sales tool to sell yourself. A marketing-savvy cover letter entices the reader to want to read your resume and can actually intrigue hiring managers to call you even before they review your resume. Catch their attention with a cover letter that clearly shows your value proposition (that you developed in ***Step 4: Develop Your Personal Brand and Professional Summary***), explains how your qualifications match the position requirements, includes a summary of your key accomplishments, and states why you feel you can be an asset to the firm.

Here are some guidelines:

- Start your cover letter by including your value proposition and/or other components of your personal brand. Consider using your *Elevator Pitch* you developed in ***Step 4***. Include the position title you are seeking and where you heard about the job opening.
- The second paragraph should sell yourself as a qualified candidate based on your experience, education, and skills. Explain what you have to offer through your matching qualifications, and include the primary requirements in the job posting insofar as how they pertain to your expertise and skills in those areas.
- In the third paragraph, summarize some related achievements (in bulleted or paragraph form) to exemplify how you can be an asset to their firm and help them achieve their goals. When stating your achievements, leave out the details and indicate *"See resume for details."*
- A fourth paragraph could include additional information about your primary attributes and skills, a related story of why you are passionate about or interested in the profession, and/or other compelling information that might be of specific interest to a prospective employer in your industry.
- In the last paragraph, close with a statement of interest, include your call-to-action, and thank the reader for their consideration.
- Keep your cover letter to one page (4 to 5 paragraphs work well). Be sure it includes all of your primary keywords.

For more information on how to compose a superb cover letter, my book, ***Step-by-Step Cover Letters: Build a Cover Letter in 10 Easy Steps Using Personal Branding*** *(JIST Publishing)*, takes you step by step through the process and includes a CD containing a number of cover letter foundations you can load into your computer and use to fill in your related information.

19. PRINT OUT YOUR RESUME AND COVER LETTER.

Use a high-quality (28 to 32 lb.) resume paper found in office supply stores for printing and mailing your resume and cover letter to prospective employers. If the targeted position includes both a physical and email address, use both methods to send out your resume. And always bring extra copies with you when you go on interviews.

ACTION VERBS:
RESUME BULLET STARTERS

- [ ] Abate
- [ ] Abstract
- [ ] Accompany
- [ ] Achieve
- [ ] Add
- [ ] Admit
- [ ] Affirm
- [ ] Ambulate
- [ ] Animate
- [ ] Apprehend
- [ ] Archive
- [ ] Ascribe
- [ ] Assist
- [ ] Auction
- [ ] Automate
- [ ] Batch
- [ ] Bisect
- [ ] Brainstorm
- [ ] Brief
- [ ] Budget
- [ ] Calibrate
- [ ] Capture
- [ ] Cash out
- [ ] Categorize
- [ ] Champion
- [ ] Check
- [ ] Cite
- [ ] Climb
- [ ] Co-administer
- [ ] Co-contribute
- [ ] Co-develop
- [ ] Co-invent
- [ ] Combine
- [ ] Compensate
- [ ] Composite
- [ ] Conclude
- [ ] Configure
- [ ] Conserve
- [ ] Constrain
- [ ] Contemplate
- [ ] Converge
- [ ] Co-present
- [ ] Correct
- [ ] Count
- [ ] Counterplea
- [ ] Craft
- [ ] Cross-file
- [ ] Cultivate
- [ ] Cycle
- [ ] Debug
- [ ] Decode
- [ ] Deduct
- [ ] Defray
- [ ] Delineate
- [ ] Demount
- [ ] Deport
- [ ] Describe
- [ ] Detect
- [ ] Diffract
- [ ] Disallow
- [ ] Abbreviate
- [ ] Accelerate
- [ ] Accomplish
- [ ] Acknowledge
- [ ] Address
- [ ] Adopt
- [ ] Affix
- [ ] Amend
- [ ] Answer
- [ ] Apprise
- [ ] Arraign
- [ ] Assemble
- [ ] Assure
- [ ] Audit
- [ ] Award
- [ ] Begin
- [ ] Blend
- [ ] Brand
- [ ] Bring about
- [ ] Build
- [ ] Call
- [ ] Care for
- [ ] Cast
- [ ] Cater to
- [ ] Change
- [ ] Check in
- [ ] Claim
- [ ] Clip
- [ ] Co-arrange
- [ ] Co-coordinate
- [ ] Co-direct
- [ ] Co-lead
- [ ] Commence
- [ ] Compete with
- [ ] Compound
- [ ] Condense
- [ ] Confirm
- [ ] Consider
- [ ] Constrict
- [ ] Contest
- [ ] Convert
- [ ] Co-produce
- [ ] Correlate
- [ ] Counteract
- [ ] Countersign
- [ ] Create
- [ ] Cross-index
- [ ] Cumulate
- [ ] Deactivate
- [ ] Decide
- [ ] Decompress
- [ ] Defeat
- [ ] Dehydrate
- [ ] Deliver
- [ ] Demystify
- [ ] Depose
- [ ] Deselect
- [ ] Determine
- [ ] Diffuse
- [ ] Disarm
- [ ] Abide
- [ ] Access
- [ ] Account for
- [ ] Acquire
- [ ] Adhere to
- [ ] Advance
- [ ] Affray
- [ ] Amplify
- [ ] Appease
- [ ] Approach
- [ ] Arrange
- [ ] Assert
- [ ] Attach
- [ ] Augment
- [ ] Backtrack
- [ ] Bestow
- [ ] Block
- [ ] Break down
- [ ] Broach
- [ ] Bulk
- [ ] Cancel
- [ ] Carry out
- [ ] Catalog
- [ ] Centralize
- [ ] Channel
- [ ] Check out
- [ ] Classify
- [ ] Clock
- [ ] Coat
- [ ] Co-create
- [ ] Co-edit
- [ ] Collaborate
- [ ] Comment on
- [ ] Compile
- [ ] Compress
- [ ] Condition
- [ ] Confiscate
- [ ] Consign
- [ ] Construct
- [ ] Contract
- [ ] Convey
- [ ] Co-promote
- [ ] Correspond
- [ ] Counterbalance
- [ ] Couple
- [ ] Credit
- [ ] Cross-link
- [ ] Curtail
- [ ] Deal
- [ ] Decipher
- [ ] Decorate
- [ ] Defend
- [ ] Delay
- [ ] Demagnetize
- [ ] Denote
- [ ] Deposit
- [ ] Design
- [ ] Develop
- [ ] Dig
- [ ] Disassemble
- [ ] Abolish
- [ ] Acclaim
- [ ] Accredit
- [ ] Act as
- [ ] Adjudicate
- [ ] Advise
- [ ] Aid
- [ ] Analyze
- [ ] Apply
- [ ] Appropriate
- [ ] Arrest
- [ ] Assess
- [ ] Attain
- [ ] Authenticate
- [ ] Bag
- [ ] Bid
- [ ] Board
- [ ] Break up
- [ ] Broadcast
- [ ] Bundle
- [ ] Canvas
- [ ] Carry over
- [ ] Catalyze
- [ ] Certify
- [ ] Characterize
- [ ] Check up
- [ ] Cleanse
- [ ] Close
- [ ] Co-author
- [ ] Code
- [ ] Co-handle
- [ ] Collate
- [ ] Commit to
- [ ] Complete
- [ ] Compute
- [ ] Conduct
- [ ] Conform to
- [ ] Console
- [ ] Consult with
- [ ] Contribute to
- [ ] Cooperate with
- [ ] Copy
- [ ] Corroborate
- [ ] Counterbid
- [ ] Cover
- [ ] Critique
- [ ] Cross-reference
- [ ] Cut
- [ ] Debate
- [ ] Declare
- [ ] Decrease
- [ ] Defer
- [ ] Delegate
- [ ] Demise
- [ ] Densify
- [ ] Depreciate
- [ ] Designate
- [ ] Deviate
- [ ] Digitize
- [ ] Disband
- [ ] Absolve
- [ ] Acclimate
- [ ] Accrue
- [ ] Activate
- [ ] Adjust
- [ ] Advocate
- [ ] Align
- [ ] Anchor
- [ ] Appoint
- [ ] Approve
- [ ] Articulate
- [ ] Assign
- [ ] Attend
- [ ] Author
- [ ] Balance
- [ ] Bill
- [ ] Book
- [ ] Breed
- [ ] Broaden
- [ ] Buy
- [ ] Capitalize on
- [ ] Carve
- [ ] Catapult
- [ ] Chair
- [ ] Charge
- [ ] Choose
- [ ] Clear out
- [ ] Close out
- [ ] Co-chair
- [ ] Co-defend
- [ ] Co-head
- [ ] Collect
- [ ] Communicate
- [ ] Comply with
- [ ] Concentrate on
- [ ] Confect
- [ ] Congregate
- [ ] Consolidate
- [ ] Contact
- [ ] Contrive
- [ ] Coordinate
- [ ] Copy Write
- [ ] Co-sponsor
- [ ] Counterdemand
- [ ] Co-write
- [ ] Crop
- [ ] Cross-section
- [ ] Cut back
- [ ] Debit
- [ ] Declassify
- [ ] Dedicate
- [ ] Deflate
- [ ] Delete
- [ ] Demolish
- [ ] Deny
- [ ] Depute
- [ ] Detach
- [ ] Devise
- [ ] Direct
- [ ] Disburse
- [ ] Absorb
- [ ] Accommodate
- [ ] Accumulate
- [ ] Adapt
- [ ] Administer
- [ ] Affiliate with
- [ ] Allocate
- [ ] Anesthetize
- [ ] Appraise
- [ ] Arbitrate
- [ ] Ascertain
- [ ] Assimilate
- [ ] Attest to
- [ ] Authorize
- [ ] Base
- [ ] Bind
- [ ] Brace
- [ ] Bridge
- [ ] Browse
- [ ] Calculate
- [ ] Captivate
- [ ] Cash
- [ ] Catch
- [ ] Challenge
- [ ] Charge off
- [ ] Circulate
- [ ] Clear up
- [ ] Close up
- [ ] Co-compose
- [ ] Co-design
- [ ] Co-here
- [ ] Co-manage
- [ ] Compare
- [ ] Compose
- [ ] Conceptualize
- [ ] Confer with
- [ ] Connect
- [ ] Consort
- [ ] Contain
- [ ] Control
- [ ] Co-partner
- [ ] Copyright
- [ ] Counsel
- [ ] Countermand
- [ ] Crack down on
- [ ] Cross-check
- [ ] Cross-sell
- [ ] Cut down
- [ ] Debrief
- [ ] Decline
- [ ] Deduce
- [ ] Deflect
- [ ] Deliberate
- [ ] Demonstrate
- [ ] Deploy
- [ ] Deputize
- [ ] Detain
- [ ] Diagnose
- [ ] Disable
- [ ] Discard

☐ Disclaim	☐ Disclose	☐ Disconnect	☐ Discontinue	☐ Discount	☐ Discover
☐ Discuss	☐ Dismantle	☐ Dismiss	☐ Dispatch	☐ Dispense	☐ Disperse
☐ Display	☐ Dispose of	☐ Disprove	☐ Dispute	☐ Dissect	☐ Dissipate
☐ Dissolve	☐ Dissuade	☐ Distribute	☐ Disunite	☐ Diversify	☐ Divert
☐ Divest	☐ Divide	☐ Dock	☐ Document	☐ Dodge	☐ Dogmatize
☐ Double	☐ Draft	☐ Draw	☐ Drive	☐ Duplicate	☐ Edit
☐ Educate	☐ Elect	☐ Elevate	☐ Eliminate	☐ Embrace	☐ Employ
☐ Encourage	☐ Endure	☐ Energize	☐ Enforce	☐ Engage in	☐ Engineer
☐ Enhance	☐ Ensure	☐ Enter	☐ Entertain	☐ Entrench	☐ Entrust
☐ Enumerate	☐ Equalize	☐ Equate	☐ Escort	☐ Establish	☐ Estimate
☐ Evaluate	☐ Examine	☐ Exceed	☐ Execute	☐ Exemplify	☐ Exercise
☐ Exhibit	☐ Expand	☐ Expedite	☐ Explain	☐ Explore	☐ Fabricate
☐ Facilitate	☐ Fasten	☐ File	☐ Fill	☐ Finance	☐ Fine-tune
☐ Fix	☐ Follow up on	☐ Forecast	☐ Formulate	☐ Foster	☐ Founded
☐ Frequent	☐ Fulfill	☐ Furnish	☐ Fuse	☐ Garnish	☐ Gather
☐ Generate	☐ Give	☐ Govern	☐ Greet	☐ Grow	☐ Handle
☐ Harmonize	☐ Heighten	☐ Help	☐ Hire	☐ Identify	☐ Illustrate
☐ Impact	☐ Implement	☐ Improve	☐ Incorporate	☐ Increase	☐ Induce
☐ Inform	☐ Initiate	☐ Inspect	☐ Inspire	☐ Install	☐ Instill
☐ Instruct	☐ Instrumental in	☐ Integrate	☐ Intensify	☐ Interact with	☐ Interface with
☐ Interpret	☐ Intervene	☐ Interview	☐ Introduce	☐ Invent	☐ Investigate
☐ Invite	☐ Involved in	☐ Irrigate	☐ Join	☐ Juggle	☐ Launch
☐ Layout	☐ Lead	☐ Learned	☐ Lend	☐ Lessen	☐ Link
☐ List	☐ Litigate	☐ Locate	☐ Lower	☐ Maintain	☐ Manufacture
☐ Mark	☐ Market	☐ Maximize	☐ Measure	☐ Mediate	☐ Meet
☐ Mentor	☐ Merchandise	☐ Minimize	☐ Model	☐ Moderate	☐ Modify
☐ Mold	☐ Monitor	☐ Motivate	☐ Mount	☐ Negotiate	☐ Network with
☐ Nullify	☐ Observe	☐ Obtain	☐ Offer	☐ Open	☐ Operate
☐ Optimize	☐ Orchestrate	☐ Order	☐ Organize	☐ Orient	☐ Originate
☐ Outline	☐ Overcome	☐ Oversee	☐ Package	☐ Paint	☐ Participate in
☐ Partition	☐ Penetrate	☐ Perform	☐ Perpetuate	☐ Persist	☐ Persuade
☐ Place	☐ Plan	☐ Plant	☐ Post	☐ Practice	☐ Preapprove
☐ Prearrange	☐ Pre-establish	☐ Prep	☐ Prepare	☐ Present	☐ Preserve
☐ Prevent	☐ Price	☐ Print	☐ Prioritize	☐ Problem-solve	☐ Process
☐ Produce	☐ Project	☐ Promote	☐ Proofread	☐ Protect	☐ Prove
☐ Provide	☐ Publish	☐ Purchase	☐ Pursue	☐ Quadruple	☐ Quantify
☐ Question	☐ Raise	☐ Rank	☐ Reach out to	☐ Realign	☐ Rearrange
☐ Reassemble	☐ Reassess	☐ Reassure	☐ Rebuild	☐ Recalculate	☐ Receive
☐ Recheck	☐ Recommend	☐ Reconcile	☐ Recondition	☐ Reconstruct	☐ Reconvert
☐ Record	☐ Recreate	☐ Recruit	☐ Rectify	☐ Recultivate	☐ Redesign
☐ Redevelop	☐ Redirect	☐ Redistribute	☐ Reduce	☐ Reengineer	☐ Reestablish
☐ Reevaluate	☐ Re-examine	☐ Re-explore	☐ Refer	☐ Refill	☐ Refinance
☐ Refute	☐ Regenerate	☐ Rehabilitate	☐ Reinforce	☐ Reinstall	☐ Reintroduce
☐ Reinvent	☐ Relate	☐ Relay	☐ Relocate	☐ Remanufacture	☐ Remarket
☐ Remerchandise	☐ Remind	☐ Render	☐ Reorchestrate	☐ Reorder	☐ Reorganize
☐ Repackage	☐ Repair	☐ Replace	☐ Replant	☐ Report	☐ Repossess
☐ Represent	☐ Reprint	☐ Reprioritize	☐ Reprocess	☐ Reproduce	☐ Rerun
☐ Reschedule	☐ Research	☐ Reselect	☐ Resell	☐ Resend	☐ Resolve
☐ Respond to	☐ Restructure	☐ Resurvey	☐ Retest	☐ Retouch	☐ Retrain
☐ Reuse	☐ Review	☐ Revisit	☐ Rewrite	☐ Ride	☐ Run
☐ Safeguard	☐ Sample	☐ Satisfy	☐ Saturate	☐ Save	☐ Scale
☐ Scan	☐ Schedule	☐ Screen	☐ Script	☐ Search	☐ Secure
☐ Seize	☐ Select	☐ Selected to	☐ Sell	☐ Send	☐ Separate
☐ Serve	☐ Serve as	☐ Service	☐ Set up	☐ Settle	☐ Ship
☐ Sign	☐ Simplify	☐ Solicit	☐ Solve	☐ Sort	☐ Spearhead
☐ Specialize in	☐ Specify	☐ Split	☐ Standardize	☐ Strategize	☐ Streamline
☐ Strengthen	☐ Structure	☐ Study	☐ Sub out	☐ Substantiate	☐ Succeed
☐ Successful in	☐ Summarize	☐ Summon	☐ Supervise	☐ Support	☐ Surpass
☐ Survey	☐ Synchronize	☐ Synthesize	☐ Tackle	☐ Tailor	☐ Take
☐ Teach	☐ Test	☐ Testify	☐ Thwart	☐ Track	☐ Train
☐ Transition	☐ Translate	☐ Transmit	☐ Transport	☐ Treat	☐ Triple
☐ Troubleshoot	☐ Turn around	☐ Tutor	☐ Uncover	☐ Underwrite	☐ Unify
☐ Unite	☐ Upsell	☐ Use	☐ Utilize	☐ Validate	☐ Verify
☐ View	☐ Visit	☐ Vote	☐ Warn	☐ Work as	☐ Work out
☐ Work with	☐ Write				

DESCRIPTIVE ADJECTIVES & ADVERBS

DESCRIPTIVE ADVERB SAMPLES

- [ ] Accurately invoice...
- [ ] Analytically review...
- [ ] Carefully inspect...
- [ ] Concisely edit...
- [ ] Creatively develop...
- [ ] Dramatically reduced...
- [ ] Encouragingly assist...
- [ ] Finitely define...
- [ ] Independently test...
- [ ] Patiently cater to...
- [ ] Proactively provide...
- [ ] Regularly monitor...
- [ ] Strategically plan...
- [ ] Succinctly write...
- [ ] Thoroughly investigate...
- [ ] Voluntarily serve...
- [ ] Actively explore...
- [ ] Appropriately allocate...
- [ ] Clearly communicate...
- [ ] Consistently attain...
- [ ] Diligently perform...
- [ ] Effectively enhance...
- [ ] Expediently route...
- [ ] Fruitfully completed...
- [ ] Intriguingly captivate...
- [ ] Persistently follow up on...
- [ ] Professionally greet...
- [ ] Significantly improved...
- [ ] Successfully coordinated...
- [ ] Tactically manage...
- [ ] Virtually eliminated...
- [ ] Warmly greet...
- [ ] Actively network with...
- [ ] Architecturally design...
- [ ] Collaboratively tackle...
- [ ] Continuously improve...
- [ ] Diplomatically negotiate...
- [ ] Efficiently conduct...
- [ ] Financially manage...
- [ ] Impartially determine...
- [ ] Intuitively foresee...
- [ ] Persuasively present...
- [ ] Quickly intervene...
- [ ] Simultaneously tackle...
- [ ] Successfully spearheaded...
- [ ] Tastefully decorate...
- [ ] Vividly demonstrate...

DESCRIPTIVE ADJECTIVE SAMPLES

- [ ] Allocate appropriate resources...
- [ ] Create vogue fashions...
- [ ] Devise captivating presentations...
- [ ] Implement seasonal planograms...
- [ ] Negotiate diplomatic negotiations...
- [ ] Prepare accurate records...
- [ ] Recommend analytic solutions...
- [ ] Conceptualize creative designs...
- [ ] Develop contemporary programs...
- [ ] Execute successful new policies...
- [ ] Make a visible difference...
- [ ] Offer encouraging support...
- [ ] Prepare essential reports...
- [ ] Showcase attractive displays...
- [ ] Conduct regular reviews...
- [ ] Develop effective solutions...
- [ ] Facilitate timely negotiations...
- [ ] Make thorough recommendations...
- [ ] Perform preventive maintenance...
- [ ] Present stimulating ideas...
- [ ] Write succinct outlines...

ADD COMPANY & POSITION DESCRIPTORS
FOR YOUR "PROFESSIONAL EXPERIENCE" SECTION

INTRODUCTION

Adding a "Position Descriptor" under each of your jobs encapsulates your company and job responsibility information into a few lines to make it easier for hiring managers to get a full perspective of what you are/were engaged in before reading all of your function- and achievement-related bullets. It is especially beneficial if you have quite a number of bullets listed under your positions where you can cull out some of this information to include in your Position Descriptor and condense some of your bullet content.

This short italicized (two- to five-line) sentence or paragraph will describe the purpose for which you were hired, your primary responsibilities and accountabilities, and specific information about your firm, such as its size, revenues, number of locations and/or employees, products and services it offers, and so on. You can obtain company information from your employers' websites, annual report, and/or marketing materials.

Below are some foundations to use as a guide in developing your own company and position descriptors for each of your positions. Add or adjust information as appropriate for your position and company.

COMPANY & POSITION DESCRIPTOR FOUNDATION #1

Recruited as ______ *[what function or title?]* **to** ______ *[do what?]* [☐ for ______ *(whom or what?)* | ☐ with focus on ______ *(what?)*] **and to** [☐ lead and direct | ☐ manage and oversee | ☐ conduct | ☐ perform | ☐ other: ______] **all aspects of** ______, ______, **and** ______ *[your primary keywords]* **as well as** ______ *[what areas?]* **for this** [☐ multibillion-dollar | ☐ multimillion-dollar | ☐ $______ *(revenues)*] ______ *[type of]* **firm with** ______ [☐ locations | ☐ employees | ☐ other: ______] **that provides** ______ *[type of]* [☐ products | ☐ services | ☐ other: ______] **to (the)** ______ *[type of clients or industry]*. [☐ ______ *(additional information)*.] **(**______ *[#]* **direct reports |** ______ *[#]* **indirect reports)**

SAMPLE FOR A FINANCIAL VICE PRESIDENT

Recruited as Vice President of Finance **to** revamp financial support and control **for** the Portfolio Solutions Group **and to manage** all aspects of investment, overhead, research and development, and a $9 million sales support budget **as well as** all financial aspects of the Service Delivery Center **for this $**3 billion investment **firm that provides** investment portfolios **services to** middle- to upper-income clients. **(**5 **direct reports |** 25 **indirect reports)**

SAMPLE FOR A UNION LEADER

Recruited to lead the expansion of the Nationwide Operations' Business Unit **with focus on** new business development in the Northeast markets **and to manage and oversee** operations and spearhead new projects **for this** multimillion-dollar construction management **firm. Provide** representation **services to** union members **including** contract negotiations and enforcement, grievance handling, collective bargaining, union organizing activities, **and** development and enforcement of health and safety procedures. **(**7 **direct reports |** 15 **indirect reports)**

SAMPLE FOR A TURNAROUND SPECIALIST

Recruited as part of the Turnaround Team **to** direct and manage strategic planning and operations for front- and back-of-the-house operations including restaurant supervision, kitchen management, inventory control, food cost control, and staff training and development **for this** full-service fine dining restaurant **with** 3 **locations,** 75 **employees,** a seating capacity of 250, **and** annual sales of $25 million. **(**14 **direct reports and** 20 **indirect reports)**

COMPANY & POSITION DESCRIPTOR FOUNDATION #2

[☐ Appointed by the ______ *(title)* | (☐ Selected / ☐ Recruited) as ______ *(what function?)*] **to** ______ *[do what?]* **in support of** ______ *[what?]* **for this** ______ *[type of]* [☐ company | ☐ agency | ☐ organization | ☐ other: ______] **with** [☐ revenues | ☐ locations ☐ employees ☐ other: ______] **of** ______ *[number / amount]*. [☐______ *(additional information)*.] **(**______ *[#]* **direct reports |** ______ *[#]* **indirect reports)**

SAMPLE FOR AN ASSISTANT VICE PRESIDENT

Appointed by the President **as** a special representative **to** lead Far East operations and to serve as interim Chief of Staff **in support of** organizational restructuring vis-á-vis a holistic approach **for this** governmental agency **with revenues of $**2.9 Million ensuring all program activities operate consistently and ethically within the mission and values of the firm.

SAMPLE FOR A HIGHER-EDUCATION MENTOR / LEADER

Selected by the Administrator **to** help facilitate this brick-and-mortar, traditional college's learning communities with a student body of 3500 **in support of** providing academic advisement, mentoring, and coaching to an adult student body of nontraditional, first generation college students with different learning styles **for this** higher-education facility. Spearheading various strategic initiatives drove the student body population to 18,000.

SAMPLE FOR AN OPERATIONS DIRECTOR / GENERAL MANAGER

Recruited as turnaround specialist **for** the corporation's multiple holdings of 3 **locations** including ABC, Inc.; DEF Corporation; and GHI Company establishments. 7 **direct reports and** 150 **indirect reports.**

COMPANY & POSITION DESCRIPTOR FOUNDATION #3

Provide ______ *[what?]* **to/for** ______ *[whom or what?]* **including** ______, ______, ______, **and** ______ *[what activities?]* **for this $**______ *[revenues]* ______ *[type of]* **firm** [☐ with ______ *[#]* locations and ______ *[#]* employees | ☐ serving the ______ *(what?)* industry]. [☐ Manage and oversee a $______ *(amount)* ______ *(type of)* budget.] [☐______ *(additional information)*.]

SAMPLE FOR A CLIENT FINANCIAL MANAGEMENT ANALYST

Provide key support **to** the P&L budgeting and forecasting process **including** detailed analytics focused on expenses, taxes, **and** net income **for this** multibillion-dollar global management consulting, technology services, and outsourcing **firm with** 12 **locations and** 25,000+ **employees**. Assist with the preparation of engagement, project, program reporting, and finance control processes. **Manage and oversee a $**12 million department **budget.**

SAMPLE FOR AN OWNER & PRINCIPAL STRUCTURAL ENGINEER

Provide structural engineering and drafting services **to** architects, contractors, developers, and owners of commercial and industrial facilities with client goals driving every design solution **for this** engineering **firm serving the** energy, manufacturing, and process industries. Blending architectural creativity with practical engineering solutions, manage all phases of development—from renderings to completion.

SAMPLE FOR A POWER GENERATION MANAGER

Provide power plant maintenance and operations management **including** safety and environmental oversight, manpower planning, process improvements, energy reductions, and outage coordination **for this $**26 billion paper, packaging, and forest products **firm.** Maximize production growth and opportunities through strategic planning, prioritizing, and scheduling.

COMPANY & POSITION DESCRIPTOR FOUNDATION #4

[☐ Manage and drive | ☐ Lead and direct | ☐ Strategize | ☐ Perform | ☐ other: ______] ______ *[what?]* **of** ______, ______, **and** ______ *[what?]* **for this** ______ *[type of]* **firm with** [☐ $______ *(amount)* in revenues | ☐ ______ *(#)* locations | ______ *[#]* employees | ☐ other: ______] **that** [☐ serves | ☐ provides | ☐ includes] ______, ______, **and** ______ *[what?]*. [☐______ *(additional information)*]. **Direct reports:** ______ *[#]*. **Indirect reports:** ______ *[#]*.

SAMPLE FOR AN AUTOMOTIVE SALES & TECHNICAL MANAGER

Manage and drive regional sales of all automotive refinish products and computer systems, generate and support new business, conduct field sales, and provide technical support **for this** national platinum distributorship **with $**275 million **in revenues,** 25 **locations, and** 325 **employees. Direct reports:** 5. **Indirect reports**: 13.

SAMPLE FOR A CHIEF OF DENTISTRY / CLINICAL DIRECTOR

Lead and direct the continuous strategic planning **of** innovative business model development and issue management; **and oversee** Fiscal Management, Human Resources, Administration, Facility Management, **and** Information Technology **for this $**25 million multispecialty diagnostic and treatment center **that provides** a wide range of specialty health care services including medical, dental, mental health, rehabilitative, and support services **to** 3,000 patients annually. **Direct reports:** 15. **Indirect reports:** 23.

SAMPLE FOR AN IT REGIONAL MANAGER

Strategize and lead execution **of all** field sales and sales support **for** Optical Transport, IP RAN, and Metro Ethernet product lines **for** the new ABC brand including calling on science and technology organization, product management, **and** network operations across 9 states. **Direct reports:** 10. **Indirect reports:** 28.

COMPANY & POSITION DESCRIPTOR FOUNDATION #5

[☐ Founded | ☐ Co-founded | ☐ Built | ☐ Started] **this** ______ *[type of]* **firm from the ground up** [☐ to a leading ______ *(type of)* firm specializing in ______ *(what?)* | ☐ and championed the growth of the firm to ______ *(#)* offices, $______ *(amount)* in annual sales, and ______ *(#)* employees]. [☐ Lead and direct | ☐ Oversee | ☐ Perform | ☐ Conduct | ☐ other: ______] **all aspects of** ______, ______, **and** ______ *[what?]* [☐ that provides ______ *(what?)*]. [☐______ *(additional information)*].

SAMPLE FOR A MORTGAGE BROKER / BANKER

Started this mortgage bank / brokerage **firm from the ground up and championed the growth of the firm to** three offices, **$**156 million **in annual sales, and** 90 **employees. Oversee all aspects of** mortgage sales, marketing, **and** brokering—from new business development and loan originations through to sale closing, loan underwriting, and processing—tackling changing market conditions.

SAMPLE FOR A SENIOR MEDICAL ADVISOR / CHIEF EXECUTIVE OFFICER

Co-founded this firm from the ground up to a leading full-service medical claims evaluation firm specializing in independent medical evaluations and medical claims solutions, management, and staffing. **Lead and direct all aspects of** new business, joint venture, **and** physician panel development **that provides** second opinion diagnostic reviews and medical evaluations in all medical specialties.

SAMPLE FOR A PROJECT MANAGER

Founded this construction management **firm from the ground up to a leading full-service construction firm specializing in apartment rehabilitations,** managing the $2.5 million, 75-unit ABC apartments rehabilitation project on time and within budget. **Manage and monitor** key outside personnel, wages, bidding, purchasing, budgeting, scheduling, permitting, change orders, lien releases, and contracts for the construction of all units.

100 COMPONENTS OF AN EXEMPLARY RESUME:
HOW DOES YOUR RESUME FARE?

Did you know that a full 98 percent of the general public prepares their resume incorrectly? That's because resume writing is an art and a science that takes even professional resume writers years to perfect.

Job seekers generally do not target their resumes precisely to the positions they seek, match their qualifications with the position requirements, incorporate all of the relative resume keywords, showcase their value proposition and matching achievements to prospective employers, and they do not know how to brand themselves. These and other areas are critical to demonstrate to prospective employers how suitable of a candidate you are for them.

If your resume and cover letter are well crafted, it will help you increase your interview odds manyfold, heighten your confidence level, gain renewed enthusiasm for the job search, feel empowered in the interview stage, land the position you seek sooner, and obtain your highest salary potential possible.

The following list of requirements for successful resumes focuses on all of the critical resume and cover letter areas to help you make your presentation the best it can be in order to maximize your interview odds and salary potential. As a Certified Resume Writer and Career Coach, these are the areas I personally include in all of my clients' resumes.

A. Overall Targeted Resume and Cover Letter Strategy

A building is only as strong as the foundation on which it sits. Similarly, resume strategy is key in developing your resume to ensure it is a success. The correct resume format should be used, your overall resume should precisely target the position for which you seek, any "red flags" must be skillfully handled, and it should portray how you can help prospective employers reach their goals.

CRITERIA CHECKLIST:

1. Resume and cover letter target prospective employers' needs with matching qualifications and demonstrate a fit between your qualifications and their needs.
2. Correct resume format (Chronological, Functional, Combination, or Curriculum Vitaé) is used for your situation.
3. Most important targeted information is contained in the top one-third of your resume.
4. All of your key transferable skills (skills used in one profession or position that can be transferred over to another) are included in your cover letter and resume.
5. Work history goes back 10 or, max, 15 years (if relative experience cannot be shown in the past 10 years).
6. Employment related to your targeted profession is documented under "Professional Experience." Any earlier, unrelated experience is listed under "Earlier Career Development," "Additional Experience," or "Other Employment" at the end of your resume.
7. No employment gaps are evident or are skillfully handled.
8. "Red flags" are omitted or tactfully handled by turning them into assets wherever possible.
9. Resume plays up strengths and minimizes weaknesses.
10. Unrelated jobs include targeted job functions wherever possible. *(Example: Someone applying for a railroad conductor might include customer service and money handling functions in an unrelated position.)*
11. Activities, hobbies, professional affiliations, and/or special interests are included when relative and omitted when not.
12. Promotions are included and demonstrate progressive experience in your field.
13. Resume incorporates all relevant information and omits or de-emphasizes irrelevant information.
14. All resume and cover letter components meet strict Resume-Writing Standards.
15. Ensure that all pertinent qualifications (those targeted to your goal) are included.

B. Your Cover Letter

Your Cover Letter, if written well in marketing-savvy language, attracts your audience to want to read your resume and can even compel hiring managers to call you in for an interview based on your cover letter's content alone.

CRITERIA CHECKLIST:

16. The first paragraph attracts your audience via your personal brand message (your assets, benefits, competitive edge, value proposition, and return on investment) or other "wow" factor.

17. First paragraph also includes position sought and where heard of.
18. The second paragraph explains what you have to offer through your matching qualifications and value proposition.
19. The third paragraph validates your value proposition by summarizing your related achievements.
20. The fourth (optional) paragraph sparks additional interest via a related story or eye-opening comment that shows hiring managers why you are interested in and/or passionate about the position.
21. The last paragraph closes with a statement of interest, includes your call-to-action, and thanks the reader.
22. Overall cover letter uses benefit-driven sentences to entice the reader to want to read your resume, and if it's a really good cover letter, to call you in for an interview before even reading the resume.
23. Shows how you are a match for a position opening by including the primary requirements in the original job posting and noting your expertise and qualifications in these areas.
24. Portrays how you can help prospective employers reach their goals with an explanation of how your assets and benefits can serve the firm.
25. Provides a human touch for the person behind the piece of paper so hiring managers can envision you in their firm and its culture performing the position they need filled.
26. Cover letter should be kept to within one page (4 to 5 paragraphs work well).
27. Summarizes your major achievements in brief statements, substantiates how you can be an asset to their firm, and sells you as a qualified candidate based on your experience, education, skills, and qualifications.
28. Contains persuasive benefit-driven statements that make hiring managers want to meet with you.
29. States what your return on investment is to prospective employers if they were to hire you.
30. Includes all of your primary industry-specific keywords. (Check Job Descriptions found on the Internet for your position title, and include all keywords in which you have experience.)
31. Includes specific ways you might be able to help the prospective employer. (View their website to get a feel for what the firm's mission and goals are and any other information where you might be able to fill a need.)
32. Contains any additional compelling information as to why this particular field or position is important to you.

C. Professional Summary Section

The "Professional Summary" section is an encapsulated first paragraph of your resume that states what you have to offer in a concise format. The purpose of this section is to match your qualifications with your prospective employers' requirements, to demonstrate you are a good fit for the position you seek, and to invite the reader in to want to read the rest of your resume.

CRITERIA CHECKLIST:

33. "Professional Summary" is well constructed and summarizes your experience in a nutshell (one to two paragraphs work well).
34. Includes your Personal Brand Message (your assets, benefits, competitive edge, value proposition, and return on investment).
35. Invites the reader to want to read the rest of your resume.
36. States your targeted position in the first sentence (so it is not necessary to include an "Objective" section in your resume).
37. All primary targeted skills and qualifications are included.
38. Primary personal attributes are contained within your "Professional Summary" section.
39. Matches your qualifications with the prospective employers' requirements to demonstrate you are a good fit for the position.
40. Includes all of the primary keywords for the targeted position.
41. Contains heavy-hitting, marketing-savvy, and impactful statements.
42. Includes good use of varied sentence types.

D. Core Competencies or Areas of Experience Section: Resume Keywords

Many firms scan in resumes to search for all relative keywords that match the position opening to determine if you are a qualified candidate. The purpose of including resume keywords is to pass the first electronic screening of your resume so that it is put in the hands of a hiring manager. If your resume does not include all relative keywords, it may not be read or even seen by a human.

CRITERIA CHECKLIST:

43. All related keywords are including in list form under a *"Core Competencies"* or *"Areas of Experience"* section of your resume right under your *"Professional Summary"* section.
44. Infuses the important industry-specific keywords for your profession within your resume and cover letter.

45. Profession-specific keywords are included within responsibility bullets wherever applicable.
46. Transferable skills you may have used in other positions are also included.
47. All technical skills pertinent to the position are identified and included.

E. Professional Experience Section: Job Responsibility and Achievement Bullets

Most jobseekers who prepare their own resumes just list their job functions under each employer. That's what job descriptions are for. Your resume, on the other hand, must showcase how well you accomplished these job functions in order to demonstrate that you are a qualified candidate for the position, or it will not generate many interviews. Achievements are the most important part of your resume. They should target the position you seek and showcase measurable employer benefits.

CRITERIA CHECKLIST:

48. Job years are placed to best advantage: before job title if there are no employment gaps, tucked at end of employment line if gaps are evident.
49. Primary profession-specific bullets start with responsibilities that target the position you seek.
50. Action verbs are used (in their natural sequence) to start each resume bullet, such as manage, develop, and implement...
51. Resume bullets for each position are in good sequential order relative to the targeted position you seek: most relevant bullets appear first, companion bullets thereafter, less important bullets last.
52. Wherever possible resume does not show job hopping. Jobs held for less than a year can be omitted if unrelated to position sought and employment gaps are explained as an asset, wherever possible.
53. The number of jobs included in your resume does not exceed five, or when there are more, they are categorized differently to provide the "look" of five or less. For example: older jobs with the same position title can be categorized as one by listing the three employers followed by bullets related to all three.
54. Job promotions are included and skillfully handled and/or progressive experience in your field is evident, if applicable. Job promotions are included in a way that shows progression under one employer, not as separate positions.
55. Management or supervisory bullets, if applicable, are included to demonstrate how well you can lead, manage, mentor, and train staff.
56. Bland job function bullets are converted into action-packed **CAR (Challenge-Action-Result)** achievement statements. They state the challenge you were faced with, the action you took to meet that challenge, and the benefits your employer or clients derived from your efforts.
57. Job functions are quantified with measurable employer benefits (how much, how many, how big, how fast, how well, how often, and so on) in percentages and dollar amounts.
58. Current and most relevant positions contain the most bullets; older and less relevant positions contain fewer bullets.
59. Bullets are worked up comprehensively so anyone who reads your resume has a full understanding of what you accomplished.
60. Each achievement bullet is concisely edited down to its "lowest common denominator" so it is impactful and does not leave out any important content.
61. Bullet line length is varied throughout resume from one to four lines.
62. Resume includes a "Key Accomplishments" section when achievements are many (such as for Executives, managers, and/or technical positions).

F. Resume Format and Design

For your resume to stand out and be read, it must first attract interest. Using graphic elements and rules and a resume format and design that invites the reader in will help it to stand out from your competition and get read.

CRITERIA CHECKLIST:

63. Resume immediately attracts attention through exceptional formatting and design that helps it stand out from your competition and entices the reader to want to read your resume.
64. Incorporates effective marketing, design, and presentation strategies.
65. Resume design is suitable for your profession and targeted market.
66. Placement of most important information (that which targets your audience and the position you seek) is in the top one-third of your resume.
67. Job titles are clearly indicated in bold, caps, and a larger font size.
68. Proper use of fonts and font sizes has been applied for headings and body copy.

69. There is good organization and division of material and content flows well.
70. Important information is bold-faced (section titles, job titles, employers).
71. There is sufficient white space around content so resume does not look crowded.
72. Individual pages end with full paragraphs, or better, full positions.
73. Spacing is consistent throughout and formatting looks professional.
74. Resume sections are organized and titled well *("Professional Summary," "Areas of Expertise," "Key Accomplishments," "Professional Experience," "Education and Training," etc.).*
75. Contact information is clear and readable (be sure to verify accuracy).

G. Education and Training

All relative education and additional training are important to include in your resume. The way your education is presented plays an important part in your resume.

CRITERIA CHECKLIST:

76. Education includes college or university name, town and state, and degree received (or related coursework, if none).
77. Include Grade Point Averages of 3.0 or above or GPA in major when overall GPA is less than 3.0 and it is higher. Otherwise omit GPA altogether.
78. Year of completion is included if within the past 10 years; omitted if earlier in life.
79. All Degrees are included except when both a Bachelor's and Associate's Degree have been attained, in which case the Associate's Degree can be omitted.
80. When a new grad, education belongs up front. When experience is more relative than education, education belongs towards the end of the resume.
81. Any additional training you received related to your targeted position is included in your resume. Include training course titles and where received. Add years attained if recent.

H. Resume Grammar, Punctuation, Spelling, and Editing

There are few, if any, excusable mistakes allowable in a resume. Grammar, punctuation, and spelling are not any of them. Many firms toss resumes with misspellings and misuse of grammar and punctuation. Be sure your resume has no typos and each sentence flows well.

CRITERIA CHECKLIST:

82. Information is comprehensive but concise; one gets a complete understanding of what you are capable of and have achieved in your career.
83. Your resume does not include personal pronouns. "I," "me," and "my" are understood and do not belong in resumes.
84. Bullets are prioritized within each position in order of their importance to the targeted profession.
85. Action verbs start off each resume bullet and are used correctly (unless they are preceded by an adverb to show how well you handled that function). Such as "Finitely edited..."
86. Descriptive adjectives or adverbs are included, but not overused.
87. Resume is edited down without losing content.
88. Redundant or superfluous words are eliminated.
89. Irrelevant information is omitted.
90. Quantifying information (in numbers) is included wherever possible.
91. Your resume and cover letter contains powerful, persuasive marketing phrases.
92. Personal information (marriage status, children, etc.) is left out.
93. Your resume engages reader and maintains interest through well-written content, compelling copy, and concise editing.

I. Personal Branding

Personal Branding is critical in today's world of work. It sets you apart from your competition and actually helps position you in the top 2% of candidates who are called for interviews and receive job offers.

CRITERIA CHECKLIST:

94. Your cover letter should include all elements of your personal brand: assets, benefits, competitive edge, value proposition, and return on investment.
95. Your personal brand message is finitely written and edited and makes a "wow" statement.
96. Your resume must back up your personal brand with matching achievements.
97. Some use of Visual Branding (Occupational Icon™, graphic elements, charts, graphs, work samples, etc.) is contained within your resume and cover letter, if applicable.
98. Good use of Verbal Branding (slogan, testimonials, mission statement, success stories, case studies, etc.) is included in your cover letter and/or resume.
99. When you read your finalized resume and cover letter, you say ***"Wow! I'd hire me!"***
100. To ensure you have left no stone unturned in making you shine, modify any areas that can use enhancement.

With your resume complete, you are now ready to market yourself!

RESUME DESIGN LAYOUT SAMPLES

RESUME DESIGN LAYOUT #1

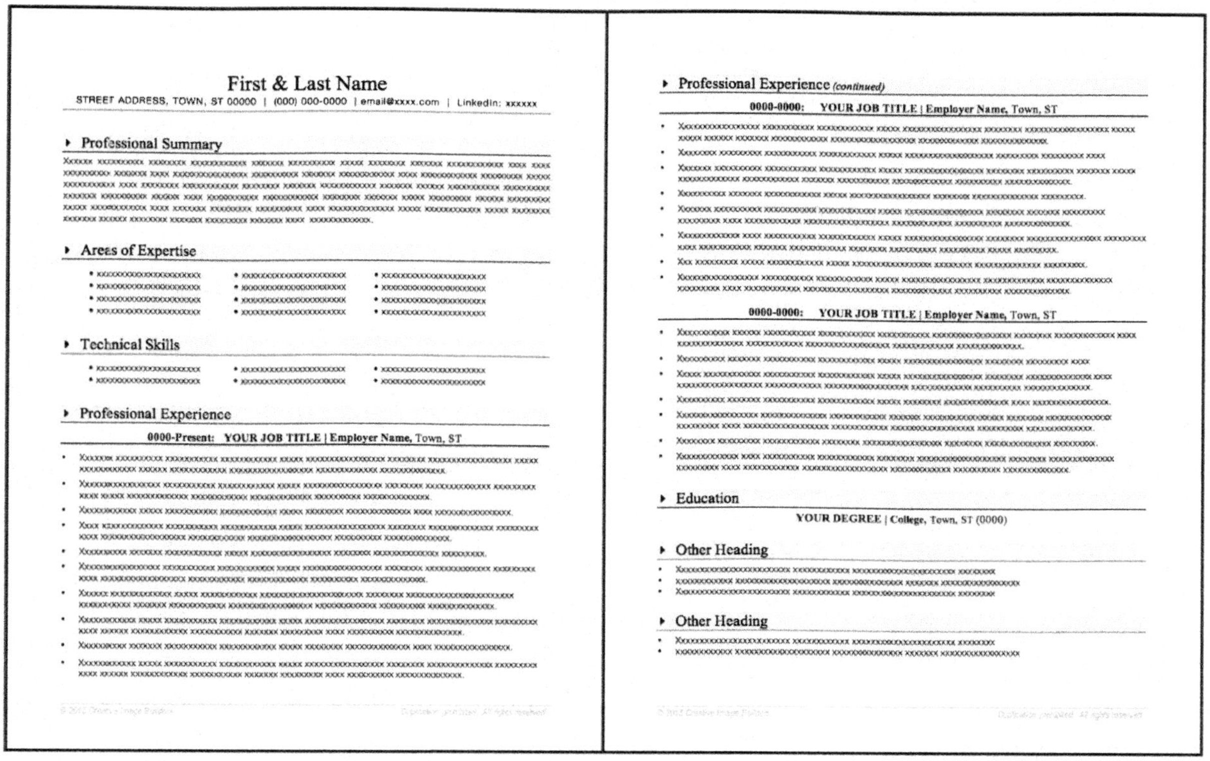
First & Last Name

STREET ADDRESS, TOWN, ST 00000 | (000) 000-0000 | email@xxxx.com | LinkedIn: xxxxxx

Professional Summary

Areas of Expertise

Technical Skills

Professional Experience

0000-Present: YOUR JOB TITLE | Employer Name, Town, ST

Professional Experience (continued)

0000-0000: YOUR JOB TITLE | Employer Name, Town, ST

0000-0000: YOUR JOB TITLE | Employer Name, Town, ST

Education

YOUR DEGREE | College, Town, ST (0000)

Other Heading

Other Heading

RESUME DESIGN LAYOUT #2

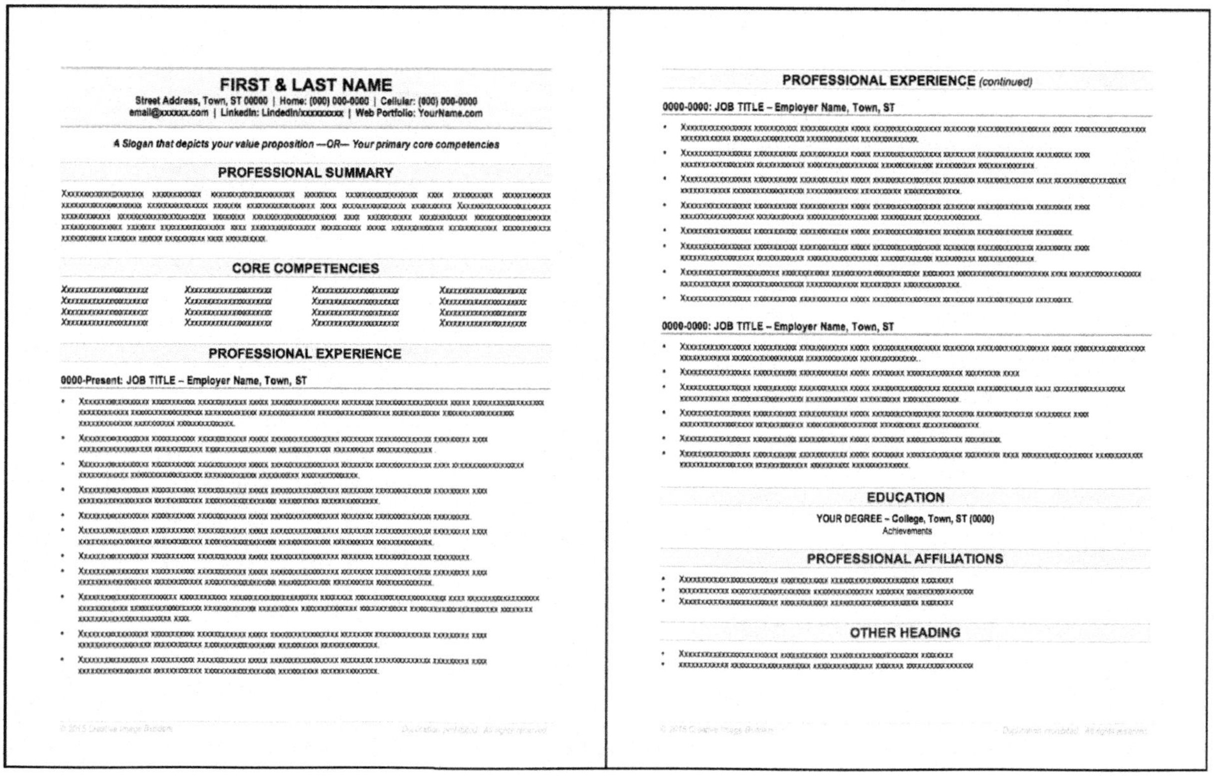
FIRST & LAST NAME

Street Address, Town, ST 00000 | Home: (000) 000-0000 | Cellular: (000) 000-0000

email@xxxxx.com | LinkedIn: LinkedIn/xxxxxxxx | Web Portfolio: YourName.com

A Slogan that depicts your value proposition —OR— Your primary core competencies

PROFESSIONAL SUMMARY

CORE COMPETENCIES

PROFESSIONAL EXPERIENCE

0000-Present: JOB TITLE – Employer Name, Town, ST

PROFESSIONAL EXPERIENCE (continued)

0000-0000: JOB TITLE – Employer Name, Town, ST

0000-0000: JOB TITLE – Employer Name, Town, ST

EDUCATION

YOUR DEGREE – College, Town, ST (0000)

Achievements

PROFESSIONAL AFFILIATIONS

OTHER HEADING

RESUME DESIGN LAYOUT #3

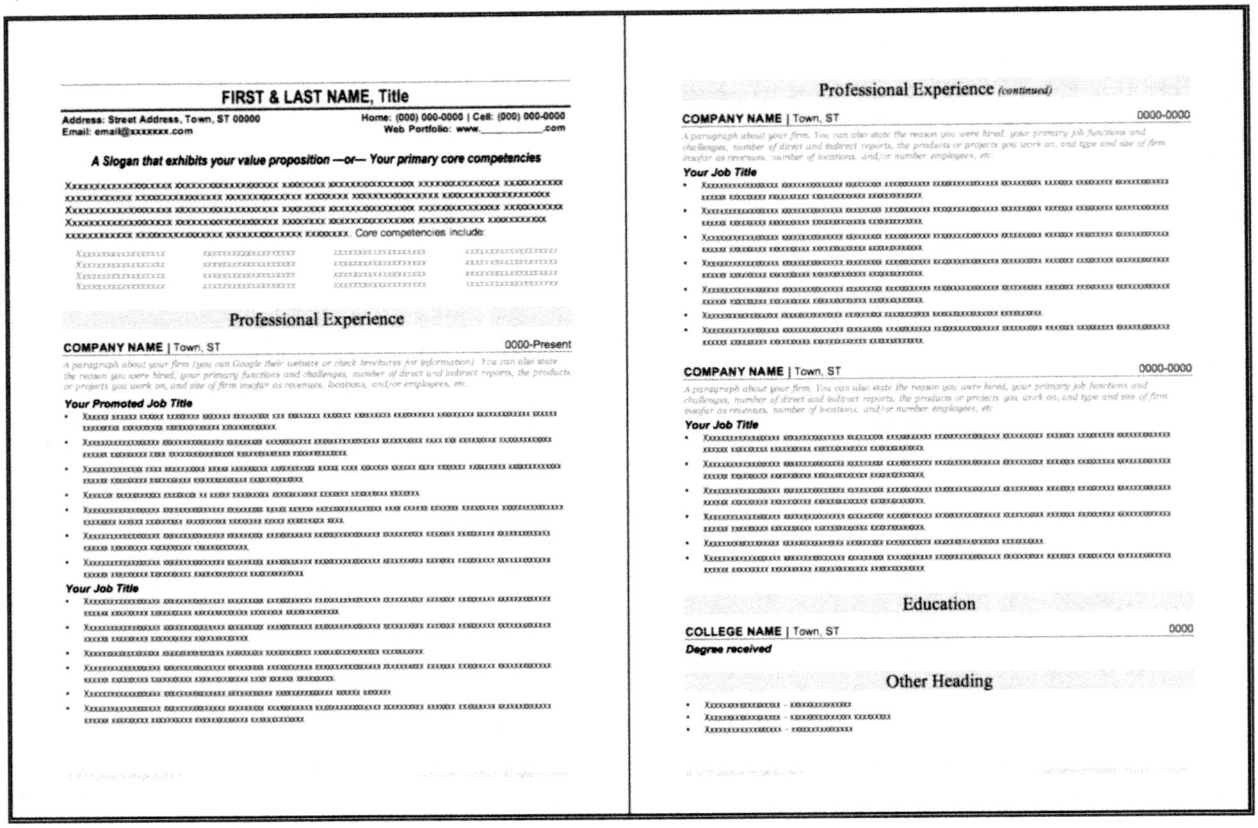

RESUME DESIGN LAYOUT #4

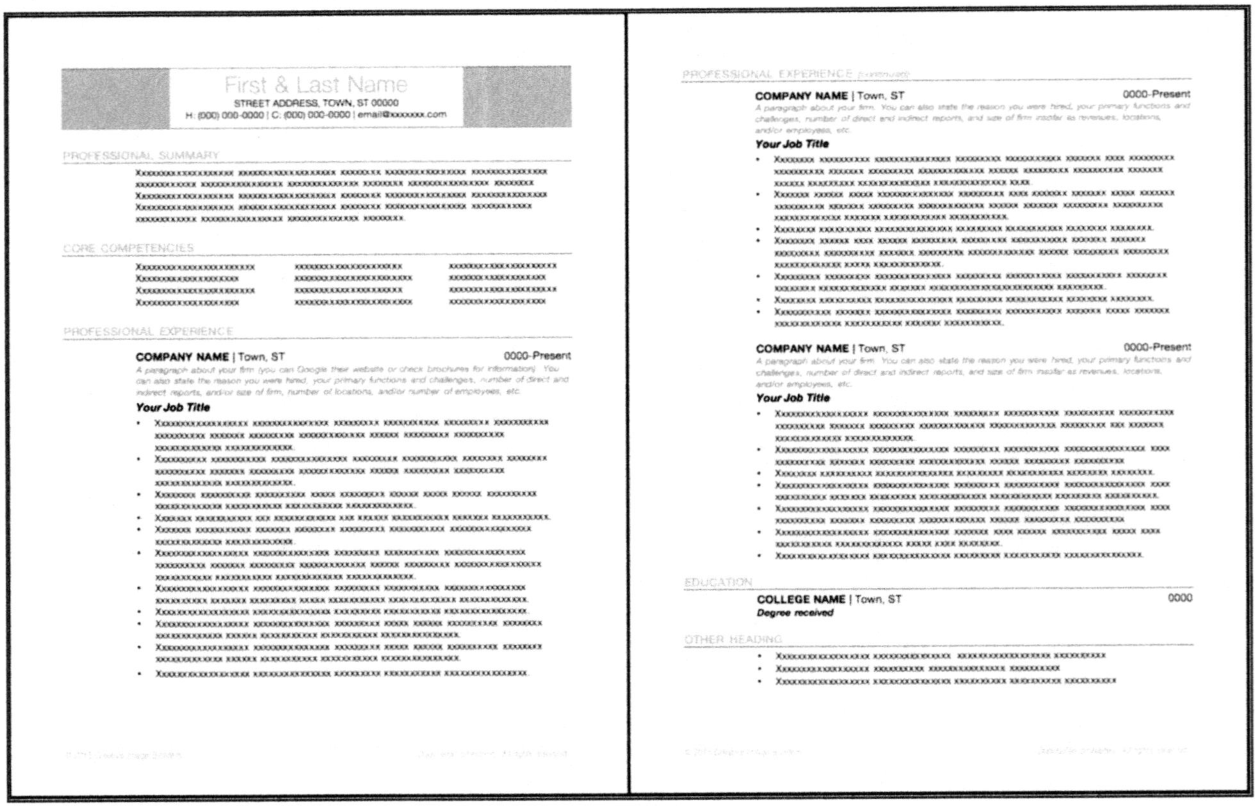

RESUME DESIGN LAYOUT #5

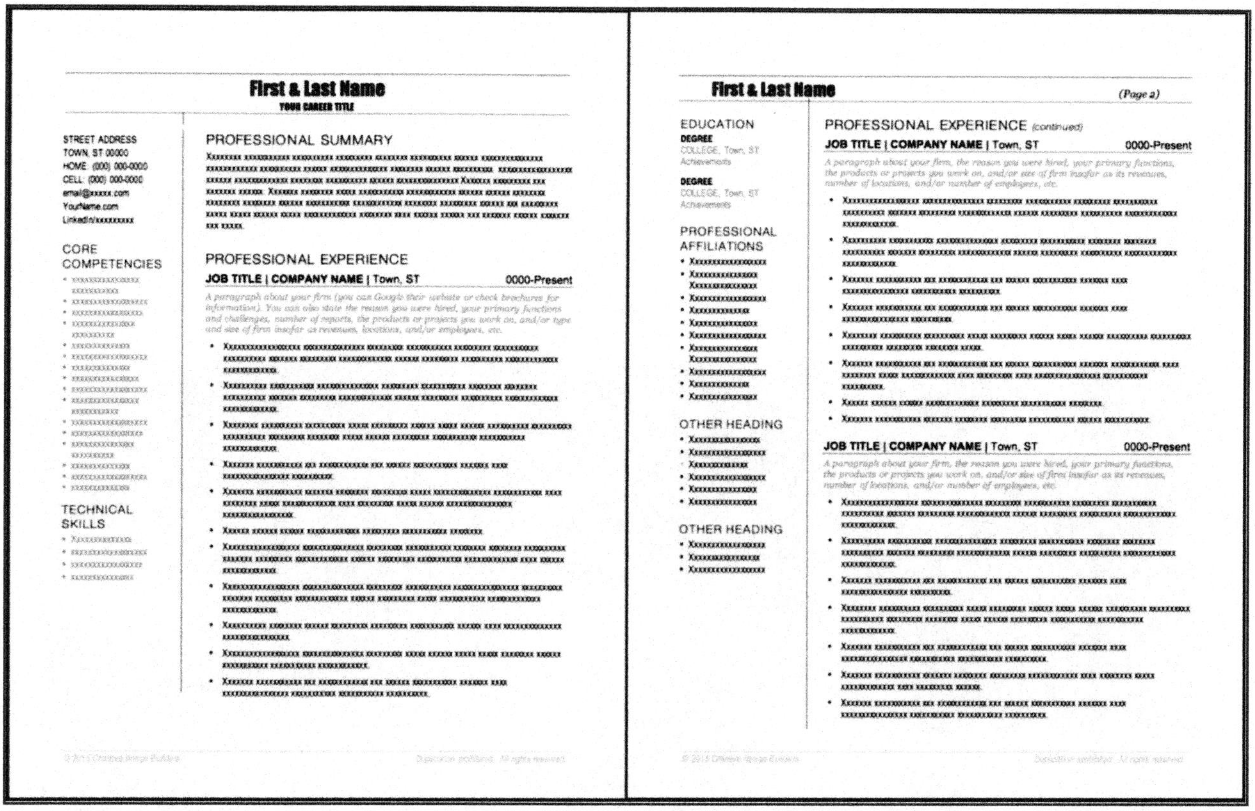
First & Last Name
YOUR CAREER TITLE

STREET ADDRESS
TOWN, ST 00000
HOME: (000) 000-0000
CELL: (000) 000-0000
email@xxxxx.com
YourName.com
LinkedIn/xxxxxxxxx

CORE COMPETENCIES

TECHNICAL SKILLS

PROFESSIONAL SUMMARY

PROFESSIONAL EXPERIENCE

JOB TITLE | COMPANY NAME | Town, ST 0000-Present

A paragraph about your firm (you can Google their website or check brochures for information). You can also state the reason you were hired, your primary functions and challenges, number of reports, the products or projects you work on, and/or type and size of firm insofar as revenues, locations, and/or employees, etc.

First & Last Name *(Page 2)*

EDUCATION

DEGREE
COLLEGE, Town, ST
Achievements

DEGREE
COLLEGE, Town, ST
Achievements

PROFESSIONAL AFFILIATIONS

OTHER HEADING

OTHER HEADING

PROFESSIONAL EXPERIENCE *(continued)*

JOB TITLE | COMPANY NAME | Town, ST 0000-Present

A paragraph about your firm, the reason you were hired, your primary functions, the products or projects you work on, and/or size of firm insofar as its revenues, number of locations, and/or number of employees, etc.

JOB TITLE | COMPANY NAME | Town, ST 0000-Present

A paragraph about your firm, the reason you were hired, your primary functions, the products or projects you work on, and/or size of firm insofar as its revenues, number of locations, and/or number of employees, etc.

STEP 7

MARKET YOURSELF!

CONTENTS OF STEP 7

Decide on Your Marketing Campaign:

- ☐ Develop or Enhance Your Positive Online Identity.
- ☐ Set Up Your LinkedIn Account and Include Your Branded Profile.
- ☐ Clean up Your Facebook, Twitter, and other Social Networking Posts.
- ☐ Create a Blog in Your Area of Expertise.
- ☐ Have Your Web Portfolio (YourName.Com) Created.
- ☐ Compile a Career Portfolio that will Impress Hiring Managers.
- ☐ Consider Having a Logo Created that Depicts Your Personal Brand.
- ☐ Have Your Branded Business Cards Printed.
- ☐ Design Your Stationery to Showcase Your Brand.
- ☐ Use Your Personally Branded Slogan Everywhere.
- ☐ Ensure Your Screen Name is Professional.
- ☐ Set Up a Professional Voice Mail Message.

DECIDE ON YOUR MARKETING CAMPAIGN

INTRODUCTION & INSTRUCTIONS

Before you begin conducting your job search, you will need to decide on your personal marketing campaign and what it will encompass. This chapter covers various ways you can market yourself. The more methods you use, the better your chances for success in getting the position you want quickly—*and* at your highest earnings potential. Check off the various components you will be including in your campaign.

In this step you will most likely find methods you may not have considered using to promote yourself. Know this: Back in 1990 when I was writing and designing branding materials for businesses, I started creating visionary, strategic marketing materials (resumes and cover letters) for individuals using the same branding methods I used for businesses; and clients repeatedly received many interviews despite—and because—those methods were interesting, out of the norm, and memorable to hiring managers.

Those marketing materials branded jobseekers in their profession, just like marketing materials brand businesses, thereby positioning them in the top two percent of applicants because they showcased job candidates as experts in their niche with a high value proposition and an edge over their competition. Decades later, other professional resume writers started applying some of these marketing concepts and found they helped their clients achieve success very quickly; and those methods have since become the "norm."

So, as a pioneer of Personal Branding, I behoove you to not ignore any of them should you find them different or out of the "norm." They will help you stand out and shine over your competition to succeed quickly.

Decide on the career marketing methods you would like to include in your campaign repertoire; and develop an action plan to make each of them happen.

☐ DEVELOP OR ENHANCE YOUR POSITIVE ONLINE IDENTITY.

Google™

Today, approximately 93 percent of hiring managers solidify their hiring decisions based upon an applicant's Web presence. Prospective employers Google applicants to get a more well-rounded view of their skills and achievements before calling them in for an interview or making a job offer. Finding positive affirmations of what you have to offer can help hiring managers determine your overall fit within their company and can clinch the "deal."

Having a positive Web presence is a necessity for all careerists. You want an online identity that showcases you in your very best light, exhibits your strengths and qualifications, demonstrates your expertise, and shows how you are a qualified candidate to meet prospective employers' needs and help them solve their challenges.

If you haven't done this already, find out what type of online identity you have: Google your name *in quotes* and scroll through a number of pages. What comes up? Depending upon whether you have a common or unique name, you may find a few or many results...or none at all. You might be surprised at what you find—or don't find. Perhaps entries you were unaware existed. Some might be helpful to your career goals, others might not. If you are known in your targeted industry, you may find entries on Websites you didn't know were there. Perhaps an article you wrote or were quoted in, a profile that hasn't been verified by you, associations you are a member of, speaking engagements you may have conducted, and so on.

If you do not already have a positive Web presence that has been built through your professional network and experience —and even if you do, you can take hold and start creating or enhancing it for yourself now.

Three primary ways to create or enhance your positive online identity are by having a LinkedIn account, a Web Portfolio, and/or a blog—each of which should include your personally branded message *(as created in **Step 4: Develop Your Personal Brand & Professional Summary**)* to help you attain career success. Be sure to include your LinkedIn, Web Portfolio, and/or blog URLs on your resume, business / networking cards, email tag lines, articles you write and/or are cited in, and so on. These methods increase your career opportunities as they compel hiring managers to call you ahead of your competition. Each is discussed in this step.

☐ SET UP YOUR LINKEDIN ACCOUNT AND INCLUDE YOUR BRANDED PROFILE.

Linked in

LinkedIn is hiring managers' social networking site of choice. Serious careerists are expected to have a LinkedIn account. Potential employers seek candidates to fill their open positions using resume keywords. They also post their open job positions there. If you do not already have a LinkedIn account, be sure to set one up to include your personal brand message you created in ***Step 4: Develop Your Personal Brand & Professional Summary***. Be sure your LinkedIn URL is included in the header of your resume before you attach it to LinkedIn or distribute it. Other social networking platforms, such as Twitter and Facebook, are more incidental but are generally checked when prospective hiring managers Google you, so you can elect to include them in your resume header as well. *(See also "Use Your Social Media to Locate Positions and Make Connections" in **Step 8: Conduct Your Job Search.**)*

☐ CLEAN UP YOUR FACEBOOK, TWITTER, AND OTHER SOCIAL NETWORKING POSTS.

Be careful what you post and make public online! You should only make public those posts that are not harmful to your identity, and better—topics that are related to your profession—as prospective employers *will see* your posts, which may be cause to screen you out of the mix altogether. You'll never know if you had been considered for a specific job and were screened out due to social networking posts hiring managers might find. It is suggested that you befriend or follow colleagues in your field and post like-minded professional messages that can be seen by your target audience. Make those comments public. Keep everything else private, including your Facebook Friends list (unless it only contains professionals). *(See also "Use Your Social Media to Locate Positions and Make Connections" in **Step 8: Conduct Your Job Search.**)*

☐ CREATE A BLOG IN YOUR AREA OF EXPERTISE.

Consider starting and publishing a blog (short for Weblog or Web Log) in your area of expertise where you can address matters of professional interest; write about current events in your field; share opinions, experiences, related links, and photos; and obtain comments / feedback from others. Blogs create a community of like-minded people who interact with each other sharing what's on their mind in the form of an online journal. Blogs are typically updated regularly (daily, weekly, or monthly) by the blogger. You can also subscribe to others' blog feeds where you can post comments regarding your own experiences and opinions on topics of interest in your profession. Your blog can be added to your Web Portfolio or published in WordPress, Blogger, TypePad, or other blogging software. Blogging on professional topics of interest can help position you as an expert in your field, build notoriety regarding your brand, and enhance your positive online identity.

☐ HAVE YOUR WEB PORTFOLIO CREATED.

Create (or have a professional create) a **Web Portfolio** (with a URL of "YourName.com," or if you have a common name, "YourName Title.com") that showcases your branded biography (from ***Step 4: Develop Your Personal Brand & Professional Summary***) on your Web Portfolio's home page. Be sure to include your URL in your resume header along with your LinkedIn URL.

There are several reasons I recommend jobseekers have a Web Portfolio:

1. When potential employers do a Google search for you prior to calling you in for an interview or making a job offer (and they will), having a Web Portfolio in your name generally positions the jobseeker as the ***number one*** Google entry *(see sample below)* unless you have a very common name in which case, your Web Portfolio will still generally show up on the first page. By so doing, hiring managers get to see your Personal Brand before they view anything else on the Internet and it will resonate with them as they continue their search.

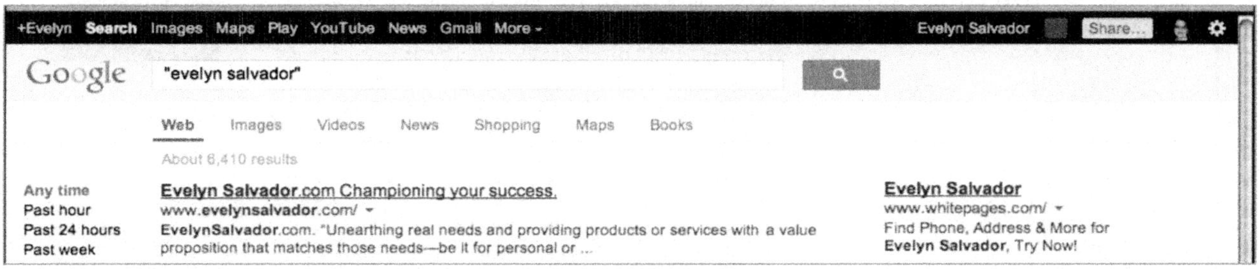

2. Not many people have a Web Portfolio, so it will be another way to help you stand out from your competition. And the more hiring managers view your brand, the more apt they are to reach out to you.
3. Potential employers can also find you when they search the Internet for relevant keywords to locate candidates to fill their open positions, so it increases your visibility and chances of being called. Be sure to optimize your Web Portfolio to include all of your resume keywords you selected in Steps 2 and 4.
4. Ongoing networking is easy when you provide your URL when you might not otherwise have a resume available. And since your URL will be in your name, it is an easy way for others to remember it.

Your Web Portfolio can include as few or as many web pages as sufficiently sells you in your field. Pages can include your *"Home"* or *"About"* page, Personally Branded *"Biography," "Credentials," "Resume," "Career Highlights"* or *"Key Accomplishments," "Work Samples," "Success Stories," "Case Studies,"* and the like. It should contain a resume hyperlink option to download your resume as MS Word, PDF, and/or ASCII (text only) versions and provide a Call To Action for hiring managers to contact you. (If you need help in this area, Web Portfolios are available at CareerCatapult.com.)

Web Portfolio Samples

Following are Web Portfolio Samples in various professions including Realtor, Talent & Leadership Development Director, Elementary Teacher, Information Technology Director, Accounting Vice President, Executive Secretary, Quality Assurance Manager, Travel Agent, International Sales Director, Telemarketing Supervisor, Horticulturist, Information Technology Manager, Vice President of Manufacturing, Vice President of Sales & Marketing, Internet Marketing Specialist, Retail Sales Manager, Nurse Manager, Architect / Project Manager, and Telecommunications Director,

WEB PORTFOLIO SAMPLE FOR A REALTOR

The following Web Portfolio was developed for the Realtor whose Personal Brand Biography was included in ***Step 4: Develop Your Personal Brand & Professional Summary.*** In Jane's case, her Web Portfolio was used both for obtaining employment at a Real Estate firm (to showcase her selling methods and techniques) and also for buyers looking to purchase a home and homeowners seeking to sell their house.

JaneMurphyRealtor.com

"This is the Moment. This is the Time."

JaneMurphyRealtor.com

- LICENSED REAL ESTATE SALESPERSON
- CERTIFIED BUYER'S REPRESENTATIVE
- REAL ESTATE TURNAROUND EXPERT

WELCOME | SERVICES | BUYER PROCESS | SELLER PROCESS | REAL ESTATE TERMS

Did you know it takes on average 1.5 years to sell a house today?
Do you have that kind of time to waste?

Anyone can put your house on a multiple listing, sit back and wait for calls, and call themselves a real estate broker. Sitting back and waiting is not part of Jane Murphy's repertoire. Slow economy or not...there are homes for sale and buyers looking to purchase. Joining the two full circle is what she does best. And as a top real estate performer, Jane uses multiple methods, techniques, and connections to help buy or sell houses as quickly as possible ...generally 50 to 75 percent faster than the average realtor.

Most people see a house they like and go with whomever advertised that home. Truth is, most agents have access to the same homes in their region. (Jane's covers all of Suffolk County.) The better method is to interview and select the realtor you feel will work hard for you and then go forward with your search for a home or a buyer. If you are a buyer, Jane will take you through more homes; and if you are a seller, she will bring by more prospects than you would obtain from other realtors.

As a Top Real Estate Producer who is often in the TOP 10 of Long Island's NO. 1 producing office of the largest real estate firm in the industry, Jane is more experienced, trained, and able to help you buy or sell your home than 90% of other agents and within a much shorter time-span. How? She just doesn't stop. Because she keeps going, and going, and going, some call her "Ever Ready" and her colleagues joke they are going to give her Imodium because she's always running out the door saying, "I gotta go! I gotta go!"

As a Licensed Real Estate Salesperson and a Certified Buyers' Rep, Jane works equally hard for her buyers and sellers without favoritism to one or the other as you may find in the field. As an expertly skilled realtor who has saved her clients tens of thousands of dollars, you'll have the BEST OF THE BEST working with you side by side to achieve the BEST OF THE BEST for you...and have fun in the process!

Using a Talented Agent = Your Success!

Buying or Selling Your House? Interview me.
Call or email me and I will walk you through a house or two or bring you in leads before we even talk contract!
000.000.0000 Email Me

START YOUR HOME SEARCH:
MLS Search

MEMBER, LONG ISLAND BOARD OF REALTORS & NEW YORK BOARD OF REALTORS

Not all Realtors are Alike

Jane Murphy is a Real Estate Turnaround Expert who accelerates results, gets the best prices for her buyers and sellers, and ensures the whole process runs smoothly—while making your house buying or selling experience enjoyable.

On average, Jane:

- Provides 50-75% faster turnarounds
- Saves clients $10s of thousands
- Is both a buyer's and a seller's rep
- Shows more houses to buyers
- Brings more leads to sellers
- Is the best of the best to bring you the best of the best!

Branding and Website by CareerCatapult.com

WEB PORTFOLIO SAMPLES FOR VARIOUS PROFESSIONS

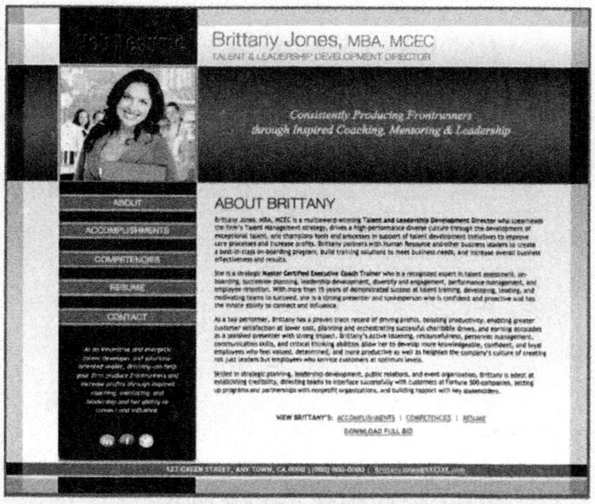

TALENT & LEADERSHIP DEVELOPMENT DIRECTOR

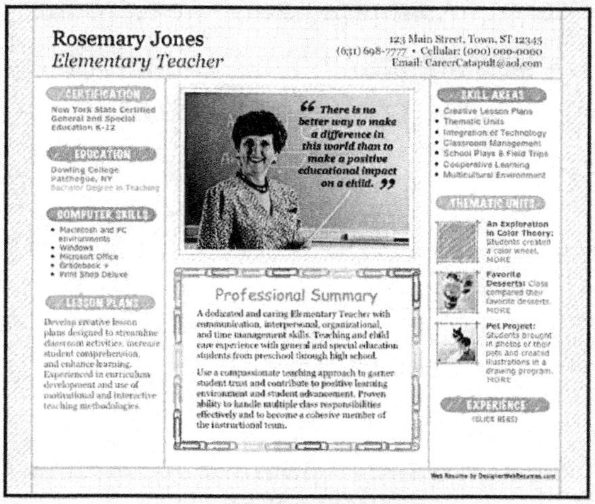

ELEMENTARY TEACHER

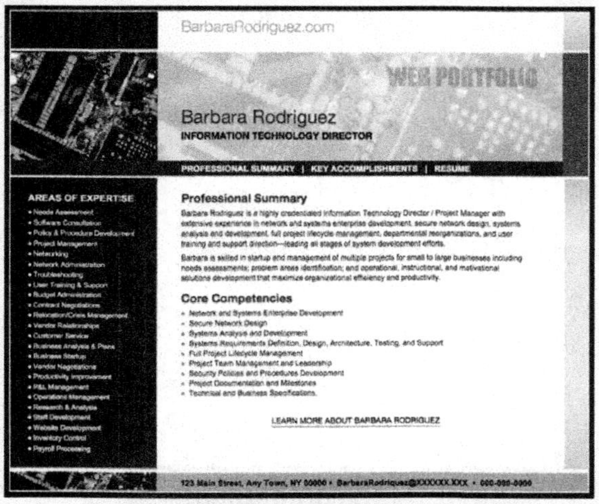

INFORMATION TECHNOLOGY DIRECTOR

ACCOUNTING VICE PRESIDENT

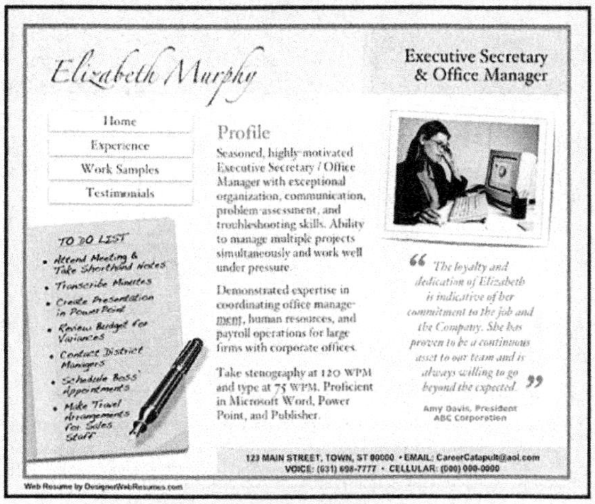

EXECUTIVE SECRETARY

QUALITY ASSURANCE MANAGER

WEB PORTFOLIO SAMPLES FOR VARIOUS PROFESSIONS *(Continued)*

TRAVEL AGENT

INTERNATIONAL SALES DIRECTOR

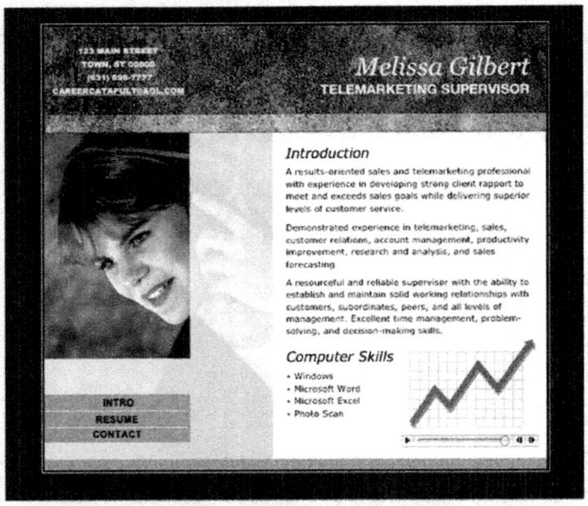

TELEMARKETING SUPERVISOR

HORTICULTURIST

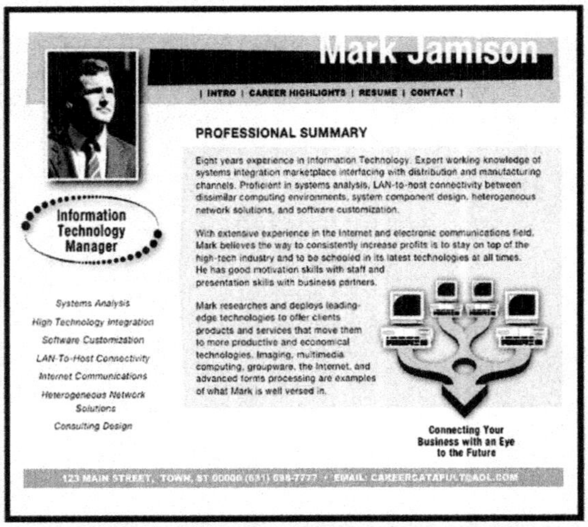

INFORMATION TECHNOLOGY MANAGER

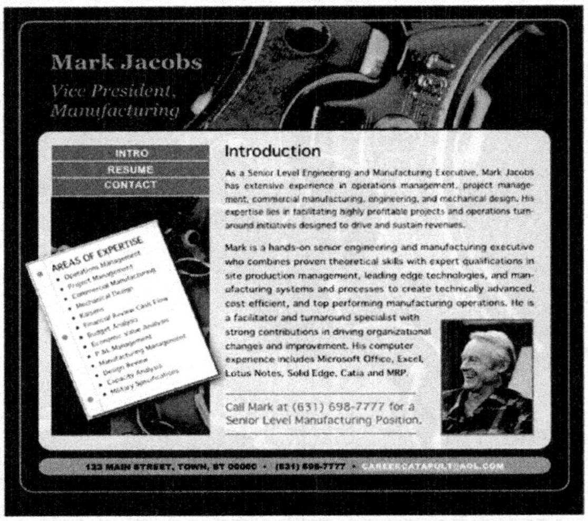

VICE PRESIDENT OF MANUFACTURING

WEB PORTFOLIO SAMPLES FOR VARIOUS PROFESSIONS *(Continued)*

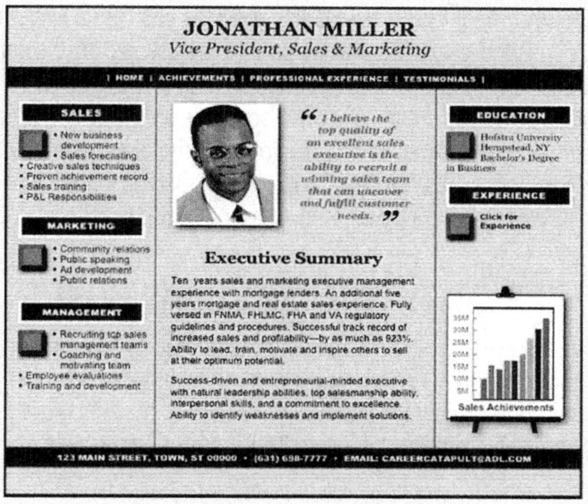

VICE PRESIDENT, SALES & MARKETING

INTERNET MARKETING SPECIALIST

RETAIL SALES MANAGER

NURSE MANAGER

ARCHITECT / PROJECT MANAGER

TELECOMMUNICATIONS DIRECTOR

☐ COMPILE A CAREER PORFOLIO THAT WILL IMPRESS HIRING MANAGERS.

Creating and exhibiting a **Career Portfolio** (or **Interview Portfolio**) during all of your interviews is a professional and impressive way to showcase what you have accomplished and how you can help a prospective employer meet their goals. It also provides you with a systematic way of discussing your background and expertise and helps alleviate stress on the part of the candidate with the ability to hone in on challenges you may be able to tackle for a prospective employer and showcase how you solved them. You can also create a PowerPoint presentation on to use as a leave-behind at your interviews. Include your resume along with any licenses, certifications, awards, success stories, case studies, project (work) photos, and/or other relative career-related information. Try to keep the number of pages to a dozen or so.

☐ CONSIDER HAVING A LOGO CREATED THAT DEPICTS YOUR PERSONAL BRAND.

Just like business branding, having a targeted and memorable Logo increases your chances of being remembered by hiring managers and those with whom you network. This is another way to shine above your competition. To etch your name and what you do in the minds of hiring managers, a logo that exemplifies your personal brand and includes your slogan / tag line can be used in all of your career marketing materials. Include it on your resume, cover letter, business cards, blog, Web Portfolio, Interview Thank You Letters, and more. *(Logo creations are available at CareerCatapult.com.)*

Jane Murphy

LICENSED REAL ESTATE SALESPERSON &
CERTIFIED BUYERS' REPRESENTATIVE

*This is the Moment.
This is the Time.*

☐ HAVE YOUR BRANDED BUSINESS CARDS PRINTED.

Careerists should have their own personal business cards (preferably with a logo) they you can give out whenever they network and use as a leave-behind at interviews. It shows you are serious about yourself and what you do; and it is preferable to hand out a personal business card than a company one or, worse, to have to find a piece of paper to jot down your number when you network. Be sure to include your tag line. The back side of your business card is an excellent place to bullet your areas of expertise or include your Elevator Pitch. And the cost is incidental.

☐ ENSURE YOUR SCREEN NAME IS PROFESSIONAL.

I once had a client whose screen name was "SleepsAlot@xxxxx.xxx." Needless to say, this would have been a turn-off to hiring managers, and I recommended she change it. If you prefer not to change your existing screen name, I suggest you set up a separate email account with a professional ring to it that you can use just for job search and/or professional purposes. Be sure your resume includes the new screen name.

☐ SET UP A PROFESSIONAL VOICE MAIL MESSAGE.

Listen to your current voice mail message. If you were a hiring manager calling to schedule an interview, what would that message convey to you? If it is less than appropriate, change your greeting to one that is more professional—and better, on brand.

☐ USE YOUR PERSONALLY BRANDED SLOGAN EVERYWHERE.

Be sure to add your slogan you created in ***Step 4: Develop Your Personal Brand and Professional Summary*** to all of your marketing materials including on your Resume, Cover Letter, Web Portfolio, LinkedIn Profile, all email and online messages, business cards, letterhead, blog(s), Career Portfolio, Interview Thank You Letters, and any other professional communications. Slogan samples are included in ***Step 4.***

☐ DESIGN YOUR STATIONERY TO SHOWCASE YOUR BRAND.

Also consider having your branded stationery designed and printed with your logo (or you can print it yourself on quality resume paper). You can use your letterhead for your Cover Letter, Interview Thank You Letters, and other professional correspondence. Showcasing your brand will help you stand out from your competition and can detract from possible negatives in your resume *(such as in the case of the example that follows).*

Sample Letterhead for a Teacher

The following letterhead was designed for a teacher who had been stagnated in substitute teaching positions for a long time. Though it doesn't contain a logo, it includes the areas she is skilled in. To prevent from being screened out by school districts due to her lengthy time without a permanent position, I designed her letterhead to exhibit her creativity and numerous interests in the margin of her cover letter so it is the first thing that is read. By the time prospective employers read her resume and saw that she was a substitute teacher for five years, they would already have a positive impression of her. As a result, this client received many calls for a full-time teaching position.

SPECIAL INTERESTS I CAN BRING TO YOUR CLASSROOM:

READING / LITERATURE

CREATIVE / JOURNAL WRITING

PAINTING / FINE ARTS

MUSIC

DANCE

TRAVEL

PHOTOGRAPHY

THEATRE PRODUCTION

KATHY GARDNER

123 MAIN STREET, ANY TOWN, NY 65432
(000) 000-0000 • EMAIL: XXXXX@XXX.XXX

Dear Superintendent:

I believe my Master's Degree in Special Education and Bachelor's Degree in Child Study coupled with five years of teaching experience has amply prepared me for an Elementary Education or Special Education Teaching position in your school district. I am enclosing my résumé for your review.

During my substitute and student teaching experiences with varying elementary grade and academic levels, I have been involved in all facets of teaching — from developing creative and functional lesson plans and producing productive thematic units to effective classroom management. I have utilized my interpersonal, communication and team-building skills to work effectively and cooperatively with colleagues, students and parents, resulting in a well-rounded, knowledgeable and resourceful teaching approach.

I have earned the respect and recognition as a substitute teacher who is organized and adaptable. Working with various school districts and grade levels has allowed me to develop the ability to effectively manage a classroom of varying behavioral levels.

I believe my creative interests (noted in the margin), can be combined in creative lesson planning to enhance content, promote retention, and add a three-dimensional approach to learning where children participate and are motivated to learn and grow.

While I have enjoyed substitute teaching for several years, I am now seeking a permanent teaching position at a school I can call "home," and would appreciate hearing from you to discuss any existing or future openings you might have. Thank you for your consideration.

Sincerely,

Now You Are Ready to Start Conducting Your Job Search!

STEP 8
CONDUCT YOUR JOB SEARCH

CONTENTS OF STEP 8

- ☐ Target Companies You Would Like to Work for.
- ☐ Mail Your Resume and Cover Letter to Targeted Employers.
- ☐ Search the Internet for Available Job Postings in Your Targeted Area.
- ☐ Use Your Social Media to Locate Positions.
  - LinkedIn Jobs
  - Twitter
- ☐ Consider Using a Resume Distribution Service to Distribute Your Resume.
  - Targeted Direct Mail Campaigns for Executives and Senior Professionals
  - Email Campaigns for All Jobseekers
- ☐ Post Your Resume on Job Boards or Use a Service to do it for You.
  - General Job Boards
  - Resume Posting Services
  - Niche Job Boards and Career Resource Sites
- ☐ Join Professional Associations In Your Industry
- ☐ Consider Registering with an Employment Agency / Recruitment Firm.
  - Private Employment Agencies
  - Public Employment Agencies

CONDUCT YOUR JOB SEARCH

INTRODUCTION

Keep in mind that regardless of the economy there are jobs available in most all industries. However, most position openings are not advertised to the public for a number of reasons including that they are being filled from within the firm, employers hire referrals from employees, the company is using an employment agency, an in-house resume database is used to select candidates, and so on. Therefore, the more methods you use to get your resume in the hands of hiring managers, the better your chances are for success.

This chapter covers various ways to conduct an effective job search including targeting companies of interest to you, mailing and emailing your resume and cover letter to hiring managers, using your social media platforms to locate positions and make connections, posting your resume to job boards, joining professional industry-specific associations, and registering with an employment agency.

☐ TARGET COMPANIES YOU WOULD LIKE TO WORK FOR.

Since most job openings are not advertised, it would behove you to be proactive and research various companies in your targeted area, visit their Websites to get a feel for the work culture, check their directory (if there is one) for position titles within the firm and the people who hold them, and view their career opportunities to determine which ones, if any, would be a good fit for you if a position were to become available. By sending your resume to a select group of targeted firms and expressing an interest for any current or future openings, you will be included in their resume database for future reference should a position become available.

Good sources to find out about firms that may interest you include reading local newspapers, trade magazines, business periodicals, and professional journals. Also check the want ads in these publications. You can contact the firm to ask them to send you information about the company, such as their promotional materials, annual report, new product offerings, and so on. The more you can learn about the companies that interest you and their current or future endeavors and how your skills and qualifications might help them, the better your chances for success.

Once you have targeted several companies, call them to find out the names and titles of the hiring manager and department head with whom you would work under and send them both your resume. They may or may not have a position opening at that moment but you never know if one would open up shortly and they will have your resume on file. Follow up in a week to see if they received your resume and the possibility of any current or future openings.

☐ MAIL YOUR RESUME AND COVER LETTER TO TARGETED EMPLOYERS.

Though you may consider snail mailing your resume "old school," DON'T. Here's why: Hiring managers today are flooded with jobseekers applying for positions online—many if not most of whom do not even fit the criteria for the position. It is a daunting task for employers to search for just the right candidate.

If you mail your resume, it makes an impact that you are genuinely interested in *their* position and it may get in the hands of the hiring manager quicker than if you just posted it online.

You can use a resume distribution service (see below) to mail your resume and cover letter out to prospective employers in your field or you can check the Internet and local directories and/or ads for companies in your targeted geographical area that hire candidates in your profession to do this yourself. Whenever possible, mail your resume out to the company's hiring manager and/or department head—both if you can obtain their names. If not listed, make that call to find out. That extra effort matters. And if you are responding to an Internet job posting and there is an address listed or you can find it out, also snail mail your printed resume to them. Needless to say, the more resumes you send out, the higher your chances of getting called in for interviews and getting the position you seek sooner.

☐ SEARCH THE INTERNET FOR AVAILABLE JOB POSTINGS IN YOUR TARGETED AREA.

Google

Check the Internet for available positions by Googling your position title with the word "jobs" in quotes, such as "Human Resource Jobs." You will find entries for both individual positions and those on job boards that match what you are seeking, such as "Human Resource Jobs on CareerBuilder.com," "Human Resource Jobs – Monster.com," "Human Resource Jobs in New York | LinkedIn," "New York Human Resource – craigslist," and so on. Apply to all those that interest you by following the instructions on the post. See also ***"Mail Your Resume and Cover Letter to Targeted Employers"*** *(above)* and ***"Post Your Resume on Job Boards or Use a Service to Do it for You"*** *(below)* for additional information. Before distributing or posting your resume, check these job descriptions and the ones you researched in ***Step 4: Develop Your Personal Brand and Professional Summary*** to make sure that all of the functions your targeted job descriptions contain and that you have handled are contained in some fashion within your resume.

☐ USE YOUR SOCIAL MEDIA TO LOCATE POSITIONS.

LinkedIn JOBS

LinkedIn has one of the largest job boards where you can search available job postings and post your resume. Click on "Jobs" and enter the location(s) you would like to work in and industries you are interested in. You can discover jobs in your network and reach out to your connections to ask them to make a referral for you. All job activity is private.

twitter

Used in conjunction with LinkedIn and job search boards, Twitter can be an effective job search tool in finding job listings since employers post job openings on Twitter as well. You can search by position title and/or by company name to locate specific firms. You can also receive targeted job tweets forwarded to your Twitter feed.

☐ CONSIDER USING A RESUME DISTRIBUTION SERVICE TO DISTRIBUTE YOUR RESUME.

Using a resume distribution service to snail mail, fax, and/or email your resume out to hundreds, even thousands, of prospective employers can result in getting your resume in the hands of more prospective employers, increase your interview odds, provide a competitive advantage, and ultimately save you a lot of time. For an effective job search campaign, jobseekers should focus on including several distribution channels in their job search marketing endeavors.

The following resume distribution services provide Direct Mail Campaigns, Resume Email Campaigns, Resume Fax Distribution, and/or Resume Posting services to a targeted list of hiring managers who recruit those in your profession.

Targeted Direct Mail Campaigns for Executives and Senior Professionals

Profile Research | Resume Distribution Master.com

The two resume distribution services I recommend that **snail mail, fax,** and/or **email** resumes to targeted employers for executives and senior professionals are: **ProfileResearch** and **ResumeDistributionMaster**. Both services work one-on-one with their clients to develop a customized targeted mailing list that meets your specifications.

Your resume will be sent directly to a select group of hiring managers, proprietary executive recruiters, and/or private equity / venture capital firms based on your selected industry, geographical area, company size, resume keywords, and/or customized criteria, and will help you get your resume in the hands of decision makers quickly. Each service provides a complete list of all recruiters who are sent your resume, along with their contact information for you to make follow-up calls.

Email Campaigns for All Jobseekers

There are a number of resume distribution services that will **email** your resume to thousands of hiring managers and/or head hunters that seek and recruit people with your qualifications in your targeted industry and location. The primary resume distribution services today include: **ResumeRabbit**, **ResumeSpider**, **ResumeViper**, **ResumeDispatcher**, and **ResumeZapper**.

A note of caution: *do not use a service that blasts your resume to **all** hiring managers on their list regardless of whether or not these companies seek candidates in your profession.*

POST YOUR RESUME ON JOB BOARDS OR USE A SERVICE TO DO IT FOR YOU.

Although Job Boards have a 15% success rate for matching candidates with open positions, including your resume in some of the top Job Boards *(such as Indeed, LinkedIn, SimplyHired, Monster, CareerBuilder, Glassdoor, and/or Execunet)*, may very well help you find the perfect position for which you would like to apply; and you can set up to receive job search alerts via email so you don't have to check the boards regularly. If you are inclined to post to only one or two job boards, it is recommended you do so on either Indeed, SimplyHired, and/or LinkedIn as they are the largest job boards with many available positions. There are also niche boards specific to your career *(see "Niche Job Board and Career Resource Sites" below)*, that are beneficial to post your resume and seek job openings. As there are more than 100,000 job boards worldwide, following is some guidance in deciding where to post your resume and seek position openings.

Resume Posting Services

You can save a lot of time if you use a resume posting service to electronically post your resume to job boards for you. Sites that provide this service include the following:

General Job Boards

Many job boards allow you to post your resume as is and will use the contents to fill their appropriate fields. Others ask that you type in or cut and paste your resume components into various fields. For the latter, use your ASCII (text only) version you created in ***Step 6: Pull Your Resume Together***. Following are the top job boards:

Here's a current list of additional job boards as of this writing where you can locate positions and/or post your resume:

☐ Beyond	☐ BilingualCareer	☐ Career	☐ CareerMag
☐ Craigslist.org	☐ DiversityJobs	☐ EmploymentGuide	☐ HireFlyer
☐ Hound	☐ idealist	☐ internships	☐ JobBankUSA
☐ JobFox	☐ Jobing	☐ Jobs.aol.com	☐ JobShouts
☐ LinkUp	☐ LocalHelpWanted.net	☐ NationJob	☐ Net-Temps
☐ ProfessionalJobBoards	☐ Recruiters Online	☐ ThingaMaJob	☐ TopUSAJobs
☐ TrueCareers	☐ US.jobs	☐ Vault	☐ YahooHotJobs

Niche Job Board and Career Resource Sites

In addition to the above general job boards, there are numerous industry-specific niche sites available where you can post your resume, read about current industry trends, network with others in your profession, and/or obtain advice. There are several benefits to posting to a niche job board as opposed to the large, well-known boards listed above:

1. Targeted sites, such as the ones that follow, often include job openings not otherwise found on the larger job boards as hiring managers find that candidates who apply to position openings on these boards are often more qualified in matching their required skill sets.
2. Some niche sites are specific to the location you are seeking and you won't have to wade through numerous positions that are not within your targeted search area.
3. You will find less competition than you would on the larger job boards because the applicant pool is smaller, which can equate to increased interview odds in your favor.

4. Plus you will receive fewer untargeted emails about irrelevant job openings you are not interested in when you sign up for email updates on these niche sites.

A number of niche sites in various professions are included below under their specific industries: (All are .com unless otherwise indicated.) Please note that these are current as of this writing, but job boards tend to come and go.

Niche Job Boards

CONSTRUCTION INDUSTRY JOB SITES

☐ASPENational.org	☐BuilderJobs	☐BuildFind	☐ConstructionEquipmentJobs
☐ConstructionExecutive	☐ConstructionJobs	☐ConstructionWork	☐ConstructionIndustryCentral
☐iHireConstruction	☐OnlyConstructionJobs	☐SkilledWorkers	☐TheConstructionJob
☐TopBuildingJobs			

TRADE POSITIONS JOB SITES

☐ACDoctorPro	☐AirConditioningJobs	☐ANLA.org	☐AWS.org
☐BlueCollarJobs	☐Careers.ch2m.com	☐CarpenterJobsite	☐ElectricalAgent
☐ForConstructionPros	☐GetWeldingJobs	☐HVAC-Industry	☐HVACJobsCenter
☐IEEE.org	☐iHireBuildingTrades	☐Jobs.NDT.org	☐LandcareNetwork.org
☐LandscapeCareerSearch	☐LCAMDDCVA.org	☐MEPJobs	☐PlumbingAgent
☐PlumbingGigs	☐PlumbingHelper	☐RedSealRecruiting	☐SkilledWorkers
☐TradesJobs	☐USTradesLLC		

UNION JOB SITES

☐HelmetsToHardhats	☐UnionJobs

Niche Job Boards – Diverse

CONTRACT JOB SITES

☐CJHunter	☐ContractCareers	☐ContractedWork	☐ContractedWork
☐ContractingCareers	☐ContractJob.net	☐ContractJobHunter	☐Contract-Jobs
☐ContractJobSite	☐FindaCrew.net	☐GoingGlobal	☐Project4Hire

FREELANCE, FLEXIBLE WORK & SEASONAL JOB SITES

☐AllFreelanceWork	☐ASTD.org	☐AWASummerJobs	☐BackDoorJobs
☐Coolworks	☐Elance	☐GetaFreelancer	☐FlexJobs
☐IFreelance	☐JobMonkey	☐Jobble.net	☐Net-Temps
☐ODesk	☐QuintCareers	☐SnagaJob	☐SummerJobs
☐Telecommute-Jobs	☐WAHM	☐WeWorkRemotely	☐WorldwideWorkAtHome
☐WorkAtHome	☐WorkAtHomeCareers		

GOVERNMENT & POLITICAL JOB SITES

☐AllCountyJobs	☐CareersInGovernment	☐FederalGovernmentJobs.us	☐FederalJobSearch
☐GovernmentJobs	☐GovtJobs	☐JobsFed	☐Taegan Goddard's Political Wire
☐USAJobs.gov			

INTERNSHIPS & ENTRY-LEVEL JOB SITES

☐AfterCollege	☐CampusCareerCenter	☐CareerRookie	☐CollegeGrad
☐CollegeJobBank	☐CollegeJobBoard	☐CollegeRecruiter	☐Experience
☐GraduateJobs	☐InternJobs	☐InternMatch	☐Internships4You
☐InternWeb	☐IntershipPrograms	☐MyFirstPaycheck	☐UrbanInterns
☐WorkReadyGrad	☐YouTern		

NONPROFIT JOB SITES

☐ASAECenter.org	☐ASAP-Jobs	☐BoardNetUSA.org	☐CharityChannel
☐DotOrgJobs	☐ExecSearches	☐FundRaisingJobs	☐Idealist.org
☐Nonprofit-Jobs.org	☐NonprofitJobs.org	☐NonprofitCareer	☐OpportunityKnocks.org
☐OpportunityNocs.org	☐Philanthropy	☐PhilanthropyNewsDigest.org	☐YouTern

VETERAN JOB SITES

☐CivilianJobs	☐CorporateGray	☐GIJobs	☐HireAHero.org
☐HirePatriots	☐HirePurpose	☐HireVeterans	☐iHireVeterans
☐Jobs2Vets	☐JOFDAV	☐Military	☐Military2Career
☐Military-Civilian	☐MilitaryConnection	☐MilitaryHire	☐TAOnline
☐TAOnline	☐TransitionCareers	☐TransitionCareers	☐VeteransEmployment.net
☐VetJobs	☐VetReady.org	☐WeHireHeroes	

VOLUNTEER POSITIONS JOB SITES

☐BackDoorJobs	☐Idealist.org	☐VolunteerMatch.org	☐WWOOF.net

☐ JOIN PROFESSIONAL ASSOCIATIONS IN YOUR INDUSTRY.

Most industries have their own specific trade associations. Joining professional organizations in your industry; participating in their events, conferences, and/or online discussion boards; attending regular meetings; receiving their periodicals; and/or becoming an active member are all excellent ways to network with colleagues and other professionals in your area of interest and obtain information about member companies that might appeal to you. Obtaining a copy of their membership directory will provide a resource of professionals with whom you can network.

☐ CONSIDER REGISTERING WITH AN EMPLOYMENT AGENCY / RECRUITMENT FIRM.

Registering with an employment agency in your targeted geographical area is a good resource for job leads. Some employment agencies specialize in specific professions while others are more generalized. They typically handle permanent, full-time, direct-hire, and/or contract positions. Check if the agency you select handles your industry, has a good reputation, and that their contract is clear as to what you might expect. If possible, get recommendations from other professionals for reliable agencies. Because position openings handled by search firms are generally not publicly posted, you will not be privy to those jobs unless you avail yourself of the services of an employment agency or recruitment firm.

There is a difference in recruitment firms. Some work on a contingency basis, while others work on a retained basis, and still others do both retainer and contingency work. With the exception of some private employment agencies though, employers generally pay the fee so you have nothing to lose.

Private Employment Agencies

Private employment agencies handle a large variety of positions at various levels in many different industries. Conversely, temporary agencies generally specialize in a particular profession or industry. Once you register with either, they will keep your resume on file for current and future job openings. In most cases, the employer pays the fee for the recruit, while at some private employment agencies the candidate is responsible for paying the fee, so inquire about this.

Public Employment Agencies

Public employment agencies are your Departments of Labor, Bureaus of Employment Security, and state Workforce Development Agencies. They have all types of job openings obtained from employers within various industries; and you can search their computerized job bank for available positions to which you can apply. Many public employment agencies offer workshops in resume writing, job search skills training, and interviewing techniques and/or provide career counselling at no cost to the candidate. In fact, several states in the United States (that is, Connecticut, Delaware, and Florida) use my ***Career Worksheets For All Professions™*** to build comprehensive resumes for their patrons.

Now Proceed to Network! Network! Network!

STEP 9

NETWORK! NETWORK! NETWORK!

CONTENTS OF STEP 9

- ☐ About Networking
- ☐ Use Social Media to Network Online.
  - LinkedIn
  - Twitter
  - Facebook
- ☐ Locate Face-to-Face Networking Events.
  - Ryze
  - Meetup
  - Eventbrite
  - Eventful
  - eWomenNetwork
  - DamesBond
  - CraigsList
  - LinkedIn Events
  - Twitter Tweetups
  - Facebook Events
  - RileyGuide
- ☐ Attend Career Networking Events.
  - Business Networking Events
  - Career Expos and Job Fairs
  - Chamber of Commerce Events
  - College Career Networking Events, Alumni Programs, and Reunions
  - Community Service Groups / Organizations
  - Diversity Career Networking Groups
  - Job Club Meetings and Job Search Support Groups
  - Professional Association / Trade Organization Events
  - Professional Conferences and Expos
  - Speed Networking for Professionals
- ☐ Ace Your Networking Efforts.
  - Prepare for Your Networking.
  - Make a Memorable Impression.
  - Selectively Distribute Your Career Marketing Materials.
  - Follow up.
- ☐ Now Go Out and Network! Network! Network!

ABOUT NETWORKING

INTRODUCTION TO NETWORKING

Networking is a scary word for some but doesn't have to be. This chapter is written with the intent to take that scare feeling out of networking so you can feel confident and go forward with ***your most critical component of your job search*** by providing you with sound, comprehensive but concise information on the many ways and methods you can network and build connections online and in person. It also includes how to prepare for, conduct, and follow up on your networking.

Start by networking at a few events that are more within your comfort zone, such as networking online, then go forward with attending others. All of the research has been done for you, so you can view each method or site and decide whether or not it is applicable to helping you meet your goals.

NETWORKING DEFINED

Networking is about building new contacts and nurturing relationships that can ultimately lead to word-of-mouth referrals. It helps you make connections and develop genuine, lasting relationships that can help you achieve your career goals. Networking not only allows you to connect with people but also the people they know to whom they can provide introductions and/or referrals.

Since most positions are filled through networking *outside* of job boards and position postings, it cannot be stressed enough to network everywhere you go when you meet up with people. Network with colleagues, friends, family...everyone...using your ***Elevator Pitch*** you developed in ***Step 4: Develop Your Personal Brand and Professional Summary.***

DETERMINE YOUR NETWORKING GOALS

While your primary goal is to make connections in order to help you land a position quickly, examine the various networking methods contained in this chapter and set up a plan for yourself based on the specific goals you would like to achieve.

Example: You may first wish to increase your social networking connections and network online, then obtain Information Interviews from some of those connections while simultaneously advancing your knowledge in your profession and marketplace, followed by attending face-to-face career networking events.

NETWORK! NETWORK! NETWORK!

☐ USE SOCIAL MEDIA TO NETWORK ONLINE.

Networking is still by far the most successful way people find jobs; and today social media participation is an essential tool toward that end. By connecting with all those you know and staying in touch with your professional contacts can enhance your career brand and professional image, connect with others in your field, and help you with your job search efforts. It is also a more relaxed way to start out your networking in the comfort of your home at your own pace.

Be sure you are consistent on your personal brand message and image throughout all of your online platforms. Following is a guide on how to use the top social networking sites—specifically, LinkedIn, Facebook, and Twitter—to network with other professionals and enhance your job search efforts.

LinkedIn

Since LinkedIn is an online forum of professionals and companies, you can network with other professionals, research companies, connect with affiliates, conduct your job search by viewing the numerous high-quality professional job postings it contains, and join a variety of business-related groups.

There are several ways you can use LinkedIn to conduct your job search and increase your visibility so prospective employers and recruiters can locate you:

- Joining various industry-specific LinkedIn groups allows you to connect with professionals in your industry and have access to the group member job listings, thereby increasing your job opportunities.
- Conducting targeted searches by location, industry, or number of employees can help you locate the types of firms you are interested in. You can also use the "Advanced Search" feature to get more specific search results. When you conduct your search, locate professionals you are connected with to connect with others who may be influential to you by asking if they can make a connection for you. Send them a message that includes your Elevator Pitch you developed earlier.
- View the job postings in your specific field and geographic area, and respond to all those you are interested in.
- Consider sending emails to your contacts to let them know of the type of position you are seeking and ask them if they can put you in touch with anyone who might be able to help you.
- Link your blog post, if you have one, through LinkedIn's Blog Link. Your blog posts will then be updated on your profile and included in weekly update emails that are sent to your connections.
- If you have a Twitter account, your tweets can also be linked to your LinkedIn account as well.
- Consider adding visual elements to your LinkedIn page, such as a background photo that depicts your brand on your profile page, your Career Portfolio as a PowerPoint presentation (addressed in ***Step 8: Market Yourself!***), a slideshow presentation from a speech you conducted, and so on to attract additional opportunities and connections.
- LinkedIn's "Endorsements" component showcases your expertise that is validated by others who know you.
- And don't forget to upload your resume to LinkedIn!

twitter

Include the Elevator Pitch you developed in ***Step 4: Develop Your Personal Brand and Professional Summary*** and a link to your Web Portfolio on your Twitter page. Posting tweets on industry topics can help you establish yourself as an expert in your field thus enhancing your personal brand. Be sure to follow industry experts and engage in tweeting topics of interest with other professionals in your field. It is also a good idea to create a custom background that exemplifies your personal brand and includes your qualifications.

facebook

You can use Facebook for professional networking when you are job hunting by following the guidelines in ***Step 9: Market Yourself!*** Also, consider posting a message on your timeline, or private message to any of your colleagues or friends you think might be able to help you if you are more comfortable. Let them know you are seeking a career transition and ask them if they are aware of any positions that might be available in your industry or if they know anyone you might be able to network with. Friends are genuinely more apt to help you meet your goals than outsiders. *(See also **"Facebook Events"** below.)*

☐ LOCATE FACE-TO-FACE NETWORKING EVENTS.

To make new connections and learn about new opportunities, the first step is to locate the type of events you would like to attend. To find professional networking events in your area, follow this guide by looking into the sites and what each has to offer insofar as how they might benefit you with your career goals. You can start out by searching the Internet for local "Networking Events (town)" or "Business Networking Events (town)" in your area where you will find a mix of networking event types such as job search support groups, networking organizations, career fairs, special interest groups, business social events, trade shows, and so on. The following sites provide a host of networking opportunities from which to select:

ryze
Business Networking

Ryze is an online business networking site where you can connect with like-minded professionals. Ryze allows you to "build a free networking-oriented page; get practical advice, tips, and resources from people in your field; make quality business contacts; and build your network." Members find Ryze very useful and supportive in meeting many people and ideal for making new business connections.

Meetup

Meetup, the world's largest network of local groups in various capacities (such as social events, business networking events, photography groups, singles meet-ups, various hobbies and interests, and so on), allows you to meet up with people to make new connections and build relationships. For careerists, you can search by your profession for industry-specific networking events in your area. You can sign up to receive weekly emails containing all the Meetups in your locale; and you can even start your own Meetup events.

Eventbrite

(bringing "The World Together Through Live Experiences")

Eventbrite facilitates gatherings that bring "passionate, driven, and curious" people together to "learn, grow, get inspired, feel connected, get healthy, give back, and celebrate." As soon as you load the page, Eventbrite brings you to events and experiences in your area. You can scroll through the various categories to locate areas of interest or click on "See More" on the bottom of the page, then "Event Type" and key in "Networking Events" to view details on upcoming get-togethers and find out who will be attending. You can register for particular events (some free, some not) while on that page or set up your own events that can be published to your Facebook. You can also subscribe to RSS feeds for particular events of interest.

eventful

Eventful is a social media platform / events site with more than 21 million members that connects its members with events as well as other users. Like Eventbrite, it immediately brings you to events in your area. Key in "Networking Events" in the search category, and all upcoming networking events will be listed, such as local networking meetings, round table luncheons, business professionals networking events, entrepreneur networking social events, professional and business networking mixers, talent connections, innovation events, conferences, resume and career help, and so on, as well as networking events geared towards your specific profession. You can also invite friends to join.

eWomen NETWORK *("The Complete Success System for Businesswomen")*

eWomenNetwork is an international business women's network that helps empower success-minded corporate women to succeed through support and guidance, one-on-one coaching sessions, online forums and discussions, and webinars, along with access to opportunities, member database, and resources. The organization hosts "Accelerated Networking™" events (see also "Speed Networking for Professionals" under ***Attend Career Networking Events*** below), workshops, summits, conferences, and business expos where women can market and promote themselves. Producing more than 2000 women's networking events annually, they claim to be "the largest women's business event company in the world" run by skilled Managing Directors. You can post your profile on their site. The cost to join is a $357 initiation fee and a $19.95 monthly membership fee.

damesbond
A Business Community for Women Entrepreneurs *("A Business Community for Women Entrepreneurs" / "When Dames bond, Dames thrive")*

Dames Bond is a women's networking community that helps "women thrive personally and professionally through networking, collaborations, and learning experiences" by developing connections, building relationships, and "leveraging the resources, connections, and marketing to thrive and prosper in business." While you can network online on this site, its leaders also host social-based, motivational, inspirational, and educational events and meet-ups. You can also attend events posted by its members in the community "Calendar of Events"; some are free others charge a nominal fee. The average gross income of their members is $61,000 to $406,000; and the annual membership fee is $30 or $125 dependent upon the membership you select.

craigslist

Craigslist.org, a large local community-moderated classifieds and forums site, allows you to search listings of "Events and Classes." Key in "Networking Events" and select "Career," and the site will provide you with a list of local events such as Open Networking Groups, Business Networking, Women for Women Networking Events, various events in your industry, and so on. Though the site is generally noncorporate in its nature, it claims to list approximately one million job openings per month (search "Jobs") where you can send your resume to the contact person. Craigslist also contains various discussion forums and supports many languages including Catalan, Danish, Dutch, English, Filipino, French, German, Italian, Norwegian, Portuguese, Spanish, Swedish, and Turkish.

LinkedIn Events

LinkedIn contains an Events section that you can access by searching "Networking Events." Sample events on LinkedIn include business and social networking events and meet-ups, networking for young professionals, network after work, professional development, and so on. Attending these events can help you make face-to-face networking connections. Just select your industry and location, and scroll through the various events to find ones that interest you.

twitter Tweetups

Search **Twitter's** "Tweetup" (a word merged from "Twitter" and "Meetup") to browse through events and gatherings in your area. Tweetups are face-to-face organized or impromptu gatherings of people on Twitter who share similar interests and arrange to get together in person to network, share ideas, become friends, and/or socialize with regularly. Often attendees at conventions who tweet about speakers and topics arrange to meet with other attendees after hours for get-togethers, dinner, and/or drinks. Tweetup meets (also called Offline Networking) can help you increase your networking.

facebook Events

There are several ways to find events on **Facebook:**

1. Click on "Events" on your news feed page to see if there are any upcoming events scheduled that you may be interested in attending. Facebook notifies you when your friends are hosting or attending various types of events and you can share those and your own events with other friends.

2. Click on "Find New Groups" under GROUPS and browse through the various categories. Join all groups of interest so you will be aware of any new events scheduled.
3. Search "Networking Events" or "Business Networking Events (town)" and scroll through the various postings.

Riley Guide.com/support.html *("The Web's premier gateway for job search, career exploration, and school information")*

The **Riley Guide** provides information on career networking, job search support groups, online groups, networking Websites, interviewing and salary negotiation tips; and nationwide job listings, organizations, and other helpful links. In their "Job Search" section, you can also read up on *"How to Job Search," "Before You Search," "Job Listing Sites," "Worldwide Job Search," and "Handling a Job Loss." Specifically check "Sites with Job Listings."*

☐ ATTEND CAREER NETWORKING EVENTS.

In addition to attending events of interest in the sites you located above, there are many other types of networking events you can explore and attend. They are listed alphabetically below.

Business Networking Events

Business Networking Events, sometimes called Cocktail Mixer Networking Events, are the most common of professional networking gatherings. Typically held in bars or restaurants, they are generally well attended and are a good way to get together to exchange information and experiences with like-minded professionals to build your contact list. You can Google "Business Networking Events (town)" and click on various sites to obtain a list of events in your area.

Career Expos and Job Fairs

Career Centers of colleges and universities typically sponsor Career Fairs throughout the year. Career Expos and Job Fairs provide excellent opportunities for jobseekers to connect and speak with a number of prospective employers in one day to whom they can submit their resumes. To get the most out of your Career Fair experience, prepare in advance by researching the attending employers' websites and their current career opportunities, select firms of interest, practice your Elevator Pitch, and print out multiple copies of your resume and cover letter to hand out.

women for hire, a recruiting site for talented professional women that connects members with hiring managers, also hosts free Career Expos and events throughout the United States where you can meet with prospective employers and distribute your resume to hiring managers and recruiters.

Chamber of Commerce Events

Chambers of Commerce hold various event types in your area including business card exchanges, networking mixers, a variety of workshops, charity fundraisers, and so on. By attending Chamber of Commerce events, you can meet prospective employers and other professionals in your industry. Be sure to bring with you your career marketing materials you developed in ***Step 8: Market Yourself!***

College Career Networking Events, Alumni Programs, and Reunions

College and university Career Service Centers and Alumni Affairs Offices sponsor Career Networking events and programs for students and alumni to interact and get to know each other. These career networking events, sometimes organized by industry, are typically hosted on campus or in surrounding towns of the college. Speed *Networking (see below)* has become a popular event structure at colleges. You can check for the schedule of events on your college Website or with the Career Service Center where you can request a list of event sponsors, participants, and any employer affiliations.

Colleges and universities also host other event types where you can informally socialize and network with others, such as lectures, museum tours, social cocktail mixers, happy hours, and sporting events that can ultimately provide you with opportunities to share your career status and goals and possibly set up information interviews (see ***Step 11: Prepare for and Ace the Interview!***). For alumni in career transition, College Reunions are another great source to attend to reconnect and network with former classmates and share what you have been doing since graduation.

Community Service and Advocacy Groups / Organizations

Community Service Groups include organizations such as the Rotary Club, Lions Club, and Kiwanis as well as community boards, advocacy groups, environmental groups, civil rights groups, fraternities and sororities, and houses of worship—each formed for a specific cause. Becoming a member of a Community Service Group provides you with the opportunity to get the word out as to your career status. Volunteering your services, such as for fundraisers and event coordination, allows you to interact with others and be more visible in your profession.

Diversity Career Networking Groups

Diversity Career Networking Groups, such as women's and men's networking organizations, are based on gender, race, and/or ethnicity. Following are some sites where you can locate various career networking groups in your area and specificity:

- **Professional Diversity Network** **(ProDivNet.org)** *("Better Jobs for All Americans")*

Dedicated to serving diverse professionals in the United States, the **Professional Diversity Network** is a professional online networking group for diverse groups (including the Women's Career Channel, Military 2 Career, Asian Career Network, Black Career Network, iHispano, Out Professional Network, and Pro Able) that provides members with access to career resources and opportunities to connect with top employers who seek diverse candidates. You can also attend their national events and career fairs to connect with those in your industry.

- Job Diversity Network *Developing Opportunities - Building Connections* **(JobDiversityNetwork.org)** *("Developing Opportunities – Building Connections")*

The **Job Diversity Network**, a "leading professional consortium of higher education institutions, government agencies, business for profit and not-for-profit organizations dedicated to advancing diversity and inclusion in (the) workforce and workplaces," inspires a feeling of unity. It holds online Career Fairs for various diversity groups where you can access career opportunities. The site contains a listing of hundreds of diversity groups you can join and attend in-person events.

- PDN **(prodivnet.com/events)**

Professional Diversity Network holds diversity conferences and career fairs where you can build your network. The site contains a listing of network leaders and like-minded professionals with whom you can connect and network and includes job postings in your area.

- QC QUINTCAREERS.COM **(QuintCareers.com/minority_networking_organizations.html)** *("Empowering Jobseekers Since 1996")*

The **QuintCareers** *(Quintessential Careers)* site contains a host of career networking opportunities and professional organizations for diversity groups including career networking resources for disadvantaged jobseekers, retired persons, African-American and Hispanic professionals, and so on—some specific to your profession, such as accountants, engineers, programmers, scientists, law enforcement, business owners, and so on. On its *"Careers Content Index"* page, you can locate job-search articles and tutorials.

Job Club Meetings and Job Search Support Groups

Job Clubs and Job Search Support Groups are formal or informal networking groups where jobseekers and career-changers help fellow club members with their job search and networking endeavors through regular monthly meetings. Formal Job Search Clubs are moderated by a career coach, Human Resource professional, recruiter, or other job search expert. Members assist each other with their job hunt by providing job search advice, helping with networking to build relationships, offering job leads and referrals, making connections and introductions, and working on and practicing their Elevator Pitch. The camaraderie helps jobseekers get started in their job search, learn how to start networking conversations, and build ongoing relationships through these structured or nonstructured networking events.

Professional Association / Trade Organization Meetings and Events

To create strategic alliances with people in your profession, first join and start to become an active member of one or more Professional Associations in your industry. You can attend their meetings, connect with and learn from members, go to their conferences, apply for leadership roles, volunteer to participate in projects, or submit articles for their newsletter or website. All are excellent ways to network with like-minded professionals in your field; enhance your personal brand by learning more about the industry; and get your name out. You may even be able to connect with company decision-makers and hiring managers.

Professional Conferences and Expos

Attending conferences, conventions, expos, and/or workshops held by professional and trade associations are wonderful opportunities to meet up and network with others in your field. Formal or informal networking opportunities, extracurricular activities, and/or events are typically included in the agenda to connect with others. Go to them. You can also submit presentations to speak at conventions or volunteer to help organize one. The best course of action when attending a conference is not to try to meet up with everyone in attendance, but rather to engage in conversation with a select number of people with whom you may be able to build ongoing relationships.

Prior to attending, visit the conference Website to know the event schedule and opportunities where you may be able to connect with others, review the speaker and attendee list to get an idea of who will be attending, learn about the exhibitors, and select certain individuals with whom you would like to network based on your own goals. Check their Websites, Web Portfolios, and/or online presence to find out more about their expertise and how you might benefit by networking with them. Consider shooting them an email to introduce yourself and letting them know you look forward to meeting them. Be sure to bring with you your career marketing materials (business cards, biography / sell sheet, and/or resume).

While at the conference, enjoy the opening reception, attend the key note speech and workshop sessions of interest to you, visit the exhibit hall, and chat during coffee and lunch breaks to network with colleagues and new contacts.

There are also ***Professional Networking Conferences*** specifically for Career Development. Typically hosted by Career Development Centers of colleges and universities, these conferences provide career advice, address related topics such as industry trends and career paths, and help attendees to navigate their career path and expand their professional network.

Speed Networking

Speed Networking uses the same premise / structure as speed dating, that is, to accelerate the meeting of a lot of new contacts within a short timeframe through the rotation of participants so that all attendees have a chance to meet with one another. Basically, you skip all of the small talk. While speed daters narrow down their choices in these get-togethers, speed networkers wish to increase their exposure and contact pool. Depending upon the number of participants and length of the session, each attendee is allotted from one to 15 minutes to interact with others and sessions generally last from one to two hours. Use your ***Elevator Pitch*** as a conversation starter.

These events are held by business clubs, networking organizations, Chambers of Commerce, trade associations, college alumni groups, and various professional organizations that may also host monthly ***Shakers and Stirrers Events*** where attendees can network in a more casual, relaxed environment. Note that college alumni groups set up Speed Networking Events with employers themselves who wish to make quality connections to consider college grads for internship positions. These events are generally set up in groups of three participants so prospective employers can see how potential candidates interact socially. Search the Internet for Speed Networking Events in your area.

☐ ACE YOUR NETWORKING EFFORTS.

Now that you know which events you would like to attend, here is how to prepare for your networking, make a memorable impression, follow up with your contacts, and make the most out of your connections:

Prepare for Your Networking.

Because your time is valuable, carefully select the events you would like to attend that can help you network with the right people for the purpose you have in mind. Don't spread yourself too thin.

By now you should start feeling comfortable with your unique personal brand. When attending networking events, try to showcase your brand in the appearance you portray to leave a lasting impression before you even meet others. You can accomplish that visually through not only your stature and professional demeanor but in your choice of clothing color and accessories, such as your eyeglasses, scarf, tie, jewelry, attaché, and the like. Select a brand color or colors you can call "you," and wear those colors at all events. (Selecting your brand colors is covered in ***Step 4: Develop Your Personal Brand & Professional Summary.***)

Practice your ***Elevator Pitch*** you developed in ***Step 4*** to use with all of your contacts so they know what your unique personal brand and qualifications are and what you are seeking. You never know if someone you meet will run into someone else who may be hiring, and because you networked with them, he or she can pass on your name and qualifications.

Before attending any events, see if you can find out who is attending so you can view their profile and online presence and have a feel for the people you will be meeting. Prior to the event, prepare a list of questions you may wish to ask them. Arriving at the event early allows you to mingle with people as they arrive before it becomes too crowded. And hanging around at the end of the event, you might be asked to join others for a drink or dinner where you can have more casual, relaxed conversation.

Make a Memorable Impression.

Be friendly and upbeat with everyone you meet. Smile and offer a firm handshake while introducing yourself through your ***Elevator Pitch***...at the table you are sitting, during session breaks, in the elevator, on the lunch or bus line, and so on. If you are at a conference, wear your name tag on your right shoulder or lapel so it is visible when you shake hands.

Ask your contacts to tell you about themselves and the most rewarding aspects of their career, and take an interest in what they have to say. People generally enjoy talking about what they are passionate about, and it can help you feel comfortable with mingling and starting conversations with others by putting the spotlight on them first.

In order to transform conversations into eventual opportunities, carefully listen to and understand the needs and interests of others with whom you network (remember, they are networking with you, as well) while being genuine in all of your interactions. Speak conversationally as you would in your professional norm. To create the best impression, don't try to be someone you are not, just be yourself, exhibit what you are passionate about, and always use eye contact. It's easier for you and comes off more genuine to others.

Keep a note pad on you so you can jot down the names of people you meet and notate who they are, what they do, and the topics of conversation so you can remember them going forward.

Selectively Distribute Your Career Marketing Materials.

Be sure to bring with you your ***Personal Brand Biography / Sell Sheet*** you developed in ***Step 4: Develop Your Personal Brand and Professional Summary,*** as well as the various marketing materials you created in ***Step 8: Market Yourself!***, such as your Business Cards, Resume, and/or Career Portfolio (if you are bringing your laptop, otherwise burn it to CD or DVD); to hand out to select individuals with whom you network.

Follow up.

Follow up with the contacts you make after each event by timely mailing out a personalized card (see ***Step 8: Market Yourself!***) or sending an email. Within your communiqué, remind them of who you are by recalling what you discussed and what your goals are, letting them know you enjoyed meeting with them, thank them for any advice they provided, suggest you connect online, ask if you could help them in any way, and/or consider sending them a link or an article that may be of interest to them based on what you discussed and learned about them. If appropriate, you might even inquire about conducting an Informational Interview (addressed in ***Step 11: Prepare for and Ace Your Interviews***). They will be more likely to remember you for future reference and possible referral should a job lead or other opportunity arise, and doing so will help nurture your ongoing relationship building. Stay in touch with your select contacts through phone or email. Connect with them on LinkedIn, Twitter, and/or Facebook. And don't forget to refer them when an opportunity arises where you may be able to help them!

☐ NOW GO OUT AND NETWORK! NETWORK! NETWORK!

Get the word out repetitively as to what you are seeking. Use your Personal Brand everywhere: in person, on the phone, in your email tagline, online, and in all of your correspondence...while networking, when making phone calls, in your Web presence, in your PowerPoint presentation, as a part of your recorded phone greeting. Include your Personal Brand Message in everything you do in the professional world. **TIP:** The easiest way to start to memorize and feel comfortable using your Personal Brand Message is when you are on the phone. Keep the message in front of you so you can read from it until it becomes natural.

Next, start preparing for your interviews...

STEP 10

PREPARE FOR & ACE YOUR INTERVIEWS

CONTENTS OF STEP 10

PREPARE FOR & ACE YOUR INTERVIEWS

INTRODUCTION

This chapter covers various ways to prepare yourself for and conduct your interviews, as well as the follow-up steps you need to take after the interview along with effective salary negotiation strategies to use when offered a position.

It contains informational interviews and different job interview types and styles, and includes various online interview resources you can refer to for additional information. It also contains a *Job Search Log* you can copy to maintain your job search records, an *Information Interview Request Letter Foundation* and a *Thank You letter Foundation* to use after your interviews.

☐ SET UP INFORMATIONAL INTERVIEWS.

An **Informational Interview** is a valuable source to garner occupational information in your career or industry. It is *not* a job interview, nor should it be conveyed that that is your purpose for requesting one. It is an informal learning opportunity for you to connect with professionals in your field and interview *them* by asking relative questions so you can learn more about a specific firm, position, career, or industry. Setting up Informational Interviews is also a good way to build confidence in handling your upcoming job interviews.

While you are conducting your networking, you will be making connections with a number of professionals in your field. Select a few you believe might be helpful to you in meeting your career goals. Contact them (by phone, email, letter, or through social media) to see if you can set up an appointment to meet or have a phone conversation to discuss topics of interest to you. Let your potential interviewees know the purpose of your interview request insofar as the type of information you are seeking, such as salary expectations for your profession, required skills, career paths, advancement opportunities, important personal attributes required for the position, job search advice, possible leads, and so on.

By meeting with individuals in your chosen career, you can discover first-hand the types of functions a person in your profession performs, what it's like to work in a particular firm, what a typical day or week is like, the most satisfying aspects of a particular job, what the culture is like, typical work hours, types of work-related pressures and challenges, technology used, best resources to find related jobs in your area, opportunities within the firm they work, and so on.

Formulate your questions ahead of time based on your genuine interests with respect to the field, and take some notes regarding things you will want to remember after the interview. Within a day or two after your interview, send a thank you letter or note (addressed below).

Sample Informational Interview Request Letter / Foundation

Dear ______,

While attending the ______ *[which?]* **networking event, I was impressed with your knowledge and abilities in the ______** *[which?]* [☐ profession | ☐ industry] —OR— ______ *[Name]* **from ______** *[Company]* **referred me to you as a good source of career information regarding the ______** *[type of]* [☐ position | ☐ profession | ☐ industry | ☐ field], **and I am** [☐ calling | ☐ writing] **to ask if we could set up an informal Informational Interview, either on the phone or in person, to discuss ______, ______, and/or ______** *[topics].*

Since I am seeking a ______ *[type of]* **position in the ______** *[field]*, **I believe I could benefit from any insight or information you could provide regarding tapping into your** [☐ career | ☐ industry] **knowledge regarding any job search tips or hidden job opportunities you might know about.**

I will call you in the next few days to see if you are available to set up a time to meet or phone call to chat, or you can reach me at (000) 000-0000 | (your email address). Thanks in advance for your consideration.

Warm regards,

Your Name

☐ GAIN AN UNDERSTANDING OF THE DIFFERENT JOB INTERVIEW TYPES AND STYLES.

Hiring managers use different styles and methods to conduct interviews in order to determine the best candidate matches for their position openings. Generally speaking, all interviews fall into the first two categories below, that is, ***Traditional Job Interviews*** and ***Behavioral Job Interviews.*** Though each firm may conduct their interviews differently, hiring managers are trying to determine if you have the ability to perform the job, if you would fit within the firm's work culture, if you are a team player, your ability to communicate well, what your work ethic is, and if you have enthusiasm for the position.

The types of questions asked will be different; but no matter the interview style, convey your skills and qualifications for the position, how well you believe you can fit within their work culture, how you've tackled similar challenges in the past, and your passion about your profession. Preparing for your interviews in advance is key to acing the interview, no matter the type or style used (discussed next under ***Prepare for Your Job Interviews***).

Traditional Job Interviews

In ***Traditional Job Interviews***, hiring managers ask a number of broad and position-related questions to determine what you have to offer as a candidate. Sample questions would be to tell the interviewer about yourself (use your ***Elevator Pitch*** you developed in ***Step 4: Develop Your Personal Brand and Professional Summary***), what your strengths and weaknesses are (addressed under ***Prepare for Your Job Interviews*** next), why you left your previous position, what your goals are, why you chose that career, challenges you were faced with and how you tackled them (see ***STAR Interview Technique*** below), why you want to work for the firm, how others might describe you, the type of work environment you are most comfortable in, how well you work independently and/or as part of a team, and so on. For more information, see ***Check Out Various Interview Resources*** (below) for many types of questions interviewers ask.

Behavioral Job Interviews

In ***Behavioral Job Interviews***, hiring managers seek to understand your past performance in order to predict future performance and your potential for success on the job. They will probe into your answers to get to the core of your behavior to understand your detailed thinking process and route of your decision-making. According to *Quintessential Careers,* these interviews are *"said to be 55% predictive of future on-the-job behavior, while traditional interviewing is only 10% predictive."*

Every position requires a different set of skills and attributes, and different firms might seek a distinct set of attributes for the same position. From the job descriptions you Googled in ***Step 4: Develop Your Personal Brand and Professional Summary,*** review the requirements for your targeted position(s) and keep those in mind. In ***Step 3: Check Off Your Personal Attributes*** where you identified your primary attributes, hone in on those. Lastly, you can always ask the interviewer what skills and traits a desirable candidate requires in that position to give you a heads up on how to proceed with your answers.

STAR Interview Technique

The ***STAR (Situation | Task | Action | Results) Interview Technique*** (also called **SAR** and **PAR** techniques) is a form of a ***Behavior Job Interview***. In these, hiring managers are seeking the same type of responses you already included in your resume (from ***Step 5: Select Your Resume ClipBullets***) as **CAR** (**C**hallenge | **A**ction | **R**esults) statements. Explain the situation or challenge you were faced with, the actions you took and tasks you performed to meet the challenge, and the end results of your efforts as it relates to benefits derived for your employers or their clients. By now you should be comfortable with this as that is the way you constructed your resume bullets under your *"Professional Experience"* section.

Case Interviews

Answers to ***Case Interview*** questions are similar to how you would respond to a ***STAR Interview*** question, but in future tense. A situation or challenge is presented and the candidate would respond as to how he or she would tackle it. Relate it to your own background if you tackled something similar or first ask relative questions to find out needed information, then come up with your best answers using problem-solving methods based on your knowledge and experience. According to the *Wharton MBA Case Interview Study Guide,* interviewers are looking for the following skills: "numerical and verbal reasoning skills, communication and presentation skills, and business skills and commercial awareness."

Situation Interviews

Similar to ***Case Interviews***, in ***Situation Interviews***, hiring managers ask how you would handle certain hypothetical situations given a set of circumstances. These interviews test candidate's competency level and help the hiring manager learn about the applicant's skills and abilities. Candidates are asked how they would tackle certain challenges, such as how you would use your communication, conflict resolution, customer service, negotiation, or other skills the position requires to resolve it. Try to determine what the interview is attempting to learn from their questions and form your answers accordingly. Review the skills required in the job posting before going on the interview and hone in on those.

Simulation / Hands-on Job Interviews

Simulation Interviews test the applicant's abilities and thought process to see how candidates "think on their feet." They can be hands-on interviews where you will be asked to perform a certain function to prove your ability in a specific area, or candidates can be asked how they would tackle a certain challenge, such as in ***Situation Interviews*** above. Brainstorm various options so the interviewer can see your thought process, then select what you feel might be the best-case-scenario solution under the given circumstances and state why you selected that answer.

Panel or Board Interviews

In ***Panel Interviews***, sometimes called ***"Board Interviews,"*** you meet with several interviewers at once where one or several will ask you questions. Those in presence typically include a human resource professional, the department head you would work under, and the hiring manager. These interviews are formal and organized and use the same set of prepared questions to ask each candidate they interview. The benefit of the panel interview is that you would be meeting with the various managers who would ordinarily interview you in a second or third interview. It saves time for both the firm and the candidate.

Be sure to shake hands and make eye contact with everyone in the room and show your interest in the position. Start off by providing your *Elevator Pitch* you developed in ***Step 4: Develop Your Personal Brand and Professional Summary.*** As in other interviews, present opportunities to have a two-way discussion to showcase your qualifications for the position, value proposition, and matching achievements; and ask your list of questions as discussed in ***Prepare for Your Job Interviews*** below.

Group Interviews

During Group Interviews, candidates are participants in a large group of other applicants where each interviewee is typically asked the same question around the table and/or you may be asked to participate in group discussions or exercises. These interviews can include other techniques, such as in ***Simulation / Hands-on Interviews*** (above) where you may be asked to perform a hands-on task to see how well you can problem-solve.

Group Interviews generally start with a presentation by the hiring manager and end with a question and answer period. Group Interviews help employers observe how candidates interact with others, how adept they are in their communication skills, their interpersonal ability, if they can be a team player, and how persuasive and competitive they may be. Be prepared to take constructive criticism without being defensive and provide praise to other candidates when duly noted. Avoid any power struggles or conflict with others. Don't be overpowering or interrupt when others speak. As in all interviews, act poised and professional.

Competency-based Interviews

Some employers use highly structured ***Competency-based Interviews*** in their selection process. These are a form of the ***Behavioral Interview*** (above) where hiring managers seek to determine critical competences in candidates based on those identified by the employer as important in the position. Competency-based Interviews help employers increase the efficiency of their employee selection process by delving into the details of candidates' top accomplishments. For example: the hiring manager might ask you to describe an accomplishment, what you did to make it happen, what your role was, why you were chosen, how long it took, why it was important to the firm, and so on. Again, use your CAR statements discussed in ***STAR Interviews*** above.

Phone Interviews

When ***Phone Interviews*** are used by hiring managers, they generally take place as part of the initial screening process and serve to narrow down the candidate pool. Just like in-person interviews, Phone Interviews can take anywhere from ten minutes to an hour or so. After a number of candidates are chosen and the Phone Interviews have been conducted, the hiring manager then selects only a portion of candidates to interview in person.

As you await your call, be sure you are comfortable in your setting by eliminating any distractions that could potentially occur, turn off computer and telephone sound, make sure your phone is charged, and instruct those around you to give you privacy during your scheduled call. Keep your resume and any support materials handy (such as your list of questions from ***Prepare for Your Job Interviews*** below). Show enthusiasm in your voice and smile often.

Video Interviews

Video Interviews are on the rise. When a Video Interview is used to screen candidates, Human Resource professionals generally prepare a set of (10 to 15) questions to ask all selected applicants. In this way, the hiring manager and department head can view the interview again after they have narrowed down their candidate search to make comparisons. Video Interviews use the same premise as in-person interviews but they save time for both the employer and the candidate.

Typically, you can perform your interview using your own computer Webcam and the prospective employer will provide instructions for its proper use. Wear the same type of attire you would at an in-person interview, make sure your desk is neat and any background clutter behind you is cleared up, and make eye contact with the interviewer.

Restaurant Interviews

Restaurant Interviews, sometimes ***Breakfast, Lunch,*** or ***Dinner Interviews,*** might occur in the second or third interview stage where the hiring manager or several senior managers want to observe another side of you. Restaurant Interviews are conducive to a more relaxed setting and can be more conversational; however, don't let down your guard. Typically, the hiring manager has already been sold on your qualifications for the position; but, just like any other job interview, respond to questions as noted above in the various interview types and ask some of your own. A few notes of caution: don't order alcohol or finger food and use your table manners. Act genuine and be your professional self.

Stress Interviews

Stress Interviews are not often used in today's world of work (thank goodness, as interviews can be stressful enough for most interviewees). The hiring manager is testing you to determine what your ability is in handling stress, as the position itself may include work-related, on-the-job stress. They may fire multiple questions at you in quick sequence before you have a chance to respond or might dispute your statements. They may even say derogatory things to or make accusatory statements about you to see how you would respond. You can politely challenge them by asking why they feel that way. If you find yourself in such an interview, try to relax. Think as you would on the job. Perhaps envision an irate customer or dissatisfied client and how you would go about appeasing them. Recognize when you are purposely being put under stress, and try not to become defensive. Be your professional, poised self, despite the interviewer's rudeness.

Good Cop / Bad Cop or Team Interviews

The ***Good Cop / Bad Cop or Team Interview*** combines the ***Panel Interview*** and ***Stress Interview*** methods. During these interviews, one person or both people may fire questions at you while one of them takes notes. Answer one question at a time and remain professional even if one of them—the "bad cop"—is not. Each interviewer generally uses a different style but for the same purpose: to see if you are a suitable candidate for the position. One of them is polite, the other sets out to make you uncomfortable. Though you may feel on the defensive, try to stay cool and answer each question professionally in a way that exhibits your qualifications and value. Sometimes if you speak up for yourself to acknowledge their rudeness, you may actually be offered the position because you were assertive. It's a gamble, but when you leave, by no means let it get you down; they were jerks for presenting the interview in this style!

☐ PREPARE FOR YOUR JOB INTERVIEWS.

To make a memorable impression with hiring managers and feel comfortable and confident during your interviews, prepare for them in advance. Following are steps you can take the days before and day of the interview. If you need to build confidence to ace your interviews, apply for positions you may not actually want so you can feel more comfortable when you interview for the jobs you are actually seeking.

The Days Before the Interview

1. Conducting research on the company is critical. Review their Website, its online presence, and any marketing materials you can get your hands on to find out as much as you can about the firm including the type of products or services it offers, who their clients / customers are, what their mission and goals are, and so on. While conducting your research, think about ways you might be able to help the firm or department achieve their goals.

2. Assess your qualifications and expertise against the job posting requirements; and determine how you can demonstrate you are a good fit within their firm by exhibiting your competitive edge, value proposition, and matching achievements and any way(s) you might be able to help the organization solve challenges as they relate to the position.

3. Hiring managers will ask you a number of questions to determine your ability to perform the job functions, your fit within their work culture, your ability to communicate, if you are a team player, and your enthusiasm for the position. Prepare some responses to possible questions hiring managers might ask you keeping this in mind. Practice them until they resonate with you.

4. If you have any gaps in your employment history, held positions for less than a year, or there are other possible red flags, carefully prepare your responses to these questions before going on your interviews. Try to convert a possible negative into an asset such as in the sample Web Portfolio provided in ***Step 7: Market Yourself!***

5. Prepare a list of a dozen or so questions you might want to ask the hiring manager, such as details about the firm, its culture, and the position responsibilities; why the position is open; the types of challenges the firm or department faces and what role the position

would play in helping to solve them; what a typical day is like; who you would report to; what the average work hours are; the types of assignments you would have; the company's mission and goals as well as its strengths and weaknesses; what constitutes an ideal candidate for the position; and so on.

6. Jot down notes regarding your achievements so that you can recall them and provide success stories when discussion involves challenges the position or firm needs to solve; and exemplify how you tackled similar types of challenges by providing achievement stories that showcase your value to the firm.
7. Typically, human resource professionals will ask candidates what their greatest weakness is. Prepare your response to this question in advance so you don't respond with an answer that could convey a possible hindrance in your job performance and ultimately screen you out. Rather, bring up a minor weakness or one that has nothing to do with performing your job and say how you are working to improve it.
8. Practice your *Elevator (Sales) Pitch* you developed in ***Step 4: Develop Your Personal Brand and Professional Summary*** again and again until you are comfortable using it, and keep in mind your matching achievements that will prove your value.

The Day of the Interview

1. First and foremost...breath! You have prepared for your interviews in advance. Remember, interviews are two-way conversations. You, too, have to find out if the position is right for you. So try to relax.
2. Prepare to arrive 10-15 minutes prior to your scheduled interview. Make sure you have good directions and check if your route is unencumbered by traffic or accidents. If so, leave earlier than you would normally.
3. Dress appropriately in professional attire suitable for your industry, one notch above what you would wear on the job, but not above what a hiring manager or department head in your field would wear. Use your personal brand colors you chose in ***Step 4: Develop Your Personal Brand and Professional Summary.*** Stay away from cologne and large jewelry, unless there is an item (such as a brooch) that exemplifies your brand.
4. Carry an attaché or (faux) leather folder. Within it, bring several copies of your resume and cover letter, your list of questions, work samples you may have, business cards, your Bio / Sell Sheet you created in ***Step 7: Market Yourself!***, a list of professional references, and a pen and note pad. Also bring with you your Career Portfolio (and/or CD) you developed in ***Step 7: Market Yourself!***

☐ FOR ADDITIONAL INFORMATION, CHECK OUT VARIOUS INTERVIEW RESOURCES.

There are a number of resources available on the Internet if you seek additional help on any career-related information. Following are various sites that contain a host of career-related articles with advice and tips on conducting job interviews, types of job interviews, interview questions and answers, interview preparation, interview skills, and more.

On **About.com** (scroll down and click on **AboutCareers)**, Alison Doyle, *Job Searching Expert,* and other career experts discuss job interview preparation, interview tips, career planning, job search advice, internships, salary negotiations, career assessments, job applications, references, networking, professional portfolios, background checks, job interview follow-up calls, and more. AboutCareers also includes information and guidance regarding a number of different professions.

Other sites for career information include:

☐ ACE THE INTERVIEW.

Consider the interview a meeting where both you and the hiring manager wish to determine if there is a fit within their organization. You are in need of a job and the firm needs someone with your qualifications, so try to relax by making it conversational and show your interest in the position. Keep in mind that hiring managers select candidates who are likable, fit in with the company's culture, and have the ability to do the job. Be your genuine, professional self.

Use these Interview Tips as a Guide

1. Make a good first impression with everyone you meet at the firm. Smile and be friendly and courteous. When you meet the interviewer, provide a firm handshake, make eye contact, and use his or her name.

2. Often a first question asked by a hiring manager is for you to tell them a little about yourself and what your career goals are. Respond by using your *Elevator Pitch* that you developed in ***Step 4: Develop Your Personal Brand and Professional Summary***. In this way, you are stating what you do as well as your value proposition to the firm and the competitive edge you have over other candidates.
3. Maintain good posture, be alert and focused, and listen carefully to your interviewer, asking questions when you need further clarification on what he or she says. Lean in a bit toward the interviewer to exhibit interest and enthusiasm.
4. Show your passion and enthusiasm about your profession and interest in the position. Smile often. Act confident, professional, poised, and modest; and be honest and genuine in your responses.
5. If the hiring manager didn't start the interview by explaining the position, ask what it entails and what qualifications the perfect candidate would require in order to be considered. If you don't already have one from a job posting, you can ask for a copy of the job description.
6. Turn the questions asked of you into opportunities to showcase your skills and communicate your value. Use success stories to show how your achievements have tackled similar challenges. Again, use your CAR Statements by explaining the CHALLENGES you were faced with, the ACTIONS you took to meet the challenge, and the RESULTS of your efforts.
7. If you find yourself needing a break from answering a lot of questions, ask some of your own at that point relative to the discussion and/or from your prepared list.
8. Make opportunities for yourself to provide information about your related skills, attributes, qualifications, accomplishments, and competitive edge insofar as how they relate to the position and can benefit the firm.
9. Communicate your Assets, Benefits, Competitive Edge, Value Proposition, and Return on Investment—the five critical components of your Personal Brand that you developed in ***Step 4: Develop Your Personal Brand and Professional Summary***—by exhibiting ways you can help the organization meet its goals, such as by elevating sales and/or profitability, improving productivity, enhancing customer satisfaction, decreasing costs, minimizing turnover, strategically solving problems, and so on.
10. Try not to talk about salary until a job offer is made (see next).
11. At the end of the interview, ask the hiring manager what the next step in the interview process is and when the firm expects to make a hiring decision. Ask if you are a viable candidate for the position, how your skills compare to others, and if there is anything that could prevent the firm from offering you the position. If so, hone in on any qualifications you may have missed during the discussion.
12. Shake the interviewer's hand and thank him or her for meeting with you. If you are genuinely interested in the position, say so and let him / her know you feel you would be a valuable asset to the firm and a good fit in their culture.

Try Not to Talk Salary Until a Job Offer is Made

The one who speaks salary first during an interview (before a job offer is actually made) generally loses. Hiring managers will want to know what salary you are seeking so they can see if you fall within their ballpark and/or come up with a number that works for them in later negotiations. However, if the salary you seek is lower or higher than the position offers, two things can happen if you give them a number before learning the salary range the position actually offers:

1. In a tough job market, candidates often undercut their worth in the hope that it will help them receive the job offer. This method can work in reverse. It decreases your perceived value and may actually cost you the position.
2. If the salary you seek is much higher than the salary range, it can automatically put you in the "screened out" pile.

To prevent either from happening and to position yourself on the short list, strategic candidates will first find out the salary range the position pays. Try to procure this information *before* going on the interview, such as by calling Human Resources anonymously to ask them, researching what the market rate is for that position, or if you were referred by an employee having them find it out for you.

When asked during an interview before a job offer is made what the salary you are seeking is, try to divert the topic until such time as a job offer is made. You can respond in a number of ways:

- say that if you both find you are a good fit for the company, you feel confident a number can be worked out;
- ask what the salary range for the position is or the budget they have allocated for it;
- tell them that based on your research, the position pays in the range of X dollars, and ask if that is correct;
- state your salary is negotiable and dependent upon the overall compensation package;
- tell them you would feel more comfortable discussing salary at such time as a job offer is made; and/or
- say you would consider any fair offer.

If the hiring manager continues to press you for a number, you can respond with several of the answers above. If he or she insists they at least know the range you are seeking, provide a salary range (based on your research and the salary range the position pays) that comes somewhere between 15% below and 15% above the maximum, allowing yourself room for negotiation when the time comes if you are offered the position. (More on this below under ***Salary Negotiations***.)

☐ ALWAYS SEND INTERVIEW THANK YOU LETTERS.

For both Job Interviews and Informational Interviews, *always* send an **Interview Thank You Letter** or note to the interviewer(s) within a day or two of your interview thanking them for the interview and reiterating your interest in and qualifications for the position to keep your name fresh in their mind.

Sending an Interview Thank You Letter will not only help you to stand out from your competition, but those who do are hired more frequently than other candidates. In a survey conducted by Accountemps, a specialized service for temporary professionals, 97% of Human Resource Managers liked receiving Thank You Letters, with more than half feeling it was helpful in making their candidate selections.

Interview Thank You Letters—*follow-up sales letters per se*—provide you with the opportunity to restate your matching qualifications and why you believe you are an excellent candidate for the position. Hone in on the areas you discussed during the interview and any you may have left out, and include your value proposition. Keep it brief.

A thank you letter sent by postal mail provides more of a personal touch and allows you to send it on your personally branded stationery (discussed in ***Step 7: Market Yourself!****)*; however, if the firm plans to make an immediate hiring decision, sending it by email ensures you are timely. Here is an example:

Sample Interview Thank You Letter Foundation

Dear _____,

I appreciate the time you took to interview me [☐ today | ☐ yesterday | ☐ this week] **for the _____** *[which?]* **position within your firm. I am** [☐ sincerely interested in | ☐ enthusiastic about | ☐ passionate about filling] **this position and believe I would be a perfect candidate for it.**

As a(n) _____, _____, and _____ *[your primary attributes and/or skills]*, **I feel my** [☐ expertise and qualifications | ☐ background and education | ☐ knowledge and experience] **in _____, _____, and _____** *[primary areas]* **would allow me to _____** *[do what?]* **in helping your** [☐ firm | ☐ organization | ☐ department] **meet its goals and objectives by way of** [☐ elevating sales and/or profitability | ☐ improving productivity | ☐ enhancing customer service | ☐ decreasing costs | ☐ strategically solving _____ *(type of)* problems | ☐ other: _____]. **By the way, I neglected to mention that I also have experience in _____** *[what, if anything you didn't already mention]*.

If there is any additional information you might need from me, please email or call me *[include your contact information in the header]*. **I look forward to going on a second interview and/or hearing from you regarding your decision. Thank you again for this opportunity to meet with you.**

Warm regards,

Your Name
Your Tag Line / Slogan

☐ MAKE FOLLOW-UP CALLS.

Making a follow-up call to the interviewer about a week after the interview to find out the status of the position is an opportunity to again express your interest in the position and find out about the decision status. If you need to, jot down your phone script before making the call and have your resume available so you can refer to it. Keep your conversation to a few minutes.

If you have an opportunity and the position has not yet been filled, reiterate some of the information you discussed in your interview and included in your Thank You Letter as to why you feel you are a good match. Thank him or her again for interviewing you, and ask if there is any additional information they may need and when the hiring decision is expected to be made.

☐ KEEP DETAILED JOB SEARCH RECORDS.

Keep detailed records of all positions you apply to and/or are interviewed for including contact names, titles, addresses, phone numbers, email addresses, interview notes, and any comments you receive on your follow-up calls. You can make copies of and use the following ***Job Search Log*** for this purpose. Also keep an accurate record of all places you have networked, sent your resume, and/or solicited. Be sure to include all follow-up information.

JOB SEARCH LOG

Keep an accurate record of all places you have networked, sent your resume, and/or solicited. Be sure to include all follow-up information, including names and dates.

DATE SENT	COMPANY NAME & ADDRESS	NAME	RESPONSE DATE	COMMENTS (Interview, Follow-up, etc.)

☐ WHEN A JOB OFFER IS MADE, USE EFFECTIVE SALARY NEGOTIATION STRATEGIES.

Once a job offer is made, you will need to use effective salary negotiation strategies to earn your highest salary potential. Prepare for job offers in advance by following this guide.

Prepare for Upcoming Job Offers

1. First, thoroughly research salaries in your field to get the fair market value for the position before going on interviews so you know what to expect for someone with your qualifications and experience. This information can be obtained at:

salary.com® PayScale HUMAN CAPITAL

2. Identify a salary you feel would make you a "happy camper" based on your worth and keep this figure in mind. Don't under or over value yourself.
3. Prepare some responses in advance to various salary amounts that may be presented so you can feel confident about negotiating. Refer to the ***Salary Negotiation Tips*** below.

Selling Power Using Your Brand: 6 Steps to the Job Offer

The graphic below bases your sales strategy (remember, you are the product you are selling) on your prospects' Achilles heel—that is, what it is they need the most or where they are most vulnerable and you can help them solve their challenges:

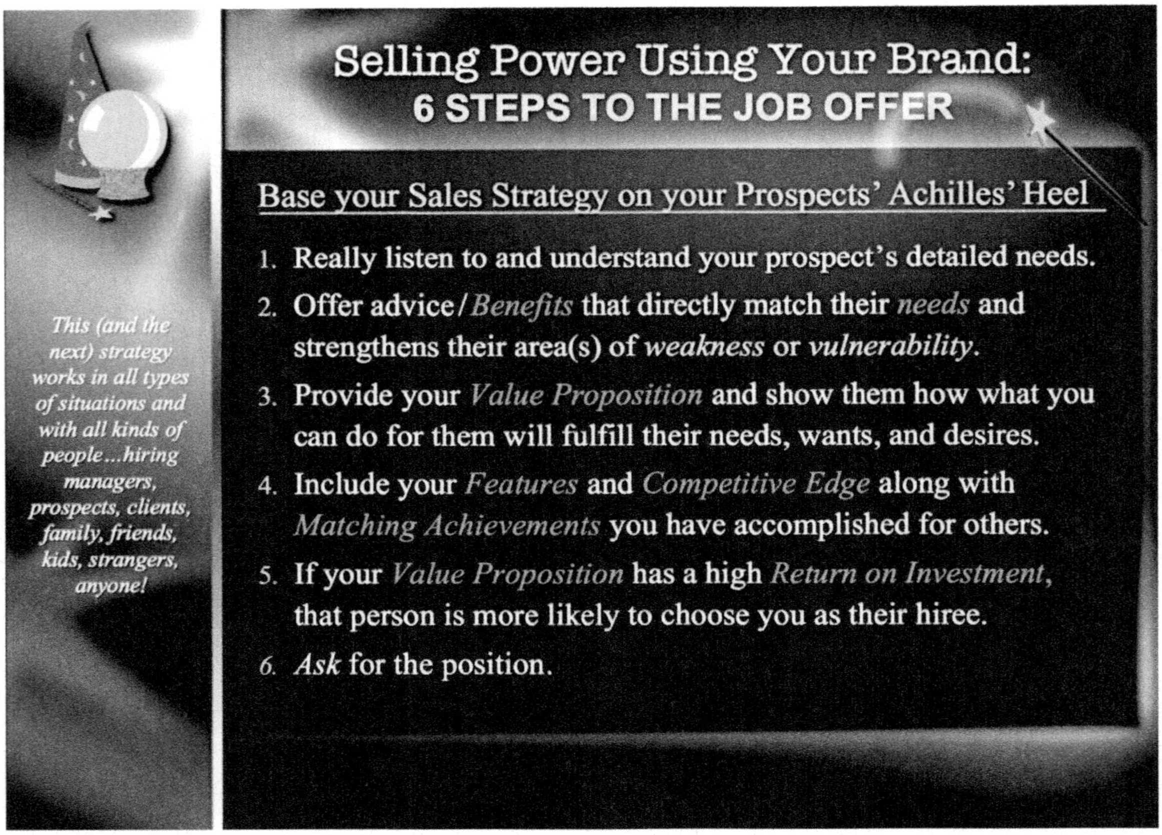

Asking Power: 4 Steps to a "Yes"

This second graphic depicts steps to get what you want in most *any* type of situation or circumstance in life.

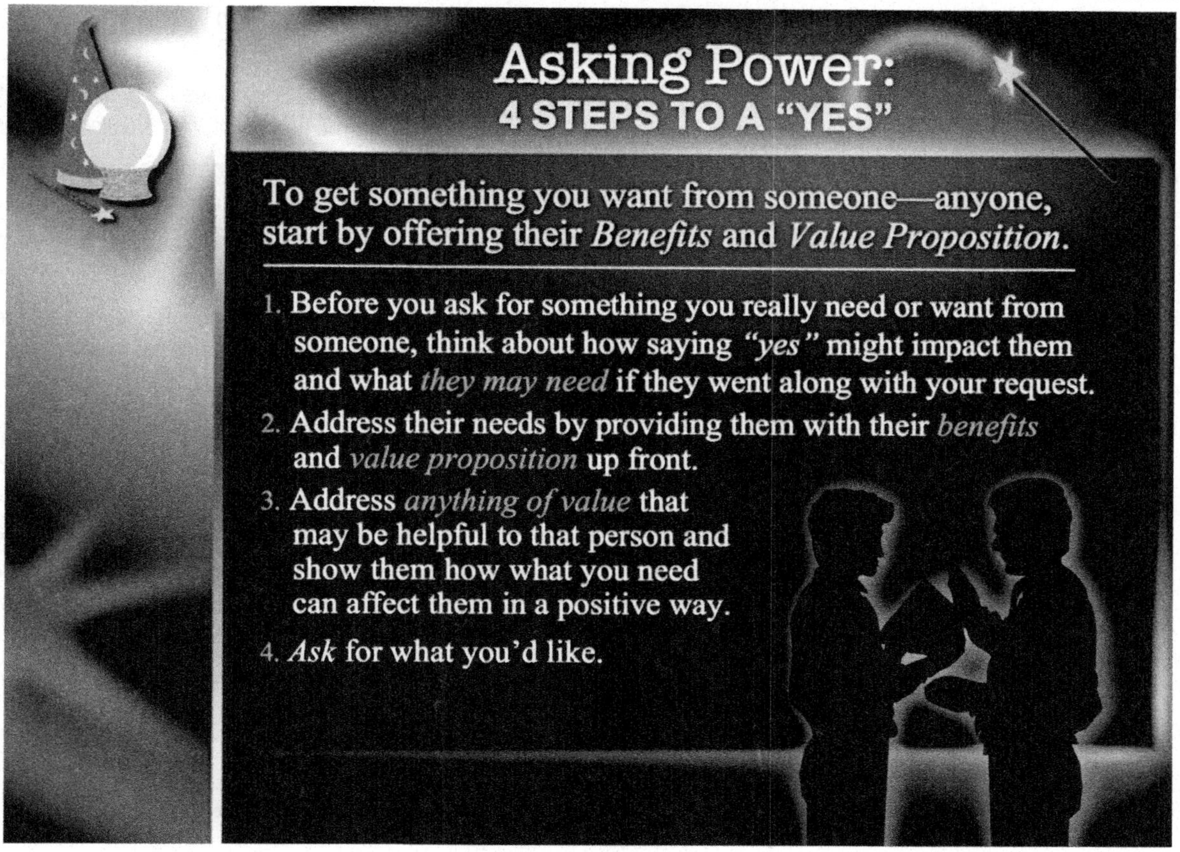

Use these Salary Negotiation Tips as a Guide

1. Typically, the first salary offered by the employer is the lowest paid for the position and there is room for negotiation. Hiring managers expect candidates to negotiate and are surprised when they don't.
2. Don't say "yes" to the first job offer. It's like throwing away money. That's why it's called "salary negotiation." Know that in any economy there is usually room for negotiation.
3. Remember, when discussing salary with a hiring manager, it is not about what *you* need, it's about the value you bring to the table for the prospective employer. Don't make it personal.
4. Stay positive, show your interest in the position, be genuine, and assert yourself with confidence. Don't feel intimidated or act apprehensive, demanding, emotional, or argumentative.
5. After you fully understand what the position has to offer, determine an amount you would feel comfortable with and happy to come to work for every day, not the least amount you would accept.
6. Decide how much you'd like to work for the organization, and let that play into your salary negotiation. Don't be afraid to ask for what you feel you are worth and a salary that is fair. The old adage, "you'll always get a no if you don't ask," holds true in salary negotiations.
7. Once an offer is made, let the hiring manager know that you are excited about working for the firm and can provide a lot of value but that you were seeking a salary in a higher range. State what you feel you are worth.
8. Defend your worth by reiterating your qualifications. Show how your achievements can benefit an employer. For example, if you are seeking $75,000 and you saved your previous employer $100,000, in essence your value has already paid for your salary!
9. If the amount offered is lower than the market range generally pays, consider letting them know the difference based on the research you conducted. If it is less than you had expected, you can ask them how they came up with that amount.
10. Once a salary amount is offered, provide a number that is higher than you would actually seek, knowing you can bargain down. A good rule of thumb (as mentioned earlier) is to provide a salary range that comes somewhere between 15% below and 15% above the maximum the position pays, allowing yourself room for negotiation. Typically, firms will not offer more than the salary range the position pays and may come in at a number somewhere between the midpoint and maximum, allowing room for growth.

11. Sell yourself. Justify the amount you are seeking by capitalizing on a win / win strategy solution by providing a vision of how you can help the company based on your unique value.
12. If unsure the amount is right for you, ask if you can think about it and get back to them. Sometimes a higher offer will be made at that time. Or, if you have other job offers, you can negotiate between them stating you had an offer for X dollars from another firm.
13. Ultimately, the best salary range you might expect is one that falls somewhere between the mid-point and maximum the position pays. If you are more qualified than others in your profession, there may be additional room for negotiation.
14. If the final amount offered is firm and you still find it a bit low, you can ask about additional compensation going forward, such as by requesting an evaluation in six months with the potential for an increase at that time.
15. Before agreeing on an acceptable salary, discuss the compensation package. There may be room for negotiation there as well, such as in your benefits, vacation time, stock options, having a flexible work schedule, educational reimbursement, commission or bonuses, relocation assistance, company car, and so on.
16. Weigh your risk and reward before accepting the offer and decide how much you are willing to compromise.
17. Once you settle on an amount, get the job offer in writing. You don't want to quit a job or turn down other job offers and later find out that the position you accepted has been eliminated or offered to another candidate. You can also use the written job offer to gain leverage at your current employer should you want to stay in your existing position if your salary were to be increased.
18. If you find the salary is too low and they are not negotiable, thank them for the offer and walk away if you feel you need to. But if you really do want the position, be careful not to turn it down as they may pursue another candidate.

Note: To read more on the subject of salary negotiation, Jack Chapman's book, ***Negotiating Your Salary: How to Make $1000 a Minute,*** provides excellent advice. One of my favorite tips is that when a job offer is made, instead of answering right away, give a brief silent pause or say "hmmm," as hiring managers will typically offer more.

Much Success in Your Career Endeavors! Here's to hearing the words, ***"You're Hired!"***

INDEX
OF ALL POSITION TITLES

Concrete Swimming Pool Installer
Construction & Estimator Assistant
Construction Administrator
Construction Carpenter
Construction Customer Service Manager
Construction Estimator
Construction Field Estimator
Construction Form Setter
Construction Journeyman Electrician
Construction Manager
Construction Materials Technician
Construction Operations Supervisor
Construction Project Engineer
Construction Project Manager / Site Superintendent
Construction QA / QC Engineer
Construction Quality Specialist
Construction Services Manager
Construction Superintendent
Construction Tradesman
Contract (Site) Manager
Cost Analyst
Crane Manager
Crew Chief
Curb Builder
Customer Service Representative – Construction
Deck Installer
Demolition Foreman
Directional Bore Operator
Dirt Foreman / Superintendent
Dredge Operator
Driller
Drywall & Make-ready Technician
Drywall Carpenter
Drywall Installer
Drywall Sander
Drywall Worker
Dump Truck Driver
Electrical Construction Foreman
Electrical Engineering Technician
Electrical Project Manager
Electrician
Electrician Foreman
Elevator Installer
Equipment Operator
Estimating Assistant
Estimator – High-end General Construction
Estimator / Assistant Project Manager
Excavating Contractor
Excavator Operator
Facilities Construction Trades Worker
Facilities Maintenance Mechanic
Facility Operations Project Manager
Field Foreman
Field Install Site Supervisor
Field Manager – Residential Construction
Field Superintendent
Field-based Construction Manager
Finish Superintendent
Fire Sprinkler Fitter
Flat Glass Glazier Technician
Floor Laying Contractor
Foreman / Foreperson
Framing Carpenter
Garden Center Worker
Gas Welder

Concreting Supervisor
Construction & Service Coordinator
Construction Area Manager
Construction Coordinator
Construction Electrician Journeyman
Construction Expeditor
Construction Field Supervisor
Construction Inspector
Construction Labor / Equipment Operator
Construction Manager
Construction Office Manager
Construction Project Administrator
Construction Project Manager
Construction Project Specialist
Construction Quality Assurance Inspector
Construction Representative
Construction Site Manager
Construction Supervisor
Construction Trainee
Contract Administrator
Cost Estimator
Crane Operator
Crew Leader
Custodian
Customer Service Superintendent
Deck Worker
Demolition Superintendent
Directional Drill Operator
Door & Window Installer
Dredger
Drilling Foreman
Drywall Applicator
Drywall Finisher
Drywall Mechanic
Drywall Stripper
Drywaller
Electric Service Worker
Electrical Contractor
Electrical Foreman
Electrical Systems Design Engineer
Electrician Apprentice
Electrician Helper
Engineer – Electrical Systems Design
Estimating / Bidding Assistant
Estimating Supervisor
Estimator – Specialty Construction
Estimator / Purchaser
Excavating Machine Operator
Facilities Construction Coordinator
Facilities Foreperson
Facilities Superintendent
Fence Builder
Field Helper
Field Manager
Field Operations Supervisor
Field Supervisor
Field-based Facilities Manager
Finish-Pour Assistant
Fire Sprinkler Helper
Floor Installer
Floor Systems Carpenter
Forklift Operator
Front-End Loader Operator
Gardener
General Building Contractor

Construction & Building Inspector
Construction Administrative Coordinator
Construction Assistant Superintendent
Construction Cost Estimator
Construction Equipment Operator
Construction Field Engineer
Construction Foreman
Construction Journeyman
Construction Laborer
Construction Mason
Construction Operations Manager
Construction Project Coordinator
Construction Project Manager / Designer
Construction Project Supervisor
Construction Quality Control Manager
Construction Services Assistant
Construction Site Superintendent
Construction Supervisor
Construction Worker
Contractor
Craftsman
Crane Rigger
Crew Leader – Maintenance
Custodian Engineer
Deck Builder
Demolition Contractor
Demolition Worker
Director, Labor Relations
Dragline Operator
Dredging Inspector
Drywall & Ceiling Tile Installer
Drywall Boardhanger
Drywall Hanger
Drywall Metal Stud Worker
Drywall Taper
Dump Truck Backhoe Operator
Electrical Apprentice
Electrical Design Engineer
Electrical Inspector
Electrical Systems Supervisor
Electrician Contractor
Electrician Supervisor
Engineering Equipment Operator
Estimating / Change Manager
Estimator
Estimator – Structural & Miscellaneous Steel Fabricatic
Estimator Project Manager
Excavator Foreman
Facilities Construction Project Specialist
Facilities Generalist
Facility Maintenance Specialist
Field Construction Coordinator
Field Inspector
Field Manager – Homebuilding
Field Representative
Field Survey Specialist
Finish Carpenter
Fire Sprinkler Designer
Fire Sprinkler Installer
Floor Layer
Foreman
Framer
Furniture Maker
Gas Inspector
General Construction Equipment Operator

General Construction Laborer
General Engineering Contractor
General Highway Worker
General Maintenance Technician
General Superintendent
Glass Fitter
Glass Technician
Glazier Supervisor
Golf Course Laborer
Grader Operator
Greenhouse Foreman
Greens Foreman
Greenskeeper
Ground Worker
Groundskeeper
Hand Arc Welder
Hazardous Materials Removal Worker
Heating Mechanic
Heavy Civil Project Engineer
Hedge Trimmer
Highway Foreman
Highway Maintenance Laborer
Highway Maintenance Worker
Home Building Superintendent
Home Remodeling Contractor
Housing Inspector
HVAC Foreman
HVAC Mechanic
HVAC Specialist
HVAC/R Mechanic
HVAC/R Technician
Indoor Gardener
Inspecting Engineer
Installation Supervisor
Insulation Installer
Inventory Control Assistant – Construction
Irrigation Project Superintendent
Joint Finisher
Journeyman Carpenter
Journeyman Fire Sprinkler Fitter
Junior Site Surveyor
Labor Foreman
Labor Relations Director
Laborer
Land Development Manager
Landscape Foreman
Landscape Laborer
Landscape Technician
Lath & Plaster
Lather Apprentice
Lawn Mower Operator
Lawn Sprinkler Servicer
Lead Glazer
Lead Superintendent
Leadman Construction Laborer
Loader Operator
Maintenance & Operations Supervisor
Maintenance Contractor
Maintenance Groundsman
Maintenance Mechanic
Maintenance Project Supervisor
Maintenance Specialist
Marble Setter
Mason Laborer
Masonry & Stone Setting Contractor
Masonry Outfitter

General Contractor
General Foreman
General Laborer
General Maintenance Worker
Glass & Glazing Contractor
Glass Installer
Glazier
Glazing Project Manager
Gradall Operator
Grass Cutter
Greenhouse Worker
Greens Laborer
Greenskeeper Foreman
Grounds Caretaker
Groundskeeper Foreman
Handyman
Heating Foreman
Heating Specialist
Heavy Equipment Operator
Helliarc Welder
Highway Inspector
Highway Maintenance Lead Worker
Highway Safety Specialist
Home Improvement Contractor
Horizontal Directional Drill Operator
HVAC / Skilled Tradesman
HVAC Helper
HVAC Project Manager
HVAC Systems Foreman
HVAC/R Service Technician
HVAC-R Inspector
Industrial Brick Mason Foreman
Inspector
Installer
Insulation Worker
Inventory Control Manager – Construction
Janitor
Joint Setter
Journeyman Construction Carpenter
Junior Construction Estimator
Junior Superintendent
Labor Organization Representative
Labor Supervisor
Land Assistant Project Manager
Landfill Heavy Equipment Operator
Landscape Gardener
Landscape Maintenance Worker
Landscaper
Lath Hand
Lawn Caretaker
Lawn Service Worker
Lead Carpenter
Lead Plumber
Lead Welder
Licensed Journeyman Electrician
Loading Machine Operator
Maintenance Aide
Maintenance Electrician
Maintenance Helper
Maintenance of Traffic
Maintenance Repair Worker
Maintenance Worker
Mason
Mason Tender
Masonry Contractor
Masonry Specialist

General Contractor
General Foreman – Civil
General Maintenance Mechanic
General Manager – Construction
Glass Combo Technician
Glass Setter
Glazier Contractor
Golf Course Keeper
Grade Checker
Grass Mower
Greens Cutter
Greens Superintendent
Ground Crewman
Grounds Cleaner
Groundskeeping Maintenance Worker
Handyman / Service Technician
Heating Installer
Heating Technician
Heavy Equipment Operator Apprentice
Highway Construction Inspector
Highway Maintenance Foreman
Highway Maintenance Technician
Highway Technician
Home Inspector
Horticulturist
HVAC Contractor
HVAC Installer & Service Technician
HVAC Service Technician
HVAC Technician
HVAC/R Specialist
Independent Contractor
Industrial Electrician
Installation / Service Technician
Installer Technician
Interior Finish Carpenter
Iron Worker
Job Superintendent
Journey Lineworker
Journeyman Electrician
Junior Estimator
Labor Business Representative
Labor Organizer
Labor Union Business Representative
Land Construction Manager
Landscape Design & Build Project Manager
Landscape Irrigation Project Superintendent
Landscape Management Technician
Landscaper Helper
Lather
Lawn Maintenance Laborer
Lawn Sprinkler Installer
Lead Electrician
Lead Project Coordinator
Leadman / Lead Person
Licensed Plumber
Low Boy Driver
Maintenance Carpenter
Maintenance Engineer
Maintenance Journeyman
Maintenance Project Superintendent
Maintenance Repair Worker Assistant
Manager Construction Projects, Facility Engineering
Mason Carpenter
Mason-Plasterer
Masonry Foreman
Masonry Superintendent

Masonry Tuck-pointer Laborer
Master Electrician
Metal Framer
Metal Roofing Technician
Midlevel Estimator
Multifamily Superintendent
New Homes Superintendent
Office Administrator – Construction
Operations Manager – Construction
Painter
Painter – Residential
Painter Leader
Painting Foreman
Park Caretaker Worker
Park Keeper
Paving Inspector
Pesticide Sprayer
Pipefitter
Planning & Coordination Specialist
Planting Foreman
Plastering, Drywall, Acoustical & Insulation Contractor
Plumbing / Mechanical Inspector
Plumbing Designer
Plumbing Inspector
Plumbing, Heating & Air Conditioning Contractor
Prefabricated Structures Carpenter
Project Associate – Construction
Project Coordinator
Project Environmental Engineer
Project Leader
Project Manager – Electrical
Project Manager – Plumbing
Project Manager / General Contractor
Project Manager Assistant
Project Scheduler
Project Superintendent
Property Compliance Inspector
Property Manager – Groundskeeping
Public Works Inspector
Purchasing Administrator
Purchasing Trade Agent
Refrigeration Installer
Refrigeration Technician
Regional Purchasing Manager
Resident Project Representative
Residential Electrical Foreman
Retail Construction Manager
Rockboard Lather
Roofing Apprentice
Roofing Foreman
Scaffold Erector
Senior Building Maintenance Mechanic
Senior Building Technician
Senior Facilities Maintenance Mechanic
Senior Plant Maintenance Mechanic
Services Manager
Sheet Metal Worker
Sheetrock Finisher
Sheetrock Layer
Sheetrock Worker
Shrub Planter
Siding Foreman
Site Supervisor
Skid Steer Loader Operator
Skilled Trades Specialist
Solar Installation / Production Manager

Masonry Worker
Master Plumber
Metal Furrer
Metal Stud Framer
Motor Grader Operator
Multiskilled Craftsman / Remodeler
Nursery Helper
Office Manager – Construction
Operations Supervisor
Painter – Commercial
Painter / Crew Leader
Painting Contractor
Park Caretaker
Park Crew Chief
Park Worker
Pay Loader Operator
Pile-Driver Operator
Pipefitter Helper
Plant Maintenance Mechanic
Plaster Lather
Plumber
Plumbing Contractor
Plumbing Foreman
Plumbing Inspector / Plans Reviewer
Preconstruction Manager
Principal Landscape Architect
Project Control Coordinator
Project Engineer – Electrical
Project Foreman
Project Management Administrator
Project Manager – HVAC
Project Manager – Residential Remodeling
Project Manager / Installation Manager
Project Material Coordinator
Project Specialist
Project Superintendent / Engineer
Property Maintenance Worker
Property Manager – Landscaping
Public Works Manager
Purchasing Agent – Construction
Refrigeration Apprentice
Refrigeration Mechanic
Regional Property Manager
Remodel Contractor
Residential Construction Estimator
Residential General Contractor
Roadway Construction Laborer
Roofer
Roofing Carpenter
Scaffold Builder
Scenic Carpenter
Senior Building Maintenance Technician
Senior Estimator
Senior Field Manager
Senior Project Manager / Estimator
Sheet Metal Contractor
Sheetrock Applicator
Sheetrock Hanger
Sheetrock Nailer
Sheetrocker
Shrub Trimmer
Site Manager
Site Surveyor
Skilled Carpenter
Skilled Trades Worker
Solar Photovoltaic Installer

Master Carpenter
Material Coordinator
Metal Lather
Metal Welder
Multi-Family Construction Project Supervisor
Multiterrain Loader
Nursery Manager
Operations Manager – Construction
Owner / Operator (Contractor)
Painter – Industrial
Painter Helper / Prepper
Painting Contractor
Park Caretaker Keeper
Park Foreman
Paving Equipment Operator
Pesticide Handler
Pipe Welder
Pipefitter Trade Foreman
Plant-Care Worker
Plasterer
Plumber Apprentice / Helper
Plumbing Contractor
Plumbing Foreman (Multifamily)
Plumbing Installer
Preconstruction Manager – Renovation
Project Assistant – Jobsite
Project Coordination Specialist
Project Engineer / Finish Carpenter
Project Lead
Project Manager
Project Manager – Metal Construction
Project Manager – Sheet Metal
Project Manager / Site Superintendent
Project Principal Work Planner
Project Superintendent
Project Supervisor
Property Manager – Construction
Pruner
Purchasing / Estimating Assistant
Purchasing Manager – Construction
Refrigeration Foreman
Refrigeration Specialist
Regional Purchasing Administrator
Remodeling Tradesman
Residential Construction Project Manager
Restoration Carpenter
Rock Lather
Roofing & Siding Contractor
Roofing Contractor
Scaffold Construction Manager
Senior Building Facilities Technician
Senior Building Maintenance Worker
Senior Estimator, Home Building Construction
Senior Maintenance Mechanic
Service Plumber
Sheet Metal Helper
Sheetrock Applier
Sheetrock Installer
Sheetrock Sander
Shop Steward
Side Boom Tractor Operator
Site Superintendent
Sitework Manager
Skilled Trades Apprentice
Solar Heating Cooling System Installer
Solar Project Manager

Special Trade Contractor
Sprinkler Fitter
Stonemason
Structural Contractor
Structural Tradesworker
Superintendent – Installation
Superintendent – White Paving
Support Specialist
Swimming Pool Installer
Terrazzo Contractor
Terrazzo Setter
Tile Installer
Track Hoe Operator
Trades Specialist – HVAC
Tree Maintenance Worker
Tree Surgeon
Truck Driver / Equipment Operator
Union Negotiator
Union Staff Representative
Utility Maintenance Worker
Waterproofer
Weed Sprayer
Welding Contractor
Wiring Technician
Working Superintendent
Yard Worker
Specialty Contractor
Steamfitter
Stonesetter
Structural Superintendent
Subcontractor
Superintendent – Specialty Construction
Superintendent of Facilities Maintenance
Surfacing Equipment Operator
Tack Welder
Terrazzo Finisher
Terrazzo Worker
Tile Setter
Trade Professional Manager
Tradesworker – Bridges
Tree Pruner
Tree Trimmer
Union Business Representative
Union Organizer
Union Steward
Utility Worker – Heavy Equipment
Weed Controller
Weeder
Window Washer
Wood Lather
Working Superintendent – Retail / Commercial
Zone Chief (HVAC)
Spot Welder
Steward
Structural Concrete Superintendent
Structural Trades Superintendent
Superintendent – Concrete
Superintendent – Steel
Supervisor of Building Trades
Swimming Pool Installer
Tamping Equipment Operator
Terrazzo Grinder
Territory Facilities Manager
Torch Welder
Trade Union Representative
Tradesworker – Welding
Tree Specialist
Trencher Operator
Union Carpenter
Union Representative
Utility Line Locator
Vocational Assistant / General Laborer
Weed Inspector
Welder
Wire Lather
Working Foreman
Yard Work Laborer
Other related positions

OTHER RESOURCES

NEED MORE CAREER MANAGEMENT TOOLS?

Visit:

StepByStepResumes.com

FOR RESUME BOOKS IN ALL PROFESSIONS

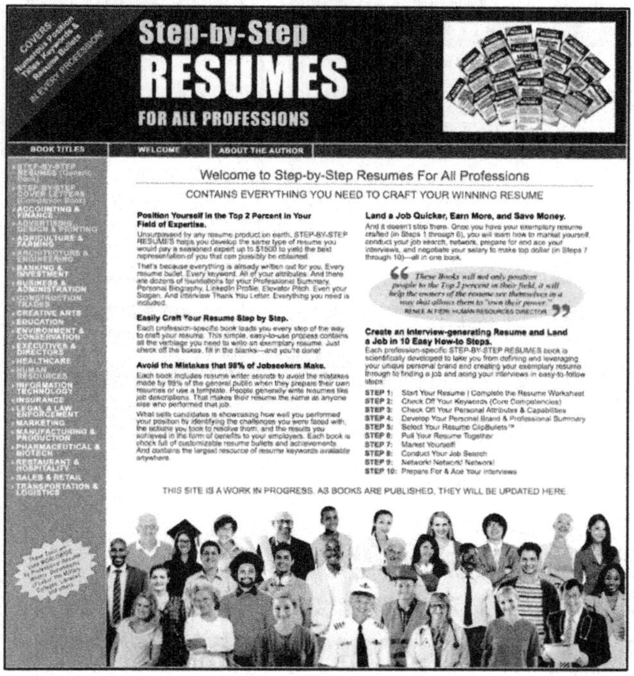

CareerCatapult.com

FOR OTHER RESUME & CAREER PRODUCTS

See next page for all Step-by-Step Resume book professions.

STEP-BY-STEP RESUMES: Build an Outstanding Resume in 10 Easy Steps! *(Evelyn Salvador, JIST Publishing)*

This book, first published in 2008 with its second edition in 2011, was the first Step-by-Step Resumes book. It is applicable to all professions in a more generalized nature.

STEP-BY-STEP COVER LETTERS: Create Your Cover Letter in 10 Easy Steps Using Personal Branding *(Evelyn Salvador, JIST Publishing)*

Like the Step-by-Step Resume books, this companion book explains exactly how to write your cover letter to gain interviews in easy-to-follow steps. It is loaded with foundation templates and examples.

If you need clarification on or help with any of the steps contained in this Book or if you see ways to enhance its contents, contact the author at CareerCatapult@aol.com.

Step-by-Step Resumes For All Professions

Books are in various stages of completion. Visit **StepByStepResumes.com** for more information.

CPSIA information can be obtained
at www.ICGtesting.com
Printed in the USA
LVOW02s1042120616
492277LV00011B/303/P

9 781682 131633